The
AVIATOR
and the
SHOWMAN

The
AVIATOR
and the
SHOWMAN

AMELIA EARHART, GEORGE PUTNAM,
AND THE MARRIAGE THAT MADE
AN AMERICAN ICON

Laurie Gwen Shapiro

VIKING

VIKING
An imprint of Penguin Random House LLC
1745 Broadway, New York, NY 10019
penguinrandomhouse.com

Copyright © 2025 by Laurie Gwen Shapiro

Penguin Random House values and supports copyright. Copyright fuels creativity, encourages diverse voices, promotes free speech, and creates a vibrant culture. Thank you for buying an authorized edition of this book and for complying with copyright laws by not reproducing, scanning, or distributing any part of it in any form without permission. You are supporting writers and allowing Penguin Random House to continue to publish books for every reader. Please note that no part of this book may be used or reproduced in any manner for the purpose of training artificial intelligence technologies or systems.

VIKING is a registered trademark of Penguin Random House LLC.

Image credits may be found on page 481.

DESIGNED BY MEIGHAN CAVANAUGH

LIBRARY OF CONGRESS CATALOGING-IN-PUBLICATION DATA

Names: Shapiro, Laurie Gwen, author.
Title: The aviator and the showman : Amelia Earhart, George Putnam, and the marriage that made an American icon / Laurie Gwen Shapiro.
Description: New York : Viking, [2025] | Includes bibliographical references and index.
Identifiers: LCCN 2024043042 (print) | LCCN 2024043043 (ebook) | ISBN 9780593295908 (hardcover) | ISBN 9780593295915 (ebook)
Subjects: LCSH: Earhart, Amelia, 1897–1937—Marriage. | Putnam, George Palmer, 1887–1950—Family. | Putnam family. | Women air pilots—United States—Biography. | Publishers and publishing—United States—Biography. | Domestic relations.
Classification: LCC TL540.E3 S43 2025 (print) | LCC TL540.E3 (ebook) | DDC 629.13092/2—dc23/eng/20250304
LC record available at https://lccn.loc.gov/2024043042
LC ebook record available at https://lccn.loc.gov/2024043043

Printed in the United States of America
1 3 5 7 9 10 8 6 4 2

The authorized representative in the EU for product safety and compliance is Penguin Random House Ireland, Morrison Chambers, 32 Nassau Street, Dublin D02 YH68, Ireland, https://eu-contact.penguin.ie.

For my spirited daughter, Violet O'Leary.

Soar high, stay curious, and keep surprising yourself.

I love you.

Everyone has oceans to fly if they have the heart to do it. Is it reckless? Maybe. But what do dreams know of boundaries?

AMELIA EARHART

Truth is such a *rare* thing it is delightful to tell it.

EMILY DICKINSON

The only thing new in the world is the history you don't know.

HARRY S. TRUMAN

CONTENTS

A Note for Readers — xi
A Word on Name Usage — xv

Needle in a Haystack — 1

1. The Kingmaker — 7
2. Saturday's Child — 32
3. The Golden Twenties — 53
4. Amelia Takes Off — 78
5. The Right Sort of Girl — 91
6. Lady Lindy — 121
7. The Mitten — 136
8. Under Whose Rooftree — 147
9. Something Had to Give — 176
10. Pilots and Plunges — 196

11.	The Truth to the Rumor	*213*
12.	An Attractive Cage	*233*
13.	A Kind of the Dithers	*248*
14.	Call of the Wild	*285*
15.	Morning Becomes Electra	*310*
16.	Dead Reckoning	*323*
17.	Whistle in the Dark	*343*
18.	Slow Circling Down	*387*
19.	Who Came to Dinner	*411*
20.	Veiled Ventures	*418*
	Epilogue	*439*
	Acknowledgments	*441*
	Notes	*453*
	Bibliography	*469*
	Image Credits	*481*
	Index	*483*

A NOTE FOR READERS

Sex, violent death, and mystery. If your life has one of these things, people might be interested. If it has two, now you're tabloid fodder. If it has three, you're Amelia Earhart.

Because of these titillating elements, more people have gotten Amelia Earhart wrong than perhaps any other person in the last century. Wrong "facts" about every single aspect of her life. Wrong conclusions about her personality, her career, her goals, her sexuality. And her disappearance.

My first encounter with Amelia Earhart was through a squeaky-clean Scholastic biography that my mother helped me choose from a flyer in third grade. I was wowed by her story, and I well remember my dad's admiration for Amelia when we all discussed her at dinner. Decades later, Amelia Earhart floated back into my world while I was researching my last book, which is about a kid who stowed away on Richard Byrd's storied 1928 expedition to Antarctica. Byrd's publisher, George Palmer Putnam, had organized a national competition for a Boy Scout to join Byrd's crew and then write his own Putnam book for young boys. I was aghast: What kind of person sends an untrained boy on a life-threatening expedition to the bottom of the globe? Well, the kind of person who would marry the heiress of the Crayola empire, and then hire Amelia Earhart to write a book, and then have an affair with Amelia Earhart. Those juicy details were somehow absent from my childhood Scholastic book.

So here was Amelia, buzzing over the Hudson River to help promote Commander Byrd's departure (with the Boy Scout and the stowaway aboard). It's been said that the story you should write is the one that sticks in your head. I realized I knew very little about Amelia Earhart. Was she the wholesome role model depicted in biographies for children, or did she have a tarnished political background and a secret, messy family legacy, like Charles Lindbergh? Was she a great flier or merely brave? What was her inner life like? And what was her later marriage with George Palmer Putnam—her manager, publisher, and business partner—like? I wanted a fleshed-out narrative, an Amelia Earhart book for adults.

Everyone I asked, from cousins to cabbies, had a strong take on Amelia Earhart. The more I dug in, the more I realized that she had been a lightning rod for almost a century of projections and agendas: chauvinists who wanted to belittle her abilities; those who wished to skew her sexuality and ambition to align with nonexistent reality; well-meaning historians who bought into all sorts of whitewashed narratives (supplied by family, estate overseers, museums, etc.); historian frauds who used Amelia's disappearance as a point of departure for their own smart-sounding yet evidence-free theories; and outright crackpots whose speculations about her fate belong in science fiction yet grab headlines even today.

I find truth much more interesting than nontruth. In striving to illuminate who Amelia Earhart really was, I found myself not only a researcher but also something of an avenger—it was astonishing how much time and effort I spent just debunking Earhart lore that had been repeated for generations, not to mention coming up against influential people who had a stake in hiding crucial facts.

What stands out is that Amelia Earhart—the real woman, not the one of fantasy—was ambitious, courageous, intelligent, curious, sexual, overconfident, lazy, kindhearted, shrewd, and flawed. One quality doesn't negate another. You can be all sorts of things simultaneously, which drives lightweight and unscrupulous chroniclers batty—it's hard to write a simple narrative when your subject contains multitudes. Another Jazz Age great, F. Scott Fitzgerald, famously observed that "the test of a first-rate intelligence is the ability to hold two opposed ideas in the mind at the same time, and still retain the ability to function." But how fascinating and inspiring the truth is, as opposed to nonsense!

So I approached my work as a trained journalist with one overriding focus: to uncover and report the truth without any personal agenda. The truth will lead you to how Amelia Earhart's story is deeply intertwined with that of George Palmer Putnam, once a boldface name who continues to fade from memory as the years go by, all while Amelia's legacy rises.

This is a story of ambition and marriage. Amelia Earhart and George Palmer Putnam together exploited the freewheeling climate of the Jazz Age and the more sobering Great Depression for their personal gain but at the same time inspired countless young people—especially young women—to fulfill their own ambitions. My narrative delves into the relationship between Amelia, a boundary-pushing woman, and George, a talented mythmaker eager to mold her legacy. Their partnership crafted the polished, iconic image of Amelia Earhart that still emboldens everyone from young children reading their first Amelia Earhart biography to women astronauts, moved by Amelia's spirit since youth and now embarking on groundbreaking space expeditions.

Laurie Gwen Shapiro—New York City, 2025

A WORD ON NAME USAGE

During my research on Amelia Earhart and George Palmer Putnam, I considered the naming conventions appropriate for a detailed narrative nonfiction book. Some writers before me have used "AE" for Amelia and "GP" for George. However, I found that Amelia adopted "AE" as a public persona at the strong suggestion of her manager and future husband, and those closest to her continued to call her Amelia or Millie, openly disregarding George's affects.

George, when mingling with the hoi polloi, insisted that he be called "GP," pronounced "Gee-Pee." To be fair, the nickname helped differentiate him in an industry where many of his relatives had similar names, like his powerful elderly uncle, George Haven Putnam, a book publishing legend. At G. P. Putnam's Sons, the company his grandfather founded, underlings respectfully addressed him as Mr. Putnam, and his later California business partner, Cap Palmer, revealed that the inner circle always called him George. Amelia's endearments for him were "Gyp" and "Gyppy" and, by many trustworthy firsthand accounts, rarely GP.

In George's embellished revisionist memoir from the 1940s, ghostwritten by his young, loyal hire, Cap Palmer, there's a striking inclusion: a prenuptial agreement, handwritten by Amelia and given to him on the eve of their wedding—included in an adulterated form later on in this book.

Amelia signed the original document as simply "A." However, in the typed version used for his memoir, George changed the signature to "AE." This swap wasn't the only adjustment; the published letter, as recrafted by George, included several other intriguing modifications that served his preferred narrative.

For authenticity, clarity, and consistency in this narrative, I've gone with "Amelia" and "George." This decision not only supports historical accuracy but also offers a smoother reading experience in a narrative filled with Earharts and Putnams. I've also occasionally used first names for other figures to enhance reader connection.

NEEDLE IN A HAYSTACK

Amelia Earhart was sitting across from George Palmer Putnam. He was on the phone, not acknowledging her, taking his sweet time. He was a flamboyant, career-making publisher who liked to be in the news. Putnam was always photographed with swells of the era: standing next to Charles Lindbergh, the first man to fly solo across the Atlantic; posing with Commander Richard Byrd, the man who conquered the South Pole; smiling with Howard Carter, the man who discovered King Tut.

Amelia was thirty-one years old, a Boston social worker. She was not a famous person. But unknown to her that spring of 1928, Putnam had decided he wanted to create a new hero—the first woman to cross the Atlantic in an airplane!—the counterpart to the world's most famous man, Charles Lindbergh.

Putnam sent out feelers to find candidates for such a heroine, who merely had to be the first female Atlantic passenger to get famous. The idea was familiar: sponsor the wildly risky adventure, find someone physically attractive and willing to imperil their own life, sign them to an exclusive tell-all deal, publicize the thing to the max, and make a fortune on book sales.

Soon word came from Boston: George Putnam's old friend, a PR guy named Colonel Hilton Howell Railey, had found a perfect candidate: Miss

Earhart was an experienced flier, she was well spoken, and she had pleasing looks. George's response was swift and decisive: "She must be in my office by the start of the next morning!" When George Palmer Putnam wanted things done, there was no room for argument.

Railey told Amelia that someone in New York City wanted to see her about a possible flying venture. She was a committed full-time social worker and only a part-time aviator, but Amelia's heart beat faster at the prospect of sponsored flying, a rarity for any woman, even the most accomplished pilot. She agreed to go to New York.

Railey escorted her down from Boston by train. At 2 West Forty-Fifth Street, just off Fifth Avenue, a colossal PUTNAM banner fluttered from the rooftop. A landmark of New York's Jazz Age publishing district, the Putnam Building reached sixteen stories skyward. An elegant retail bookstore graced its lobby, and its prime location was often touted in newspapers as "just 100 feet off Fifth." Times Square, now ablaze with neon, was just a couple blocks west and had recently eclipsed Herald Square as the energetic heart of Manhattan.

On the day of Amelia's arrival, thirty skyscrapers had already reshaped the Midtown skyline, transforming the area into a bustling hub aglow with light. The district housed titans like *The New York Times*, the city's most respected newspaper, and *The New Yorker*, a sharp-witted rising star on the media scene that, even in 1928, held outsize influence among the cultural elite.

Railey brought Amelia to the elegant reception room of G. P. Putnam's Sons and introduced her to George's neat and professional brunette secretary, Miss Josephine "Jo" Berger. Dressed in the day's standard attire for working women in publishing—back-seamed stockings and practical T-strapped low heels—Jo exuded an air of efficiency, and in her respectable brown day dress, with a powdered nose and a touch of rouge, Amelia, too, seamlessly blended into the office's urbane ambiance. An Episcopalian bluestocking, she easily could have pursued a secretarial career in publishing had she desired.

Jo had explained to Amelia and Railey that Mr. Putnam, eager for their meeting, was held up in another discussion. After Jo assured Railey that she would look after their special guest, Amelia replied that it was no problem at all for her to wait. Railey gave Jo a curious look and headed to the building's third floor, where he had a satellite office for his Boston-based PR firm. "Come get me if needed!" he said.

Amelia, having arrived on the dot, saw the wait as a glaring sign of negligence. Why endure an overnight trip from Boston if only to be kept waiting? But, in reality, it was a calculated chess move. Railey and Jo had recognized this for what it was: a deliberate delay meant to assert dominance before the game even began. George Putnam, one of the numerous Putnams in the building and not nearly as powerful within the family firm as people might assume, was nonetheless making waves in the publishing world. Critics might have grumbled, but post-Lindbergh, George's rise to industry prominence was evident to all. By deftly securing the rights to Charles Lindbergh's story with a blend of charm and dogged determination, George had turned its success into a springboard for a slew of bestselling adventure tales.

Unbeknownst to her at that moment, Amelia Earhart was poised to become his next great triumph.

George, the peacock at the handsome desk, was still conducting his power phone call, his deep voice filling the office. Impeccably dressed in a flawless double-breasted suit, he was well versed in commanding the room—and absorbing the admiring glances that often followed.

To kill more minutes, Amelia's eyes might have scanned what the bookcase held: there was Lindbergh's famous G. P. Putnam's Sons' book, *"WE"* (those peculiar quotes around all caps), probably signed by the fabled Lindbergh himself. Should she confess to having a clipped newspaper picture of Lindbergh tacked up in her social worker's bedroom? Would that be seen as genuine admiration or as an overly starry-eyed gesture for a woman her age?

At last, the publisher ended his call, allowing dramatic silence before inquiring, "And how about you? Do you consider yourself a risk-taker?" Amelia replied, "It depends. I'm here to learn more."

Weighing how much to disclose, and after securing her promise of secrecy, he shared glimpses of the confidential project: he was scouting for a female passenger to be the first across the Atlantic.

A widely read piece in *The New York Times* had recently announced the end of the brassy, high-voltage flapper era, signaling the rise of a more subdued and sophisticated modern archetype, and Amelia Earhart perfectly encapsulated this transition. Her role as a Boston social worker lent her a wholesome allure reminiscent of the great Charles Lindbergh's all-American aura. To George, who'd done some quick homework, Amelia was a fresh narrative, embodying class, poise, and captivatingly elusive independence—qualities he believed the world would eagerly embrace.

As she shared stories about her years studying science at Columbia and her experiences setting records in air rodeos in California, George considered how she might appear in a publicity photo. While Amelia didn't fit conventional beauty standards, she had a striking presence: tall and slender with almond-shaped gray eyes. Her smile, revealing a gap between her front teeth, added an unexpected touch of charm, though he wondered how this would photograph. But that perfect patrician nose! And her hands were lovely, with long fingers. Her unpainted nails were unlike those favored by Ziegfeld showgirls, hotly pursued by married men in his circles. He had weighed the option of some well-known aviatrixes, such as his neighbor, the elegant debutante Ruth Nichols of Rye, New York. But Amelia's pleasant, straightforward demeanor aligned precisely with what Mrs. Guest, the feminist financier behind the risky venture, was looking for. Amelia was also well bred and embodied values of wholesomeness, Christianity, and Puritan lineage, but she was new, unknown, which the public loved.

If Amelia Earhart survived a flight to become the first female passenger to cross the Atlantic, he'd go big. Very big.

Like George, Amelia was processing rapidly. Behind those rimless spectacles was a man with a solid history of making shrewd choices. Would he catch her in a lie? Did he know she had shaved two years off her age (from thirty-one to twenty-nine)? Lots of women did that, though—surely he would understand. Did her eyes betray her vulnerability—that she looked at this not only as an adventure but also as a chance to indelibly etch her legacy while time was still on her side?

This was a whirlwind for her. The afternoon before, Railey had giddily called George to report that he'd found the ideal candidate. George often hesitated to acknowledge it, but Railey's talent for promotion outshone his. Unlike George, Railey was no mere salaried family man tied to dividends and modest pay; he was a trailblazer in public relations, answering to only himself at the helm of his own successful firm. George trusted him implicitly; theirs was a bond forged in the wake of the Great War, rich with shared confidences. For Railey, collaborating on George's ventures was more than just business—it was an exhilarating diversion from serving his routine corporate clientele, a world of airlines, railroads, and tobacco companies. Despite Railey's lucrative roster, it wasn't money that drove him; it was the thrill of the chase, the pleasure of the game, that drew him to these unorthodox challenges alongside Putnam.

As for the secretive task at hand, steel heiress Amy Guest, whose staggering wealth sat at a rumored $1.9 billion in 1928 dollars (equivalent to nearly $35 billion today), had initially planned to be a passenger herself, aiming to bolster feminist movements and enhance US-Britain ties. Yet faced with her family's fears for her safety, she felt compelled to search for an alternate flier, one whom she would back.

The first tantalizing bulletin reached George Palmer Putnam through Railey, a man with countless connections who liked to keep his name out of newspapers. The intelligence was delicate: One of Railey's prominent clients, Commander Richard Byrd, had leased a surplus plane—the very one used for his North Pole expedition—to Guest for the flight. Although Byrd's connection had to remain clandestine, Railey had given George a golden tip-off and trusted that his friend could come up with a good spin. George was thrilled, and they both knew a bestseller could come of it if the gal selected made it.

That gal was still in George's office two hours after Railey had dropped her off. Though he had gone up to his third-floor office, his curiosity finally wore him down, and he decided to personally investigate the cause of the delay.

Railey's sudden entrance prompted George to swiftly gauge Amelia's reaction to the man with whom she had just shared a train ride—someone whom many women found utterly captivating. Did her eyes linger a little too long, her smile a tad too bright? Railey, tall and sporting a mustache, his black hair neatly combed back, still carried the unmistakable aura of his military past, even a decade after transitioning to civilian life.

"Did you show George your pilot's license?" Railey prodded Amelia with his genteel Southern cadence, adding, "Has she mentioned she's the first American woman to own one?"

"I hold the sixteenth license issued to a woman in the world," Amelia chimed in. She was taken aback by George's understated response to her impressive paperwork, which bore the signature of Orville Wright, the hallowed aviation pioneer himself.

In contrast to George—a brazen opportunist who had by 1928 already garnered the tongue-in-cheek nickname "Lens Louse" from the press—Railey operated as a quiet mastermind, often choosing to work from the shadows. This discreet nature would be an asset when he later co-commanded the Ghost Army, America's most clandestine unit during World War II. George Palmer Putnam, self-mythologizer, would soon write Railey out of the narrative of that first meeting with Amelia. Railey, always valuing results over recognition, would not object.

However, years later, when Amelia's name rang louder than even George's, Railey candidly admitted—off the record—that he had been in that room the day the very married George Palmer Putnam met Amelia Earhart. Thinking back to that significant meeting, Railey would muse all those years later: For George, it was undeniably "love at first sight."

One

THE KINGMAKER

The George Palmer Putnam of the Jazz Age may have been the flashiest Putnam, but he was only the latest in a long, winding road of famous Putnams. He wasn't the first George, or even the first George Palmer Putnam.

In 1887, he entered the world as a son of the second heir to the family's publishing empire, and all Putnam males were expected to contribute to keeping the empire strong.

The rise of American letters owed much to the Putnams. Their publishing company revolutionized the industry by nurturing homegrown talents such as Washington Irving, Herman Melville, Harriet Beecher Stowe, James Fenimore Cooper, and Edgar Allan Poe. Beyond their literary contributions, the Putnams had a storied history, with ancestors playing notable roles in events like holding down the fort during the American Revolution and, far less commendably, pointing fingers during the Salem witch trials. In the Revolutionary War's Battle of Bunker Hill, Israel Putnam, another direct forebearer, is said to have declared, "Don't shoot until you see the whites of their eyes!"

Long before the days of celebrity pilots and publishing giants, George's lustrous grandfather, George Palmer Putnam the First, laid the foundation for their family's publishing legacy. In 1825, he left his home in Brunswick,

Maine, to apprentice at his uncle's carpet company in Boston. Then, in 1838, after working as a bookstore clerk and as a messenger for a religious book firm, he cofounded Wiley and Putnam near Broadway's Trinity Church in New York City. George Palmer Putnam I was the driving force behind the prestigious *Putnam's Monthly* and eventually ventured out on his own, expanding their reach across the Atlantic. By establishing an office in London and securing American publishing rights to the finest European authors, he aimed to showcase the quality of American publishing to a European audience, which often viewed the former "revolting colonies" as lacking in cultural sophistication. His success in distributing high-quality European literature in America also helped to elevate the standing of American publishers both at home and abroad, challenging the stigma that American literature was inferior and proving that the "revolting colonies" had indeed become revolutionary in the realm of letters.

After the sudden 1872 death of the hallowed founder, which happened at his beloved basement bookstore just after five in the evening, the publishing firm's mantle was taken up by one of George's sons, George Haven Putnam, our George's uncle. Despite the challenges of managing complex familial ties, he brilliantly navigated the firm through various economic downturns with steely resolve. George Haven Putnam, a Union veteran of the Civil War, was aptly nicknamed "the Major." Every day in the Roaring Twenties, the spirited, elderly Major, still a hard-liner for tradition and etiquette, walked into the latest of several Putnam buildings early in the morning with the same vigor he once brandished on Civil War battlefields. Despite his age, his step remained spry and assured, a testament to his well-lived life in a rapidly modernizing world of radios and skyscrapers.

Like any man nearing the end of his glory, the Major kept careful track of his potential successors, weighing their strengths and weaknesses, then marking out those who seemed most suited to carrying on the legacy. The George that Amelia Earhart knew from the papers was not the sole heir to the Putnam empire: he was fifth in line, strategically vying for the top spot in an age-old game of succession. Although George's father, John Bishop Putnam, was long dead, George still had a waiting elderly uncle and a slew of cousins to contend with. The daily sight of the four other founding Putnam descendants, each a potential successor and often riding the same elevators as they rose through the ranks, fueled George's ambition to emerge victorious.

The Major surely recognized that despite his flashy nephew's occasional triumphs, George was a wild card—cunning but rogue, often succeeding more by luck than by judgment. With Palmer Cosslett Putnam, the Major's talented engineer son, currently in Africa and showing no interest in the family business, and Irving, his septuagenarian brother, out of contention, the Major pondered the future of the family legacy.

From the gleaming silverware in his home to his tailored suits at work, George Palmer Putnam epitomized the refined upper-middle-class world from which he hailed. Yet George was not one to follow the crowd. Captivated by novelty, he quickly lost interest when results did not come swiftly. His journey through the prestigious Gunnery School (now the Frederick Gunn School), Harvard's hallowed halls, and breakfasts with his father at the Union League were merely steps along an uncertain path. As the always-reading loner at boarding school, he longed to stand out, even from the taller boys who bullied him, surviving on his wit and occasionally cruel jokes. How could he prove his true self to everyone? With his family lightly dismissing his mediocre grades at Harvard as the result of "health concerns," he dropped out after just a year. Avoiding the buttoned-down security of a family job, he then tramped around California, taking any job he could find. Under family pressure, he briefly attended Berkeley—only to drop out there as well.

In 1908, on a Sierra Club excursion up Mount Whitney, George, who was now trying his hand as an outdoorsy Ivy League guide, took a shine to a young climber named Dorothy Binney, a well-bred athletic girl visiting from back East. At twenty, the tall brunette in a long skirt with petticoats was intelligent, handsomely pretty, and, even better, an heiress to the Crayola empire. As they walked, George learned about her father, Edwin Binney, who had invented Crayola crayons when Dorothy was fifteen. She had grown up at Rocklyn, a six-bedroom fieldstone mansion in Sound Beach (now Old Greenwich), Connecticut, a millionaire's showplace complete with two hundred feet of Long Island Sound shoreline, dramatic spiral staircases, and a magnificent swimming pool—a home that would fetch more than $14 million in 2019. Dorothy's mother, Alice, had even named the crayon company Crayola, merging *craie*, the French word for "chalk," with *ola*, from *oleaginous*, to suggest oiliness. While the Putnams were steeped in a heritage that resonated deeply with many Americans, their fame was rooted more in history than in wealth. By contrast, the "new money" Binneys, with their serious wealth, enjoyed a thick financial cushion.

George was an excellent marksman in the wild, thanks to childhood outings with his father, John, and now he had a pretty heiress in his sights. Dorothy returned to the East Coast, flattered by the "swell guy" she'd met but uncertain if he was the one—plus, he wanted her to leave the East Coast for California. When he learned about the Ivy League suitors competing for her hand, determined to reel her in, he upped the ante with relentless, heartfelt letters and weekly bouquets of red roses. Dorothy was not the first, nor would she be the last, woman swept off her feet by George's unwavering pursuit—a behavior that contemporary therapists might label "love bombing." His attention cast a dreamy spell, and it was easy to fall for the intensity. Yet face-to-face, his ardor seemed to wane. Though undeniably attractive, Dorothy had deep-seated insecurities, a consequence of her mother's hurtful comments during her younger years. Her mother had suggested that she was one of those girls whose looks alone couldn't retain a man's attention; she needed to do more to make herself attractive to suitors.

Even before accepting George's proposal, she felt a nagging unease, which she recorded ambivalently in her diary: "A strenuous letter from George, and two apologies in next mail. So, do I love him enough to wear his ring? Oh, heavens. Why this?" Young Dorothy wrote all in her diary, adding, "I wish someone would love me." Dorothy soon discovered, perhaps a bit shockingly, that George's family wasn't very monied at all, but to her parents, the Putnam name, steeped in American history, was an ideal match for their nouveau-riche crayon fortune. The Binneys appreciated the arrestingly handsome young man's willingness to wait until her college graduation; his patience in waiting reflected a broader societal norm during an era when long courtships were not only common but often seen as a sign of respect and genuine commitment. For them, his flexibility and pledge to their daughter sealed the deal. Let him prove to them what he could do out West.

In the late 1800s, trains were the hallmark of American progress and bridged the expanse between the coasts, playing an instrumental role in changing the face of the landscape. By the early twentieth century, nearly all intercity travel relied on this network of steel and steam. Against this backdrop, a young George relocated to Bend, Oregon, determined to show his prospective in-laws his mettle. This promising town in the Cascade Mountains was a blip on the map, accessible only by stagecoach. Yet, at just twenty-one, George sniffed opportunity in the prospective extension of the rail lines there. He wrote the occasional squib for Eastern newspapers, advocating for Bend's inclusion in the national rail grid, and thanks to his tireless advocacy, Bend was soon serviced by two major rail lines. By 1910, an entrepreneurial George had bought *The Bend Bulletin* from then-owner J. M. Lawrence, the sole newspaper voice in town.

"I had no idea of settling in any one place until I reached Oregon," he later recalled for the *Brooklyn Eagle*. "I liked the country better than any other place I had ever seen, and I decided to stay there. That was when I was twenty-one. When I was twenty-two I was elected Mayor of Bend. I think that I was among the youngest Mayors of any Western town. For a good all around education I would recommend being the Mayor of a small town. I had a perfectly swell time."

On October 26, 1911, Dorothy and George were married in front of over four hundred guests at Rocklyn. Delmonico's, one of New York's oldest and most time-honored restaurants, catered the event, and the Binneys generously covered all expenses—to the cash-poor Putnams' great relief. The newlyweds then set out on a six-thousand-mile honeymoon, another fine gift from Dorothy's parents, and journeyed through Central America, visiting Panama, Costa Rica, and Guatemala. It was an underwritten opportunity for George to conduct research and to network, although he involved Dorothy in the process by having her record and organize his notes. She felt an exhilarating sense of purpose, even though she typed up her ambitious groom's notes during her long, hot honeymoon. Yet her diaries, later printed by her granddaughter, note a lack of intimacy and indicate that the trip felt more like an "extended business venture" than a "romantic excursion." More doubts crept into Dorothy's mind—had she misjudged their connection? Committed and literally at sea, she felt ensnared by her choice.

The transition from a wanderlusty, business-oriented honeymoon to settling down did little to ease Dorothy's concerns. Backed by more Binney family funds, George and Dorothy bought the most impressive house in Bend—a town of just 536 people, far from the bustling city it would later become. George's lack of intimacy, first noticed during their travels, persisted, leaving Dorothy feeling increasingly sidelined. Their marriage seemed more focused on bolstering George's career than on building a shared life of adventure and affection. His relentless networking and creation of self-serving stories only magnified her unease. As a result of small-town politics and a lack of suitable candidates, Ivy-educated George was elected "Boy Mayor" at twenty-four by a six-to-one margin. His embellished story about his unexpected election—a humorous tale in his Bend newspaper that claimed his only rival had fallen out a window—was soon a nationwide syndicated hit.

As prominent figures in a tiny community, the Putnams relished their status and soon celebrated the birth of their first son, David. They introduced a touch of East Coast sophistication to local conventions by hosting tennis games and social gatherings at their home, following Sunday services they didn't even attend. In November of 1912, Dorothy, an advocate for women's rights, nearly became the first woman to vote in Oregon. She stepped aside, possibly at George's suggestion, allowing the governor's wife to claim that honor. His debut book, *The Southland of North America: Rambles and Observations in Central America during the Year 1912*, was published by his family's company the following year; it was neither outstanding nor terrible. Over time, George secured small contracts as a West Coast correspondent for several wire services, and when genuine stories were scarce, he supplied fabricated narratives—the bigger the lie, the more he got paid.

Under old Major Putnam's adept leadership, the family's publishing business back in New York was just fine, even without the energetic presence of the Major's nephew George, who did not want to be where he was not needed. George's father, John, had managed the New Rochelle printing plant, affectionately known as Knickerbocker Press, or KP, a name inspired by Washington Irving. Besides running the plant, John also led the firm's educational department and served as its treasurer. Following John's death in 1915, George's oldest brother, Robert, took over these responsibilities.

In 1915, the Bend newspaperman and small-town mayor worked with Governor James Withycombe, switching from the Democratic Party to the Republican Party. During World War I, he enlisted in the Oregon National Guard and briefly served on the Mexican border before returning to Oregon. Despite never serving overseas, he later served the Department of Justice in Washington (and sometimes New York) as an undercover agent who monitored soldiers suspected of vice. While working undercover for the anti-vice squad, George became friends with the tall and imposing Lieutenant Hilton Howell Railey, just two years older than him but his superior. George was jealous that Railey had also made a name for himself as a writer, and that a widely read *Saturday Evening Post* story about his war years had caught the eye of the Major, who, as he soon found out, was mentoring Railey and giving him freelance assignments at the family firm.

So at the beginning of their connection, George was one of Railey's lowly enforcers. "I spotted him," Railey recalled, "as I was raiding some kind of dive. On the rear seat of a Department of Justice staff car, he had slid down to almost the nape of his neck when I began to chat with him." After realizing who George was, Railey mentioned his connection to the Major, and they frequently crossed paths in their covert roles and even at publishing parties. The more they interacted, the more Railey pegged George as a "bored and lazy" scion with a slippery grip on honesty. However, George's unconventional publishing ideas, met with skepticism by his uncle, intrigued Railey, who found himself adding his own ideas and getting roped into schemes and nights at the private men's clubhouses George enjoyed, like the informal Coffee House Club. George was well read but bawdy, always up for the new, and, if you were with him, quite fun. An unlikely bond built on shared secrets formed.

In October 1918, George's thirty-six-year-old brother, Robert Faulkner Putnam, husband to the widely admired feminist writer Nina Wilcox Putnam, fell victim to the flu pandemic at their mother's Rye residence. Robert's shocking death left a void in the family business, prompting George's mother to urge him to take on his big brother's duties. Feeling valued, George heeded the call, promptly moving his family to Rye and jumping back into New York publishing, which would soon define him. Through Robert, George had seen a marriage that valued a woman's intellectual autonomy, and while Dorothy was bright and fun, not to mention rich, he envied men with wives who made headlines beyond society pages. "While I was out West I worked on a paper," he recalled later, "took some courses at the University of California, and generally found plenty to keep myself busy. Still I had not definitely decided whether I wanted to go into the publishing business. But when the business was left without a head because of death of my father and brother I came to New York. It was my own inclination and circumstances that decided me. And generally that is the way most things are settled."

While the Major appreciated George's dutiful return to the firm, he hesitated to hand over the reins of the family business to a brash and cocky college dropout, regardless of George's West Coast achievements, and sought harder evidence of George's capabilities. As George familiarized himself with a complicated business, the Major monitored him closely, assigning tasks as deemed appropriate and hinting that with proven diligence, he might earn a stint in the London office and see how they did things there.

Soon, the family welcomed son number two, George Palmer Putnam III, lovingly nicknamed Junie for "Junior," a nickname Dorothy's brother shared. When the crayon heiress felt that a bigger house was needed and asked her parents for the money, George couldn't be more pleased. They needed a place to entertain.

Things were going swimmingly at the office too, and with his first notable professional challenge set by the Major, George was dispatched to Europe with a mission: persuade Ignacy Jan Paderewski, the world-famous pianist and then Polish prime minister, to write a book for their firm. Though he didn't secure Paderewski's commitment, George forged invaluable contacts and secured writing opportunities. Throughout their European trip, which started in Paris and ended in Poland, Dorothy was again far more than just a travel companion. As George's literary right hand, she transcribed his notes and immersed herself in his desire to be taken seriously in the literary world. Their teamwork paid off when George's article on Poland graced the front page of the *New-York Tribune*, a fine upgrade from *The Bend Bulletin*.

By 1924, just as once hoped at the dinner table, the ascent of Dorothy and George in literary circles was unmistakable. Yet after his European sojourn, George decided to replace Dorothy as his de facto secretary with a real secretary, an attractive brunette named Josephine "Jo" Berger. At the office, rumors swirled about the nature of their initial relationship. Though never publicly confirmed, recorded evidence points to an early office romance that, following Jo's marriage, transformed into a steadfast friendship. George, ever loyal to those close to him, ensured she was generously compensated for her continued support. Meanwhile, as George and Dorothy's shared life was touted in the society pages, Dorothy's role in his professional life receded.

In Rye, after tapping into Dorothy's inheritance once more, the young couple built a sixteen-room Spanish-style pink stucco mansion. Dorothy, asserting some independence, employed her own chauffeur. Yet beneath the luxuriant surface, there bubbled quiet tensions and silent spite. In that era, conjugal sex was not merely a marital expectation but a legal obligation; failure to comply could even serve as grounds for divorce. Dorothy's diary entries from this period subtly reveal their emotional chasm and George's indifferent yet lawful demands in the bedroom. Her writings also expose a profound loneliness, exacerbated by George's frequent absences. Even though the couple lived in the suburbs of New York, George often chose to stay overnight in Manhattan hotels, citing business demands that stretched late into the evening or began unusually early. His trips to London, necessitating lengthy voyages by ship, further deepened Dorothy's sense of isolation.

It wasn't long before the maverick became the driving force behind G. P. Putnam's Sons' surprise bestsellers, and with a sharp eye for what was in vogue, he reinvigorated the company's image. He drew in fresh, modern authors and rubbed shoulders with the rest of the crème de la crème. While sipping cocktails with like-minded buddies during Prohibition, George expressed his unfiltered opinions about the Major: He compared his uncle's antiquated thinking to the Statue of Liberty's tarnished green. While the rush was on for Great War stories, the old Major stubbornly clung to the Civil War era, even regrettably passing up the profitable translation rights for *All Quiet on the Western Front*. When speaking to potential authors, George confidently asserted that *he* was the man with the golden touch at the firm, with a growing list to prove it.

Books that outperformed those signed by his uncle were not merely commercial triumphs but personal victories. With each announcement of a new bestseller, he began to view himself as the sole possible successor to the venerable Putnam legacy. This first half of the Roaring Twenties saw George develop a new fondness for publishing adventure literature, which he pursued through blatant social climbing and grand soirees in Rye, all funded by Dorothy's wealth. On any given evening, ordinary guests might mingle with the day's remarkable figures, such as North Pole explorer Admiral Peary or Carl Akeley, the pioneering taxidermist behind the majestic ape displays at natural history museums. In one corner, you might find the playboy Danish explorer Knud Rasmussen nursing a drink while Roy Chapman Andrews—the janitor turned adventurer, often cited as the inspiration for Indiana Jones—held court from the sofa. Could that be Howard Carter, who unveiled Tutankhamun's tomb in 1922, discussing his find near the grand piano? A glittering lot.

One night, a wild idea would take root in George's mind: to transform his spirited eleven-year-old son, David, into a celebrity explorer. He would send the little devil exploring, just like his adult clients. And get a book out of the popular, if lousy, student. Teach his worried teachers a lesson or two.

While most people dismiss the fleeting whims of 4:00 a.m. brain waves by daylight, George was the type to seize even the wildest notions. David Binney Putnam's rise to extraordinary fame began in 1925, when, on a chilly February day, thirty-eight sailors and eighteen scientists boarded a steam yacht from Brooklyn led by Bronx Zoo director William Beebe, one of G. P. Putnam's Sons' bestselling authors signed by George. Using the largest vessel ever built for oceanic exploration, Beebe and his team would start off on their groundbreaking Arcturus Expedition, heading from New York to the Galápagos Islands and south to a drifting oceanic realm that had puzzled voyagers and scientists for centuries: the Sargasso Sea, the only sea without a land boundary and one whose mysterious deep waters had never been explored for new animal life. Several of the forward cabins had been transformed into an oceanic land with cages and tanks for the live aquatic creatures they hoped to bring back. The deck held cables three miles long, ready to be sent down into equatorial waters. Beebe had even outfitted a section of the *Arcturus* with a novel glass bottom, an unprecedented feature for expeditions. He had also introduced the bathysphere, a compact submarine designed for deep-sea observation. The skipper remarked, "This is the queerest equipped vessel that has ever set off from a New York port."

George's eleven-year-old son, David, and his wife, Dorothy, joined the expedition on March 23. They had traveled from Rye to Panama just so that David could experience the Galápagos. With a youngster aboard, the adventure of the *Arcturus* and its leader, Beebe, the kind of person people spoke about in that knowing, reverent way, became compelling enough to attract frequent press coverage. However, the daily reports on the young sixth-grade cabin boy, David Binney Putnam, soon captured the hearts of young readers and their parents. To a bewildered Beebe, George Palmer

Putnam justified the accompanying juvenile's narrative as serving a dual purpose: it would disrupt the publishing status quo and act as a prelude to Beebe's anticipated adult exploration narrative in the months to come. Beebe laughed and was thrilled by the promotional potential. Go ahead, George. Whatever sold more of his books!

While some in the publishing industry dismissed the bold move as mere nepotism, others, including thirty-one-year-old Harold McCracken—a youthful, good-natured explorer and recent addition to George's firm—recognized it as genius. Their alliance had been sealed at New York's storied Explorers Club over Manhattans, with George offering the self-funded explorer a cushy position. On McCracken's first day, George set the tone with a clear mandate: "What I want to publish are books with original ideas. You find them. I don't care how badly the manuscripts are written. I can hire plenty of Phi Beta Kappas at a nickel a dozen who know where to put all the periods and commas, but don't have an original idea in their head."

McCracken's first big assignment was to make George's son a star, and by golly, he did. By September, McCracken had placed excerpts of David's book (his voice brightened by ghostwriters) in youth magazines like *St. Nicholas* and the more important *Boys' Life*, captivating readers with the notion that it was authored entirely by a kid. By the all-important Christmas season of 1925, *David Goes Voyaging* had become a sensation, topping the children's book charts and ranking fourth on the adult bestseller lists. "People are reading the hell out of this stuff!" George exclaimed to McCracken. The overwhelming success quickly led to the creation of an exciting sequel, *David Goes to Greenland*, which managed to outsell its predecessor with 28,500 copies. The lousy student David Binney Putnam had become a phenomenon.

Given the stupefying success, why stop at one boy star? At George's directive, McCracken regularly supplied him with newspaper clippings about adventurous boys and suggested privileged others whose parents could become valuable contacts if their kids were given a whiff of fame. Thirteen "jaw-dropping, all-true" stories, handpicked by George and McCracken, soon captured global attention, and the formulaic Boys' Books by Boys series became a highly profitable mill for the family firm.

Next up after George's son was thirteen-year-old Deric Nusbaum, stepson of Jesse Nusbaum, the respected superintendent of Colorado's Mesa Verde National Park. His "self-authored" book, *Deric in Mesa Verde*, focused on the cliff dwellings and interactions with the nearby Pueblo tribe. Following him, sixteen-year-old Henry Bradford Washburn, from the Groton School in Massachusetts, recounted his adventures in *Among the Alps with Bradford*. Like all the young men picked, Washburn had a cosseted upbringing of private schools and house servants, but unlike the others, his book was entirely his own work. Even George had to concede the boy clearly had writing talent. That boy might go places long after he left the Putnam limelight.

The "boy explorers" who landed on George Palmer Putnam's growing roster went on increasingly harrowing quests to drum up publicity for possible bestsellers. One of the most dangerous adventures was undertaken by sixteen-year-old Augusto Flores, who was among a group of five brave Argentine teenagers trying to reach New York to win a locally offered prize of twenty-five thousand pesos. The contest went awry when two of the group died—one from a flood in Bolivia, the other from a snakebite in Ecuador. Two others fell ill and withdrew, but Augusto Flores carried on, facing relentless storms and wearing out six pairs of shoes as he covered forty miles a day—aside from the few days he was held back during an unjust arrest in Bolivia. He crossed alligator-infested rivers and one time faced Nicaraguan rebels.

When George received word from McCracken that Flores, the last trekker standing, had reached Texas, he was wild with excitement. "Think of the foreign sales too!" he exclaimed. George promptly secured a deal for Flores to complete the remaining seventeen hundred miles to New York on foot under the banner of G. P. Putnam's Sons, while McCracken orchestrated a sweeping publicity campaign to herald Flores's arrival. Capitalizing on his friendship with Jimmy Walker, New York's charismatic and notoriously hard-drinking mayor, George obtained a proclamation—a simpler alternative to a ticker-tape parade, yet a perfect pretext for extensive press coverage. Soon, newspapers nationwide were featuring photos of Walker welcoming the young adventurer at city hall.

Once in New York, an exhausted, threadbare Flores recounted his adventure to a bilingual ghostwriter, and the resulting book, *My Hike: Buenos Aires to New York*, quickly climbed the bestseller lists, published not just in English but also in Spanish and Portuguese. George and McCracken toasted in the office. Where could they find a story to top that? They could orchestrate danger and let the newest kids get the thrills of a lifetime.

The relentless quest for profits often overshadowed the safety of these youthful adventurers. A fifteen-year-old cabin boy, "the author," got stuck in ice on a Siberian fur-trapping boat and needed an airlift rescue (during which a pilot died). One ten-year-old boy was introduced to West Indies Vodou practices by an Episcopalian priest, Reverend Henry S. Whitehead, who, at the time of these events, was archdeacon of the Virgin Islands. Whitehead was an unvetted supernaturalist who played a significant role in introducing Vodou into popular American culture. He was later suspected of pedophilia and was a close friend of weird-fiction writer H. P. Lovecraft. Another young author under contract with Putnam climbed an unexplored Alaskan volcano and was nearly burned when it erupted; two other boys almost drowned after being trapped by a blue whale. All of this was a stark testament to the perilous nature of the adventures George endorsed—episodes of bravery and danger intermingled with unchecked ambition and peril.

One of George Palmer Putnam's longest-lived boy explorers, a kid named Robert "Dick" Douglas Jr., survived an extraordinarily age-inappropriate adventure to Africa that resulted in a coauthored bestseller called *Three Boy Scouts in Africa*. About seventy-five years later, the boy explorer was ninety years old and still sharp, recalling in detail in his self-published memoir the liability waiver his parents signed that absolved George and his firm of responsibility should young Dick be killed by lions, locals, snakes, or a transport accident. With considerable charm, George had placated Mom and Dad's fears, convincing them the journey would be a lifetime opportunity that could secure the family's future. And, in many ways, it did.

Dick Douglas's moment in the spotlight began when he won a contest that was advertised in *Boys' Life* as offering three "all-American" Scouts an unprecedented African adventure guided by the renowned explorers Martin and Osa Johnson, a married couple whose popular adventure books were already on George's list. George, master of publicity, saw an opportunity to boost sales even further by targeting the era's 625,000 American Scouts. Railey, emphasizing the importance of Southern representation, pushed for a third participant: Douglas—the great-grandson of Stephen A. Douglas, whose 1860 presidential bid and famous debates with Abraham Lincoln were etched into the annals of history.

Young Dick Douglas, just as Railey had suggested, was a promotional jackpot. The resulting book "by" the three lucky kids swiftly gained traction. Within a year, 125,000 copies were sold out of an eventual print run of 400,000, and *Three Boy Scouts in Africa* was translated into seven languages. Though an impressive feat, it is alarming to modern sensibilities: its "compelling" narrative spotlights the Scouts' degrading interactions with the underpaid Maasai people who were hired to cater to the winning boys' needs and used for racist comic relief in the book. In an equally appalling move that stirred controversy even back then, the boys strayed from the Scout code, which advocates against harming animals for trivial reasons. Yet each boy was required to kill a lion. George, sensing the promotional value, had encouraged this deviation, recognizing that many Americans were turned on by the ugly world of big-game hunting.

While Americans largely viewed the shockingly bigoted narrative as great fun, it was not received so lightly abroad; the French publication *Revue des lectures* sharply criticized it, stating, "These young Americans neither prayed nor hesitated to mock their black servants' beliefs." However, in the US of the time—deeply influenced by eugenics and mired in the darkest history of the Jim Crow era—the boys were celebrated as noble representatives of America's promising future.

George Palmer Putnam's uncanny ability to spot up-and-coming trends was indisputable, especially as his strategic marketing tapped into the public's growing infatuation with aviation with an ease that others envied.

After World War I, civilian interest in aviation soared. Daredevil pilots performing at air shows and barnstorming events became the era's celebrities, and rapid technological advances suggested thrilling possibilities for transportation and communication. By 1926, aviation was firmly planted in the public's imagination, largely due to Putnam.

Paramount Pictures' *Wings*, featuring Clara Bow, then universally known as "the It Girl," and two actors playing World War I aviators, was a silent-film sensation. With an ensemble cast of over three hundred pilots and an unprecedented $2 million budget, the film clinched the inaugural Academy Award for Best Picture, and a play adaptation enjoyed a successful Broadway run.

Wings' release resonated with a nation still processing the Great War, hungry for tales of bravery and national pride, and it marked a pivotal moment in American film history. George Palmer Putnam's contribution to this cultural shift was foundational and strategic. He marketed the surprisingly loose material from John Monk Saunders, an unstable alcoholic but gifted writer in his mix who would later marry Fay Wray, the famed actress known for her role in *King Kong*. The bits and pieces from a brilliant, if troubled, man were expertly rewritten into the screenplay for *Wings* by Hope Loring and Louis D. Lighton. After the silent film's resounding success, Putnam further capitalized on its popularity by commissioning Saunders to create a novelization of the film. This innovative move not only launched the film-to-book industry but also capitalized on the movie's acclaim to further solidify his family firm's financial success.

But just when it seemed like nothing could top *Wings*, along came 1927, and with it, Charles Lindbergh, whose sensational feat left the remarkable success of *Wings* looking positively pedestrian by comparison. The previously obscure Midwestern airmail pilot was thrust into the limelight following a 1926 newsreel that broadcast the unclaimed $25,000 Orteig Prize for the first nonstop solo flight from New York to Paris. The prize, established by Raymond Orteig in 1919 to further aviation and strengthen Franco-American ties, was reserved for aviators from Allied countries, excluding

Germans. Captivated by the challenge, Lindbergh began to strategize, laying the groundwork for what would become a historic flight.

Though just twenty-four, Lindbergh was no rookie. He'd trained at the Nebraska Aircraft Corporation, flown daredevil stunts, and handled airmail between Chicago and St. Louis. But bagging the Orteig Prize required more than skill; it called for cash. After Lindbergh was turned down by Wall Street, St. Louis backers stepped in, funding the construction of the *Spirit of St. Louis* by Ryan Airlines. Lindbergh tested his new aircraft in St. Louis before taking off from Long Island, New York. Though the press first mocked him as "the Flying Fool," Lindbergh's rugged looks and relentless drive quickly turned derision into adoration.

In 1927, as Lindbergh's bold endeavor captured the nation's imagination, Amelia Earhart found herself enthralled by his daring spirit and unshakable courage. She eagerly followed his exploits, pinning his handsome, deified face—clipped from a newspaper—to her wall. Meanwhile, in Rye, New York, George pondered the fortunes awaiting the lucky individual who would land Lindbergh's story for a lucrative book deal.

Early in the morning on May 20, Roosevelt Field on Long Island was dark and damp. As preparations for the flight progressed, a mechanic inquired if Lindbergh planned to fly with only five sandwiches and two canteens of water. Lindbergh's answer was clear: "If I get to Paris, I won't need them anymore, and if I don't, I won't need them either." Furthermore, Lindbergh had chosen to fly without a radio, given its weight and limited utility over the Atlantic. Lindbergh's flight was singular; he was setting out alone on a transatlantic flight longer than any before it.

Just before 8:00 a.m., the *Spirit of St. Louis* took off with 2,750 pounds of fuel. Anticipation gripped those watching as it ascended and vanished into the clouds.

The headlines said it all: THE BIGGEST STORY OF A DECADE. Radios and newspapers focused on the fearless young pilot. The flight was emblematic of American individualism and the nation's belief in pushing boundaries.

Meanwhile, George's mind was racing as he fixated on the idea of being the first to tell Lindbergh's story. *The New York Times* had already offered Lindbergh $60,000 for his story, and George hoped to sway Lindbergh toward a book deal with the help of his main contact there. George's foresight and risk-taking had positioned him as a groundbreaking figure in the publishing world, and Lindbergh's flight presented yet another opportunity to redefine the industry.

Immediately after Lindbergh's electrifying and historic departure from New York, George Palmer Putnam wasted no time. He tapped into his significant connection at *The New York Times*, striding purposefully from his office on West Forty-Fifth Street to Times Square to confer directly with features editor Fred Birchall. With Birchall's cooperation secured, Putnam swiftly arranged for a cable to be sent from the *Times*' New York office to its Paris counterpart, ensuring a crucial meeting with Lindbergh upon his landing. Armed with an initial offer of $60,000 in 1927, equivalent to just over $1 million today, Putnam decisively set the stage for a rapid book deal, seizing the aviator's story for a global audience and solidifying his reputation as a publishing trailblazer.

The nation closely followed Charles Lindbergh as he ventured alone across the Atlantic. Fourteen hours in, his plane a mere dot over the ocean without radio communication, the public braced for troubling news. Despite their fears, people across America held on to hope, millions picturing the young aviator navigating through the hypnotic blur of sky and sea as exhaustion began to take its toll.

At 7:15 p.m. on May 20, the Flying Fool was sighted soaring above St. John's, Newfoundland. Lindbergh was still alive but deeply fatigued, his overtaxed mind conjuring hallucinations of ghosts. In a desperate bid to maintain his focus, he slapped himself awake before opening the cockpit window to the bracing cold, determined to continue his perilous journey through the dreary skies. At 10:22 p.m. on May 21, Lindy landed in the Parisian suburb of Le Bourget after thirty-three and a half hours of flight. He had no idea if anyone would greet him, but one hundred thousand did. The euphoria of it all! When he was spotted, the crowd howled joyfully, screaming his name. People pulled at his helmet and his flight suit and terrified him. "As soon as I touched down, a human sea swept toward me. I saw a danger of killing people with my propeller, and I quickly cut it off," he recalled.

The interior of the *Spirit of St. Louis* was torn apart by souvenir seekers before it could be secured. Lindbergh went to the American embassy for the night. The following day, France roared again when he stepped out onto the balcony, perhaps the most famous living person on Earth; he hadn't even processed the information after calling his mother in Detroit.

Miraculously, Charles Lindbergh received Birchall's speculative offer via telegram at the Paris branch of *The New York Times*; the aviator was indeed in need of funds, with less than $1,500 of the initial $15,000 he had raised in America remaining, and he was eager to repay his backers. Overjoyed, George began searching for a ghostwriter almost as soon as he hung up, determined to share the story with the world as swiftly as possible. Meanwhile, he summoned his wife from Rye to Manhattan with an eager phone call, exclaiming, "Come on over!" The streets echoed with honking horns and hearty embraces. As excitement bubbled up throughout the city, envy percolated throughout New York's publishing circles. It was thought that Lindbergh had accepted George's offer, and even before all the details of Lindbergh's travels were finalized, plans for a book were taking shape. Anyone with a piece of Lindbergh was minting money, and every nuance was fastidiously arranged; by a twist of fate, the chosen ghostwriter, an American journalist, had shared the ship journey home with Lindbergh. This writer was poised to chronicle Lindbergh's adventures in a forthcoming autobiography that bore the working title *His Own Story*. The epochal flight had sent Charles Lindbergh into the stratosphere, and he returned to an ecstatic welcome in the United States. Millions of Americans were glued to their radios, listening to NBC's live broadcast of Lindbergh's conversation with the president at 11:30 a.m. The fervor spilled over into New York City, where over one hundred thousand people watched the ticker-tape parade on Broadway and three hundred thousand gathered in Central Park. In total, more than four million New Yorkers thronged the streets to celebrate. The Lindy Hop filled dance floors across the nation in Lindbergh's honor. Recognizing his achievement, *Time* magazine named him its first "Man of the Year," and a commemorative airmail stamp featuring his portrait was quickly issued.

J. Carlisle MacDonald, the ghostwriter, drew from his talks with Lindbergh aboard the USS *Memphis* and in Paris, settling into George's Rye estate to write. But Lindbergh, ever the stickler for accuracy, swiftly rejected the early drafts. They were littered with mistakes and lacked his distinct voice and flair. Faced with an eager readership behind one hundred thousand preorders, George, typically a man who needed to ask for nothing, found himself pleading with Lindbergh for a solution. Uncompromising, Lindbergh resolved to take over, vowing to rewrite the story himself to ensure that it truly reflected his experiences. After a grueling parade schedule, Lindbergh finally had a chance to retreat from the public eye.

The task ahead was no less daunting: he had three weeks to refine MacDonald's rough draft into a polished manuscript. His writing sanctuary, however, was nothing short of luxurious. Lindbergh settled into Falaise, a neomedieval mansion in Sands Point, Long Island. Owned by Harry and Carol Guggenheim—Harry hailed from a line of mining magnates and harbored a deep passion for aviation—the estate spanned ninety private acres, providing Lindbergh with luxury and privacy.

George's anxiety grew with each passing day, especially given the rapid turnaround he had promised buyers. Inspired by Lindbergh's habit of treating his aircraft as a collaborative partner in his journey, George suggested changing the title to *"WE"*—italicized and set in quotation marks. "I didn't realize the scope of this undertaking," Lindbergh later admitted. After immersing himself in the project, he found himself spending fourteen-hour days transcribing his thoughts onto yellow legal pads. George marveled at Lindbergh's almost mechanical manner in crafting the narrative about his iconic flight, stretching it to forty-five thousand words as the contract required. Though MacDonald might have felt overshadowed, his substantial $10,000 kill fee likely offered some consolation.

Pedal to the metal, in three weeks, Lindbergh delivered work that was unmistakably direct yet somewhat restrained. Given the flier's snowballing commitments, George was grateful for any manuscript in his hands and expedited it through Knickerbocker Press, his family-run imprint, adding in a sappy foreword by the American ambassador to France, Myron T. Herrick, that likened Lindbergh to legendary figures such as Joan of Arc, Lafayette, and the young biblical David. And though some rivals had their hopes pinned on that supercilious George Palmer Putnam's stumble, the outcome defied them. *"WE"* was another tour de force for the executive, with sales of 650,000 copies in its inaugural year alone.

George later recounted handing Lindbergh his first eye-wateringly large royalty check—$100,000, just half of what was to come and just under $2 million in today's dollars: "I couldn't get the time of day out of him until I came around with his first royalty check. It was for an even $100,000. This will open him, I told myself. I was partially right too. He glanced at the check, smiled briefly, and commented, 'On that basis, you can come around more often.'" Such a coup not only rocketed George to new heights in the publishing realm but also earned him the nickname Kingmaker among some of his friends and rivals. A bespectacled man with the Midas touch, capable of turning narratives into gold.

Reinvigorated, Lindbergh again commandeered the *Spirit of St. Louis* in a flying project this time lavishly bankrolled by Harry Guggenheim. Over the next three months, the "Lone Eagle," as he was now dubbed, soared across eighty-two cities in all forty-eight states, meeting the cheers of thirty million Americans. After the culmination of his journey at Bolling Field, his iconic aircraft was bequeathed to the Smithsonian and is now in the collection of the National Air and Space Museum. A head-spinning 25 percent of Americans caught a fleeting sight of Lindbergh during his 1927 odyssey, thrusting him from relative anonymity into unparalleled fame. This trek didn't merely serve to elevate Lindbergh; it supercharged a budding aviation sector, marking the advent of the golden age of air travel.

"People set down their glasses in country clubs and speakeasies and thought of their old best dreams," F. Scott Fitzgerald wrote in a 1931 essay,

"Echoes of the Jazz Age," reflecting back on the dazzling, just-bygone era. "Maybe there was a way out by flying, maybe our restless blood could find frontiers in the illimitable air."

Lindbergh, now a lionized author under Putnam and a globally recognized pilot, visited Dayton, Ohio, on his eighty-two-city tour, which now held particular significance. His earlier meeting with aviation icon Orville Wright at the Brevoort Hotel had been brief, overshadowed by the excitement and fuss surrounding his receipt of the Orteig Prize. However, upon touching down in Dayton, the immense legacy of the Wright brothers—whose flight twenty-four years earlier covered 852 feet in fifty-nine seconds—loomed large. The Wrights had not only pioneered human flight; they had catalyzed an entire industry. To Lindbergh, they epitomized the origins of all human flight, a pursuit that had become almost sacred to him and a beacon of human innovation. His stop in Dayton transcended a mere visit; it was a heartfelt tribute. In a solemn gesture, Lindbergh laid a wreath at Wilbur Wright's tomb, deeply aware of the intertwined legacies: the pioneering spirit of the Wrights and the audacity of his own transatlantic journey.

The twentieth century marked a time of transformation, with aviation reshaping travel and the publishing landscape undergoing its own evolution. In the previous century, established, genteel firms like G. P. Putnam's Sons, Henry Holt, Macmillan, and Doubleday dominated the field. Yet these "venerable" houses were not free from the prejudices of the period, including socially sanctioned antisemitism. Jewish entrepreneurs such as Alfred A. Knopf, Richard L. Simon, and M. Lincoln Schuster, facing barriers simply due to their ethnicity, pioneered new avenues and redefined the publishing industry with their innovative ideas and approaches. Meanwhile, George Palmer Putnam worked within his family institution to not so quietly lead a revolution of his own. Guided by the success of Lindbergh's book and a dedication to his family's legacy, Putnam sought innovative ways to marry the venerable with the modern in the art of publishing.

George, that irrepressible idea addict who could never let a single shiny stone rest in peace, lunged into new Jazz Age territories with the fervor of a gold rush prospector. He plunged into the nightlife too, throwing his chips into a high-stakes game with an upscale nightclub not far from the luminary Stork Club. And, yes, to achieve this, he once again dipped—dove!—into Dorothy's well-lined coffers, a salaried man making unsalaried moves, thus etching his name into the throbbing, pulsating social heartbeat of New York City.

On many nights, George stayed away from Rye, preferring to sleep in the Putnams' pied-à-terre, an extended hotel rental in New York. During the same period, Dorothy busied herself with plans for her emotional escape—a South American adventure set for the New Year, alongside her youngest son, Junie, and her mother-in-law, Frances. As her departure date approached, friends from high society popped in to bid her farewell. Among the visitors was someone's young friend, a striking blond Chicago debutante, Annie Laurie Jaques, who brought along her charismatic Yale boyfriend, George Weymouth. At a towering six foot one, with rich-brown hair and mineral-blue eyes, the twenty-two-year-old Weymouth was a sexy addition to the party. To Dorothy's giddy surprise, there was an unexpected and forbidden spark with this younger George—it *felt* like something. The love-starved heiress in a well-rotted marriage was sure that he was flirting with her, but her initial reaction was self-reproach—what drew her, a mature woman, to a man almost twenty years her junior? His playful talent for walking on his hands captivated her, evoking in Dorothy the lightness she deeply yearned for.

During their first conversation, charged with a bewildering chemistry, she learned that he hailed from Narberth, part of the prestigious Philadelphia Main Line. A reversal of fortunes had forced him to attend public school, but his tenacity earned him a scholarship to Yale. Despite being in a relationship, the boyish Weymouth felt compelled to revisit Dorothy alone—a surprise, to say the least. Dorothy's maturity and sophistication starkly contrasted with the youthful exuberance of the college-aged women he usually dated.

During her three-month sojourn in South America, Dorothy's thoughts constantly drifted—not to her increasingly estranged husband but to the young man with an enchanting smile and athletic build. Upon returning to Rye, she was surprised to discover that George had not only met her recent fascination at a dinner party but also sought Weymouth's assistance for their oldest son, David. With his academic performance waning in the wake of his adventures and book promotions, David could use a bright Yalie's guidance. George had even invited Weymouth to live at their Westchester estate so that he could tutor David and prep him for his latest offering as a "gifted" young writer—a boy's-eye view of an upcoming Arctic expedition to the remote Baffin Land (now Baffin Island). George was already publicizing this voyage, hinting at an ensuing book, *David Goes to Baffin Land*. However, he discreetly omitted mentioning to the press that while the book might reflect the guileless tone of a young adventurer, the skilled hand shaping the narrative would be George Weymouth's. Before starting this dual literary and exploratory endeavor in June, Weymouth's primary task was to bolster David's scholastic performance.

Before the Baffin Land departure, while Dorothy's husband was often away on short corporate trips to New York and Washington, she and her young paramour grew closer, their early flirtations escalating into what could only be described as a full-blown kissathon. By May 19, 1927, the rainy night before Lindbergh's historic flight, the collegian, fresh from his fraternity initiations, sat before the fire and tenderly touched the strands of gray in the heiress's hair. That night, they consummated their affair, celebrating with a rare bottle of 1859 wine, unfettered fun, and passion. Dorothy later chronicled and underlined their intimate encounter in her diary: "An evening never to be forgotten—music—wine—content!"

When the summer day came that Weymouth, young David, and Dorothy's husband headed off way up north to Baffin Land, she was "allowed" to join the boys as far as Brigus, Newfoundland, but was expected to return after that, since there was a strong superstition about having women on a ship too long. She would be alone but tended to by servants, including Harold, the Putnams' chauffeur, whose wage was paid out of Dorothy's trust fund. One day at the tail end of June in the empty estate, Dorothy was putting away George's summer clothes when she found an incriminating letter tucked into one of his pockets; it was from the very enamored woman with whom he was then having an affair. Dorothy unfolded the letter from George's jacket pocket, each word striking like a cold slap. The elegant, looping script of another woman's words mocked her, and a cold realization crept in—her secret liaisons were mirrored in George's hidden life. This was not someone like a convenient secretary, taking "dictation" behind a closed door, but, rather, a mysterious lady she had never heard of. There was cocktail talk, and Dorothy knew the places her husband, a creature of habit, liked, such as the speakeasy Jack and Charlie's (later known as the 21 Club). Dorothy realized she would eventually have to address this adultery, but even if she did not, she had ammunition up her sleeve, and a terrible conversation and possible row over her indiscretion could be neutered with a counter offense. The very next day, she bought a snappy Dodge roadster as shopping therapy—in her words, "an antagonism against George."

Given the emotional distance between George and Dorothy (who viewed intimacy with him as more of a duty than a pleasure), George might have sought relief elsewhere. As a connected Times Square publishing circle member, he could have frequented Polly Adler's discreet, upscale roving brothel, which reportedly hosted many of George's acquaintances. Adler's biographer even speculates that Franklin D. Roosevelt, a family acquaintance of the Putnams, may have visited during marital strain. Such were the hidden secrets beneath the veneer of their seemingly ordinary lives.

The Jazz Age peaked in 1927 and 1928, and people sought release from existential pain through alcohol, sex, and laughter.

Two

SATURDAY'S CHILD

In 1897, on the cusp of the twentieth century and six years before the Wright brothers' maiden flight, Amelia Earhart was born on a stormy night in Atchison, Kansas—a prospering river town about fifty miles northwest of Kansas City. The rain lashed against the family's sprawling seven-bedroom house perched on the bluffs of the Missouri, as if nature itself was heralding the arrival of a girl destined to soar above it all. Owned by her affluent grandfather, Judge Alfred Otis, since 1861, the brick-and-clapboard house featured a glass-enclosed walkway leading to an elegant round dining room with multicolored glass windows, a distinctive feature in Atchison. Outside Amelia's bedroom window, sugar maples and lindens framed scenic views of the property, which was enclosed by a quaint picket fence. In the spring, the air was scented with the sweet fragrance of lilacs in bloom.

The birth of Amelia Mary Earhart, bearing the names of both her silvered grandmothers, represented renewed hope for her mother, Amy Otis Earhart. The previous year, at twenty-three, Amy had suffered the heart-wrenching loss of an infant girl, who remained nameless and was carried away as swiftly as she came, following a Kansas City streetcar accident during pregnancy. Edwin Earhart, Amelia's father, a fledgling lawyer with roots in a Lutheran ministry rather than in wealth, had no cushion of affluence to soften life's blows. It was against this backdrop of loss and longing that Amy returned from Kansas City to the protective fold of her parents' stately home in Atchison to give birth.

Two and a half years after Amelia's birth, the Earhart family welcomed another daughter, Grace Muriel, known as Muriel. The newborn's arrival brought an intensified mixture of joy and responsibility to the young parents. Seeking to lessen the stress of having two young kids at home, as well as to ease the sorrow of Amelia's namesake, who had recently lost an adult son, the three-year-old was sent to cheer up her grandmother. In the lively presence of her granddaughter, Grandma Amelia found solace that neither her garden nor her church attendance could provide. Meanwhile, Atchison's secure and familiar environment presented little Amelia with a world rife with exploration and discovery. And in Atchison, the Otis name commanded respect.

Amelia's grandfather embodied the nineteenth century's pioneering American spirit. A University of Missouri alumnus, he cofounded the thriving white-shoe law firm Otis & Glick, and the judge's local influence remained strong. Atchison blossomed with grand residences after the Atchison and Topeka Railroad Company's lines arrived in 1860. Even after retiring from the bench in 1880, the judge's civic engagement was apparent; he led the Atchison Savings Bank and had significant sway in the Episcopal Church. A savvy investor, he had assets that included several town buildings. The grand home he secured for his wife, Amelia Harres, a descendant of a steady and upright Pennsylvania Quaker lineage, was among the finest in Atchison.

Yet for all the grandeur and heritage, the Otis and Earhart homes were not strangers to hidden strains. Before the birth of her daughter Amelia, a young Amy found herself in an emotional tug-of-war between her conservative parents and the man she deeply loved. Judge Otis had already attempted to stop Edwin Earhart from marrying his daughter a few years prior, after the two met at Amy's society debut. Amy couldn't understand the resentment. Edwin had worked hard to achieve his status as a lawyer, overcoming obstacles and financing his education through odd jobs. His drive was evident; at age eighteen, he was the youngest to graduate from

Thiel College, where he enrolled at age fourteen. To Amy, this was impressive. But Judge Otis saw things differently, disapproving of Edwin's Lutheran faith and relative lack of wealth and status, with a position in the railroad sector that was viewed as beneath the family's standards.

The judge tested Edwin's resolve, setting financial goals for his son-in-law. The situation worsened when he learned that Edwin had pawned some law books, a precious gift from the judge himself. This was no minor faux pas; it was an affront, a black mark splattered across Edwin's already wobbly reputation in the high court of the Otis household.

In the comfort of her grandparents' fine Atchison home, Amelia was shielded from family tensions and low bank accounts in Kansas City. Her effervescence brought joy, especially during her grandmother's low periods. The nice-size gardens and stables were Amelia's playground, with horses being her favorite. However, the household relied on staff: a German housemaid, a white yard worker, and a Black cook who earned just one dollar a week. Weekends and holidays served as happy reunions for the Earhart siblings, separated by just over fifty miles. As daughters of a railroad lawyer, they enjoyed complimentary train trips, turning each journey into a swift and luxurious outing. Amelia eagerly anticipated visits from her uncle Mark. An adventurer in his own right, Mark Otis had been part of the turn-of-the-century Baldwin–Ziegler expedition to stake the American flag at the North Pole—a journey marked by the hunting of sixty-two walruses and thirty-two polar bears. His polar bear rug and tales of distant escapades left young Amelia spellbound, dreaming of far-off lands she might explore if she ever left Kansas.

The girl everyone in town called Millie (occasionally "Meelie") was, as each year passed, still an active, opinionated, and enthusiastic kid in love with adventure and life—a thin, sprightly tomboy, she could climb to the top branches to pick the ripest cherries.

Amelia was the unofficial leader of a group of local kids who congregated by a playhouse down over the bluff east of the Otis house. Her little sister and shadow, Muriel, was nicknamed Pidge because of her never-ending habit of singing "Sleep Little Pigeon," a Eugene Field lullaby. "Amelia was always the leader; I was always a follower," Muriel remembered. "We used to get rough, and she could get as rough as we did," Balie Waggener, one of the boys who never left their hometown, recounted in his later years. The ladies of Atchison recalled that Amelia was a mentor who taught younger girls how to roller-skate and ride a bike.

Amelia, Muriel much later recollected, was given a beautiful black cocker spaniel in Kansas City when she was about eleven. "His name was Mark Anthony, and mine was Cleopatra from the same litter. Amelia and I loved them dearly, but sadly, Amelia had to give Mark up, as she was scheduled to spend the winter term with Grandmother in Atchison, and there was no room for voracious puppies in the dignified Otis home."

In 1910, after a minor legal windfall of about a hundred dollars, Edwin chose to treat his beloved children to a memorable summer weekend. His father-in-law, the stern judge, felt the funds should cover bills and was taken aback to learn that Edwin had spent it all at the 1904 St. Louis World's Fair. But for Amelia, the fair was a realm of wonder: Sioux Indians performing bareback equestrianism, an elephant ride, and turns around the Ferris wheel. The only damper on her enthusiasm was being denied a ride on the roller coaster. Not accepting this dreadful fate, Amelia recruited her four-year-old sister to help her build a miniature roller coaster in the backyard of their parents' modest Kansas City house. Two young neighbors, Freddie and Ralphie, and Amelia's uncle Carl all helped. Two small girls propped loose boards against a six-foot shed across from their parents' house. The boards and the wooden wheels were greased with fresh lard and butter from their mother. Amelia raced down the fourteen-foot slide first, in a wooden crate with wheels from a baby buggy. Her homemade contraption was too steep, and she fell and bumped her head. With a bruised lip, she exclaimed, "Pidge! This is just like flying!"

When Amy heard the outside clamor, she stopped the event, but Uncle Carl (nicknamed "Uncle Nicey" by his nieces) promptly fashioned a miniature foot-powered merry-go-round to quell the girls' disappointment.

Amelia soon concocted an aerial tramway stretching from her front porch to Ralphie's bedroom window. This allowed them to exchange messages and treats without the risk of injury, a pastime that kept them busy for days. Next on her list was a gadget to catch the neighbor's wandering chickens. Edwin couldn't help but see his mechanical aptitude reflected in his darling Millie. He often mused that mechanics would have been a more satisfying path than law. The year before, Edwin had designed a signal flag holder for caboose cars, believing it would be his ticket to wealth and freedom from his father-in-law. He'd journeyed to Washington, hopeful, only to discover that a Colorado inventor had patented a similar idea two years prior. Soul-crushing. Amy was not supportive upon his return; she'd had enough of his misty talk when he had a law degree to lean into.

In Atchison, when Muriel reached school age, she rejoined her elder sister, Amelia, her partner in countless escapades. Beneficiaries of an unconventional upbringing, the Earhart girls enjoyed freedoms unknown to most Victorian youngsters. Along with their mother, who was born before the birth of the phonograph, they existed on the cusp of modernity in a world transitioning from buggies to buses. Edwin and Amy admirably rejected the ossified Victorian norm of giving a good hiding by cane or belt, preferring to send their kids into closets or corners to encourage their daughters' reflection on their actions.

Yet the girls' Christmas gifts were juxtaposed against such progressiveness: one year, Amelia unwrapped a Daisy BB air gun; the subsequent year, she unveiled a .22-caliber Hamilton rifle. "We decimated bottles off the back fence and diminished the rat populace in Grandma's barn," Muriel later recalled, and how Amelia's eyes sparkled when the rifle, paired with a football, appeared beneath the tree. Amy's aspirations for her daughters diverged from the period's norms; she envisioned them as strong and athletic. Inspired by her forward-thinking sister Margaret, an ardent feminist who championed "bloomers" beneath dresses, the Earhart girls, too, sported their blue flannel "gym suits." Bloomers, unconventional in Atchison, mirrored the more extensive societal shift toward women's rights led by the safety bicycle's rise in the 1890s. The feminist cause was further advanced by Annie Londonderry, a reinvented self for Annie Cohen Kopchovsky, the young Jewish cyclist who toured the globe in bloomers, setting societal conventions aside. Bicycles didn't just symbolize mobility; they propelled feminism, granting women the freedom of self-transportation and, with attached baskets, liberation from waiting at home until a carriage came calling.

Other mothers were scandalized to see the Earhart girls playing tennis, basketball, and football. Yet Amy smiled broadly as her daughters explored river caves, sledded down snow-covered streets, and fished. Under Amelia's guidance, the sisters collected pebbles, toads, and moths, and a well-worn copy of *Insect Life* helped them identify tiny creatures on their grandfather's porch. Was there any harm in that? While many Midwestern parents of the era clung to chaste Victorian mores, Amy and Edwin Earhart were no fossils.

After several years of private tutoring for Amelia and Muriel, Judge Otis's savings allowed the girls to enroll in Atchison's college preparatory school with three dozen students across twelve grades. Privileged kids in the area attended first grade through high school, and graduates matriculated at elite East Coast colleges like Wesleyan and Harvard. Virginia "Ginger" Park was Amelia's best friend there, where the kids all called her Millie. This banker's kid from the upper middle class remained close to Amelia for the rest of her life, and together they made a comical-looking pair: Ginger, the class shorty, and Millie, always so tall. The girls with mismatched heights always giggled together and stood up for each other. There was value in solidarity.

One year, Amelia was without the customary recital attire at her prep school's youth dance class. Once her Quaker grandmother caught wind of this, a package soon arrived from Kansas City: inside was a modest velvet-trimmed dress. The garment's simplicity contrasted starkly with the ornate ensembles of her peers, but Amelia embraced it. She looked like no other girl in town as she twirled and twirled in delight, and her pride in her distinctiveness hinted at an iconic look that would later become her hallmark.

Most days in Atchison unfolded as peacefully as a summer afternoon. But then came 1908, the year Amelia turned eleven. Her parents had relocated to Des Moines after a company transfer from the Rock Island Railroad Company that offered a salary twice what Edwin was making before. His wife joined him immediately, leaving her girls with her parents. Then, in 1909, Amelia and Muriel journeyed nearly three hundred miles to move to Des Moines. Despite their distress at their new lot, which they had been cautioned not to express, the two girls quickly adapted to their new life, which was a bit lonely at first. Concerned about potential issues in public schools, like lice, their mother initially opted for homeschooling. An Iowan governess took charge, emphasizing poetry and French but neglecting subjects like geography. Despite this unsatisfactory arrangement, the sisters spent much time together and had confidential chats about sisterly stuff.

Thinking way back to this time, Muriel would one day recall how she said to Amelia, "I would think it would be fun to run down the street in the moonlight without any clothes on to show how pretty my legs are!" Amelia replied, "If you think of doing naughty things like that, your face will grow like Scrooge . . . but it would be fun to do, maybe just with panties on!"

Given their limited social connections and a curriculum so sorely lacking in math and science, their mother soon felt that public school would serve them better. Amelia was subsequently enrolled in the seventh grade, while Muriel began fifth grade.

It was an "absolute embarrassment" for Muriel when, during the first week of school, she saw Amelia wearing the same discount dress from a downtown department store as a young Black girl named Lulu May; Muriel worried that the other kids would think their parents were church-mouse poor, but Amelia headed over to Lulu May in the recess yard, seeing the shared frock as an opportunity to make friends. She never shared with her new schoolyard friends what was happening at home, that before the Earharts' big move to Iowa, Edwin had taken to social drinking, partly as a respite from his judgmental in-laws back in Atchison, and this habit had gradually morphed into an addiction. Nonetheless, Edwin upheld his professional responsibilities, and by 1910, his diligence was rewarded with a promotion, and he became the head of Rock Island's claims department. For a time, though his drinking occasionally disturbed the home's peace, he safeguarded his family's well-being. Edwin and his wife cherished their newfound financial autonomy, which enabled them to move near Drake University, close to the most sought-after neighborhood in the city. Amy Otis Earhart, former debutante, could now afford things a nineteenth-century debutante considered a God-given right: a Japanese cook, a housemaid, and cultural outings.

Amelia, as the oldest child, was most aware of the domestic strife amplified by her father's alcoholism, and it took a toll on her emotionally. She soon crafted a private facade in Des Moines to shield her vulnerabilities, a self-protecting act her mother saw through and called "putting on herself outside."

Back in Kansas, the family's concerns intensified. Despite suggestions from the family for Amy to leave Edwin because of his escalating alcoholism, Amy stuck by him. However, as his drinking worsened, it was decided that teenage Amelia would go to Atchison to assist her ailing grandmother. Meanwhile, Edwin's behavior undermined the fragile safety measures established to protect Amelia and Muriel. And then, in 1911, to safeguard Amy's own future from Edwin's erratic conduct, her parents revised their wills. Amy's inheritance was placed in a trust managed by her brother Mark, with the rest of the assets allocated to Mark and her sister Margaret.

The year 1912 was marked by even more extreme upheaval. In February, Amelia's maternal grandmother died, and her assets were distributed among her children and husband. Then, in May, Judge Otis was found dead in his bed following a recent nervous breakdown. While Grandma Amelia had a sizable trust fund from her Philadelphia ancestors, it was modest compared with Judge Otis's holdings worth roughly $6 million in modern dollars. Grandma Amelia's deliberate decision to exclude Edwin from Amy's inheritance exacerbated his bitterness. Upon learning that Amy's portion would be placed in a trust, just so he could not get at it, Edwin chose not to attend his father-in-law's funeral. His aggravation, fueled by alcohol, led to erratic behavior, frequent absences, and eventually the loss of his job. Facing personal and financial challenges, the Earhart family left Des Moines for good. Their only consistent income came from Amy's monthly trust, managed by Mark. When Muriel later recalled this unseemly period in Des Moines, she said she believed that the family disorder had deeply affected Amelia, revealing itself in her later aversion to alcohol and a need to not rely on men for support. Edwin's alcoholism destabilized his children's lives, resulting in job losses and numerous relocations. By the time they were young adults, Amelia and Muriel had moved eleven times.

After 1914, the family's financial problems continued, magnified by tensions between Edwin's affluent relatives and their Kansas relatives. Amelia was forced to make do with stopgap solutions, like crafting clothes from curtains and selling bottles. Edwin's drinking worsened, resulting in an incident where Amelia poured out his whiskey, inciting his rage until her mother intervened. Every afternoon, after navigating her daily misery at St. Paul's Central High, Amelia would return home to moments of fragile calm. Amid the chaos, Amelia found refuge in physics and languages, chasing order in an unsteady world.

In 1915, a promising Chicago, Burlington & Quincy Railroad Co. gig for Edwin lured the family to Springfield, Missouri. Amelia was crushed by the news. Just as her social life was taking off, blossoming with invites and hard-won friendships, she was yanked away. But fate played a cruel trick: upon arrival, they discovered that the job had vanished into thin air. Edwin, crestfallen, was handed a ticket back to St. Paul. While Edwin scoured St. Paul for work, Amy shepherded the girls to stay in Chicago with the Shedds, family friends who opened their doors in this time of upheaval. Meanwhile, a disheartened Edwin retreated to the familiar, if pitying, embrace of his extended Earhart family in Kansas City.

At seventeen, Amelia was underwhelmed by the science room when Muriel enrolled at Chicago's Morgan Park High School. Amelia didn't hide her dissatisfaction, so her mom suggested that she do her own research. After interviewing several principals, she chose Hyde Park High. However, enrollment depended on the proximity of a prospective student's residence to the school. In search of housing, they shared a dingy, threadbare apartment with two middle-aged sisters, a stark contrast to Amelia's early years with her grandparents.

During these trying times, Amelia and Muriel found strength in each other and through poetry. The editors of *Aitchpe*, Hyde Park High's yearbook, chose a line from Wordsworth for Amelia's farewell quote after she came from St. Paul in 1914: "Meek loveliness is round thee spread"—not, as many early Earhart books state, the more depressing "the girl in brown who walks alone." Though Amelia, the perpetual new kid, was seen as reserved by some, Muriel later suggested that her sister's fervor for academics made her stand out—even made her seem an oddball—in a school system that prioritized decorum over achievement for girls.

Years later, Muriel would admit that their parents always thought Amelia had a sharper mind, which hurt her, and she felt it hard to measure up. She also maintained that although Amelia believed she was intellectually gifted, looks-wise, she felt awkward and plain. Still, Muriel remembered that Amelia was less concerned about her looks than her determination to set herself apart from those she didn't consider intellectual peers. Getting into Vassar was an obsession for Amelia, fueled by her father's belief in her and shadowed by their relentless financial struggles.

In 1915, when Amelia returned to Kansas City, Edwin saw defeat on his eldest daughter's face. Having graduated from high school, Amelia seemed lost, unsure of how to attain the life she aspired to have, and Edwin knew all too well that his wife's family possessed wealth that should, in part, be available to his children. Acting on Edwin's advice, Amy initiated a lawsuit against her brother Mark, accusing him of mismanaging the family's assets. During the proceedings, allegations arose that questioned Grandmother Amelia's mental capacity at the time she amended her will. Evidence revealed Mark's substantial financial improprieties. Observing silently from a portrait in the courtroom was Amy's father, Judge Otis, a voiceless witness as Amy's legal challenge proved successful, bringing significant financial gain to the family.

Despite the ensuing familial strife, the victory in 1916 enabled both sisters, who were keen on education, to pursue spots at esteemed East Coast schools. However, Amelia faced a discouraging obstacle: she was considered too young for Vassar. Determined to find a solution, the Earharts enrolled her in the Ogontz School for Young Ladies in the Philadelphia area, a finishing school for the elite founded in 1850. Set on sixty-five acres of picturesque land in Elkins Park, Ogontz offered a city-level education in a rural environment, with courses in current events, languages, literature, music, art, history, and science, along with what some might call fuddy-duddy subjects like Bible study and "tidiness." Amy assured Amelia that performing well at Ogontz could potentially lead to a transfer to Vassar, as Ogontz was a feeder school. Additionally, Amelia's aunt Margaret would be nearby for emergencies. Amelia traveled there by rail in early October, ready to put an end to her uneven past.

A year older than most Ogontz students, Amelia Mary Earhart entered classes on October 3, 1916. Her parents paid $1,200 yearly for tuition and board, a considerable expense they could now mostly afford if they budgeted. Although the girls were taught how to curtsy and pose by their well-groomed teachers, the academics were also solid. In addition to French and German, Amelia took various other subjects that mirrored the coursework at Vassar, such as English literature, chemistry, philosophy, and logic. Toffee-nosed ladies with Old Vic accents stressed correct pronunciation, word choice, and acceptable subject matter. As a result, Amelia was commended for her polished and cultivated vocalization for the rest of her life. The Ogontz School arranged chaperoned trips to Philadelphia, only twenty minutes away by train; the girls also visited New York, Washington, and Chicago for cultural events.

In the summer of 1917, the young but maturing Amelia Earhart's life took a formative turn when she attended Camp Gray, a lakeside Presbyterian retreat nestled in Saugatuck, Michigan, near the mouth of the Kalamazoo River. Away from the watchful eyes of her parents, Amelia was free to socialize with worldly young men for the first time. Among them was Gordon Pollock, son of a Pawnee tribal member and Rough Rider—a cavalryman with Theodore Roosevelt's ethnically diverse and gallant volunteer cavalry unit that was stationed in Cuba during the Spanish-American War. Pollock Senior, a painter, a warrior, and Roosevelt's orderly, had a passion for photography before enlisting. It was Amelia who fascinated Pollock Junior most. Alongside her friend Sarah Treadwell, Amelia enjoyed swimming and walking to the beach with these young men, relishing first flirtations.

But it was her romantic dalliance with Kenneth Griggs Merrill that gave Amelia new confidence as a young woman. Merrill, known for his literary, athletic, musical, and ambitious pursuits, would later publish short stories in esteemed magazines like *The American Mercury* and *The Atlantic Monthly*, appearing alongside famous writers such as Sherwood Anderson, Ernest Hemingway, and F. Scott Fitzgerald. He was deeply enamored with Amelia, and although there were whispers of marriage, she was firm in her desire to graduate and chase her own ambitions. In letters home to her mother, Amelia kept the most intimate details to herself, describing her summer as "a wildly exciting time." Sadly, the couple drifted apart when Merrill enlisted in the US Navy for World War I, though they remained in sporadic communication; even after he married another woman in 1925, Merrill kept Earhart's tender letters until he died in 1963.

Amelia returned to Ogontz that fall, combing her long hair back from her forehead and with a more buoyant attitude. She joined the field hockey team as an offensive player, excelled in most subjects for the first time, and contributed to the school's poetry magazine, the *Ogontz Mosaic*. Thanks to a nudge from Merrill, Amelia began to view reading less as a chore and more as a wild roller coaster, diving into the cerebral realms of George Bernard Shaw, Theodore Dreiser, and Fyodor Dostoevsky. Although she was as lean as a beanpole, her cheeky classmates now called her "Butterball"; later, they would remember that she loved philosophy, science essays, and Charles Dickens's *The Pickwick Papers*. Former Ogontz students also cited her unassuming manner, though some had clearly not been impressed by her at all: "She cared little for music or art or anything of that sort," sniffed one Ogontz alum.

When Amelia pulled teenage stunts that landed her in hot water, like scampering onto her dorm roof in her nightie, the school rang up her nearest relative: her no-nonsense aunt from Germantown, forty-four-year-old Margaret Otis Balis, who would stop by to straighten things out. By senior year, Amelia snagged the title of class vice president and crafted the class motto, earning some serious bragging rights for her folks. Not just sticking to school politics, she also donned the hat of secretary for the Ogontz Red Cross chapter and knitted up a storm, churning out sweaters for the troops during World War I.

Ogontz was no ordinary school; it maintained a legacy of "physical culture" with military drills that were considered revolutionary when introduced in 1888. These exercises—featuring knee bends, posture drills, and other regimented movements—instilled confidence, built discipline, and gave students a bit of swagger, coming as they did with snazzy navy blue uniforms adorned with brass buttons, Civil War–style belt buckles, faux muskets, and engraved swords for those with rank. As one of Amelia's peers later recalled, "We felt like hotshots because we knew we could do anything they could, and it was a pleasant feeling." With a smirk, she added, "The guys we dated couldn't believe we could drill." While the school garnered a reputation for being forward-thinking, dynamic, intellectually invigorating, and democratic, it's notable that the concept of structured youth drills later found a much darker expression in Europe, when, as evidenced by a fan letter to the school penned by a young Adolf Hitler, the structured discipline of Ogontz directly influenced his idea of the Hitler Youth—an extreme and unintended legacy of such educational innovations.

At Ogontz, Amelia also crafted a scrapbook of women who defied conventions, documenting those who broke free from their constrained lives, a project that could be seen as her first feminist awakening. One of the clipped-and-pasted heroines was Bessie Raiche, an inventor's daughter and a dentist who became the first American woman to fly solo without any formal training when she ingeniously crafted a bamboo-and-silk biplane in the cozy confines of her Mineola home's living room. Raiche completed twenty-five triumphant flights in a single week. Another clipped story featured a brave firefighter perched atop majestic Harney Peak (now Black

Elk Peak) in South Dakota, diligently surveying the borders of four states from her watchtower. Amelia celebrated Mrs. E. E. Abernathy, a trailblazing bank president from Oklahoma City, and Mrs. Mithan Tata, the first woman to gain admission to the prestigious Bombay Bar. Helen Hamilton Gardener, the first woman to serve on the US Civil Service Commission, believed that balancing a career and a family is challenging but not impossible. On that clipping, Amelia scribbled: "Good girl, Helen!" Every story, every clipping, stood as a symbol of hope and inspiration, a reminder that women's potential is limitless. Friends said that she wanted to submit it to a publisher as an anthology when she found the time.

During her senior year at Ogontz, as the chaos of the Great War raged overseas, Amelia and her mother traveled by rail over the Christmas break to visit Muriel, who was studying to become a teacher at St. Margaret's in Toronto. They checked into the modest four-story St. Regis Hotel on Sherbourne Street, a place designed specifically for "gentlewomen." Wrapped in their snow-dusted cloaks, the sisters and their mother shared a reunion filled with overwhelming joy. Yet as Amelia wandered the city's snowy streets, she found herself coping with unexpected sights and thoughts.

Although the United States did not enter the fray of the Great War until April 1917, Canada, tethered to the British Empire, had been on the European front lines since August 1914. It was in Canada that Amelia's perception of war underwent a remarkable transformation. The ravages of fierce confrontations like the Battle of Vimy Ridge were plainly visible on the bodies of returning Canadian soldiers. One day, as she stood on King Street, a sight ahead was seared into her memory: "Four men on crutches, doing their heartbreakingly jaunty best to walk together down King Street, changed the course of existence for me . . . and in that instant, I truly came of age. I understood that war wasn't just knitting sweaters and selling Liberty bonds."

In 1917, the Royal Flying Corps' Canadian branch was based at Wycliffe College at the University of Toronto. As the Great War dragged on, aircraft became increasingly important. According to some estimates, one-third of all pilots died in combat, and both sides of the conflict began to laud the status of their pilots. The air war was a novel and romantic development of the war. In addition to cooking up the Fokker triplane, the Germans designed planes for aerial photography. In parallel, British builder Thomas Sopwith built the single-seat Sopwith Camel biplane for combat. Pilots would mark their planes when they shot down another aircraft in this new form of close-range dogfighting. They knew the risks, but many men still yearned to be nothing less than an ace. Dashing air cadets, would-be aces, and a few airplanes for teaching crowded the campus.

At nineteen, Amelia felt uneasy about returning to boarding school, viewing it as a morally questionable choice during such turbulent times. She was inspired by her volunteer work with the Red Cross, but she yearned to move beyond the tame tedium of knitting socks and rolling bandages. By the time she turned her back on Ogontz, the senior class had dwindled to just twelve girls. Though she could have worn a cap and gown in June 1918, Amelia returned to the institution in January only to collect her belongings and, as an almost-graduate, lingered for just a few weeks before joining her sister in Toronto.

The Earhart sisters found a room at the St. Regis Hotel, where they had stayed the previous Christmas with their mother. Amelia, recharged with a new purpose, set out to make a difference. She trained with the Voluntary Aid Detachment (VAD) and began serving as a nurse's aide, first, briefly, on a children's ward at the Hospital for Sick Children (then called Victoria Hospital for Sick Children). She witnessed a tonsillectomy that fascinated rather than repulsed her. Seeing her resilience, her superiors reassigned her to the Red Cross at Spadina Military Hospital on the University of Toronto's campus. This military hospital, once an age-old Presbyterian college edifice, now housed survivors of the Third Battle of Ypres (commonly known as the Battle of Passchendaele), infamous for its catastrophic conditions and continued use of poison gas, and the Battle of the Somme, which marked the ghastly debut of tanks. She witnessed firsthand the trauma of those with shell shock, horrid gas injuries, shrapnel lodged in their lungs, and those in the unyielding grip of tuberculosis. As she remembered, "The day I arrived, someone pulled the fire alarm. Perhaps it was an accident, perhaps a cruel joke. The outcome nearly killed some patients. They screamed, cried, and rolled out of bed, and as we returned them, they rolled out again, pleading for an end to their agony." This Toronto chapter brutally exposed Amelia to the barbarism of war, tearing apart the sheltered worldview she knew. Her exposure to global atrocities sparked an unwavering determination to do good in the world, and she perhaps saw herself as part savior. Despair was now a luxury.

Amelia's unit was directed by Dr. Margaret Patterson, a former missionary to India and a pioneer in the Canadian feminist movement whose eloquent discourses on women's wartime roles deeply impacted Amelia. Now affectionately known as "Sister Amelia," the young Midwesterner worked tirelessly under such mentorship. Fueled by new dreams of attending medical school and driven by her proficiency in chemistry, she was admired by staff. When they realized this child of an alcoholic never touched liquor, she was allowed to work in the locked medical dispensary, where there was a supply of whiskey needed for medical purposes; a person's upbringing is the bench from which they can pull.

Amelia's social circle soon included the gallant officers of the Royal Flying Corps (RFC)—a connection initially sparked by her love of horses, a passion inherited from her mother. During a casual ride with Muriel, Captain Spaulding noticed Amelia's skillful handling of Dynamite, a horse locals dubbed "a man-eating bronco." Drawing a parallel between her equestrian prowess and flying, he was the first to invite the sisters to view an RFC training aircraft, the Curtiss JN-4 "Canuck," the Canadian variant of Curtiss's American JN-4 "Jenny" model. Consequently, watching biplanes gracefully land at Armour Heights became a routine pastime for the Earhart sisters.

During one thrilling air circus held during this Toronto stretch, Amelia and a friend watched the handsome devil dogs and their airplanes, made of bamboo and baling wire, in a small clearing away from the crowd. Onlookers were oohing as one of the flying aces buzzed down for a bit of theater.

Except for Amelia, everyone darted to safety. "I'm sure he thought, 'Watch me make them scamper,'" she later wrote, adding, "I didn't understand what he meant at the time, but I think he was saying something to me."

Just once in the last years of her life, Muriel suggested in print that Amelia took a clandestine flight or three with dashing pilots billeted at the University of Toronto, despite the strict prohibition of civilians on military flights. If this onetime slip was truthful, it challenges the belief that Amelia Earhart's maiden flight occurred several years later in California. Regardless of the exact truth, Amelia always credited her Toronto experience with her aviation passion, writing, "I can attribute my aviation career to what I experienced here in Toronto. . . . Despite my long hours, I made time for the flying fields. . . . [The pilots'] youth, their charisma, those takeoffs—it all left an impression. I remember . . . I hung around in [my] spare time and absorbed all I could." The sensation, she noted, of snow flung onto her face by propellers remained vivid.

It was a remarkable transition from the cloistered halls of an all-girls school, under her mother's nurturing umbrella, to what was then the second-largest city in Canada; she was suddenly surrounded by men—heroic men, valiant pilots—and the most gut-wrenching horrors. She must have been swept up in the literally uplifting spirit of aviation.

World-weary people were about to get wearier when, in the early months of 1918, a cluster of influenza cases erupted at an army base in Kansas. The cluster exploded into a pandemic that would kill around one hundred million people before it finally subsided. The flu virus killed more people in twenty-four months than AIDS killed in twenty-four years, and more in a year than the Black Death killed in a century. One-third of the world's population, or five hundred million, caught the virus. Modern medicine was confronted with a pandemic for the first time, and though health experts put forth countless proposals for how to manage the worsening crisis, they ultimately saw limited success.

Reverberations from the flu were felt everywhere. In cities from New York to New Delhi, streets became ghost towns. The eerie silence of the outside world juxtaposed with the inside turmoil of overwhelmed hospitals, including, by the end of September 1918, Spadina Military Hospital in Toronto. One hundred and fifty thousand residents succumbed to its grip as the flu savaged the city. Amelia served the wounded and the ailing, but her compassion came at a personal cost. After being exposed to a plethora of sick individuals, she, too, developed pneumonia. Complications arose, leading to maxillary sinusitis, an agonizing infection of the sinuses near the cheekbones. The era's lack of advanced medical treatments meant a prolonged and difficult recovery for Amelia and many others. Their stories, though harrowing, exemplified human resilience in the face of one of history's deadliest pandemics.

Amelia was hospitalized in Spadina in early November 1918, becoming a patient in the same hospital where she had tended to wounded soldiers. She was bedridden on the day the armistice was signed. The war had taken a heavy toll on both sides of the Atlantic. The United States lost "only" 112,000 soldiers. But 900,000 people were lost in the United Kingdom, 1.3 million in France, and 1.8 million in Germany. With news of the war's end, cities and even back-pocket towns erupted with joyous shouts and cheers, leaving indelible memories of raucous all-night parties. Even the esteemed citizens of Toronto couldn't resist the allure of postwar festivities, eagerly joining in lively snake dancing and mischievously tipping their hats. Amelia observed the drunken melee from her window with glee and irritation, unwavering in her commitment to abstinence from alcohol. It was a spontaneous carnival, with a bonfire at the intersection of Queen and Bay Streets, drawing people circling around its mesmerizing flames. Animated bands, jubilant parades, and the piercing steam whistle atop city hall's bell tower brought the city to life. Flags fluttered from every corner, and the scent of trampled confetti mingled with the smoky air from street vendors. Bay Street roared with a ticker-tape parade, while other streets turned into dance floors where shoes clattered against cobblestones. Hotel lobbies buzzed with off-key singing and laughter that echoed into the night. On Yonge Street, crowds spilled into the road, their cheers drowning out the hum of streetcars, forcing factories to shut down as no one had any desire to work during the revelry. Within the confines of the hospital ward, Amelia found her own way to commemorate the consequential occasion—if not with champagne, perhaps with ginger ale.

Hospital beds were in high demand, so Amelia was discharged a month after her admission. Although now outside, the American do-gooder faced severe pain around one eye, worsened headaches, and intense mucus drainage. Her treatments included agonizing procedures known as "washings out," which involved draining her sinus cavity through small tubes inserted into her cheeks. Much like today's long-term COVID sufferers, Amelia was plagued for years with chronic sinus issues stemming from the 1918 pandemic.

She left Toronto in 1919, a committed pacifist unsure about her future. Following a surgery, she returned to the US and settled in Northampton, Massachusetts, for a year of recovery. As Muriel prepared for her Smith College entrance exams, Amelia focused on healing physically and mentally. She spontaneously bought a twenty-five-buck banjo from a pawnshop and enrolled in a five-week mechanics course at John Charlebois's auto shop. There, she joined other women and Smith students. Her attendance was less about formal education and more about satisfying her innate curiosity, wanting to understand "what makes the wheels go round."

The next step in Amelia's recovery journey took her to a tranquil resort in Lake George, New York. A modest rental cottage by the lake's crystal-clear waters provided her peace, punctuated by only occasional wild storms. The Earhart sisters mixed with diverse vacationers—from well-to-do travelers to artistic souls seeking a city getaway—and enjoyed picnics, games, and theatrical tales. Marian Stabler, a twenty-three-year-old New Yorker visiting her well-off family that summer, was especially drawn to Amelia, the tall, recovering sister with a distinctive "Western" accent. Although she had traces of postpandemic fatigue, a pale complexion, and shadowed eyes, she was laid-back and engaged daily in broad discussions on topics ranging from the arts to politics and science.

Residing that summer in a nearby cabin, the openly gay avant-garde poet Mark Turbyfill was a refreshing presence during a dynamic era of literary experimentation in American culture. It was a moment of existential introspection for many artists, preceding a time when more commercial interests beckoned them. While Amelia and her straitlaced sister weren't exactly postwar bohemian types, they were avid readers of *Poetry* magazine. Amelia crafted verses in the quiet corners of her life, dreaming of seeing them in those esteemed pages. She was head over heels for Dante Gabriel Rossetti, that true maestro of beauty. Muriel would later stumble upon a few lines written beneath a Rossetti sonnet, and she was sure she recognized Amelia's handwriting.

> *Beauty is not the hue and glow of the right*
> *Nor for man's pleasure given;*
> *For hell itself is beautiful at night*
> *From the far windows of heaven.*

Turbyfill was undeniably the better bard at the lake, and he would later become well-known as a dancer, abstract expressionist painter, and esteemed published poet. One day, *Poetry* would dedicate an entire issue to him. Any young woman who loved beauty would have appreciated his simple, lovely works, and Amelia loved hearing him read his work aloud.

She had loved writing since she was five, but she'd kept most of her poetic scribblings private. She may have published under a pseudonym in still-unknown journals using the name Emil Hart, and she sent a quartet of poems to *Poetry*'s editor, Harriet Monroe, with the titles "Palm Tree," "To M_____," "My Friend," and "From an Airplane." On April 6, 1921, all were sent off with a cover letter: "Enclosed are four small efforts of a novice."

> *Palm tree.*
> *Like crackling icicles,*
> *your brittle sword-branches*
> *rattle in the small breezes*
> *of thick warm nights.*
> *Knowing nothing of cold,*
> *is it with the malice of ignorance,*

*that you chill
the thick, warm dreams
of souls uneasy at discomfort*

Monroe wrote Amelia this heartening rejection note: "Not quite—as yet. But we consider these unusually promising. So please send us some more when you have some you like."

After, Amelia long reflected on the challenge posed by those words, wondering, like many with grand ambitions, whether she could elevate her innate talents from good to great.

Three

THE GOLDEN TWENTIES

As the Great War raged, with millions of men stationed overseas or in training, capable women adeptly stepped into roles in manufacturing and agriculture. Many also played crucial parts on the front lines as nurses, ambulance drivers, and translators. Having tasted newfound agency, many women dreaded the prospect of returning to domestic confines and traditional societal expectations.

Then, after the war, as the turmoil of conflict and disease receded in 1919, the cultural landscape of North America and Europe underwent a radical transformation. Historically, women worked as teachers, nurses, librarians, and seamstresses in textile mills, but the postwar period saw a significant uptick in their corporate participation. There was a high demand for typists, mail clerks, stenographers, and secretaries—roles for which there were insufficient male applicants; this uncharted era marked a surge in young, single women being recruited for such positions.

The dawning Jazz Age was a time of liberation; it now became feasible for ambitious men and women to mingle without the weight of societal gossip. Among such enterprising individuals was Amelia Earhart. Fresh from a rejuvenating summer at Lake George, she began her college journey at Columbia University, burning with the zeal to make a difference.

When she started at Columbia, the United States had a population nearing one hundred million, with New York City alone home to nearly six million, the numbers ballooning after recent waves of European immigration. Only 2 percent of Americans age twenty-three and older earned bachelor's degrees. For a woman, securing one required both wealth and tenacity. Columbia's School of General Studies provided an avenue for women previously denied access to Columbia. Intriguingly, it was here where some of the institution's first female professors were appointed. Earhart was alerted to this promising prospect by her feminist acquaintances, particularly her idol, Alice Paul, an alumna of the institution.

Yet financing Amelia's education posed a dilemma for her parents. They were reluctant to back her ambitions of entering the medical field—a profession scarcely chosen by young women.

By the time Amelia reached the city, it was packed with thirty-two thousand speakeasies and clandestine establishments that served diluted alcoholic beverages. The term *speakeasy* stemmed from the need for patrons to speak in hushed tones, thereby not drawing attention to the prohibited activities within. Remarkably, these illicit establishments outnumbered the legal bars that had existed before the Eighteenth Amendment took effect at 12:01 a.m. on January 17, 1920—a deliberately chosen moment to erase any doubt about the start of Prohibition. As Prohibition unfolded, society became polarized between the "wets," who staunchly opposed the stringent liquor regulations, and the "drys," who staunchly supported temperance.

While many were charmed by the allure of amiable bartenders swirling their glass rods in hidden rooms, Amelia had different fascinations. Living in Manhattan's Washington Heights, she dove into peculiar experiments, such as giving orange juice to mice, dissecting cockroaches, mucking about the forbidden subterranean passages of Columbia, and scaling the Low Library dome.

Still relying on her mother's dwindling trust fund but budgeting as best she could, Amelia found affordable lodging at 50 Morningside Drive. Fueled by her relentless optimism, she enrolled in inorganic chemistry at Columbia and organic chemistry at Barnard, also indulging her passion for French poetry with an elective. Despite her substantial academic load, she impressively secured a B+ grade.

On Thursdays, Amelia's only weekday off from classes, she took refuge in the posh Manhattan family apartment of Marian Stabler, the good friend she had made at Lake George. Together, they indulged in the city's exciting arts scene, attending concerts at Carnegie Hall featuring the likes of Fritz Kreisler, Mischa Elman, and Sergei Rachmaninoff. For those on a tighter budget, the Lower East Side's Third Street Music School Settlement offered affordable classical performances.

The world of visual art was also at their fingertips. Stabler fondly remembered the day Amelia introduced her to Toulouse-Lautrec's works during their visits to galleries and the Metropolitan Museum of Art. For a more relaxed outing, they might hop on a Manhattan ferry, which, for a nickel, transported them across the Hudson River to a bathing beach in the Palisades that was great for picnicking. There, an array of global delicacies awaited while accordionists, violinists, and other musicians serenaded the crowd, passing cups around for tips. Closer to home, they enjoyed watching couples steal kisses and munching on deli sandwiches while perched on Riverside Park rocks.

Although Amelia was intellectually stimulated in New York, she confided in a letter to her sister that she didn't see herself as a doctor, nor did she feel a strong drive to pursue a medical career.

Amelia's mother was a devout Episcopalian, relying daily on the Book of Common Prayer. However, Amelia's church attendance waned while she was at secular Columbia and eventually stopped altogether. She wrote to soothe her concerned mother: "Don't think for an instant I would ever become an atheist. . . . But you must admit there is a great deal radically wrong in methods and teachings and results today. . . . It is . . . the outside pressure that squeezes them into a routine."

Nevertheless, she candidly stated, "I see only with deep regret that God punishes. . . . In my opinion, only his nonexistence could excuse him." Her spiritual musings might have aligned more with Emerson, Thoreau, or even Einstein, who once said, "Try and penetrate with our limited means the secrets of nature. . . . To that extent, I am, in point of fact, religious."

Empathy for her parents during their conflict was simpler than grappling with divine concepts. Her mother was slated to undergo surgery in Boston, yet Amy considered having the procedure in California if her daughters would care for her over the summer. "One of us ought to be there for Mom and Dad," Amelia told her sister, "but after that, I will come back here and live my own life." Balancing family obligations with personal ambitions proved challenging. Observing Amelia's indecision about her career and how New York's polluted air exacerbated her sinus issues, Muriel suggested that a change of scenery might benefit her.

Understanding the delicate situation at home—with her parents moving to Los Angeles to salvage their relationship—Amelia committed to caring for her mother and maintaining some peace while Muriel stayed with East Coast relatives for the summer to save money. This decision led Amelia on a weeklong, one-hundred-hour train journey from Chicago to Los Angeles via the Union Pacific's Overland Route, switching later to the famed Golden State train of the Rock Island Line.

As Amelia acclimated to California, seismic changes unfolded nationally. Tennessee ratified the Nineteenth Amendment, granting women the right to vote. Though Amelia likely appreciated this progress, enduring societal biases meant that only a fraction of eligible women voted.

When Amelia arrived in Los Angeles in 1920, she discovered that her father had become deeply involved in Christian Science, a belief system that holds reality as primarily spiritual and relies on prayer to alleviate suffering and maladies. While this alarmed Amelia, an Ivy Leaguer with a growing scientific perspective, for her father, the congregation provided not only spiritual comfort to combat alcoholism but also occasional legal opportunities.

Other concerns preoccupied Amelia beyond family religious dynamics: her father's frequent references to a Christian Scientist named Annie. She wondered whether their bond was merely one of shared faith or something more intimate. The Earharts' financial situation added further strain. Despite drawing from Edwin's promising career and Amy's shrinking trust fund, their expenses often outstripped their earnings.

To ease their financial pinch, Amelia's parents decided to rent out two rooms in their unnecessarily large rented house. They ended up with a Fuller Brush salesman, a budding lawyer, and Samuel "Sam" Chapman, a chemical engineer with baby-blue eyes and dark hair. Sam, who was educated at Tufts and hailed from the posh beachside enclave of Marblehead, Massachusetts, caught Amy's attention immediately, and she was positively itching to have a chat with him. As she watched young women of her acquaintance start families, she was concerned that Amelia might miss out on a happy marriage, so she subtly nudged the conversation, hoping for a spark between Amelia and Sam. Initially, their introduction might have felt orchestrated, but a genuine connection blossomed. Sam loved baseball almost as much as Amelia loved horseback riding. Their shared pacifist views added depth to their bond, as did Sam's time in the Massachusetts Naval Militia during World War I and his stint at the American Smelting and Refining Company in Monterrey, Mexico. In Clifton, a Marblehead district populated by fishermen and sailors, Sam had grown up as the postmaster's son. He didn't own a yacht, but he had a good degree, career aspirations, and an assured inheritance of a big New England home near the ocean. The engineering background he possessed was also promising for a healthy financial future.

Not only did their political ideals overlap, but they also had a shared compassion for the underprivileged. One evening, donning their unassuming "slumming" clothes, they tiptoed into a secret gathering of the Industrial Workers of the World, held within a vacant shop in the market district. Going down a narrow alley, past cruddy windows, they soon walked into a room of young activists discussing their beliefs. But the assembly was short-lived, halted by the police, who seemed to view the activists with disdain. "Time to head home and gear up for a productive day," an officer snapped. The mockery in their slogan, "I Won't Work," contrasted sharply with their forward-thinking ideologies, like advocating for pensions at sixty—an idea even more radical than FDR's later policies. The trailblazing Wobblies dreamt of a democracy molded by a working class with proper agency.

Back on the East Coast, Amelia's sister pored over letters from home, some mentioning Sam. Amelia was no great writer, not even a great letter writer, but her dashed-off notes do give glimpses of their adventures, such as the secretive Wobblies meetings, and she wrote about how Sam was an intellectual, not flaunting his smarts but effectively harnessing them. In one note, Amelia confided about a spirited debate they had on socialism—a subject Amelia's conventional sister recognized as close to her heart. "The concept of pensions surely trumps the bleakness of poorhouses come sixty," Amelia wrote. "The government should mandate a portion of savings from wages, to be returned in one's twilight years. . . . Tonight, our voices should have resonated in discussions, not [been] stifled and dismissed as if we were errant children." Amelia's leanings toward socialism weren't news; even her previous headmistress, Abby Sutherland, recollected Amelia, fondly nicknamed "Millie," as gravitating toward socialist beliefs during that period.

Sam, a quiet, loyal, and well-read thinker, was a perfect foil for Amelia's quirky intellectual spirit. The whole family saw it: her parents, his sister, and even Amelia. But while Amelia somewhat embraced the idea of matrimony, doubts crept in. Sam was everything she could have wanted in a partner: enjoyable, considerate, and bright. In an era when many men recoiled at the thought of opinionated wives, Sam stood out, championing her independent thinking. But a gnawing question persisted: If she married now, would she be sidelining her aspirations? The world was just beginning to open to her. Would marriage, at this juncture, undermine her pursuit of individual accomplishment? She decided, for the moment, that any marriage could wait and begged her surprised father to take her to air shows, which he did.

On a clear California day, Amelia's father finally agreed to sponsor her (supposedly) first-ever flight at Rogers Field on Wilshire Boulevard. She took to the skies with a former Great War pilot, Frank Hawks, who would later set astonishing cross-country speed records. For now, like many underemployed vets, he was making a quick buck on short flights with the air-curious. Tradition called for students to sit in the front cockpit, but Amelia couldn't sit there alone due to Edwin's conservative views. Hawks, who once humorously told a reporter that he believed all women were nervous Nellies, nodded when Edwin insisted that a male presence was necessary. After, Edwin handed Hawks five dollars for the ride. Transactional. But for Amelia, the emotional and spiritual payoff was enormous, and that evening, she mentioned in passing to her family: "I think I'd like to learn to fly."

The 1921 Los Angeles landscape that Amelia flew over was starkly different from today's. The city was just on the brink of an explosion, with oil derricks dotting the beaches and Venice Beach still in its nascent stage. Houses were springing up across the transforming terrain, and the early foundations of the film industry were being set, though the iconic Hollywoodland sign had not yet graced the Hills. Between her waning interest in medicine and her parents' financial woes and rocky marriage, Amelia found herself unexpectedly drawn to flying. "Two major hurdles stood before me: the tuition fee I needed from my father, and my preference to learn under a woman's guidance to avoid feeling dwarfed by the typically more experienced men," she reflected.

Then, in her father's office at Third and Hill, she worked for any hours he could spare, earning a modest stipend to fund her flying lessons. Los Angeles felt lonely without the stimulating discussions of Columbia, but Amelia stayed dedicated to keeping the peace at home, shelving any immediate plans to return to New York.

Just after New Year's in 1921, merely six months since her exhilarating flight with Frank Hawks, Amelia Earhart was ready to make her greatest resolution a reality at Kinner Field, a modest airstrip south of Los Angeles. Unlike the busier Rogers Field, this quieter runway on the west side of Long Beach Boulevard and Tweedy Road became a focal point for the twenty-four-year-old Amelia. Since hosting the world's first air meet at Dominguez Field in 1910, Los Angeles had evolved from a sprawling country town into an emerging aviation hub, though it was still very much in its infancy. With the postwar surplus of aircraft, new opportunities for exhilarating flights and private lessons became accessible, even to daring women like Amelia. Standing beside her, in a nondescript business suit, was her fifty-five-year-old father. Amelia, ever poised, donned white gloves and wore her hair in braids. When she inquired about female instructors, she was introduced to Neta Snook—a short, freckled woman with fiery red hair, streaks of grease marking her face, and piercing Irish-blue eyes. Neta Snook, affectionately known as "Snooky" or "Curly," was a pioneering female aviator who had been flying since 1918 and was the first woman to graduate from the Curtiss School of Aviation. Thanks to mentors like Glenn Curtiss and Glenn Martin, California had become a breeding ground for aviators. In those early days, when airplanes were still a novelty, pilots often found work crop-dusting, delivering mail, or performing at air shows.

Amelia's desire to be taught flying by another woman struck a chord with Neta. Amelia, in turn, was charmed by twenty-five-year-old Neta's outsize confidence. She was a tiny woman with an imposing flying dog, a Great Dane named Cam (after the aviation term *camber*), who liked to go up in the air with her. The two aviatrixes, only a year apart in age, shared a love for animals and even had uncannily similar Midwestern backgrounds. Amelia's can-do attitude further elevated her in Neta's eyes.

Amelia contemplated whether her snug brown riding breeches, designed to prevent chafing, would also serve well for flying. Neta affirmed that they would work but warned of the colder temperatures at higher altitudes, suggesting an additional sweater. Moved by Amelia's enthusiasm, Edwin agreed to cover the cost of her initial flying lesson, though he made it clear that she would need to finance her future flights, either through work at his office or elsewhere.

Subsequently, Amelia took a position as a clerk at a telephone company, handling routine duties among her male colleagues. She also secured a role at a photo lab, mirroring Neta's prior job in Iowa. "The family barely saw me," she later recounted. "I worked all week and spent every weekend at the airport, just a few miles from town."

On January 4, after a frustrating trolley ride that left her short of her destination, Amelia faced a sweltering three-mile walk to the airport. Upon arrival, Neta welcomed the eager new pupil and introduced her to the training aircraft: a Curtiss "Canuck," the same plane that had been crucial in training scores of Canadian pilots during World War I.

With a surge of deep excitement, Amelia began her aviation journey. Their initial task was mastering the ground maneuver of figure eights, a demanding half-hour exercise in taxiing. As Amelia's training with Neta progressed, so did her bond with the skies—each flight ignited her passion and offered a precious respite from the everyday drudgery below.

Amelia logged a measly four hours of flight over two months, often grounded by fickle weather or commitments at her part-time jobs. Neta, however, took Amelia's occasional absences in stride. Despite economic strains, Neta consistently filled her passenger seats after the war. Her festival gigs, which involved barnstorming feats over two days, earned her a commendable one grand. Charging fifteen dollars for each flight lesson, she quipped, "I charged fifteen dollars, and we got fifteen dollars—a dollar a minute." But Neta's vision soared beyond just lessons. Aerial advertising over Los Angeles, like banners promoting WILSHIRE GASOLINE, netted her an additional one hundred dollars per flight.

Amelia's drive to keep learning satisfied Neta, and their shared love for aviation deepened their bond. Recognizing Amelia's ambition, Neta allowed her to pay with liberty bonds or credit. Amelia even pawned personal treasures to fund more flight time.

In a letter to Helen "Lev" Le Vesconte, one of Amelia's friends from her Toronto nursing days, she confided about her shift away from traditional goals, writing, "[I] fear the name of Amelia Earhart will be taboo.... However, flying is great and is worth, I believe, the blow to respectability sustained. I contemplate falling *still lower* within the next few weeks."

During Amelia's close-knit chats with Neta, she shared details about her tough stint at Columbia. She admitted that even with her passion for science, premed wasn't her fit. She believed that there was a right path for her somewhere, just not there. Yet her thirst for learning persisted. While unwinding at Kinner Field, Amelia indulged in Christina Rossetti's romantic verses, Carl Sandburg's contemporary poetry, and the weighty reflections of Omar Khayyam's *Rubaiyat*. Her eclectic reading choices often surprised Neta, whose Jehovah's Witness beliefs leaned more conservative than Amelia's broad literary tastes.

One morning, Neta's eyes widened as she glanced at the book's title Amelia had brought for downtime—the Quran! Neta recalled Amelia's enthusiastic greeting: "You MUST read it! I've devoted the whole weekend to it." Neta couldn't help but express her surprise, reiterating her belief in only one God, Jehovah, and her unwavering faith in the Genesis creation account.

Amelia responded nonchalantly. "We can learn from what other people believe," she said, brushing off her friend's remarks.

Over time, Amelia's perception of Neta evolved: she became the kind of valued friend with whom you'd share secrets during sleepovers and build hope chests rather than an enduring intellectual confidante. Much later, Neta—who may have never picked up on the fact that Amelia regarded her as an intellectual inferior—would paint them, through the gauze of years gone by, as far closer than they really were. In interviews and writings, Neta reminisced about their double dates to still-young Los Angeles's hidden gems, places where the presence of a man provided an added shield against unwanted attention. But there were plenty of outings with just the two of them; they dined in Chinatown, then seen by insular Westerners as a world of exoticism with its back-alley opium dens and secret gambling parlors.

They'd visit the Pantages Vaudeville Theater for a dose of popular culture, relishing its comedic acts, concerts, and theatrical productions. Amy was elated to see the two tomboys—Amelia and Neta—dressed to the nines. While Amelia's ensemble of choice was a brown dress paired with gloves, a scarf, and a simple purse, Neta often opted for one of her black gowns. Their outings, whether to elite events (under the escort of a respected matron) or elsewhere, typically concluded with fits of shared laughter. Neta fondly recalled Amelia's guiding phrase: "Let there be peace on Earth, and let it begin with me." Amelia, ever jovial with young suitors yet careful to maintain her distance, once remarked about Neta's beau, Bill Southern, "I think he has the mating instinct." She warned, "Are you ready to sacrifice your career? Because you will." And, in time, Neta did.

Under Californian skies, Amelia found an unlikely sidekick in Leland Brusse, the twelve-year-old brother-in-law of Bert Kinner, aviation engineer and manager of the airfield. Often seen kicking around the airfield, Leland, destined to later captain a United flight deck, recalled their quirky rabbit-hunting escapades near the early aircraft, a .22 rifle in hand. He mused that Amelia was a quiet spirit but always up for a good flight and a touch of flair. And while Leland remembered their airborne adventures, Amelia always made her own statement on the ground.

Influenced by the fashion-forward choices of New York flappers like Zelda Fitzgerald, she slyly snipped away her locks without her parents' knowledge, who feared that a daring cut might put a dent in her matrimonial chances. But for Amelia, it was all about the practicalities of flight. Her long tresses had become a nuisance, tangling in collars and caps during her aerial escapades. In the tight confines of the cockpit, a windswept short 'do under her leather helmet was simply logical.

After her exhilarating first flight lesson, Amelia decided that "life was incomplete" unless she owned her own plane. She was set on acquiring a Kinner Airster, a compact two-seater with a seventeen-foot wingspan and dual controls. Bert Kinner, viewed by Amelia's father as both farsighted and somewhat impractical, touted it as "America's foremost sport plane." But Amelia didn't have the funds yet and picked up whatever extra work she could get.

A few weeks later, as she was figuring it all out, she crossed paths with Thomas Humphrey Bennett Varney, a sixty-three-year-old socialite with, as one politely says, marital complications.

In Neta Snook's rare self-published memoir, dotted with iffy facts, she delicately describes a "friend"—without referring to him as Amelia's lover or suitor. Even so, Neta portrayed Varney with evocative details: a bowler hat, a cane tipped with gold, and an odd habit of draping travel rugs over his legs when he went anywhere by car, suggesting that he might have had a physical ailment. Neta, among others, skeptically assessed the amount of attention this man lavished on Amelia. She nicknamed him Powell Ramsdell to protect his identity in her writings—a red herring, as there were a lot of rich Ramsdells at the time, mainly on the East Coast. Some other snippets revealed seem plausible—for instance, the story of how Amelia and Varney met. According to Neta, Amelia, who was a big reader and frequent library patron, crossed paths with Varney's befuddled chauffeur at a Los Angeles library and helped him find a book about California history on Varney's behalf. As Amelia walked home, arms laden with her checked-out books, Varney's splendid black Cadillac pulled up beside her, and he offered her a ride home.

Varney's exact relationship with his second wife, Ella, in 1921 remains unclear. Was he separated from the ailing Ella, whom he married after his first wife died in 1883? A free agent? It is determinable that after weeks of private get-togethers, Varney's appeal to Amelia was strong enough to prompt a proposal to the Earharts. In a recently rediscovered 1970s interview with Muriel that needed much audio enhancement to make out content and clues, Muriel was cagey, especially as she recalled that Amelia was still dating Sam Chapman. She was unnerved by what was being asked but claimed she couldn't remember the other fellow's name, dryly adding, "All Sam lacked was money."

As the son of an ultrawealthy family in Petaluma, California, Varney built a successful business on his inheritance. Ramble Bicyclorama, a bicycle store in San Francisco, was born of his early affluence. His many assets included a Northern California home and, in Los Angeles, an elegant residence at 672 Orange Street, which later became part of prestigious Wilshire Boulevard, then lined with mansions. Although never a pilot, he bankrolled his ambitious son Walter Varney's Redwood Aviation School, which laid the groundwork for Walter's later ventures—founding Varney Air Lines, the precursor to United Airlines, and Varney Speed Lines, which eventually became Continental Airlines. Amelia's aviation passion must have surprised and impressed the elder Varney at that first meeting in his limousine. He'd often chauffeur her to Kinner Field for training and intently watch her flying sessions from the sidelines. Varney's wit, support, and wealth slowly swayed Amelia away from Sam, who may not have even been aware of this elderly rival.

Those regular appearances at Kinner Field in his Cadillac didn't escape notice, leading to whispers among the field's regulars. Cora Kinner, wife of Bert Kinner, offered a dimmer view of the situation in a (lost but transcribed) 1980s audio interview with researcher Doris Rich for the Smithsonian. "Those girls exploited him for his money," Cora asserted, recollecting, as Neta did, that Varney was possibly ailing, since the millionaire never left his car. (Perhaps he was just embarrassed by the age gap.) After much prompting, Muriel finally recalled the nickname Amelia used for Varney—"Fuzzy."

Yet their relationship must have had depth beyond financial appeal; she wouldn't have introduced the charming man to her family without genuine feelings. (Even though she was a ripe old twenty-four, she came from a Victorian family.) In many ways, Varney's visions resonated more with Amelia's aspirations than did Sam's ideas of a comfortable future back East in the Marblehead home.

Amelia was well into her twenties, but Varney, from an older era, understood the Earharts' Victorian sensibilities and sought the traditional route of securing her mother's seal of approval before moving forward. As Muriel remembered, "He came to Mother to ask for Amelia's hand, and she said, 'Well, don't expect my support. You won't have it.' Mother didn't foresee any happiness for Amelia with [Varney]; she was very fond of Sam." Muriel was personally rooting for Sam Chapman too, although she acknowledged the gentlemanly demeanor of Varney and the lavish gifts—such as flowers, theater tickets, notes, and clothes—he routinely showered on Amelia. Despite Muriel's initial claims that Amelia's Victorian upbringing prevented her from accepting these presents, evidence suggests that she did. There was even the promise of a luxury car—one that would later alter the course of her life.

Even in her eighties, Muriel remembered riding in a limousine with Amelia—her first time in such a fancy car—to meet Varney. Muriel was surprised, because she had expected to meet the young engineer named Sam, whom Amelia and her mother had mentioned in letters.

Earlier accounts of Amelia Earhart's life missed Varney's crucial role as a benefactor and never named him. This may have been to protect her legacy and not connect her to an early "sugar daddy" relationship, but Muriel's words hint at something more—actual love—and Varney's role was indeed a father substitute in many ways, a more successful one. The discovery of his influence, based on these recently unearthed interviews and memoirs, offers a fresh perspective on Amelia's private life, revealing complexities that previous biographies overlooked or ignored.

Neta revealed that Amelia preferred the company of mature companions over that of youthful Jazz Age boys. Muriel, meanwhile, shared that Amelia was deeply troubled when their parents disapproved of her potential marriage to Varney—a man Neta discreetly referred to without naming when declining to respond to the Smithsonian's inquiries about Amelia's "special man," mentioned in a 1981 interview with the *Los Angeles Times*.

Details about the forgotten role of Varney are drawn from a multitude of sources, including Neta Snook (her book and interviews), Cora Kinner, and Muriel Earhart. When Neta was having a recorded conversation in the 1970s with researcher Elgen Long—who was more focused on solving the enigma of Amelia's disappearance than on understanding her inner life—she requested that the recording be stopped. Long complied, seeing no issue with omitting parts of her story, even if they might hold key insights into Amelia's personal life. Before the recording ceased, however, a few revealing words were captured that hinted at a man who could only be Varney, given the contextual clues. Though the full extent of Amelia's relationship with Varney remains somewhat veiled, it's clear that as early as 1921, Amelia was seeking a partner who would support her ambitions.

In stark contrast with Amelia's parents' negative reaction to Varney, Neta received her family's blessing when it came to her relationship with Bill Southern, a union that blossomed despite Amelia's reservations. "Why should I have to give up flying?" Neta once challenged after Amelia cautioned her about the future. "Because you will," Amelia replied softly. "He is the kind who will insist on being the boss." However, as Amelia anticipated, Neta's priorities shifted, and she soon married Bill, a decision that distanced her from her flight student. Neta's choice to leave aviation and start a family with Bill highlighted the growing divide between their paths; Neta wanted kids and didn't envision herself as a flying mother.

In 1922, Neta let it be known that Amelia needed an even more experienced instructor to qualify for the Fédération Aéronautique Internationale's (FAI) newly introduced pilot's license. Many barnstormers, who captivated crowds at fairs with their aerial theatrics, flew without this license. Before the FAA's structured regulations, flying was less constrained, with no formal permits required. During wartime, barnstormers piloted biplanes and triplanes, often mentoring newcomers without proper oversight. However, the FAA was now steering aviation into mainstream travel. The air shows, while entertaining, were primarily designed to demonstrate the safety of flying. With the proper license and enhanced training, Amelia could have well-paid opportunities in air rodeos. Neta anticipated limited prospects for unlicensed pilots, a sentiment Amelia took to heart.

Just before Neta left the scene, Muriel temporarily dropped out of Smith to save money and secured a teaching job in Huntington Beach. Amelia had learned to fly before her sister arrived in California, but now Muriel joined her on Sunday morning with their mother's chocolate cake for the field and even met Neta more than once.

If she was going for rodeo work, the only air work available to female pilots, Amelia would also need a polished and standout look. With some money she'd initially set aside for a raincoat, she instead purchased a leather coat, a flying helmet, and goggles. Her family laughed hard when they found out that she'd slept in her leather coat for three nights to give it a lived-in appearance. (The first time she wore it to the field, as Neta witnessed, her friends called her a "dude" aviator.)

Varney's proposal had been knocked back, but another unexpected rival to the intellectual Sam Chapman emerged: Lloyd Royer, a handsome mechanic with black hair and long lashes hailing from Iowa. Royer was already a friend of Neta's, thanks to their shared time at a flight school in Davenport. Like many seeking employment in aviation, Royer had relocated to the West in pursuit of any prospects and, after engaging in barnstorming adventures, found employment at the Douglas Aircraft Company with a ground-based role. Alongside his work at Douglas, Royer ran a truck-hauling company to supplement his income. As Amelia grew closer to Royer, she discovered his courageous service during World War I, when he fearlessly navigated the skies of France. Amelia went in on Royer's truck-hauling company—for money (she was still dating Sam, who couldn't say much if he didn't want to lose her again). But her mother was appalled that she was going against social norms. Women driving trucks, let alone giant Mack trucks, was virtually unheard of in 1922. Amy begged her daughter to give up this unladylike work.

Lloyd, like Sam and Varney, was besotted with this pretty nonconformist who had an unexpected fire in her belly. In old photos, he appears devastatingly handsome, but that wasn't enough for her—she declined his proposal, which left him yearning for more than friendship. Even so, they remained close for years, and most of the surviving correspondence from this period exists because he chose to keep her notes, despite their connection being, to his regret, strictly platonic.

With family encouragement, Amelia found herself committing more to Sam. However, dating an aviator came with exasperating asterisks, and Sam lived in fear that he might one day discover his sometimes-girlfriend, whose commitment he was finally winning over, had perished, despite spending hours in the field. Her father shared similar concerns, but at the dinner table, she echoed the steely-eyed aviators she admired—those who saw death as "growing pains." This stoic perspective contrasted sharply with Neta's evolving psyche; she would later recall that someone these brave lady aviators knew was killed almost every week. She was glad she got out and would live to tell the tale of early Californian aviation.

Amelia dismissed Sam and her father as worrywarts—nothing could halt her determined course. And, finally, she was getting paid to fly: on

Saturday, March 17, 1922, Miss Amelia Earhart, in her helmet and self-distressed aviator jacket, was billed as part of the 1:00 p.m. air rodeo for the dedication of the Glendale Municipal Airport. An event heralded as "the Lady Sportsplane Special" included "Miss Amelia Earhart's Flying Kinner Airster" and "French airwoman Mademoiselle Andree Payre." That banner day, right in front of her family, who had no idea what was coming, Amelia set an altitude record of fourteen thousand feet, though Payre would smash that record a few days later in her Farman Sport.

To raise funds for a better plane, Amelia sold her canary-colored Kinner Airster, which she'd bought in 1921, to Maynard Morley, a young war veteran and aspiring pilot. On June 6 at Lynwood Field, Morley, who lacked proper training on such a craft, recklessly took the plane for a spin with Jackson Underhill, a twenty-three-year-old student, also a veteran. Right before Amelia's eyes, Morley attempted figure eights, and the plane pancaked, landing right side up, killing Underhill instantly and injuring Morley, who later died at a local hospital. Grim stuff, but Amelia, like many early aviators, was learning to compartmentalize. Theirs would not be the last air deaths she would witness, and that day, the bloody scene did not deter her. Young, reckless, and air-minded, she still wanted to fly in a newer, better plane.

With the Kinner Airplane & Motor Corporation needing funds and the Earhart family's finances stretched, Amelia finally got the newer model she desired when her family and Kinner negotiated a mutually beneficial deal. Amelia would purchase the plane at a steep discount and allow Kinner to use it for field demonstrations. In return, she'd receive complimentary hangar space, mechanical aid, and added flight time. With a loan of $1,000 from her mother, a contribution from her sister, and a promise that she would leave her part-time truck business and embrace a more ladylike demeanor, Amelia secured the superior Kinner aircraft on July 24, 1922, her twenty-fifth birthday.

"Amelia always wanted to go cross-country," Neta later said. She paused, her mind on a lost youth. "Well, there wasn't any cross-country place we could go to within a reasonable distance with that Airster. . . . I wasn't anxious to fly across the city of Los Angeles with a motor that was likely to lose one cylinder anytime." When asked if Amelia would be game to do that, she said, "Oh, she would, yes, she would."

Amelia resumed her aviation career that August under the guidance of another one of Neta's skillful friends, John Montijo, a former army pilot, test pilot, and stuntman for Goldwyn Pictures. One of America's first Latino pilots, Montijo trained students referred to him by Kinner at his restaurant stand just across from Kinner Field. He was impressed by the student Neta delivered to him, as she was undoubtedly motivated, and in seven lessons and seven hours of training, Amelia mastered maneuvers such as loops, spins, and barrel rolls with Montijo in the rear pit. But what about Sam? her mother asked.

What about him?

On April 10, an engagement announcement appeared in the *Los Angeles Times*, declaring "Mr. and Mrs. Edwin S. Earhart of Hollywood announce the engagement of their daughter, Miss Amelia Earhart, to Mr. Samuel Chapman of Marblehead, Mass. The date for the wedding has not yet been set."

The astonishingly faithful Sam tried to be a good sport about his fiancée's career, but his fears only intensified after their engagement was publicly announced in newspaper ads purchased by his future in-laws. In Los Angeles, having a car was essential, especially for someone as independent as Amelia. Using a rented Model T, Neta had taught her to drive in 1921. Now Sam, with an engineering degree from Tufts and a stable job in the city, wanted to show Amelia he could care for her. Though he couldn't match Varney's wealth, he bought Amelia a 1923 Ford coupe for $750, a significant portion of his salary. They affectionately named the car "Triscuit"—likely after a forgotten cartoon of the time. The vehicle, which had wooden spokes on its wheels and detachable metal rims, was a reliable ride, if not a glamorous one.

Despite Sam's hopes that Amelia would give up flying as they planned their future together, Amelia's passion for aviation remained strong. She worked tirelessly, saving money, waitressing, and even trying her hand at portrait photography—all to keep her dream of flying alive.

Amelia's next significant milestone was reached on May 16, 1923, after numerous focused training sessions in her sixty-horsepower Kinner airplane. Only sixteen people received (what was believed to be) a pilot's license from the FAI, the leading authority in sports aviation. It was only in October of the previous year that the FAI had begun awarding these certificates. Media coverage of Amelia's accomplishments was widespread. She was celebrated by the *Los Angeles Times* and several other national news outlets. She was even written up in her hometown newspaper, *The Atchison Daily Globe*. Her license tests were challenging. She had to glide down from 2,000 feet without her engine. She also had to navigate around two pylons 1,600 feet apart and complete five figure-eight turns at 650 feet, landing within 35 feet of a mark. Her skills impressed both male officials who assessed her performance. The *Los Angeles Times*, which called her a youthful beauty, also noted that she had only started flying in December 1922, an early Amelia fib. What was not a lie was that in 1923, she practiced religiously several times a week, and she was good.

Meanwhile, Edwin's growing involvement in his Californian religious denomination and his friendship with Annie, a fellow member of his Christian Science church, contributed to the disintegration of his marriage in 1923.

Victorian-raised Amy was gutted by Edwin's request for a divorce—a marriage she had believed was meant to last forever. It went uncontested, leaving her and her daughters to start anew. They moved to a two-story house at 5314 Sunset Boulevard in East Hollywood, a temporary refuge as the trio vowed to rebuild their lives together, united in their resolve to leave Edwin behind. Through a Smith College connection, Muriel quickly found a teaching job at Lincoln Middle School in Medford, a suburb of Boston, and went ahead by train, renting a nice-size Queen Anne Victorian on Brooks Street in West Medford, a lively historic working-class neighborhood on the outskirts of the city. That year, Amelia faced long-term health issues stemming from the pandemic; her sinuses were once more infected, and she was bandaged again around the area where a small tube was inserted to drain the infection. As a result of their unwise investments and poor financial management, the Earharts now had little money to pay for medical care.

Months after the wedding announcement, the mystery surrounding Amelia and Sam's relationship perplexed many, including Sam himself. Why the reluctance to fix a wedding date? Despite Sam's evident infatuation with his fiancée, whom he dotingly described as a "REAL GIRL," extolling her unaffected demeanor and natural allure, doubts lingered.

Looking back, Muriel, with the wisdom that comes from years lived, told a reporter in the 1980s that Sam, who was very liberal for his time, still held certain expectations for Amelia: a future in which she would embrace the traditional roles of wife and mother in Marblehead, the quaint community where they would set down roots. Amelia feared that Sam's desires for a semblance of a normal life would constrain her, limiting her freedom to pursue her own aspirations. She worried that in seeking stability, Sam might inadvertently stifle her independence, "clipping her wings" and curtailing her potential.

Instead of traveling to Boston by common train, as Muriel had, Amelia and her mother decided that Amelia would drive the two of them across the country on an exciting adventure. The $750 Ford coupe that Sam had bought for her would never be able to make the road trip. Although the car was Sam's gift, he was gracious enough to let her take all the money from its sale, which she told him was going to go toward the purchase of a better car. Soon, Amelia did have a much better car, a luxurious canary-colored Kissel Kar with wire wheels, cutaway doors, and outrigger side seats. It was not the kind of ride owned by people with part-time jobs; in fact, it was favored by celebrities like Fatty Arbuckle, who also owned the 1923 Kissel Model 6-45 "Gold Bug" Speedster. Amelia nicknamed hers "the Kizzle." She would later claim that she sold her second airplane and Ford coupe for this Kissel, a story that long ago made its way into gospel. In truth, the car was an enormously expensive parting gift from the man her parents had forbidden her to marry: billboard king Thomas Humphrey Bennett Varney.

Still tormented by the threat of disaster, Sam was tickled pink by the sale of her plane and harbored hopes that his future bride might retire from aviation. He was a Massachusetts boy, and Marblehead was not far from Medford. He could get a good engineering job in the city and simply head there by train. Amelia heard him out and clarified that she wasn't ending their relationship, but for now, marriage still wasn't in the cards for her. If he was willing to wait, the decision was his. Undeterred, he promptly chose to return to the East Coast as soon as he could.

That spring, Amelia took the wheel in Los Angeles, navigating the roads despite her novice driving skills. For Amelia and Amy, this was an unforgettable adventure. Their solo expedition as two women, especially in a conspicuous bright-yellow Kissel, made them an unusual and intriguing sight when cross-country drives were a novelty. With unpaved roads and limited infrastructure, the duo faced the challenges of their trek without the comforts of modern roadside assistance, but they had a grand time sightseeing up the West Coast and went to several national parks, including Sequoia and Yosemite in the Sierra Nevadas before heading on to Yellowstone. The travelers then headed east toward Chicago and, finally, Boston, arriving six weeks after they set off.

"The yellow boat rolled into Boston yesterday morning," Amelia said in a letter that week to a friend. "It had been modest enough in California but was a little outspoken for in Boston, I found."

As he said he would, Sam followed Amelia to Massachusetts by train and soon secured a night-shift position at the Edison Light Company on Boylston Street. At times, she seemed more concerned about her car and the weather than a wedding date, even building a garage for the Kissel at the back of the rented house to ensure her prized sports car's safety. Acute sinus pain led to another series of operations at Massachusetts General Hospital; after Amelia recovered, she taught English to foreign students in the University of Massachusetts's extension program.

Now determined to earn an engineering degree, Amelia returned to New York and reenrolled at Columbia's School of General Studies for the 1925 spring semester. This time, she took a lighter course load, but expenses remained high. To address this financial challenge, she pursued a degree in aeronautical engineering at Cambridge's Massachusetts Institute of Technology, which would cover boarding expenses. Even in the Jazz Age, MIT was known for its progressive stance, admitting women on the same basis as men. However, Amelia faced disappointment when she failed to secure a scholarship, which she crucially needed to attend. During this time, to alleviate some of the debts she was incurring, Amelia took a job at a mental hospital and then as a companion to elderly patients. In an additional side hustle with her Brookline friend Grace Miller, she even imported high-quality sausages from Chicago to Boston.

Then, in 1926, Amelia applied for a position at the Women's Educational and Industrial Union. Limited aviation opportunities for women led her to a part-time English-teaching role at Denison House in what was then Boston's South Cove neighborhood. "I fell into settlement work because I had to get a half-time job of irregular hours to supplement the one I already had," Amelia explained. At the settlement "house," comprising five brick buildings, she tackled issues ranging from illiteracy to tuberculosis for sixty dollars a month.

Amelia's days brimmed with purpose. She devoted herself to teaching English to immigrant children from diverse backgrounds—Jewish, Syrian, and Chinese—fostering connection and inclusion with every lesson. Beyond the classroom, she drove a Syrian boy to the Perkins School for the Blind, ensuring he had access to the resources he needed to thrive.

Amelia devoted her extra time at the settlement house as an assistant to the drama director, striving to bring solace and joy to those around her—a brief escape from life's hardships. In these moments of service, she found a sense of purpose and fulfillment, forging meaningful connections with the young people she worked with. Years later, her genuine kindness left a lasting impression. Mrs. Roberto, a disabled woman, fondly recalled how

Amelia had carried her to treatment sessions as a child, crediting her unwavering support as the reason she could walk at all.

At first, Sam reveled in Amelia's newfound passion for social work, envisioning a settled life in Marblehead. However, his hopes were dashed in 1927, when, worn down by societal pressures, Amelia made the bold decision to live as a full-time worker at Denison House. This move incensed Sam; in his eyes, if she longed for a home, why not marry him and create one together? Despite his inner turmoil, Sam displayed remarkable grace, assisting Amelia in her transition to Denison House. He helped her set up her new living quarters, and before long, the walls were filled with a lively collage of photos featuring Abe Lincoln and Lucky Lindy.

Meanwhile, a bookshelf groaned under the weight of philosophical tomes that Sam had helped her unpack. Works by Hume, Kant, Spinoza, Hegel, Darwin, Goethe, Voltaire, Schopenhauer, and Rousseau—all a testament to Amelia's early intellectual curiosity and Sam's dedication to a life together.

While Amelia deeply valued her relationship with the devoted Sam, she still often questioned her identity and place in society. Struggling with societal norms and feminist ideals, she wanted more than just love. After moving into the settlement house, Amelia juggled multiple roles, from providing childcare to teaching flying lessons, and quickly became invaluable. The board of directors recognized her efforts and elected her secretary. Amelia's boss, Marion Perkins, appreciated her unconventional yet dedicated approach. No longer the shy girl of her Chicago high school days, Amelia confidently represented the settlement at national conferences and was known for giving local kids thrilling joyrides in her bright-yellow Kissel Kar, which had fallen into disrepair.

Amelia was soon approached by a Boston architect named Harold Dennison at the recommendation of Bert Kinner, her old "visionary" aviation friend from back in Los Angeles. Kinner had told Dennison that she learned to fly at his school in Los Angeles and had owned two of his biplanes. Dennison was forming an airfield in Quincy, on the south side of the Squantum

Peninsula, and needed, for almost no pay, "a director" and chief bottle washer for three privately owned ships and one commercial hangar. Despite the lack of a good salary, the already-employed social worker jumped at the chance, overextending herself once again, primarily because she could now, at no cost, glide a Dennison plane over Lynn marshes and coastal beaches during her downtime.

Dennison's longtime sourpuss secretary, Evelyn Johnson, frowned again one morning when she walked into his real estate office to see a strange-looking new woman "mannishly" crossing her legs. Everything about the visitor—her casual, boyish windblown bob, fatigues, and peculiarities—just outright annoyed Johnson. As she eavesdropped on Amelia's conversations in the office, she realized that Amelia's life was all about planes, while hers was all about women's clubs and homelife.

In addition to holding the title "Director of Dennison," Amelia was also Kinner's new East Coast sales representative. Directing at the fledgling airfield also meant hands-on involvement, including selling hot dogs and crafting window curtains. Her social work career was taking off too; she had been asked to join the board of Denison House, partly because of her aviation skills, which leadership saw great value in. The *Boston Herald* soon featured a photo of her soaring over Boston, air-dropping admission passes to Denison House's Cedar Hill Carnival. She wore her helmet, coat, breeches, and boots—the look she had honed for publicity in California. *The Boston Globe* included the part-time flier in a July 1, 1927, article on the newly opened airport. The nationally syndicated piece read, in part: "Miss Amelia Earhart, social service worker, teacher, sportswoman, and a member of the board of directors of the corporation, will be a member of the airport flying staff. Miss Earhart for years held the altitude record for women. . . . Though but 29 years old, Miss Earhart has been a pilot for nearly 10 years, and through most of that period has owned her own plane." In another *Globe* article, she stated, "I started flying as a sport. I had ridden horses, played tennis, enjoyed yachting and all that—and flying, by the way, is much akin to sailing. . . . I am very fond of riding, but I have often given more thought to a high jump than I have to stunting in the air."

Not long after, she was in the news again as a passenger on the first flight out of Dennison Airport. Identified as the only professional "aviatrix" in the Boston area, she now flew a baby monoplane called *Miss Providence*. As her name recognition grew, she was asked to write about her experiences as a flying social worker for local papers.

It was her varied, if frenzied, activities in Los Angeles and Boston before she met George Palmer Putnam that would soon bring her name to mind at Hilton Howell Railey's PR firm, and even though many other flying women would grumble about how she came out of nowhere, Amelia had made her own luck.

Four

AMELIA TAKES OFF

Who wanted a humdrum life in the age of anything goes? Toward the end of the decade, parents couldn't stop their media-deluged kids from wanting to escape the dreaded life of the ordinary, yet after Charles Lindbergh's triumph in 1927, only the bizarre could shock an increasingly jaded nation that yawned at hidden whiskey and bobbed hair. Stunts were a spectacular Jazz Age way to leave middling lives behind and offered a life change within hours if successful. Stowing away on a ship, sitting on a flagpole overnight, or completing an outrageous swimming challenge could lead to astonishingly quick fame. Like social media influencers today, those who had seen new worlds in the flickers (movies) and newsreels dreamed of nothing less than fame and fortune. With the growing reach of radio and newspaper coverage, countless attempts at novelty became common, primarily by desperate youth born into the wrong families.

The famous Flaming Youth of the era were not the only ones with bolder ambitions. Due to the outstanding efforts of suffragist movements worldwide, many women could vote for the first time at the beginning of the decade, but seven years later, that wasn't enough for many middle-aged women. Was it too late to be spectacular? Flight-minded women, young and old, were in the right place at the right time.

As always, the American attention span proved short. After Lindbergh's exploit, a man's attempt at an Atlantic crossing lost its allure, but daring women sought glory crossing the pond, even as passengers. These aviation pioneers constitute a forgotten chapter in history, as Lindy's success inspired half a dozen to try and fail—either drowning or being rescued at sea. Though now lost to time, their names were once synonymous with daring feats.

The first lady to try was a sixty-two-year-old English princess named Anne Löwenstein-Wertheim-Freudenberg, also known as Lady Anne Saville. The princess, an iconoclast who invented the "automatic balancing bed" to ease seasickness on ocean voyages, was a fervent devotee of aviation—a passion that unsettled her family and friends. Using her considerable inheritance, she secured a seat on the Fokker F.VII named *St. Raphael*. In a friend's car, the regal aviator snuck up to the plane as it readied to cross the Atlantic. After her family discovered her plans, she hid in the bushes, waiting to jump on when given the alert. The first minutes in the air were fine, with Lady Anne's well-paid pilots navigating as she made herself comfy in her seat—that is, until the craft was swallowed up in the fog off the coast of Ireland. A botched Atlantic attempt with a prominent woman drowned triggered a public outcry regarding suicide missions.

The next woman to attempt the conquest of the mighty Atlantic was Ruth Elder, a stunner setting her sights from New York's Roosevelt Field. At twenty-three, this brunette dental assistant turned student pilot with a reed-thin aviation résumé (but fantastic teeth!) was always picture-perfect for the cameras, taking seductive steps in high heels and striking seductive poses under the relentless, often lewd gaze of aviation reporters. The "eligible bachelorette" was, in fact, Mrs. Lyle Womack of Lakeland, Florida, cleverly hiding her marital status to appeal to the broadest audience. Although her plane, the *American Girl*, took off from Roosevelt Field with her flight teacher on a publicity stunt, she had enough skill as a flight student to fly part of the way under supervision. Due to headwinds, their gas supply ran out thirty-six hours later. They ditched the plane 325 miles east of the Azores after an oil pressure failure and a burst hose; like Lindy, they were headed for Paris but, unlike Lindy, wound up way off course. After lowering a lifeboat, a Dutch tanker picked up the crew. Captain Goos watched in awe as the gorgeous Elder reached into her bag for a mirror and lipstick. Goos's captain's hat was an appropriate prop for the inevitable photo shoot. Soon after the rescue, the Dutch ship tried to lift the *American Girl* onto the vessel, but the plane burst into flames; though she'd landed in the drink, Elder was inundated with movie contracts within hours. Stardom followed after newsreels of her rescue spun, and the minx was soon cast as a lead in the Paramount silent film *Moran of the Marines*. Her flight sparked a craze for "Ruth ribbons" that mimicked the kind she wore in her hair, and other endorsements she landed brought in a quarter of a million dollars. Rich pickings.

Wouldn't any would-be movie star try something outlandish for results like that? A Viennese film director egged on his wife, Lilli Dillenz, a young, pixie-haired singer at the Cabaret Fledermaus, to become another east–west passenger. She, too, barely eluded Neptune's clutches and was rescued at sea.

Mrs. Frances Wilson Grayson, a petite woman of undeniable charm, was widely described in her time as a thirty-five-year-old niece of the late president Woodrow Wilson—though the family connection remains unclear and is likely apocryphal. In truth, she was thirty-nine, a bold adventurer who, after a nine-year marriage without children, divorced in 1923, seeking a life that was ne plus ultra. Freelancing as a journalist and show dancer, she ventured into real estate on a whim, reportedly making a fortune speculating in Garden City, New York. Shortly before Christmas 1927, Grayson and her hired crew took off from Roosevelt Field, New York, but were lost soon after clearing Cape Cod, overmatched by the fickle Atlantic. Their amphibious Sikorsky S-36, christened *Dawn,* was nowhere to be found, despite an all-night search that included the navy dirigible *Los Angeles*.

But foolhardy ladies didn't stop there. Elsie Mackay, the cultured thirty-four-year-old actor daughter of Lord Inchcape and heiress to his shipping fortune, made the fifth attempt on March 13, 1928. To her fans, she was Poppy Wyndham, a name chosen to protect her family name from her liberated adventures. Sadly, Poppy and her hired pilot and navigator barely left home before they met their fate. It is still unclear where her team was headed, but it was probably New York.

The men were not exempt from such newsworthy stunts, although their attempts got less ink than those of the gals. In the Jazz Age Atlantic crossing frenzy, twenty-one lives were lost, nineteen in 1927.

Not every lady wanted to be a passenger. An Atlantic crossing was an expensive endeavor. A newspaper sponsorship would have allowed the most experienced female pilots to try flying themselves over with the added safety that money can buy. Gifted pilots like Ruth Nichols and Thea Rasche became hopeful that times were changing after *The New York Times* published an op-ed titled "Fair Play for Women Fliers." (The paper of record had, of course, famously sponsored Lindbergh's successful flight.) Even with the *Times*' official tribute to aviatrixes, the paper's owner, Adolph S. Ochs, harbored deeply misogynistic views and believed that women were better off governing households. Female fliers pleaded for sponsorship dollars after Lindbergh's success, especially following the publication of that magnanimous op-ed. Ochs turned them all down, including Rasche, as evidenced by the *Times*' own archives, which contain this revealing reply to Rasche's request: "Regarding Fräulein Rasche, I respectfully decline to sign this German lady, or any other lady, for a transatlantic flight in advance of her making it. In other words, I decline to aid and abet any lady to attempt a dangerous feat which may result in her death."

Rasche remained steadfast in her desire to fly her Bellanca monoplane from Europe to America, despite the limited sponsorship opportunities, and joining her in this ambitious endeavor was Mabel "Mibs" Boll, whom the press dubbed "the Queen of Diamonds." Boll's unconventional journey included a stint at a convent school to temper her spirited nature as the daughter of a Rochester bartender. She married an American at sixteen, became a mother at twenty-one, and remarried a Colombian coffee merchant at twenty-eight. Boll, who'd embraced a new persona and adorned herself with diamond baubles, planned to cross the Atlantic in a Parisian sweater woven from gold links.

Rasche and Boll were the only "Atlantic crossing" contenders whom aviation reporters could write about in the early spring. However, fate took a sharp left turn during an auspicious April week in Manhattan.

Meanwhile, in his Midtown office, forty-year-old publishing scion George Palmer Putnam was ready to pounce on his next big deal. True talent was unimportant for a short memoir or magazine piece that could lead to a movie; a fellow or gal just needed a riveting tale to work with. On one cool mid-April morning, George made time for his old friend Hilton Howell Railey, who was equally calculating in different ways but admittedly better liked and, for the sake of his PR business, more under the radar. Railey had popped in to check on his sometime partner in crime before returning to his headquarters in Boston and to his wife.

Well, Hilt said to George, he had some intel about their shared client, something Commander Richard Byrd had heard. Top secret. Byrd had emerged as one of Putnam's bestselling authors following his leadership of a 1926 expedition to the North Pole, which ultimately earned him the esteemed title of commander of the navy, something that proved to be another great publicity asset. (Eventually, he would end up an admiral.)

Hoping to extend his fading legacy, Byrd had sought advice from his trusted adviser, Railey. Why not lead a "scientific" summer expedition to Antarctica in 1928? They would gather boats from New York, where the newsmen were, and equip themselves with planes and huskies. Byrd's experienced North Pole pilot, Floyd Bennett, would fly him over the South Pole. This expedition would show off American prowess in an area that had not seen significant exploration before. They would demonstrate to the Europeans how it could be done by air. With government sponsorship for expeditions unavailable in the 1920s, Railey proposed that his client could cover the expenses through fundraising efforts and promotional deals. True to Railey's rosy predictions, Byrd's Antarctic expedition quickly became a topic of national conversation.

A hushed discussion unfolded in G. P. Putnam's office. Railey had secured a rugged and reliable Ford trimotor from Henry Ford for Byrd's South Pole expedition. Byrd had owned a spare Fokker F.VII trimotor from his 1926 North Pole expedition, but as Railey informed Putnam, he'd sold it to Donald Woodward, a passionate aviation enthusiast and one of the heirs to the Jell-O fortune, for $60,000.

News of Woodward's deal spread among privileged circles, reaching Amy Phipps Guest, the fifty-six-year-old daughter of Pittsburgh steel baron Henry Phipps and the wife of the Right Honourable Frederick Edward Guest, PC, CBE, DSO, MP, who had once served as the British secretary of state for air and was a member of His Majesty's Most Honourable Privy Council—and if that wasn't enough, he was Winston Churchill's cousin. The American socialite was rumored to be worth $1.9 billion in 1928 dollars.

As Railey learned from Byrd, Lady Guest was horrified by Boll's Atlantic venture. With big blue eyes and a love of flashy jewelry, the Queen of Diamonds from Central New York had married money and was now a happy-go-lucky young woman long separated from her wealthy husband. High up on her perch, Mrs. Guest couldn't bear the thought of such a tart basking in the spotlight and got to thinking: With his flight from New York to Paris, Lindbergh had improved relations between the United States and France. Couldn't she do the same, but as a passenger? Passengers like herself had their own money and could get whatever they fancied. David Layman, Mrs. Guest's startled but dutiful financial adviser, muttered that he would investigate what he could for her. She offered to lease the plane from Woodward and insure it for loss. Nobody could say she couldn't afford that insurance.

Railey's brain was churning after he got wind from Byrd that a flight with a female passenger was in the works—inklings of news too hot for him to touch but not too hot for his enterprising friend George. The tight-lipped Byrd had only mentioned that the operation was happening in Boston Harbor. That's all Railey knew—that Mrs. Guest was leasing Byrd's old orange Fokker and had added pontoons for safety, paying for everything herself. Railey and George both knew that Byrd was a stickler about controlling information, and if George wanted more details, they would need to do some gumshoeing, like they had back in the old vice squad during the Great War. Granted, Amy Phipps Guest was not a flying ingenue like Ruth Elder, but she was already a boldface name in society pages. George could get an early start on a book, just as he had with Lindbergh. Railey had ideas, but he needed to learn more before playing chess. Plus, with all that steel money at play, there would be no unpaid bills.

George wanted to home in on Byrd's world and promised Railey that he, as Byrd's publisher, would handle it if Byrd ever got wise to their meddling. Get creative! Fish for more! A new project together!

When Railey arrived in Boston after dark, with his ear to the ground, he took on the challenge and hailed a taxi to the wharf, slipped money to the right people, and posed the right questions. A plane with pontoon floats was being worked on for Byrd's polar team by Wilmer Stultz, a seasoned pilot who often moonlighted as a member of the Gates Flying Circus in New Jersey. Railey discovered that Stultz could be found in the evenings at the Copley Plaza Hotel's bar. With Scotch paid for by Railey, Stultz would only give up the name of Mrs. Guest's financial adviser, David Layman, in New York.

Railey briefed George from his Boston office the following morning. Now they had a name to play ball with. With a burst of energy, charged up by the game, George reached out to this fellow, Layman, and demanded an exclusive, making not-so-subtle threats that he'd still horn in on the story if Layman didn't comply.

George's bravado and thorough knowledge of Layman's personal matters surprised the private banker, who was, at first, wholly put off by this vulgarian, skilled predator. However, after the initial shock of the call wore off, he grudgingly revealed that he had a big problem and openly contemplated whether a man like George, with his connections, could help.

George was listening.

For Mrs. Guest's children, their mother's decision to fly across the ocean was nothing short of "total crackers." Layman took a breath and disclosed that Mrs. Guest was no longer slated to be on this flight; she'd been put under the restraining influence of all her relatives after one of her billionaire sons heard about her plans. Her daughter was afraid that she would be found floating in the ocean, and her son was furious that she would fly during his law exams. The siblings had enlisted John Phipps, their equally wealthy uncle, to stop their irresponsible mother. Since this intervention, the Phipps family had been seeking a young woman of honorable character to replace their mother.

Would the publisher be familiar with a young female pilot? George pounced and said he would get back to Layman as soon as possible while he checked on some names that sprang to mind. But for his help, this had to be a secret. Layman agreed. Seconds later, George called Railey with his wild update. He didn't care that Railey had someone significant in his office and insisted to a secretary that it was an emergency. When Railey reluctantly picked up, George updated him quickly, adding, "Now get me an attractive young woman to be the flier. Someone new and fresh!"

As it happened, the prominent individual in Railey's office was retired rear admiral Reginald Rowan Belknap, who represented Railey's highest-paying client, the chairman of the Massachusetts Bay Colony Tercentenary Commission. When Railey hung up with George, he decided he might as well ask Belknap, who had deep connections in the Boston aviation community, on the off chance Belknap would know someone good.

Yes, he did! Belknap instantly thought of a well-spoken young pilot, Miss Amelia Earhart, whom he'd met at local National Aeronautic Association meetings. It wasn't just her consistent attendance and attention to lectures filled with aviation jargon that impressed him. He recalled reading about her dual role at Denison House: a social worker with wings who helped promote the settlement house's cause by dropping pamphlets about the charity from the sky in her spare time. Belknap assured Railey that the pretty flying social worker was also the epitome of grace.

It was good luck. Railey waited for their handshake and then, rivaling his pal George's hustle, immediately called Denison House. She was content to keep the job until she could figure out her future, but it turned out that her future was about to be figured out.

Amelia was teaching a drama class just before 3:00 p.m. when her colleague informed her that she was wanted on the phone. Amelia hesitated to answer, as some schemers who knew from local articles that she flew part-time had called with the intent of getting her to smuggle liquor into the country by plane. Amelia quickly warmed when Captain Hilton Howell Railey name-dropped Rear Admiral Reginald Rowan Belknap, the almost-senatorial gentleman she often spoke with about aviation.

Giving only subtle hints about a mysterious "flying proposition," Railey invited her to his office at 80 Federal Street, just twelve blocks from her settlement house. She arrived within twenty minutes, accompanied by an older chaperone, Marion Perkins—a single woman and the prim head of Denison House, who had hired the spunky gal on a whim, despite her haphazard education and spotty résumé.

Amelia's decision to hear the PR executive out was life-changing, opening a portal to a new self. Amelia leapt out like a found diamond, but Railey coolly said a bit more: "Would you be willing to do something meaningful for the cause of aviation, such as flying a plane across the Atlantic?" Marvelously unfazed, she said she might be but admitted she could not fly with instruments alone and her experience with trimotors had been inconsequential. Railey said that none of this was disqualifying. There would be a qualified pilot on board. He had calculated what would resonate most with Amelia and encouraged her to do this for herself and other women pilots. The feminist angle was music to her ears, and she finally decided to fly with these experienced men if she could "pull her load." Could she get a few minutes of flying? Railey tentatively agreed to this proviso.

Triumphant, Railey called George and reported on Miss Earhart's charm, good looks, and astonishing potential. Already? In hours? George admitted he had put other feelers out, but Railey was to be commended. One caveat, Railey added: "She said she'd go if she could pull her load. The young lady wanted to fly the ship 'one-third' of the way." Well, George wasn't sure about that, but he wanted her there as soon as possible. "Railey, call her back and pay her fare on the midnight train to New York. You'll travel with her, won't you?"

At the end of his morning meeting with Amelia, George admitted he had other meetings booked for the afternoon; Railey was again needed as chaperone to escort Amelia to the East Side, where she would meet Mr.

Layman and Mrs. Guest's brother. Nothing was final without their approval, he even let out.

Downstairs, the doorman of the Putnam Building hailed a black-and-yellow Checker cab, and Railey and Amelia rode to 787 Fifth Avenue, a ritzy ten-story building designed in 1903 as an apartment complex for wealthy New Yorkers, and went up to the Phippses' palatial apartment. There, they were greeted by the fifty-year-old Layman, once a wunderkind bank manager but now the full-time overseer of the Phippses' considerable Jazz Age fortune. Layman liked Amelia right off, and he happily led her into a private room with John Phipps, Amy Phipps Guest's brother, who explained that his sister had just boarded a liner bound for Southampton, England, to meet the flight of a female passenger. Amelia, cautious not to show too much excitement or entitlement, nodded politely.

Phipps clarified that his sister would have the final say on Amelia's hiring. She had decided to rename the plane the *Friendship* to emphasize a strengthening of ties between the United States and the United Kingdom, and Amelia, as his sister saw it, would be serving as a flying ambassador between nations.

After Phipps asked Layman to join them, questions flew at Amelia again: Would she sign a release so that the company wouldn't be on the hook in a disaster? Would she be miffed that she was a passenger, not a pilot? The pilot would receive $20,000 for the flight, and Slim Gordon, the copilot, would get $5,000. But she was a passenger and was expected to be grateful for the opportunity to travel, despite risking death. To defray the costs of the flight, she was obliged to give Putnam any loot she got for newspaper exclusives—possibly as much as $10,000.

Even though she was shocked by the stingy terms, Amelia still focused on getting the gig. She looked at each man in the room as they asked her more questions.

"Why would you want to fly the Atlantic?"

Amelia didn't hesitate to respond. "Why does a man ride a horse?"

Layman thought. "Because he wants to, I guess."

After they laughed, he said it was her chance to ask questions now.

Was it true that despite her pilot's license, she would not be able to use it on the flight?

Phipps would later say that he almost stopped the flight from taking place because he liked her so much and felt as if he were meddling with human life. After handshakes, Railey brought Amelia back to the Putnam Building by cab so that she could say goodbye to George. Power his ego, Railey might have advised. Make him feel important.

This time, George stopped everything when Amelia walked in, and Railey said he was pleased with how things had turned out. Good work! George told the candidate that he wanted to do one more discreet background check but would report back as soon as he could. (Now was the time to dial in Richard Byrd. And, of course, Mrs. Guest had to say yes.)

When he gleaned that Amelia was traveling back to Boston alone this time, George jumped up to accompany her on the short walk to Grand Central Terminal, where trains headed to Boston hourly on the New Haven Line. Railey noted the wolfish George's sudden close attention to the young woman; he was a secret keeper who knew his friend too well.

In the absence of Railey's watchful eye, George effortlessly charmed and flirted his way through the short walk to the station. Standing tall at five foot eight, Amelia was accustomed to towering over men, but here was burly Putnam looming above her. Handsome and exciting, he cut a striking figure, impeccably dressed and worldly-wise from his extensive travels throughout Europe. And then there was that cleft chin, which added a touch of rugged charm to his already distinguished appearance. With a confident stride, he regaled Amelia with tales of his recent expedition to Greenland, funded by none other than the American Museum of Natural History. George painted a glowing picture of adventure, emphasizing the potential for significant financial gain and the empowerment it could offer to modern women like Amelia. A risk-taker by nature, he exuded confidence in his instincts, assuring her of prompt updates from his team as they embarked on their daring journey.

When Amelia finally said goodbye, she found herself rethinking her initial dislike of the man. He wasn't without his charms, sporting a droll sense of humor that reminded her of her talkative father, Edwin.

George's pulse likely pounded as he returned that night to his mansion in Rye. Behind closed doors, tension simmered between him and his wife, who accused him of splurging on her dime. She felt neglected, only needed for hosting parties when George desired to impress. Although many, even his own friends, viewed him as the publishing world's P. T. Barnum, George yearned to be taken seriously by them.

By April 1928, George and Dorothy had faced a daily communication chasm, both feeling trapped. Did she sense his intensity? Despite the press clippings highlighting his accomplishments, George still occupied a relatively minor role in the renowned Putnam enterprise. He was a salaryman with some stock, relying on his wife to cover many household expenses and memberships. George's enthusiasm for Dorothy had long ago dwindled, and the charm he held over her had faded too. His constant sulking, outbursts, and lack of empathy wore her down. Whenever he couldn't foot the bill for his hedonistic Jazz Age lifestyle, he passed it on to her. Over time, she began to view her husband as a dependent lodger who was emotionally neglecting her. She had no desire for him, and he knew it, and notwithstanding her hidden affair, he, in turn, saw her as a cold fish. Despite their grand house and staff, it was hardly a happy home.

Sleep rejuvenated him, and after a breakfast prepared by his cook in Rye, George hopped on an early commuter train to Grand Central. If the stars aligned, he might close the year with another bestseller, cementing his already successful publishing year.

After hanging up his coat, he called in his secretary, Jo Berger. "Get Dick Byrd on the phone!"

Byrd answered the call and, like many, was startled by George's meddling in his affairs, but he already knew what was happening from Railey. He'd play ball, as the two Machiavellian careerists found each other mutually beneficial. *Skyward*, Byrd's just-released "elaborately illustrated" book about his flight to the North Pole, with a last-chapter plug for his upcoming Antarctic expedition, also needed attention. It was good to keep George Palmer Putnam happy.

Meanwhile, in Boston, Amelia filled in her Denison House boss, Marion Perkins, on the latest developments. Over the next few days, Amelia worried about how well she had handled the intimidating men's scrutiny. And after several more days passed with no word, she wrote a kind yet ambitious letter to Railey absolving him of any blame for introducing her to Mr. Putnam and his risky offer—a short missive Railey would reread many times in years to come.

In a tale George later concocted for the media, he claimed to have been aboard the Staten Island Ferry with Bernt Balchen, Commander Richard Byrd's first-choice pilot, journeying toward Miller Airfield in New Dorp when Balchen mentioned a wealthy Boston woman intent on becoming the first female pilot to cross the Atlantic by air. According to Balchen, George went on, pontoons were being added to her plane at the East Boston Airport for potential water landings—a novel feature for Fokkers that would inevitably reduce their speed.

However, this narrative was, like many of George Palmer Putnam's stories, full-on fib. While the pontoons were indeed installed in Boston, the ferry trip was invented. Balchen, who in private correspondence described George as "aggressive, profane, and publicity-hungry," avoided public confrontations with him, wary of the vindictive nature of a narcissist. If George said he was on the ferry, he'd let it slide. George was good to him in other ways and had valuable contacts.

Similarly, Railey was reluctant to challenge George's fabrications publicly, though the truth is revealed in long-filed-away letters he typed in 1958. Railey had played a more central role than George's narrative suggested, just as he had been very present at George's inaugural meeting with Amelia Earhart. But for a man like George, even credit was a commodity. In his retelling, George also portrayed himself as initially indifferent to Amelia's charm, emphasizing that any romantic inclinations arose later.

Five

THE RIGHT SORT OF GIRL

In the days leading up to Amelia's official selection, George Palmer Putnam woke with even more nervous energy. Just how was he going to pull this stunt flight off? What a disaster if she died! If she succeeded—and that was always an *if*—she wouldn't get paid, but the real windfall lay in future endorsements, a potential gold mine he intended to secure for her—and, in taking a cut, for himself too. Her financial future hinged on not only the weather but also the media coverage, and Putnam had to have one of his signature "instant books" ready to roll.

Having successfully obtained Commander Richard Byrd's thumbs-up, George was pleasantly surprised by his active advisory role on the flight. However, ear to the ground as always, George had heard troubling rumors that Wilmer Stultz, the chosen pilot for the transatlantic flight, was a boozer. George sought the unfiltered opinion of Byrd, who had personally recommended Stultz to Mrs. Guest; he reassured George that Stultz was a remarkable pilot when sober and their job was to keep him that way. And it was also Byrd, as it turned out, who had recommended a twenty-seven-year-old Texan named Louis Edward "Slim" Gordon, whom Railey had met at the Copley Plaza Hotel's bar, for the *Friendship*'s flight. Even the technical advisory committee for Mrs. Guest had been selected by Byrd.

Well, if Byrd was that involved in picking staff, what did he think of Rear Admiral Reginald Rowan Belknap's recommendee, Amelia Earhart? Yes, he was aware of her in Boston. The job was right for her, he said. A fine reputation locally and her standing as a flier was solidly on the up and up.

Amelia finally received the hotly desired job offer around May 2, and unbeknownst to her, she had been the top choice from the beginning. She eagerly embraced the opportunity without informing her family, not even her mother. There was slight uncertainty regarding flight timing, depending on Wilmer Stultz's decision. Nevertheless, Amelia could now plan her part and contemplate her future.

After learning that his friend Hilton Howell Railey was coaching "the girl" in Boston during his wife's absence, George ached to be alone with her. Consumed by irrational jealousy yet wisely keeping it to himself, he resolved to make his way to Boston as soon as possible. Railey's wife, Julia, was supportive after returning from a trip to the South to discover a fetching young lady sitting on a rug in her living room. She was soon introduced to the social worker, who was reluctantly helping Railey and his secretary pound out a colorful sketch of her life in shorthand to prepare for the inevitable press. Amelia, Railey explained to his wife, had insisted, "But I don't know how to make myself interesting to order!" She questioned whether anything about herself would capture people's attention—school, college courses, wartime nursing, and a sprinkle of flying. Railey beckoned Julia to the kitchen to fill her in on how Amelia had been like this for two days, barely appreciating her unique background, and he underscored the need for her to play the game for media fodder.

"Take her to dinner, Julia!" Railey urged his wife, a writer who, through her husband's connections, had a Southern-themed novel published by G. P. Putnam's Sons under her belt and, Amelia was happy to hear, a former social worker herself. Soon, Julia and Amelia dined alone at Fenway-Kenmore's enormous Child's Old France, a cafeteria-style restaurant. Julia implored Amelia, as she nibbled on her salad, to tell her if she wanted to back down and insisted that Amelia could; her Hilt was a good man, and she would personally see to it that there was always an off-ramp if Amelia needed one. The former social worker knew how to talk to the young flier and built a real connection with her. "This is how I look at it," Amelia finally said. "My family's insured, and there's only myself to think about. And when a great adventure's offered to you—you don't refuse it."

In a swift maneuver, George cited urgent flight arrangements in Boston as the reason for his sudden departure, leaving Dorothy to ponder his true motivations. Shrewd as ever, Dorothy recognized an opportunity for a clandestine rendezvous with her secret lover, George Weymouth. Their affair, born out of circumstance and discontent, thrived in the shadows, flourishing only in the absence of Dorothy's unsuspecting husband. Weymouth had become a familiar presence in Dorothy's life through his role in David Binney Putnam's Baffin expedition, offering an alluring escape—a slosh of color in an otherwise muted life.

Seizing the chance to orchestrate a clever ruse, Dorothy playfully suggested that Weymouth, with his Yale pedigree and familiarity with her husband's endeavors, could stand in for her spouse at an upcoming lecture in Sound Beach, New York, while her husband attended to Amelia in Boston. Though rarely an attendee at her husband's lectures, Dorothy found a certain satisfaction in bolstering her young lover from the sidelines, further weaving the intricate tapestry of their affair.

Soon, George Palmer Putnam nervously but eagerly reentered Amelia's presence. The increased time spent with her had heightened not just his admiration but his sexual attraction; she was even more captivating than when they first met. George, fueled by a desire to outshine any potential rival, such as Railey, was eager to share what he had accomplished on her behalf. Despite ongoing efforts to secure a *New York Times* sponsorship—complicated by Adolph S. Ochs's reluctance to fund any flight by a woman that might lead to negative press—George's excitement couldn't be contained. He was bursting to reveal that he had successfully sold the rights to Paramount Pictures.

Amelia, too, would do almost anything he asked—and it was nice to have a woman listening to him again. After careful instructions from George, Amelia kept working at her day job during weekdays so that nobody would get suspicious of her doings. With George now temporarily based in Boston, he placed her in a room under his wife's name at the Copley Plaza Hotel; this way, he could be close to the fake "Dorothy Binney Putnam" on weekends when she returned from work. Dorothy was a bit taken aback by that update, but George assured his wife that David Layman, Amy Phipps Guest's financial adviser, and his wife had arrived from Manhattan and checked into the hotel too. No funny business.

Amelia also obediently kept her mother and sister in the dark, with only her boss, Marion Perkins, who had accompanied her to Railey's office, dialed in on the coming flight. During the day, George checked goings-on at the field and mostly spent time in Railey's office. Given a desk, he turned his spot into a new headquarters for the *Friendship* project. Amelia was told not to set foot on the airfield while the *Friendship* underwent remodeling. As George explained, reporters still thought the craft was being prepared for Byrd's Antarctic expedition, which Railey also promoted.

Eyes were everywhere, but George intensified his flirtation, and with that sort of focused attention, Amelia found it challenging to resist flirting back. After learning that she had loved Chinese food since her days in Los Angeles, he took her to chop suey joints, and in return, she would drive her handsome business adviser around in her 1923 Kissel "Gold Bug" Speedster. Railey and Julia only sometimes joined them on outings.

Well past the formalities, George had shed his corporate veneer and become "Gyp" to the prospective passenger, a play on his initials and his "Gypsy" ways of deception (an "innocent" nickname derived from a harmful stereotype that reads as derogative through a modern lens). When barking orders at his subordinates over the phone, he exuded power and intimidation. Yet in Amelia's company, George was as friendly as he'd been on their brief stroll to the train station in New York. George gushed over her, not unlike how he had during his initial courtship of Dorothy. It marked Amelia's first encounter with a man who seemed to know everyone important. Though high-strung and combustible when not getting his way, he possessed a wit and a racy charm that kept him intriguing. They even shared an oddly similar sense of wordplay. On the flip side, George reveled in Amelia's uniqueness—especially her use of invented words like *harye* (how are you), *sprize* (surprise), and *berries* (a dollar), a practice she had maintained since childhood.

She told George that his jumble of ideas reminded her of Simpkin, the cat from Beatrix Potter's *The Tailor of Gloucester*. Just like the tailor and Simpkin, George was always into something. Like Simpkin with a teacup of mice, he always had an exciting new project in reserve. If one thing slowed down, another popped up. George laughed hard at the funny comparison, and he even signed "Simken" [*sic*] in his early messages to Amelia. More inside jokes and tender exchanges were shared each day, and a closer friendship grew between them, with George endlessly pleased by her bright smile, bouncy walk, and, most of all, her open-minded approach to living large despite her conservative upbringing. He pointed out repeatedly that both of them enjoyed aviation, the outdoors, and books.

Tensions arose when George voiced his unease about Amelia's close interactions with Railey. "It's not that I distrust Hilt," he clarified, "but he's merely implementing the plans I've designed." As Amelia processed this, George unveiled a thrilling update: Emanuel Cohen, editor of *Paramount News*, had secured the experienced Jake Coolidge for a covert photo session atop Boston's Copley Plaza Hotel. A veteran of the era of wet plates and tintypes, Coolidge was prepared to capture Amelia in a secret shoot, contingent on the success of their imminent flight. So no one would suspect he was working as he entered and exited the hotel, Coolidge would keep a lockable paint cooler on the hotel's roof that contained his extra photo equipment.

Atop the building, readying for the session, Amelia learned that Coolidge was calling it "Remember Lindbergh!" She already owned the high-laced boots, brown breeches, helmet, and goggles she'd been wearing since her Los Angeles days; from the get-go, they had acted as a transformative armor, fortifying her once shy and quintessentially reserved Midwestern nature, empowering her to embody the spirit of a daring and dauntless woman who fearlessly defied the boundaries of the skies. Phil, Coolidge's twenty-seven-year-old son, assisted him in taking a reservoir of shots, positioning her near the hotel's rooftop ventilators to provide more visual whomp. Both posed her just so to add a hint of sex appeal. Amelia's image was forever defined by these photos, smartly commissioned by George, who had a keen understanding of the potent impact of visual storytelling.

Coolidge also captured George Palmer Putnam making goo-goo eyes on the hotel rooftop at his soon-to-be star.

Meanwhile, the team worried that Wilmer Stultz was hungover nearby during daily check-ins and meetings, and at George's suggestion, Layman sent a letter from Mrs. Guest stating that although Amelia was not the pilot, she would be captain of the hired crew and would make any final decisions about when to leave. This did not sit well with Stultz.

Late into the preparations, Slim told Railey and George that Stultz had gone to Manhattan to meet with Mabel Boll. She still had no idea he wasn't traveling with her across the pond. The wealthy Mrs. Guest had offered him a much higher salary, and Stultz had only attended the meeting with Boll because he felt he owed his former employer something. Afterward, he returned to Boston (sober this time!), where Byrd advised him to stay true to Amelia and George and, above all, keep the secret.

Lampooned in the press for being ostentatious, Boll didn't find out about Stultz's decision until they left for the Atlantic. She represented every stereotype that we unwittingly reinforce and despise in women, and like many women, she was unfairly maligned for her naked ambition, which was never problematic in a man. "I'm tired of being called 'Queen of Diamonds.' It's such an absurd title. But 'Queen of the Air'! I should be very proud to deserve that," she once said.

Holding the developed "Remember Lindbergh!" photos in his hands, George immediately saw that the images had a special something—Amelia's face was undeniably captivating, and her steely gray-blue eyes simply popped, even in black and white. Like a smitten schoolboy, he even raved to Coolidge about Amelia's grace, smarts, and humor. Amelia looked at them with pride but also a bit of shock. That was her? She did look brave, but she hardly looked like Lindbergh. Enough with that nonsense!

Then came another surprise: an inscribed leather-bound diary trimmed in gold that George had picked up for Amelia in Boston; it was just like the one his cultured wife owned. Having spent a week of ambitious planning in Boston, George called Rye in a giddy, slightly guilty state and said he might be taking on the biggest project of his life. But when he told Dorothy, she had plenty of romantic distractions of her own. She certainly wasn't thinking too much about a missing husband on May 19—a date on which George probably ate dinner with Amelia—while she celebrated the first anniversary of her ongoing sexual affair with her son's youthful tutor. "A delicious soft rain just saturating my lovely ferns and garden! I watched two thrushes building in the dogwood on the terrace. And it made me a little breathless for various reasons," Dorothy told her diary. She recorded the significant date using codespeak, referring to the affair as her "child": "The child is one year old, the darling, and I adore it."

Despite the heady mix of frisky banter with his new infatuation, just four days later, he wanted Dorothy to join him. Whether driven by guilt or the need for a facade, he said, "You can be her female companion."

It certainly calmed things down, and for six days, the Putnams played the role of a married couple (with a phony surname at the Copley Plaza Hotel) keeping Amelia company. The trio also shared a memorable lunch with Commander Richard Byrd and his wife, Marie, at their elegant Beacon Hill home on Brimmer Street. There, the legendary musher Scotty Allan regaled them with tales from the Klondike Gold Rush and his renowned dogsled adventures. The day was capped off with a trip to Kimball's on Cohasset Harbor for a lobster dinner. They also enjoyed an evening at the Hollis Street Theatre. There, they watched the maritime drama *The Good Hope*, starring Eva Le Gallienne. Set in a fishing village, the play depicts the tragic consequences of a treacherous boat and a widow's heartbreak. An owner driven by profit pockets insurance money and moves on with his life due to his greedy impulses. The line "The fish are dearly paid for" resonated with Dorothy, leading Amelia to gift her a fish pendant engraved with this phrase. Dorothy's diary entries for that week in Beantown also reveal George's curious late-night conversations with Amelia, during which he seemed deeply engrossed, nurturing a gratifying intimacy. The thought that "the girl" might be a female Lindy intrigued Dorothy, and while she appreciated Amelia's bravery and good nature, it astonished her to see just how malleable the young flier was. When George told Amelia how to flog her own mythology—and how to cut her bobbed hair to more closely resemble Lindbergh's—she did what he said.

Zipped tight about her Atlantic flight, as promised, Amelia told only her on-again, off-again fiancé, Sam Chapman, and three colleagues back at Denison House what was at play. Sam wasn't thrilled, especially after she handed him a key to a lockbox at the Atlantic Bank of Boston in Medford and explained, unemotionally, that it contained her will. While Amelia seemed excited about the trip, Sam reasonably feared for her life.

Sarah Layman, another wife in on the secret flight, was shocked that Amelia didn't have a watch; she, bless her heart, generously gave her the one on her own wrist, and her husband, David, gave Amelia an expensive Kodak camera. Amelia had two handkerchiefs, a comb and toothbrush, a tube of cold cream, a pair of binoculars, and a borrowed camera in her small knapsack, ready for the big day when her team would first fly out of Boston. Commander Byrd also handed Amelia an autographed copy of *Skyward*, his Putnam book, to give to Amy Phipps Guest if she reached Southampton. George beamed at the ask, for Dick was a natural promoter like himself, and he had his own book for her, a logbook, in high anticipation that she could take notes for the quick-turnaround book he hoped to publish if she made it.

The large island of Newfoundland, then a self-governing British dominion strategically located in the North Atlantic, was the closest point to Europe in North America, and it would serve as the starting point for the *Friendship*'s flight. Before the attempt to depart Boston for Newfoundland, Amelia wrote sealed letters to her parents and sister, entrusting these missives to Marion Perkins at Denison House, just in case anything went wrong during the upcoming journey. With a touch of cheekiness, she referred to them as her "popping off" letters. It's difficult to imagine that this was a thrilling game for her, but her bold decision to embark on a mission that had seen many before her vanish marked an era when women were breaking free from the constraints of dinosaurian Victorian norms. One prominent figure of this era was Mrs. Irene L. Luce, who was known to Amelia. Fearlessly seeking a divorce from her husband, Oscar B. Luce, she unabashedly declared, "I can't be bothered with a husband." Her most iconic quip—"I intend to live a fast life, die young, and be a beautiful corpse"—embodied the spirit of newfound liberation. Amelia's goodbye letters had the recipients' names on the outside of the envelopes, ensuring that her story would be delivered to the right people if needed.

> *Dearest Dad,*
>
> *Hooray for the last grand adventure! I wish I had won, but it was worthwhile anyway. You know that. I have no faith we'll meet anywhere again, but I wish we might.*
> *Anyway, goodbye, and good luck to you.*
>
> *Affectionately, your doter, Mill*

Her letter to her mother read, in part:

> *Even tho I have lost, the adventure was worth while [sic]. Our family tends to be too secure. My life has really been very happy, and I didn't mind contemplating its end in the midst of it.*

The third "popping off" letter was mailed to her little sister. Muriel unsealed it and showed it to the press on June 4, the morning Amelia and her *Friendship* crew left Boston Harbor.

> *Dear Snappy,*
>
> *I have tried to play for a large stake, and if I succeed all will be well.*
> *If I don't, I shall be happy to pop off in the midst of such an adventure.*
> *My only regret would be leaving you and mother stranded for a while.*

. . . Sam will tell you the whole story. Please explain all to mother. I couldn't stand the added strain of telling mother and you personally. If reporters talk to you, say you knew, if you like.

*Yours respectfully,
Sister*

Amelia also listed her debts and meager possessions in the short will she left to the care of Sam, ending with: "My regret is that I leave just now. In a few years, I feel I could have laid by something substantial, for so many new things were opening for me."

Several attempts were made to take off toward Newfoundland, but the aircraft, fitted with pontoons for water landings, struggled to gain enough speed on the harbor's surface. The added weight and choppy waters hindered acceleration. Amelia crouched on the fuselage floor after every short trip on the tugboat, which had been maneuvering the plane into position for each attempt. Dorothy left town after the last failed effort. George would stay, of course.

After more frustrating no-gos in the following days, the *Friendship*'s crew and official cheer squad, including photographer Jake Coolidge, Commander Byrd, and David Layman and his wife, convened again, driving to Boston Harbor's T Wharf, which leads to the northern side of Long Wharf. Their destination was the secluded Jeffries Yacht Club in East Boston, then accessible by chartered tugboat. George felt relieved that Dorothy wasn't accompanying him on the tug *Sadie Ross*; he wanted to spare her from seeing the pain evident on his face when he said his goodbyes to Amelia.

Should Stultz, known for his drinking habits, be unable to pilot the plane, Byrd's alternate, Lou Gower, was on standby, positioned in the plane's rear seat.

Amelia had previously advised Sam and her ground-based friends from Denison House to forgo this umpteenth send-off. But Sam, along with some of Amelia's colleagues, wouldn't hear of it. They rented rowboats, setting off into Boston Harbor to wave their farewells to Amelia, uncertain if this might be their last sight of the brave aviator who faced her journey with unmatched pluck.

On June 3, takeoff was a battle against gravity. After three failed water attempts and with time running out, Stultz made a decisive move. In Boston, Gower disembarked near the *Sadie Ross*, shedding crucial weight from the *Friendship*. The crew then shifted to a land-based runway, where they could build enough speed for liftoff. This allowed them to accelerate to fifty miles per hour. At 6:01 a.m., they finally lifted off, bound for Newfoundland. Watching the aircraft rise, its silhouette cutting through the morning clouds, George felt a surge of relief that quickly turned to dread. Once the plane vanished, he caught a train back to New York. A warm embrace from his wife and their sons awaited in Rye.

George hastened to his Midtown office the next day. With his releases flooding the wires, the world was met with the blockbuster news that a "humble girl" was headed to Trepassey, a tiny fishing village on the Atlantic coast of Newfoundland, the easternmost part of North America. Amelia Earhart was launching into the public eye, challenging Mabel Boll to a race across the Atlantic.

In the sky, Slim struggled with a malfunctioning door lock just minutes after takeoff, and Amelia reached for a loose gas can, nearly teetering on the edge herself. To secure the door and ensure a safe landing, they resorted to an ingenious but careful solution: tying it to a brace with twine. Meanwhile, within the aircraft's cold interior, where temperatures barely reached forty degrees, the flight posed significant challenges. Amelia's initial excitement about departure gave way to an excruciating headache, possibly linked to her ongoing postpandemic sinus condition or simply caused by fuel fumes. She resigned herself to her less-than-comfortable seat between two sizable gas tanks, as her cushions had been jettisoned to lighten the *Friendship* for takeoff.

Unexpectedly, instead of reaching Newfoundland, the crew made an unplanned stop in Halifax, Nova Scotia, due to blinding fog. To escape the prying eyes of reporters, they arranged for an isolated hotel stay in Dartmouth, a suburb of Halifax. To compound matters, Slim had fallen ill from bad clams back in Boston and remained queasy during their Canadian stopover.

Astute Boston reporters quickly picked up on the fact that the plane had taken off before George's official announcement. They pressed on; there was no hoodwinking them. It became evident that this plane wasn't suited for an Antarctic expedition, as they had initially been led to believe. Sam attempted to convey word of Amelia's departure to her mother and sister, but unfortunately, he didn't arrive in time. Instead, it was local reporters who broke the news to both women, leaving them in a state of shock and disbelief.

> Dateline: Boston, Mass., June 3, 1928: The newest entrant in the transatlantic sweepstakes is striking both in personality and physique. She is tall and slender, with a head surmounted by wavy, curling blonde hair, which is surprisingly short when it is plastered down, but unless she has been in swimming, never is.

Sam stood outside Amy Otis Earhart's door, a sense of unease likely settling in his stomach as he heard her sobs from within. However, the news had already broken, and Amy had read in reports that Amelia was part of a team that had departed Halifax at precisely 8:36 a.m. on their journey across the Atlantic. On June 4, George made their names public, announcing them side by side in the media. The aircraft, outfitted with "high wings and pontoons" and powered by three formidable Wright Whirlwind engines, soared confidently through the skies. Amy Phipps Guest and Putnam were also supporters of this endeavor. "Miss Amelia Mary Earhart" was described by George as a woman with Lindbergh-inspired modesty. Her age was inaccurately given as twenty-nine, leaving some uncertainty as to whether George knew her actual age at the time.

Years later, Muriel still recalled the day: "I remember my mother's looking with shock and disgust at the first headlines in a Boston newspaper telling of Amelia's takeoff from Boston Harbor. Her remark that nice women's names appeared in the papers only when they were born, married, or died was genuine. But of course, in this case, her love for Amelia conquered her prejudice, and she had me send a 'Wish I Were with You' wire, which received a flurry of publicity at this end." Until Amelia's safe landing, they would stay glued to the radio. Muriel also remembered that this was the first time George Palmer Putnam emerged as the project's spokesman and was sometimes misidentified as the wealthy backer himself.

NOT A FLY-BY-NIGHT OPERATION, said the *Daily News*, still misspelling the intrepid social worker's name as "Miss Amelia Earhardt." The enigmatic "Mechanical Science Corporation" had received a startling £8,000, the equivalent of nearly $650,000 today, from its equally mysterious donor. (Mrs. Guest was not yet named.)

Amelia was a front-page sensation nationwide. An uncanny resemblance between the female passenger and Charles Lindbergh was noted by journalists. As Amy Phipps Guest hoped, the media played up a wholesome-as-cherry-pie rival to Mable Boll, the "unsavory" Queen of Diamonds. A race was news with a Lindbergh look-alike, no less.

After an unforeseen night in Halifax and a four-hour-and-twenty-four-minute flight, the *Friendship* touched down in Newfoundland on June 5. Located on the Avalon Peninsula, Trepassey was one of Newfoundland's key aviation staging points, already a historic one known for persistent winds. Before starting the perilous journey across the North Atlantic, the *Friendship*'s crew patiently waited for better weather conditions.

In 1928, English-speaking Newfoundland was a mystery to most Americans. Its coastal waters, where the Labrador Current meets the Gulf Stream, were renowned as among the globe's wealthiest fishing grounds, sparking centuries-long disputes between European powers like France, Portugal, Britain, and Ireland over the ancestral fishing territories of the Indigenous people.

The village of Trepassey, several hours' journey from bustling St. John's, played a crucial role in the daring west-to-east transatlantic crossing of Curtiss seaplanes. Its calm, protected waters provided an ideal refueling point for seaplanes, while for those flying aircraft with wheels, Harbour Grace became the more practical option.

Amelia, seemingly unoccupied during the approach to the village of Trepassey, sketched out the shapes of Newfoundland's lakes in her logbook. Later, she quipped that one bore an uncanny resemblance to a plesiosaurus.

The Americans' arrival in the village wasn't exactly a surprise, as Dr. Fred Gill, Trepassey's doctor and magistrate, had been informed by George's New York team about their impending visit after Stultz and his crew, stranded in Halifax, got good news regarding the clear skies in Trepassey. The orange-and-gold monoplane was easily visible as it emerged from the western harbor, circling twice before landing in rough conditions. A group of men with ropes in hand awaited the plane, hoping to guide it into town, and Amelia later humorously dubbed them "maritime cowboys."

On June 5, Dr. Gill and his two sons waited in dories near the aircraft to escort Amelia and Stultz to the dock. The pilots were introduced to local fishermen and subsistence farmers who crowded the wharf in anticipation. Trepassey's Catholic schoolgirls, initially glued to the windows, eventually ran down to shore in white pinafores and aprons, leading Amelia to compare the girls to breasted robins.

"Where will you eat? Where will you stay?" Richard and Fanny Devereaux approached the American lady pilot. The sight of her stunned Fanny, a forty-nine-year-old midwife with three hundred births to her credit; overwhelmed by emotion, she reached out to touch Amelia's skin, as if to confirm she was real. Richard offered to let the fliers stay in their two-story house, which had a convenient general store in front, while the fog cleared. Fanny said she would send Amelia to a friend's house across the street so that she could have her own room; Stultz and Slim would share a room. Amelia hurried to Mike Jackman's house when she learned he had a telegraph: she had to let George Palmer Putnam know they had arrived safely and comfortably.

A foggy day turned a one-night stay into two days, and as the men fished for trout, Amelia strolled around the picturesque outpost. Her inquisitive nature and the Ciné-Kodak K camera from David Layman helped her make friends and take photos. The grounded aviators appreciated the baymen's free meals, but the land's simple food quickly grew old. Newfoundlanders, often engulfed in pea-soup fog and battered by North Atlantic storms, had developed essential survival dishes over the years. The meat was preserved by salting it during the harsh winters. Because of the island's poor soil and short growing season, root vegetables were stored in root cellars. The local "Jiggs' dinner" consisted of salted beef, cabbage, and root vegetables. That was a fancy meal if you were lucky to get it! Fish cakes, mainly fried cod, were a community staple. Local delicacies included deep-fried cod tongues and cheeks, partridgeberry jam, and bakeapple jam.

Given persistent howling gales, fog, and mechanical mishaps, their plans for a transatlantic flight were consistently hampered; their heavy plane remained grounded in Trepassey's bay waters. During one severe storm, Stultz forced Slim to drain the pontoons, risking his life. This near-death experience caused a fight between the men that concerned Amelia. Slim declared he wouldn't be involved; beneath Stultz's mild, good-looking blond exterior, a vindictive side lurked, unsettling Slim and altering the trio's dynamic. Captain Earhart mended fences and got Slim back aboard their mission.

Marooned in cruel monotony on the far eastern shores of Canada, the beleaguered visitors indulged in ceaseless rounds of gin rummy while the newspapers scrambled for spicy updates beyond the fliers' authentic Newfoundland dinners.

In later years, Amelia would refer to canned rabbits as the prime delicacy of the local larder, probably arctic hares preparing their warrens for winter. "Appetizing but tiring if seen too often," Amelia said. Slim wouldn't eat seafood after his grievous experience with clams, so he now lived on candy bars from the general store. Stultz lived off the booze.

Meanwhile, thirteen hundred miles south, as agreed to beforehand with Mrs. Guest, George now made himself available for interviews in Manhattan as "the publisher and explorer" and backer of the flight. Questions?

Ask him! If he was grating, his expert promotion made Amelia the topic of many a dinner discussion even before she crossed the Atlantic.

With only sketchy details about the flying social worker, Mabel Boll gathered what intel she could and grew more determined than ever to beat this woman across the Atlantic. When Boll learned that Stultz, who she thought was leaving with her that summer on *Miss Columbia*, had quit on her, she openly sobbed. "I can't understand it. Wilmer promised to be here today . . . and now he has gone and taken another woman." The enraged Boll took off in *Miss Columbia*, which used to belong to Charles Levine, who flew it in his challenge against Lindbergh and Byrd for the 1927 Orteig Prize. Her mission, she openly stated, was more dangerous than that of the *Friendship*. Boll's *Miss Columbia* didn't have the pontoons found on the *Friendship* and lacked other safety features, like life rafts, gear, and a radio.

In place of Stultz, Boll hired aviation daredevil Oliver Colin "Boots" LeBoutillier. The hotshot stunt pilot had volunteered to join the Royal Air Force before the United States declared war on Germany. Boots had even witnessed the crash that killed Manfred Albrecht Freiherr von Richthofen, the infamous Red Baron. The classically debonair, thickly mustachioed Great War ace recruited Arthur Argles, a less-ranked pilot, as his navigator. Boll's hastily assembled team soon left Long Island, stopping briefly in Maine before continuing toward Newfoundland. The Queen of Diamonds gave a true-to-form parting statement to the press: "If I go down, they [my jewels] go down with me."

As Boll set off toward Newfoundland, a discernible shift was observed in Amelia's demeanor. Her yearning to take off was palpable. For a span of nearly two weeks, a contest raged between the two women, both vying for the title of the inaugural female passenger across the Atlantic. The media reveled in the suspense, framing Boll as somewhat crude compared with the ladylike Amelia. Misogyny, more than maybe, as Amelia was no less ambitious than Boll.

Doc Kimball, Lindbergh's weatherman, transmitted weather data three times daily; yet, even with favorable conditions, mechanical issues continued to hold both crews back.

Newsmen became bored with George Palmer Putnam's bloviating—as appealing as a two-hour organ drone in a continuous loop—and exclusives with Lady Lindy's family and friends filled the slow news days.

Two old friends from Des Moines recalled "Millie" as a girl who would rather be outside—bicycling, swimming, climbing trees—than anywhere else. When they were asked if she had a beau back then, their hearty laughter was followed by an explanation: "Why, Millie never thought of boys. High school girls in 1912 and 1913 were wearing long hair, long modest skirts, and didn't even powder or rouge. But even if Millie were in school now, she wouldn't be the kind of girl who would be given a rush by the masculine sex." They said she was neither a tomboy nor a shrinking violet. "She was just different. She never went out of her way to pick friends, but if she wanted you for a friend, you somehow knew it and were glad."

George was none too pleased to learn of Amelia's undisclosed (purported) fiancé, who had been rooted out by reporters. Who the heck was this guy? One of those friends of hers who came along to say goodbye? George had mistaken him for a fellow social worker. But, yes, it seemed that Amelia really was engaged—and not just recently either! Sam told one reporter he was "as scared as a witch." As for Amelia, she was modest, charming, winning, and sweet, and Sam blushed when he added, "Who wouldn't love a girl like that?"

"Nothing to say about the boyfriend," George firmly replied to inquiring press, but the spirited promoter enthusiastically yammered on record about the virtues of his crush: "Did you notice Amelia's gorgeous white teeth? And the way she smiled like a child at a picnic when she took off from Boston last week? It's amazing how her hair always looks perfect without any effort. She's not the type to fuss over clothes or be overly particular, but somehow, she always looks great." The long-winded George also noted Amelia's resemblance to Lindbergh, and with his pushing, *The New York Times* soon front-paged a sketch of a painting in progress by Norwegian artist Brynjulf Strandenaes; the portrait of Amelia had been arranged by George's most loyal disciple, Harold McCracken. "Why, she looks more like Lindbergh than Lindbergh," Strandenaes was quoted as saying. He had followed George's instructions to make her look like Lindy, though George firmly denied making such a request.

Hilton Howell Railey, catching his slick pal's ever-growing yarns, was more amused than mad about the breathless hyperbole—just typical George. But the claim that Amelia had racked up five hundred flight hours? That was a stretch even Railey found hard to swallow, though he let it slide. Dealing with George always meant sifting through a lot of noise. Already on edge, George was quick to snap at any pushback. His mood took another dive when *The New York Times* called Sam Chapman Amelia's true love. Sam, in his rare chat with the paper, said, "I am very proud of her. She's a real girl, and I am confident she will be successful. But I thought we could keep the engagement to ourselves. I did not know the world was going to be interested in it. We have been engaged for about four years."

Whenever Sam's name was mentioned, George's demeanor shifted. To him, Sam was an obstacle, a footnote. Even by June 1928, it was clear that his admiration for Amelia wasn't just professional.

On June 10, one reporter pressed George about his intentions, asking, "Isn't this merely a perilous venture for your personal gain?" George stared icily before responding. "There will be no post-flight book published, and we have no intentions of exploiting this accomplishment," he said. "If Miss Earhart decides to write a book, Putnam will handle its publication, but that's not currently under consideration, and any book she authors will be a result of her exceptional writing abilities, not solely because of her achievements in aviation."

Around this time in June, George admitted to Dorothy his itch to decamp to a New York hotel. There he could wire directly to Amelia, the team's linchpin, and use the *Times*' wire services room to do so. Though there was truth to George's claim, being away from Dorothy's scrutiny also allowed him to flirt with his crush unreservedly.

As everyone awaited suitable weather, George learned that Amelia hadn't packed a change of clothes. He teasingly wired: SUGGEST YOU GO INTO RETIREMENT TEMPORARILY WITH NUNS AND HAVE THEM WASH SHIRT ETC—STOP.

Amelia's cheeky response: THANKS [FOR THE] FATHERLY TELEGRAM. NO WASHING NECESSARY. SOCKS [AND] UNDERWEAR WORN OUT. SHIRT LOST TO SLIM AT RUMMY. CHEERIO, AE.

Intertwined with their playful banter was George's underlying drive to secure a narrative from this adventure, despite the public denials. He suggested: FOR OCCUPATION, WRITE A SKELETON THOUSAND-WORD STORY. HALIFAX TO TREPASSEY WITH NAMES AND DETAILS TO ELABORATE LATER.

Amelia's reply conveyed her mounting frustration: GOING NOWHERE FAST.

Yet weather wasn't the only concern in Trepassey. Stultz's drinking habits had worsened after their arrival. We all have layers of reference we carry with us, and Amelia, drawing on her experience handling an alcoholic father, struggled to control Stultz's pub visits. "He was a brandy addict, neat, downing a water glassful in one go," Railey remarked. Though Prohibition had ended in Newfoundland in 1924, Stultz's drinking needed intervention, but Amelia's repeated sermons had yielded minimal results. They had a standby pilot, Lou Gower, but Amelia worried that reports of alcoholism would taint Stultz's career.

Newfoundland reporters claimed Amelia had to hold back tears when she heard that Mabel Boll was stepping up her actions to be the first woman across. But the later news that German aviator Thea Rasche was also gearing up to cross the Atlantic terrified her. "Rushing Thea," as she was known to her countrymen and women, had more credibility as an aviation talent than as a passenger. In three days, the green-and-red Bellanca monoplane would arrive on Long Island, and the craft had no pontoons to weigh it down. "Fräulein Rasche will take the long hop nonstop to Berlin after June 10 if all goes well," Amelia read to the crew, and her log shows her nervousness: "Our competitors are gaining on us by delay. Rasche is the one to fear. I wish we'd have a break."

Boll soon landed at Harbour Grace's airstrip; Newfoundland's celebrated first aerodrome was on a grassy plateau over historic Conception Bay. It had already launched many men and their magnificent flying machines, as the eastern third of the field had a 4 percent incline, and the other two-thirds were perfectly level; aircraft carrying heavy loads were greatly benefited by this grade during the golden age of aviation. The Queen of Diamonds' crew was greeted by the whole town and taken to Cochrane House in St. John's for dinner and a reception. Boots, her hired ace, said they would rest for a few days and then "take on" the Atlantic.

Fearing these ladies, Amelia was determined to escape Trepassey that same day, despite two looming storms. Three weather forecasts from Doc Kimball were sent an hour apart by George. The hungover Stultz tried for four hours to get the *Friendship* airborne but was thwarted by the weight of the passengers and equipment. A tightening competition prompted the crew to recalculate fuel and count every ounce of weight.

George wired Amelia again on June 15: ANYWAY, BYRD REMINDS ME... WEATHER HELD HIM UP TWO WEEKS. YOU'LL MAKE IT TOMORROW OR SUNDAY. WE REALIZE FULLY HOW DESPERATELY TRYING TO DELAY FOR YOU. HOPE YOU EAT AND REST. IF YOU LOSE AS MUCH WEIGHT AS EYE HAVE, FRIENDSHIP COULD TAKE TEN OF US. TELL ME EVERYTHING WE SHOULD KNOW. He signed it with her cutesy name for him—Simpkin.

As soon as the blasted weather cleared, a new wrinkle emerged: the fully fueled plane was too heavy, the crew was exasperated, and morale was low.

A dramatic twist occurred the next day: Thea Rasche had withdrawn from the unofficial competition after a disagreement with her now-jittery sponsors. Still, Amelia's crew had to worry about Boll and Boots. Stultz knew that *Miss Columbia* was faster than the safer *Friendship* with her clunky pontoons.

"Is it possible we have been here so long?" Amelia wrote in the black leather journal that George had gifted to her. "We are just managing to keep from suicide.... All of us are caged animals."

Thirteen days into their Trepassey tenure, on the seventeenth of June, Amelia was shaken awake at the ungodly hour of 3:30 a.m. by Kimball's wire—proclaiming a rare patch of favorable dawn weather, with calm seas and tides. Slim served Stultz a steaming cup of wake-up brew—a sobering salvo from him and Amelia. The press had sniffed out a whiff of discord between Stultz and Amelia. Yet despite Stultz's manning of the controls, Amelia clung to her "flight captain" title with a firm, unyielding grip.

If there was no fog to thwart takeoff at Trepassey, Captain Amelia was willing to risk the brewing storms that Doc Kimball was concerned about. But Captain Boots, more cautious, decided it was too much of a crapshoot and that *Miss Columbia* should not leave Harbour Grace. The half-sober Stultz was bitter. A few lucky villagers witnessed the contracted captain of the mission, Amelia, arguing with the crew's pilot—all while she clutched a camera, a small army-navy knapsack, and a large black notebook. Amelia had ordered Slim to put Stultz in a cold shower at 7:00 a.m., dress him, and bring him coffee upon coffee. She was not taking no for an answer.

Chow on the Atlantic crossing would consist of egg sandwiches, ham sandwiches, five gallons of water, a crate of oranges, a box of chocolates, and a bottle of malted milk tablets. As the three aviators packed a communal duffel, Captain Amelia reminded all that Railey awaited them in Britain as the team's advance man. He was ready for the press if they made it, and Mrs. Guest had arrived in Europe by ship from New York and would greet them there.

After six attempts that morning, characterized by brief liftoffs and immediate touchdowns, the aviators boarded their aircraft just shy of 11:00 a.m. They faced the challenge of trimming the plane's weight, shedding everything from extra clothing to Amelia's curling iron, and deliberated over the fuel load. Initially, they had planned for 830 gallons of fuel for the journey to Britain, but they briefly considered a more modest trip to the Azores. Eventually, they settled on 700 gallons of fuel, as they believed it would still allow them to reach Ireland—and they hoped a landing there would still garner significant global attention.

At 11:21 a.m. Newfoundland time—an hour and a half ahead of Eastern Standard Time—they took off, with Amelia inconspicuously crouched beside the fuel tanks, her silhouette faintly visible. She later confided to pilot Jacqueline "Jackie" Cochran that she had been angrily told by Stultz to sit in the john. "She told me that part of it. They got mad at her." If any second thoughts beset Amelia, it was too late to act on them.

The three hours following Amelia's departure from North America, when she and her crew braved clouds, fog, and fierce winds, were nerve-jangling enough. But as the latest woman to cross the Atlantic, she found herself in a humble position between the gas tanks in the cabin, closely examining Stultz. His cheeks had the unwavering red spots of an alcoholic... Was she next in the melancholy roll call of aviation deaths?

At first, Slim could communicate via radio despite the roar of engines. George alerted reporters that he'd received the coded message VIOLET CHEERIO to confirm they were officially out of radio range from Mike Jackman.

EARHART PLANE SOARING OVER ATLANTIC shouted the front-page headline of *The New York Times*.

When Railey heard that the *Friendship* had finally hopped, it was already nightfall in London, so he was on alert, ready to promote and chaperone. In mid-May, after promising to help his young friend navigate a world that was new to her but comfortably familiar to him, he'd left his wife, Julia, and sons, John and Kenneth, behind in Brookline. George had not hired him for this job, which was contingent upon Amelia making it, and he'd brought his assistant. With his young PR associate, A. K. Mills, and a *New York Times* reporter named Allen Raymond in tow, he headed for Southampton as fast as possible. Well, that's where the plane was supposed to land, at least. Railey would be identified as H. H. Railey, European representative of the *Friendship* flight, until Amelia returned to New York. Then, as agreed, George would take over.

Midflight, earplugs in place, Amelia was grateful for finally being able to look skyward. For most of the flight, the "captain of the flight" was still kneeling between the two extra gas tanks, forbidden from taking a turn in the cockpit. There was little to do but see if they would live; to help the odds, she furtively threw the pint of whiskey that Stultz had smuggled on board into the clouds.

In addition to taking a few shaky photos of the kaleidoscopic patterns of the clouds through a low window, Amelia also attempted to jot down notes for George Palmer Putnam. She tried her best to be poetic: "Marvelous

Millie Earhart at six years old, showing signs of defiance and curiosity. Taken in her hometown of Atchison, Kansas.

Summer 1917: Twenty-year-old Amelia paddles down the Kalamazoo with her first real romance, Kenneth Griggs Merrill, savoring the freedom to flirt, swim, and enjoy "a wildly exciting time."

Sam Chapman on Mount Wilson, 1923—captured around the time his engagement to Amelia was announced by the Earharts in the *Los Angeles Times* on April 10.

Fresh out of Chicago's Hyde Park High, likely before heading off to the exclusive Ogontz School. (Labeled by family as 1915.)

Amelia had her first taste of aviation in Toronto, circa 1918. Muriel once hinted to a journalist that Amelia may have taken off with a pilot or two here—allegedly without permission. However, according to 1928 press releases and later biographies, her "official" first flight was recorded in California.

George and his "boy explorer" star, son David Binney Putnam, aboard the *Effie M. Morrissey* in 1926. George sent David on wild adventures and had ghostwriters help turn his notes into "self-authored" Jazz Age bestsellers.

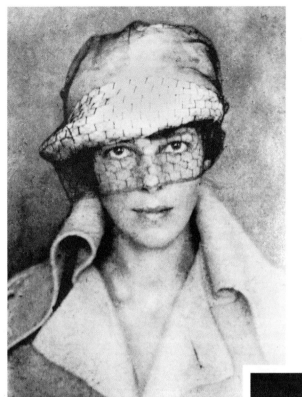

This rare self-portrait captures Amelia Earhart honing her photography skills long before she became a household name. Misplaced for decades, it resurfaced among the belongings of her mother, Amy Otis Earhart, in Berkeley—an intimate and unexpected discovery.

Thomas H. B. Varney, Amelia's wealthy suitor, sixty-four years old in 1922. Newly available recordings reveal Varney asked her parents for Amelia's hand when she was twenty-five and bankrolled her legendary yellow sports car—the one George liked to say she'd saved up for.

Millionaire aviation pioneer Grover Loening, who sold his company just before the stock market crash, and his pilot, B. A. Gillies. When Loening couldn't accompany Amelia during their relationship in 1929, he'd send Gillies as her escort—Amelia, newly monied, fit right in with the high-flying crowd.

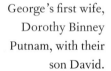

George's first wife, Dorothy Binney Putnam, with their son David.

Major George Haven Putnam, the elder statesman of publishing, a Civil War vet, and a friend of Mark Twain, ruled his desk into his eighties while keeping a steady eye on his potential successors in the family legacy.

George, just twenty-one years old, stands second from left in front of the office of *The Bend Bulletin*, which he took over as publisher after dropping out of Harvard and Berkeley, transforming the small-town paper into a scrappy voice of the Wild West.

A rare business card from the Heigh-Ho Club, launched on New Year's Eve 1928 by George, Dorothy, and legendary Jazz Age impresario Don Dickerman. Marketed as a "dry" club, it combined art moderne elegance with a strictly enforced Ivy League vibe and an antisemitic door policy.

Surviving copies of George's once-famous kid-explorer series: Boys' Books by Boys. Initially tested on his son David with the first installment, *David Goes Voyaging*, the series later evolved to include girl explorers, reflecting Amelia's influence. Parents were required to sign liability waivers, and some tales, like that of Augusto Flores, even hit bestseller lists.

After a harrowing eighteen-thousand-mile journey and the loss of two companions, sixteen-year-old Augusto Flores finally arrived at New York's city hall, where Mayor Jimmy Walker signed his record book. George saw in this young adventurer's survival the perfect story for a bestseller.

Amelia and George on the rooftop of Boston's Copley Hotel, 1928, for a private photo session arranged by George, who couldn't hide his growing infatuation with the daring flier.

George Palmer Putnam hired artist Brynjulf Strandenaes to paint Amelia Earhart's portrait, leaning hard into her "Lady Lindy" image.

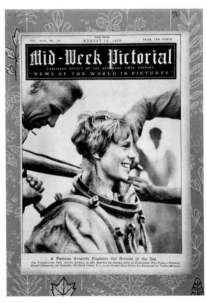

There was no escaping George's marketing genius. As his focus turned to Amelia, he strategically placed her on the covers of *Mid-Week Pictorial,* the precursor to *The New York Times Magazine,* featuring her in stunts like scuba diving and cavern climbing.

The "Female Lindbergh" campaign hit full throttle with George's push. Helmet, goggles, intense gaze: America's newest Lindy was primed for takeoff.

Amelia in Southampton, England, in 1928, after becoming the first woman to cross the Atlantic by air as a passenger. With her on her left was honorable Amy Phipps Guest, her supremely wealthy financial backer who'd initially wanted to make the journey herself.

On the rooftop of London's Hyde Park Hotel in June 1928, with Captain Hilton H. Railey—the suave Southern gentleman who persuaded her to take on the transatlantic flight as a passenger. Railey harbored suspicions about George Putnam's intentions toward Amelia, whom he viewed as a new ward.

Stepping ashore at Burry Port, South Wales, on June 18, 1928, after a twenty-hour Atlantic crossing in the *Friendship*. Though she was officially "just" a passenger, Amelia's arrival made her an instant icon.

Front-page news coast to coast: LADY LINDY FLIES ACROSS ATLANTIC! With George's publicity magic at work, Amelia's face was everywhere, setting the stage for her legend.

Back in Boston, in 1928, cruising in her flashy yellow Kissel roadster, Amelia is surrounded by the children she'd mentored as a social worker at Denison House—a triumphant return.

When Amelia visited Hyde Park High in 1928, she stood atop a piano to thunderous applause. This celebrated alum had once slipped by unnoticed—a shy, lonely teen grappling with her father's alcoholism and discord at home.

November 1929: Founding members of the Ninety-Nines, including Amelia, gather at Curtiss Field, New York. Fierce and determined, these pioneering women aimed to shatter aviation's "boys' club."

Amelia arrived in Delaware in 1929 with George's secret $25,000 check—part of a quiet bid to buy the powerful Bellanca CH-300, threatening Elinor Smith's record-breaking plans.

Elinor Smith—the "Best Female Pilot" of 1930 and the first woman on a Wheaties box. Her soaring fame made George sweat over Amelia's "Queen of the Air" title.

Amelia arrived late by train at her sister Muriel's wedding in June 1929 after a plane mishap. She turned heads in green chiffon and bold lipstick, including ex-fiancé Sam Chapman's.

Mabel "Queen of Diamonds" Boll—an ambitious socialite who married into money—was set to beat Amelia as the first woman to cross the Atlantic in 1928.

Amelia Earhart with Ludington Line VPs Eugene Vidal and Paul Collins. As VP herself, she inspired women to fly, adding star power to the new commuter service.

shapes in white stand out, some trailing shimmering veils. The clouds look like icebergs in the distance."

The aircraft's radio was their lifeline, but soon interference from poor conditions severed this connection. Amelia's last recorded transmission, marking their position relative to the SS *Rexmore*, a British steamship bound for New York, came through at 5:37 p.m. Eastern time. Later, after a brief rest, she woke to Stultz's voice calling out to any nearby ships. The radio remained silent. With sixteen hours of flight time behind them and an estimated four hours of fuel left, they found themselves isolated in the scary expanse of the Atlantic. Without radio guidance, Stultz was left to rely on his navigational instincts while the world below anxiously awaited any sign of the crew's whereabouts.

Then there was plenty of excitement when the crew spotted the massive SS *America* steamship. At this point they were seventy-five miles southeast of Cobh, Ireland, off the southern coast, but they had no clue as to their position. The plane was next supposed to be over Ireland, but where was Ireland? Stultz worked on pinpointing it and asked for Amelia's help. As he circled the liner, Amelia attempted contact by wrapping a note around an orange with a silver cord pleading for the latitude and longitude to be painted on the deck. Frustration mounted as she failed to hit the ship in two ridiculous attempts.

Nevertheless, Captain George Fried of the *America* quickly wired shore that he had seen the plane above seventy-five miles southeast of Cobh at 11:00 a.m. (6:00 a.m. New York time). Hoping to be the first at sea to spot it, Captain Fried, an aviation enthusiast, had plotted the monoplane's probable course so that he might be the first to make contact. He used a special searchlight at night and a heavy smoke screen to attract its attention. Perhaps the *Friendship* would even dip her wings.

As the advance man in Southampton's harbor, Railey eagerly awaited news. Minutes turned into hours, and a juicy twist emerged in George's ongoing plot to protect Amelia and their shared interests. While Railey was visiting the London office of G. P. Putnam's Sons, a friend leaked a letter filled with George's trademark paranoia. In it, George urged a representative to keep a close eye on Railey, as he was convinced of Railey's infatuation with Amelia. The rascal! Despite Railey's admiration of Amelia's courage and kindness, he had no romantic interest in her, and unlike George, he was happily married. Railey, confident in his superior writing and sleuthing skills, relished the prospect of settling the score when the right moment arose.

The *Friendship*'s fuel was running low—there was only enough for about an hour. The radio had been dead since the crew left Trepassey. As Stultz descended through the clouds, they could see the ground below. Stultz spotted a blue shadow emerging from the mist as Slim munched on an egg sandwich. Holy moly, was that Ireland?! Slim was so pumped he tossed his half-eaten sandwich out the window, and Stultz grinned wide. They had finally reached land.

On June 18, 1928, after nearly twenty-one hours, the fuel-depleted *Friendship* touched down in Wales, becoming the eleventh heavier-than-air aircraft to traverse the Atlantic. After an arduous journey of nearly two thousand miles from Newfoundland, Amelia Earhart and her crew touched down at 12:40 p.m. local time on the muddy beach of Burry Port. The flight, which lasted twenty hours and forty-nine minutes, would later inspire the title of Earhart's subsequent book for George: *20 Hrs. 40 Min.* Witnesses observed their narrow miss of the Burry Port Copper Works' chimney stack. Despite Slim's attempts, he couldn't catch the attention of three Welsh men on a nearby railroad. Ossie Roberts, a boat pilot from Burry Port (Porth Tywyn in Welsh), was among the first to respond. Within an hour, a curious swarm of local fishing boats had gathered, soon attracting crowds from far and wide to the newly famous plane. Amid the excitement, a fortunate six-year-old was carried across the river to touch the miraculous Fokker, a plane that had come from American soil. Another awestruck youth etched his initials under the plane's flap with his penknife.

John Daniels, standing on the beach, heard Amelia call out from the plane, "We ran out of petrol!" With his strong Welsh accent, he asked in surprise, "Are you from America?" Indeed, she was. Amelia, her short, floppy hair wrapped in colorful silk, opened the plane's door. A photo from that day shows her tired but happy, dressed in a gray sweater, riding breeches, and high-laced boots. "Are we in Ireland?" she asked. Daniels laughed and clarified their location, though his thick accent initially made it difficult for her to understand. Later, Stultz attributed their accidental overshooting of Ireland to unpredictable winds.

As soon as Stultz contacted Putnam's London office and reached Railey, the anxious PR executive let out a whoop. Stultz received Railey's hearty congratulations by wire, and Amelia was instructed to remain aboard in her photo-worthy flight garb until Railey reached them. Expert press handling was required for the young woman involved.

Starving and bone-weary, Amelia dutifully waited with the crew by the open plane door. Stultz, admitting it had been a spine-chilling ride, was visibly tired and not eager to engage in much conversation. However, under the impression that he needed to fabricate a story for public relations, he falsely claimed that "Miss Earhart took her turn at piloting the plane" while he was refueling. "We are all well, but could certainly use a few hours of sleep," he added, also admitting that he mistakenly thought Carmarthenshire was England's Land's End.

The unexpected landing tossed Railey into quite the pickle. To reach Amelia's remote landing site, he embarked on an adventure nearly as daring as the aviator's own: a chartered flight from Southampton to Swansea, capped with a choppy motorboat ride out to where the *Friendship* bobbed gently on the waves. Meanwhile, back in the bustling hub of New York, George was spinning his own webs and finally convinced *The New York Times* to feature Amelia's victorious saga. When Railey at last made landfall in Wales, he secured an exclusive interview with a London-based correspondent for the paper. There, by the aircraft's door, they found Amelia, the picture of serenity, her calm demeanor anchoring the storm of celebration swirling around her.

All this was wonderful, but out of earshot, Railey asked Amelia about her cheerless mood. Her face fell further as she acknowledged that Stultz had made the right decision not to let her fly under the rough conditions of blind flying—a skill she had not mastered. "I'm just baggage," she confessed, a hint of bitterness in her voice. She explained that she had spent her time lying on her stomach taking pictures of the clouds, feeling like a faker due to George's excessive promotion of her as a pilot. Celebrated for feats she hadn't achieved, Amelia resolved to seriously train upon her return, determined to truly earn the accolades for her flying.

To mollify her, Railey encouraged her to briefly engage with reporters and mull over these feelings more fully after some shut-eye. Despite her exhaustion, Amelia managed to address the reporters: "I am very glad we have done it and very happy we've landed. I am too tired to say more." Stultz, also weary, stressed the need for rest, postponing any further plans.

Local Welsh reporters squeezed in a few questions before the fliers were allowed to rest. Amelia, gathering her thoughts, modestly denied competing with the Queen of Diamonds and quipped, "I've never met Colonel Lindbergh, and I'm sure I don't look like anyone else, especially right now!" As the day drew to a close, Railey oversaw the filming of these interactions, capturing the moment they were officially greeted by Carmarthenshire's high sheriff. The trio was then whisked away by volunteer-driven cars to the historic Ashburnham Hotel in Burry Port. Once checked in, the fliers could finally unwind in rooms that offered views of the picturesque Gower Peninsula. The prospect of a hot bath was particularly enticing.

Amelia, exhausted, peeled off her flight jacket and collapsed into bed. Meanwhile, Railey, ensuring everything was in order for the following day, learned that Stultz had been flying blind for eight hours before losing his bearings at 4:30 a.m. Now they could all finally rest and recover from the ordeal.

As Amelia slept soundly on June 18, America was wide awake, especially George Palmer Putnam, who had endured a restless night in Rye without any news. Now the impossible had clicked, and the triumphant George held a press conference in New York. Not much was said about Wilmer Stultz or Slim Gordon. The flight was successful because of Miss Earhart's "indomitable courage and will." Tell that to the men who flew!

Vaudeville, he bragged, had already offered her $3,000 a week in a year that headliners made $1,000; George insisted that she said, "Thirty thousand dollars wouldn't be enough!" and laughed. "This gal's heart is all wrapped up in aviation," he said. "She loves flying and made the flight for no other reason. Right now, I'm proud that I chose that girl for the flight."

In her fine leather journal, Dorothy Binney Putnam genuinely rejoiced in her younger friend's success, recording that Amelia had realized her dream. Was she the one who reminded George not to forget the men? The following day, George (perhaps feeling a twinge of guilt) would eventually cable Stultz at the Hyde Park Hotel: GRAND JOB, HEARTFELT CONGRATULATIONS.

As cheering crowds gathered outside American newspaper offices to celebrate, many people scooped up first editions of newspapers with amusing, happy quotes from Amelia's gray-haired mother. "Now that that's over, I can catch up on my mending."

Back in Wales, Railey rousted each flier after six hours of sleep. The lady hotelier Alice Jones proudly served the now-ravenous trio bacon and eggs with toast, marmalade, clotted cream, and a pot of raspberry jam. When Railey returned with alarming schedules, the flying Cinderella barely had time to digest the meal. Once she landed in London, Mrs. Guest would lend her fanciful Parisian gowns and shoes. Gowns? Yes, there were many in England waiting to greet her. Luncheons and dinners were already planned . . .

After Amelia took the jolt of that in, Railey prepared her to speak with a local reporter, and the new star started in by admitting that she had eaten only two oranges and six malted milk tablets on the trip. "How lovely your country is," Amelia said. "To think that forty-eight hours ago, I was in America, and now I am in Wales!"

An article that bore Amelia's byline but was probably cranked out by Railey or his assistant soon appeared on the first page of *The New York Times*. Now that a woman pilot was safely ashore, Adolph S. Ochs had agreed to pay Putnam's fee for Amelia's exclusive story, which earned Mrs.

Guest $12,460. All of Amelia's earnings from this flight were promptly returned to the project's coffers, as warned. Amelia had crossed the Atlantic but was, for the moment, still broke.

In the *New York World*, Frank Sullivan, an anchor of the cliquey Algonquin Round Table, had immediate fun with the *Friendship*'s surprise landing. "When Miss Earhart asks how to get to Southampton, she's told: 'Southampton? Well, I tell you. You take your first right and then your left until you come to Braich-y-gwynlwynnglan. Don't stop there, but go on to Ddinllaentrwynoclynnlayn and then take the first left turn, which will bring you through Mryndd, Caer-g-wrie, and Llanfrrhaladrpenmachnin.'" (This continues for a long while, as one would imagine.)

But there was no lightness in the *Evening Standard*'s biting stance. A correspondent for the London-based paper caustically remarked, "Her presence added no more to the achievement than if the passenger had been a sheep." (Though Amelia joked it off, that barb hurt her for many years to come, and she was determined to avail herself.)

By the third week of June, articles ghostwritten by Railey and cronies for Amelia were everywhere—all placed by Putnam under her byline. (With a bit of abracadabra from George, the pilot and social worker was now a newspaper journalist too!) In one obviously ghosted piece for *The New York Times*, Amelia Earhart "the writer" claimed that women did not lack the stamina to make a solo Atlantic crossing. However, they would need to learn how to fly blind, with instruments alone, an art that few alive had mastered.

The New Yorker's wags, those all-seeing writers who had paid their dues at their typewriters, got their licks in at Putnam: "As was to be expected, the *Times* took Miss Amelia Earhart on its staff immediately after she had landed in Wales on the successful George Palmer Putnam flight. On June 19 it ran, in the old Lindbergh spot, an exclusive story signed by her and an endorsement by Mr. Putnam."

While the crew was still in Wales, Railey seized a rare moment alone with Amelia to deliver a direct yet earnest warning: she should exercise caution upon her return by sea, as their companion Gyp seemed nonchalant about his marital vows while actively wrestling for her affections. As someone acquainted with George's virtues and vices, he told her about the letter he had read. Someone had been enlisted to spy on him due to George's interest in Amelia. Did she fully grasp the gravity of his message? Despite her faint nod, Railey couldn't shake the doubt that his words hadn't fully registered.

On her first day in England in 1928, Amelia blazed through endless receptions. Her day began in a loose-fitting flowered dress borrowed from her benefactor, Mrs. Guest. Still buoyant from a recent awards ceremony in Southampton, Amelia dazzled as the British ate up her humility, admitting, "All my clothes are borrowed, but I'm not vain." This statement earned her widespread praise for her modesty. Her schedule was packed: a luncheon hosted by the American ambassador's wife, Mrs. Alanson B. Houghton, followed by another with the Air League of the British Empire's women's section. Her day also included a shopping spree at Selfridges, meetings with admirers, lunch with Mrs. Guest, and interactions with enthusiastic spectators. Amelia's busy itinerary was rounded out with teas, interviews, a tennis exhibition, and a visit to Parliament.

Across the Atlantic in Medford, Amelia's sister, Muriel, though once deemed "less accomplished" in an article, was busy teaching civics, English, and civilization. The Earhart family was increasingly in the spotlight, with Muriel asserting, "It was perfectly natural for her to enter into aviation." Their nearly deaf mother, Amy, added to the fascination by admitting in public, "I have flown with Amelia," a statement that amazed many. Amy expressed regret at not being able to accompany Amelia, not-so-humbly recalling how her firstborn daughter was reading Dickens and playing tennis at an age when most children were far less advanced.

But where was Amelia's dad? Edwin Earhart was tracked down in California at his Los Angeles law office in the Fay Building, where he worked on Southern Pacific Railroad cases. Now sixty-one, he was photographed in thick, round black glasses and a bow tie when he called the stunt a "foolhardy sporting adventure that will not advance aviation in the slightest degree. But I'm trying to take a philosophical view of the whole thing. If my daughter doesn't get killed in some crazy airplane flight, she might die of pneumonia, and that would be a more lingering end." Telegrams of congratulations littered his desk. Relatives he'd never heard from before the flight had contacted him by wire to express family pride, which greatly amused him. "Amelia will be surprised that the family tree has branched out so remarkably."

The busy attorney also admitted they had communicated by wire after her flight plans were revealed in Boston. He shared some of their amusing exchanges with reporters.

"Amelia, I am expecting you to do your stuff."

"Dad, I did my stuff."

"Amelia, I knew you would do your stuff."

Edwin's voice swelled with emotion as he confessed that he had not seen his daughter in five years, admitting that he had once "strongly disapproved" of her flying career. "Just why she should make such a dangerous flight is something that I don't know," he continued, expressing natural parental worry. "I wish now that she would give up flying and come to live a peaceful life with me." It was all water under the bridge now, wasn't it? Her goal had been achieved. "Am I proud? My God, yes!" Edwin said. "That's a daughter to be proud of. She has everything—brains, courage, and beauty." Amelia, he continued, had automobiles ever since learning how to drive and bought an airplane when ground speed bored her. Truth be told, he was worried that she was planning to fly *back* over the Atlantic. He felt it would be a jinx to do so and dreaded the repetition of suspense. As she had crossed the sky once already, waves would carry her home.

Six

LADY LINDY

Amelia's triumph led Sam Chapman to retreat from the limelight, his reflections on past interviews tinged with regret. From the porch of her Marblehead home, Emily Chapman, Sam's protective mother, addressed the press, affirming, "We both love Amelia and are grateful for her success."

As the press clamored for more details, the *Boston Herald*, in a desperate move, resorted to using the only photo it could obtain—one from Sam's high school baseball days. Coaxed back into speaking, Sam briefly reminisced about the affectionate notes he received from Amelia while she was up in the sky, recalling how he was rooted to his radio all night. (One can imagine George in Rye brooding intensely, thinking hard about how to deflect this affectionate narrative.)

Yet Sam wasn't the only one caught in the media's crosshairs. Reporters also turned their attention to Ruth Nichols, the debutante aviator recognizable by her purple flying suit. Living near George Palmer Putnam on Grace Church Street in Rye, Nichols had more than a passing acquaintance with him. She harbored deep feelings of regret about being passed over for the opportunity that Amelia Earhart seized. By 1928, Nichols had distinguished herself as the first woman to secure a hydroplane pilot and transport license. She was no flash in the pan; her talent and achievements in aviation had soared to notable heights. Nichols would have given anything for the chance that Amelia received. Wisely, she presented a poised front and expressed "joy" for her fortunate peer.

Meanwhile, mired in jealousy over her rival's success, Mabel Boll faced further dismay when her last-minute hire, Boots LeBoutillier, refused to cross the Atlantic after hearing that the rival team had left from Trepassey. As her aspirations crumbled, she provided an official comment in Newfoundland while packing her bags for home: "I congratulate them all and am delighted to see them succeed." Gracious words accompanied by tears, but what choice did a woman of ambition have? Then, perhaps to protect her legacy, she smartly contributed $500 to Harbour Grace's "world-class airstrip." In a scene reminiscent of a Hollywood movie, Boots angrily drove off in a car moments after *Miss Columbia* touched down in New York.

Fine coverage of the *Friendship*'s triumph continued in Britain, but only for "the girl" and occasionally with cartoonish reduction of the brave woman. "Amelia Earhart, what a remarkably quaint name!" a sniffy British newspaper reporter quipped, while a rival reporter gave the finishing school dropout a country bumpkin's drawl.

Captain Hilton Howell Railey, long at ease in rarefied settings, served as Amelia's official chaperone in military attire. It was Amelia alone—not Wilmer Stultz or Slim Gordon—who had tea with George Bernard Shaw, received a box of honor at Wimbledon, and dined with American-born Lady Astor, the first woman to sit in the House of Commons. Her solo appearances at these prestigious events underscored her newfound status as an international celebrity, once again setting her apart from her male counterparts.

During a well-attended luncheon for the Women's Committee for the British Empire, Amelia sat beside Winston Churchill, a cousin of Amy Phipps Guest's husband and a current backbencher. Railey, a social connection of Churchill's, proudly introduced him to her. When Churchill drank two stiff highballs, Railey caught Amelia's glance—he had warned her. Railey later remembered, "Amelia was at ease with Winny as she would have been with the traffic cop at the corner of State and Federal Street in Boston."

Before leaving the United Kingdom, Amelia toured Toynbee Hall, a respected British charitable organization founded to fight poverty. Railey had shrewdly arranged this photo op to show she had retained the values she displayed as a social worker. Away from the gaze of George Palmer Putnam, they had long, relaxing conversations, and he was tickled to find that his young friend wrote secret poetry too—a pastime they shared! (His pen name for his many poetry submissions was Peter Cameron.) The time he spent with Amelia was lovely, but he dreaded his other duties as the *Friendship*'s self-appointed European tour manager, especially watching over an alcoholic. Once, when Stultz languished in a fog of alcohol at London's Hyde Park Hotel, Railey pulled down the shades and somehow managed to get through to his hazy consciousness by telling him that his mother would not want him to die.

Pale and beat, Amelia attended one last event on European soil: a private dinner hosted by Imperial Airways at the South Western Hotel. At this dinner, her upcoming plans were revealed. With credit (extended to her because of her contract with Putnam for an upcoming book), she had purchased Lady Heath's Avro Avian Moth, a biplane that would hitch a ride on their ship home, the luxurious SS *President Roosevelt*. After further discussion with George, she planned to tour parts of the country before resuming her social work and showing naysayers she could fly. She was also bringing back souvenirs from her British sojourn, including a shawl made of old lace, a rubber cat with gleaming eyes, a butterfly made from coral beads, and a sofa cushion embroidered with a scene from the *Friendship*.

On the voyage day in 1928, Railey and his aviators tried to make a discreet entry onto the *President Roosevelt* but failed to do so, instantly drawing attention and cheers from the eager crowd at the dock. Amelia's mind raced as the triumphant fliers finally boarded. What was she going home to when, eight days after leaving Southampton on June 28, the ship docked in New York on July 6?

When Railey did his first checkup on his team aboard the SS *President Roosevelt* before the departing whistle, he found Stultz undressed in his cabin, holding a glass of cognac with one hand while bracing himself against the washbasin with the other, gazing at his inebriated reflection. As the ship lurched, Stultz knocked himself unconscious against the bulkhead. Railey put him to bed and later heard him remark, "Drunkenness is the only true form of happiness," revealing, as Railey saw it, "his inner gloom and despondency."

As the ship set off on its journey to New York, it rocked with the ocean's rhythm. Romantic things can happen in the shifty and moony beauty of an ocean crossing, and this journey was setting the stage for just that: Captain Harry Manning, a rakish thirty-one-year-old German-born American commander, stood ramrod straight when meeting the newly famous Amelia Earhart. With his wavy brown hair and steel-blue eyes, he was dreamy on his own, but even more so beneath a sky brimming with stars and wind blowing off the ocean. Manning, who had a bit of a caddish reputation for charming the boatloads of blue-blooded ladies aboard his ship, found a definite spark with his famous guest. After a long chat, he even reserved a secluded deck for her that would serve as a sanctuary on the ocean. Their playful glances and laughter over toasts hinted that this transatlantic journey would be anything but ordinary. By the time they neared New York's skyline, it was clear their bond had grown beyond that of shipmates. She even confided in him her concerns about Stultz's alcoholism back in New York—how would the pilot make it through any events when, in an alcoholic stupor, he had already caused great embarrassment on British soil with his outbursts, once publicly calling British ships unseaworthy. (The solution was that he would stay at George Palmer Putnam's home in Rye under heavy watch.)

Just before Amelia and Railey stepped into the dining quarters for the Captain's Night Dinner, Railey paused, struck by the transformation before him. In just a few short weeks, Amelia had metamorphosed from a modest aviator into a splendid vision clothed in the finest from England's distinguished shops. That evening, she didn't just enter a room; she owned it, her every move exuding a newfound self-assurance. This moment, this striking evolution of Amelia, would forever be etched in Railey's memory.

But the Captain's Night Dinner, tendered by Captain Manning in honor of the aviators, had an unintended consequence—it again made Amelia self-conscious about the attention directed solely at her name, overshadowing her colleagues' collective accomplishments. She was mortified after seeing the menu, which included Liberté's Délice and Tornadoes à la Miss Earhart—nothing had been cooked up and memorably named for the men, of course. Captain Manning's handsome good looks and gentlemanliness greatly appealed to Amelia, just as they did to many women who'd sailed with him under moonlight. Sam Chapman who? Could a budding romantic connection from these intoxicating nights at sea grow after they docked? Nothing was too improbable in Amelia's new life.

Things were going gangbusters for her, but all was not well in Rye, where at the tail end of June, Dorothy recorded in her diary an all-night row just before Amelia's triumphant arrival on the SS *President Roosevelt*. Why was she indifferent to George? "Why and wherefore!" George wanted answers and emotional access. Even more telling was her emphasis on his "insistence" (underlined boldly in her journal). Dorothy's agitation over what she was legally expected to do for a husband who wanted sex was evident in her additional note: "As tho' one ever brought back romance—or could order it. . . . To hell with conjugal rights!"

After the SS *President Roosevelt* arrived on American shores on July 6, the *Macom*, New York's trusty official welcoming tug, which had picked up Lindbergh, set off to collect the fliers under gray skies and persistent drizzle. Anchored near the Statue of Liberty since midnight, the fliers had cleared quarantine by morning, and it was time to pick them up. Mid-ride, the *Macom* sounded her siren, and the SS *President Roosevelt* acknowledged her back with a long whistle. At 9:10 a.m., Amelia hopped aboard the tug wearing a hideous and tight-fitting feather cloche. (George decided right on board he would have a word with her about the hat later.) She was accompanied by her two air companions and Railey, beaming widely and not yet ready to confront George about his outrageous letter. That time would come.

On board the famous tug were over a hundred relatives and friends of the fliers, including Amelia's sponsor, Amy Phipps Guest, and the rest of the Phipps family. (Mrs. Guest had said hello to her in England before cleverly setting sail to New York to get in the papers again.) George was there with his favorite house ghostwriter, Fitzhugh Green, who by 1928 had written twenty-three books; he had ghosted for polar adventurer Richard Byrd and penned the introduction to Lindy's bestseller; Green would now be Amelia's ghostwriter for the book George had planned. And there was Dorothy Binney Putnam, who later that night, in her journal, expressed gratification that Amelia threw her arms around her and kissed her as she boarded. This, she proudly claimed in her private pages, was the only kiss Amelia gave when she stepped aboard.

After disembarking from the steamship, Wilmer Stultz saw his pretty wife cry happy tears while Mama Stultz welcomed her brave son with open arms; he answered with a heartfelt "Mother!" As the famous tug bounced back to Manhattan's shore in rough waters, there on its upper deck was Amelia, flanked by her co-fliers, the also-flew men nobody seemed to notice. People did, however, notice George Palmer Putnam, as by June 1928, he had a familiar face and a name that mattered.

The most famous person on the boat was thirty-nine-year-old Commander Richard Byrd, sporting his white navy ducks and happily participating while promoting his upcoming Antarctic voyage and recently released G. P. Putnam's Sons book, *Skyward*. Amelia, once his young, unassuming, unknown acquaintance, was now a prominent figure and a useful one. Byrd warmly saluted her as an American hero, aware that his every action was noted too. His appearance was a double publicity win for George, who, with Railey's help, arranged for the commander to appear at both the parade and the 10:00 a.m. city hall ceremony. Byrd took the opportunity to talk privately with Railey on the tug, begging for more support for his upcoming August expedition to Antarctica and outright suggesting that Railey halt his involvement with the Earhart situation now that its objectives had been achieved. While Railey still harbored concerns about George's inappropriate behavior toward Amelia, he had already cautioned her. His work with Amelia was unpaid, but Byrd had secured funding for a generous bonus up front. On the spot, Railey agreed to assume a more significant role, relinquishing his self-appointed volunteer position as Amelia's chaperone. After a two-day rest, Railey would raise an extraordinary sum of $1 million in funds and sponsorships for Byrd's Antarctic expedition—equivalent to nearly $20 million in today's currency.

George was all too happy to hear that Railey was bowing out of the ring—with Amelia on American soil, he could now call all the shots without second-guessing. The weeks away from her and the excitement in the air had skyrocketed his interest in Amelia, and George had even arranged for a plane to drop a lavish bouquet onto the tug *Macom*. He relished watching her break into a smile. This was his doing, he admitted; he knew it would be an excellent photo op for the lady of the hour. With cunning strategy, George had orchestrated the absence of Amelia's mother, sister, and fiancé, justifying their nonattendance by emphasizing their indispensable roles in planning Boston events. While Amelia was still navigating her journey, he had taken the initiative to contact her mother and sister personally. He'd described the scene in New York as a frenetic three-ring circus, stressing that the city required Amelia's undivided attention. Asserting what he believed was best for her career, George had then sent a forceful telegram that ultimately led Amelia to agree to the plan. A released statement explaining the absence of Sam Chapman and Amelia's family from the New York City festivities ran nationally. "Please tell them that I shall see them Monday Morning," Amelia said. "I am looking forward with the keenest desire to my return home on Monday, and then I shall be happier than ever." With each passing hour, the possibility of a life with Sam slipped away, just as George had intended. Her new life seemed a planet apart.

Despite being away from her family and fiancé, Amelia was comforted by the presence of a few familiar faces at her welcoming party. George had given approval for Amelia's friends from her 1919 Lake George summer, Marian and Dorothy Stabler of Great Neck, to attend. He also sanctioned the presence of Elsie Owens, a social worker and friend from Stonington, Connecticut. Regrettably, the media unkindly referred to them as Amelia's "three spinster friends."

Everyone shushed and gathered on the tugboat when "The Star-Spangled

Banner" was performed by a volunteer band. Tall and a little less pale from a week at sea, Amelia paused her laughter, feeling an unexpected surge of emotion. Soon after, the three stars of the moment were escorted to the private aft cabin for a brief press conference aboard the *Macom*. As horns blared in the background, reporters wasted no time bombarding Amelia with questions. Wearing a flowing dark-blue coat accented with white fur, a gift from Britain, she also sported the matching cloche with tiny dark-blue feathers.

A reporter started the press conference with "Are you engaged to Mr. Chapman of Marblehead?" Amelia replied with a soft but fury-tinged voice: "Wouldn't that be a personal matter, not for discussion?"

"Would you mind revealing your salary?"

"I most certainly would mind."

Tense and unaccustomed to these pushy American reporters and their flashbulbs, she accidentally confessed to keeping a diary for future grandkids. A reporter then boomed, "You are going to get married!" Amelia briefly cast her gaze downward. "Every woman hopes to get married someday," she said self-consciously. "I don't know. I haven't seen him since the day I departed from Boston. . . . We've been cautious of newspaper reporters and photographers. It will be just him and me, so I'm afraid I cannot divulge the details of where or when."

In his blue flannel suit and soft-collared shirt, Stultz silently observed the scene. So, it was all Amelia again, even on American shores. Reporters now depressingly directed their attention toward Amelia's coat.

"This thing? Oh, it's just a fur coat given to me in London. I'm not keen on shopping for clothes. . . . By the way, I intend to return to my job as quickly as possible. I hope it's still waiting for me! Social work takes precedence over aviation for me. That's my job. However, I won't abandon flying entirely. I'm too deeply intertwined with it. I would like to promote light plane clubs, like the ones they have in England."

That noble line of talk was less appealing to reporters. One wanted to know if she thought she looked like Lindbergh.

"I don't know whether I look like him," she answered, wondering aloud whether women could simply enjoy flying as sport, as men did—was there anything strange about that?

Ignoring her concerns, the press sharks pounced on her again about Sam. Again? She responded firmly: "Please! I said I have not heard from him. I don't have to be engaged to everyone who sends me roses except to get some roses. I've had them lots of times. Suppose we let it stay at that. Shall we? That's really private life."

Despite reporters' unwillingness to question her male companions, she was relieved to be asked if she ever felt scared. That was about flight, after all.

"I wish I had been. I would have liked to have thrown a fit in the middle of the Atlantic, but I didn't."

But soon it was back to Miss Earhart.

How did she look so chic after leaving in a flight suit with no baggage? The woman, still scrimping her way out of debt, admitted she'd returned with two trunks of gifted clothes, including three evening dresses, two sports suits, half a dozen hats from Paris, a fur coat, and an evening coat. One reporter noted that the New England social worker's steel-buckled shoes were probably the only things she owned just a month before this bonanza.

"Aren't there any questions for the men who did the flying?" Amelia asked as politely as she could.

Stultz was now dutifully given a turn at the mic and revealed that the inductor compass was out of order.

"But you can't make a trip like that without a magnetic compass!" a reporter said. "Maybe I can't," Stultz replied, "but I did." A cheeky reporter asked if "Dusty" Stultz bought any hats. Stultz guffawed and answered: "I didn't buy any hats."

A *New York Herald Tribune* headline from the day summed up the scene:

CITY WELCOMES MISS EARHART, PALS IGNORED

An insightful journalist aboard the *Macom* that day later wrote that Amelia had not yet realized that when you fly the ocean, you bid goodbye to privacy. Another aviation reporter's initial impression up close was that she appeared almost delicate at first blush. "Her face is pale and thin, her figure slight. Until she laughs, she appears prim. She has a grin, however, that runs almost from ear to ear, and when she removes her hat, her blonde hair becomes a flying tumble."

Only two hundred people were present in the disheartening drizzle thirty minutes before the aviators' arrival, when the *Macom* shoved off toward New York shores. The *Daily News* reported that it was probably the quietest Gotham reception for transatlantic fliers yet. George was disappointed—tens of thousands had strained for a first glimpse of Lindbergh, Chamberlin (the record-breaking pilot of the *Columbia*), and even teen swimming sensation Gertrude Ederle. Were New Yorkers finally worn out by parades—or was it just the rain?

That's not to say that no one was captivated by her story. As the *Macom* docked at Pier A, located at Manhattan's southern tip, an estimated two thousand people gathered at the Battery. (George's overly generous estimate inflated the crowd size to five thousand.) It was a far cry from the Lindbergh mania, and the police, perhaps overly prepared, found themselves with more resources than necessary. One reporter with a heart called it "sincere." But then again, who could resist those cheers?

Hey for Amelia! Ray for Amelia! Laaaady Linnndy.

A sizable, if not gargantuan, ticker-tape parade followed. A rainy 10:00 a.m. start to the celebration was not ideal. In the 1920s, most heroes' parades were held during Wall Street's lunchtime. A start time of 12:05 meant that even the busiest stockbroker could shout congratulations and toss ticker tape from a lofty window. The timing was a shame, but enough Broadway windows were crowded with people trying to catch a glimpse. Businesspeople's faces filled every window of the many skyscrapers. Photos could be taken. But like any spinmaster, George could work with the pictures of a few thousand onlookers.

Then, two motorcycle officers led the police escort for the Girl Who Dared. Slim sat on her right and Stultz on her left. They were first in the line of the fleet of automobiles, followed by a police car with screaming sirens. In the shadow of the towering, mist-covered skyscrapers, Amelia carried yet another massive bouquet of roses, baby's breath, and ferns.

The *Friendship*'s crew arrived at city hall half an hour late. Several thousand people had waited impatiently as the band played lively tunes in the poor weather, and many had left. When the fliers were spotted, the band broke into "The Star-Spangled Banner." "There they are!"

The once familiar (now long-forgotten) journalist Hector Fuller was announced as the designated master of ceremonies and prepared to hand each of them a handwritten scroll. Amelia's champion, Commander Richard Byrd, still clad in his formal white naval uniform from the *Macom*, stood ready for the ceremony. Despite George's prior snubbing of her for the Atlantic flight, he had arranged for Ruth Nichols, his Rye neighbor and Amelia's air rival, to attend. One can't help but wonder: Did he derive some satisfaction from that invitation? Nichols, with her customary grace, confirmed her attendance. Clarence Chamberlin, Lindbergh's rival, who crossed the Atlantic with less fanfare, was also present.

New York's then iconic "official greeter," Grover Whalen, was unmistakable with his square jaw, black mustache, and red carnation affixed to his suit. This convivial self-appointed "Chairman of the Mayor's Welcoming Committee" bowed to Byrd; at that moment, Byrd and Lindbergh were America's two greatest living aviation heroes.

The official ceremony was succinct. Acting Mayor Joseph McKee stood in for the absent New York mayor, the showy and "wet" Jimmy Walker, who was reveling in style at William Randolph Hearst's San Simeon castle out West. A newsreel from that day depicts Amelia once again stealing the show as McKee lavished even more glowing praise on her. "New York is used to big things. New York itself is big. New York is great. Aviation is one of the great things of the age, and it has been New York's proud privilege to pay honor to the greats of aviation. We welcomed here Lindbergh, Byrd, Chamberlin. On behalf of the City of New York, welcome back to your native land," McKee began.

All three aviators received formal keepsake scrolls. Before departing westward by train, Mayor Jimmy Walker had signed only Amelia's—the others received McKee's signature. Amelia alone addressed the audience. "This is the most glorious reception I ever had," she said in her girly voice with enunciated diction. The others faded into the background, including George, who couldn't take his eyes off her every move. "Most of the credit must go to Mr. Stultz," she added behind the lectern.

As the token key to the city was handed to Amelia alone, she glanced over her shoulder, and George took it from her. A smile passed between them. Finally, he was the majordomo again, not his (perceived) romantic rival, Hilton Howell Railey. George had orchestrated a luncheon hosted by his other star client, Commander Richard Byrd, immediately following the parade.

She was handed a schedule as she was whisked away in a car. George had overseen a team of staffers working full-time, making calls and securing favors. They were on his home turf now, and he had his publicity machine in high gear. He occasionally checked in with staff for press-worthy updates. There was a long list of other obligations.

Amelia and the two others were to stay that night at the Biltmore Hotel next to Grand Central Station "as guests" of Commander Byrd; the Biltmore was covering his stay for publicity. Byrd had been given a donated office to plan his Antarctica expedition with George's help. He had happily secured more freebies so that he and this young flying lady could get good press together.

In their free rooms, the three aviators rested briefly before two o'clock. Then Byrd threw a massive Biltmore luncheon for the fliers, attended by all the luminaries of aviation and exploration. In the place of honor at the long dais with a white tablecloth, the overwhelmed social worker, who was barely making ends meet, now sat next to the aviation greats she had once only read about in Boston newspapers. Perhaps coached by George, Amelia modestly said that she planned to relegate her aviation to Sundays and holidays and do social service work the rest of the week. "If I haven't been fired," she joked.

In an effort to keep Stultz sober until the Boston events, all three fliers would be briefly housed by the Putnams at their Rye estate, where the butler could keep an eye on Stultz.

The next day, Amelia's itinerary was Putnam-packed. A bit more energetic the next morning, she convinced her motorcycle cop escort to let her ride in the sidecar from her first event to her second; he was waiting with Dorothy and George to take her downtown. Her hair flying, Amelia rode with Officer Millett as he drove hell-for-leather down Riverside Drive, then past the lawns and trees of Central Park, taking a sharp turn down Fifth Avenue and another left onto Forty-Second Street to reach her suite at the Biltmore. And, yes, it was a thrill. George undoubtedly envied the officer and Amelia's youth as he rode toward the Biltmore with his wife in their boring car. Oh, to be giving her that ride!

On her second night back in the city where she had once traveled the subway incognito, Amelia was chauffeured alongside the Putnams to the newly opened Ziegfeld Theatre. Their destination was the premiere of the musical adaptation of Edna Ferber's bestseller, *Show Boat*. This musical sensation, composed by Jerome Kern with lyrics by Oscar Hammerstein II, marked a significant departure from the era's usual light entertainment, and it etched its place in history by allowing both prominent Black and white actors to share the Broadway stage for the first time. Once again, Amelia's transformation was nothing short of remarkable. The woman who had previously been seen in jodhpurs and a flight helmet was now nearly unrecognizable—she was dressed to the nines, with just the right amount of ladylike makeup for the occasion.

Amelia's big night at the theater was anything but ordinary; it was an affair marked by extraordinary touches. As she was the personal guest of the legendary impresario Flo Ziegfeld himself, even the iconic chorus of "Ol' Man River" was altered to "Ol' Man Ocean" in a nod to Amelia's aerial feats over the waves. This unique tribute set the stage for an evening where the spotlight, quite fittingly, turned her way. Upon her arrival at the theater, Amelia was immediately surrounded by an eager press corps, all clamoring for details about her engagement. She answered with a hint of weariness: "Yes, I have heard from Mr. Chapman that there were roses waiting for me. . . . He expects to see me on Monday." Aware of her new manager's disapproval of this disclosure, she cleverly added, "But I have received many flowers from those to whom I am not engaged."

Wherever Amelia went, she ignited a frenzy of excitement that not only enraptured audiences but also allowed George to revel in her reflected glory. Tethered to his corporate duties, he was invigorated by her carefree and glamorous aura. Amelia was the "it girl" of the moment—urbane, relaxed, and effortlessly charming, enlivening every space she entered.

Even in the midst of this excitement, George found room for critique. "Talk into the microphone. . . . Be a little looser. . . . Don't let your voice drop at the end of sentences," he instructed firmly, coaching her on the subtleties of public appearances. For her early public outings, he also guided her on how to smile for the cameras despite her gap-toothed grin, how to walk and talk while giving slide lectures, and how to keep her tone steady and engaging throughout.

Amelia also quickly learned to downplay her avid feminism to make it more digestible for the broader public. The country wanted her prettied up too. Her hastily combed hair and makeup were restyled for bewitching new photos that must have startled even her "fiancé" left behind in Boston; they subtly crafted an image that softened her revolutionary ideals without silencing them.

Word was she was sincere, despite her theatrical modesty. She had the unmistakable aura of a clean romance, the reporters said. Although *The New Yorker*'s highbrow mockery was often weaponized in the 1920s to dismiss crass ambition, the staff first wrote about the young social worker with a notable display of low snark: "It is our deliberate judgment that Amelia Earhart is an awfully nice girl. After all, it is not her fault that the papers call her 'Lady Lindy.'" Perhaps they agreed about her disposition at the Algonquin Round Table; it's fun to imagine that Dorothy Parker was the one giving her the pass.

The irony of Amelia's situation was that, during an era when women were routinely excluded from opportunities, she received a break solely because of her gender. Witnessing doors open for her left many other highly qualified female pilots feeling disheartened. An exclusive luncheon at Rye's Westchester-Biltmore Country Club, intended for hardworking women aviators, had attendees like Amelia's German rival, Thea Rasche, and George's often-overlooked neighbor, Ruth Nichols, both great sports about it all.

Meanwhile, reporters had moved on to Boston, where Amelia's sidelined mother had been contacted and located. She was working at Denison House, preparing for local receptions. She feared that her daughter, who came "from a long line of Philadelphia Quakers," would find the New York experience difficult. (She had that wrong!)

In one of his last interviews, a humiliated Sam Chapman said he had planned to go to New York initially but had since decided that this was her reception, not his. He graciously made no mention of the fact that Amelia had told him not to come after speaking with George. He said he "was taking a back seat" until the hoopla was over and helping her mother with local celebrations in Massachusetts.

In Midtown, George was busy trying to scotch bothersome reports that Amelia's relationship with Sam was real. She soon read what he had prepared: "My status so far as any engagement is concerned is identically the same as it was before the *Friendship* left Boston. Whether or not there is any understanding, informal or otherwise, is, after all, a purely personal matter and of interest to no one except those directly concerned. Please let us say no more about it."

Seven

THE MITTEN

The weary aviators readied themselves for their journey to Boston after spending the night with the Putnams in Rye. As a passenger once more, Amelia boarded a private Ford trimotor with Dorothy and George. A hired pilot would take them to a Boston airport. Wilmer Stultz, thankfully sober following the vigilant watch of the Putnams' staff, piloted a Fokker that carried his wife, Slim Gordon, and Slim's fiancée.

Both planes landed safely in Boston at 11:30 a.m. on July 9. After the spectacle in New York and the emotionally draining hours leading up to it, Amelia managed to catch some much-needed sleep during the flight. Before facing the eager crowd of a thousand people enduring the sweltering summer heat at the airfield (including the perspiring Boston mayor, sporting his top hat and morning coat), Amelia shared a tender moment with her mother and sister, who awaited her inside an office at the airport.

"I'm so glad you're home, my darling daughter," her mother said. This made Amelia cry some more, as her tearful mother was referencing the old nursery rhyme they used to recite together: "O Mother Dear, may I go out to swim? / Yes, my darling daughter. / Hang your clothes on a hickory limb, and don't go near the water!"

Muriel had her own hug and kiss and told her sister to wear a hat in the hot sun, or she would get more freckles too. A proper reunion had to be postponed until they could be alone. Sam Chapman had agreed to meet up with her at the hotel after the official Boston parade, which, with Hilton Howell Railey as the architect, was expected to draw a massive crowd that would outshine the somewhat disappointing crowd in New York—a result of bad weather and, though George would never admit it, poor planning.

The grand parade route unfurled from the airport, weaving through Chelsea and Charlestown, and culminated in the pulsing heart of Boston, where three hundred thousand spectators thronged the streets. Railey, in a stroke of genius, saw to it that Amelia was riding in the very Cadillac that had once ferried Lindbergh during his own heralded visit. *The Boston Globe* perfectly captured the electrifying atmosphere in its headline: BOSTON ROARS WHILE AMELIA EARHART RIDES IN TRIUMPH.

Once more, ticker tape descended upon Amelia as she wore her smart blue coat from Britain, and countless telephone book pages had been torn into confetti. Following the pageantry, a large crowd gathered outside the Boston Chamber of Commerce. George Palmer Putnam's voice boomed through the crowd as he tried to shoo them away: "You can't have her now!"

Obediently, Amelia accompanied George to the thirteenth floor of the building, where he had arranged for her to be photographed alongside two local celebrities before her twelve thirty luncheon in the main dining room. There, a grand assembly of seven hundred men celebrated Amelia, with Commander Richard Byrd and Mayor Malcolm Nichols by her side on the dais. Notably absent was Sam Chapman, and whether he was overlooked in the invitations remains unknown.

When Amelia finally withdrew to the sanctuary of the Ritz-Carlton by limousine, seeking another much-needed respite, the hotel itself was a hive of anticipation, busily preparing for an evening reception destined to entertain two thousand guests in her honor. Upon her arrival at the Ritz-Carlton, Amelia was greeted in the marbled grandeur of the lobby by her long-suffering fiancé. As Dorothy chronicled in her diary, Sam, seizing a quiet moment, slipped upstairs to visit Amelia in her suite—a move that soon made its way through the grapevine of eager newsies. Despite the prospect of a future together, Amelia's tightly packed schedule permitted only a fleeting connection. Recognizing the need for added discretion, she arranged a longer meetup in her lavish Ritz-Carlton suite.

The transformed Amelia descended to the lobby in a swirl of elegance, dressed in a midnight-blue chiffon gown, her feet adorned in glistening silver slippers and a matching scarf draped gracefully around her neck. As she approached the cluster of reporters, the first question cut through the murmur: "Could you have flown across the Atlantic alone?"

"Absolutely not," she replied firmly. "I don't believe there is a girl flier anywhere who could handle a plane alone across the Atlantic."

"And do you object to being called Lady Lindy?"

"I certainly do. It makes me feel like apologizing to Colonel Lindbergh! Remember, I am primarily a social worker. Social work is my vocation, aviation my avocation. I recently told friends that I'm merely a social worker on a whim—it's a fitting description. In six weeks, I'll return to my old job at Denison House. Though I plan to fly more than ever, there are no immediate plans for any specific flights. If given a choice, I'd prefer a novel route, previously uncharted. Whether that leads me across the Atlantic or Pacific remains to be seen."

"Do you think your flight will boost women's interest in aviation?"

"I hope so; that was part of my intention in making this flight. Women face significant barriers in aviation—they can't join the army or navy and be paid to learn flying, as men can. But I am convinced that eventually, women will fly as frequently and competently as men. It's no different than driving a car—some are good at it, and some aren't."

"When is your new book coming out?"

"Oh, am I writing a book?" she said slyly. "That's more news to me than it is to you." Despite her deflecting smiles and bonhomie, she was pressed into admitting that she would be spending the rest of the week at the Westchester home of Mr. George Palmer Putnam, the publisher who had supported the *Friendship*'s flight. She added that many questions regarding her future would be decided during her stay there, including those around any rumored book.

She could not evade the oft-asked last question: "When will you marry your honey?"

"Please," Amelia snapped, "let me have just a few secrets of my own.... I've seen him today, and I expect to see him tomorrow, and that's that."

It wasn't the only important order of business she'd have to sort out in the hubbub. Before the trip, while processing paperwork for Amelia's new biplane, which she'd bought on credit from Lady Heath, George's assistant had discovered that Amelia's much-touted 1923 license, which she presented as proof of being the sixteenth female aviator licensed by the Fédération Aéronautique Internationale, was merely an FAI certificate. The horror! Amelia now learned she had been flying without proper credentials since 1923. To further complicate matters, George had inflated her flight hours to the press, claiming over five hundred—a good-sized lie, with the actual number being hundreds of hours less than the figure ascribed to her.

Quick-thinking George had already invited Lieutenant Commander Porter Adams—president of the National Aeronautic Association and guest of honor for the grand evening reception at Boston's Ritz-Carlton—partly to help prevent negative media coverage if the truth emerged. George managed to get Adams alone in a room and persuaded him to assist Amelia. However, Adams could offer only limited help. Amelia wanted to hone her skills and really fly.

In Adams's view, Amelia had two options: fly the aircraft without a license or quietly take a few refresher lessons and sit for the test. Officials at Westchester assured George that any refresher lessons would be held in the strictest confidence. Wisely, Amelia, after a candid conversation with George, chose not to fly her new Avro Avian unlicensed and instead opted for catch-up lessons near the Putnams so she could start flying in the fall. While her long-term aspiration was to navigate the Atlantic solo—a lofty goal for someone so untrained for what that required—her immediate objective in the summer of 1928 was to obtain a bona fide basic pilot's license.

She was still far from the skill level needed for the advanced transport license, a qualification that top women fliers like Ruth Nichols proudly held. When George happily toasted the guest of honor at the dinner, it would not be the last time he would rely on his networking to help cover up Amelia's actual flying ability before proper training.

In yet another private space that night, Railey had a few moments with Amelia—their first solitary moment since sailing back over the Atlantic on the SS *President Roosevelt*. He'd warned her about George Palmer Putnam and his less-than-honorable intentions in Europe. Now, after Railey had observed his married friend's laser focus on Amelia, all while standing next to his devoted wife, his apprehensions were understandably growing.

On a sheet of high-end Ritz-Carlton stationery from his room, Railey scribbled the words BRUSH FIRE, folded the note, and handed it to her, urging her to telegraph or telephone that code to him, wherever he might be, if George got out of control. "Smiling sweetly and with apparent complete understanding," he later wrote in a private letter, "she stuffed this code in the costly pearl-beaded dress." After their week in Boston, Railey believed he'd given her all the caution he could muster. He would later reflect: "An obscure social worker in Boston, Amelia was a superior young woman. But she was not 'big' in any sense whatsoever. In fact, she was gullible, and subject to flattery; and for that frailty she paid with her life. After she had ignored my advice, vehemently expressed, and had fallen for the wiles of that son of a bitch, as everybody called him, George Putnam." Amelia now officially called George her manager and sometimes her agent. While Railey generously offered his services for nothing, George was more pragmatic, already there, and all too happy to cash in on his 10 percent cut.

Spotting another opportune moment during the reception, George cornered Railey in the Ritz-Carlton's men's room and, perhaps after a word with Amelia, accused him of being "in love" with "their" Amelia. So much for gratitude for Railey's invested effort and unpaid work. Railey later dismissed the ugly conversation as "vague guff," the clumsy ramblings of "a fool."

Meanwhile, Sam Chapman and Dorothy Binney Putnam somehow found each other that night in the hotel and had a "fine talk" about being sidelined from the formal ceremonies, and the flies on the wall talked openly about Sam's relationship with Amelia. Dorothy added in her diary: "Such an insight in to [sic] a human being as I've only seen a few times before. I like him, but Lordy, what a problem he is facing." (As was Dorothy, even if she had not yet admitted it to herself. She would soon head back to Rye by private car, leaving George with his pageantry and obsessions to head back to her lover's arms.)

Boston provided George with the opportunity to meet and size up Amelia's fiancé, but he remained composed as they dined together, the table divided into two couples: Dorothy and George, Amelia and Sam. A dullard, a nonentity—so devoid of color he nearly blended into the upholstery! No threat there, George mused, his mind already racing ahead. He resolved to have a serious talk with Amelia about her dazzling future, one that shouldn't be dimmed by the shadows of a lackluster past. Could she picture what he saw—the mouthwatering success that could be their shared adventure?

On Tuesday, July 10, Amelia and Sam Chapman had a private breakfast in her Ritz-Carlton suite, with the doors closed to the outside world. What they discussed over breakfast stayed between them, leaving others to speculate. Outside, a wry reporter, notebook in hand, couldn't resist speculating with a smirk: "A secret tryst! A quiet hour with the boy she loves."

Contrary to press speculation, there was no clandestine rendezvous; Amelia simply sought a candid and private conversation with Sam. Their once-harmonious relationship now suffered irreparable tides; she hoped he understood that things were different now.

Muriel's later octogenarian memories shed more light: "Sam opposed the Atlantic flight from the beginning." Her voice, fragile yet resolute in an old recording, continued: "He thought it was outrageous that she was risking her life. And when she returned, he longed for a simpler New England life, overwhelmed by the constant adulation she received." She had to leave Sam again, off to yet another George-orchestrated Boston photo op, a return to Denison House. What else could he say but "Yes, fine"?

And there, at her settlement house, hundreds of children touched by

Miss Earhart's influence gathered, screaming with excitement, clinging to her dress. *Their* Amelia was famous! Sam showed up this time when Medford threw a massive celebration for her, a celebration that he had helped his would-be mother-in-law and sister-in-law plan, the festivities attracting twenty-five thousand attendees. Yet it was all just too much. Seeking a fleeting escape, he proposed a drive to Marblehead. Unexpectedly, she acquiesced. Their discussion during that drive remains shrouded in mystery. However, their shared warmth couldn't persuade Amelia to rethink their future.

A week after returning to New York, Amelia made her national speaking debut at Madison Square Garden and dramatically arrived onstage by driving in a Plymouth, the new low-cost model from Chrysler that made its own debut that night. Wearing a simple blue chiffon gown with silver slippers and a matching scarf, she began her address with a touch of humor, saying, "Flying the Atlantic is one of those things you decide to do in a moment and then forget the danger, just like a trip to the dentist."

As a break from her busy schedule, Amelia spent another peaceful week at Rocknoll, the Putnam home in Rye. "Peaceful" came with an asterisk: with eyes on the gal and the publishing prize, George persuaded Amelia to let him personally help her write the book on her flight. All she had to do was move for the summer into his family's house, where he'd give her all the help a beginner needed. In his fine house, there was plenty of room for her, as well as servants to indulge any whim. Plus, his top ghostwriter, Fitzhugh Green, a former navy commander with a knack for adventure writing, would talk to her, extract her accounts, and, with the assistance of a typist also staying with the family, convert them into a compelling narrative. Green and Amelia's collaboration, George assured, would remain discreet. She was to tell no one that she was not actually writing her own book.

Green, who had already moved in, was soon introduced to Amelia, and after the next breakfast, he spent the first hour pulling stories out of her, encouraging her to share her best recollections and most exciting experiences. This task, as Railey knew all too well, could be as challenging as flying across the Atlantic.

Right off, Green sensed that Amelia had some beautiful poetic thoughts but didn't possess a writer's mindset. So where could he find drama? Might he have to invent some? In the meantime, Green gathered enough material to at least start working. The rest of the discussions he might plumb could wait until after more celebratory obligations, like Chicago, where yet another exhausting parade and lecture schedule awaited. "Have some quiet time, Amelia," Green must have assured. "We'll call you when we need you."

George privately assured Green that others could fill in the blanks.

On July 13, Amelia's maritime suitor, Captain Harry Manning, was in his Upper West Side apartment, preparing for another Atlantic venture, when he got quite the surprise: his most recent ocean flirtation, Amelia Earhart, invited him over for dinner at Rocknoll. He could even stay the night. To George's unhappy surprise, Amelia's anticipation for the evening was apparent, and he was secretly seething.

George had seemingly managed the Sam Chapman matter, but on closer observation, was Manning another hurdle? George kept a close eye on Amelia and Captain Manning, even when he left the room—he was quick to notice any change in their demeanor upon his return. Later, Green spoke with Manning, gathering material for the book, but when he presented Manning's recollections, he conveniently left out the heavy flirtation between Manning and Amelia, which Railey had witnessed firsthand.

The *Friendship* crew reunited in Midtown and began their journey to Chicago via the Pennsylvania Railroad. Their first stop on July 18 took them to Altoona, Wilmer Stultz's hometown, where Amelia Earhart continued to attract attention. On July 19, they were slated to participate in a parade at Chicago's Union Station. George had secured sleeper cars for their trip, and this time, bored by it all, Dorothy wisely decided not to accompany the crew.

Before the train arrived at Union Station at 9:55 a.m., the Loop district was festooned with flags. The fliers hurried into waiting cars, including one with Ann Bruce, Slim Gordon's Brookline-based fiancée. This time, Mayor William Hale Thompson presided over the parade. New town, new mayor.

George's quick thinking proved vital on that chaotic morning when Stultz disappeared just before the city hall festivities, likely in search of a drink. Slim, evidently tired of the "Amelia Show," was AWOL too. George leapt into the fray by putting on Stultz's well-worn leather helmet and ditching his wire-rimmed glasses; somehow, he convincingly impersonated him. Meanwhile, Amelia's old Hyde Park classmate Reed Landis—who had made a name for himself as a World War I ace—happily stepped in to play Slim. Since Amelia was the face everyone recognized, their ruse went unnoticed. A pretty good trick.

Later, Amelia and George roared with laughter over the day's successful masquerade, especially over how "Mr. Putnam's whereabouts" remained an amusing mystery throughout the day, and how George cheekily apologized for his (feigned) absence in a letter to the mayor.

Amelia's return to Chicago after a long absence stirred up some fond memories, but the trip pained her at times, as it reminded her of her father's hidden struggle with addiction and brought back strong recollections of her nomadic upbringing, which was shaped by Edwin's unspeakable battle with alcoholism. It also dredged up her long-ago disappointment with school staff who, due to their indifference, failed to connect with their students, even on a fundamental level. After her years as a social worker, Amelia believed that the key to engaging and inspiring youth was understanding and connecting with them on their own terms. And she was determined to demonstrate this approach.

On July 19, to deafening cheers, Amelia, dressed in brown, entered her old high school auditorium and confidently stepped onto the piano. Her bold move surprised the school's longtime principal, Hiram B. Loomis, who had also been Amelia's principal. However, the thunderous applause that filled the auditorium swept away his unease. The flier was no longer the shy girl who once hid behind a locker. She spoke into a waiting microphone with confidence: "If only I had known that Hyde Park would embrace my transatlantic flight with such fervor . . . ," she began.

With candor rarely seen in her typically guarded exchanges, Amelia spilled some of her history to a Chicago journalist, and with a mix of irony and magnanimity, she offered up effusive thanks to those schooltime shadows—once blind to her existence, now front-row enthusiasts.

Stultz and Slim slept in and missed the high school event too. She would see those fellow fliers just once more before they completely disappeared from her life. Amelia joined over five thousand guests at Slim Gordon's civil wedding to Ann Bruce. The wedding was held in the grand (and air-conditioned!) Trianon Ballroom, built in 1922. The carnivalesque celebration was one of George's "genius" press events. However, it left a sour note when George neglected to pay the $100,000 bill, a gesture of disdain toward the resentful men he no longer needed. He was simply cutting them loose from his life. The unpaid wedding bill, like many others to come, was someone else's mess, a pattern George would repeatedly follow, absolving himself of responsibility.

It was back to Rye and Dorothy, who certainly wasn't going to pay *that* bill.

Now, George thought, how to finally finish off that pesky Sam Chapman. Why wouldn't that topic go away too? He was more than pleased to hear it when Amelia agreed that all the marriage talk was wearying.

While Amelia was always enthusiastic about discussing her career and advocating for gender equality, it was the romantic speculation surrounding her love life that still, much to her chagrin, captivated readers. A female reporter even playfully suggested that no news about the fiancé meant Sam had been given "the mitten"—a quaint slice of linguistic Americana, hearkening back to the days of horse-drawn buggies and tightly laced corsets, a quip that meant he'd been dumped. When she was spotted in town, Amelia refused any commentary beyond "I do not intend to get married today or any other day. I'm never going to get married. I am more interested in science than romance."

A listless reporter from one of the Hearst papers, grasping for a headline, pressed Amelia: "Miss Earhart, when will you marry Lindy?"

She blushed and composed herself before calmly stating, "I have never met Colonel Lindbergh." She then left the room. Nevertheless, the clever correspondent had his headline: AMELIA WON'T MARRY LINDY.

One July evening, Sam received an unexpected phone call from a reporter for the *Daily News* who asked if he was concerned that Amelia's expanded circle of elite acquaintances would threaten their relationship. Caught off guard once again, Chapman's response was disjointed and hesitant: "Well, whatever she says is right. Everything is just as it was."

Eight

UNDER WHOSE ROOFTREE

To Amelia, Sam Chapman, with his yearslong wholehearted affection for her, seemed like a lifetime ago now. On Rye's Locust Avenue, she turned a decisive corner and found herself in the gilded embrace of the Putnams' Spanish mission–style mansion, an oasis of calm. A snug reading alcove, tucked near a modest bookshelf, became one of her favorite retreats during her transition to authorship, even if it wasn't the legitimate path she had once envisioned. It is a Darwinian world, and it always has been.

Dorothy's garden featured brightly colored zinnias, fragrant prized roses, and gardenias. Amelia was amused to learn that Dorothy was "an avid gardener" with a live-in gardener for pruning and other grunt work. Amelia often lingered in the garden alone, secretly relishing this temporary life of luxury, perhaps meditating over whether such opulence would ever reach her again. She must have reflected on her privileged childhood years in Atchison before her family's financial spiral began. And with the parades behind her, Amelia's life was calmer here. While her ghostwriter and his staff crafted sentences based on whatever she could remember, her workload was minimal. There might be a lecture or two to attend each week, but she'd be chauffeured to them. She also secretly practiced her flying skills at the nearby country club, even dreaming of a cross-country trip in her Avro Avian Moth when she felt skilled enough.

The day they met, George had boasted about the bold spirit of his much-lauded eldest son, David. Now, she had weeks to spend with the spirited boy she'd first been introduced to upon moving in. Recently, the fifteen-year-old had shot up in height and now spoke with a deep, froggy voice. Despite Amelia's own height, he, like his father, towered over her. Shyer but undeniably sweet was his younger brother, George Jr., who she discovered was affectionately known as Junie by his family, his namesake being Dorothy's adored older brother. At seven years old, Junie remained a tiny, skinny child brimming with adorable interests. In the tranquility of his bedroom, he sat curled up in an oversize armchair, clutching in his small hands a model airplane Amelia had given him. She observed him from the doorway, a protective smile gracing her face as memories of her own childhood curiosities flooded back. With her background as a social worker who specialized in children, she felt an immediate connection with him too.

Although Fitzhugh Green, the principal ghost behind the Putnam machine, never spilled a syllable on record about the clandestine scribblings he fashioned into a semi-compelling hack narrative for George and Amelia, a window into what it might have been like to mimic Amelia's voice was provided in a secret 1980s interview with another one of her ghostwriters, Helen "Roses" Weber, a publicist and former Curtiss aviation employee who wrote articles for her. Weber painted Amelia as a paradox wrapped in an aviator's jacket: shy yet amiable, and fiercely private outside the lecture halls. Writing good poetry, not prose, was her one-day writing dream, Weber recalled. "She disliked shopping too, which I did for her, but she had a good mind, mechanically and technically."

As the spotlight on Amelia intensified with her many public appearances and her first wave of endorsement deals, George and Dorothy plotted to further elevate their Midwestern guest's image. They aimed for a sophisticated, big-league makeover—a transformation befitting the emerging star. With strategic flair, Dorothy chauffeured her to Stamford, a haven of high-end shopping, where gleaming store windows promised luxury and exclusivity. A notable photograph captures Amelia and Dorothy in Amelia's newly earned Chrysler roadster, en route to Stamford for a rendezvous with Sam Chapman. Still? While this meeting was recorded in Dorothy's diary, it evaded local press coverage, perhaps hinting at its private and intriguing nature. One can't help but wonder if George was even aware of this encounter.

By midsummer, photographers captured Amelia, always hatless, with the short, tousled hair that she and George had agreed would become her signature look.

George felt that some of his new client's openly feminist remarks needed to be toned down for a broader audience. Despite his deep respect for strong-willed women, he advised Amelia to exercise caution and temper her "radical" feminist views. During the Jazz Age, youth and beauty were celebrated, but ambitious women faced expectations of tact that their male counterparts never encountered.

George's caution was not unfounded. Although 1920 marked a historic moment for American women with the suffrage movement, by 1923, prominent feminists faced mounting resistance. While innovative, Henry Ford, among other influential figures of the day, not only held deep prejudices against Jewish and Black people but also harbored antifeminist sentiments and used his platform to label feminists "Communists," intensifying hostilities. The publication of the "Spider Web Chart" in Ford's self-published weekly newspaper, *The Dearborn Independent*, featuring inflammatory content crafted by Lucia Maxwell, an intelligence officer, falsely linked various women's groups to "International Socialism." This deceptive chart had far-reaching consequences, even affecting mainstream organizations like the National League of Women Voters. It sowed fear among politicians, prompting them to swiftly distance themselves from any associations with feminism.

For Amelia, a staunch feminist since her Bloomer years in Kansas (later, as a plump-cheeked teenager, she revered radical feminist Alice Paul and now supported birth control and the Equal Rights Amendment), this atmosphere was troubling and outright depressing. Yet Amelia had always been astute. As early as 1927, in a letter to aviator Ruth Nichols, she had hinted at this internal conflict. She wrote, "I cannot claim to be a feminist but do rather enjoy seeing women tackling all kinds of new problems—new for them, that is."

By the summer of 1928, Amelia had taken George's advice to heart and began to exercise more restraint in her public discourse regarding the new freedoms modern women should enjoy. She made calculated statements such as "Well, that's why I took up aviation; I did it simply because I wasn't considered beautiful and was determined to do something to offset it." It wasn't until her fame was secure that she openly rallied for the National Woman's Party and the Equal Rights Amendment.

In July, Dorothy Binney Putnam organized a celebratory luncheon at the Westchester-Biltmore for the "lovely, modest" aviator—a tribute mentioned in the papers that was likely more his design than hers. Of course not. The twenty attendees, carefully selected by George, included Thea Rasche and Ruth Nichols, Amelia's gracefully reserved and highly skilled aviation contemporaries. George had a habit of requesting that Nichols, the close neighbor whom he had spurned for a paid ride across the Atlantic, publicly praise the emerging Amelia. Because of her debutante background, Nichols concealed her deep-seated resentment behind a wide smile. As for crossing the powerful Gyp Putnam? Few dared to do so.

As the summer heat intensified, Amelia often swam with Dorothy and relied on her fashionable hostess as her conduit into an unfamiliar realm. At dinners hosted by the Putnams and at their haughty country club gatherings, Amelia encountered artists, explorers, and famous writers from the storied Algonquin Round Table—bold names she might have never crossed paths with otherwise. But in the Putnams' private bedroom, the strain of prior disputes lingered, especially as it became evident that George was more attentive to Amelia than to Dorothy, who found his preferential treatment humiliating in front of their friends. At any given dinner party— a laugh too loud, a touch too long—George's attentions to Amelia were like spotlights, casting Dorothy in unwanted shadow. With each of George's overtures, was Amelia keenly aware of the glances that seemed to whisper betrayal?

On a painfully hot August day in Rye—before air-conditioning was standard in private homes—Hilton Howell Railey and George's talkative, bosomy mother, Frances Putnam, sought respite in the shade, enjoying Scotch before their luncheon. As another marital spat between the Putnams unfolded, the two remained silent spectators. In a hushed tone, Frances confided in Railey that George had the worst childhood tantrums imaginable. "Pure cussedness," she described them. But after a lighthearted chuckle, Frances also admitted her son's early fascination with the opposite sex. "Charm he possesses a lot of," she told Railey. "And he knows how to turn it on—provided he gets what he wants when he wants it, pronto! But what a whining, snarling SOAB [sic] he is when he doesn't." Her guffaws resonated with a mother's unconditional love.

That day, Frances openly remarked to Railey about George's evident infatuation with their guest, Amelia, making no effort to hide her observations. The atmosphere grew increasingly strained, especially for Amelia. Though hemmed in by marriage, George's fascination with the "it girl" only deepened, exceeding the intensity of their private moments in Boston and his flirtatious messages to Trepassey. Though Amelia offered a refreshing change of pace for George, she might not have fully grasped her own allure. George, however, was unmistakably enchanted; in his words, she was "very lovely to look at." Amelia was attracted to him, but navigating these feelings was complicated by his marital status. His blatant advances, especially in front of Dorothy—a respected and friendly figure to Amelia—were troubling. Just a month after Amelia settled in Rye, Dorothy recorded in her diary: "George is absorbed in Amelia. . . . Maybe he's in love with her."

Meanwhile, George's pretty "new friend" left a mark on the Putnam children; sometimes, they even seemed to prefer Amelia's company. Dorothy also wrote, "The minute he laid eyes on Amelia Earhart, he had eyes for no one else." With the growing distance between them, Dorothy's thoughts wandered toward new possibilities—perhaps not with her son's young tutor but certainly with someone else. If George found comfort elsewhere, why shouldn't she? "Why should we continue on this path for the rest of our lives?" she asked herself. The fabric of their marriage had worn thin, with betrayal casting shadows from both sides.

George was capable of spinning many plates, and as a publisher, he was thrilled that America couldn't stop talking about Commander Richard Byrd's upcoming expedition, which Railey had been promoting almost full-time since returning on the SS *President Roosevelt*—and which George had long ago secured the book rights for. Three ships, readied by funds that Railey had drummed up from the nation's tycoons, were slated to ferry planes and dreams to those frigid expanses. Several newspaper reports speculated about what Byrd might spot from his upcoming bird's-eye view as the first to fly over the South Pole after his ships arrived and he built the first town on ice, Little America. Some hitherto unknown antlered creature in Antarctica? Lost dinosaurs, maybe? Lost tribes? (This folly was even pushed by Byrd for more press.) But, heck, this was the age when the world was introduced to the Komodo dragon, and anything seemed possible.

During this tumultuous month, Amelia and Dorothy struggled to hold their fragile friendship together. To warm things up between them, Amelia offered Dorothy a spin in her newly acquired Avro Avian, which she'd been stealthily practicing in all summer at the nearby out-of-the-way country club. Dorothy readily said yes, as sharing a two-woman ride with the country's most famous female aviator was still a thrill. Yet the day had its plot twist. Amelia later went off with George on an errand, leaving Dorothy in the curious spot of playing hostess to their drop-in guest, Laurence "Larry" McKinley Gould—a central figure in Byrd's Antarctic endeavor. Late that night, Amelia, returning with George, murmured an offer to a drowsy Dorothy: "I'd like to dedicate my book to you, Dottie, if you think it's good enough, and if you don't, I won't. But I'd like to." Dorothy's diary captured her bewilderment: "This was a surprise; does she really want to? Or was it a sop to me because she monopolized George all summer?"

Over these weeks, before Commander Richard Byrd's ships left New York Harbor for the faraway ice, George even thought of promoting two of his clients with one event. On George's advice, Amelia agreed to fly over the *City of New York*, Byrd's romantic, newly famous nineteenth-century barkentine that would be sailing for Antarctica. Dorothy listened quietly at the dinner table as they discussed how the newly born Queen of the Air would fit into one of the summer's most significant events. "It's wonderful," Dorothy said. "Congratulations." She'd had enough. This time, Dottie Putnam did not want to be in town.

As detailed in her diary entries, she fled Rye on August 23, bound for the rugged expanses of a Wyoming dude ranch run by Carl Dunrud, an outdoorsman and trusted guide from happier days in her marriage. George and Amelia accompanied her to the station, and Dorothy's final glance through the train window confirmed her suspicions. There they stood, George and Amelia, unmistakably a pair, their proximity in the chill morning air speaking volumes without a word.

In Dorothy's absence, the emotional landscape shifted. Relieved of the burden of discretion, Amelia found George's intensified attentions increasingly tricky to parry. With no watchful eyes to temper their interactions, what was once guarded became palpably intimate.

The grand polar send-off for Byrd occurred two days later, on Saturday, August 25. Amelia followed George's instructions. Byrd, who would later depart from America but would for now go only as far as the Statue of Liberty, climbed the mast to wave to Amelia buzzing overhead in her Avro Avian Moth, the plane she had acquired from Lady Heath back in England. Hidden from view, three stowaways destined for instant fame were still secretly tucked away on board as Amelia gave a friendly wing dip to Byrd's crew. For the crowds lining the urban shorelines, watching these first forty men in Byrd's team depart felt like witnessing people blast off to the moon years later. With the book deal secured for the heroic Commander Byrd, George had little guilt; he was feeling confident about delivering another success for his family. Juggling Byrd as a client and a blossoming romance with Amelia, he had his hands full.

While Dorothy took a break in Wyoming, George and Amelia caught up with Railey alone. Railey buried the hatchet with George, despite past tensions from the Ritz-Carlton incident. Amelia was clearly close to him, but this was her situation to handle. Since George wasn't one to ever apologize, Railey had no choice but to rise above it all. Their get-together at Rye Town Beach marked a fresh start in their friendship and is documented in many cheerful photos.

But in Wyoming, solitude didn't bring Dorothy the peace she sought. Once again, her diary revealed her emotions, indicating that she often felt useless and unaccomplished compared with Amelia. She was no longer interested in her husband's bombast. And what was the point of trying when her husband and her young friend had "become a couple"? She was depleted, lifeless, and ready for separation or divorce. The "charm" of suicide even crept into her thoughts. Did she have the courage to leave him and her marriage behind? To leave the world behind? If you have experienced pain, it is because you have experienced joy.

After months of promotion by George, Amelia, in stark contrast, was seen as anything but useless. America's top syndicated columnist, O. O. McIntyre, wrote (with prescience) around this same time: "Amelia has become a symbol of a new womanhood—a symbol, I predict, that will be emulously patterned after by thousands of young girls in their quest for the Ideal."

It was perhaps fortunate that Dorothy, the matriculated English major, was out of town on August 27 when *Cosmopolitan* announced Amelia as its permanent aviation editor. Amelia had previously been published in *McCall's*, whose star editor, Otis Wiese, put out two trial articles under her name.

It ended in a mess when (as the story goes) she endorsed Lucky Strike for $1,500 to support Wilmer Stultz and Slim Gordon. The copy was dicey—just at the line of saying she smoked them herself: "Lucky Strikes were the cigarette carried on the *Friendship* when she crossed the Atlantic. They were smoked continuously from Trepassey to Wales. I think nothing helped so much to lessen the strain for all of us." But what had seemed like a top-notch idea at first caused immediate fallout. What kind of all-American gal smoked? This was the stuff of flappers. Following public outcry, Wiese ended Amelia's trial run immediately. Railey advised George on how she could quickly distance herself from smoking, and from then on, she claimed she never lit up—which was almost the truth. (As noted by several impartial observers, she smoked occasionally.)

Under Railey's wise counsel, Amelia donated $1,500 to Byrd's Antarctic expedition to repay his support of her *Friendship* flight. Railey had the young flier's back by using his connections to secure two printed letters in *The New York Times*—one from Amelia announcing the donation and another from Byrd expressing gratitude.

After the dizzying backlash resulting from his bad decision-making, George was satisfied and proud that he had reached a much better agreement with *Cosmopolitan* for Amelia—one that came with a steady salary and an office she could call her own. (Undoubtedly, George also hoped to prevent her from rekindling her romance with Sam. He reasoned that giving her a legitimate reason to be in the city would also allow them to meet without raising suspicion.)

Amelia was proud, too, and wrote to her mother, excitedly telling her that she could now use her Filene's credit card in Boston. (And sit down for this, Ma!) She was about to become a New York magazine editor. How she could write and edit articles when she had never done so before was the least of her worries. The biggest challenge was getting through her daily circus. Amelia addressed the New York State Fair on August 28 after traveling upstate to Syracuse with George, little Junie, and boy explorer David, the latter old enough, at fifteen, to sense what was going on between his father and the new family friend. He was intelligent enough to keep his father's betrayal of his vacationing mother from his younger brother.

A few days later, on August 31, Amelia and George commenced a "flying vacation" to celebrate the publication of her book and her participation in the National Air Races in California. George's official statement suggested a cross-country promotional tour, with him delivering speeches about his explorations as a warm-up act. However, the start of this ambitious trip almost became their Waterloo. Disaster struck near Pittsburgh after an early-morning departure from the Westchester-Biltmore's polo grounds in Rye. At 6:15 p.m., Amelia's front wheel hit a rut while touching down in Rodgers Field. This broke the landing gear and caused the Avro Avian Moth to overturn, splintering the propeller and lower left wing.

Amelia couldn't believe her bad luck when, after emerging unscathed, she found a reporter on the scene. Without informing Amelia, George had alerted the local press that the pilot would be in town. Coached by George on what to say, she laughed off the accident, deeming it a minor error to miss her ditch and falsely claiming never to have been in a crash in her ten years of flying. (Neta Snook might have had something to say about that!) Despite the technical mishap, photos captured George, clad in a leather jacket and holding binoculars, looking quite enamored. That night, there may have been discreet encounters at Pittsburgh's first skyscraper hotel, the Schenley. If so, as with many aspects of her life, Amelia kept it secret. While George did not admit to a new love as a married man, he called their trip a "pleasure flight" during a refueling stop in Bellefonte, Pennsylvania. Infidelity was either brewing or had already occurred.

The next day, another Avro Avian was flown into Pennsylvania for the new star, and she crashed that one too, saying, "I don't profess or pretend to be a flier. I am just an amateur, a dub, flying around the country for the amusement there is in it for me."

Amelia likely did not know that George slipped off somewhere in Pittsburgh to send an urgent telegram to Dorothy. Dorothy had traveled west, from Wyoming to Seattle and even to her erstwhile home in Bend, to see old friends. George had just heard damning rumors, relayed by Railey, that he and Amelia were having an affair, and in an odd accusation, he said he strongly felt that Dorothy's absence from the East Coast was fueling the rumors. She must ride home on the Sunset Limited. He was coming home, too, and letting Amelia head to California without him.

Feeling cornered and slighted, Dorothy obliged, truncating her own adventure to escape such nonsense. To her surprise, upon her return, with Amelia finally out of the house, George seemed momentarily recommitted to their relationship, even treating her to a night out with dinner and a movie—

the groundbreaking talkie *The Jazz Singer*, with Al Jolson. However, beneath the surface of this seemingly pleasant evening was ever-present marital tension. After the movie, George was uncomfortable explaining his recent actions: the crash, his decision to let Amelia proceed to California alone, and the resulting delay in her arrival at the National Air Races. They could sort things out later. They had investments together and children. He begged for unity and a joint trip to the Arctic the following summer, which he would announce, hopefully batting down the growing rumors. But Dorothy, feeling more like a pawn than a partner in this charade, vented her frustrations in her journal, unabashedly labeling George a "passion-scalded pig."

That fall, she also wrote about his "obsession for" Amelia and his constant need to be with her every moment, using any excuse to stay close. She saw this as the perfect opportunity for a separation—if not a divorce. "Eight years ago, April, I asked for a break; anything as long as I didn't have to live with him. And he broke down and cried, and swore he couldn't imagine living without me . . . I wish, almost, I cared."

On September 14, Amelia traveled to Los Angeles without George. After a five-year gap, she met her father and his second wife, Helen. Though absent from their 1926 wedding, Amelia warmly embraced Helen, known as "Annie." The reunion was both joyous and poignant.

When Amelia returned from the West Coast, several advance copies of *20 Hrs. 40 Min.: Our Flight in the* Friendship; *The American Girl, First across the Atlantic by Air, Tells Her Story* were ready for her review—the first she saw of them. What she thought of the rush job under her name is unknown. Perhaps after the Pittsburgh scare, Amelia dedicated "her" book to Dorothy, not George, likely a misguided suggestion from George himself: TO DOROTHY BINNEY PUTNAM, UNDER WHOSE ROOFTREE THIS BOOK IS WRITTEN.

Dorothy was drawn to the dedication page when she opened an advance copy. She had many opinions but was too well bred to express them publicly.

During a September barbecue, in the still-warm early-autumn air,

Dorothy Binney Putnam abruptly departed from the estate, seemingly for good, on the same day George released one of his books. The outdoor deck gathering included many famous explorers and luminaries, among them aviator Clarence Chamberlin. Railey, present at the event, noted a distinct shift in Dorothy's demeanor—a psychological detachment that perhaps marked a breaking point.

Decades later, in the 1970s, Dorothy, then in her eighties and comfortably ensconced in her Florida home, made a rather startling confession (on tape!) to researchers Elgen and Marie Long, claiming to have caught George and Amelia "having sex" in her own bedroom. Although the Longs were terrific and dogged researchers, their sights were set on what they considered to be the ultimate prize: the recovery of Amelia's plane. Determining whether Dorothy actually walked in on her husband having sex with Amelia Earhart wouldn't help the Longs in that pursuit. Their book contains few personal nuggets . . . and that is quite the nugget. The Longs were also careful not to ruffle the feathers of George's descendants, whose goodwill was crucial to their ongoing research. In their minds, preserving the dignified legacy of Amelia Earhart took precedence over any potential scandal.

Though referenced a few times in other extant tapes among the Amelia Earhart Project Recordings, held by the Smithsonian's National Air and Space Museum Archives, that particular "sex tape" has gone missing from the collection. Elgen notably mentions Dorothy's taped claim to newly divorced David Binney Putnam, interviewed a few days later in Naples with his new girlfriend, Pat. However, with no transcript or recording, the exact date of her rather shocking surprise allegation remains unclear. Could it have been recorded by Long just before this 1970 discussion with her son?

But the most colorful account comes from one of George's authors, Corey Ford, a Jazz Age humorist who hobnobbed with the Algonquin Round Table wits. Remembering George as "the diametric opposite of Max Perkins"—referring to the notoriously patient, rigorous editor who stewarded Jazz Age greats like F. Scott Fitzgerald—he also recollected how he had first met George via a brash phone call in which the publisher announced that he had sold Ford's short parody as a book without getting him involved. Ford described the publisher as "always calculating, always figuring out how to make use of people, always with a commercial end in mind. Everything was for sale. His enthusiasms were strictly mercenary; he seemed incapable of genuine affection. I think he was the loneliest man I've ever met."

In piercing detail, Ford recalled George wearing a white chef's hat at the September barbecue as he tended to the grill. Nearby, a truck was parked for movers carrying Dorothy's trunks. Dressed for travel, she asked Ford, "Didn't you know? I'm divorcing George. He doesn't need me anymore." Horrified and amused, Ford returned to the party, where George was "gaily spearing frankfurters for . . . Amelia Earhart."

Further insight into this day comes (without Ford's sarcasm) from Dorothy's eldest granddaughter, Binney Dudley, who told a reporter in 1976, a year when Grandma Dorothy was still alive and could fact-check, that Dorothy "begged him to leave New York and go to Oregon but he wouldn't go, so she just up and left."

Railey was still determining if this was a permanent break but was not surprised by the shambles unfolding in real time. An heiress does not have to grovel for her husband's attention, and family money gives her an easier exit than most women. Railey felt that Amelia was equally responsible for these consequences, as she had never heeded him when it came to George. He was disgusted by Amelia and George's unscrupulous conduct, especially since Railey was also good friends with Dorothy. "AE and GP left a bad taste at Rye," he wrote confidentially. "I observed their conduct in Dorothy's presence and under her rooftree." (The latter comment was, of course, a humorous jab at Amelia's book dedication to Dorothy forced on her by George.)

And as Railey had predicted, this wasn't the precise end of Mr. and Mrs. Putnam; after spending a few angry weeks apart from George to regain her sense of self, fun-loving Dorothy decided to occasionally join her husband (and his unofficial girlfriend) for fun outings rather than get left behind. (It took a lot of work for friends, let alone the public, to figure out where Dorothy and George stood as a couple.) Dorothy, after all, had her own money and felt that an inevitable divorce was looming. Without a sexual connection to George, she played the field under her husband's nose.

Critics gave Amelia's ghostwritten book lukewarm reviews—a typical result for George's hastily produced works. Despite his bulgy ego and marketing prowess, George was not a skilled editor, often creating pedestrian content in a flurry of frenzied publications.

By the fall of 1928, despite emotional challenges, Project Amelia was in full swing. George secured a position for her in New York and now helped "Miss Earhart" find accommodation at the esteemed Greenwich House, a downtown settlement house.

When Amelia had returned from the West Coast on October 13, she'd settled into this negotiated arrangement. For $42.07 a month, she enjoyed the top floor of the men's residence, complete with a fireplace. This setup would soon also accommodate Amelia's mother, an arrangement that offered Amy Earhart a break from assisting Muriel and allowed her a taste of life in America's cultural epicenter. Amelia's residency application listed her occupation as "aviatrix/editor at *Cosmopolitan*." It was a rental, yet George exaggerated the narrative, insisting she resided there at no cost as she continued her social work in New York, rather than in Boston, alongside her glamorous editorial role. But records from Greenwich House reveal a different picture. While Amelia, who lived on the top floor and had dinner with the staff every Tuesday, was well liked, she was often seen as a celebrity transient—someone with commendable ideas but mostly absent and without the time to implement them. An anonymous note about her potential as a staff member read "NO."

Despite the lackluster follow-through on George's marvelously rich promises of social work contributions in exchange for reduced rent, Mary Kingsbury Simkhovitch, Greenwich House's director, held Amelia in high regard. She recognized Amelia's inquisitive nature and her sincere commitment to justice. "Amelia had strong scientific interests, which gave her an inquiring attitude into every aspect of life," Simkhovitch reminisced. Indeed, Amelia's presence was felt. At an outdoor neighborhood event, she told the local children tales of her adventures and even let them hold her aviation helmet and goggles.

Even an enlightened chat at the corner store made for a nice change from conservative Boston. The local bohemians in the Village were into Freud and bandied about words like *repressed* and *maladjusted*. And they left her alone. Her time living in Greenwich Village was brief, but according to one dog obedience trainer who saw her self-servicing her clanking car, parked on Barrow Street near Greenwich House: "I think most of the people in the neighborhood knew who she was, but nobody took much notice. She ate in a café with a courtyard—one a lot of us went to—and someone said she liked to talk about Edna St. Vincent Millay's poetry. She didn't seem different from us—just an ordinary person."

In a letter to an old friend, written uptown on fancy *Cosmopolitan* stationery, she allowed herself a mild brag about her new, Hollywood-style magazine office. Her desk was decorated with a long line of eight yellow porcelain elephants, cascading in size, which she explained symbolized good fortune from "a friend." At work, she always wore only one "obvious" piece of meaningful jewelry, a gold-link bracelet—from whom, she wouldn't say.

What could George Palmer Putnam say when other men showed interest in Amelia? She was not only a glamorous and famous single woman but also one of the most sought-after bachelorettes of the time. While George had managed to distance her from both Sam Chapman and Captain Manning, he felt powerless regarding her newest admirers. Among them was Grover Loening, one of New York City's most eligible bachelors. After Loening's aircraft company merged with Pennsylvania's Keystone in October 1928, he became flush with cash, pocketing $4,300,000—a tremendous sum for that era. Introduced to high society in 1928, the same year Amelia emerged as an aviation enthusiast, Loening had his pick of New York's "finest" women, and he got around. But he dated Amelia as well, finding her sweet nature, love of aviation, and lack of guile refreshing.

Loening encouraged his personal pilot, Bud Gillies, to go out on dates with her too. (Gillies sheepishly recalled on tape that his famous womanizing boss didn't want Amelia to feel lonely!) Gillies also did not think he was playing with fire by dating Amelia while his boss was too: "Oh, he had more girlfriends than he could take care of, but they could talk aviation, and they fired each other's imagination and did enjoy each other's company.... I had numerous dates with Amelia while Loening was busy with another woman, but sometimes I was just a chauffeur in the air. Grover also flew, but he never liked to carry passengers." Gillies flew Loening and Amelia (on their dates) to events such as the Preakness Stakes. "I flew Grover and Amelia down to the Curtiss airport on the northwest side of Baltimore Airport; we all went to the races as guests of Mr. Sylvester Labrot."

When pressed in the 1970s, Gillies described dating Amelia as a pleasant but entirely unsensual experience, noting, "She wasn't a romantic type, though. We'd go to places at the Aviation Country Club for dinner, ride on top of the Fifth Ave. bus, and up to Grant's Tomb and back after dinner to get some fresh air. It was a very happy, easy, pleasant relationship; she was a very charming person, very easy to know . . . very intelligent, but she was very straitlaced and didn't appreciate even the mildest off-color jokes." (It was not until being told her age during this recorded interview in the 1970s that Gillies realized she was a woman raised in the Victorian era and seven years older than him. "Seven?!")

While Amelia's aviation feats and personal life soared, she harbored a valid insecurity: she wasn't a natural magazine writer. Her fondness for poetry aside, Amelia recognized her *Cosmopolitan* assignment as a privileged opportunity, yet she wasn't the writer behind her columns. Ella May Frazer, a budding journalist who met Amelia during one of her Red Cross membership drives at Fifth Avenue's Arnold Constable & Company, later disclosed that all of Amelia's *Cosmo* pieces (like her books) were ghostwritten.

Frazer was married and four months pregnant then, and she feared her dreams of adventure were dashed with a baby on the way. Amelia, unaware that Frazer was pregnant, invited her to be the actual writer. Frazer was hell-bent on flying with Amelia, but her doctor nixed the plan. George probably found a quick replacement.

Frazer recalled Amelia being on the cusp of national recognition when they met. Interestingly, not many women thronged around the flier that day, affording the two plenty of conversation time. Amelia expressed her astonishment at having been given the opportunity to write an aviation column for *Cosmo*, admitting her deficiencies as a writer. "She knew she was a terrible writer, but now she had to write for *Cosmo*," Frazer remembered. "We were just becoming friends, but she knew I could write. I had two long pieces in the [*Sunday Magazine of the New-York Tribune*] and *The New York Sun*."

That month, in a gimmick aimed at driving up readership, *Cosmopolitan* added another new hire: the infamous Italian premier Benito Mussolini, already branded by many as ruthless, bigoted, and unmistakably Fascist. While Amelia was undoubtedly the more endearing personality, Mussolini, known to the world as Il Duce, was the better writer. Amelia's articles, though written by someone else, were bland—her own efforts might have been even blander. Meanwhile, the Fascist leader's punchy first column, headlined "Woman," featured such disturbing pearls of wisdom as "A woman's very nature imposes on her a willing submission to the power and strength of the male."

The official press release for Amelia's *Cosmopolitan* position, approved by George, stated that her writing career would not impact her aviation career. One cynical reporter wrote, "Those associate editors everywhere will read this and dream of what other firms offer with just one article a month. By the way, did Long have any vacancies?"

Though insiders within the building may not have taken her seriously as a writer, the public certainly did. Hearst's Midtown offices were soon inundated with thousands of letters from readers, young and old. To George's credit, the pieces churned out by the first aviation columnist in a popular magazine inspired many women readers to take to the skies. Amelia's ghostwritten articles read stilted and were saturated with clichés, but she often suggested the topics. Headlines included "Shall You Let Your Daughter Fly?," "Is It Safe for You to Fly?," "Mrs. Lindbergh," and "What Miss Earhart Thinks When She Is Flying."

Despite press releases and newspaper coverage, neither Mussolini nor Amelia could boost circulation. But between her column, celebrity endorsements, and speaking engagements lined up by George, she netted $50,000 after George's 10 percent cut. (Adjusted for inflation, that's almost a million dollars.) George finagled lavish gifts for the social worker too, like that blue Chrysler roadster from her Madison Square Garden appearance and a fur-lined "Amelia Earhart Flying Suit," which she was supposed to strut up and down Fifth Avenue.

In August 1928, she wrote to her mother with pride: "Please throw away rags and get things you need on my account at Filene's. I'll instruct them. I can do it now and the pleasure is mine."

While she was a good worker bee, giving press interviews and lectures for the new book she was supposed to be concentrating on, the seemingly cheerful dedication to Dorothy, forever etched in print, served as a constant reminder of her internal conflict—a praise hymn to the wife of a man with whom she shared more than a professional bond. Harold McCracken, George's most trusted assistant, often journeyed with Amelia, acting as George's steadfast aide when she delivered her well-paid "Adventurer in the Air" lectures. After Amelia's return from California, McCracken recalled, George once asked him if he would go down, "pick her up in taxi," and bring her back to the office. At Greenwich House, McCracken, who had been exploring Alaska at the time of Amelia's flight as a passenger, met her for the first time. He found her doing some social work, examining the throat of a young Black boy who clearly adored her. Her sincerity shone through. McCracken had been adventuring at sea in June and July. He only got to know her now that he was back in town and at George's beck and call. But he had a copy of her new book and, at first, did not understand why she wouldn't sign it on the dedication page. Eventually, in private, she admitted shame and agreed to sign a small silk American flag that she claimed to have carried in her shirt pocket during her 1928 flight.

On October 10, George and Dorothy made another perplexing appearance together, this time as coinvestors in the Heigh-Ho Club at 35 East Fifty-Third Street. They had launched the club on New Year's Eve in 1928, touting it to be "dry"—wink, wink—with avant-garde artist Don Dickerman, a Jazz Age personality known for themed nightclubs like the kitschy Pirates' Den in Greenwich Village, as their partner.

George envisioned the Heigh-Ho as an ultrasmart class act for the high society set, requiring elegant evening dress. Located at the former site of the Lido-Venice, the club embodied an "Art Moderne-ish," "Park Avenue-ish" elegance, combining Dickerman's eccentric flair with George's more exclusive sensibilities. Ivy Leaguers, with buddies piled into their rumble seats, were the target clientele. The club also played a role in launching the career of one of the era's iconic crooners, Rudy Vallée, a Yale alumnus. However, as the "all-American" crooner Rudy Vallée himself would attest, its polished facade belied a darker reality. Under instruction from George and Dickerman, the maître d', George Ott, enforced discriminatory rules, ensuring that only those who fit the Ivy League mold were allowed entry—meaning that, among other prejudicial rules enforced by America's elite gentleman racists of the 1920s, Black and Jewish people were not welcome.

That evening, Dorothy and George hosted an event at the club honoring three renowned aviators: American airman Captain Henry "Harry" Lyon, British pilot Captain Bill Lancaster, and Jessie "Chubbie" Miller, an Australian aviation pioneer. Despite the club's "officially" dry designation, clandestine libations swirled in glasses. Dorothy Binney Putnam noted in her diary the excessive drinking: "Too much drinking and poor dancers." She also observed how the aviators, loosened by booze, openly mocked Amelia's supposed technical skill: "Gosh, how these three flyers loathe Amelia! It's a shame."

Maintaining this veneer of marital bliss as Mr. and Mrs. Putnam led to even more uncomfortable social encounters. On October 21, Dorothy, George, and Amelia attended a Yale-Brown football game. The Putnams traveled from Rye to Yale and met up with Amelia for a buffet lunch. Dorothy later drove solo back to Rye, where she spent the evening by the fire. In Amelia's presence, George's demeanor changed noticeably, a fact not lost on Dorothy. The next day, October 22, George and Amelia went horseback riding. By Sunday night, George and Amelia likely spent the night together, an intimate fillip that left Dorothy to confront flabby excuses and tears the following morning. That night, George didn't sleep with his wife—a detail that, while self-evident given his absence, underscores the strain in their marriage. Adultery was confusing even for George. Two weeks later, Dorothy wrote in her diary that he was determined to "woo me and win me all over again, and he's certainly concentrating. He's even breaking dates with A. E."

While Amelia, George, and Dorothy were trying to power through that fall, over in the small town of Freeport, Long Island, Amelia Earhart's success in 1928 had ignited bold ambition in her 112-pound superfan, Elinor Smith.

The pint-size dynamo had been passionate about flying from a young age. Her father, Tom, a vaudeville star, was known for his role as the Scarecrow in stage productions of *The Wonderful Wizard of Oz*. He moved the family to the actors' colony of Freeport and began flying to reduce travel time between shows. While growing up in Nassau County, Elinor had the privilege of family dinners with celebrities like W. C. Fields and Buster Keaton but also faced the troubling influence of the Ku Klux Klan, whose presence in suburban Long Island was noticeable, and whose influence reached community affairs and local law enforcement. Elinor's non-Catholic peers often ostracized her for being Catholic.

Having few willing playmates, she spent her time with pilots and mechanics at her father's airfield. The sky provided a reprieve from prejudices on the ground, and in 1927, she became the nation's youngest licensed pilot (of any gender) at age sixteen. In her first year as a licensed pilot, Elinor earned $30,000. Despite her petite stature, which required her to sit on cushions so that she could reach the controls, she had a commanding presence in the air. Elinor performed stunts that drew large, rapt audiences. Among her feats was a three-hundred-foot loop during which she picked up a handkerchief lying on the ground. Her aviation antics soon earned her the nickname "the Flying Flapper of Freeport."

Without a wealthy promoter like George Palmer Putnam to support her, Elinor struggled to devise a way to make her grand public debut unforgettable. Her moment came on October 21, when, at seventeen years old, she ascended in a Waco 10 from Roosevelt Field, responding to a daring challenge by her friend Herbert McCrory of the *Daily News*. Well acquainted with her exceptional skills from his time at Roosevelt Field, McCrory watched in awe as Elinor deftly guided her plane under New York City's East River crossings: the Queensboro, Williamsburg, Manhattan, and Brooklyn Bridges. In his insider article, McCrory described a heart-stopping moment when the young pilot tilted the plane sideways under the last bridge to dodge an approaching tanker. Her daring feat earned her a front-page feature and sparked controversy at city hall. Realizing the gravity of her actions, Elinor feared losing her license. To her surprise, Mayor Jimmy Walker, an outgoing socialite who recognized her as a showbiz friend's daughter, opted for a public reprimand and a lenient retroactive ten-day probation. Elinor was free to fly immediately. Soon, she posed with the mayor's team for photos. "It was easy as pie!" she confessed, and anyone from Roosevelt Field would confirm that the flying prodigy was telling the truth. Her official reprimand even came with an autograph request from a female clerk.

Amelia stepped off the Pittsburgher in her glamorous new fur coat on the morning of November 16, ready to begin a busy day in Pittsburgh. Her first stop was KDKA's studio for a Friday morning broadcast, followed by a luncheon in her honor at the Pittsburgh Chamber of Commerce. In front of a crowd of aviation-minded businessmen, the most famous lady in town talked about her Putnam book. Another book signing and talk would soon follow at a local bookstore, and as evening fell, hundreds of Boys Scouts, Girl Scouts, and Camp Fire Girls gathered for an auditorium event. Joining Amelia and George on that lively G. P. Putnam's Sons bill was Dick Douglas, that sixteen-year-old explorer whom Putnam had sent to Africa under a risky contract with lion hunter Martin Johnson for the juvenile tale *Three Boy Scouts in Africa*; George hoped the famous teenager's presence would divert gossip while simultaneously promoting his book.

While George was occupied outside the Chamber of Commerce, a talented Black journalist from the syndicated "Negro" press approached Amelia Earhart, seeking an unscheduled private word. Amelia granted the request, which resulted in a revealing article titled "Amelia Earhart Discusses the Negro: Transatlantic Woman Flier Believes in Race's Ability." The article appeared in *The Pittsburgh Courier* and was syndicated in leading African American newspapers. The journalist, Blanche Taylor Dickinson, would become a Harlem Renaissance poet.

"I shall be very glad indeed if one word of mine is accepted by your race as a sincere token of my faith in its ability to do worthwhile things," Amelia told Dickinson.

Initially planning to hold back on difficult questions, Dickinson saw an opening for pressing Amelia's beliefs. "Then capability regardless of color—you would deny no one an even break?"

"Certainly not," Amelia replied. "The capability of the individual only should be considered."

Dickinson responded, "Well, it is gratifying to know that you do not believe achievements of distinction serve to unbalance us."

"Why, I do not see how distinguished achievement could unsettle the Negro race. Rather, achievement should be an inspiration."

Addressing a contentious issue, Dickinson inquired: "Miss Earhart, what do you think of discrimination?"

"Discrimination, in general, I think unfair!" Amelia began, then added with some hesitation: "I am not enough of a biologist to say definitively whether discrimination against intermarriage is justifiable. . . . But by the slow process of breeding to the best, we should emerge presumably, mentally, morally, and spiritually, that is, biologically better than we are today."

Mindful of the topic's sensitivity, Dickinson shifted the conversation to Bessie Coleman, a groundbreaking Black aviator who shattered racial barriers in aviation before tragically dying in a plane crash—years before Amelia's rise to fame. Despite Coleman's remarkable achievements, Amelia offered little comment. Dickinson then brought up Hubert Julian, a distinguished Black aviator whose race barred him from securing sponsorship for an Atlantic flight.

"I do not advocate stunt flying," she countered. "If anything is to be proved, it would not matter to me who the pilot was, if he had the ability."

Their conversation was cut short when George returned and reminded Amelia that she had a book signing. Amelia promised Dickinson a signed photograph and added, "And tell your people that I believe them capable of accomplishing in aviation the same as they have done and are doing in other pursuits. Goodbye." The exalted aviator then departed for the bookstore.

Eugenics' influence on prominent figures from this era cannot be understated. Alexander Graham Bell, Margaret Sanger, and even leaders in the Black community, like W. E. B. Du Bois, made notable contributions to their fields while also being touched by this ugly ideology. Brands like Ivory and Del Monte utilized eugenic themes in their campaigns, illustrating the prevalence of these beliefs. It serves as a sobering reminder of the dangers of pseudoscience.

In print, Dickinson acknowledged Amelia's progressive stance for a white woman of her time. While helping to promote George's controversial Africa-set book, she wouldn't have seen herself as prejudiced. Time would show that Amelia, unlike many of her contemporaries, went on to regret some of her views on eugenics.

As Amelia relaxed on the road with George, her festering guilt easing by the second, the duo undoubtedly contributed to the national mood evoked by Eddie Cantor's 1928 song "Makin' Whoopee." After intimate days together, George told Amelia it was high time she formally pulled the plug on Sam Chapman (even though he, at the same time, was crafting letters to Dorothy and still telling her that he didn't really want their marriage to end). Sam was still living in West Medford when Amelia next spoke to him. George had her announce their split after giving Sam a few days to process what she said.

Around this time, during the Cleveland National Air Races, a news item gained wide attention: the first woman to fly across the Atlantic, Amelia Earhart, had "officially" ended her engagement to Sam Chapman in Boston.

The report also mentioned her upcoming trip to Chicago for the International Aeronautical Exposition—commonly referred to as the "Chicago Air Show"—before she would return to New York. "I am not engaged to be married. If I was sure of the man, I might get married tomorrow," Amelia said.

She was particularly eager to meet Elinor Smith at the show, and Elinor was thrilled when George called, his voice dripping with charm, to say that Amelia wanted to meet in their private suite. He, too, was quite eager to meet Elinor. The possibility that someone as influential as George might be interested in managing her career was enticing, especially after Elinor learned that an appearance by Amelia could bring in more than $500. Opportunities were clearly on the horizon.

During their eventual breakfast in Amelia's suite, Elinor's initial nerves melted away under Amelia's genuine warmth, but she was taken aback by the depth of Amelia's knowledge about her flying feats—not just the daring flight beneath New York's bridges but her whole past, like her hushed solo flight at just fifteen. It was as if Amelia had been briefed. In their first face-to-face conversation, the freckled Elinor became highly cognizant of little details, like the soft, tiny freckles on Amelia's nose, which never showed up in photographs. "You have freckles too!" Elinor exclaimed. Amelia laughed, and Elinor's candid remark about Amelia's distinct gap-toothed smile drew another hearty laugh from the famous aviatrix. "That's why GP makes me practice smiling with my lips closed," Amelia said. "There's so much to learn about this publicity business."

George, so tall and impeccably dressed, cut an imposing figure to Elinor, just as he had to Amelia when the two first met. At the meeting's start, he was gracious and impressed young Elinor with a glib remark: "Meeting you is one of my career highlights." The conversation weaved through Elinor's aerial feats and her role in delivering Waco planes. They even knew the story of Elinor's escapade with Jimmy Walker, which was great fun to recount. But then George grew gruff. He began almost pumping her for commentary on her future or on any ideas she had about women in aviation.

When the topic turned to a rayon tycoon's proposal for a high-fashion flying dress endorsement from Amelia, George wanted her take. Her take? A kid who wore her brother's knickers and warm sweaters?

"But what if you were in an enclosed plane?" George asked. "Would you like nice flying apparel? What would you envision?"

"Well, I don't see that being an issue," Elinor said. "Has any woman flown one of those powerful Fokkers or Bellancas? Now that would draw real attention—and I'd love to be the first at the controls." The fleeting glance exchanged between Amelia and George spoke volumes. Had they found the information they were after?

The intimate undercurrents between Amelia and George did not escape Elinor's keen eye for detail, a skill that served her well in the air. She noted the subtle electricity that seemed to pulse between the pair. Their discreet exchanges—fleeting hugs and barely-there kisses—spoke volumes. Most telling, however, was the arrangement in Miss Earhart's suite. It featured only a double bed.

The aviatrix rendezvous ended ambiguously. While George dangled the idea of representing Elinor (pinkie promise?!), it remained only an idea. She departed clutching a vague assurance of a call in the future, hoping for a solid offer.

On December 2, Dorothy wrote in her journal that she and George hadn't had sex since his return from the Chicago Air Show trip. By month's end, their intimacy had cooled to such an extent that she questioned if they'd ever share a bed again without animosity.

In an extraordinary move—likely spurred by her husband's pleas over their faltering joint venture—Dorothy hosted a cocktail soiree at the nightclub she and George co-owned with Don Dickerman, the Heigh-Ho. Strangely, she chose to honor Amelia, fresh from her ten-day lecture tour with George, which had been spotlighted in *The New York Times*. At the event, Amelia crossed paths with Neysa McMein, the renowned illustrator celebrated for her work in *McCall's* and *The Saturday Evening Post*. Embodying bohemian flair, McMein might have divulged tales of her unconventional "open marriage" in between the jazz band's sets. Originally Marjorie McMein from Illinois, she'd metamorphosed into a paragon of New York femininity, championing modernism and autonomy. She feverishly advocated for women's suffrage and lent her talents to US and French wartime propaganda. With an apartment overlooking Carnegie Hall, she entertained luminaries like Irving Berlin and Dorothy Parker. Her artistry distilled the essence of the 1920s woman—case in point: a precocious depiction of a female aviator that foreshadowed Amelia's feats. Unsurprisingly, McMein would soon celebrate Amelia's unwavering spirit through a beautiful *McCall's* portrait.

As 1928 drew to a close, Americans were still exploring new venues for enjoyment. In stark contrast to the Heigh-Ho, with its sophisticated gatherings, the Nutshell Jockey Club offered its own brand of Jazz Age bacchanalia. Tucked away in Norman Bel Geddes's apartment on Thirty-Eighth Street, this exceptionally unique speakeasy had no hatcheck girl, presenting an informal and intimate setting that even the most imaginative novelist might find hard to conjure.

Bel Geddes was a novice bettor at the Belmont Park racetrack and came up with an idea that took months to develop but was immediately successful. In the center of a twenty-eight-inch table, he displayed a miniature green turf racing track powered by electricity, with eight hundred individually painted cast-iron horses and sixteen tiny boxes for them. Every Wednesday and Saturday, he held "live" races every half hour, and a large crowd gathered in the apartment to bet, drink, and cheer on the miniature thoroughbreds. Over a hundred insiders regularly blew off steam in this Manhattan apartment's illegal stable: Mayor Jimmy Walker, Cole Porter, Douglas Fairbanks, Charlie Chaplin, and *The New Yorker*'s Harold Ross each owned a diminutive horse. Alexander Woollcott, the wisecracking correspondent, owned horses named after Dickens. The horses cost a dollar each, so maintaining a toy stable wasn't expensive. Three other unexpected celebrity owners of toy horses included Amelia Earhart; her on-again, off-again boyfriend, George Palmer Putnam; and her on-again, off-again boyfriend's wife, Dorothy Binney Putnam. Sometimes, they all bet together. Amelia passed on the illicit booze but loved the spectacle. This was especially true when sixteen horses were brought from the stable to the starting gate every Wednesday and Saturday night. A mini starting gate was raised, and the mini horses took off! Bel Geddes's machinery was enclosed in glass for everyone to see. To authenticate the experience, he played recorded sounds of chaos on a racetrack. The bidding got loud and earnest. All night long, taxis screeched up with more inebriated gamblers.

Nosy neighbors eventually shut it down, which Amelia thought a shame. It was always about the fun at the Nutshell, never the money. At the tail end of 1928, she didn't need money anyway. Though her memoir wasn't a publishing sensation like Lindbergh's, it did well. Was it possible for the once financially strapped social worker to remain in the field? With all the money and ego-boosting attention she received, pretending that social work was still her future was a farce. But she had new clarity that she could promote aviation and improve women's lives by using her growing platform. It would become her life's work. She would be a social worker in the sky. "I still do public service—by lecturing, writing, speaking over the radio," she told a reporter then. "My previous social work was more than teaching the correct use of English words."

She was also becoming more and more of a fixture in the most prominent aviation circles. In December 1928, a ceremony was held to honor aviation pioneers Orville and Wilbur Wright on the same spot and day of the world's first successful flight in 1903. Orville Wright's twelve seconds in the air in Kitty Hawk changed perceptions of human flight. Interestingly, Amelia and about two hundred aviation enthusiasts reached the event by ship, as planes couldn't land at the location. Lindbergh agreed to attend only if he could arrive by plane. The event attracted aviation standouts such as Igor Sikorsky, Glenn Curtiss, and even Orville Wright—marking his first return to Kitty Hawk since 1903. (Wilbur had died in 1912.)

Around three thousand people attended the dedication ceremony, which was held in front of a monument resembling a granite boulder. Delegates from fifty countries listened intently to the tale of this pioneering achievement.

Amelia's history was forever altered in 1928. Her astonishing year was ending with eyes on her personal life. On December 8, a syndicated gossip columnist asked her readers: "Does it mean that Amelia, home from across the foam, feted, kowtowed to, confronted by opportunities for fame and money of which she had never dreamed before, found the life outside matrimony too glamorous? Was it a case of her Samuel not seeming to fit into the picture?"

(Yes.)

The reporter added, "Being gentlefolk, both, they don't give us the inside dope. One wonders if Amelia, or Samuel, will ever be sorry for their decision. . . . We humans are usually sorry we didn't do the thing we might have done."

Amelia's mother, Amy, joined her in December to live in the top-floor apartment at Greenwich House. As one of her Christmas gifts, along with perfume and woolly slippers, they took a five-dollar, fifty-mile flight over New York with Colonial Transport Lines, preferring a night ride for its unique view. Despite Amelia's concern about being recognized at the airfield, they soared over New York Harbor, the Statue of Liberty, and Manhattan's towering skyscrapers. Wisely, Amelia declined the captain's offer to take the controls, knowing that her lack of recent practice could lead to mortal danger.

This exhilarating experience was overshadowed when, just a few days later, Amy discovered George Palmer Putnam's intentions to divorce his wife and propose to Amelia. Marjorie B. Davis, Amelia's friend (and cousin to her boss, Harold Dennison, at Dennison Airport), was visiting during this time, trying to make herself invisible as she overheard the intense argument between mother and daughter. To diminish Amy's influence, George suggested Amelia move to her own apartment, possibly at a new residence for professional women that was opening in the spring. For all he cared, Amy could damn well move back to Boston.

All the while, George tried to quell persistent gossip about his relationship with Amelia. He scheduled a timely media interview centered around a call from Dorothy inviting Amelia to Rye for the weekend. George and Dorothy appeared publicly yet again, and reports were fed to the press about the couple being spotted at the Coffee House Club enjoying cocktails with friends. They were seen at the Plymouth Theatre taking in the play *Holiday*, marking their first public outing alone in 1928. All of it was aimed at dispelling gossip.

Yet this time, George's PR stunts appeared transparent to the public. Attempts to project an image of marital bliss with Dorothy only amplified whispers about his relationship with Amelia. The more George tried to control the narrative, the deeper he dug his hole. Trying harder still, he organized a lavish sixteen-day Christmas cruise aboard the *Duchess of Bedford*, a Canadian Pacific liner, for himself, his wife, their two children, and 275 other passengers. The trip, which included stops in Kingston, Cristóbal, Havana, and Nassau, was designed to portray a united family front. Despite the tension, Dorothy found solace in the time she would get to spend with her children and the luxurious escape that the West Indies trip, financed by her family's wealth, would provide.

While she no longer harbored romantic feelings for George, she looked forward to the upcoming cruise. This was, if nothing else, a chance for her to enjoy some peace on her deck chair in the sun. However, the trip was marred midway when, on New Year's Eve, she received a cablegram in Havana with the heart-wrenching news of her brother's passing. This left her grieving in isolation until her return to her family on January 7. When her parents learned how miserable she was in her marriage, they begged her not to leave George just yet. After the loss of their son, a star swimmer and professor of geology at Yale, an embarrassing divorce was too much to bear.

Nine

SOMETHING HAD TO GIVE

The year 1929 opened with financial optimism for most Americans. Even the average worker was dabbling in the stock market, buoyed by radio advertisements and thriving newspapers that reached every corner of the country. The publishing world flourished alongside Wall Street, producing bestsellers like *The Art of Thinking*, *The Bridge of San Luis Rey*, and Little, Brown's English translation of *All Quiet on the Western Front*— a title the Major, to his family's embarrassment, had dismissed. But those paying close attention to the markets saw the cracks beneath the surface. Something had to give.

Despite prosperous times, flight was still an expensive profession for civilians, and pilots like Amelia Earhart were looking for creative ways to gain wealthy sponsors' attention. In 1929, a man flying solo across the Atlantic was already old hat. Could a woman attempting it alone gain attention if she had the financial backing and ability to accomplish that daring feat? It was clear to Amelia that even after more training, she was still not yet good enough to try for that honor. But how could she practice and meet all her work obligations? If she didn't up her skills, friendly rivals like Ruth Nichols and maybe even that upstart Elinor Smith could beat her to the solo Atlantic crossing she had coveted since her *Friendship* flight.

In January 1929, Dorothy Binney Putnam wasted no time distancing herself from George after their face-saving family cruise. She was deep in mourning following the sudden loss of her brother, and her wealthy parents facilitated her move into Mugo Court, a spacious home located directly across from Rocklyn, the grand estate owned by her affluent parents in Sound Beach, soon to be renamed Old Greenwich. In due course, Dorothy would rename the house "Journey's End."

Separated but not yet divorced from his wife and facing financial struggles without Dorothy's steady income to support his lifestyle, George was contending with his changed circumstances but continued to shepherd Amelia's growing fame, including devising an "expedition" to Carlsbad Caverns in January 1929.

During a scheduled appearance in Rochester on January 24, Amelia reunited with the plane she had used for her famous Atlantic crossing. The *Friendship*, which had since been restored by Donald Woodward for a sum of $62,000, now took center stage at his private airport. Dressed in a chic suit and fur stole paid for by her lecture tours, Amelia graciously posed for photos. Her admiration of the plane's restored condition was evident, and George ensured she was duly compensated for her appearance.

In February, acknowledging Amelia's flying aspirations and recognizing her skill gaps, George organized training sessions with Edward Weatherdon at Newark Metropolitan Airport. Here she'd learn to handle a Ford trimotor. Yet on March 3, a mishap occurred: Amelia's aircraft met with an unfortunate muddy patch near New York, resulting in it nosing over. This unsettling event underscored her need for more training and attracted unwanted media attention.

A shared sentiment began to emerge among those in the close-knit aviation community. C. B. Allen, a close friend, candidly noted that while Amelia's celebrated passenger trip had reanimated her long-held ambitions, her piloting skills at this time were "decidedly mediocre." He rightly believed that for Amelia to realize her dream of solo Atlantic flights, she required more hours in a powerful aircraft. George recklessly presented a more favorable image to the media, overstating Amelia's experience—a potentially perilous embellishment, given that flying an advanced aircraft without proper preparation could have deadly outcomes. Still, George was determined to establish Amelia as the Queen of Aviation—his catchphrase of choice—in the public's eye.

On March 9, another big moment in aviation history unfolded as Charles Lindbergh landed in Brownsville, Texas, after a groundbreaking flight from Mexico City. This occasion signified the grand opening of the Brownsville Airport. Amelia, who traveled there by train, was among the notable attendees. While Lindbergh was the star attraction for the twenty-thousand-strong crowd, Amelia had her own memorable moments in this border city, such as riding in a powerful Fairchild plane piloted by Major Bernard Law. Later, Amelia used a mic to express concern for a lost child and rejoiced with the crowd when the child was reunited with his parents. Eventually, the press reported, she departed by train to fulfill her speaking commitments. With the spotlight heavily on Lindbergh during that visit, few realized that Amelia had spent hours testing her skills away from the public eye.

In the following week, there was notably no official record of Amelia undergoing any specialized tests. However, George, that master at shaping narratives, planted press stories that Amelia had effortlessly passed her license tests in Brownsville under the guidance of Captain Paul F. Baer, a renowned World War I veteran and influential figure in New York's aviation community. This misleading narrative had George's familiar flair and gained credibility when an influential man, William P. MacCracken Jr., assistant secretary of commerce for aeronautics, endorsed it. MacCracken—whom Amelia had known since they were among the first passengers on a January 29 Pan Am flight to Havana, a high-profile inaugural route—lent his support, facilitated by George, making the fraud less easily detectable. Despite stories in papers, seasoned insiders like C. B. Allen remained skeptical that she really got that license the year George claimed she did; their skepticism primarily stemmed from her weak flying skills that year and the fishy absence of photographic evidence.

Throughout the years, many biographers, even some affiliated with the Smithsonian, have continued to promote the claim that Amelia was awarded American transport license 5716 in March 1929. If true, it would have been a significant feat, making her the fourth woman after Phoebe Omlie, Ruth Nichols, and Lady Heath to do so. However, this was all fiction. Yes, she would eventually earn that license but not until a year later, training under false credentials. To deflect potential flak should the truth emerge, George seeded predictable whispers in the press that the aviation bureau hadn't received her paperwork—a handy dog-ate-my-homework ploy.

Amelia herself never explicitly claimed to possess the transport license she didn't acquire that year—a subtle omission that revealed her inclination to stretch the truth (or simply keep quiet when George did so on her behalf) to advance her ambitions.

In late March 1929, while training at Bellanca's headquarters in New Castle, Delaware, Elinor Smith experienced a revealing turn of events. Elinor had always held Amelia in high regard, considering her a friend since their first meeting in Chicago, when she mentioned that there would be big press for the first woman to pilot the more powerful aircraft only available to men.

A year prior, Elinor had met Giuseppe Mario Bellanca, who recognized her innate talent and encouraged her to get in touch when she felt prepared to pilot one of his premium aircraft. Bellanca carefully chose the aviators he permitted to fly his planes; esteemed pilots like Clarence Chamberlin and Bert Acosta were among the chosen few.

In early 1929, Evelyn "Bobbi" Trout nabbed the women's endurance record with a flight lasting seventeen hours and sixteen minutes, topping Elinor's record by four hours. Elinor, spurred on to reclaim her spot, contemplated a borrowed Bellanca monoplane for her comeback. Even though Charles Lindbergh had been knocked back by Bellanca in the past, Elinor received the call she was hoping for: Bellanca was on board to lend her a plane worthy of recapturing the record, so long as her parents were also on board.

After arriving in New Castle, Delaware, Elinor relocated temporarily and began training under George Haldeman, the pilot of Ruth Elder's aborted transatlantic endeavor in 1927. He had since restored his reputation and now held esteemed positions as chief test pilot and technical adviser for the Bellanca Aircraft Company. Learning under Haldeman was a demanding affair, but Elinor understood that becoming a competent pilot required countless hours of commitment.

On April 3, during one of her training sessions, Elinor was taken aback to see the globally acclaimed Captain Bill Lancaster touching down in New Castle, Amelia Earhart by his side. Elinor was familiar with Lancaster through their aviation networks and mutual friendship with Lady Heath. Elinor was happy to see Amelia again. Their last meeting had been at the Chicago Air Show. Now, free from George Palmer Putnam's watchful gaze, the two could reconnect. Elinor congratulated Amelia on her supposed transport license achievement and exchanged pleasantries with Lancaster. A handsome British aviator with a Royal Air Force record, he had gained global recognition after his pioneering flight from England to Australia.

Meanwhile, back in New York, George seized an opportunity from Lancaster's financial troubles. He craftily brokered a deal: for a modest sum, Lancaster would secretly pilot Amelia between cities, and she would be publicly credited as the sole pilot. This arrangement forced Lancaster to work for pennies, keeping his skilled yet financially burdensome involvement behind the scenes. Although this was demeaning work, Lancaster's pressing financial woes left him little choice but to accept George's terms. With cunning mastery, George ensured that Amelia remained the celebrated aviator in the public eye, while the true dynamics of their flights stayed under wraps.

Had Elinor been privy to George's covert motives to secure the very Bellanca CH-300 monoplane she was training on for Amelia, her demeanor toward Amelia and Lancaster likely would have been more guarded. The Bellanca CH-300, with a forty-six-foot wingspan and a potent 225-horsepower Wright J-5 engine, was specially outfitted for endurance flights.

George was determined to acquire the powerful aircraft for Amelia, even if it meant keeping it out of Elinor's hands before any record attempts or thoughts of an Atlantic crossing. With specialized training, Amelia could hone her skills in secluded Rye until she was prepared to take on the challenge. It is plausible that Amelia was aware of George's machination, but we can't know for sure. George had called Bellanca, expressing his desire to purchase the aircraft before Elinor could fly it. He wanted it right now and told Bellanca that he was very friendly with Henry B. du Pont, the man who dominated Bellanca's board. Why play around with a kid? His goal was clear: to divert the spotlight from Elinor and shine it squarely on Amelia. He had a $25,000 check ready. Cash it!

Entangled in this intricate situation, Bellanca sought advice from his trusted colleague, Lauren D. "Deac" Lyman, a Pulitzer Prize–winning aviation editor. Bellanca expressed his concerns: he found Amelia amicable but doubted her piloting skills and feared negative publicity if an accident occurred. Lyman concurred, suggesting that Amelia might not possess the license and that George would be furious if his assumptions were challenged. Any move against that man might backfire. Lyman then diffused the crisis by advising Bellanca to delay—he wouldn't want to jeopardize the aspirations of a spirited young pilot, nor would he want to risk bad press if his prized plane was cratered by an uncertain pilot.

In a calculated move, George sent Amelia directly to Bellanca's headquarters with a substantial, persuasive check for $25,000. In his Delaware office, Bellanca consulted with his seasoned test pilot, Haldeman. They decided that Haldeman would assess Amelia's prowess firsthand. Following their discussion, Haldeman courteously asked Amelia to accompany him and Elinor on an evaluation flight. Once they were airborne, with Amelia and Haldeman in the lead and Elinor observing from the rear, Amelia hesitantly assumed control at around one thousand feet. The plane's erratic movements were evident almost immediately. Embarrassed and flustered, Amelia gestured for Haldeman to regain control. Once grounded, Amelia approached Elinor for a second attempt; she hesitated but agreed. Yet the same issues persisted during their retry. Elinor was left perplexed. Since she had carefully set up Amelia's controls earlier, the plane's operation should have been straightforward. Doubts about Amelia's piloting proficiency emerged. "Hearsay!" some might exclaim, but was she adept at flying? Could it be that Amelia had grown rusty from her years as a social worker—and from her packed schedule, with her book signings, lectures, radio interviews, public appearances, endorsement deals, and magazine photo shoots—or were Putnam's claims of her five hundred flight hours grossly exaggerated?

Amelia and Lancaster, who had furtively flown her to Delaware and would furtively fly her back, departed without finalizing a purchase. This unexpected turn posed a nasty wrinkle for George, leaving him furious after defeat. After Elinor underwent an additional week of intense training, Bellanca and Haldeman finally informed her that she, Elinor Smith, a terrific pilot, was ready to go.

Amelia finally sent her mother back to Boston and, on April 13, moved from her homey Greenwich Village digs at Greenwich House to a Midtown spot. Having faced private humiliation in front of a respected colleague, she was determined to improve her flying skills, a goal she couldn't achieve while simultaneously providing bandages to children and writing an aviation column. (And she wasn't doing much writing anyway, as Ella May Frazer was her literary Lancaster. But even one's notes to another writer are time-consuming.) She happily checked into her room at the new twenty-four-story American Woman's Association's residential clubhouse on Fifty-Seventh Street. The sleek, plush hotel with its women-only surroundings pleased her greatly, and George was elated; she was now close to his Midtown office, making it easier to fend off the gossipmongers.

The driving force behind this progressive establishment was Anne Morgan, the unmarried feminist (and lesbian) daughter of financial tycoon J. Pierpont Morgan. Her clandestine relationship with the fantastically loaded Mrs. William K. Vanderbilt and their exquisite taste ensured that the $7 million clubhouse was nothing short of luxurious. Amelia, now within walking distance of her job at *Cosmopolitan*, even had George propose shared accommodation with Norah Alsterlund, a fresh Smith English graduate, to help her write articles.

As Amelia navigated life shifts, Elinor's world became a whirlwind of activity. On April 24, she made a grand entrance at Roosevelt Field, stunning onlookers as she skillfully piloted a massive aircraft and set a solo endurance record—twenty-six hours, twenty-three minutes, and sixteen seconds—that would stand unchallenged for decades. The press couldn't get enough of her. Offers poured in, including one from Long Island rayon tycoon Sam Savage, who had previously courted Amelia for an endorsement deal, hoping to launch a line of women's flying attire. Amelia had declined, and now the same offer was being shopped to Elinor.

While Elinor similarly turned it down, preferring practical attire over the flashy designs favored by her friend Lady Heath (who once commissioned a designer leopard coat made from her own African hunting trophy), an unexpected call from George took her by surprise. This was no laughing matter. She again reflected on her first meeting with Amelia and George in that Chicago hotel room, where George had peppered her with what seemed like flattery. Could those compliments have been sincere? Perhaps Lady Heath and Elinor's other aviation acquaintances had been too quick to judge George duplicitous.

A year had passed since Amelia confidently stepped into the spotlight as a boldface name and became part of George's professional circle; Elinor yearned for a similar professional relationship—minus the romantic complications. George's history of endorsing aviation giants like Byrd and Lindbergh lent authenticity to his new interest in Elinor. Despite the success she had already achieved flying her father's Waco and the borrowed Bellanca, both wangled on her own, Elinor saw George's potential to elevate her career even further.

Alas, her hopeful illusions crumbled in just a short conversation within the confines of George Palmer Putnam's office. George's agenda, wrapped in phony charms, was clear: to exploit her talents.

This time, after George attempted to extract plans from her, Elinor heeded the warning Lady Heath had given her at their last meeting. "You tell him everything," she had hissed, "and then he knows exactly how to cut the ground out from under you." Elinor kept her plans to herself. His proposal was a debasing one—a paltry seventy-five-dollar weekly salary for two years to transport Amelia. Further, she would be bound by a four-year silence clause, forbidden from interviews and writing. "For the Derby and tour, you would do all the difficult cross-country flying. AE is not physically strong, but of course, she must appear to be doing it," he explained, making it clear that Amelia's public image was a carefully crafted false persona, one George was determined to uphold at all costs. The manipulation extended further: In each photograph, Elinor would be positioned to Amelia's left, guaranteeing that Amelia's name took precedence. How power perverts. With a smug expression, George slid a prepared contract toward her and steepled his fingers. "Please proceed and sign! Secure an income for yourself!" This contract had been expertly prepared in advance by Jo Berger, his ever-loyal and unfazed secretary, who had greeted Elinor warmly upon her arrival.

George might have believed he would encounter little resistance. However, Elinor would not be cowed by him and refused to sign. That stumped him. He gave her a cold, piercing look and delivered a savage reply. "You may think you have other plans, but believe me, if you don't sign this, you will never fly professionally and certainly never again in the New York area."

The idea of a grown man threatening to blackball a teenager was as terrifyingly repugnant then as it is now, yet the young woman did not cower; rejecting any notion of being marginalized, she slammed the door behind her as she left. This act, he felt, was an invitation to an all-out war.

Elinor took a brief taxi journey to the building that housed *The New York Times*. Like Bellanca, Elinor frantically sought advice from her family friend, the aviation editor Deac Lyman. Lyman was infuriated, referring to George as a "son of a bitch" and telling her how that sly dog had sent Amelia to Delaware with a $25,000 check, intent on usurping the Bellanca CH-300 before Elinor could even fly it. As for the contract, Lyman had that seat-of-the-pants sense that the schemer had been bluffing. Indeed, the press would have known that Elinor was doing the flying; he suspected George's real aim wasn't to replace Lancaster with the teenage aviation star but to entrap her with a contract, embroil her in prolonged legal battles, and effectively sideline her.

Lyman swiftly contacted his confidant, C. B. Allen, a towering six-foot-two aviation reporter and editor for the *New York Herald Tribune* and a flying officer in the National Guard, to apprise him of the young aviator's predicament before orchestrating a coffee rendezvous with Elinor. While Allen and many other reporters viewed George as a jackass, they still held Amelia in high regard, admiring her friendliness and courage. Yet despite their aviation influence, even these seasoned reporters trod carefully around George Palmer Putnam, whose clout extended to the uppermost echelon of the publishing world. George often broke bread with powerhouses like Adolph S. Ochs, the notoriously chauvinistic publisher of *The New York Times*, and other journalism giants. Management frequently directed reporters to sidestep questions about who helmed the controls during Amelia's flights, especially when she was accompanied by aviators like Bill Lancaster. Any skeptics were met with a steely gaze followed by a stern reminder of Amelia's stature—too eminent to warrant justifying to any doubter.

Unfortunately, George was a master at getting people blacklisted too. In that regard, he wasn't just bluffing. Elinor was close to tears upon hearing that. Well, what to do, fellows? They told her to avoid stunt flying. Amelia held no current records other than her flight to Wales, which she'd spent lying on her belly. Impress the world with your flying skills! They assured her they would continue to give her publicity if she kept breaking records. They would think some more. Elinor remembered what her mentor, Bellanca, liked to say in Delaware: "Whoever said life was fair?" Elinor would also later say, thinking back to this trying time, "You ran into a lot of evil in a lot of ways."

George was up to no good. According to Lindie Naughton, the esteemed Irish biographer of Lady Heath, her research revealed that George, under the guise of a casual nightclub invitation to discuss plans, was actually scheming. He maneuvered behind the scenes to ensure that Amelia, not Lady Heath, received the coveted invitation to speak at the 1929 Chautauqua lecture series, deliberately sidelining her rival for the spotlight. Was it humiliating? You bet. Lady Heath had also set her sights on piloting the inaugural flight to Cuba. However, Amelia, presumably given the George Palmer Putnam boost, was chosen. Naughton's revelations find support in a January 9, 1929, article highlighting Amelia's participation in what was touted as the first Pan Am flight to Havana; she is described as being accompanied by merely a "mechanic." While Naughton acknowledges Amelia's charisma and heroism, she says that in 1929, Amelia's flying expertise was still in its infancy. This was evident when, after acquiring Lady Heath's 1927 Avro Avian Moth—a plane with an impeccable service record over Africa—Amelia brought it back to the US only to crash it shortly after. "She had multiple mishaps in the air; her actual flight hours were surprisingly limited," Naughton concludes.

Elinor Smith was the first to publicly challenge George Palmer Putnam's character, revealing her disturbing experiences after his death through many consistent accounts well before the digital era. Her allegations that he was an egomaniacal liar and a terror to other women pilots, actively seeking to erase any threats to Amelia's path to dominance, were initially dismissed by some experts, who pointed to Amelia's 1929 transport license as evidence contradictive of Smith's narrative, casting a woman speaking up as an untrustworthy rival. Why they would do so is baffling; this author's extensive research not only supports but also reinforces Elinor's version of events and includes validation from credible figures like John Frogge, a seasoned *New York Times* aviation reporter with firsthand industry insights and access to confidential sources. Frogge's testimonies and those of other insiders lend substantial weight to Elinor's integrity and affirm her status as a truth-teller, challenging earlier dismissive perspectives and shifting the historical understanding of George Palmer Putnam's influence in the aviation world.

Although some researchers—relying on the goodwill of living Putnam descendants eager to protect his legacy—have accused Elinor of dishonesty, the enduring pattern of disbelieving women who speak out highlights the need for thorough, independent verification of her claims. Such scrutiny only reinforces their plausibility. Elinor has alleged not only that Amelia was flying with a fudged license due to her celebrity status but also that George's manipulations cost her a contract with Standard Oil. As Standard Oil's preferred aviator, Amelia was central to George's reported threat to sever ties with the company if it proceeded with a radio broadcast deal involving Elinor, which was subsequently canceled—an event that seared her, especially considering that over $26,000 in today's dollars was at stake. A deep dive into Elinor's most sensational claim, including research at the Smithsonian to look into the licensing issue, supports her credibility and bolsters her reputation for truthfulness among those who knew her well as an older woman. Therefore, there's little reason to doubt her other disturbing tales about her tormentor, which were printed after his death. To assist her, Elinor also claimed that Lyman introduced her to Bellanca, who recommended that she fly for Leslie L. Irvin's parachute company, Irvin Air Chute. While George schemed to blacklist a young woman half his age, Elinor seized the moment, determined to propel her career forward on her own terms.

By Elinor's believable account, when George learned Elinor was in the running for a new role at Irvin Air Chute, he stormed down to the company's Wall Street office by cab. The company was financially sound after a recent sale valued at what today would be $68 million. George wanted some of that pie and acted like a brute as he tried to tarnish Elinor's reputation by suggesting she was a reckless youth chasing vaudevillian dreams like her father, not a respectable lady like Amelia Earhart. It got ugly in there. Galled by what they were witnessing, Irvin Air Chute's dumbfounded directors quickly showed their nakedly self-serving guest the door. Despite his bulldozing attempts to undermine Elinor, her position with Irvin Air Chute remained secure, and she rapidly ascended to become the company's premier female pilot. Nevertheless, George's relentless meddling hinted that their feud was far from over.

While entangled in these manipulations, George simultaneously seethed with anger upon discovering his wife's affair with Frank Upton, a decorated World War I Medal of Honor recipient who had served as a navy en-sign. Upton was more than a fleeting fancy to Dorothy; he was a real threat, an authentic hero, honored with a ticker-tape parade following his daring rescue aboard the USS *Stewart*, and George felt overshadowed in every way. While his emotional and romantic focus remained fixated on Amelia, his deflated ego had him wondering if he should pay more attention to his wife and show Upton who was the alpha dog. Their mutual connections with Upton via the Explorers Club added fuel to the flames.

In fact, George had all of this and more on his mind. Amelia's younger sister, Muriel, was set to marry World War I veteran Albert Morrissey, affectionately called Chief, on the last Saturday of June at Medford's Grace Episcopal Church. During the celebrations for the upcoming wedding, Amelia was poised to reunite with her former fiancé, Sam Chapman; hours alone for intimate conversations loomed, and George felt powerless to intervene.

Family tension brewed beneath the wedding's surface. Muriel's discontent peaked when Amelia missed the prewedding dinner. But Amelia had her reasons: a stone had chipped the propeller of her Avro Avian Moth biplane during a warm-up. She informed Muriel that she'd be arriving, less glamorously, by train. On her wedding day, a mollified Muriel donned a white chiffon dress, and beside her, in a green chiffon dress adorned with pinned yellow roses, stood Amelia. Guests exchanged puzzled glances when Muriel chose Amelia's ex, Sam, to act as an usher, and throughout the ceremony, Sam seemed more engrossed by Amelia than by the ongoing nuptials, especially noticing a bright red sheen on her lips—a departure from her usual cosmetics-free ways. Cornered by a journalist questioning whether matrimony with Amelia was on the horizon, Sam blurted out, "Leave me alone!" Faced with the same question, Amelia responded contemplatively: "My constant travels hardly suit the role of a good wife." She jokingly told Reverend Hadley, who presided over the wedding, that committing to marriage required more bravery than flying across the Atlantic—an observation that everyone (except, perhaps, Muriel) found amusing. The celebration gently wound down with an intimate home reception at 15 Vine Street, which provided a welcome respite from the day's tensions.

Just two days later, the aviation press shifted its focus when Wilmer Stultz, the twenty-nine-year-old pilot of the *Friendship*, met with an accident during a flight stunt. He and his two passengers, also his friends, tragically lost their lives on what turned out to be their first and final stunt ride together.

Much of the New York area aviation community gathered solemnly at the Reformed Church of North Hempstead in Manhasset, Long Island, to honor the fallen pilot. Among the attendees were George and Dorothy, with Amelia seated close by. Notably, Lou Gower, the backup pilot for the *Friendship* in case Stultz couldn't perform, was also present. However, the navigator, Slim Gordon, was away in Buenos Aires. Adding gravitas to the occasion were esteemed members of the Vanderbilt and Whitney families, alongside pallbearers drawn from the Quiet Birdmen—an exclusive fraternity of World War I aviators, as famous for their secretive, whiskey-fueled camaraderie as for their daring feats in the air, a brotherhood bound by loyalty and legend.

Throughout, Amelia remained a picture of grace and restraint. She spoke of Stultz's unmatched expertise during their 1928 transatlantic journey, offering little comfort to his young mourning wife, Mildred, who, overwhelmed by grief, later fainted during the service. Soon after the funeral, an article emerged—syndicated through George's efforts and bearing Amelia's name, though it was most likely ghostwritten—that lauded Stultz's professionalism: "I'm certain there was no wrong decision that led to this deadly accident." The portrayal presented Stultz as a diligent pilot whose tragic end resulted from unforeseeable circumstances. While rumors had circulated about Stultz's alcoholism even during their famous 1928 flight, the article tactfully sidestepped the issue, preserving the integrity of their shared achievement and protecting both of their reputations. The aviation community, understanding the delicacy of the situation, chose discretion over scandal when, after examining Stultz's remains, a toxicologist at Bellevue Hospital stated: "The man was very drunk at the time of his death."

Stultz's body was transported to Pennsylvania Station aboard the Whitney family's luxurious Pullman railcar, fittingly named Adios. His gray coffin, draped in an American flag, was accompanied by representatives of the Whitney family, his widow, and a nurse.

Amelia had little time for reflection, for she was thrust into the spotlight again, this time as the assistant to the general traffic manager for Transcontinental Air Transport (TAT). Her role was demeaning: no flying, just delivering speeches, inspecting facilities, and "suggesting" improvements. TAT valued her celebrity, not her piloting skills, a reality that could distort anyone's sense of self.

In the striking market upswing of the late 1920s, even Charles Lindbergh threw his hat into the ring, allowing his name to grace the airline—soon commonly called (and later rechristened) the Lindbergh Line. Aviation stocks had been buoyed by Lindbergh's widespread acclaim and the nation's newfound infatuation with flight, and by 1929, shares in a notable plane manufacturer had rocketed from $80 to an astonishing $300, drawing close to $400 million in investments for aircraft enterprises (about a wild $7.4 billion in today's dollars).

Lindbergh explained to potential investors and customers that his airline, TAT, would introduce an innovative service, combining daytime flights with pitch-black nighttime journeys aboard Pullman railcars, which were known for their comfort and premium amenities. A passenger would start the journey by rail, going from New York's Pennsylvania Station to Columbus, Ohio. A Ford trimotor aircraft would then carry them from Columbus to Waynoka, Oklahoma. Following an overnight stop with breakfast at a Harvey House, they'd board a train to Clovis, New Mexico, and finish the journey by flying over the mountains to Los Angeles. It was an ambitious venture that featured a fleet designed to carry ten passengers. Male couriers on TAT's Ford planes provided box lunches, gum, and cotton to ease differential pressure pain and block excessive noise. Pilots from TAT's mail service were promoted to captain positions, adding to its charm. The airline's acronym would half-jokingly come to stand for "take a train." While TAT flights saved time, trains couldn't crash into mountains. But the future looked bright days before launch, when this forty-eight-hour service cost an air-minded passenger $352, equivalent to about $6,225 today, adjusting for inflation from 1929 to 2024—not a small fee, yet it reduced coast-to-coast travel time by a third. Despite the cost, and in no small part due to Lindbergh's backing, a thousand applicants were vying for the first fourteen seats, which generated a substantial cash flow of $350,000.

No one knew economic free fall was around the corner when, on July 7, Lindbergh finally pressed the ceremonial button in Los Angeles, launching the new airline and initiating the first eastward passenger train. Meanwhile, on the other coast, at New York's Pennsylvania Station, Amelia Earhart took center stage. With all the pomp of the occasion, and in a symbolic gesture during the Prohibition era, she smashed a glass bottle filled with nonalcoholic grape juice against the propeller of a Ford trimotor. Photos from that day underscore the massive size of the *City of New York*, a plane so big that men disassembled it for transport into the waiting room and then painstakingly reassembled it for the display.

With the plane christened, the world's most famous assistant to the general traffic manager addressed the crowd: "I've been instructed to offer cheerful remarks for precisely one minute and twenty-five seconds. Soon, daily flights will traverse our nation, acquainting all with the marvels of aviation. As I christen this craft, I aim for a sound that resonates with the live audience and radio listeners." Wearing a snug cloche hat and sharing a light moment with Police Commissioner Grover Whalen, formerly the official New York City greeter, Amelia decisively swung the bottle toward the Ford plane's propeller, proudly declaring, "The *City of New York*—I christen thee!"

New York City's silky showman, Mayor Jimmy Walker, also played a role in the event. As Amelia prepared to travel westward to meet up with Lindbergh in California, Walker presented her with telegrams intended for the mayors of Los Angeles and San Francisco.

After the final speeches, nineteen passengers, including Amelia, were ushered underground to a train bound for Columbus, Ohio, where silent-film icon Gloria Swanson would christen another TAT Ford aircraft. Another one of those passengers was, of all people, Dorothy Binney Putnam, which baffled those who knew the bad blood behind the scenes. Despite the Putnams' ongoing and complex separation, George had managed (via Amelia) to secure an invitation for Dorothy to be the first female passenger to step aboard the plane on this inaugural TAT flight. To their mutual credit, Amelia and Dorothy maintained a friendly rapport during the fifty-one-hour trip across the continent, even if they knew that George had ulterior motives to use the event (and Dorothy's Crayola heiress status) to publish a ghostwritten article under Dorothy's byline in an influential magazine. Dorothy's *Sportsman Pilot* article (not penned by her, of course) extolled Amelia's flying.

Several thousand people gathered in Los Angeles to see Amelia and Lindbergh meet in 1929. Eyeing Amelia's thirteen bags, the Lone Eagle ribbed her about traveling light, telling his wife not to ask Amelia for packing tips. Amelia, who was traveling with her reliable twenty-five-year-old secretary, Norah Alsterlund, explained that the luggage contained their summer and winter wardrobes, their "itinerant office," parachutes, and emergency rations. "During our explanation," she said, "I sensed he was making a comparison with the impedimenta of a typical Lindbergh journey."

Amelia and Dorothy amicably parted ways in California. Still, Amelia spent alone time that week with the Lindberghs at the luxurious 49 Fremont Place estate of TAT's president, Jack Maddux. It was a chummy get-together of aviation supernovas that further solidified Amelia's stature in aviation circles.

One evening, as they sat close to the icebox, Anne Morrow Lindbergh and her "enchanting" new friend, Amelia, were enjoying glasses of buttermilk and learning about each other for the first time as Charles was nearby, indulging in a tomato sandwich. In what he called a playful jest, he let a few drops of water fall onto his wife's precious blue silk dress. Amelia was taken aback to see Anne's initial lack of reaction, sensing her restrained anger. However, Amelia was even more stunned when the petite, well-mannered woman swung around decisively and poured her glass of buttermilk onto Charles's blue serge suit. While Charles laughed hard, Amelia couldn't help but be less impressed by the man than by the aviator, feeling sympathy for his dutiful wife. Anne would later write in her famous diary: "Damn,

damn, damn! I am sick of being this 'handmaid to the Lord'. . . . Where is my world, and will I ever find it?"

After returning to New York, with zero time to rest, Amelia was instantly drawn into one of George's more screwy plans: a cutting-edge double-hulled submarine developed by Simon Lake, often called "the Edison of the Sea" during the Jazz Age. Together with some friends, George had bet on a unique compact submarine designed by Lake. Engineered for deep-sea salvage operations, this twenty-foot steel tube had a five-foot dive chamber. The team was convinced that unimaginable treasures, amounting to billions, were waiting to be discovered on the ocean floor. After the navy didn't invest in their compact submarine, George contemplated an exit strategy. He saw an opportunity for Amelia; generating publicity from a deep-sea dive was perfect, especially after the Fourth of July. The public was desperate for any kind of light story, and media attention would be huge for such a daring feat, he explained to Amelia, who wasn't so sure she should be doing this. But, as usual, she agreed, and on dive day, a converted minesweeper was sent to Block Island's New Harbor on standby. In a loose-fitting deep-sea diving suit, she pulled a signal cord during her first descent and was dragged back. Her wrists were considerably thinner than those of the master diver who had lent the suit, and a gap caused dangerous valve leakage. She resolved to try again, especially after some reporters claimed she had chickened out.

She was checked into the Narragansett Inn on Block Island and had gotten a night's rest, but there were more social obligations that weekend, valuable time wasted instead of doing what she most wanted and needed: practicing flying. She dared not gripe to George, who had once again invited Dorothy along. Maybe Dorothy was lonely, too, and sniffed fun. They had an enjoyable evening of swordfishing, where the always-second-fiddle Dorothy openly flirted with a handsome, widowed state senator. After a solid night's sleep, Amelia suited up and reboarded the *Defender*, descending back into the Atlantic. She remained underwater for much longer this time—twenty minutes. Then Amelia walked on the bottom of New Harbor for twelve minutes in fifteen feet of water. There was not much to see except an old milk bottle, but she paused at the bottom to pick up a clam for evidence.

George was pleased by Dorothy's participation, which kept gossip at bay, and by the media coverage he had correctly predicted, including an odd but beautiful giant photo of Amelia in diving gear on the cover of *The New York Times*' widely distributed *Mid-Week Pictorial*, which ran with the coverline A FAMOUS AVIATRIX EXPLORES THE BOTTOM OF THE SEA.

The press was already nibbling at every curious angle of Amelia's life, feeding the flames of her growing celebrity. Yet on one point, Amelia and George surely agreed: she needed to solidify her aviation credentials. Initially considered a sideshow to the men's race, the upcoming Women's Air Derby quickly took center stage. George was determined to make sure no one else would steal Amelia's spotlight. But it was already July 23, and Amelia didn't have a powerful plane suitable for the event. Though George had made progress in securing a plane, Amelia hadn't practiced with such an aircraft, nor did she have the appropriate license. On July 30, under George's guidance, Amelia sold her Avro Avian aircraft and acquired a used Lockheed Vega 1 from Myron Hutchinson of Air Associates in New York, Lockheed's eastern distributor. This plane, powered by the impressive 225-horsepower Wright J-5 Whirlwind engine, had a top speed of 135 mph.

Thrilled by her newly acquired powerful plane, she still couldn't shake her nerves, aware of her limited experience. On July 31, she headed to California with Lieutenant Orville Stephens, a US Army pilot and Lockheed aircraft expert. Stephens, like Bill Lancaster earlier in the year, secretly piloted the Vega across the country, all while sharing his expertise with Amelia during their flights. George had played a crucial role in facilitating this arrangement, even securing leave for Stephens from Langley Field so that he could fly Amelia. Press releases immediately issued by George's office highlighted Amelia's upgraded plane and "undeniable flying expertise," which positioned her as the "top contender" for the upcoming Women's Air Derby.

Stopping in Pittsburgh on August 3, Amelia, at George's request, broadcast messages to Commander Richard Byrd's Antarctic team. They were stationed at Little America, a remarkable village built entirely on the Ross Ice Shelf in Antarctica. This audacious base was more than just a research station; it was a fully functioning icebound village, complete with a library, living quarters, and workshops, all constructed to withstand the harsh polar conditions. This frosty enclave, surviving in perpetual darkness during the winter months, symbolized human ingenuity and resilience in one of the earth's most extreme environments. Byrd and his team greatly appreciated the encouragement during their formidable expedition. Meanwhile, Amelia's cross-country flight revealed the secondhand plane's lamentable condition. Upon landing at Burbank's Lockheed airstrip, she humorously dubbed her plane a "thirdhand clunk," and discussions with Lockheed confirmed its dire state. Wiley Post, then a Lockheed test pilot and not yet a household name, generously offered Amelia the use of a brand-new demonstrator Vega 1 for the 1929 Women's Air Derby on behalf of his company.

Following a test flight of the new plane that took them east of Los Angeles back to Clovis, New Mexico, Stephens, eager to try some dangerous solo stunts, wanted to briefly borrow the replacement Vega up in the sky, just for fun. Amelia nodded that it was fine and remained on the ground, talking to her mother, who, thanks to Amelia's insider connections at TAT, had traveled for free to witness the opening festivities of the Women's Air Derby. But calamity struck when Stephens's stunts culminated in an unplanned tailspin and heart-wrenching crash from fifteen hundred feet, witnessed by Amelia and her shocked mother. Learning of this by wire, George issued a statement praising Stephens as "one of the finest pilots I have ever known." And Amelia, long desensitized to even death up close, compartmentalized again. Of course, she would go on, she told George, and Lockheed soon quietly produced another replacement Vega.

Ten

PILOTS AND PLUNGES

No men need to apply. "No men will be allowed to fly in this derby race." Women were to fly solo; female mechanics were okay if they had never soloed. Those were the startling rules of the Women's Air Derby. This was a sub-event of the National Air Races, promoted in other parts of the country by Ohio's Cliff Henderson.

Behind these groundbreaking rules was the indomitable spirit of advocates like Elizabeth Lippincott "Queenie" McQueen. A fifty-year-old feminist and founder of the Women's International Association of Aeronuatics, Queenie was a leading force in early aviation, even without a pilot's license. She was often seen with her opera-singing parrot, Dick, perched on her shoulder, and the bird would cheekily chime, "Hello girls, can you fly? I can!" Recognizing a surge of enthusiasm among female aviators, Queenie reached out to women nationwide, discovering a collective eagerness to assert their right to the skies. Armed with this knowledge, she convinced Cliff Henderson that the first women's air race would be a publicity gold mine.

Air races of the early twentieth century were the equivalent of today's NASCAR races—thrilling spectacles of agility and speed. And in that era, pilots were revered celebrities.

On August 18, 1929, the inaugural nine-day Women's Air Derby kicked off. Amelia, with her notable financial backing, joined eighteen other skilled female pilots in the race. Whispers among the competitors suggested that the famous Amelia had an edge, flying the "fastest plane," which her shrewd manager, George Palmer Putnam, had procured for her.

Applicants needed three days' worth of provisions, a parachute, and a pilot's license. Cross-country flying experience of at least twenty-five hours was required, including one hundred hours of solo time. Twenty-three women were accepted; nineteen would fly. Americans included Florence Lowe "Pancho" Barnes, known for her exceptional flying ability as well as her sexual appetite and saucy comments, and Ruth Elder, who, if not for that ruptured oil line, would have been the first woman to cross the Atlantic. Since her student pilot days, Elder, that instant silent-movie star, had worked hard at her skills and, like Amelia, yearned to be taken seriously.

For some overseas flavor, the aviation reporters mentioned German stunt flier Thea Rasche, Amelia's onetime rival in the quest to be the first woman across the Atlantic, and the cute Aussie pilot Jessie "Chubbie" Miller. Lady Heath, Amelia's old friend from England, was also scheduled to appear but barely survived a rooftop crash just before the race.

Amelia had joined the race to sharpen her skills, with an eye on future solo flights across the Atlantic. George wanted her to be seen as the nation's number one woman flier. In a race with powerful commercial planes and agile sports aircraft, Amelia knew that the advantage went to the more robust crafts like hers. However, her decision to participate by fudging a transport license was risky, both for her reputation and her safety. Rumors were already circulating that George had inflated her flight hours to an improbable 560, what insiders jokingly called "Parker P-51 time"—after the expensive desk pen. But she arrived at the gates in the iconic red Lockheed Vega. Designed by John Knudsen Northrop and Gerard Vultee, this state-of-the-art aircraft was highly desired in the golden age of flight. With its shift from wood and fabric to high-powered engines, it was a marvel when flown correctly but deadly if mismanaged. Elinor Smith—who, after failing to secure a plane, became a much-listened-to radio announcer for the race—voiced private concerns that Amelia, always heralded by George as the "leading woman flier," might struggle with such an advanced aircraft. Others privately worried she was right.

Amelia was the odds-on favorite to win, despite any such fears or jealousies. For once, more attention was paid to women fliers than to men in the derby run-up. In 1929, only 34 of 4,690 licensed pilots were women, and they gained novelty status. The Women's Air Derby, the first official air race for women, proved that women could fly long distances and compete seriously in aviation. Hundreds of women from all over the country gathered in Santa Monica to see these "girl pilots" rebelling against the norms. Yet coverage of the event also highlighted the broad societal discrimination they were up against, the kind that always chafed Amelia. Newspapers noted their hair color, wrote about the challenges of balancing aviation with housekeeping, and dismissively called them Petticoat Pilots, Ladybirds, and Flying Flappers. When the exceedingly popular humorist Will Rogers nicknamed this race the Powder Puff Derby, the little dig stuck, and it's how the race is still popularly known almost a century later.

Once the starter dropped his flag, the race was on, and the nineteen "Powder Puffers" took off one minute at a time. Every one of these women was no less than valiant, and even those listening on the radio were in awe. The pilots were heading toward Cleveland's municipal airport, the main grandstand for the National Air Races and almost three thousand miles away. Local exchange groups provided lap prizes at seventeen stops, with eight "night stops" until Cleveland. From sunup to sundown, they flew roughly three hundred miles a day. A media frenzy descended at every stop, with Amelia always the center of attention—Amelia Earhart had a stranglehold on publicity, often due to her boyfriend's effective, if underhanded, promotions. She weakly grinned and signed autographs for her throngs of fans. Nonetheless, she remained content. Despite the disparaging nicknames, reading about women pilots in the news was beautiful.

Next, the racers convened at the California Hotel, sixty miles distant, for a communal meal and a sequence of protracted speeches. Pancho had personally performed daring stunts in the exciting aviation-themed film

The Flying Fool, an early talkie. The film screening heightened the excitement. Unfortunately, the late-night festivities stretched until midnight, sabotaging everyone's chances of getting a good night's sleep.

But the real challenges were just beginning. The disoriented "Miss America of the Air" landed in a cow pasture after a whirlwind snatched Ruth Elder's map from her grasp. Despite the fanfare, Amelia had barely enough flight hours to make her comfortable piloting her swift, hefty monoplane. At a scheduled stop in Yuma, Arizona, her plane nosed over, the crack-up contorting its propeller. Miraculously, she emerged unscathed with just wind-ruffled hair. Amelia dismissed what went far beyond a "glitchy" start as a minor misstep, though she narrowly escaped a fatal outcome. Later, in a display of camaraderie, her rivals voted to delay their departure by three hours instead of the customary ninety minutes to allow her propeller to be repaired. That night, they pressed on to Phoenix.

Tragically, not all fared as well. Marvel Crosson, sister to the then well-known Alaskan bush pilot Joe Crosson and a record-setting aviator herself, didn't make it to Phoenix on the race's second day. She was reportedly seen plunging to earth near Wellton, Arizona. The next morning, search teams found her body three hundred feet from her mangled aircraft in a rugged valley beside the Gila River, her partially deployed silk parachute tangled around her feet, the rip cord tragically activated too late.

In the wake of this macabre discovery, there were calls to cancel the race, but the women on the race committee and the racers themselves voted to press on. Men routinely gambled with their lives in the skies, and Amelia was adamant that women deserved no less a stake. "We all feel terrible about Marvel's death," Amelia declared to the assembled press, "but now more than ever, we know we have to finish." Her statement, veiled in mourning, belied a deeper desire—for women to be given the same options as men, even in taking life-or-death risks.

Sabotage fears escalated among the participants. Rasche had been grounded east of Calexico, in the Imperial Valley of Southern California, right on the border with Mexico, when her engine failed. She blamed "dirty gasoline" and revealed sand in her fuel as evidence of foul play, supported by a cryptic telegrammed warning she had received. Bobbi Trout also experienced terror near Los Algodones in Baja California. Her aircraft plummeted, shedding its propeller and landing gear, yet she walked away unharmed. Trout, too, suspected sabotage, later saying that her altimeter had been tampered with and her Golden Eagle monoplane unexpectedly ran out of fuel.

Blanche Noyes faced her own crisis when a cigarette was tossed into her cockpit, forcing an emergency landing. Another forced landing involving Claire May Fahy's OX-5-powered Travel Air occurred near Calexico, California. Snapped center-section wires were the culprit. After inspecting the damage, her test pilot husband, Herbert, suspected that acid had been applied to her struts, corroding the wires. Heeding his warnings of continued tampering, she withdrew from the race. Even though race officials dismissed these claims as unsportsmanlike and unfounded, a closer examination of history suggests they may not have been so baseless after all. This pattern of sabotage hints at a broader resentment toward women advancing in what was then a male-dominated field.

Despite the crowds of curious spectators (predominantly women) at each stop, only eleven competitors crossed the finish line in Cleveland, Ohio, after nine days. Eight thousand spectators were waiting to see who outblazed the others. Flying her large, swift Travel Air J-5 biplane, Louise Thaden of Pittsburgh claimed the $8,000 prize in the Powder Puff Derby. In just over twenty hours, she shattered the women's world records for speed, altitude, and endurance in a single flight. Thaden was crowned with a garland of roses as she took the highest honors—but the thorns proved too much. She quietly whispered to an official, who swiftly removed the prickly prize.

Flying into town with her Waco, Gladys O'Donnell came in second place and won $1,950, a considerable sum during the era. Wild cheers erupted when Amelia Earhart appeared in view. There she was, scatheless, the Queen of Aviation in her formidable plane. Amelia had finished behind Thaden by two hours, with a pitiful bumpy landing in front of the Cleveland crowds. She had finished a "respectable" third, as George later spun it, earning $875. Starstruck fans rushed the field, and she lost the already-iconic leather helmet she had worn across the Atlantic in 1928, snapped up by a young man wishing to impress a girl.

After seeing Amelia falter at the controls while riding with her, Elinor Smith could admit how brave Amelia was to participate without proper training: "I was filled with admiration for her.... It was barely five months since the New Castle incident.... This was gut courage that transcended the sanity of reason." Although all the women competing well knew that Amelia wasn't a natural pilot, despite the unending publicity blitz around her, there was no denying her progress; there was no doubt that she had guts, and everyone hoped she would improve as she logged more flight hours.

At a breakfast gathering in the Hostess House following the 1929 races, Peggy Rex, the forty-five-year-old governor of the Cleveland chapter of the Women's National Aeronautical Association, conceived the idea of forming an official organization with historical importance. Inspired by Peggy's proposal to sustain the momentum of the races, a group of women pilots, yet to be named, engaged in spirited discussions. The welcome mat would soon be unfurled to women pilots worldwide. Due to her New York–based secretary and her proximity to many pilots on the East Coast, Amelia was chosen to be the first host for this possible organization in either New York City or Rye. But because Amelia was busy, the wealthy Opal Kunz called the first meeting at her home on Riverside Drive.

A few months later, Amelia was invited to christen a Goodyear pony blimp, a small dirigible capable of carrying a few passengers. "I christen thee the *Defender*," she proclaimed in front of sixty thousand people in the grandstands. Afterward, she invited some of her air derby rivals for rides in the *Defender*. Gladys O'Donnell, Blanche Noyes, Bobbi Trout, Thea Rasche, Phoebe Omlie, and Ruth Nichols took her up on the offer. Despite the fierce competition up in the air, they remained friends on solid ground. For some of the ladies, it was their first-ever ride in a blimp, and a thrill was only afforded because of Amelia. It was clear why she was asked to christen everything—she helped bring in an audience. Having christened another

Goodyear blimp, the *Volunteer*, back in May, it was not even her first blimp ride—but she wanted her friends to experience the fun. Amelia would later say that the true legacy of the Cleveland National Air Races was the bond formed among a juggernaut of pioneering pilots. Soon after the first determined discussions, all 117 licensed women pilots in America were invited to a meeting at Curtiss Field in Valley Stream, Long Island. Though busy as a bee, Amelia lent her name to add prestige to the invitation. The purpose of the gathering was simple: to get to know each other, discuss work and sport opportunities for women pilots, and share insights about the industry.

The seemingly endless summer of 1929 closed on a high note, with optimism soaring after the late-August highlight, that remarkable Women's Air Derby. Soon, though, a chilly fall arrived. Things were cooling on Wall Street as well: speculation peaked on September 3 as stocks reached a perilous high, followed by a shocking decline when many share prices nosedived. Despite the downturn, the market eventually recovered, with blue chips holding their ground. Nonetheless, people were already shaken.

Start-up airline TAT had been flourishing until September 3, when a westbound plane left Albuquerque at 10:00 a.m. and ominously fell silent. Six days later, searchers discovered the plane's wreckage in the sierras of New Mexico—a grim site with no survivors. A stealthy photographer tailed TAT executives to the crash site, having cleverly eluded their attempts to misdirect the press, and captured the horrific aftermath of charred bodies, propelling TAT into a PR catastrophe.

As the aviation industry contended with TAT's disaster, pilots like Elinor Smith continued to navigate their own turbulent skies, literally and figuratively. Elinor returned to Freeport, Long Island, concluding her four-thousand-mile Irvin Air Chute Tour. During the tour, a terrible error in a parachute stunt had resulted in the death of Helen Williams, a Wichita stenographer. Elinor had been flying the plane, but she bore no blame for the parachute's failure. Still, the incident overshadowed her recent accolades, and nothing could shield her from the glare of media scrutiny.

After a short but well-received paying stint in Miami, Elinor dealt with uncertainty about her future. Alone in her childhood bedroom on Long Island, she indulged in a private moment of tears. Her mother knocked on the door, announcing a call from a "Mr. Sarnoff." Was her mother serious? David Sarnoff, the head of RCA? Days later, in Sarnoff's smoke-filled office, flanked by NBC's Merlin Aylesworth and General Electric's Owen Young, Elinor was reassured of Irvin Air Chute's endorsement. They proposed making her the flier for a luxury craft, a joint project between NBC and RCA Victor, offering a well-paid gig piloting a plane that parachutists would jump out of.

Then, somehow, George Palmer Putnam gleaned the details of her arrangement, a confidence she had shared solely with Deac Lyman of *The New York Times*. Their shared elation was cut short by the news that the venture had been "financially" grounded. Stunned by the abrupt suspension of the project—especially considering the immense profitability of the participating companies—Elinor couldn't shake the nagging suspicion that George had outfoxed her once more. Or was she merely succumbing to paranoia? Could he really be at it again? Seeking truth, she turned to her mentor, C. B. Allen, at the *New York Herald Tribune*, who she knew wouldn't lie to her, even though he was Amelia's friend too. Allen agreed to poke around, and his probing uncovered unsettling insights: The sheer balls! Yes indeedy, George had orchestrated a rendezvous with Sarnoff's team and, with his poisoned take on the Wichita parachute incident, launched a calculated smear campaign to sully Elinor's reputation and pivot the focus toward Amelia for any aviation engagements. Yet when his girlfriend's inconsistent record was brought up by executives, a vexed George Palmer Putnam made a hasty exit. (A few years later, when NBC hired Elinor as a star radio reporter, Aylesworth would back up this intel and beg forgiveness for the mess.) Allen had followed the penetrating scent of deceit, and his gloomy report on George's doings left Elinor weepy until a timely telegram from Bobbi Trout, a pilot friend from the air derby, lifted her spirits. Bobbi was planning to attempt a new women's endurance record using midair refueling, aiming to stay aloft for more than forty-two hours. The ambitious feat tempted Elinor, though she couldn't help but wonder if George might try to sabotage her, even from afar. Elinor crumpled. Lyman and Allen determined that she had to set a goal and get her spirits back. Despite lacking a powerful patron, she had the backing of these two stalwarts who adored her spunk and admired her skill, and with their cheering, Elinor eventually resolved to leave New York on her terms.

Her loyal friends even orchestrated a memorable coordinated press send-off at Penn Station as she prepared to head west. A radiant Elinor, clutching flowers and dressed in a chic raspberry-colored suit, posed for a photograph, poised for her next challenge. Her departure was memorialized with the headline ELINOR SMITH OFF FOR HER RECORD.

At the airport, far from George, Amelia and Elinor met up at Columbus, Ohio, one of the westward TAT stops. Like Elinor, Amelia had many irons in the fire, and she was in town as a vice president of the airline, representing TAT at a general traffic conference. Snapshots of the two of them together show them smiling. Even though she considered Amelia's boyfriend and manager a stinkard, Elinor still admired her and counted her as a friend. A Columbus aviation reporter caught some of their banter: "If I stay up long enough," Elinor told Amelia, "I may grow my hair long. I can't weaken and go to the beauty parlor up there." Amelia let out a big laugh when Elinor said the best thing about endurance flights was that women didn't have to shave their armpits and legs.

Just before Elinor boarded her TAT aircraft heading west, Amelia pulled a dollar from her pocketbook. "Give this to Bobbi. I've owed it to her for a long time, but I've never been able to see her."

After the bull market peaked in what papers called "the wildest speculative orgy in history," the following weeks saw worrisome volatility. Though it wasn't a full-blown crisis, people were becoming uneasy; George shifted his frustrations from Elinor to the spiraling financial situation enveloping the nation. On September 22, Dorothy received a disconcerting letter from George, ominously warning that he had "certain things in his possession" that could "prevent a divorce in any court." Dorothy was horrified when she realized that George had invaded her privacy, going so far as to snoop through her personal items to find messages sent to LA. The recipient was not specified, but it was likely her recent lover, Frank Upton.

As October 18 introduced further precipitous market declines, the stock market frenzy was the talk of even average Americans. By the old New York Stock Exchange Building, a dazed and ashen crowd gathered. American history had never seen a stock market like this. Market panic escalated on Monday, October 21, with a significant downturn, although financial experts predicted a rally. However, by October 23, stocks had crashed again, shattering any remaining optimism.

Not so curiously, as the market situation worsened, George's tone toward his wealthy wife shifted. According to Dorothy's diary, realizing the economic disaster that only Dorothy's family money could save him from, he began sending her daily letters, trying to rope her back in, "suddenly realizing" the value of having an "anchor" in life. One moment, he was "alternately furious" at her "damn foolishness," and the next, he was tenderly pleading for her to return.

By October 24, known as Black Thursday, the market had hemorrhaged 11 percent of its value, with a breathtaking 12,894,650 shares changing hands. Both Kennecott and General Motors kicked off trading with sizable twenty-thousand-share volumes, but stability was fleeting. Within the first trading hour, stock prices plummeted, throwing brokers into tumult nationwide. The market wasn't just awash in shares due to panic; rampant short selling exacerbated the freefall. By midmorning, there was a frenzied rush to liquidate. Even the stalwarts weren't immune: US Steel, previously at 205.5, staggered at 193.5, and General Electric, which had traded at 400 just weeks prior, had plummeted to a concerning 283.

Stockbrokers' telephone lines were overwhelmed.

To play the soothsayer and stave off disaster, Richard Whitney, then vice president of the New York Stock Exchange, took dramatic action on Black Thursday: backed by powerful Wall Street bankers, he bought twenty-five thousand shares of US Steel at a price significantly above the going rate. The move temporarily stabilized the market and earned him the nickname "White Knight of Wall Street," but the respite was fleeting.

Four days later, on Black Monday, October 28, the market plunged again, losing nearly 13 percent of its value. Then came Black Tuesday, October 29.

Fear gripped the nation, triggering frenzied trading that resulted in an unprecedented sixteen million shares changing hands. Billions of dollars were wiped out, as were countless people's hard work and savings. It was all over. Finished. The end. In just two days, the market lost more than 23 percent of its value, setting the stage for the Great Depression—the most severe economic downturn in Western history. It would take more than two decades for the economy to recover.

In the aftermath of the crash, fortunes dissolved overnight, sending shock waves far beyond the stock market's inner circle. Initially, those untouched by investments seemed sheltered from the storm, but the illusion was short-lived. Within a year, the ripple effects had doubled unemployment, from 1.6 million to 3.2 million. Nearly one out of every four Americans found themselves without work, their prospects dim. The stock market, once a tower of strength and certainty, crumbled, shedding most of its value by the bleak midsummer of 1932. By the following year, over thirteen million were unemployed, a shadow that would not lift until the drums of World War II began to beat. The relentless downturn carved deep scars into the American psyche, unleashing a wave of hopelessness that manifested in rising suicide rates and deepening alcohol dependency. The bright, buoyant days that preceded this dark chapter faded, growing as distant and pale as an old, sun-bleached photograph—once vivid, now forgotten.

As the exuberant spending of the late '20s curdled into a pervasive gloom, Ruth Nichols—an unmarried aviator and both friend and foe to Amelia—witnessed the dissolution of her once-lucrative role promoting aviation clubs tailored to the wealthy. With fortunes wiped out overnight, she knew that "few people would be able to afford to fly airplanes for a long time to come. The social and sports aviation era had to be filed under finished business." She was terrified. Alone.

When George's two sons matured, they painted a grim picture of their father's circumstances during the week of the crash, both believing that banking on Amelia's fame was perhaps his only lifeline. Unbeknownst to them, George was simultaneously trying to charm their mother—whom he had recently threatened with incriminating information to prevent her from pursuing a divorce. David Binney Putnam later recalled that on the crash's first day, George could still cover his stocks. However, by the third day, he couldn't even provide for his family. In the wake of financial ruin, they leaned on the generosity of their mother's wealthy Binney lineage. After all, even in the throes of the Depression, children still had simple needs, such as crayons.

George's onetime prosperous business associate, Don Dickerman, wasn't spared either: having divested his remaining assets in the cratered nightclub industry and with debts nearing $70,000 (including $9,800 owed to George), he was in dire straits. Despite desperate attempts to recover money, the Greenwich Village pirate didn't have two buffalo nickels to rub together and declared bankruptcy, claiming only "a few suits of clothes three or four years old." His previously successful nightlife ventures, once fueled by the Roaring Twenties' exuberance and the allure of prohibited alcohol, had lost their charm. By December 1929, flappers in the Zelda Fitzgerald mold had receded into history, and Dickerman's once-trendy "atmospheric" concepts were outmoded in a rapidly changing New York.

In the latter part of the 1920s, the real excitement was unfolding uptown, where the A train could whisk you away to Harlem. This exciting hub emerged from the Great Migration, as over one million Black people made the collective decision to escape the Deep South's rampant racism, driven by World War I–induced labor shortages in the North. Originally a white, middle-class enclave, Harlem transformed dramatically. Its African American population swelled from 50,000 in 1914 to 165,000 by 1930, igniting the Harlem Renaissance in its heyday—a dazzling explosion of novels, poetry, art, plays, and music. Jazz, born from this cultural surge and the complexities of the Great Migration, became a defining genre, leaving an indelible mark on music and dance worldwide.

By 1925, Harlem had become a hot spot for middle-class white thrill-seekers looking for a taste of the "exotic."

Guidebooks, dripping with a sense of daring, advised thrill-seekers to visit at night, heightening the air of forbidden excitement. The hottest spots, like the Cotton Club, Connie's Inn, and Smalls' Paradise, proudly showcased

Black performers while hypocritically barring Black patrons, a glaring reflection of the era's deeply entrenched racist attitudes.

Despite its cultural vibrancy before the crash, Harlem was not spared by the economic downturn of the late 1920s. A decline in white patronage and reduced discretionary spending posed financial challenges, even for venues that had thrived during the Renaissance's peak.

With the crumbling interest in the Village's bohemian scene, the popularity of George's adventurous boys' series dwindled. The economic downfall following the postwar boom resulted in a significant decrease in readers who could afford books. Furthermore, the can-do-anything attitude of the Jazz Age, which had thrived during the prosperous years, evaporated. As the nation struggled with widespread unemployment, enthusiasm for tales depicting privileged teens wielding rifles in Africa waned.

Although the boy explorers were not stirring audiences anymore, Amelia Earhart (remarkably) still was. Yet George feared that her carefully crafted image had slipped after her less-than-impressive performance in the Powder Puff Derby. He remedied that fast when Amelia granted an exclusive interview at her newly established Hearst office on 959 Eighth Avenue. Despite the advantages her celebrity status afforded her, which had caused discontent among other participants, she poured on the praise for all the women who competed alongside her, firmly stating: "No pilot took unfair advantage of anyone."

The female journalist assigned to puff Amelia had received a tip, possibly from George Palmer Putnam himself, regarding Amelia's decision to carry Louise Thaden's luggage during the Women's Air Derby, effectively reducing the weight of Thaden's plane and inadvertently contributing to her competitor's victory while sacrificing her own chances. When this appalling matter was raised, Amelia swiftly dismissed it, cautioning, "But let's not bring that up!" She justified her actions by explaining, "I needed something to secure my plane. It could have been her baggage or any other weight." She added, "Of course, I could have taken a passenger, but all of us preferred flying solo. There were mechanics trailing us, officially listed as copilots, regardless of their level of involvement. It's customary for men flying with women to be called 'copilots.'"

As Amelia embraced this new chapter of camaraderie and adventure, the personal life of her promoter and partner was unraveling. By late September, Dorothy had moved to Reno with her and George's youngest son, Junie, to take advantage of Nevada's lenient divorce laws. Although their sons would later characterize their separation as amicable, Dorothy's diary during this month exposes a more contentious split, with unsettling hints that George threatened blackmail over things he found while riffling through her diary. Was the man she had shared her life with truly the owner of such a cold, spiky heart?

George once ominously wrote, "I could prevent a divorce in any court." Intensely creepy stuff! Dorothy suspected he had something from her belongings that he could use against her, particularly as she contemplated remarriage. Despite this, she held significant power in negotiations. Even after she faced losses in the recent stock market crash, her wealth as an heiress remained intact, while George's finances had dwindled to $1,000. Both sought high-profile legal counsel for their divorce: George secured the services of Cooke & Stoddard, and Dorothy retained Kendrick Johnson. (In the end, they settled on joint custody of their children. Dorothy would receive $5,000 in cash, cover David's annual expenses, and cover half of Junie's. George, on the other hand, would retain their house and the staff.)

Reminiscing on the financial dynamics of the situation years later, in a candid 1970s interview after his own challenging divorce, David, the firstborn son, remarked: "My mother was pretty well fixed financially. She could do what she darn well pleased. You get to the forties, and everyone gets sidetracked."

The media picked up on Dorothy's Reno move, culminating in another *Daily News* piece on September 27 that further fanned the gossip flames.

DOROTHY PUTNAM MOVES TO RENO

"Mrs. Dorothy Binney Putnam, wife of George P. Putnam jr. [*sic*], treasurer of G. P. Putnam's Sons, publishers, arrived here this week, supposedly to establish a residence. Her home is in New York. She declined to see reporters."

She was determined to see it through this time, as the kind of love you need to stay married had long been knocked out of her heart. Better yet, Frank Upton was waiting for her in Florida, ready to marry her when she was free of this six-foot baggage.

MRS. G. P. PUTNAM, IN RENO, TO SUE NOMAD PUBLISHER
PUTNAM'S WIFE SEEKS FREEDOM FROM PUBLISHER

"Reno, Nev., Nov. 28—Nomadic George Palmer Putnam, distinguished millionaire publisher who has spent so many months exploring the wastes of Baffin Land, is to be divorced quietly here by Mrs. Dorothy Binney Putnam, she revealed today."

The *Chicago Daily Tribune* soon reported that George had failed to keep in touch with his wife during his "long cruises after walrus" with their older son, David. The report mentioned that an out-of-court financial settlement had been arranged for the children's care. Dorothy accused George of being incompatible and falling short of a "dutiful husband." Another reporter noted that Dorothy, being wealthy, had no need for money. George, reportedly in Europe, would be represented by his counsel there. Meanwhile, his two sons were occupied: David was at Roxbury School in Connecticut, and Junie, a polio survivor, was in Reno with his mother, ensuring his well-being. Whatever sordid goods George held over her likely saved him from a protracted public divorce that might have included his wife taking the stand to testify about his affair with Amelia and the uglier side of a man who did not want his gentleman's mask ripped off.

As they duked out the final settlement, Amelia set eyes on her own agenda. On December 18, 1929, in aviator Opal Kunz's Manhattan apartment overlooking the Hudson River at 137 Riverside Drive, eighty-six names were called out among the gathered group of lady aviators. First, they would be the Eighty-Sixes. But more fliers had been licensed since the initial get-togethers. As a result, Amelia teamed up with Neva Paris, a pilot with organizational skills, and wrote a letter to recruit them. The official name would be the number of total acceptances plus eighty-six to represent those already on board. It looked like they would be the Ninety-Sevens. Then two more letters with earlier postmarks arrived after a Christmas delay.

The Ninety-Nines were born, the first flying fraternity for women.

But not all top female pilots joined. Neta Snook, who taught Amelia how to fly, chose not to, saying, "I had no idea aviation would advance as it has—all our friends were killing themselves; they were just falling in crashes." Elinor Smith and Lady Heath had safety concerns after seeing the risks taken during the Women's Air Derby. They believed that too many pilots favored dangerous stunts over proper training. These women would be up against skilled male pilots like Jimmy Doolittle, Frank Hawks, and Roscoe Turner. Only a few women had in-depth training on the most powerful planes. Smith and Heath, concerned for those who didn't fully grasp the dangers, believed that for less experienced pilots, joining could be a death trap, with the responsibility falling on the organization.

A day later, Dorothy Binney Putnam almost got cold feet before she formally split from George Palmer Putnam. Her final entry on the last day of her marriage was one word: "Misery!"

The following entry, made on December 20, was by an obviously scared and newly divorced woman: "So, I released him just so he could marry her. She's to get my husband, my house, my lovely garden—but not my furniture! Odd fate! This country has been whispering with suspicious gossip! Now it's over."

Settlement terms revealed that she and her children, David and Junie, would be provided for under a joint trust, which was George's demand, as he feared her boyfriend, Frank Upton, would go right through his sons' inheritances.

Dorothy's diary entry that day captured an emotion familiar to anyone navigating a divorce: "How scared and empty I feel!"

With the formalities concluded, Dorothy and Junie went to Florida, traveling by ship via the Panama Canal. Amelia, after learning about Dorothy's divorce, expressed her sympathy and called the situation unfortunate.

She was deeply conflicted about her role. Speculations about her marrying George surfaced only a day after the divorce. By the year's end, George had fled to Paris, eager to escape the public eye, which had exposed him as an unfaithful husband unable to provide for his family. His objective was also to secure a unique manuscript on Fascism. With an economic downturn looming, he transferred the manuscript to the family office in London. Intent on controlling his narrative, George contemplated how he might reshape his image from struggling spouse to successful publisher.

Just before the new year, working from G. P. Putnam's Sons' Bedford Street office on the Strand, George strategized on how to dominate London and American papers with news he could dictate. What he wanted to speak about to the press was that under his guidance, Francesco Fausto Nitti, nephew of the former Italian premier and an early opponent of Fascism, was set to publish an anti-Fascist book with G. P. Putnam's Sons. Nitti's dramatic escape from Lipari Island's penal colony and his establishment of Giustizia e Libertà in France had drawn attention. His memoir, *Escape: The Personal Narrative of a Political Prisoner Who Was Rescued from Lipari, the Fascist "Devil's Island,"* provided a rare glimpse into Mussolini's regime. George had secured the translation rights during a more stable time in publishing but was determined to ensure its success amid the market's downturn.

When the news broke, Amelia was in Los Angeles—a guest in the extravagant home of TAT head Jack Maddux and his wife. She publicly maintained a distance from George's harebrained scheme, stating, "He's simply my publisher."

Eleven

THE TRUTH TO THE RUMOR

As the new decade turned, George wove a dark fantasia of danger that ensnared the public's imagination. With a poker face and self-satisfied glint, he flaunted two counterfeit letters to the British press—one in English, the other in Italian—postmarked from Paris, December 29, 1930. With nary a pause, he claimed they had landed at G. P. Putnam's Sons' London office on Bedford Street just as his plans to publish Francesco Fausto Nitti's book in five weeks' time came to light.

One letter said, "Mr. Putnam risks his life to gain some dollars. A cunning Fascist vengeance will find him wherever he may hide himself." The other forged letter shown to the police was signed "the Fascists of Paris" and warned that publishing a book exposing Italian prison conditions would lead to the obliteration of George Palmer Putnam's New York office by two bombs. The Italian letter derisively called George "the pig who publishes the book of the other pig, Francesco Nitti," and was accompanied by a detailed sketch of a black hand adorned with a dagger, a pistol, a coffin, and fasces—bundles of rods from ancient Rome that symbolized authority during the Fascist era. It was evident that someone had put a lot of time and effort into the elaborate creation of these angry missives.

Soon, a new batch of unsettling, off-kilter letters arrived for George to show anyone interested. One threat, so mysteriously scrawled in perfect

English, starkly warned: "PIG! YOU WILL NEVER REACH NEW YORK ALIVE." It seemed that George's Fascist antagonists were zealous not only in their convictions but also in their affection for swine-based insults.

However, insiders long familiar with George Palmer Putnam's antics were not deceived by the dramatics, and soon, *Publishers Weekly* published a snort-worthy headline: PUTNAM TO BE BLOWN UP! And beneath it, they listed George's absurd claim: that on January 31, the publishing house would face two bombs due to the book *Escape*, a work that some factions deemed offensive to Fascism. "Allegedly," the magazine said with great restraint, the global Fascisti organization had warned Mr. Putnam to halt the publication if he valued his safety.

The Major, George Haven Putnam, head of the family firm, found nothing funny in this hokum, fully realizing the gravity of his nephew's exploits on the family's storied reputation. Despite the scheme driving some much-needed sales after the October market crash, the Major demanded answers. What the hell was going on? As he walked the firm's halls, his nephew rolled his eyes and winked at staff, dismissing the seriousness of the situation.

After returning to his small corner office in New York, George found himself on the receiving end of practical jokes within hours—first, a heavy carton designed to spark when opened, revealing a false fuse connected to an eggplant that George soon after proudly displayed on a bookshelf. Another package, wrapped tightly and making a ticking sound, emitted the loud noise of a dollar-store alarm clock and was cleverly timed to give George a jolt. That went on the bookshelf too.

"We'll publish this remarkable story on January 31 despite the threats George Palmer Putnam received as he returned from Europe with the manuscript," proclaimed his firm in mid-January advertisements. That ad must have taken some convincing behind closed doors! Lies galore and misuse of police resources, but George's bold deceit succeeded when *Escape* hit the bestseller lists. He appeared indifferent that this had cost him respect among his family and peers. He'd won again. G. P. Putnam's Sons had secured another smash hit during an economic crater. Yet the office antics reflected a growing consensus: George's showmanship spiraled into a sideshow far removed from serious business.

As George reveled in his latest literary victory, Amelia, by stark contrast, was charting a course that favored the skies over sensationalist fiction, laser-focused on the fledgling Ninety-Nines organization. At the first January meeting, a president was to be determined as the group gave shape to its vague goals of solidarity and working together to fight sexism. But then, on January 9, disaster struck when a Curtiss Robin Challenger monoplane ferrying thirty-six-year-old Neva Paris, the organization's presidential hopeful, on her way to Miami for the annual air derby, plummeted into the marshes near Woodbine, Georgia. Paris's body was found in the cockpit with her head crushed. The untimely tragedy of her death cast a somber tone, prompting a temporary halt to the Ninety-Nines' leadership decisions.

The question of leadership loomed after Paris was mourned. Following the first loose club meetings in the wake of Paris's death, Louise Thaden became national secretary. Once Opal Kunz was named president pro tem, the debate continued for almost two years, although from the start, Amelia was championed by many. Some saw her as polite with a hidden ruthless streak, but Amelia took time to amplify other voices. Amelia's advocate, a non-pilot PR executive, Clara Studer, spearheaded a campaign to draft her for president. After Paris's passing, the mantle of leadership within the Ninety-Nines became contentious, with Amelia's candidacy gaining momentum.

Despite the turbulence of her professional life, Amelia found meaning in mentoring the next generation, imbuing them with her passion for aviation despite its challenges. She sat on a bench at Roosevelt Field one day with one of the youngest members she was mentoring, Edna Gardner Whyte, who was determined to beat the odds and make an aviation career. Amelia cautioned her about the industry's sexism. She said military men could train for free, paid by taxpayers, then move on to well-paying corporate airline jobs. No matter how diligently women worked, they never got that leg up. Whyte later recalled Amelia as "a beautiful woman inside and out" who was genuinely interested in promoting women and aviation, but she also backed up Elinor Smith's claim that Amelia didn't have the hours like the other women. She recalled that Amelia had "very, very few" hours of flying and didn't race. "But she always tried to improve herself," Whyte acknowledged. Though aware of more skilled pilots, she wanted Amelia to run for president because she thought that Amelia was what women in aviation needed—someone to inspire them.

Fay Gillis Wells was another charter member who knew Amelia well in this era. Gillis was later sure that what drove her friend was the same thing that compelled Charles Lindbergh: "She wanted to PROVE IT and encourage others (particularly women) with the spiritual joys she had found."

On January 12, after waiting for the romantic twilight, Dorothy and her war hero, Frank Upton, finally exchanged wedding vows aboard the SS *El Salvador* in the West Indies, where the ship's captain officiated their union under a moonlit sky. The news blindsided George. It was this very man with whom Dorothy had been involved in Florida, a liaison that inflamed George's jealousy despite his own transgressions. After hearing about the new bride and her manly groom, Amelia wrote to her friend Marian Stabler: "Dottie got what she wanted. A physical specimen. George was too intellectual for her."

While George Palmer Putnam may have been intellectually astute, he was further destabilized by life-altering events, as his leathery uncle, Major George Haven Putnam, nearing his eighty-sixth year, succumbed to pneumonia. Newspapers nationwide noted the Major's death as the end of an era for one of the luminaries of America's literary scene. The stewardship of the Putnam legacy now shifted to Irving, the formidable Major's younger brother, who had often been outshone within the family's second generation. Despite their close relationship, Irving had experienced his share of marginalization, his voice frequently suppressed in the Major's presence, perhaps most notably during the critical decision to reject *All Quiet on the Western Front*. The decision haunted Irving, especially since the novel made a mint in translation under a rival publisher's banner. He would leave clippings about its success on his brother's desk, a silent testament to what could have been—a fact the Major would never come to learn.

Although Irving had finally ascended to the top, his health was failing in his late seventies. George had bided his time: he was poised to lead the next generation of literary scions. The Major's will divided his estate among his wife, Emily; five children; and other direct descendants. The Major left his sword, his prized Civil War books, and, in a surprising twist, a significant one-sixth share of the company to his only son, Palmer Cosslett Putnam, who was then in Africa. Drawn by tales of his cousin George's accomplishments and keen to tap into his own network of doers, Palmer expeditiously returned to the US, eager to dive into the publishing game despite its diminishing returns in the economic downturn.

As George slowly grasped the new dynamics, he flipped his lid, his angry voice erupting throughout the office. Were they all out of their minds? Ever since his brother had died in 1919, George had invested his soul in the family business, envisioning himself as the rightful successor. He had brought massive hits that provided huge financial boons to the company. He aspired to acquire Uncle Irving's shares and rise to the presidency upon the elder's retirement.

Was he not the expected heir, especially after being mentored by the Major? Still and all, his imperfections couldn't be overlooked.

Later, in midcentury, Howard Cady, then editor in chief at G. P. Putnam's Sons, wrote off the record that he'd carefully examined old files and learned the coup in the clannish family was just as much caused by uneasy feelings about George's frequent in-office rages and his funhouse distortions about being hounded by Fascists. The Major had feared not only his nephew's careless and ludicrous stories but also his apparent boredom with the daily grind and less exciting literary fare, the lifeblood of any working firm. True, he was a hitmaker, but was he morally fit to lead the company into the future? The Major hadn't thought so. In an illuminating off-record letter, Cady called him "a great dreamer who often got carried away by ideas." George would later tell friends that in a fit of temper, "he let them have it," but the pesky truth, Cady said, is that he was pushed out. As Cady added, he left a "bad taste."

Even in the first few weeks after the Major's demise, with Uncle Irving now at the helm, George realized that Palmer was the Putnam being groomed for the top. They were in the firm together briefly when George saw that he was getting the old heave-ho. Teeth-grittingly humiliated, he sold his one-sixth interest to his cousin. The agreed-upon price was $100,000, $25,000 of which was paid at signing. In hushed tones, the office staff wondered how George would spin it this time. The public knew him as a millionaire publisher. He had gotten the extravagant Rye house in his divorce settlement, but now there were servants' wages and utility bills he couldn't ask Dorothy to pay. House rich, cash poor. And no one was buying houses.

In a later published account of his life, George naturally portrayed Palmer as an inept executive who not only forced his ouster but also then singlehandedly led the firm to bankruptcy. He claimed that Palmer's mismanagement wiped out the $75,000 still owed to him. However, the legendary publishing historian John William Tebbel openly contested this depiction, suggesting that Palmer's exit in 1932 was more analogous to a planned retirement and that after Palmer helped orchestrate a merger with Minton, Balch & Co., an old army friend of George's, Walter Balch, subsequently took the reins, concluding the family's control over the company. Far from being a nitwit, Palmer Cosslett Putnam was, in his lifetime, celebrated as the "Edison and Marconi of turbine wind energy technology" and earned numerous accolades, including a medal from Eisenhower for technical contributions that shortened the war. Known for his brilliance and straightforward demeanor, Palmer left a legacy that differed sharply with George's portrait of him. Assessing the exact truth is always challenging, especially when the narrative is shaped by someone like George. News of the shake-up, no doubt placed by Palmer's loyalists, included these acerbic lines: "Last winter he received threats that said his publishing house would be blown up if he persisted in bringing out an anti-Fascisti book. The bombing never materialized."

Another account of this turbulent time comes from George's publicity protégé, Harold McCracken, who witnessed the firm's inner workings. McCracken noted in his memoir that his friend and boss "was financially ruined by the stock market crash. [George] had no alternative but to sell his interest in the publishing firm to the other members of his family." McCracken remembered a wealthy friend who committed suicide after losing a fortune. Post-separation from his wife's wealth, George had "lost the important prestige he had once enjoyed."

Amelia Earhart, not yet George's wife, watched sadly as his world crumbled, realizing that the ongoing economic crisis jeopardized her potential as a solo aviator. Still, thanks to George, her presence was sought after at aviation events, and like any person, she longed for close companionship during trying times. As George departed from the family business, McCracken, who had been given a new career opportunity by George, didn't celebrate like many in his office did. He later said, "It was a sad day when G. P. moved out of his office." George soon faced the brutal reality of his situation head on. "He had not been able to adjust himself since being compelled to leave the publishing firm that bore his family name," McCracken said. Despite feeling crushed by shame, George was determined to overcome his setbacks. He had McCracken set up a favorable article (in a trade publication) about his career and the many choices that still lay ahead, teasing an "exciting future." With a hint of defiance, he told a reporter, "If you played golf for twelve years, you wouldn't stop all at once, would you?"

The strategy seemed to work, as George soon landed a vice president position at Brewer & Warren. Yet the firm was willing to rebrand itself as Brewer, Warren & Putnam to capitalize on George's reputation, offering him a lifeline. His loyal longtime secretary, Jo Berger, and Amelia Earhart, his girlfriend (and now the secret backbone of his financial survival), followed him to the new venture.

McCracken joined him too. They had previously collaborated on promoting the Heigh-Ho Club with Don Dickerman, a surprising ally known for running a "clean" operation, though he was also involved in the risky liquor trade during Prohibition. They navigated a world where Dickerman's speedboat, a remnant of the Great War, dodged federal agents along Long Island's coast, ensuring that their literary events were never dry. At one infamous book launch, George humorously suggested eels as a replacement when the planned rattlesnake entrée was compromised, endearing him to McCracken despite the circumstances.

As the decade's ebullience gave way to the harsh realities of the Great Depression, Amelia became an indispensable ally and confidante to George. She encouraged his optimism and saw potential in new markets. Noticing a gap, she suggested targeting young female readers. "Goings-on of this sort are typically left to masculine characters, joyously relived by boy readers," she told him.

Seizing the idea, George reached out to Grace E. Murphy, wife of Robert Cushman Murphy, curator of birds at the American Museum of Natural History. Could their daughter, fifteen-year-old Alison—a confident swimmer and adventure enthusiast they'd boasted about at parties—be the protagonist of a new series for young girl explorers? The Murphys agreed, seeing an opportunity in challenging times, and George assured them that seasoned ghostwriters would polish her journal entries, ensuring a professional sheen, with all profits duly directed to them.

Robert Cushman Murphy had nominated George for the Explorers Club in 1924, and this was his return favor when the Murphys needed money in dicey times. Their son was already a published boy explorer at his old firm, and their younger daughter was determined to become a well-paid author like her big brother.

Soon enough, the Girls' Books by Girls series launched with Alison Barstow Murphy's *Every Which Way in Ireland*. Thanks to George's connections, Alison met the legendary Lady Gregory and her friend William Butler Yeats, who was near mythical even then. Yeats was an unplanned guest who had knocked on Lady Gregory's door for a shared tea, and upon learning of Alison's literary project, Yeats said to her mother, "I hear your daughter is writing a book. Are you writing it for her?" Despite this, he engaged in a lively conversation about fairies with the young American girl, providing delightful historical vignettes for the book. Alison's Irish adventures took her from kissing the Blarney Stone, to attending a wedding on the Aran Islands and exploring druid circles, to delving into the history of the Book of Kells. She toured Northern Ireland before the onset of the Troubles. A charming encounter occurred when she spotted Slats, MGM Studios' lion mascot, in Phoenix Park.

Despite such a magical cameo, most readers found that the rest of the book offered bland, childlike perspectives. After its release, Alison's work received mostly muted praise and was also met with biting critiques, including one from *The Irish Book Lover*: "To us older countries the whole plan of these books is unattractive—we feel it is not good for young people to imagine their conclusions and impressions of any permanent value."

The book's lack of impact meant that George, who had once found Alison "so fascinating," never contacted her again. Over time, Alison grew resentful, and according to her still-living daughter, she long remembered how the boys under contract with George, including her brother, received more aggressive promotions and multiple book deals.

Undaunted by Alison's anemic sales, which also disappointed Amelia, George believed that a younger female protagonist might garner more public interest. He hypothesized that Alison's maturity was perhaps too advanced for the public's taste. Continuing the trend of calling in favors, he contacted another Explorers Club associate, the father of Mary Remsen North—a ten-year-old sixth grader from Walton, in the Catskills, and a recent victor of the junior canoe championship on the Delaware River. Mary's elder brother had been successfully published by G. P. Putnam's Sons in the previous decade, during the boom.

After the wild sales of his *Three Boy Scouts in Africa* book, which had outperformed even his famous son's juvenile works, George was counting on the bonus of featuring a Girl Scout. By 1930, the Girl Scouts of the USA, founded by Juliette Gordon Low in 1912, had a membership of two hundred thousand. Recognizing the marketable appeal of a Girl Scout, George was convinced of the sales potential. Amelia, endorsing his renewed attempts, welcomed his decision to continue.

On her publisher's dime, the pint-size explorer and her parents soon embarked on a foreboding, extraordinary journey for a family of that era. Mary navigated 350 miles of the perilous lower Colorado River by flat-bottomed rowboat, confronting dangerous rapids. Although she was accompanied by her parents, the mere thought of endangering a child's life in such a way was inconceivable to most families then. Following the river adventure, the North family journeyed to Yuma, and from there, they traveled overland to Baja California. They endured a harrowing three-day trek across the San Felipe desert, braving the intense sun and hazardous conditions on foot and by burro. Nights were spent on the abrasive desert sands, their laundry done in infrequent streams. With her tiny hands, Mary dispatched rattlesnakes that presented danger. The relentless heat and merciless landscape pressed down on her, leaving a quiet, unshakable fear that stayed with her for years.

One of George's influential contacts, New York governor Franklin D. Roosevelt, provided Mary with a letter of introduction to document her journey and interview state governors along the way. She did! The exciting emprise, however, allowed for little rest, especially when Mary's parents diligently fact-checked her journal entries and critiqued her grammar and spelling, much to her annoyance. Before George's involvement, her journal was a source of pride—a young girl's cherished passion for writing. From an early age, she had maintained a journal, and by the age of ten, she was contributing to naturalist publications on topics like Mount Marcy and Mount Vesuvius.

True to form, George Palmer Putnam rapidly brought *Down the Colorado (by a Lone Girl Scout)* to market, pricing the book at $1.75. The jacket blurb enticingly described the book as "written in the present tense, day by day in wonderful surroundings, this journal reveals a child's fascination with life." The press was told that she was the youngest white child to ever navigate the treacherous lower Colorado River.

George, distracted by legal wrangling over his nightclub and divorce, neglected the promotion of the two young "Girl Explorer" authors.

Mary was deeply unsettled by seeing her "work" in print. Her father had preemptively altered her narrative, infusing it with his perception of a ten-year-old girl's emotional journey. Discovering the editorial liberties taken with her words led her to tears; the book, now alien, distorted her genuine experience beyond recognition. To make matters worse, her parents privately disparaged her as an ungrateful child. Despite her objections, they insisted she promote "her" book to respect the contract and secure the needed income. This childhood ordeal imprinted a lasting emotional scar, one that her parents could not comprehend, nor one her intimidating six-foot publisher would ever care about.

In therapy as an adult, Mary revisited the pain of being a forgotten Putnam Girl Explorer by journaling in a voice that echoed her childhood tone: "I had to go to a book signing in New York. The book wasn't my idea. I did not like being put on display. I didn't like anything about it. Mr. Putnam and another man showed me to my table in a big room full of tables and grown-ups. They spoke to me for a few minutes and then walked off to other duties. I wished I were at home in the woods with the dogs. On the table a stack of *Down the Colorado*. My father had changed all the words in my journal. I always try to say what's true. I try so hard, and now everybody will think I told a lie."

Following a tepid reception, Mary was dropped from the roster after just one book, as George turned his promotional efforts back toward Amelia's career. Mary later wrote in her journal: "Amelia, wherever you are, thank you! Thanks to you, I was spared another book ordeal. And Amelia, may I ask? You flew distances in the silence of the wind and the stars, but did you hate the publicity as much as I did?"

George Palmer Putnam's capricious publishing decisions often placed young children in danger, only to be forgotten after brief notoriety. Yet these airy young women, lesser known than their male counterparts, warrant recognition in the chronicles of women's and American history.

That year, in April, another brave young woman, Elinor Smith, was declared the youngest man or woman to earn a transport license, a remarkable achievement after rigorous testing at LeRoy Airport in Genesee County,

New York. Amelia, who understood the significance of this achievement more than anyone, was among the first to call and congratulate Elinor. She invited her to lunch, supposedly to discuss the possibility of Elinor joining the Ninety-Nines.

During the meal in a Midtown Manhattan restaurant, Amelia conceded that she needed more flight practice, though George considered it undignified for her to be seen honing supposedly mastered skills. She mentioned her attempts to foster reconciliation between Elinor and George. (Did Amelia realize how poorly he behaved in her absence? Was she playing the role of good cop, or was he shielding her from his worst behavior?) Now alone and without the stress of an imminent flight, Elinor shared with Amelia the details of how George menaced her in his office. She confessed to Amelia her complete lack of desire to see George again, expressing utter contempt for him. Amelia's surprise was evident; she insisted that she was unaware of Elinor's distressing encounter with George, and Elinor believed her.

"He'll do anything he thinks will protect my interests," Amelia offered in what seemed to Elinor a half-hearted apology after her mortifying account of bullying. Elinor liked Amelia but pointed out that, as many would agree today, there's a difference between protecting interests and sick and twisted intimidation. Amelia, now uncomfortable, acknowledged that Elinor's comments complicated the additional reason for their meeting.

Amelia hesitated, then said, "You've always had a good relationship with New York aviation journalists like Deac Lyman and C. B. Allen. How do you think they would react if I married George?" Taken aback, Elinor blurted out that the aviation reporters would probably "rather see her married to Genghis Khan."

Amelia blushed, revealing that her sister and mother opposed any marriage to George because he had already been married, prompting Elinor to recall Amelia's earlier aversion to marriage.

Before parting ways, Elinor implored Amelia to refuse risky ventures without proper training. Amelia noncommittally agreed, citing George's demanding schedule, which left her little time for herself.

Just then, Elinor spotted Fitzhugh Green, the part-time explorer who had collaborated on the Lindbergh book's introduction and also ghostwritten Amelia's debut book. Learning of Green's presence from Elinor, Amelia turned pale with the fear that he might report this stealth meeting, and pondered the exit door. After Elinor cupped her hand and reassured Amelia that the man had joined some friends and was heavy in conversation, Amelia quickly left the restaurant without greeting Green.

Although the meeting is documented, it is impossible to determine if Amelia had any motivations to pump her friend for information. We do know that she was constantly gauging Ruth Nichols's possible Atlantic plans via "innocent" social visits, and that this grand goal had never strayed from her sights.

But Elinor Smith never mentioned this in her colorful recollections of that day, and the two occasionally met after that encounter in 1930. Yet their connection waned as their paths diverged. Elinor respected Amelia's unquestionable courage, despite her reservations about Amelia's lack of flying hours. Elinor would soon be named the "Queen of Aviation" by the American Society for the Promotion of Aviation, with the dazzling flier Jimmy Doolittle recognized as her male equivalent. Some had already called Amelia the "Queen of Aviation," thanks to George's relentless promotion, but Elinor's title came with formal recognition from her peers—a major difference.

In June, the *Boston Traveler* inaccurately reported that Amelia had wed her former suitor, Sam Chapman, during her summer in Marblehead, Massachusetts—a mention that likely perturbed George. Despite later claims in George's ghostwritten biography of Amelia that he had proposed six times since his divorce in 1929, his efforts to marry Amelia began while he was still married, as early as the summer of 1928. The first documented instance of George's attempts came when Amelia was overheard by a visiting friend, Marjorie B. Davis, in a heated December 1928 argument with her mother at New York's Greenwich House; the two were debating whether she should marry a man who would divorce for her. After the false report on Amelia and Sam surfaced in 1930, George, perhaps to finally sway Amelia, whisked her away to a secluded bungalow in Garrison, New York, on the scenic east bank of the Hudson River. Upon learning of the escapade through George's phone calls, Dorothy remarked sardonically, "Well, I'm glad he has someone to sleep with and be 'gay' with occasionally." Despite the romantic setting, Amelia's resolve remained firm. She clarified her stance in a candid note to her mother after the trip: "I am not marrying anybody." She did sign that one AE.

Despite the challenging financial climate in the US, the burgeoning commercial airline industry was poised for expansion. In the summer of 1930, Amelia Earhart was appointed vice president of a new venture led by her friend and former TAT colleague Eugene "Gene" Vidal. Funded by the Ludington brothers of Philadelphia, the airline—officially named New York, Philadelphia, and Washington Airway Corporation but soon nicknamed "the Ludington Line"—was set to revolutionize regional travel. It offered hourly flights, akin to the frequency of train services, between New York, Philadelphia, and Washington using Stinson trimotors, a novel approach at the time. Operating from the modern Newark Airport, which served as New York's terminal in the absence of any in the five boroughs, the airline launched on September 1 with a $24 round-trip ticket.

Alongside Vidal, a former army pilot, and Paul F. Collins, an airmail veteran, Amelia was instrumental in promoting women's involvement in aviation, using her position to advocate for and inspire future female aviators. Despite the precarious economics of the industry—where airlines without mail contracts often failed—the Ludingtons were daringly prepared to operate at a loss for up to five years, challenging the dominance of mail-subsidized competitors like Eastern Air Transport.

Amelia reveled in her role; her office, located in the bustling fifty-six-story Chanin Building—a beacon for airline execs with its Art Deco flair—featured a proudly displayed "Vice President" plaque. The skyscraper was not just a workspace but a lively hub, equipped with a private movie theater and an observation lounge. Regular encounters with industry peers in the elevator fueled a dynamic environment, mirroring the progressive energy of aviation that Amelia actively shaped. Alongside her, George played a crucial role in drumming up publicity by organizing complimentary flights for reporters and supporting the team's efforts. However, Amelia was the linchpin of their publicity efforts, often flying as a passenger every other day to maintain visibility and promote the airline.

Just as the buzz started on the new airline in mid-September, Amelia received a shocking cable from her stepmother, Helen Earhart (called Annie). Her father, Edwin, had stomach cancer and was dying. He wished for one final reunion with his beloved daughter. Swiftly, a flight to California was arranged using Amelia's connections at TAT. It was during this intense period that Amelia developed a friendship with Annie, whose unwavering devotion to her father was evident in every gesture and glance. However, Amelia couldn't shake off the anger that her father, a devout Christian Science follower, rejected medical interventions.

"I saw Dad on the coast, desperately ill and starving to death. Some kind of stricture prevents him from taking in enough nourishment." (She later wrote that she would prefer a blood transfusion over watching him starve; due to his adherence to Christian Science doctrine, he had shrunk to 105 pounds.)

For a woman with many (often hackneyed) ghostwritten articles and books in her name, some of Amelia's finest writing by her own hand appears in a letter she wrote to her mother:

"About Dad. The diagnosis was correct. When he had the haemorage [*sic*] the doctor said he practically knew. . . . He grew thinner and thinner and waited for me to come and change doctors or get him to a sanitarium or change diet because he didn't want to go. I tried and had X-rays to please him, and he hoped he could not move his poor hands. He didn't miss (me) when I left, and we gave morphine at the last so he wouldn't worry about my leaving. His big case was lost, and we told him he won. He couldn't have stood the disappointment, so it was for the best. I wrote up the little history and paid the hundred little debts he always had. Stationery, etc.—you know. He asked about you and Pidge a lot, and I faked telegrams from you all. He was an aristocrat as he went—all the weaknesses gone with a little boy's brown puzzled eyes."

Edwin's second wife viewed him as a bighearted man and claimed that he drank very little after they married and never spoke of Amelia's mother, Amy, as anything but a good woman. Annie added that Edwin had never considered divorce until he met her in 1924. While Annie and Amelia took turns caring for him on his deathbed, Annie shared that Edwin was aware of the Otis family's perceived superiority over the Earharts, a sentiment that caused discomfort and strain for both Edwin and the family. Any marriage is a crapshoot, and Amelia could see that Edwin and Annie were a better match than her parents had been.

The year of Edwin Earhart's death would be a turning point for Amelia, and George offered emotional comfort after she returned. Despite their differences and a past riddled with alcoholism, Amelia had felt close to her father and, in many ways, was more like him than her mother. She knew how inventive he was and how he'd had to settle in life doing claims work they both felt was beneath him.

She threw herself into work and then, perhaps, into George's arms—who, a decade older than her, was the remaining father figure for her.

While Amelia's recognition as a player in the industry was on the uptick, her personal life was also taking a new turn. George, who had already proposed several times—once at Greenwich House and again in June before Amelia met with Elinor Smith—tried again. Instead of relying on Elinor's reaction, Amelia contacted Deac Lyman at the *Times* and C. B. Allen at the *Herald Tribune* herself and invited them to her hotel suite, where she asked them directly if she should marry George Palmer Putnam.

The men were baffled at the ask, and the room fell into a hushed silence. "We stared at her . . . united by what I believe was a shared belief," Allen wrote in an unpublished account of the meeting. They advised Amelia to decide, urging her to weigh her reluctance against potential financial implications in these economically unstable times. While neither man favored George, they understood Amelia's ambition and the challenges faced by women in aviation. Allen suggested she might consider uniting with George as a team through marriage.

Viola Gentry, an aviator close to Amelia, had just as strong opinions about George as Lady Heath and Elinor Smith. As the first woman to set an endurance record and a charter member of the Ninety-Nines, Gentry respected Amelia but abhorred George. Many of her Ninety-Nine colleagues joined in this appraisal.

While George's narcissism often overshadowed his better qualities, those close to him, especially his children, could attest to the genuine compassion he could display when in an undeniably swingy mood. Blanche Noyes, a member of the Ninety-Nines and the widow of Dewey Noyes, who had taught Blanche to fly, was the only woman flier in Amelia's circle who deeply admired him. In 1936, when Blanche's world collapsed after Dewey's untimely death in a plane crash, Amelia invited her to come along on a six-week lecture tour, hoping to lift her spirits from a lonely space. During this period, Blanche, enveloped by good company, discovered a kindness in George that Amelia was often privy to.

Like George's mother and sons and even Hilton Howell Railey, Amelia knew she could have a terrific time with him if she kept his mood in check. They enjoyed many of the same pastimes together—tennis and the outdoors—and could have a fine laugh. Living between settlement houses and hotel rooms, Amelia longed for a stable home. She knew George was crazy about her, and she wanted a supportive partner but only on her terms, starting with separate finances.

After her father's death and the much-publicized denial of her engagement to George in late 1930, Amelia was soon photographed flying with George and Edna O'Brien, a former debutante and con artist stockbroker. The stock market crash had devastated George, both mentally and financially. And the money they made! And the fun they had! All the fame! What was once a decade of confetti had turned to dust; now, cash-strapped, he was detached from his family business and without the consistent financial support of Dorothy. Amelia quickly fell victim to O'Brien's Ponzi schemes, losing much of the savings she had amassed since her transatlantic flight as a passenger. With no inheritance and the Depression looming large, Amelia began to consider a partnership with George that extended beyond mere romance. Indeed, could she?

"As Amelia weighed marriage, this time thoroughly, she chose to say yes. Despite financial losses and lopsided love, she saw the strategic benefits of a union," Muriel, Amelia's sister, later observed. "She was careful to choose the man that would allow her to keep flying."

George groveled and groveled some more; after another proposal, Amelia finally agreed at the Lockheed aircraft factory in Burbank, California, in October 1930. She begged her press-release-addicted fiancé and manager to keep quiet about the development. He did, miraculously, for a while.

Because of their secret engagement, George's mood changed dramatically, and he decided to exploit the betrothal in his latest book, supposedly self-authored. *Andrée: The Record of a Tragic Adventure* recounts the true story of Salomon August Andrée, who died trying to reach the North Pole by balloon. Published on October 27 by his new firm, Brewer, Warren & Putnam, it was another rush job not penned by him, but his overall ideas were dictated to his ghosts, who got to work at his request, and with a nod to those in the know about his romantic partner, the flyleaf read: "To an aeronaut about to embark on a new journey."

The couple obtained their marriage license at Groton Town Hall in Connecticut on November 8. In the spring of that year, George helped move his strong-minded and beloved mother from her Rye estate to a small house in Noank to save money during the growing national financial crisis.

Groton town records show that Judge Arthur P. Anderson legally declared that the couple did not need to wait five days or take blood tests, as was customary. His legal words were dutifully typed by the town clerk, Henry L. Bailey, into the license: "This marriage can be celebrated without delay." Elated by the judge's decree, George realized they could wed immediately that afternoon. However, Amelia was less than pleased, chiding him for his eagerness to alert the press about their personal matters. He'd promised not to! The tipped-off local reporters loitering near town hall soon filed rumors that Amelia and George might tie the knot at Frances Putnam's house on that crisp autumn day. Adding to the speculation, Judge Anderson admitted he had been led to expect a call to officiate at George's mother's residence on November 8, yet the day passed without any summons.

Reporters casing Mrs. Putnam's boxy home, fittingly called the Square House, even noticed bright lights and flowers inside and parked themselves on neighboring lawns. Locals who saw the scene as outlanders invading their little village were rankled, and the reporters scuttling around in dark suits were not helping George's case with his would-be bride. With Frances in the car, they drove to the judge's home on the corner of Brook and Elm and asked if they might get married there for more privacy. Happily, he said yes. The judge's sons were in the house and could witness.

But when the moment to exchange vows came, Amelia Earhart found herself emotionally paralyzed. Weeping and clinging to George simultaneously, she shook her head no. He was shocked and tried very hard to comfort her; eventually, he was able to get her to sit and chat with his mother and the judge's twenty-five-year-old son, Robert "Chip" Anderson.

Another witness to this scene, the judge's younger son, William, heard Amelia ask for a rare (though, as evidence shows, perhaps not so rare after all), much-needed cigarette and a private room to think more about what she was about to do. Postponing the wedding was a difficult decision but one that was made, and the papers were overflowing with conjecture.

"To marry Miss Earhart would be swell," George said stoically when a reporter cornered him outside his home. "But while it seems pretty definite that a marriage license has been issued, we have not been married and cannot say when we will be. Nothing in this vale of tears is certain."

"There's no truth to the rumor," Amelia said to the press a few days later. "I'm not engaged to anyone. Mr. Putnam is my publisher, that's all." So, when would she get married? Curtly, she replied, "Sometime within the next fifty years."

Marriage, an institution Amelia had long wrestled with, became an even more complex decision when George entered her life. Muriel recalled that Amelia would often quote from A. S. M. Hutchinson's *If Winter Comes*, a novel examining the tribulations of marriage. She once referenced the book by saying, "Do you remember how Mabel always tried to get her husband a den, how he hated it? He said he wasn't a bear. . . . A den is stuffy—I'd rather live in a tree."

Amelia's contemplation of marriage intensified with George's unpredictable presence. His Janus-faced nature—capable of both kindness and cruelty—was recognized not only by enemies but also by friends and relatives who didn't want to air dirty laundry or had an interest in preserving his reputation. Muriel and Amelia's cousin Lucy Challis saw their affection; Lucy described George as "a most attractive person" with a "delightful mind, a sense of humor" that could make him "a charming companion," and she affirmed that Amelia truly loved him. Nevertheless, George's complex disposition was evident to all, including Lucy, who once worked as his assistant and wryly observed that keeping track of his moods was enough to make one "cross-eyed." Muriel much later divulged her private take on George's ever-fluctuating moods: "(Lucy) was cross with him because it was always the social affairs that GP wished to attend, that he and Amelia went to, no matter whether she had just flown in from California or not." In her own 1958 note to a novice biographer, Lucy confessed her regrets over revealing what she now chalked up to George's gruff disposition due to a poor sinus condition (an interesting ailment to blame, as her cousin Amelia was in fact the one with the documented condition): "It was unkind and disloyal of me to have recounted incidents which showed GP in a poor light. . . . I am asking you to be more discreet than I was." (The stories were omitted.)

Despite Amelia's desire to control her destiny, marriage to a publicist would give her the emotional protection and edge that she needed—and that other female aviators only dreamed they could have.

Twelve

AN ATTRACTIVE CAGE

Noank
Connecticut
The Square House
Church Street

Dear Gyp,

There are some things which should be writ before we are married—things we have talked over before—most of them.

You must know again my reluctance to marry, my feeling that I shatter thereby chances in work which means most to me. I feel the move just now as foolish as anything I could do. I know there may be compensations but have no heart to look ahead.

On our life together I want you to understand I shall not hold you to any medieval code of faithfulness to me nor shall I consider myself so bound to you. If we can be honest about affections for others which may come to either of us the difficulties of such situations may be avoided.

Please let us not interfere with the others' work or play, nor let the world see our private joys or disagreements. In this connection I may have to keep some place apart—where I may retreat from even an attractive cage—to be myself.

I must exact a cruel promise and that is you will let me go in a year if we find no happiness together. (And this for me too.)

I will try to do my best in every way and give you fully of that part of me you know and seem to want.

—A

February 7, 1931

The day before their intended wedding, George received a candid letter from Amelia, hastily scribbled on the gray stationery of Frances Putnam's Square House. What might now be called a prenup outlined the conditions he must accept to marry her, including her insistence on certain freedoms. George agreed, and her original note, signed "A," now resides in the archives at Purdue University. However, in subsequent publications, George revised the signature to "AE" and made further alterations before the first publication of *Soaring Wings*, his 1939 hagiographic (and ghostwritten) biography of her. Later editions omitted the phrase "affections for others," perhaps to soften the implications of her request.

With her apprehensions laid bare in pencil, Amelia woke up to confront the wintry day destined to seal her union with George. Persuaded to reconsider the nuptials, Amelia nervously drove to Noank, haunted by her previous last-minute retreat.

Many of the same people who had convened for the November attempt—Amelia; George; Judge Arthur P. Anderson and his son Chip; George's mother, Frances Putnam; and Charles Faulkner, Frances's brother—reunited for the occasion. The February air in the summer town was crisp, and this time, two black cats were part of the wedding ensemble.

Calm and collected, Amelia sat with Chip on Mrs. Putnam's couch, not dwelling one second on the imminent ceremony. Instead, she was eager to share the particulars of her recent trip to Washington, DC. There, she had advocated for military use of an innovative aircraft called an autogiro, which she'd recently test-flown on December 20 at the Pitcairn Aircraft Company in Willow Grove, Pennsylvania. This adventure garnered significant press attention. The autogiro, or gyroplane, was distinct in aviation technology, with its unpowered rotor creating lift through free autorotation, unlike engine-driven helicopter rotors. Its forward motion, driven by an engine-powered propeller, spun the rotor blades, generating lift. The autogiro's simple mechanics, stability, and low-speed flight capabilities made it a remarkable innovation in 1931, with mastery of it offering significant media coverage opportunities.

Amelia envisioned the autogiro's military potential and hoped to work with George to boost media exposure. Despite her enthusiasm, the army was not receptive, a setback that frustrated her. However, she found a more receptive audience in the navy, a detail she shared with Chip, highlighting the service's openness to innovative ideas.

As George entered the sitting room, Amelia was promptly ushered into the dining room. George's mother, Frances, extended a temporary platinum wedding band for Amelia to use during the ceremony. Judge Anderson remained stationary in the dining room as Amelia and George took their suggested places in the interconnecting corridor. Frances, elegantly attired in a gray canton crepe dress, and Chip were poised to serve as official witnesses, and completing the scene, the pair of black cats, siblings in mischief, frolicked at their feet.

Judge Anderson agreed to Amelia's request for a secular vow exchange, omitting traditional mentions of "God" and "obedience." No church bells here, no hymns or prayers to punctuate the moment—just the quiet words of two people agreeing to a union on their terms. When it came time to exchange vows, the judge addressed George: "Mr. Putnam, do you take this woman as your wife?" George confidently replied, "I do." When the officiant turned to Amelia, she quietly echoed the affirmation with a "Yes," and with that, they were pronounced husband and wife.

After the solemn vows, the mood lightened as Amelia, surprising Chip, immediately resumed her intense critique of the army's rejection of her proposals. Shortly after, Judge Anderson approached to extend his congratulations to the new Mrs. Putnam. "Please, sir, I prefer Miss Earhart," she corrected him, and in a display of levity, the judge, standing tall, declared,

"That marriage was short but effective!" before making his exit, never to cross paths with Amelia Earhart again.

When Amelia's mother-in-law leaned over the couch to drape a gift of amber beads around her neck and kiss her, Amelia kissed her back with genuine warmth. Yet, true to her feminist principles, she soon returned the borrowed wedding band, firmly resolved never to wear a symbol of marital possession. As Amelia wrapped herself in a brown fur coat, she signaled that she was ready to leave. Once the famous couple had left, Frances called George's primary secretary, Jo Berger, in New York to inform her of the nuptials so that she would be prepared for any further calls. When a reporter who was casing the house asked Frances where the couple was going, she deflected, as coached by her son, saying, "I shouldn't be able to tell, since they didn't tell me."

Amelia sent a telegram to her sister: OVER THE BROOMSTICK WITH GP TODAY—STOP—BREAK NEWS GENTLY TO MOTHER. Amelia understood that her mother—whom she had previously battled over marrying George, and who was now in Philadelphia tending to Margaret Otis Balis, her dying, cancer-ridden sister—might not be in a receptive state.

Years later, George, revisiting the day, confessed: "Why she married the man she did was often a matter of wonder to me. And to some others."

Chip later shared with Noank's local historians his belief in the genuine affection between the couple, despite Amelia's outwardly cool demeanor. Yet within their circle of female aviators and friends, there was speculation that the marriage was merely a business arrangement.

Lucy Challis, Amelia's cousin from Atchison, shared Chip's perspective, noting, "AE married GP because she loved him. . . . His only drawback was a difficult disposition." When prompted to encapsulate George in a single word, she settled on "unpredictable."

Perhaps a January 1932 article in *The Illustrated Love Magazine* captured Amelia's sentiments about George best (despite its ghostwritten origins): "We came to depend on each other, yet it was only friendship between us, or so—at least—I thought at first. At least, I didn't admit even to myself that I was in love . . . but at last, that time came; I don't know when it happened, when I could deceive myself no longer. I couldn't continue telling myself that what I felt for GP was only friendship. I knew I had found the one person who could put up with me."

Indeed, George orchestrated Amelia's endorsement lectures, but many moments of laughter and tenderness early in their marriage were witnessed mainly by family members, leaving the intimacies of their bedroom to speculation.

Muriel, Amelia's sister, recounted Amelia's complicated feelings for Sam Chapman, whom her mother had desperately wanted her to wed: "They wanted to marry and had much in common; Amelia felt that the traditional home in exclusive Marblehead on the North Shore and the social life of the yacht club set were not for her. It would have been a beautiful existence with Sam, but she had to make a decision. . . . She chose George, not for the sake of her career but because she also loved him."

The newlyweds had their first photo shoot in mid-February at the Wyndham Hotel on 42 West Fifty-Eighth Street. Their temporary abode was a book-filled three-room suite before moving to George's luxurious house in Rye. The hotel, also a sanctuary for Cuban and Mexican political refugees, hosted the Maurice Beauty Salon and Jonathan's Restaurant. Those deemed important could swiftly connect with the operator by dialing Plaza 3-3500.

During the early days of her marriage, Amelia conducted interviews in their temporary home at the Wyndham. A visiting reporter noted the eclectic decor, which included a broken propeller, the frame of a motor, a typewriter used by both, and a petite upright piano. Amelia revealed her fondness for tickling the ivories—a gentle stress release she shared with her father and sister. Her surprising ability delighted George and led to cozy family concerts. In return, George delighted her by revealing his photography skills, a calming hobby known to only his close friends. He captured numerous pictures of Amelia, preserving their precious moments together.

No longer hiding their romance, the couple openly dined around town at places like the intimate Schrafft's Alexandria Room on 556 Fifth Avenue.

Two witnesses to this carefree time were John Monk Saunders, the hard-drinking silent-film writer who had provided the material George sold for

Wings, and his new wife, Fay Wray, whom he brought to Rye to introduce to the man who was still his agent and publisher. While Saunders's Broadway show, *Nikki*, fell short, Fay stood on the cusp of fame as the lead in *King Kong*. In her later years, she reminisced about Amelia, George's lively new bride, playfully wielding a can of FLIT insecticide at George.

The 1931 social register revealed the elite circles that Amelia had entered through her marriage, listing George as the vice president of the Explorers Club, a Psi Upsilon fraternity brother, a member of the Harvard Club, and a member of the Wilderness Society; he also belonged to the Apawamis Club, minutes from his home in Rye. His credentials were carefully worded; he had "attended" Harvard University and the University of California.

Amelia Earhart settled into the quiet charm of her elegantly designed Rye home, where the people, the patter, and the prices reflected a delicate balance. In this affluent town, conservative residents held tight to entrenched values, creating an intriguing clash with the progressive attitudes of celebrity neighbors. The quiet hauteur of the suburban elite was a surprising choice for someone known for her independence, but Amelia's sister, who knew her well, wasn't shocked. They had spent their teenage years moving from place to place, far from the stability and affluence of their early childhood with their grandparents. That wandering life had left its emotional scars. Despite living in a house paid for by her predecessor (and former friend), Dorothy, Amelia found her own sanctuary. The sight of dogwood flowers blooming outside her window was a simple joy. Amelia could reconcile with her past in this home and comfortably step into her role as a public figure and benefactor, leaving behind the cramped living conditions and dependence that once defined her life.

The bedroom suite Amelia shared with George was soon redecorated. It featured a large bedroom, two dressing rooms, his-and-hers bathrooms, and a comfortable sitting area with an onyx desk and chaise lounge. What she called her Red Room had red drapes, red-and-white diamond-patterned wallpaper, red-painted wood trim on windows, and a magnificent bookcase full of brightly colored books.

After stumbling from a canopied four-poster bed every morning, she never scrounged for breakfast at Rocknoll (with servants too!). Despite the economic slump, Rye had not been hit as hard as it would be later. By inviting Norah Alsterlund, Amelia's secretary, to live on the grounds in one of the many guest bedrooms, George ensured she did not have to travel to Manhattan to get help with her job duties. More than she dared hope.

Looking back at this time, Amelia's stepson, David Binney Putnam, said, "There were discussions of additions to the family. . . . Amelia's attitude was, 'Let me get some of these flights out of my system before I consider it, because I don't think with the career I am involved with, a child would be anything but a complication, and it wouldn't be fair.'"

Amelia wrote to her mother a few weeks after the wedding. Her sister, Muriel, would later admit that their mother was, as expected, less than thrilled. Amelia now expressed her belief that the decision was right and that she felt happiness she hadn't expected. Of course, Amelia often kept truths hidden or altered them—she told her sick father that his estranged ex-wife had sent a friendly letter and falsely said he had won a lost court case. In another letter, she revealed her anxiety about an upcoming visit and questioned whether George's presence would make things more challenging.

Amelia and George's parties at Locust Avenue, much like the ones Dorothy and George used to host, were always graced by famous guests. George handled the highly prized guest invitations to Rocknoll, a task that Amelia was happy to leave in his capable hands. The hospitality continued under the careful oversight of Dorothy's Austrian servant, Mary Ulsvois. Visitors to the house were often shown the Jungle Room, where lushly painted scenes of plants, birds, and flowers seemed to hum—not with actual birdsong but with the idea of birdsong, as if even the discreetly included python named Eleanor, coiled gracefully among the painted foliage, might lift her head and, in a moment of grace, whistle a tune. Another guest room featured walls hand-painted with tropical fish, exotic corals, and deep-sea fauna and flora, all depicted in a stunning kaleidoscope of aquamarine, navy, teal, cobalt, and cerulean hues. The southern wing housed a spacious kitchen and five servant rooms, while the flagstone terrace, furnished with wicker chairs and brightly painted tables, had become a popular spot for cocktail parties.

"Oh, it's pleasant here," Amelia told a *Better Homes & Gardens* reporter. "I like to live where things are growing." George's influential acquaintances entertained his new wife with stories and heartfelt songs, as they once had with Dorothy.

But money was running low, and a new promotion was needed; at George's suggestion, Amelia scaled back her involvement in the Ludington Line, which offered little pay for a preposterous amount of effort. Their thoughts turned to the autogiro, the strange helicopter-like vehicle that had animated her conversation with Judge Anderson's son Chip at her wedding. Resembling a hybrid between an airplane and a helicopter, the autogiro featured rotating blades on top to provide lift and a conventional propeller for forward thrust. While it couldn't achieve vertical takeoff like a helicopter, its design allowed for extremely short takeoff and landing distances, hinting at the future of aviation technology.

An autogiro tour needed immediate luck to pay urgent Great Depression bills. When the next autogiro was slated for release, Amelia Earhart was the chosen recipient. Her excitement, however, waned upon learning she'd get the thirteenth model. Even with her deep trust in machinery, Amelia felt uneasy about the number thirteen's aura of superstition. She was hoping for a change in the serial number, but given her fame, she inherited the autogiro meant for barnstormer and autogiro enthusiast Johnny Miller instead.

Around the same time, in May, a small news article grabbed Miller's attention. *The New York Times* detailed plans for a transcontinental autogiro flight featuring Amelia and sponsored by Beech-Nut. Puzzled, Miller couldn't comprehend how Amelia had so swiftly secured her machine. Seeking clarity, he headed to Pitcairn's Willow Grove airfield. The truth was a blow: Amelia was next in line, while he got the dreaded C/N B-13 (NC10781), which he named *Missing Link*. He was irked but determined to rectify the situation by practicing extensively away from the press and secretly leaving before her, undertaking his own daring transcontinental flight.

Amelia and her autogiro mechanic, Eddie McVaugh, launched their expedition from Newark Airport in late May. They flew nearly five hours daily, making ten stops along a northern mail route. At each landing, Amelia mingled with admirers, offered kids cockpit tours, spoke to the media, and handed out Beech-Nut gum samples—a bold yet perilous sponsorship organized by George's aide, Harold McCracken. Despite the autogiro's dicey reputation, Amelia's faith in it was unmistakable. Occasionally, she would have George's youngest son, Junie, join her on these treacherous trips, with the boy fondly remembering his role in distributing gum during stops.

Amelia's friend Louise Thaden revealed that another reason for Amelia's autogiro tours was to accumulate more flying hours to pad her logbook. While her Vega was known for its speed, the unusual autogiro presented a different challenge. Simply logging hours in the autogiro didn't necessarily translate to mastering piloting skills. Insiders, aware of the autogiro's limitations, often feared for her safety, knowing that Amelia would benefit from targeted training to refine her expertise in more conventional aircraft.

Meanwhile, George, eager to greet Amelia in California, flew commercially. By the time he arrived, Amelia was already past the Rockies and aiming to set a new speed record. Racing to see her land in Oakland on June 6, George injured his leg hopping a fence. When Amelia saw her husband hurt, their roles reversed: instead of him supporting her, she rushed to his aid.

They soon discovered that Johnny Miller had landed in San Diego in *Missing Link* nine days before Amelia, dashing their record-setting aspirations and prompting Amelia to reroute to the East Coast.

Yet the return could have been smoother, and Amelia's flight showed more than a hint of haste and lapses. On June 12, 1931, in Abilene, Texas, she crashed during takeoff. Miraculously, despite hitting two cars, nobody was hurt. A rotor replacement ensued, and she later speculatively blamed a sudden gust as the crash cause. This mishap meant she couldn't beat Miller's time; accepting defeat, she took a train back to New York.

Despite the turbulence of her own flights, Amelia remained steadfast in her belief in the resilience and capabilities of lady aviators. On her return, a syndicated column under her name stated: "Texas proved my Waterloo.... [But] a fatal accident to a woman pilot is not a greater disaster than one to a man of equal worth.... I am sure they feel they can endure their share of misfortune, whatever it be, as quietly as men."

The tour had some positives: Amelia became the first woman to cross the US in an autogiro, later taking two more such journeys. However, after her Abilene crash, the Aeronautics Branch of the Department of Commerce issued her a ninety-day suspension. George stepped in and cashed in a favor with well-placed contacts, resulting in a lesser penalty of public rebuke for Amelia's "carelessness."

Amelia's subsequent autogiro mishaps were notable. A second crash had her vowing never to fly the aircraft again. In a third incident at the Michigan State Fair, she narrowly escaped injury, but George wasn't as fortunate, sustaining cracked ribs in his rush to her aid; he was taken to the hospital in excruciating pain.

Amelia's rocky 1931 record stemmed from more hasty decisions, inadequate training, and overlooked details. It would be months before she received comprehensive training on the tricky new aircraft from ace pilots Paul Mantz and Bernt Balchen.

Amelia was undeterred, and her airborne challenges were met with equal determination on the ground by George, who worked tirelessly to mitigate the impact on her reputation. To George, the press was critical, and he was concerned that Amelia's status as a credible aviator remained questionable. One scribe even sarcastically remarked, "Amelia Earhart Putnam disappointed a lot of crash fans by failing to wreck an autogiro this week." Despite these rocky flights and scary near misses, it's hard not to be awed by her determination to get back in the air, seemingly unaffected by the last brush with disaster. Though she was still in need of training hours and more skill, nobody on land or in the sky would say she lacked raw and infallible courage.

Despite the bad press over her crashes, Amelia maintained her sponsorships using the aviation column that her heavy-hitting PR husband had secured. She got the good press when, in June 1931, she received some news from "America's Greatest Female Explorer," the globe-trotting journalist Harriet Chalmers Adams (and the only female journalist who had been permitted to visit the Great War's trenches). Amelia had been elected to the Society of Woman Geographers—a fellowship of women as dauntless as herself.

In August 1931, in her *Cosmo* aviation column, she claimed that the world would soon see autogiros used for hunting and fishing trips, quick weekend getaways, and excursions to golf and aviation country clubs. Amelia predicted that one day, "country houses will have wind cones flying from the roofs to guide guests to the lawn landing area." The autogiro would also be a convenient way to commute to work. (Pitcairn Aircraft or its advertising agency authored many similarly written autogiro magazine ads, placed in upmarket outlets like *Town & Country*, with impressive photos and dramatic, descriptive copy intended to attract the rich. They likely ghostwrote this article for her.)

The press never stopped when you were Amelia Earhart and newly married to George Palmer Putnam, who would seamlessly fit in with today's branding executives, securing sponsorships for Amelia that aligned with her modern image and—at least in the last days of the Jazz Age—also ensured a healthy financial status. Through these partnerships, Amelia supported her family members, including her sister, and struggling aviators by paying off their debts. As she soared to new heights, she conquered the skies and carved a path of financial independence and support for those she held dear. Now, with a few calls from her husband, she would test out a new medium.

That summer, years before television became widely accessible to Americans or even known to them, Amelia Earhart made her first and only TV appearance. The concept of television must have seemed like magic, a foretaste of a future world. Philo Farnsworth had demonstrated this emerging medium for the first time in 1927, when it was still in its infancy. However, long before television became familiar after World War II, Amelia had a fuzzy debut on television in early August 1931. It was quite an experience for her. She later confessed to a reporter that she was "scared to death" when she saw the flashing lights, more so than on any of her flights. Sitting in a small, vault-like room, she scratched her nose while television fans twenty-one miles away watched in awe. Meanwhile, her new husband observed her from a lower floor using a video receiver. When he joined the reporters upstairs, he expressed equal amazement, wondering aloud what chance a husband had when his wife could locate him through television and then pick him up by airplane.

That month, George also oversaw the Brewer, Warren & Putnam release of *Coconut Oil: June Triplett's Amazing Book Out of Darkest Africa!*, the sequel to Corey Ford's 1929 surprise hit, *Salt Water Taffy*, a G. P. Putnam's Sons parody skillfully shepherded by George. He convinced Ford and his colleagues to venture into offbeat, satirical territory. Although no other authors except his son and Amelia had followed him to the new firm, George promised Ford that they could recreate the magic at this new enterprise, and he would reward loyalty.

The book included two unusual photos of Amelia, both taken in Central Park as a favor to her new husband. One image depicted Amelia riding an enormous penny-farthing alongside South Pole pilot Bernt Balchen, with another woman at the wheel's base. On the following page, a humorous caption referred to Amelia as a "fair pilot" who was "mounted on her trusty heavier-than-air machine, a high-powered Swackhamer bisexual autogiro." The caption, written by Ford, clearly aimed to evoke laughter and possibly allude to rumors about Amelia's bisexuality.

Interpreting that photo would be challenging for any researcher, given that the entire book was a whimsical parody; the second photo, purportedly depicting the depths of "darkest Africa," was shot in Central Park. While some scholars have speculated about Amelia's sexuality without solid fact, such speculation is wish-casting, as it is widely accepted among her family and former biographers that her only known relationships were with men and, mainly, older men. History often surprises the next generation, such as with the uncovered love letters between Lorena Hickok and Eleanor Roosevelt and the closely guarded secret of Charles Lindbergh's three European lovers and seven additional children, a double life that was hidden from even his recent biographer. Yet without solid evidence, speculation about Amelia's personal life is merely conjecture. Furthermore, conflating gender expression with sexuality can be deeply misleading. Assumptions based on appearance often do injustice to the complexity of identity.

Despite cameos by Algonquin Round Table intelligentsia and an eyebrow-raising photo of George's explorer son shirtless with a nose ring, the book failed to achieve the hoped-for success. Thankfully, copies of this racist work are rare today.

Amelia focused on her own endeavors and did not engage in publicity for the problematic book. During this time, the National Air Races, which were being held in Cleveland for the second time, unfolded from August 29 to September 7, Labor Day. At the end of the races, Amelia Earhart was finally chosen as the first president of the Ninety-Nines—an honorable recognition of her accomplishments and a boon to the group that knew Amelia would attract members.

Plagued by her old enemy, sinus pain, Amelia flew her Beech-Nut autogiro to Battle Creek, Michigan, on September 8. She checked into the Battle Creek Sanitarium, long managed by Dr. John Harvey Kellogg and renowned for its emphasis on "natural therapies" for health. The sanitarium, with its thirty tentacular buildings, was a testament to the Kellogg family's pioneering work in wellness—though often veering into quackery—and could accommodate up to thirteen hundred guests. Recognizing the publicity value of the Queen of Aviation, George saw to it that Amelia's expenses were negotiated.

Amelia was well acquainted with "the San," as it was known, having been a regular visitor since 1928 due to her sinus issues. However, this visit was distinguished by the personal invitation of John Harvey Kellogg. Always in his characteristic all-white attire and often with a white cockatoo perched on his shoulder, Kellogg was acutely aware of the allure celebrities like Amelia brought. The 1929 financial crash had diminished the number of affluent visitors, and in response, Kellogg extended complimentary stays to notable figures such as Amelia. Other special sanitarium guests included Johnny Weissmuller, and even years later, guests remembered him for his theatrical Tarzan yells during meals.

The 1930s saw Battle Creek emerge as a beacon for health and wellness, heavily influenced by the teachings of the Seventh-day Adventist Church. Its cofounder, Sister White, who once prophesied the world's end, advocated for a "pure" lifestyle, eschewing coffee, tea, and meat.

Yet Battle Creek's pioneering legacy in health practices had its shadows, including deeply alarming beliefs in white supremacy and eugenics championed by Kellogg's Race Betterment Foundation. This advocacy had dire ramifications at the sanitarium, especially for patients from marginalized communities, who were subjected to forced sterilizations and other invasive procedures rooted in unfounded racial theories. The extent of Amelia's awareness of these practices remains uncertain. Nevertheless, much malfeasance was potentially occurring during her time there, perhaps away from prying eyes.

Amelia's visit wasn't solely about health. After handling a few preliminary PR tasks, she encouraged Kellogg to explore the world of aviation. Surprisingly, he agreed. The next day, his autogiro flight—circling above the sanitarium and its towering smokestacks—captured widespread media attention and left a lasting impression on him.

Using a speech whipped up by her husband, George, and his crew, Amelia dished out zingers and insights. Although the well-honed shtick might not have been hers, she diligently delivered her vision of aviation's promising trajectory. She envisaged an imminent future where air travel replaced trains and planes handled postal duties. Alluding to the prospects of flying across oceans, she remarked, "I feel more comfortable flying over the Pacific than the Atlantic." Recalling a past trip to Newfoundland, she amusingly shared, "We ate ham sandwiches," later quipping, "I am planning to keep flying to see what else I can find to eat."

After Battle Creek, Amelia swiftly returned to her frenetic life in the Northeast, catching it cloaked in the splendor of fall colors. The world around her evolved with new traditions. In late 1931, construction began on a skating rink at Rockefeller Center, and the jaded streets of New York stirred, the promise of something lasting in the air. Nearby, the first Rockefeller Christmas tree proudly stood, a humble twenty-foot balsam fir purchased with contributions from workers and adorned with homemade garlands. This marked the start of a ritual that would bring joy to the hearts of New Yorkers for generations.

Thirty miles north in Rye, Amelia and George were settling into their second year of marriage. As they sat by the fireplace, they reflected on their deepening bond. They agreed, both content and excited, that there were still many new traditions to create. Their future together was promising and full of potential.

In the meantime, though, Amelia's autogiro flights were losing their novelty, and it was time for something new.

Thirteen

A KIND OF THE DITHERS

In the small, conservative town of Rye, new arrival Amelia Earhart had received a reserved, gossip-tinged reception with just a few shy hellos. She had no plans to win over the town by baking apple pies for local fairs, but with George's support, she did organize a free talk at a crowded banquet for mothers and daughters at Rye High School. There, she made it clear that air travel was poised to become part of everyday life, just as cars had once overtaken horse-drawn carriages. To the mothers gathered, she posed a thought-provoking question: "How many of you would fly tomorrow if I could arrange it?" When many but not all hands rose, Amelia, with a touch of grace, said, "I am quite curious about the hesitant ones," adding that skeptics often had compelling points of view.

Amelia's friendly ways and her excitement for aviation gradually softened the initial skepticism of Rye's residents—to George's relief, since he had worried about their past loyalty to his ex-wife. Her influence even reached into his business: despite his indifference to pacifism, he accepted Amelia's push to publish Frederick A. Barber's *The Horror of It: Camera Records of War's Gruesome Glories* through Brewer, Warren & Putnam. The book was filled with brutal photographs from the Great War, from the agony of famine to the raw carnage of the battlefield—far from the usual output of the firm. George, who loved a bit of drama, falsely claimed he faced "strong resistance" from the US government, arguing, "It isn't a book the government likes. It isn't pleasant enough." Yet despite the noise he tried to create, the book's sales were disappointing from the start.

But a minor misstep in their collaborative efforts couldn't quench Amelia and George's entrepreneurial drive. With an air of resilience, the newlyweds maintained their separate finances as George cheerfully managed Amelia's 1931 lectures, still skimming his standard 10 percent commission and aiding her in refining her speeches with inspiring lines ("The important and exciting thing is to find beauty in living . . .") that mirrored her thoughts, even if she didn't write the speech.

The story that became legend recounts how, sometime this month, over breakfast, Amelia proposed her daring solo flight across the Atlantic to George. With a dramatic pause, and after a big gulp, he agreed to help. The story of her decision makes for good copy, but there is no doubt this flight was her own idea, and a conversation took place just around then. Despite his public support, George shared a common concern about Amelia's flying skills, which he had once exaggerated for the media's attention. Arranging special training was on his checklist, but first, he chose May 20, 1932, the fifth anniversary of Lindbergh's historic flight, as the date for Amelia's journey, believing the timing would bring much attention if she succeeded.

Shortly after George resolved to do whatever was necessary for Amelia's transatlantic flight, her friend Marian Stabler visited the Putnams in Rye. Stabler had missed the train and taken a taxi; she was terribly chagrined, but Amelia was comforting. During this visit, Amelia kept her secret plans secret but was, as always, very personable, cordial, and pleasant, as was George's refined mother, Frances, a guest that night too. Marian found the self-satisfied look on George's face odious: "He sort of teased me through dinner and didn't make things any easier. I was working in a place called Jackson Heights—a term for what's considered lower middle class in Queens, New York City." When Stabler mentioned that Jackson Heights was having a baby parade the next month, George did what he always did—like a toothpick dispenser, mechanically offering something small and sharp. "A baby parade. I guess you'd want me to come and be a judge." Things like that hurt.

"If they knew that I know Amelia, they would certainly expect me to ask her," Stabler snapped. Still, she was quite certain they were in love, she said years later, reconsidering the awkward evening. "I didn't like him. But after dinner, I saw them settle down together, and I could see that she cared for him and he for her."

After Miss Jackson Heights left Rye, George refocused on helping his wife plan for her secret solo transatlantic flight. He ensured that she created a formal will and established a trust fund for her mother. Amelia later said, "I wanted to fly alone again. I wanted to prove to myself that I deserved some of the praise I received. . . . I had the reputation, but I wanted to truly earn it. Maybe it's illogical, but most desires are."

With spring months ahead and other women wanting to be the first to solo across the Atlantic, Amelia and George discussed at length how to proceed with her biggest dream, and in late March, Bernt Balchen, who had gained fame flying Commander Richard Byrd—now Admiral—over the South Pole and was gearing up for another Antarctic expedition alongside Chicago's Lincoln Ellsworth, received an out-of-the-blue summons to Rocknoll from George. Living near Teterboro Airport and working as a chief consultant for Fokker, Balchen was well acquainted with George but barely knew Amelia Earhart, although they had met once or twice. Following a meal at the expansive Putnam home in Rye, Amelia asked Balchen to serve as her technical adviser for a solo flight across the Atlantic. She now owned a Lockheed Vega 5B, a more advanced and powerful aircraft than her earlier models, specifically suited for the challenges of such a journey. Balchen agreed, swearing to secrecy as he planned the extensive overhaul of the Vega 5B. He soon flew the plane to the small airport in Teterboro, New Jersey, his base near Fokker headquarters, where he led a team of skilled mechanics, including Edward "Eddie" Gorski, a former Fokker maintenance supervisor.

The well-worn aircraft demanded substantial refurbishment. Assisted by

Gorski, Balchen upgraded it with larger fuel tanks, a drift indicator, three compasses, and a fortified undercarriage. But Balchen didn't stop there; he requisitioned a state-of-the-art Pratt & Whitney engine, and the finishing touch was a repaint, with the bright signal red deepening to vermilion.

Amelia became a regular at Teterboro Airport, soaking up everything she could from Balchen, whose guidance was crucial as she prepared for her historic solo flight. Though she remained discreet, keeping her plans under wraps, her cover was almost blown when she drove back alone one night from New Jersey and got a flat tire at the new Holland Tunnel's exact midpoint. A reporter spoke to Amelia as she had an embarrassing tow, and she quickly mumbled a few words about how she was out in New Jersey chartering her plane to Ellsworth's expedition. The secrecy of her mission remained intact.

In the weeks leading up to the flight, the Vega became a familiar sight circling above the airport, carrying Balchen, Amelia, or Gorski, each taking turns at the controls. The plane's cargo hold was filled with sandbags, mimicking the weight of the fuel it would carry across the Atlantic over what is now the Meadowlands Sports Complex, used for football games and rock concerts. Gorski, tasked with the weight simulation, would release the sandbags as they neared the landing zone. Balchen's coaching extended into night flights, during which he taught Amelia the critical skill of instrument navigation after dark. Looking back on those days as an old man, Eddie Gorski said of Amelia, "A lovely lady. Not pretentious in the least." In marked contrast, his boss, Bernt Balchen, had a less kind view of Amelia's husband in a 1950s letter, recalling him as a "a very aggressive person, and very fond of personal publicity."

In April, under the guise of a casual get-together, Amelia arranged a private luncheon in Rye with Ruth Nichols, a fellow aviator recuperating from her chancy 1931 attempt to cross the Atlantic—a venture that ended in a crash and a brief coma in New Brunswick. Both women, hailing from Rye and accustomed to the thrill of competition, had been allies in advocating for women in aviation since 1927. At that time, Amelia, although primarily a social worker who flew on the side, was also an active feminist, and she had written to Nichols, suggesting they collaborate to elevate the presence of women in aviation. The decorated Nichols, celebrated as Outstanding Woman Aviator of 1931, spoke candidly about the challenges posed by the massive ocean. With George's strategic insights, Amelia skillfully maneuvered the conversation, a not-so-innocent zeroing in on her competition while expertly concealing her intentions. While Nichols was forthright about the safety improvements to her aircraft, Amelia maintained the role of a prudent confidante, fully aware of Ruth's determination to attempt the Atlantic crossing at the earliest opportunity. For Amelia, any piece of information could prove invaluable.

As the anniversary of Lindbergh's historic flight approached, Amelia's planned journey began to take shape. Once on board with her intent to cross the Atlantic, George advocated for a flight plan that aimed to replicate Lindbergh's landmark journey on its fifth anniversary, maximizing publicity. Scheduled to depart from Harbour Grace, Newfoundland, on May 20, 1932, Amelia intended to follow a northeasterly route, with Paris as the targeted destination—echoing Lindbergh's path, and precisely five years after his solo achievement. George had already tasked his team with drafting an instant ghostwritten book about this audacious, yet-to-be-completed feat, and they had written most of the material before Amelia even left the ground so that they could quickly fill in any gaps upon her landing.

Once Amelia landed in Paris, George planned to take charge, turning the moment into a whirlwind of profit and acclaim. It was the kind of savvy move that Amelia admired and one that only deepened the bond between them.

In the lead-up to Amelia's momentous journey, other female aviators, like Ruth Nichols and Elinor Smith, had encountered their own challenges. Nichols's attempt had ended in disaster, and Elinor's 1929 venture was undermined when her backer withdrew support, fearing public backlash if the flight ended in tragedy. This patron, dubbed "Mrs. Question Mark" by Elinor's mother, initially invested $20,000 for the monoplane but balked at the additional $1,500 needed for crucial instruments and extra gas tanks, ultimately grounding Elinor's ambitious transatlantic aspirations.

Harry Archibald, Harbour Grace's airstrip supervisor, was the first to learn of Amelia's impending arrival in Newfoundland, and the second to know was his sister, Rose Archibald, who owned the Archibald Hotel on Water Street, which had a restaurant on the ground floor where pilots could fuel up before departing. Soon, the entire town knew. Amelia Earhart left Eddie Gorski and Bernt Balchen at the airstrip and drove to file her flight plan. She listed "Paris" as her destination, despite uncertainty about where she'd land in Europe; Paris was a bit of a pipe dream, and wherever she touched down would make news. To her amusement, she was asked to pay a one-dollar exit fee to leave Newfoundland, as it was an independent dominion at the time. Additionally, Amelia wrote a letter to her pilot pal Louise Thaden in which she detailed her wishes for the Ninety-Nines organization should anything happen to her. Balchen later mailed this letter from Newfoundland.

As Amelia's expected arrival time approached, Rose broke out a bullhorn to round up the town's children from the playground. "Hurry up!" she bellowed. "You're going to miss Amelia Earhart's landing!" The weather was cool and overcast when Amelia arrived at Harbour Grace at 2:00 p.m.

After leaving her crew with the plane, the American aviator made her way to the Archibald Hotel, where she intended to take a nap, and as she lay down, she may have thought back to 1928, and to Mabel Boll in Harbour Grace, racing Amelia's own Trepassey-based flight. But her mind was also likely consumed by the weight of history and the anticipation of what lay ahead. She knew that the challenges she would face on her solo flight across the Atlantic would be unlike anything she had ever experienced. This realization must have weighed heavily on her mind as she drifted off into a brief but much-needed kip.

At 6:30 p.m., the rap at her door and the telegram in the hotel worker's hand snapped Amelia out of her slumber. It was from George, clear and urgent: "Time to fly!" By the airstrip, her adviser, Bernt Balchen, cast a wary eye over the Vega. He urged Amelia to reconsider the risk of ice on the wings in the chilly evening air, his concerns hanging between them, unspoken yet understood. Amelia and George had skipped the red tape, including the required sign-off from the Aeronautics Branch of the Department of Commerce—a gambit for secrecy and a big reveal. Confident in the cloudless sky above their heads, Amelia stubbornly dismissed Balchen's warnings—this was her chance in Newfoundland's often unpredictable weather. "Doc Kimball said it's now or never," she said, echoing George's telegram. The pilot bit back his response. This was Amelia's flight, her risk to take. A handful of reporters snapped photos and jotted notes, their presence minimal but focused as Amelia made her final checks.

Then, just five hours after arrival, at 7:20 p.m., Amelia, cheered on by a town crowd, told a local newsreel reporter, "I think I'm ready for a transatlantic hop," and prepared to leave. She briefly returned to the Archibald Hotel to grab a metal thermos filled with Rose Archibald's chicken soup, momentarily worrying onlookers that she was backing out. After her return, they cheered, but she sternly warned the crowd that the propellers could slice an arm off. Stay back!

Armed with tomato juice, chicken sandwiches, and Rose's chicken soup—instead of scarfing coffee, she chose sharp-smelling salts to keep her senses keen—Amelia took off in the setting sun. Having just spoken to Amelia, an eight-year-old girl watched the plane tearfully, fearing for the aviator's safety over the ocean, while the townsfolk stood in silent reverence until the Vega was but a dot in the distance.

Starting her solo flight across the Atlantic in 1932, Amelia relied heavily on her cockpit instruments for guidance. Alone in the enveloping darkness, with the vast sky and ocean stretching endlessly before her, she aimed for Paris. For the initial four hours, she enjoyed beautiful weather and clear views. "Everything was lovely," Amelia would later recall. However, about five hundred miles into the flight, as she glided over the faint outlines of icebergs below, she was hit by a sudden storm of rain squalls and gusty winds. Skirting the worst of the storm, she managed an hour of harsh weather during which her exhaust manifold burned out, spitting hot-red flames from the side. "I wasn't scared—but having flames that close is certainly not pleasant. A leak in the oil or gas could spell real trouble." The conditions worsened—dark, cloudy, rainy—and climbing higher was her only option. At higher altitudes, she noticed ice forming on the wings, just as Balchen had warned. Then, unexpectedly, her altimeter malfunctioned, an issue she had never encountered in her decade of flying.

Amelia quickly descended lower to warm the aircraft but faced more significant stakes than ever before when the phosphorescent glow of the water appeared below, and she had to make a harrowing decision. With her equipment on the fritz, Amelia decided to risk burning rather than drowning. "There was no use turning back, for I knew I couldn't land at Harbour Grace in the dark even if I could find my way. And I didn't want to roll up in a ball with all that gasoline. So, it seemed sensible to keep going. . . . I figured I had one chance in ten of succeeding."

Finally, after flying for about fourteen hours, Amelia spotted a fishing boat one hundred miles off the Irish coast. She circled it, and the boat sent up a flare—she was greeted by a "bomb" sound and a long whistle, her first human interaction since leaving Newfoundland, an elating moment coupled with the realization that small fishing boats meant land must be near.

There it was, there it lay—at the end of her journey, atop the crest of the next rise—Ireland, unfurling before Amelia Earhart as she touched down in 1932. The sight of Ireland's greenery breaking through the clouds brought euphoric relief after navigating turbulent skies. But the poor navigator had yet to learn where she was. Searching for an airport, Amelia followed the Great Northern Railway line to help orient herself, and soon, her bright-red monoplane circled near the ancient walled Northern Ireland city of Londonderry, most often called Derry by locals. The plane's sporadic ascents and descents signaled her search for a landing spot. Word quickly spread through the area—after partition, under British rule—that "the dauntless American aviatrix" had graced their skies instead of Paris's!

But soon after it was spotted, the plane vanished, as Amelia was trying for a suitable field to land in and flew on until the urban center gave way to country roads. She next found herself in Culmore, a small town near Derry. From high above, Amelia saw fields dominated by cows—too crowded and unpredictable for a safe landing. One attempted descent sent a plowman's horses into a panic. Finally, at 1:45 p.m. (8:45 a.m. in New York City), after fourteen hours and fifty-six minutes, Amelia's "Little Red Bus" landed in a pasture, empty except for a sole cow overseen by two workmen named James McGeady and Dan McCallion. The men were busy mending a fence for Robert Gallagher, the well-off owner of what locals called the "Cornshell Farm."

Her wheels kissed the ground after her exhausting, perilous flight, and a great stillness hit Amelia. Wherever she was, it was across the Atlantic, with her denouement a quiet unfolding of relief and realization. Not in Paris but alive and on the other side of the ocean, she had inadvertently set two new records: the longest nonstop flight by a woman and the fastest crossing of the Atlantic. The magnitude of her achievements, though not yet fully known to her, was a testament to her courage and a defining moment in aviation history.

After gathering herself, Amelia stepped out and approached the men in her flying attire. Her jodhpurs and the short, tight curls beneath her headgear led McGeady to assume she was male. McCallion, his mouth slightly agape like a half-open clam, edged closer to the lady, mistaking her oil-smeared face for a man's, and inquired: "Where are you from?"

A wearied woman answered. "From America. Where am I?"

The high-pitched American voice shocked McCallion, who lived near the Gallaghers' farmstead and now assumed the very peculiar woman was possibly the British aviator Amy Johnson. "You're in Cornshell!" he said with some pride and stunned respect. "Ireland," he added when she looked blank. The odd creature who'd fallen from the sky in pants then sternly asked McGeady to put out his cigarette, explaining she was concerned about a fuel leak and a possible explosion. He did.

"If you've come from America, you'll want a wash," McCallion said in his heavy brogue. He escorted her several feet away to a quaint whitewashed peat cottage that belonged to the elderly Hughie McLaughlin and his wife, humble renters on land owned by the wealthy Gallaghers. Amelia was greeted with a cup of Irish tea but desperately wanted to call America—

and learned such a simple cottage had no phone. *America.* After hearing that, McCallion quickly set off to inform the landowner of Amelia's arrival.

At the Gallagher farmstead, the great Amelia Earhart was introduced to Robert Gallagher's shocked, lovely young wife, Isobel, and their young children. The pilot was mighty groggy, but her main concern was getting in touch with the outside world. She admitted to Isobel, "George gave me just a twenty-dollar bill before I left New York." She hadn't brought anything to change into either. Isobel, touched by Amelia's simplicity, offered her a respectable dress to change into, and Robert assured her they'd take care of everything moneywise. Isobel recalled, "She said she hadn't had anything but tomato juice since she left America. We asked her to stay with us, and she agreed, so long as we didn't mind her clothes. She had nothing but what she stood up in." The Gallaghers also asked Amelia to stay with them until she was ready to continue her journey, and happy to have a warm home base, she agreed, promising to return the dress after handling the press.

There was no way the farm phone could make overseas calls, so Robert took Amelia to a grander nearby house belonging to Mrs. Francis McClure, who had the same problem—but it was in this house that Amelia told local reporters she'd made it. From Mrs. McClure's home, Amelia asked them to call her husband at the Hotel Seymour and have him call her mother and sister too, and the *Evening Standard* reporter, thrilled with a scoop, said he most certainly would. Robert thought her urgent communications could be handled efficiently by the central post office and headed to Derry in his car within minutes.

A full day of action, but it was only the beginning of an extraordinary day for Amelia.

As his wife crossed an ocean, George Palmer Putnam was grateful for Hilton Howell Railey's diversionary company in his Hotel Seymour suite. The ever-loyal Railey, after a soured connection and somewhat forgotten animosities, was ready to help again, making sure every opportunity was exploited—this time stateside; the PR executive had even recently worked for the competition on Ruth Nichols's failed solo transatlantic attempt of

1931. Railey kept the mood light, trying to distract George from the anxiety that roiled his digestion, evident from the empty milk bottles scattered around the room. Time somehow passed as they waited for news, and Railey discussed potential profit strategies for Amelia, a bubbly conversation that somewhat soothed nerves. Later, they were joined by Laurence McKinley Gould, a key player in Commander Richard Byrd's first Antarctic expedition. In true "old boys' network" fashion, Railey had helped Gould secure a lucrative book deal with George. Gould, in turn, arranged for George's son David to become the youngest Explorers Club member. Gould later remembered George as a man of sharp contrasts: brash and outspoken yet also generous to those in his inner circle. He observed George's insatiable appetite for publicity, which, to those like Gould who stood as proven allies, was overshadowed by his likability and loyalty.

One woman was permitted in the room: the young journalist Dorothy Kilgallen. At just nineteen, Kilgallen was already making a name for herself as a cub reporter for the *New York Evening Journal*, earning Amelia's admiration. Kilgallen later recounted: "I sat up with [George] all night, observing his smoking and incessant calls to the telephone, witnessing his weariness deepen as the hours slipped away." Kilgallen was right there at 9:30 a.m., when the world's teletypes flashed a message indicating that Amelia Earhart had crashed in Paris, a startling report that punctured the already uneasy mood. Pacing and clucking his tongue, part wild animal, George anxiously awaited the final confirmation from London's *Sunday Chronicle*. This arrived a punishingly long twelve minutes later.

Kilgallen watched as Railey, sparing Putnam the trouble of answering yet another call, nervously picked up the phone. "Did you say her *accomplishment*?" Railey asked, surprised that New York seemed unaware. The voice across the pond assured him that Amelia was safe in Ireland. What a relief! Railey half yelled the swell news, and the mental and physical tolls of being an aviatrix's husband melted away in a minuscule moment. Railey took the lead, jotting down notes. Londonderry, a field, farmhands . . . Where, exactly, was she?

George's grin was infectious as Railey exclaimed, "Your wife wants money!" The publisher had much to share with the British reporter, who had fulfilled his promise to Amelia by contacting her husband and letting him know she was safe. "I feel like a man who has just been handed a son, with the doctor assuring him that his wife came through perfectly," George said. "Just a few minutes ago, we received a message saying she had crashed at Le Bourget, and it devastated me. Learning that she has landed safely is the best news I've heard in years. She has more courage than anyone I know. Could you please pass on my love to her and ask her to call me as soon as possible? Let her know I'm at the Hotel Seymour, eagerly awaiting her side of the story."

The British reporter also mentioned that the deafening hum of heavy machinery from the Vega's engine had temporarily affected Amelia's hearing. "If that is all that has happened, she is very lucky," George said. "I am much luckier than she is. If there were transatlantic air service, I would be on the plane right now, heading to join her." The reporter chortled and informed George of Amelia's request to contact her mother and sister. Immediately after he hung up, George dialed Medford and made the call before the American reporters in his suite.

Meanwhile, back in the Derry post office, Amelia discovered the enormous number of telegraph wires sent since her touchdown at Gallagher's Field. There were even messages from fellow aviators Ruth Nichols, Elinor Smith, and Germany's Thea Rasche, who had each hoped to be the first woman to fly solo across the Atlantic and now saw this aspiration quashed. THAT'S THE STUFF [STOP] WELL DONE.

The Massachusetts governor wired MASSACHUSETTS IS PROUD OF YOU, and President Hoover also sent his congratulations. A cable simply reading SWELL, GENE came from Gene Vidal, Amelia's aviation colleague and handsome close friend.

From the Lindberghs, likely from Anne, was a touching message sent just over eleven weeks after their child was kidnapped: WE CONGRATULATE YOU [STOP] YOUR FLIGHT IS A SPLENDID SUCCESS.

And then there was the charming note from Amelia's Westchester dry cleaner, Phil: I WAS SURE YOU WOULD MAKE IT [STOP] I NEVER LOST A CUSTOMER.

With Amelia's access to the telegraph, George now heard directly from his wife: LANDED IN PASTURE. [STOP] 5 MILES FROM LONDONDERRY [STOP] PLANE OK [STOP] 8:35 A.M. IRELAND. She had no sooner sent it than in came George's reply: CONGRATULATIONS [STOP] DELIGHTED YOU ARE SAFE.

Just before 3:00 p.m., Railey told his best contact at the Associated Press to get a message to Amelia that George had left his home and was now in Columbia Broadcasting's Madison Avenue office and on standby for her call. Amelia was thrilled by that message and waited for Derry to connect them, which in 1932 was no easy affair.

A photographer captured an image of Amelia nearly conked out by the phone, her eyes already closed. Yet he snapped another shot when her face lit up upon hearing that her call to New York had finally been patched through. "From my husband!" Amelia squealed. As George privately congratulated his wife on her monumental achievement, he was taken aback when she mentioned spending four harrowing hours flying blind, skimming the ocean in darkness.

Railey had astutely advised George to instruct Amelia to fly for free to London accompanied by a flight team of Paramount newsmen, to whom George sold her newsreel rights. This was a shrewd move, as Paramount was the company George was discreetly negotiating with for his next position following an unsatisfactory stint at Brewer, Warren & Putnam. Emanuel Cohen, Paramount's newly appointed production head, offered George the role of chairman of the editorial board, a big-sounding title that came with a modest but much-needed $5,000 salary. George's high-placed friend recognized that his extensive connections in the publishing industry could give Paramount a significant edge in the talkies era, which needed better dialogue. While George wasn't a distinguished writer, he was adept at delegation, and his phenomenal network included Algonquin Round Tablers like Dorothy Parker and Heywood Broun, who were willing to tackle Paramount film scripts, which was no small calling card.

As they talked away from anyone else's ears, George, heeding Railey's advice, told Amelia that Captain McKenzie would fly the Vega to Croydon

Airport in South London, where it would be dismantled and shipped home. No flying back for her. She agreed but admitted she wasn't sure if she was ready to face the coming chaos alone. "Could you use some company?" he asked. She could.

The answer swelled his heart. Since his wife rarely admitted that she needed him, he told her he would make his decision public as soon as possible. To meet her, he would sail to France if he could. She could tour England alone, but they could explore Europe together. He was receiving offers from everywhere! If money meant something to her, she wouldn't need to worry about it after this success. All of it mattered, she said. What did she eat?

"A thermos bottle of hot chicken soup, two cakes of chocolate, two cans of tomato juice, which I drank by punching a hole with an ice pick and sucking up with a straw."

Six precious minutes passed, and after her bright "Cheerio," he hung up and breathed, ready to face the many reporters waiting on his end.

George had scribbled it all down and finally looked up with a foxy grin. "I want to tell you, fellows, it has not always been a cinch. When Miss Earhart flew successfully across the Atlantic before, I called around newspaper offices, phoned them, and made a general nuisance of myself. This time, I have done nothing more than keep in close touch with the weather bureau. And watch the telephone here." But he wanted them to think about what she had been through. "She had it rough as the devil. So far as I can make out, it meant the kid was about to be burned alive at any time during those ten hours." George helped himself to another half-pint of milk and mopped his brow. What would his wife do next? "It is impossible to answer. But she's the only person to fly the Atlantic twice. I hope she doesn't make a habit of it." The room laughed, and he said he would head to the North (Hudson) River pier to book the next boat to France, which, he soon learned, was the RMS *Olympic*. Leaving on May 27.

While they chatted, pandemonium arose inside and outside Derry's post office. It was even difficult for her to return to the car she'd arrived in. A Royal Ulster Constabulary officer escorted her to the Northern Counties

Hotel, and she gratefully wrapped her hands around a cup of strong, brawny coffee instead of her usual buttermilk. After recovering and preparing for a few minutes, she managed, as George had advised, to give a press conference outside. "Okay, go ahead, pop the questions."

When asked why she flew alone, she said, "I had made up my mind to fly alone because if there is a man in the machine, you can bet your life he wants to take control. Well, I had already flown the Atlantic with men in control, and I was determined that if I did it again, I was the one who was going to control the machine."

Didn't she feel scared flying blind in the dark of night over the ocean? Mighty punch-drunk as she replied, she giggled. "Well, I guess it does give one a kind of the dithers."

The press laughed loudly, and she continued, telling of how she kept on at 130 miles per hour and hoped for the best. "Believe me I was glad to see land. You know that you are facing possibly the most critical moment of your life, and there is only one thing to be done, and that is brace oneself for the ordeal. It would be fatal to get terrified. Personally, I was glad I was alone, because I can do much more hazardous flying when I feel that I am not responsible for the life of someone else."

Would she return in her Vega? No, by steamship. "I have had a terrible ordeal and am not prepared to have another going back." As a welcome gift from the astounded city, Viscount Craigavon called to offer the hospitality of the poshest address in town, Stormont Castle, then the official residence of the prime minister of Northern Ireland. The world was hanging on her every word, and when she explained that she would stay near the plane with her new friends, the Gallaghers, Mr. Gallagher beamed with pride; he, too, was history now.

Hundreds gathered in the grassy field of Mr. Gallagher's farm on Culmore Road, where Amelia Earhart had brought her small red plane to a stop. It was meant to be a surprise, but news of her arrival had already leaked to *The Londonderry Sentinel*, drawing a swarm of photographers and reporters, all primed and ready.

Back in Medford, her mother, Amy, and sister, Muriel, were tending to

Amelia's young niece and nephew when the Associated Press contacted them. Amid the bedtime routines, Muriel, changing her nine-month-old daughter's diaper, received the news of Amelia's successful but unexpected landing in Ireland—not Paris, as hoped. Overwhelmed, Muriel shared the update with her family, expressing relief and pride that Amelia had reached dry land.

That Saturday night in Ireland, Amelia found respite at the Elms, the fine house owned by Mrs. Francis McClure near the Gallagher farm. She slept deeply, only stirring when the grandfather clock chimed seven the next morning. Despite her fatigue, she faced the new day without makeup, wearing a borrowed saffron-colored blouse and her only adornments—a lucky elephant-toe bracelet and a pair of silver wings presented by the United States Air Force.

For breakfast, she received grapefruit, poached eggs, and Irish tea while seated on a low stool before the fire at the Gallagher home. A scrum of journalists and hundreds of tourists awaited her. Amid all this, Amelia reflected on her journey, undeterred by the mechanical failures—a leaking gas line and a busted exhaust manifold—that had stymied her Paris goal. "It doesn't matter. I got over it," she said wistfully. "I've dreamed of this ever since I first crossed the ocean."

Amelia posed one last time in front of a crush of six thousand cheering Irish fans. She would later laugh, remembering that all sorts of people came up with little wads of British notes, saying, "You must have something before you fly!"

"I will certainly come back! I have enjoyed my stay immensely."

"Will you come back by air?" a reporter asked.

"I certainly would prefer it, but I can't say. You better get to an airport before you invite people by air. But I've enjoyed myself much. I've heard of Irish hospitality, but its warmth exceeds all expectations."

Amelia was flown by Captain McKenzie in a Royal Air Force Desoutter, chauffeured like royalty but without the crown. At the landing, the American ambassador, Mr. Andrew Mellon, and a welcoming committee of dignitaries were ready to roll out the red carpet for the "international heroine." Amid the pomp, Ramsay MacDonald delivered a message from Lord Londonderry, the so-called prime minister of the air. A cocktail was offered, but teetotaler Amelia declined. As they spoke about the flight, the ambassador then sheepishly admitted that the royal telegram he was to deliver from King George V had been snagged by an unscrupulous someone. In a scramble to make amends, Mellon had handwritten a replacement with the king's words and signed it. Amelia's only wish: Would the ambassador please tell His Majesty that his telegram had been graciously received?

"I regretted having to land so far from London," she told the BBC, "but it was the only plane I had, and I felt it was best to take good care of it and make a safe descent." Ambassador Mellon's well-married daughter, Alisa Mellon Bruce, often served as her father's official hostess during his overseas assignments, and once back at the embassy, she gave Amelia some elegant clothing and organized a shopping trip to London for the next day.

After a light breakfast at the American embassy, Amelia headed to the West End shopping district before 9:00 a.m. As she sped through the streets, a passerby overheard a man who was craning his neck to catch a glimpse of her exclaim, "There's a woman who doesn't ride in the back seat!" She wore a blue dress with a white neckpiece during her luncheon with the Chartered Institute of Journalists. Holding a glass of water, she offered a toast to the president of the United States. Ambassador Mellon, free from Prohibition constraints, indulged in Scotch with water. Newspaperman Ralph Blumenthal, editor of the *Daily Express*, declared, "I hereby retract my theory that a woman never achieved anything truly significant." The audience rose and joyfully sang "For She's a Jolly Good Fellow."

Amelia strolled through Selfridges while her instantly recognizable red Vega, which had been shipped from Ireland, was prominently displayed—an opportunity Harry Gordon Selfridge seized not only to impress shoppers but also to curry favor with her husband, should Mr. Selfridge ever need the celebrity couple's star power in the future. Amid the spectacle, a shopper's excitement was reported by a British newspaper: "I touched her!" Meanwhile, Amelia thoughtfully selected toys, including a toy model airplane, for the Gallagher children back in Derry.

While shopping, Amelia received tragic news: Major Irwin Napier Colin Clarke had been flying to London with press photographer Ernest Victor Barton, who had just taken photos of Amelia for the *Daily Sketch* in Derry. Their plane had struck a rocky hillside near the coast, killing both men. Barton left behind a young widow. When asked about the accident by a London reporter, Amelia's face fell; sure, she felt a pang of responsibility, knowing her remote landing location had prompted their flight, but despite the grim news, she knew she had to stay focused and continue, especially when she was informed that Edward, the Prince of Wales, had invited her to tea.

The then thirty-eight-year-old royal is now remembered for his sensational abdication to marry commoner Wallis Simpson and his disturbing pro-Hitler sentiments, which he later denied.

An official car from the American embassy whisked Amelia from the store to York House, the prince's residence within St. James Palace. Dressed in a chic blue wool suit borrowed from the American ambassador's daughter, she was granted fifteen minutes with the heir to the throne. However, after he pinned a pink rose onto her suit, their meeting extended to forty-five minutes—a significant honor. Prince Edward recalled, "She came to tea with me when she flew across the Atlantic. She seemed like a remarkable person, a great woman. I had hoped to introduce her to my mother; I believed she would have greatly enjoyed meeting her. Unfortunately, court regulations made it impossible." While reserved about the specifics, Amelia shared that they "talked shop" and engaged in "ground flying" discussions with the royal aviator, whose parents had discouraged him from flying postwar.

Before leaving England, she attended the Epsom Derby and the Derby Ball at Grosvenor House. When Amelia entered the ballroom, grandly attired, Prince Edward rose at once to greet her. While wealthy, fashionable women curtsied, Amelia simply nodded. The eyebrows of Lady This and Lord That rose even higher when the prince offered her a chair, inviting her to join in the festivities with him. "We are about to have a yo-yo demonstration!" he explained after introducing the celebrated pilot to the fourteen-year-old yo-yo world champion, Joe Young from Regina, Canada, a special guest of Lady Milbanke.

His Royal Highness then asked the former high school loner to dance. And dance they did! They danced three foxtrots, she in her apple-green gown and brown velvet scarf, both of which she had purchased in London. In between dances with a celebrated lady taller than him, the prince tried his hand at the yo-yo, and a picture of the prince yo-yoing that night started a British craze for the toy.

Was it all a dream?

To reach France and her husband, George, Amelia traveled to the town of Hamble, located near Southampton, England. There, she boarded the luxurious yacht *Evadne*, owned by British aviation tycoon Charles Richard Fairey, and set course for Cherbourg.

Meanwhile, George reached Cherbourg on his steamer, the RMS *Olympic*, and after their joyful and emotional reunion, he shared the exciting news that negotiations with Paramount Pictures had been successful. Amelia was then introduced to Harry H. Smith, George's traveling private secretary, aboard the SS *Île de France*. Smith would manage the couple's extensive correspondence and telegrams during their travels.

George had long touted Amelia's abilities, claiming she was fluent in five languages. However, Amelia felt caught out when she had to rely on a translator to answer an interviewer's very personal questions, and her voice was tinged with uncertainty. "With marriage and obligations, children aren't a priority," she explained. "But the right time will come naturally."

From Cherbourg, the couple traveled by train to Paris, their arrival in the City of Light marking the next step in their whirlwind itinerary. Meanwhile, George's arrival led to some puzzlement. Although well-known in the US and UK, he was unfamiliar to the French public. Consequently, the French press dubbed him the "Unknown Husband," leading to local speculation about his identity. They referred to Amelia using her maiden and married names, addressing her as "Miss Amelia Putnam Earhart."

During their brief visit in Paris, Amelia and George stayed at the charming Hotel Lotti, located between the Place Vendôme and the Jardin des Tuileries. A small but renowned hotel in Paris, it provided a cozy and comfortable sanctuary for the couple. On their first day, they stepped onto the balcony to greet the enthusiastic crowd on rue de Castiglione. The waiting throng was eager to glimpse the celebrated modern icon; after acknowledging Amelia's adoring fans with waves, the couple retreated indoors. As the evening unfolded, Amelia tenderly clasped George's hand. It was an astonishing day long remembered in their shared journey.

On June 4, Amelia became the first female foreigner to receive France's exalted Legion of Honour from the French Senate. As George had hoped, his wife's achievement drew comparisons to Lindbergh's flight of supreme skill just five years prior. After that heady ceremony, the couple flew from Milan to Rome in a trimotor plane provided by General Italo Balbo of the Italian Air Force. They were greeted with a grandiose display that included Balbo's entire air squadron, the American ambassador and his wife, and much of the American community. The extravagant spectacle of a Big Fascist Welcome was the culmination of a packed itinerary of official activities and free time for Amelia. During their trip to Rome, the two were granted a private audience with Benito Mussolini at the Palazzo Venezia. Despite Mussolini's controversial reputation, Amelia was impressed by his graciousness. However, the Putnams later regretted the flattering remarks and headlines that suggested Amelia had an affinity for the dictator. One that stuck was the infamous AMELIA EARHART LIKES MUSSOLINI.

George took plenty of pride in his visible role as Amelia's chaperone, but being a stage-door johnny had its downsides, especially when it involved world leaders. Of course, George would soon embellish the tale of Amelia's meeting with Mussolini, adding himself to the story with a dramatic flourish. He reminded Americans of the time he had faced those "Fascist threats" by daring to publish an anti-Fascist book in the 1920s and described a moment where the still-furious Duce's "falcon eyes bore into me"—a silly exaggeration that even those who knew him best cringed at.

Belgium was their next stop after Italy, and on this Lindbergh-inspired day, the Belgian king and queen, who both spoke perfect English and were keen on aviation, hosted a private royal dinner just like they had for Lindy. A Chevalier of the Order of Leopold decoration was presented during this June 13 meal.

When she returned to France, she was sapped, craving nothing more than the quiet comfort of her beloved Rye garden. Despite the anticipation of a triumphant return and extravagant reception in America, the allure of her own bed proved irresistible. Thus, on June 14, George secured their voyage on the *Île de France*, the French Line's grand flagship, from Rouen to New York. To their shared delight, the esteemed French Line extended a first-class invitation, courtesy of George's resourceful negotiations, ensuring that their journey came without paying a penny.

When New York's newest welcoming tug, the *Riverside*, docked Tuesday, June 20, at Pier A, photographers jostled for a glimpse of the Putnams before yet another grand ticker-tape parade upon Amelia's return; the mayor's team had planned it with assistance from George's trusty assistant, Harold McCracken.

Amelia made a sheepish request to ride in a luxurious Marmon convertible—a wish Harold McCracken quickly granted. A massive crowd gathered on the streets to watch as she waved from Official Vehicle No. 1, a stunning 1931 Marmon 16 convertible sedan lent to the Woman of the Hour by popular Jewish vocalist and actor Arthur Tracy. George Palmer Putnam, relegated to the second car, appears in newsreel footage looking furious at something or someone, the reason lost to history.

Mayor Jimmy Walker was thankfully in town this time, but on the steps of city hall, in a bit of comedic misfortune, he attempted to fasten a medal onto Amelia Earhart's garment so many times that it left an accidental hole. Their shared laughter made for a lighthearted moment before the mayor then addressed Amelia and the throng: "You remember that some five years before you took off, when Colonel Lindbergh made his solo flight across the Atlantic and coined the aeronautical 'we,' that it remained of the masculine gender for some five years thereafter until you took off. And it seems to me as if you have at last cleaned up that aeronautical 'we' and taken the sex out of it. Miss Earhart, you are truly and indeed welcome in the City of New York."

Amelia made the crowd laugh after saying that the airplane engines had advanced since her last visit to these famous steps—and so had the receptions in the city. Then, for the woman who arrived in a limousine and squirrel-lined coat, it was back to the old modesty game to play down her ambition. "It was simply a personal gesture," she "clarified" about her historic flight, "and doesn't signify anything more than the parsley on a lamb chop!" Curious words that, under the coaching of her husband, seemed to serve a greater purpose than mere humility.

When she first rode down the Canyon of Heroes after the flight of the *Friendship*, she was viewed as a novelty, today's fun. Four years later, her stardom was beyond ordinary, a strange continuum that she and Lindbergh shared. As Gore Vidal would later say, it elevated them to dizzying heights, to the status of gods from outer space. (In a speech to an audience of Barnard girls, she joked, "When I was going up Fifth Avenue in a snowstorm of paper, I was really pleased that they tore up the telephone books before throwing them at me!")

Following her triumphant parade, Amelia headed to the nation's capital on June 21 to receive the highest honor in American geography, the special bronze medal from the National Geographic Society, bestowed upon her by President Hoover. In accepting the award, she joined the esteemed group of just sixteen prior recipients, including illustrious explorers such as Peary, Byrd, Shackleton, Amundsen, and the Icarian daredevil himself, Charles Lindbergh. Scientists and government officials hailed the "modest girl" from Kansas.

After Amelia's flight in May, Manhattan bookstores stocked her ghost-written book *The Fun of It: Random Records of My Own Flying and of Women in Aviation*, available for $2.50. The swift publication led some journalists to muse that George's publishing company might have capitalized on her flight as a daring marketing gamble. Despite its aim to celebrate aviation, the book disappointingly skimmed the surface in storytelling and emotional engagement. Most glaringly, it completely bypassed Bessie Coleman, the pathbreaking Black aviator who not only broke barriers of race and gender but also soared before Amelia ever took the helm. This omission was a stark gap, particularly in a work purporting to honor women's contributions to aviation. The final chapter, cobbled together by George's team from Amelia's notes and off-the-cuff remarks, did little to buoy sales, which were tepid but passable. In an inventive nod to first-edition buyers, George included a miniature phonograph record of Amelia's ninety-second broadcast from London on May 22, a creative flourish.

A flurry of accolades and awards marked her feted return to New York, including a gold record of her radio address in Ireland for her own keeping. Commercial opportunities and attention poured in, often handled by Harold McCracken, George's astute confidant, who later recognized that Amelia's motivation went beyond publicity and felt that her solo flight across the Atlantic represented the brightest moment of her flying career. Despite the overwhelming demands of celebrity and the speculation surrounding her motives, she was happy during this time.

While in Europe, Amelia had promised to bring some spark to her husband's new executive role in Hollywood, agreeing on their grand liner ride back to New York to fly him to Los Angeles, where he would meet with his West Coast editorial counterparts at Paramount, perhaps in trade for his excellent assistance with her transatlantic glory. Amelia made good on July 1, when she, George, and her stepson David began a cross-country flight in Amelia's trusty Vega. When they landed in Los Angeles, George humorously quipped that they had been "ferried" by Amelia herself in the family aircraft, just back from a flight to Ireland.

On the Paramount Pictures lot, where Hollywood big shots were commonplace and fame barely turned heads, it was rare to stir a genuine buzz. Yet as Amelia Earhart strolled through the movie sets with her unmistakable poise, even Cary Grant, Jeanette MacDonald, and Harpo Marx found themselves goose-pimply with excitement, eagerly lining up to be photographed with her. George had cleverly arranged for a photographer to be on standby, and, as told, Amelia smiled slightly for the occasion. Her cachet soared moments later, when she entered the Paramount cafeteria and all pretense of social decorum evaporated. For decades, the story of how lunch was interrupted by the likes of Bing Crosby, the rest of the Marx Brothers, and Tallulah Bankhead—all clustering around Amelia like awestruck teenagers—would be a favorite tale recounted among gossipers.

But when asked about making a movie, Amelia replied that she couldn't, as she was too frenzied and planning a trip to South America. "Can you see me making love on the screen?" she said humbly.

After wolfing down a commissary lunch, she visited more sets, including the one for *The Kid from Spain*, led by the red-hot comedic star Eddie Cantor. She was also greeted by George M. Cohan in front of his dressing room. For the afternoon, her husband had set up posed shots with Harpo Marx, Cary Grant, and Myrna Loy. She was, during this period, having great fun with George, a devoted partner who had fulfilled his promises to hustle for her dreams, and in a *Redbook* interview that month, she said, "The more one does and sees and feels, the more one is able to do, and the more genuine may be one's appreciation of fundamental things like home, and love, and understanding companionship."

During their monthlong stay in California, Amelia, recently hired as a movie consultant, earned a second paycheck working on *Wings in the Dark*, a sentimental aviation-themed romantic drama. The plot, based on a short story titled "Eyes of the Eagle," was partly inspired by her. To help Grant and Loy understand their roles, Amelia took them on a flight, an experience funded by the film company. Loy starred as Sheila Mason, a brave Lockheed Vega 5B pilot, with stunts performed by Paul Mantz, George's friend and a famous stunt pilot, in the same plane that Amelia had recently piloted solo across the Atlantic. George had known Mantz since his involvement with the 1927 silent film *Wings*. Beyond his wife's consultation fees, George also secured payment from the studio for leasing that plane.

On July 8, Amelia was honored at a banquet organized by one of her aviation rivals, Pancho Barnes, the cigar-smoking heiress, skilled stunt pilot, and founder of the first movie stunt pilots' union. Pancho had first crossed paths with Amelia at the Powder Puff Derby and was also a close friend of Mantz's. Following the event, Amelia left her husband and stepson in California to participate in a race to Newark. During her absence, nineteen-year-old David received expert flight training from Mantz, a former army flight trainee who washed out but would later become one of Amelia's trusted mentors.

The solo Atlantic crossing marked a sweet and long-awaited victory for Amelia Earhart. Buoyed by this success, she quickly set her sights higher. On July 12, she ambitiously embarked on a mission to become the first woman to fly nonstop across the United States, aiming to surpass Frank Hawks, the famed aviator who had completed the journey in thirteen hours and given Amelia her first taste of flight in 1920. However, her endeavor faced formidable challenges: terrible weather and mechanical issues forced several unscheduled stops. Undeterred by these setbacks, Amelia was determined to make another attempt in August.

Despite the snags, Amelia's fame was turbocharged by midsummer, thanks to George's expert promotion. This new status granted her access to exclusive circles and lavish gifts, such as luxury cars and mink coats. On July 25, she solidified her reputation by christening a new Essex Terraplane at Detroit City Airport, which she later gifted to her stepson David for his use at Brown University.

Her celebrity continued to grow, making her the talk of downtown Los Angeles when she landed in late July. On July 29, she was awarded the Distinguished Flying Cross amid cheers from fawning fans who had waited for hours. This honor, previously given to Lindbergh for his transatlantic flight, held special significance for Amelia in Southern California, where her passion for flying had been sparked.

Her resilience and determination shone through when, on August 24–25, 1932, she became the first woman to fly solo nonstop from coast to coast, setting a women's transcontinental speed record by covering 2,447.8 miles in nineteen hours and five minutes. This achievement likely made Amelia and George the first truly bicoastal couple in America.

On November 7, the pair attended the Explorers Club's Ladies Night at

The mythical 1929 transport license was a PR tale spun by George, who blamed missing paperwork for Amelia's lack of a license—the truth being, she didn't secure it until May 1930, shown here.

January 10, 1930, shoreside, George returns from Europe, facing divorce rumors and Fascist "threats," ready to spin his latest tale for the press.

Newlyweds in 1931: Amelia and George's official wedding portrait.

Amelia and George share a rare playful moment at their Rye, New York, home circa 1936—a glimpse behind their public partnership.

Amelia, perched on the Beech-Nut autogiro in 1931. She took this odd flying machine on a US promotional tour, handing out Beech-Nut gum.

With Norwegian aviator Bernt Balchen, secretly hired by George to boost her skills, Amelia prepped for a daring solo Atlantic flight. Site taken unknown, but likely in Teterboro, New Jersey.

On the *Île de France*, Amelia and George share a quiet moment after a whirlwind of European fanfare, including honors from dictator Benito Mussolini and the French Senate.

In New York's Canyon of Heroes, Amelia rides in a borrowed Marmon 16 convertible as ticker tape rains down—George trailing behind, visibly irritated by something or someone.

In 1933, following a dinner at the White House, Amelia Earhart and Eleanor Roosevelt took flight together—this marked their second meeting and the start of a real friendship. As they soared above Washington, DC, Eleanor marveled at the city below, exclaiming, "Fairyland!"

Often overlooked is Amelia's tender role as a stepmother to David and George Jr. ("Junie"). In this rare quiet moment with Junie is a glimpse of the warmth and affection she brought to their lives, revealing a softer side of the trailblazer often lost amid her remarkable achievements.

Amelia flew to the 1933 Chicago World's Fair with George and Junie, marveling at attractions like *The World a Million Years Ago*, which featured a giant ape that echoed the era's fascination with the King Kong craze.

Amelia Earhart's 1934 label made its debut at Macy's, flaunting her signature and a striking red plane. As usual—a bit of George's mythmaking: the real design magic was crafted by a seasoned designer behind the scenes.

Canvas-covered plywood luggage, touted as Amelia's brainchild, promised a new era of independence for women travelers. While similar bags were already making waves, none carried the powerful allure of Amelia's name—a statement of freedom, daring women to soar beyond convention!

In one of her "designed by Amelia" dresses, she embodied the practical style George was eager to market.

As Purdue's new "consultant on careers for women," Amelia chats with young students about futures beyond the ordinary.

At 10042 Valley Spring Lane in Toluca Lake, Amelia stands with George and pilot Paul Mantz, inspecting her and George's new home. Earhart planned to settle here with Putnam after completing her round-the-world flight, a journey carefully designed to secure both adventure and financial gain.

Amelia stands confidently beside Paul Mantz, the Hollywood stunt pilot and trusted adviser who expertly balanced her aircraft—and her soaring ambitions.

High above the ground, Mantz transformed flying into a breathtaking spectacle. His unmatched nerve and expertise would prove invaluable to Amelia, solidifying his role as her indispensable technical adviser.

A serene photo of Amelia in a kimono, taken in Hawaii, later sparked rumors of Japanese capture—rumors her sister, Muriel, dismissed, knowing the kimono was safe at home and that her sister had run out of gas.

On St. Patrick's Day in 1937, Amelia Earhart stood ready with her globe-trotting team—technical adviser Paul Mantz, secondary navigator Fred Noonan, and chief navigator Harry Manning—to launch her first attempt to circle the world westward from Oakland.

Amelia stands before the map of her ambitious 1937 equatorial flight route—the first attempt to circle the globe at that latitude, spanning a daunting twenty-nine thousand miles. This journey would demand all her skill and determination, with lucrative book and film deals on the horizon to help her and George weather the Great Depression.

After returning from Honolulu, Amelia sought refuge from the press and even her husband at the luxurious Cochran-Odlum Ranch. Jackie Cochran urged her to build strength and prepare for the challenges ahead there.

Amelia Earhart stands proudly beside her 1936 Cord 810 Phaeton and Lockheed Electra—lavish possessions made possible by her husband's relentless hustle and savvy.

Fred Noonan, captured here in 1937, was Amelia Earhart's navigator and a master of celestial navigation with a storied past at Pan American Airways.

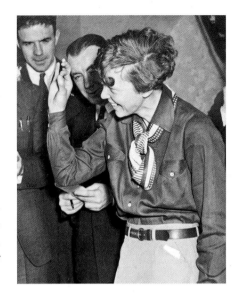

With calm confidence, Amelia dismisses reporters' concerns about the tiny size of Howland Island.

In September 1937, newly widowed George Putnam began a secret affair with stuntwoman Ione Reed, pictured here with Amelia's friend, actor William S. Hart.

In a desperate bid to save his Los Angeles publishing house and fund his new marriage, George staged his own kidnapping and fabricated Nazi threats, pulling his staff and law enforcement into an elaborate web of deception. The 1938 stunt grabbed national headlines but left him a laughingstock among his publishing peers. In this carefully staged re-creation for the press, his reflection in the window captures a man so fixated on his own narrative that the chaos and harm left in his wake seemed of little concern to him.

Jean-Marie Consigny, George's third wife, swings playfully on a rope swing he installed for her in their North Hollywood home. Just twenty-six when they wed, the young socialite was quickly swept into fifty-two-year-old Putnam's turbulent life.

After his second divorce left him feeling despairing and alone, George married USO hostess Margaret "Peg" Haviland. Their June 1945 marriage blossomed into an unexpectedly happy partnership, allowing George to step out of the shadow of Amelia Earhart.

These magazine covers highlight the contrasting narratives surrounding Amelia Earhart. On the left, *Man's Illustrated* indulges in sensational speculation, driven by conspiracy theories about her disappearance, hinting at everything from espionage to mythical captures. In contrast, *Ms.* magazine honors her legacy as a trailblazer, emphasizing her adventurous spirit.

This rarely seen family Bible entry, photographed by the author at a family member's home, marks Amelia Earhart as lost at sea about July 4, 5, or 6, in 1937. The court officially pronounced her dead on January 5, 1939—just shy of eighteen months after her disappearance—based on testimony from various witnesses, including her husband, George Palmer Putnam.

The captivating 1931 portrait of Amelia Earhart by Edward Steichen for *Vanity Fair* exudes sophistication and glamour. Her transformation from pioneering aviator to global icon was thoughtfully guided by her savvy husband, establishing her as a symbol of a modern woman.

the organization's newly inaugurated headquarters on West Seventy-Second Street. The event, attended by one hundred esteemed explorers and their partners, underscored Amelia's influence. In a powerful feminist gesture, she extended invitations to accomplished women explorers who were ineligible for club membership. Despite her private disapproval of the club's exclusionary policies, Amelia supported George, the club's vice president. The evening, among big-bellied men, showcased—just as George had envisioned—Amelia's cleverness and charm, particularly when she presented the club with a blue Persian kitten as their mascot, claiming (as George had written for her) that it was an "ancient Inca custom" introduced by William J. Morden. Laughter rose up when the kitten, anointed with oil to ensure it wouldn't stray, was christened "Amelia" after a heckling comment from the audience. Then, at an exclusive gathering thrumming with chatter, Meshie, an orphaned three-year-old chimp snatched from her forest home, took the stage. Taught to mimic human ways by Explorers Club member Henry Raven, who raised her in his home with his children, she pedaled a tricycle and deftly served fruit, even to Amelia Earhart. In everyone's opinion, including Amelia's, the evening's thrill was only heightened by the presence of a parrot named Doc, the club's feathered mascot, perched up high and observing Meshie's act. The event proved to be a hit, with Roy Chapman Andrews, the president of the Explorers Club, congratulating George Putnam, Amelia's husband, on his planning. Both men knew that such events were essential for sustaining the club's vitality, a not insignificant concern during the unspeakable hardships of the Depression.

Perhaps it was even this glorious night that George excitedly revealed to Amelia he had finally sold her signature red-and-gold Vega plane to the Franklin Institute in Philadelphia for $7,000. The shrewd transaction enabled Amelia to acquire a superior Vega—while her old plane was preserved in a display at the museum. The couple kept the sale price from Amelia's mother and sister to avoid any potential financial handouts. The aviation community praised George's decision, and a ceremony attended by Orville Wright was held to commemorate the acquisition of the Little Red Bus. This iconic plane, the oldest Lockheed, the only one of Amelia

Earhart's airships that still exists, now hangs in the Smithsonian's National Air and Space Museum, where it has captivated millions. But plenty of people saw it in Philadelphia in the 1930s, when Amelia was alive and well and always in the news for new achievements. And thanks to George, she was now perceived by many Americans as the best woman flier in America. George had promised her during their courtship that they were a harmonious match, and they were living the dream. Did he gently grasp her delicate hands as he shared the thrilling news of the museum solidifying their marriage and place in aviation history?

During the Great Depression, as people sought solace in moments of levity, the world outside continued to march forward. By 1932, the skyline of Midtown Manhattan had been transformed by the rise of the Rockefeller Center complex, a bastion of modern design in an era of economic turmoil. The building's sleek contours, intricate geometric patterns, and lavish use of chrome, gold, silver, and black reflected the cutting edge of contemporary design, sprung from shattered plans for a New York opera house after the stock market crash in 1929 and made possible when wealthy patron Otto Hermann Kahn brought in the Rockefeller family to help. They briskly found a willing partner in RCA, which developed the three-block parcel of land for its subsidiaries, NBC and the Radio-Keith-Orpheum film conglomerate.

Times Square wasn't completely darkened during the Great Depression, but it was significantly dimmed; in the Square and throughout the city, businesses and theaters reduced lighting and signage to save electricity. But there was no shortage of electricity for the December 27 opening night of Rockefeller Center's showpiece, Radio City Music Hall, when it drew in a star-studded crowd of over six thousand attendees, including luminaries like Cecil B. DeMille, Charlie Chaplin—and Amelia Earhart, with her ermine-collared silver gown and pearl-inlaid clutch. Excitement hung thick in the air as the doors swung open, and the audience settled in for a big night, yet little did the poor souls suspect the spectacle and confusion that awaited them. Curated by the Broadway impresario Samuel "Roxy" Rothafel, the program promised a full-scale extravaganza that would leave jaws dropping and heads spinning.

At 8:30 p.m., the first of many scheduled performers rose from a pit at Radio City Music Hall. In Roxy's mash-up of acts, Ray Bolger danced as if his limbs were made of rubber, the Flying Wallendas defied death on the high wire, and Martha Graham's dancers floated across the stage. A total of seventeen acts performed, including Japanese jugglers and even the Roxyettes (destined to become the Rockettes). The acts were a chaotic and crazed mix, with no clear connection between them. As the night wore on, the audience thinned, and by the time the grand finale arrived at 2:00 a.m., almost all the baffled audience members had already left (along with laughing gas—at least legal minds prevailed there).

The next morning, after the disastrous night, exhaustion claimed its toll, and Roxy collapsed, his body pushed to its limits. As he recuperated in the hospital, stunned critics typed their blistering reviews, panning the night that was once imagined as a triumphal debut but now served as a sobering lesson on unchecked ambition and the unpredictable nature of artistic ventures.

Despite the confusion and unexpected turns during the grand opening, one thing was clear: Radio City Music Hall was impressive. As a result of its modern design, it embodied the boldness and drive of a time devoted to technological advancement.

And the festive agenda for the massive new complex's opening days was far from concluded. Down the block, Rockefeller Center's Roxy Theatre opened its doors two days later, on Thursday, December 29; Amelia Earhart was back to attend the stage show and the premiere of the feature movie, *The Animal Kingdom*. An eager crowd of thirty-seven hundred swelled with an additional two hundred onlookers, who stood in line to glimpse the otherwise unreachable stars. The Roxy was designed by celebrated architect Thomas W. Lamb, and its energetic manager, Roxy Rothafel, favored Lamb's design. In the ladies' powder room, a grand six-by-eighteen-foot painted glass mural titled *Amelia Earhart Crossing the At-*

lantic commemorated Amelia's historic flight a few months earlier. The mural tickled its subject, who took glamorous photos reclined in front of it for *Vogue* and the papers.

The men's smoking room contained a twenty-five-foot-high photomural by Edward Steichen that depicted celebrated aviators, including the Wright brothers, Lindbergh, and Admiral Richard Byrd, and to make the message clear, the photographer had superimposed captions, maps, and diagrams.

Conceived in the flush of the Jazz Age, the Roxy faced severe struggles during the Great Depression and never found its place. In 1954, overwhelmed by financial losses, its executives decided to demolish it. Today, only a few photographs of that splendid glass mural commemorating Amelia Earhart's mast year in 1932 survive. And what a year it was! With substantial help from George, by the end of December, she had become one of the world's most admired women. The acclaim she had garnered since touching down in Ireland in May would later open doors to speaking engagements that sustained her through leaner years.

The financial news was only worsening—as 1933 dawned, the world was hungry for economic revival. Yet the year also brought the startling divorce of Hollywood's golden couple, Douglas Fairbanks and Mary Pickford. Hopelessly split, the duo's breakup was a bombshell that not only shook their vast fan base but also stunned close friends like the Putnams, leaving Hollywood and its admirers in dismay.

In far darker news than any celebrity split, Adolf Hitler's appointment as chancellor on January 30, 1933, slammed the door shut on the Weimar Republic's fragile experiment with democracy. Though the Nazis had gained traction in the early 1930s elections, Hitler didn't seize power through a dramatic coup; he was handed the chancellorship by President Paul von Hindenburg. Once in power, he wasted no time dismantling what remained of democracy. Just weeks later, on February 27, 1933, the Reichstag—Berlin's parliament building—was engulfed in flames. Hitler seized the crisis with chilling efficiency, using the Reichstag Fire Decree to suspend civil liberties and round up political opponents. In an instant, Germany's descent into Nazi authoritarianism shifted from a slide to a free fall.

Meanwhile, after having smoked incumbent Herbert Hoover on Election Day back in November, Franklin D. Roosevelt was inaugurated as president of the United States on March 4, 1933, three years into the Great Depression. Roosevelt swore in, his hand resting on a thirty-year-old Dutch Bible, and committed to tackling depression and poverty with decisive, immediate measures. His dynamic first one hundred days were filled with groundbreaking initiatives that left a lasting mark on American history. In his inaugural address, he famously declared, "The only thing we have to fear is fear itself." One of Roosevelt's first actions was to address Prohibition, and he signed a March bill allowing 3.2 percent beer. Investments quickly poured into industries like brewing and automobile manufacturing. By April 7, the resurgent beer industry had contributed an estimated $10 million in taxes, marking the start of economic recovery efforts.

Amelia Earhart had met the new first lady, Eleanor Roosevelt, in November 1932, just before Amelia's appearance at Poughkeepsie High School, and they'd hit it off. On April 20, Amelia became one of the first dinner guests at the Roosevelt White House, further solidifying their connection. Even though the new president wasn't present, an illustrious group gathered at the State Dining Room's table alongside Amelia: George Palmer Putnam; Gene Vidal, accompanied by his gorgeous and tempestuous wife, Nina Gore; Thomas Doe, president of Eastern Air Transport; and Hall Roosevelt, Eleanor's brother. When asked how she would feel being piloted by a woman, the first lady responded, "Just as safe. I'd give a lot to do it myself."

When a nutty idea to take a group flight that night "percolated at the table," everyone present was giddy with excitement. A night flight around Washington, DC, sounded grand, like a raucous good time. This joyride was likely a clever concoction by George, orchestrated to appear spontaneous. In front of reporters (who just happened to be there!), the first lady exclaimed, "Let's try it out!" Soon after, the group headed to an airfield near Baltimore, where a massive Curtiss Condor awaited. One surviving piece of footage shows Amelia (not so spontaneously) asking, "Mrs. Roosevelt, would you like a ride over Washington tonight?" Mrs. Roosevelt eagerly climbed aboard and watched as Amelia took the controls, her feet snug in silk slippers and her hands sheathed in white kid gloves.

"It does mark an epoch, doesn't it, when a girl in evening dress and slippers can pilot a plane at night?" Eleanor said to one of the lucky lady reporters she'd invited on board for a hard-to-beat story to beat their male colleagues at their jobs.

During her flight, Amelia switched off all the lights to enhance the beauty of the city below. They marveled at the shimmering Potomac River and the unobstructed views of the glowing capital, from the Washington Monument to the Capitol's illuminated dome, and the White House porch. Afterward, the first lady exclaimed, "It was like being on top of the world!" She also described the scene as a "fairyland."

Amelia rejoined the gang after handing over control to the pilot, but the first lady stayed in the cockpit, and after the plane made an unusual side swing, Amelia said dryly: "Oh, is that Mrs. Roosevelt on the wing?"

The day after spending the night at the White House, Amelia was poised to address the Daughters of the American Revolution. Despite her fame and fitting ancestry, her forward-thinking stances appeared at odds with the audience's anticipations. Her speech—part screed, part plea—underscored her anti-military stance. Her belief that women should be drafted alongside men—a move she thought would make the horrors of war more evident and dissuade societies from supporting it—felt foreign and radical to them. Amelia found war too awful to fall back on patriotism, a sentiment that further distanced her perspective from the hidebound views held by many in the audience.

George advised Amelia to stick to his prewritten, foolproof jokes for audiences who appreciated their humor. For instance, when a gas station customer failed to recognize her and asked for her identity, she wittily responded, "Try the air." This flawless slapstick was followed by patient answers to repetitive questions. She often explained, "A pilot is too busy on her ship to be afraid—any more than you can worry about whether your hat's on straight when you're in a tight fix in your automobile."

Amelia charmed even the most skeptical audiences with her subtle charisma, particularly when she steered clear of politics. Her eloquence and sincerity captivated listeners, leaving a lasting impression long after she exited the stage.

In May 1933, Gene Vidal, Paul "Dog" Collins, and Amelia Earhart found themselves jobless after Ludington was taken over by Eastern Air Transport. To sustain themselves financially, they hatched a plan to build a saltwater pool complex with an eight-thousand-person capacity, including a ninety-by-two-hundred-foot swimming area, a fifty-thousand-square-foot artificial sand beach, and a handball court. The project encountered problems like saltwater corrosion and unexpected weather conditions. They sought advice from Samuel Solomon, the new airport manager at Washington-Hoover Airport, who offered guidance and assistance without charge, given his past dealings with bankruptcy and his friendship with the trio. Solomon's timely intervention helped them secure a deal to sell back the lease, saving them from substantial debt.

As their relationship with Solomon strengthened, they often joined him for friendly ping-pong matches. For leisure, they ventured into investing a few hundred dollars in silver. Though only slightly profitable, this required them to diligently monitor the silver market daily.

Gathering at the Putnam residence in Rye, the friends discussed smarter potential investments and decided to start an airline in collaboration with the Boston and Maine Railroad, an idea suggested by Vidal. This venture led to the creation of National Airways. Publicly, the service was known as Boston-Maine Airways, running routes from Boston to Portland, Maine, and other cities. Appointed vice president of operations, Amelia tirelessly promoted the future of aviation. Her pulling power brought significant attention and business to the airline through her fame and passionate boosterism. Despite a packed lecture schedule, she effectively managed her responsibilities, persuading skeptical New England civic leaders to support air travel and encouraging more women to take up flying. The airline was set for an August launch, promising some summer excitement ahead.

Riding the wave of her airline's successful launch, Amelia chose to attend the marvels of the Chicago World's Fair not by train but by air, living up to her title as the Queen of the Air. On June 11, she piloted her Lockheed Vega from Newark to Chicago. The fair had commenced on May 27 on a transformed landfill near Lake Michigan. Perhaps she reminisced with her younger stepson, Junie, about her own thrilling previous World's Fair experiences, like riding an elephant and a Ferris wheel but, pointedly, not a roller coaster.

Reporters flocked to the Stevens Hotel's press room to interview the unconventional family. According to George, Junie wanted to get there early for the fair. He wasn't into aviation unless he was a passenger with his stepmother as the pilot. "Two pilots in the family are enough!" George joked. David, his elder son, who got his pilot's license at nineteen, was in South America on an expedition, and this trip, George further explained, was to spend time with his youngest one. As it was for his pleasure, Junie would decide what they saw.

In a blue blouse and white crepe skirt, Amelia told reporters that the novelty of aviation had worn off. It was now just another mode of transportation.

The Putnams' smiles in old clippings indicate they had a blissful time together during their three-day stay. Their view of the fairgrounds was from a cabled sky ride and a captive balloon eight hundred feet in the air. There were other ways to get around, and college boys pulled them in rickshaws. One exhibit, *The World a Million Years Ago*, featured old trains and a prehistoric mechanical gorilla. Apes like King Kong did not exist, but the fair debuted the same year as the titular film. Certainly they gawked at the eighty-five little people in "Midget Village." (A ride like this would never be approved today, but in 1933, it was considered a lot of fun.) Scaled-down buildings in the Lilliputian town included restaurants, a music hall, and a hotel. The World's Fair brochure even advertised a daily parade of "toy soldiers." Amelia must have stopped to smell the newly cultivated "Amelia Earhart" rose in the Horticulture Building, and Junie, like any young one, would have almost definitely wanted to see the animated dinosaurs accompanied by prehistoric audio.

As Amelia and George navigated the wonders of the World's Fair, they were reminded of the breadth of her influence when they encountered her painted image among the pioneers of women's progress in the Hall of Social Science. A likeness of Amelia graced a sixty-foot mural depicting Lucretia Mott, Elizabeth Cady Stanton, Harriet Beecher Stowe, Julia Ward Howe, Clara Barton, Emily Dickinson, Mary Cassatt, and Helen Keller. The National Council of Women had commissioned the work, called *Progress of Women*, or *The Onward March of Women*. Hildreth Meière, one of the most critical Art Deco artists, painted the impressive piece. Her imposing mural depicts women struggling to move from 1833 (the "narrow confines of home and tradition") to 1933 ("broad opportunities and freedom").

As one walked from past to present along the painted illustration of women's suffrage, the prison bars in the background got farther apart. Objects and documents about the celebrated women portrayed in the mural were displayed. Most (white) fairgoers didn't care about the mural's exclusion of women of color. These were different times.

Did George feel pride or jealousy when gazing at his wife's painted image? His fame had long been eclipsed by hers.

After the many delights of the World's Fair, Amelia pivoted back to the skies, ready in early August to inaugurate her airline's first flight just three months after the conception of the fledgling Boston–Maine Airways— touted as the "Yankee Fleet." Amelia boarded the first Stinson T flight, and the press flocked to the airport as hoped. Over ten thousand people from the surrounding towns of Bangor, Maine, showed up in the Queen City to meet the Queen of the Air. Asked to describe the thrills of her career so far, she replied, "Don't talk of aviation as a thrill. I think of it as transportation."

As an executive with National Airways, Amelia helped plan a Women's Day event in Bangor, lending not merely her name but her presence—and not as a pilot but as a celebrated passenger. Her involvement in ten-minute exhibition flights became the highlight of a whimsical jelly bean counting contest outside Freese's department store. Winners, including nineteen-year-old Alice Creamer and her cousin Marion Tuck, were treated to exhilarating aerial tours. They soared over the Kenduskeag and Penobscot Rivers, spotting familiar rooftops and landmarks from an uncommon vantage point. Amid the thrill, Amelia engaged with her passengers, her voice tinged with excitement: "Do you girls realize you're moving a hundred miles per hour?" Creamer would reminisce about that flight for years to come.

Joanne Jordan, just ten and with notable local connections—her father owned the *Bangor Daily News* and was a crucial figure in arranging Amelia's visit—was the youngest of over two hundred girls and women who experienced these flights, a subtle nod to the intertwined worlds of media and aviation. The oldest participant, a still-full-of-fun ninety-two-year-old, voiced her long-held dream to fly with Amelia. Observing the scene, National Airways's Samuel Solomon humorously suggested to Amelia: "Let her go up; she doesn't have much to lose!" After her adventure, Mrs. Cameron emerged exhilarated, ambitiously declaring, "I want to keep going and head to South America!"

After punching nine more tickets—in the air—the super-saleswoman greeted the newest passengers again. With a white hat, silk stockings, and white gloves, Sally Miller was a bulky middle-aged lady in a smart linen suit. Amelia asked her how she was doing during the ride. In a deep bass voice, Miller boomed, "Well, Amelia, here I am. Ban men all you want to, but I wanted to ride with you." To everyone's surprise, the notably unattractive lady dramatically pulled off her wig and white gloves, revealing herself as none other than Ralph Mills, a local impersonator and stage star known for his uproarious acts. Ralph's disguise had bamboozled the other passengers as he sneaked onto the airship. In fits of laughter, they now recognized him, and the joyous atmosphere continued. The mystery (and hilarity) of the situation was enhanced by Ralph's refusal to reveal who gave him the ticket. Amelia was still chuckling after landing and agreed that it had been an unforgettable and riotous stunt. After the impromptu performance that brought so many guffaws, she even posed for a photo with Ralph.

The success of Amelia's airline event paved the way for her to introduce another family aviator, her stepson David, who brought tales of adventure to the public eye. Amelia had wired her famous and always-traveling stepson that summer to say that she had a fine job for him, and in late August 1933, David Binney Putnam returned early from the ongoing LaVarre Brazilian-Guiana Expedition—once again, his well-connected father and associations at the Explorers Club had facilitated his presence as the youngest team member. The expedition aimed to search for alluvial diamond sources and collect flora and fauna in the little-known region at the headwaters of the Essequibo River in British Guiana.

David had been enticed back early from this latest adventure by a plum job offer during the Great Depression—he would be the youngest employee for his stepmother's new airline, and George had arranged a press conference in a Plaza Hotel suite for his wife and son. Now a lanky twenty-one, David, who had a shadowy blond mustache and stood over six feet tall, proudly shared thrilling tales of his adventures in northern Brazil and British Guiana, and Amelia was there to answer any questions about Boston–Maine Airways.

During the conference, perhaps with his father's coaching, David shared a wild anecdote about his failed attempt to bring over an ocelot from Martinique so that his stepmother could use it as an airline mascot. Then David presented the reporters with two preserved dead snakes and a deceased tarantula, stored in a fruit jar he'd unscrewed, and he playfully manipulated the spider's furry legs to make them appear alive.

Amelia matched David's adventurous spirit with her own humorously amped-up anecdotes of homelife, including one engaging and funny tale revolving around enigmatic bite marks appearing on every piece of fruit at her Rye house, with the stupendous riddle only solved after everyone in the home amusingly posed as furniture, unveiling a chipmunk as the true culprit. She also recounted an encounter with a flock of pigeons while piloting for her previous place of employment, the Ludington Line, just a hundred miles from Washington. Remarkably, one of the pigeons had flown through blades spinning at fifteen hundred revolutions per minute and miraculously survived, though missing a foot. Inspired by Amelia's storytelling, reporters shared their own outlandish stories, including tornadoes carrying cows and even a crowing rooster found inside a whiskey jug.

The conference concluded with Amelia playfully appointed by those present as the president of the newly formed Monday Afternoon Exaggerated Narrative Club, and the meeting was "adjourned" at 4:00 p.m. She promised to have even better tales for the next press gathering.

While Amelia's storytelling captivated the room, outside, a different kind of history was unfolding as New York celebrated the end of Prohibition on December 5. It is no exaggeration to say that the city erupted in wild celebration as the Twenty-First Amendment repealed the Eighteenth Amendment, formally declaring the end of Prohibition, and that the demise of Prohibition brought relief and jubilation. Nevertheless, the nation continued to deal with the relentless grip of the Great Depression. Roosevelt's campaign song, "Happy Days Are Here Again," had echoed with hope. Yet despite the celebrations, a lingering question remained: Had true happiness and revival genuinely arrived, or would these festivities be overshadowed by the ongoing challenges of the time?

In the same spirit of new beginnings that marked the end of Prohibition, Gene Vidal embarked on an ambitious aviation project, championed by Amelia's unwavering support. Thanks to her hearty endorsement, Roosevelt appointed Vidal to helm the Bureau of Air Commerce, and the swoon-worthy ex-Olympian soon appeared on the cover of *Time*. He had a significant platform to say that one day, air travel would be as essential as driving a car: Vidal, inspired by the affordability of Ford's Model T, explained to the magazine's readers his new "Poor Man's Airplane" project. Despite initial government backing, the idea was met with considerable skepticism, as the half-baked project needed help to overcome the inherent complexities of aviation. However, Amelia found her very close friend Vidal a strategically positioned ally, capable of granting special favors when required as she navigated a pioneering path across the skies.

Fourteen

CALL OF THE WILD

The big and unexpected fashion news of 1934 was Amelia Earhart Fashions, the pilot's new clothing line for sporting women, including lady fliers. Amelia, the first articles explained, was already an accomplished aviator, but now she had embraced a new profession, and her brilliance would soon be found at the Macy's Amelia Earhart Shop, a dedicated store within a store, with more exclusive stores to follow.

Amelia Earhart, a fashion designer? No one was more bemused than her sister, who on tape would later recall Amelia as an "unorthodox seamstress" with little to no skill in sewing. According to the first article, Amelia, a hired seamstress, was supposedly operating the old sewing machine she'd kept from her days at the Ogontz School for Young Ladies. (Seeing these photos in a Boston newspaper, Muriel simply rolled her eyes. The talk of Meelie as a "natural designer" also amused former Ogontz classmates, who later commented that she "cared little for clothes as anyone" and displayed "complete disregard of the smart clothes she affects with such grace today.")

They were not wrong. Amelia had simply been talked into the latest Amelia Earhart sideshow by her husband, just like store executives had been. George had told them, smoothly, that only Macy's would have a dedicated shop, but that would simply add prestige. Her line would be sold exclusively in one high-end department store chosen by George in each major

American city, including Jordan Marsh in Boston, Marshall Field's in Chicago, Hudson's in Detroit, Strawbridge & Clothier in Philadelphia, Meier & Frank in Portland (Oregon), Jelleff's in Washington, and L. Bamberger & Co. in Newark. The promise of the famous Amelia Earhart flying into town to promote the line was an irresistible carrot for any department store executive still on the fence.

While many in the fashion industry were abuzz at the surprising news, it also caught the aviation community's attention, and no one was more surprised than Anne Morrow Lindbergh, as after their infant son's kidnapping and just before his tragic death was revealed, the Lindberghs had shared a quiet supper with the Putnams, who offered them comfort.

The well-mannered Anne later sent a thank-you note, tacking on an ingenious "AIR SHOP" idea she had dreamed up that might help an out-of-work female pilot they both knew. Would Amelia weigh in on her idea? How about a dedicated "flying togs" store within a department store like Macy's, targeting the sports-minded too? Anne also wrote, "Shameful or not as it may be, women are interested in what to wear when flying." And now, twelve months later, Amelia's fledgling new fashion line was almost a perfect rip-off of those exact ideas. Perhaps they marveled at how Amelia shamelessly reframed this idea as her own, but more likely, like anyone who knew George Palmer Putnam well, the Lindberghs suspected George of poaching and then adopting Anne's idea. George had tinkered with it, combining Anne's suggestion with business insights he'd gleaned from fashion companies that had offered him endorsement deals. He had perhaps also extracted pearls from Amelia's discussions with designer Elsa Schiaparelli on her "active living" ideas.

With an in-store appearance from the Queen of Aviation, the flagship Macy's in Herald Square launched the third-floor Amelia Earhart Shop on February 2, 1934, right between the sportswear and the juniors' department. Silvery airplane models hung from the ceiling, and a large glass display case revealed items taken with her on her Atlantic jaunts, including a brown suede windbreaker, goggles, jodhpurs, shoes, and even smelling salts. Another case displayed objects said to inspire her designs, such as buttons, buckles, clips, wing lights, nuts, screws, suctions, valves, and a parachute.

"I hate ruffles, and when I got started, that was all I could afford. So, I decided to design clothes. They are nothing spectacular, just good lines and good materials for active women," Amelia told one reporter at the time, adding that she started with twenty-five medium-price items ranging from twenty-five to fifty dollars. As a designer of active women's clothing, she offered a "forward-looking fashion brand" that considered comfort and style. Many of the items were even washable. "I thought I was busy before, but now I am swamped.... I have five manufacturers working for me. I handle... buttons, buckles, and clips until I am dizzy. I have a skeleton in my closet too." She then stepped over to the closet and pulled out the mannequin that she draped her clothes on. "When I brought it home, my husband said, 'Do I have to live with that awful thing?'"

Tongues clucked in the Ninety-Nines meetings, where the seasoned women aviators were appalled at the growing press and wondered what that conniving George was making her do now for his cut. Wasn't flying her true passion? But there she was in the papers, plenty game, standing near a desk theatrically piled with silks and fan letters: "Some other girl should be breaking records now," she said. "I don't have the equipment, and planes don't grow on bushes.... There haven't been any sports clothes for the average woman. I can sew. I don't like to, but I can. When I saw how things were changing, with women increasingly participating in sports, I decided to see what I could do."

Reenergized and refocused on dominating the glamorous world of high fashion, George believed his slender, makeup-free wife needed the big slicks like *Vogue* and *Vanity Fair* to promote her clothing line. Perhaps that's why the perfect figure of the Jazz Age adapted to a new decade's beauty standards by downing extra cream and buttermilk to add a fleshy fullness to her face; she gained ten pounds before posing for her still-iconic shoots by the best fashion photographers in the world. String bean was out.

Even though George hyped Amelia's line, the fashion landscape of the era already had such "innovative" designs as pockets and washable materials. Styles and concepts similar to those reflected in Amelia's line could be found in the collections of established designers like Maggy Rouff and Alfred Dunhill. Furthermore, a subtle hint in *Women's Wear Daily* suggested that Amelia Earhart Fashions' Eve Bennett, previously associated with Foremost Sportswear, may have been the true creative force behind a lot of the lower-priced knockoffs of these existing designs.

Despite her overwhelming commitments, Amelia remarkably found time for cultural pursuits, especially if she was well paid for her time. During her highly publicized visit to the Museum of Modern Art, the aviator and fashion designer served as a judge for a new Machine Age exhibit that would be installed at the museum. She was joined by the venerated educator John Dewey and Frances Perkins, Roosevelt's only female cabinet member; they selected three objects—a spring, a propeller, and a ball bearing—as modern design symbols.

During one interview that she managed to squeeze in during these busy months, Amelia responded to a peculiar question about whether she'd be happier as a man: "Goodness, no. I am a woman and flier, and the two are not incompatible." Asked about children, she nonchalantly replied, "Someday, perhaps." She was not asked about her existing stepchildren, already a source of pride, especially the all-grown-up David, who excelled in flying and owned a sixth of National Airways, and they were always happy to talk company profit and aviation.

Toward the end of February 1934, family concerns overshadowed business when David learned of his mother's unbearable mistreatment by her second husband, Frank Upton. Dorothy begged her son for help after revealing the shocking extent of verbal abuse and even the brutality of horsewhipping. Determined to get his mother to safety and away from a wife beater, David, who was a trained pilot, hastily borrowed a plane from National Airways and headed to Florida. His confrontation with Upton sent the former war hero fleeing to Washington, DC. This astounding showdown was later detailed in National Airways cofounder Paul Collins's posthumous memoir. Collins recounted a curious conversation with David—then the Boston–Maine line station manager in Augusta, Maine—who had approached him with an unusual request: a quick leave of absence for an urgent trip to Florida to "find a bride." Paul, somewhat surprised, had asked, "You have a sweetheart in Florida?" To this, David confidently and mysteriously replied, "Not yet, but I'll find one when I get there."

While David's primary motive was to support his mother and ensure her safety, fate had other plans. After Upton fled, scared away by his stepson, David found himself free to pursue personal matters. In an unexpected twist, he was struck with Cupid's arrow on a blind date in Palm Beach with Nilla Ruth Shields, a recent Duke graduate from Georgia. Shields, who was visiting Florida at the time, captivated David with her blond beauty and Southern charm, marking the beginning of a significant new chapter in his life.

Within forty-eight hours, the couple decided to elope. On March 5, Dorothy nervously called New York to update George. All of this occurred during an office visit from Henry Bradford Washburn, George's favorite boy explorer, who had written about climbing the Alps. George excused himself to take Dorothy's call, and soon, his well-known temper was evident. "He was so rude to his secretary," Washburn said in an off-the-record interview, adding that George "swore and yelled" right in front of him after learning that David had married a Georgia girl right after meeting her. "Jesus Christ!" he shouted. "Is she Black or white?"

"My sister was often a buffer for David," Muriel once wrote, emphasizing Amelia's role in mediating for her stepson. After George's shock, Amelia's diplomacy was certainly needed again. She helped him write a heartfelt note welcoming his new daughter-in-law: "Anyway, I'm eager to see you, and you'll find a full measure of affection in your new dad," George wrote, revealing little of his earlier outburst. Below his note, Amelia scribbled, "I echo all that David's Dad has said, Amelia Earhart."

Following this conciliatory gesture, George didn't miss a publicity beat. He ordered formal announcements, carefully worded: The explorer, son of George Palmer Putnam, publisher and explorer, wedded the daughter of a physician from Georgia. "Friends attended." To further ease relations, Amelia and George, who had recently won a dachshund puppy named Philbert at a fancy-dress ball, gifted the puppy to David and his new bride, Nilla, as a symbol of family unity.

By late July, George and Amelia, weary from their hectic schedules, decided it was time to trade their city-slicker routines for the rugged simplicity of tent living. They chose the secluded Double Dee Guest Ranch in Wyoming for their getaway. Spanning over 3,306 acres, the ranch was managed by their old friend Carl Dunrud and accommodated just fifteen guests at a time, providing an intimate experience. Hereabouts they could enjoy serene horseback tours through the rugged backcountry, a perfect setting for relaxation.

Although George later claimed they traveled together, that was another falsehood—Amelia reached the ranch first, driving herself from New York in her current free set of wheels, an air-conditioned Franklin car, journeying the 2,200 miles to the vicinity of the ranch in Meeteetse. She managed to avoid recognition during the entire trip until she was at a gas station just under two hundred miles from her destination. An attendant, who recognized her upon taking a closer look, gaped and said, "Hey, aren't you Amelia Earhart?!"

After George did arrive (by train), he joined his wife, and they remained at the ranch for a few more days before they traveled by packhorse to Sunshine, Wyoming, and from there ventured into the towering peaks of the Absaroka Range within the Shoshone National Forest; her ride was a strawberry-hued roan named Red, and George got a horse named Peanuts. They rode under a gentle drizzle most of the time, but Amelia remained enthralled as the happy couple climbed by horse until they reached ten thousand feet above sea level and were seventy-five miles from the nearest trading post. Here was what George wanted to show her: a place light-years from Midtown Manhattan's hustle and bustle and home to deer, elk, sheep, antelope, and the Shiras moose, a local star. There was a wrangler who also cooked for them during this ten-day expedition. Their lovely stay at the Double Dee marked their longest time together since their wedding, and

George nervously hoped Amelia was enjoying the backcountry. She held his hand and assured him that she was. She smiled as she watched bighorn lambs romp on distant, unpeopled mountaintops through her borrowed field glasses and beamed widely as she trout-fished from horseback. The fish were biting, and Dunrud freed two brook trout from her hook near Emerald Creek. The steady murmur of the stream, weaving through the quiet wilderness, filled the air like a whispered lullaby. Listening to its song, Amelia turned to George and said, "I want to live here sometime." She wanted a hideout.

George was listening. They had battled the grind of ineffable fame together. There was a way forward. After all the financial turmoil, wouldn't having a getaway house here be a dream if the world returned to normal? The new dismal economy couldn't last forever; America would come back. Could they grow old together here? A haven, they were sure, where nobody would stare.

With George's assistance, Amelia would later stake a mining claim on ground adjoining Dunrud's patented mineral land. Dunrud agreed to do discovery work on her claim and build Amelia a four-room dream cabin.

During the extended drive from Wyoming to Rye, New York, this time together, Amelia took the familiar position behind the wheel, navigating pretty backcountry roads. Reporters and photographers caught glimpses of the couple outside their usual urban environs. Once, Amelia appeared at a local restaurant in a muted-green sports suit paired with an elaborate blouse, and a local reporter got a great scoop. "Oh, it was wonderful," Amelia told him. "We've been planning this trip for three years, but something always cropped up, causing a delay."

The good people of Atchison, Kansas, were soon astonished to read that the Putnams had secretly visited the happy land of her childhood during their very winding route back from vacation. Inadvertently, George said, he'd spilled the beans about her secret return home with a clipping from his pocket. At Saint Joseph's nine-story Hotel Robidoux, just over the Missouri River, a bellhop "stumbled upon" this information. (A good story, but he had almost certainly been directly told by George and instructed to call local reporters, perhaps for a bit of cash.) "Guess what?" the bellboy said to a reporter after he supposedly put two and two together. "I ushered upstairs the woman who flew the ocean." Amelia had already retired to bed. And George was happy to talk to a reporter now that the escapade was over: "I'll give you what story there is. We drove around Atchison, Kansas, this evening. That, you know, is Miss Earhart's birthplace. I'd never seen Atchison before."

Amelia let the press hound's millionth indiscretion go, and even their servants back in Rye noticed their unusual closeness upon their return. But their overcommitted lives soon resumed.

Amelia was in the spotlight on September 26 at the fourth annual Conference on Current Problems, organized by the *New York Herald Tribune*. In a lineup that boasted names like Emily Post and Fiorello La Guardia, Amelia shone as a featured speaker. The conference hummed with a lively, almost kinetic energy, especially after Eleanor Roosevelt kicked things off, calling out gender bias in aviation programs like that of New York University. As the next event in the conference began, Amelia met with Purdue University's president, Edward C. Elliott, who immensely enjoyed her talk and shared the exciting news that Purdue was trailblazing with an aeronautical science major, now open to women. Amelia was fascinated, and for George it was red meat to a dog.

Not minutes later, George proposed further discussion at the Coffee House Club, his preferred New York haunt, and there, away from the crowded conference, he peddled his grand vision for Elliott: Why not have Amelia serve as a visiting faculty member at Purdue, mentoring female students? As their discussion continued, George was already calculating the potential financial benefits, imagining a yearly compensation of $2,000. President Elliott bit.

Amelia soon captivated the audience at the university's annual banquet with her prepared "Opportunities for Women in Aviation" speech. She looked forward to joining them again so she could work directly with students during a more extended stay; until then, she would continue her regular grind of appearances and schedules.

On November 28, while Amelia was lecturing in California, a devastating fire consumed a significant part of her and George's sixteen-room house in Rye. Thanks to a watchful neighbor's swift action, the damage was not worse. Upon hearing of the blaze during her lecture tour, Amelia immediately returned to the East Coast.

Investigations suggested that the flames may have started in the basement, likely due to an oversight with the heater by Jim, their houseman. George took solace in knowing that everyone was safe and that they had good insurance coverage. However, the damage was substantial; more than five hundred of George's books, letters, and autographed memorabilia from figures like Robert Peary and Charles Lindbergh were destroyed. Treasured artworks by Rockwell Kent, an antique desk from Washington Irving, and many of David's curios from years of travel were lost. Some of Amelia's "peppers," her term for her papers, survived, but many of her childhood and social-work poems were lost in the fire.

In the aftermath, Amelia and George faced defining choices. Amelia's health had improved under the California sun, and they considered starting a new chapter on the West Coast, spurred by their budding design business. However, with George's work anchored in New York, Amelia initially found temporary accommodation, staying with airline magnate Jack Maddux near her friends Paul and Myrtle Mantz in Toluca Lake. After settling insurance matters, George joined her, albeit hesitant about a permanent move.

Post-fire, Amelia was relieved to see the end of Amelia Earhart Fashions, a project that had underperformed. The glamorous, Hollywood-inspired styles of the Depression era overshadowed her fashion line. In a candid Thanksgiving conversation with a journalist, Amelia declared, "I am not doing any designing now. It came down to choosing between designing and aviation, and I chose aviation." This decision marked a pivotal return to her passion for flying. When the fashion line folded, George's longtime assistant, Harold McCracken, took over her Hotel Seymour suite and secretly kept an unsold Amelia Earhart Fashions wicker bag as a souvenir.

Amelia threw herself back into the aviation world, beaming proudly on December 17; her now-famous friend Gene Vidal captured his own headlines when, at precisely 10:30 a.m., he ceremoniously delivered a letter from President Roosevelt to Orville Wright. The timing was deliberate, coinciding with the exact hour when Wright piloted the historic twelve-second flight at Kitty Hawk thirty-one years prior. Forty planes gracefully soared over the site in a touching tribute to Orville's achievement and his late brother Wilbur.

But Amelia would be back in the papers when rumors of a potential solo flight from Hawaii to the US began circulating—speculation that was more compelling against the backdrop of the recent mysterious disappearance of Australian aviator Charles Ulm and his Airspeed Envoy, the *Stella Australis*, leaving the aviation world intrigued and somber.

Just before Christmas in 1934, Amelia boarded the luxurious SS *Lurline*, a Matson ocean liner departing from Los Angeles to Honolulu. George joined her, as did her flying coach, Paul Mantz, and her trusted mechanic, Ernest "Ernie" Tissot. Also on board was a red Lockheed Vega, one of her two prized aircraft, securely tethered to the ship's tennis court deck. Amelia and her companions huddled in a cabin room throughout the five-day crossing, reviewing her secret flight plan—a perilous solo journey from Honolulu to Oakland.

Amelia arrived in Hawaii for the first time on December 27, stepping ashore at Pier 11 to begin her next adventure. In onshore interviews, she was still coy, saying only that she was in Hawaii for lectures at the University of Hawaii and that the Vega would just be used for "interstate travel." Suspicious aviation reporters noted that her Vega, modified to hold 460 gallons of fuel—more than double the standard capacity—was equipped for far more than "interstate travel." The departure date was unknown to even her, but in Waikiki, Tissot and Mantz sneaked her plane to Wheeler Field while she was interviewing.

Amelia and her group stayed at Queen's Surf, a dazzling estate perched on Oahu's windward shore, its architecture caught between the grandeur of a Greek temple and the sleekness of a modernist palace. This was the home of

Christian R. Holmes, the playboy Fleischmann yeast heir. Holmes was a former client of Amelia's aviation tutor, Mantz, who, for good pay, often privately ferried the rich and famous by air.

At Queen's Surf, Amelia and her entourage, including Mantz, enjoyed lavish comforts—a hidden indulgence at odds with the modest image she and George carefully cultivated. Amelia was always attended to by a team of six Japanese servants, a most privileged circumstance wisely kept secret from the American public during difficult times. While in Hawaii, as her plane underwent repairs, Amelia maintained the facade of a casual visit, engaging in lectures, making public appearances, and planting a banyan tree in Hilo. The tree stands today, marked by a wooden plaque.

On a damp Hawaiian evening, as the sun dipped behind rain-soaked palms, Amelia took off from Wheeler Field at 4:40 p.m., feeling entirely at ease despite the perils ahead. George, chain-smoking and frowning, paced anxiously in the United Press office, desperate for any scrap of news. This was the first flight to use two-way radio, and his heavy concern was eased briefly when he heard Amelia's calm, indifferent voice over the airwaves; after the advent of radio telephony, aviation accidents decreased by half. This technological advancement revolutionized aviation safety by enabling real-time communication between pilots and ground control, allowing for quicker responses to emergencies and flight issues. Before the widespread adoption of radio telephony, pilots often faced communication barriers and navigational difficulties, leading to a higher incidence of accidents. However, with the introduction of this technology, pilots like Amelia were able to receive assistance and guidance during critical moments, significantly reducing the risk of accidents. It was a good thing Amelia had the radio on board, since she found herself lost as she approached Northern California and got secret help from a local ham operator who would later receive a grateful telegram.

Officially, though, came a George story, a charming and poetic one: As Amelia approached California, the skies magically opened up enough that she spotted a boat from the Dollar Line framed by clouds. The sun rose as she touched down, offering a serene ocean dawn—a sight Amelia had never witnessed before. The final stretch of her journey had felt endless, as though she were flying from nowhere to nowhere, with only imagination to guide her toward the promise of land. "The last hour of an ocean flight is the hardest," she later remarked. "You constantly see mirages of land in the clouds that fade away quickly. You know you are near land, and imagination takes over."

Any help Amelia needed was water under the bridge when, eighteen hours and fifteen minutes after departing Hawaii, she concluded her journey and was greeted by a jubilant crowd of five thousand fans at Oakland's airport. She had once again achieved a historic feat, becoming the first person to fly solo across the Pacific Ocean. This accomplishment meant far more to her than a fashion line she had little involvement in; it was another in a growing list of aviation milestones under her belt.

Amelia wanted space, apologizing for her ask. How ragged she felt from sitting so long, and, afraid she might stink, she said she would talk to all after a bath.

This bold endeavor was more than just a flight; it was a loud rebuttal to doubts about her flying skills. Amelia downplayed her recklessness to the press, saying that hitting a continent was, in fact, easier than aiming for a solitary island. After this astounding flight, Amelia received congratulations from countless well-wishers, including President Roosevelt, who emphasized that aviation should not be limited to men.

Even so, many of her friends were simply relieved that she had survived what, in many ways, was a reckless stunt. In a letter, Amelia's close friend Louise Thaden, the 1929 Women's Air Derby winner, told her so.

"But darn your hide, I could spank your pants! Would you mind telling me sometime in strict confidence why the heck you do things like that? I'd really like to know. I was scared to death. Dammit, you're worth more alive than dead, and what profit fame when you are not here to reap the benefits? . . . Of course, your preparation is all it should be, but there is still a large element of luck, and I wish you'd rest on your laurels now that the Pacific has been conquered by women and solo at that. Oh well, you'll probably resent this, but just the same, it's the way I feel about you. When it comes down to brass tacks, I don't know you at all—I doubt anyone does."

After Amelia's flight to Hawaii, her and George's unconventional marriage seemed to expand over great distances; they sometimes shared a bed in New York or California and just as often maintained their marriage from afar through nightly telephone conversations. One of George's favorite conversations was about her ride with Eleanor Roosevelt in Buckminster Fuller's Dymaxion during a solo visit to the White House in March 1935. This enigmatic vehicle resembled a cross between a spaceship and a unicycle, its teardrop-shaped body and single rear wheel as "future-weird" as an alien pod, and its unique design allowed them to conceal their famous identities during the ride. Amelia was no stranger to the Dymaxion; in the summer of 1934, she took an electrifying test-drive of one in upstate New York alongside Australian aviator Sir Charles Kingsford Smith.

Amelia's escapades without her husband were frequent topics in their nightly phone chats, ranging from amusing stories to grave discussions. Their financial concerns had become increasingly pressing as the Depression worsened. George relied on Amelia to persevere.

In a March 4 letter on White House stationery, Amelia hinted at the tense talks, revealing that George's mentor, Emanuel Cohen, was pushed out of an executive position. "GP has departed from Paramount and is considering his next move." For now, they needed money, and that week, *Town & Country* ran an ad for a house rental, indicating that the fire insurance payout had come through and the Putnams had immediately put it to use, modernizing the house.

AMELIA EARHART – GEORGE PALMER PUTNAM RESIDENCE

Completely Rebuilt – refurnished. Rent for season. 6 master rooms, 5 baths. 5 Acres, beautiful grounds, trees, garden. Unexcelled location.

As the Putnams faced persistent financial challenges, an opportunity from the Mexican consul general in New York provided timely relief: a goodwill trip to Mexico in the third week of April, promising income generation. The offer became even more enticing when the Mexican government proposed creating a unique stamp to commemorate Amelia's flight, an idea George quickly seized and capitalized on.

While Amelia continued her lecture tour, which provided them the most dependable income, George flew alone to Mexico on a commercial flight to get things going for yet another new record she planned to set to keep herself relevant.

Arriving in Mexico before his wife, George got approval from the top: Mexico would issue a twenty-cent airmail stamp, and in an ethically hairy move, George would receive 85 percent of them, three hundred stamps, directly from the Mexican government to be used on "covers," stamped envelopes that Amelia would add value to by signing—and that George would use for his personal profit. In exchange, George promised to bring the great Miss Earhart to Mexico and get excellent press. Soon, he spent hours at the government printing office as the stamps were executed, and to prevent counterfeiting, he even destroyed the linocut blocks he had brought along on his flight.

Amelia took off from Burbank on April 20, bound for Mexico City, in her latest Vega, a 5C, carrying fifty envelopes stamped and canceled in Burbank. She intended to collect more upon her return. The intercountry flight had favorable weather, allowing her to cruise the seventeen hundred miles at an average speed of about 130 miles per hour. However, navigation was challenging, leading her to land sixty miles south of Mexico City on a dry Nopala lake bed frequented by cows. There, fifty vaqueros (cowboys) and their families met her. Despite the language barrier, they recognized Amelia and guided her toward Mexico City during her brief thirty-minute detour. Amelia, possibly echoing another less-damning narrative devised by George, blamed her detour on a bug that hindered her vision.

When Amelia touched down in Mexico City, her crimson Vega was met by a roaring crowd of ten thousand, including her husband, George, and Mexican Foreign Minister Emilio Portes Gil. The electrified throng spilled past the airport gates, shouting "¡Viva la Earhart!" in a moment as jubilant as it was chaotic. Yet, even with such an outpouring of admiration—reminiscent of

Colonel Lindbergh's celebrated arrival—Amelia remained characteristically self-effacing, insisting she hadn't quite lived up to his legacy. Her dazzling flight, however, seemed to tell a different story.

While Amelia captured the public's imagination with her daring flights, George again capitalized on these achievements for financial gain. He had previously secured fifty stamped covers in Mexico City, which he promptly canceled upon arrival. For her return flight to Newark, he arranged for thirty-five more covers to be stamped and canceled, turning these items into lucrative collectibles, a clever blend of commemoration and commerce.

During their brief stay in Mexico, the couple, donning matching sombreros, enjoyed the local cuisine. In a light moment captured by a reporter, George quipped, "Most men will wait for their wives at some time or another. . . . I regard it very worthwhile to wait while Miss Earhart is accomplishing something she really wants to do." Their visit was further honored with a reception hosted by Mexico's president, Lázaro Cárdenas, on April 23, a testament to Amelia's international acclaim.

It was supposed to be a short stay, but poor weather reports from Doc Kimball extended it by nearly three weeks. During this time, as Amelia prepared for her return flight, which presented challenges, she enjoyed jai alai, toured Xochimilco, and developed a taste for chicken tamales and enchiladas.

Needing to return to work, George boarded a commercial flight. Concerned about Amelia flying home with 470 gallons of gas at eight thousand feet, he ensured that the Mexican government built a makeshift runway on Lake Texcoco's bed. Wiley Post warned Amelia against flying over the Gulf of Mexico, but she was determined to do so.

On April 29, Amelia visited Mexico City's police headquarters to leave her fingerprints as an offbeat souvenir for the Mexican police and as a play for a bit of press attention. George, meanwhile, geared up to promote her arrival home. After a solitary stay in Mexico until May 8, preparing for a new record attempt, Amelia decided to forgo Vidal's cautious advice to stop in Washington. She set her sights on Newark Airport in New Jersey, where George waited eagerly.

At Newark, eyes bloodshot from exhaustion, she was met with a heady welcome from ten thousand fans. As George elbowed through the mad stampede, he cried out loud enough for reporters to catch every word: "Mexico is four times more civilized than Newark!" This outburst led to a New Jersey journalist advising George to refrain from insulting Mexico.

While George's eruption grabbed headlines, a significant yet underrecognized aviation milestone occurred: Ruth Bancroft Law, notable as the third woman in the United States to earn a pilot's license, arrived simultaneously but without much fanfare. This time, she was a passenger on an unnamed, newly available multiple-stop commercial flight from the West Coast, most likely operated by United or TWA on a Douglas DC-3. She was flying with her husband to visit their niece in New York City. Back in 1916, after completing a groundbreaking nonstop flight from Chicago to New York, covering 590 miles, Law commanded a jaw-dropping $9,000 per week as a stuntwoman—equivalent to about $273,000 per week in today's dollars—a sum that underscored her star power and was virtually unheard of at the time. After World War I, she passionately advocated for women's participation in military aviation, but her efforts were met with resistance and rejection.

In 1922, Law saw her flying career end abruptly when her husband cited safety concerns. Retreating to a quieter life in Los Angeles, she had immersed herself in gardening. However, a chance encounter with an older *Daily News* aviation reporter who recognized her at the airport in 1935 brought Law back into the spotlight, prompting reflections on the legacies of women in aviation. This rediscovery of Law, once a celebrated pilot, posed a poignant question: Would Amelia Earhart, the current Queen of the Air, also fade from public memory in years to come?

As Amelia checked into her own hotel suite, she stated that her Hawaiian trip aimed to inspire women in the Machine Age. When asked about risking her life, she admitted, "I expect to make quite a sum lecturing and writing for magazines about the trip."

And she was right. Her fame had grown by bounds after her solo Atlantic crossing. Even her friend Will Rogers, who had ribbed her "ladybird" friends about their "Powder Puff Derby," had stunning words to say for his millions of readers: "When you take a fast ship loaded with four hundred gallons of gas off that field, you are an aviator, be you man or woman. I bet you Amelia is the only woman that Mrs. Roosevelt could possibly in any way envy."

During the tanked economy of the 1930s, few names could draw crowds and boost ticket sales like Amelia Earhart. On May 30, she was the first female referee at the twenty-third Indianapolis 500. A guest the previous year, she surprised officials with her extensive knowledge of cars. Guests of Eddie Rickenbacker, the Indianapolis Motor Speedway's president (and World War I ace), the Putnams flew on Eastern Air Lines (formerly Eastern Air Transport) from Newark. Reporters crowded in as Amelia and George held a joint press conference at the swanky Marott Hotel. They admitted they were unwinding on someone else's dime, and Amelia added congenially, "This wasn't a busman's holiday.... On the flight, I read a detective novel. It wasn't my job to fly."

Sports reporters covering the Indy 500 were intrigued by Amelia's "surprising femininity" in her green chiffon dress and gold sandals. This year's Indy 500 was the biggest, with 155,000 fans and thirty-three cars. Rickenbacker was patted on the back everywhere he went for inviting the most newsworthy woman flier to a position previously reserved for men.

But not every opportunity George came up with was as thrilling, and sometimes they were downright depressing. Amelia groaned when her "Simpkin" hatched another plan in collaboration with New Jersey–based parachute maker Stanley Switlik, a moneymaking scheme involving an attraction where adventurers could experience parachuting without boarding a plane, all made possible by a two-hundred-foot steel tower. They believed they could secure high-value contracts by associating Amelia's name with the venture as a test jumper.

She had more fun than anticipated, and each time Amelia tried out the setup in Prospertown, hidden deep in the woods at the edge of the New Jersey Pine Barrens, she couldn't contain her scream. One reporter likened her reaction to "a woman seeing a mouse." After one jump, Amelia exclaimed,

"Loads of fun!" While she doubted the public's interest in such an attraction, the parachute stunt earned significant media attention. An action-packed photo of Amelia landed the cover of the *Mid-Week Pictorial* and ran with a quote from her: "I have never had to use a parachute in my own flying, but I suppose the day comes for all of us."

On June 7, Amelia took a break from her busy schedule for a heartfelt hometown splash, returning to Atchison, Kansas, where she was warmly welcomed with a parade and celebration that recognized her as the town's heroine. But after a grueling slate of flights and lectures, Amelia felt the wear and tear. She poured her heart out in a letter to her mother, exclaiming, "My sinuses are kicking up, and I am tired of being beaten up by washings." Shortly after fulfilling her duties in Kansas, Amelia checked into the Cedars of Lebanon Hospital in Los Angeles for surgery on her nasal cavity. The recovery proved challenging, exacerbated by a back injury. In a letter to a friend, she revealed that a wartime infection in her nose and cheek had "redoubled its vigor."

After a week with Paul Mantz and his wife, Amelia headed to Oceanside in San Diego County. She stayed at the picturesque Rancho Monserate, owned by two of George's screenwriter friends, the married couple Louis D. Lighton and Hope Loring, who had adapted George's source material for the 1927 film *Wings*. The legendary Dorothy Parker and her bisexual husband, Alan Campbell, both highly paid script doctors for Paramount, joined the fray, so the evenings were amusing, to say the least.

The mood at Rancho Monserate lifted even more on July 6 when George shared delightful news: David's wife, Nilla, had given birth to a daughter named Binney. Beaming proudly, George announced to the press, "Amelia Earhart is now a grandmother." One can only imagine Amelia's amused reaction. It's fun to picture the group's outing on July 16 to the California Pacific International Exposition in San Diego, where Amelia finally experienced the roller-coaster ride that her father had once denied her; she later confessed that the roller coaster left her "terrified."

In the waning days of summer, Amelia and George talked about a permanent place in California and found themselves drawn to a Spanish colonial–style home at 10042 Valley Spring Lane, twelve miles west of downtown Los Angeles. They had been scouting properties in North Hollywood's upscale Toluca Lake neighborhood, where Paul Mantz and his wife lived, and where boldface names like Bing Crosby, W. C. Fields, and Dorothy Lamour also resided. But more importantly, it was near Burbank's airport, the Union Air Terminal, where Amelia's plane sat in Mantz's hangar. However, the hefty price tags made George hesitant. Yet after a long drive, their eyes caught the small, stylish home on Valley Spring Lane with a FOR SALE sign prominently displayed.

Their decision was quick, and thanks to George's negotiation skills, they soon finalized the purchase with the real estate agent. Plans were set to transform the house into a nine-room residence boasting four bedrooms, four and a half bathrooms, and a sundeck. This ambitious undertaking would involve drilling and blasting. Amelia, often touring the country and thus dubbed "California-based," typically left the construction oversight to her "junior" secretary, Margot DeCarie, who openly worshipped her.

George had his hands full too, especially with the upcoming launch of his Amelia Earhart Time Saver Stationery and Amelia Earhart Luggage. A press release by an assistant to George Palmer Putnam claimed that Amelia had "thought of" using canvas-covered plywood for her bags. However, such claims warranted skepticism. Notably, Mark Cross and Hartmann Luggage already offered similar aviation-themed Irish linen luggage, frequently advertised in *The Sportsman Pilot*, a magazine the couple revered. Amelia might have had a hand in designing the "weekender bag," an ingenious creation meant to hold cosmetics, clothes, underwear, and toiletries for short trips. With such bags, women no longer depended on trunks or men to carry said trunks, allowing them greater mobility.

While awaiting the completion of their dream house, George returned east, and Amelia temporarily settled into an apartment on Hollywood Way, a block from Warner Bros. Studios. The unsightly brick building that housed her apartment was also temporarily home to Terry Minor, the girlfriend of the married Paul Mantz, who came over often when Terry cooked. Amelia frequently joined them, Terry remembered, as she had no interest in homemaking. Terry could still picture her soft-spoken friend, who would sunbathe nude on her secluded balcony until dinner was ready. Their gatherings typically took place in either Terry's or Amelia's apartment. When George was in town, he occasionally joined them in private meals, and Terry found his demeanor off-putting. Unlike Amelia, George needed to be seen while in town and would insist on taking Amelia to dine at places like Los Angeles's gossip-mill darling Brown Derby. Amelia and George would sit with stars like Marlene Dietrich, the sultry-voiced new sensation from the German talkie *The Blue Angel*. (Paramount had recently convinced Dietrich to come to America for an English-speaking role, and George had picked her up at the docks.)

In the summer of 1935, Amelia endorsed Franklin D. Roosevelt, who affectionately christened her "the Little Lady." To continue her campaigning, she demanded Gene Vidal's reappointment to the Bureau of Air Commerce, a position he lost due to a minor scandal. Roosevelt, amused by Amelia's spirited and angry appeal, reinstated Vidal, which was no small political feat.

Amelia and Vidal's relationship was an intricate one and, though often mischaracterized as a secret, passionate affair, was far from it. Since their initial meeting in 1930 at Maddux's airline, TAT, they had established a deep bond rooted in their mutual passion for aviation. They also had a shared understanding of their partners' emotional volatility. If there was any dalliance, it would have occurred while Amelia was unattached. Most insiders, except Vidal's inventive son Gore Vidal (who knew Amelia before puberty), suggest she was relegated to friendship and was never his lover after she married.

The precocious Gore Vidal, who would become a luminary novelist and essayist, increasingly romanticized his father's relationship with Amelia over the years. But his father never claimed Amelia as a lover, and in a confidential 1958 letter, Gore portrayed the relationship as fundamentally platonic. He conveyed his father's description of Amelia as too tomboyish for romantic interest, yet he also suggested that Amelia harbored unrequited love for his father, which his father reciprocated only platonically. Over time, Gore's recollections grew more embellished. He even claimed that his sister had discovered a hairbrush holding Amelia's hairs, adding a personal and poignant detail to the narrative. It's essential to approach these progressively colorful accounts with skepticism. Jay Parini, Gore's biographer and friend, observed that these embroidered stories were shaped by Gore's tumultuous relationship with his mother and his childhood longing for a different family dynamic. Aware of the compelling nature of his stories and their unverifiability, Gore tailored his later accounts to satisfy interviewers, crafting narratives that were as engaging as they were uncheckable. "As Gore aged," Parini said, "he began to craft more imaginative details—he gave interviewers what they wanted, knowing it made terrific copy and that no one could fact-check him."

Amelia's nonstop touring continued, with George arranging her engagements. She identified as a flier, photographer, and poet, intentionally leaving out "fashion designer" from her self-portrayal. Her enigmatic airs attracted large crowds to her events. Gore, commenting on the public's enduring fascination with Amelia, provided a more credible account, noting that the "circus" surrounding her was persistent—a fact that can be verified.

In August, while in DC with National Airways cofounder Samuel Solomon, Amelia was blindsided by devastating news she first overheard in a Capitol Building elevator: Wiley Post and Will Rogers, both dear friends, had perished in a plane crash in Alaska. She had dined with Post, a professional idol of hers and the first civilian to complete a round-the-world flight by a fixed-wing aircraft, just a week before he departed north with Rogers, a humorist who was gathering material for an article.

Reeling from the loss, Amelia couldn't hide from the public eye. During emotionally charged talks in Cleveland and Pittsburgh, she tearfully recounted her loss. The tragedy forced her to reevaluate her and George's nascent plans for a daring around-the-world stunt flight. Post's fatal gaffe—overloading the aircraft with extra fuel for a nonstop long-distance attempt, at the expense of safety checks and emergency gear—was a harsh lesson. Determined to avoid the same fate, she knew she needed a safer, more reliable plane. But the looming question remained: How could she possibly afford it?

On August 26, Amelia announced her intention to take a break and focus on "being a person right now." She'd paused, she claimed, to reflect on life's meaning and the joy of discovery and living. However, this rest period was short-lived. Four days later, she became the first flier to take off in the Bendix Trophy, a transcontinental race that was part of the National Air Races, at 2:52 a.m. Unfortunately, the race resulted in the death of fellow competitor Cecil Allen, leaving Amelia shaken.

Entering the race for fun, Amelia and copilot Mantz faced an unexpected outcome: they finished last, mainly due to their aircraft's slower speed. George learned of this through a telegram. In the aftermath, Amelia visited Broadway's Music Box Theatre for an inside look at the 1935 production of *Ceiling Zero*, an aviation-themed play set at a fictional airport where weather conditions often create "ceiling zero" situations—scenarios where visibility and the ceiling (the lowest altitude where clouds cloak more than half of the sky) are severely limited, making flying highly dangerous.

Amelia (or a ghostwriter) later wrote a review for *Stage* magazine. Though her writing felt stiff, she offered a positive critique of the work, drawing parallels between the play's fog-bound challenges and her real-life experiences navigating hazardous "ceiling zero" conditions.

George made sure Amelia secured a lucrative consulting role for Howard Hawks's Warner Bros. film adaptation of *Ceiling Zero*. Amelia taught navigation and parachute jumping to her students, including June Travis, a voluptuous green-eyed actress who played an aviatrix. At a ball game, Travis, the daughter of White Sox vice president Harry Grabiner, had been scouted and instructed to hide her Jewish heritage by changing her name. She and Amelia posed for several press photos to capture the fun they had working together.

Amelia was also thinking ahead to her retirement from flying, acknowledging to her husband that she couldn't do it forever. At this point, George and Amelia decided to establish the Earhart–Mantz Flying School in California.

She informed George that a safer plane was essential for her ambitions, whether they had to do with flying itself or her new flying school. Look what had happened to Post after scrimping on a plane.

On November 6, Amelia Earhart touched down in West Lafayette, Indiana, prepared to take on her new role as Purdue University's "consultant on careers for women." With a salary of $2,000 a year—a respectable sum during the Great Depression—she was ready to inspire and guide the university's female students toward their future careers. Meanwhile, George was also immersed in his own endeavors. Not five days later, as Amelia spoke with small groups of young women about careers for the mechanically minded among them, George met with Purdue's Dr. Elliott over dinner in Washington, DC, discreetly presenting a typed proposal for the confidential "Amelia Earhart Project." For Amelia to truly soar, Purdue's further financial aid was essential. Their celebrated career counselor now needed a two-motor plane, crucial for overwater flights, which her current aircraft wasn't really equipped for.

The memo, expertly crafted with Mantz's input, detailed Amelia's plan to conduct "laboratory tests" for educational purposes and advance her pioneering flights. The proposal assured Purdue a share in sponsored flights' glories and net profits if it invested $40,000 in an unnamed, yet-to-be-secured two-motor plane. However, the "laboratory tests" were merely a facade: George was promoting an unidentified plane for her global flights, but he had already received a quote of $36,089.70 for a possible Lockheed Model 10-E Electra. But Dr. Elliott didn't need to know that, did he? Mantz, instrumental in sourcing the plane, had agreed to oversee its customization should George secure the necessary funding.

Though startled by the bold request, Dr. Elliott, after a moment of contemplation, promised to discuss it with his associates.

Settling down for the time being in West Lafayette, Amelia kept the college town buzzing, her choice to walk around in slacks causing a stir among some of the more traditional "ladies" in her mix. She was occasionally spotted at the local drugstore, hamburger in hand, cigarette dangling from her lips. Staff at the esteemed university found itself sharply divided over Amelia's presence: some male critics belittled her for lacking a college degree, dismissing her as a gimmick, a celebrity counselor, but female faculty, amazed that their heroine was on campus, pushed back on the chauvinism. Amelia's revamped schedule was packed with sessions on demystifying aviation paraphernalia and engagements for more intimate off-campus talks. Many evenings were spent in South Hall, where she sat on the floor in deep conversation with a gaggle of female students.

Helen Schleman, dean of women at Purdue, later described Amelia as a tall, poised figure, effortlessly exuding grace in sleek slacks or an elegant dinner dress: "There was dignity with complete casualness and informality about her. I have never known how any woman could manage a windblown, apparently unarranged hair styling yet never appear untidy or disarranged, but Amelia could and did."

Among those captivated by her presence was Ruth Grimm, a twenty-one-year-old senior majoring in clothing design. When Grimm shared her field of study with the aviator, Amelia's eyes lit up with enthusiasm. "Design isn't just about clothes," Amelia said. "It's a thrilling world where even a can of sardines can spark creativity." Intrigued, Grimm's father, an Indianapolis businessman, called Amelia to discuss her insights. He praised her wisdom, and their conversations steered Grimm toward a new ambition. By 1943, Grimm had earned her wings and later became a lieutenant in World War II, serving with the Women Airforce Service Pilots (WASP) under the direction of Amelia's old friend Jackie Cochran.

Amelia's influence during her stays on campus rippled through the student body, becoming part of the school's folklore. One memorable incident occurred in the dining room, where the dean caught two girls with their elbows on the table. When reprimanded, one girl defiantly retorted, "Amelia Earhart puts her elbows on the table!" The dean, unfazed, replied, "Yes, but Amelia Earhart's flown two oceans."

After her inaugural stint as a counselor at Purdue, Amelia resumed her tour, arriving in Boston and Medford on December 15. This allowed for precious time with Muriel's children, her four-year-old niece, Amy, and nephew, David. (In a 2022 interview, Amy faintly recalled her aunt whisking her and her brother away on a thrilling "fast" joyride. Her aged face lit up as she exclaimed, "Fast!")

In a small booklet printed just for family, Muriel recalled the visit, claiming Amelia said, "I shall leave you with my mind at ease if you and Albert can get a slightly larger place and be willing to have our mother live with you if she wants to leave California. She seems happy sharing the apartment with (feminist) Benigna Green, but now that Dad has died, she has nothing to keep her in California. I know she loves your youngsters very much and she might like to feel she belonged, as she did when David was a baby. My own plans when I return are uncertain, to say the least. I may be working with an airline here or internationally provided that fanatic Hitler doesn't make Europe into an armed camp, in spite of Britain's attempt at appeasement."

Amy's aunt Amelia was briefly back in New York to be honored by one of the oldest literary clubs, the Lotos Club, on December 22, 1935. An outspoken ally who often stumped for Democrats, she was most disturbed to be introduced by a Republican woman who attacked Eleanor Roosevelt and the New Deal.

Closing another eventful year, Amelia and George flew via Eastern Air Lines to Hobe Sound, near Palm Beach, Florida, for a Christmas retreat. This secluded spot was the winter residence of Charles Frances Coe, a prominent sportswriter and Lotos Club president whom Amelia had encountered at the Indy 500.

During casual interviews, Amelia shifted the tone to a severe critique of Florida's outdated and sexist laws. Was it correct that grown women could not sue in court without the consent of their husbands? And that a married woman could not control her own property? She expressed her Christmas wish for gender equality in legal matters.

At an Orlando party, under the guise of masked revelers, Amelia and George toasted the New Year at midnight with a kiss. Regardless of rumors, the couple always united for the holidays, and as the clock struck twelve, they looked forward to yet another remarkable year filled with extraordinary adventures and more of George's shrewd promotion.

Fifteen

MORNING BECOMES ELECTRA

Amelia Earhart started 1936 off earning her keep. On a brisk mid-January afternoon, she made her way to the Andrew Johnson Hotel in Knoxville—once the tallest building in East Tennessee. The hotel staff, accustomed to the mundane, were simultaneously caught off guard and thrilled as they watched her step out of her car alone. Amelia, driving herself, had arrived without notice in a tailored light-brown suit accented with an orange-and-brown silk scarf tied around her neck. A world away from big-city glitz, her unexpected appearance at this sleepy local landmark was nothing short of astonishing. To the awestruck staff, familiar with her exploits, she seemed to have materialized out of thin air, a real-life Mary Poppins.

The news of her arrival spread quickly, and as she was dining in her room, immersed in preparations for her speech, an unexpected knock from an eager reporter broke her meditation. Reluctant to decline and conscious of the potential negative press, Amelia engaged with the reporter, simultaneously dining and addressing a barrage of questions. In response to a question about fear, she proudly replied, "Never!" In her opinion, the air was much safer than the ground. However, she nonchalantly added that a plane crash wouldn't be too dreadful. "Who wants to be eighty and have hardened arteries?"

That evening, before her typical crowd of hundreds—fans and the simply curious alike—she mentioned she was en route to meet her husband for a brief escapade in Bowling Green, Kansas, and then they would drive back to their Hollywood home together. She was never afraid to go alone and often picked up hitchhikers for company. "Perhaps one day I will need a ride!" The audience laughed long and hard, clearly delighted by her seemingly joyful married life.

Despite enduring numerous near-death scares and even closed-door potshots at each other, Amelia and George's marriage had reached a stable plateau. Together, they were dedicated to keeping their dreams alive and the money flowing. Currently, Amelia harbored a secret wish to embark on a leisurely round-the-globe flight to see more of the world, and she desired a powerful plane for the journey. "Wiley would still be alive if he had a more suitable plane," she confided to George over the phone, after updating him on her post-lecture discussions with Purdue.

George was keen to preserve their marriage, which also augmented his income, and knew that aiding her in these death-defying dreams would only bring more money in. But for new opportunities to arise, Amelia couldn't afford to fade from the news and become—gah!—irrelevant. One of his tactics to prevent this involved placing cozier stories that slipped in her achievements, still affirming her place as the Queen of Aviation.

Janet Mabie of *The Christian Science Monitor* was George's preferred writer for more intimate and detailed stories designed to keep Amelia's fans emotionally connected. Having worked hard to secure exclusive access to Amelia for plane rides since 1928, Mabie was a known and trusted ally, and while she harbored no fondness for George, whom she called a "boar" in a private letter, she never risked deriding him in her published work, and she consistently depicted Amelia with respect and elegance.

Thanks to another persuasive phone call from George, she had once again nabbed an exclusive story, this one about a short winter walk the couple had taken from their hotel suite to the Arden Galleries on Park Avenue, where he'd surprised his wife by presenting her with a firesafe wooden chest from an exhibit that included sculptures by Paul Manship, the artist behind *Prometheus* at Rockefeller Center. George claimed it had been his grand idea to commission the fine artisans Albert Wood and Five Sons of Port Washington out on Long Island to carve the chest.

In reality, Albert Wood had initiated contact after reading about the fire in Rye and the painful loss of Amelia's "peppers." Before even speaking with the flier's husband, Wood had drawn up a design for a hope chest and contacted George, suggesting it might make a much-appreciated gift. Seeing the potential for publicity, George loved the idea, and, possibly at no cost in exchange for publicity, Wood's family firm soon made a custom version, sandpapered by hand to a smooth finish. Albert's son, Gard, skillfully carved his father's designs in bas-relief, illustrating the course of Amelia's three most renowned flights on the front and sides. To honor her 1932 solo transatlantic flight, two more symbols adorned the front, depicting a codfish and shamrock. Her Honolulu–Oakland flight in 1935 and her Mexico City–Newark flight in 1935 were represented on the left and right ends of the chest. The impressive finished product was then secretly delivered to the upmarket Arden Galleries in Manhattan so that George could surprise his wife.

In Mabie's gushing exclusive report, when the couple stood before the intricately carved chest, the proud husband joked matter-of-factly to the recipient: "There, how do you like that?" And his startled wife oohed over the fine work and was touched when she read: "Trophy chest for Amelia Earhart, designed and executed on commission for George Palmer Putnam by Albert Wood and Five Sons 1935." Amelia later confirmed to Mabie that she had no prior knowledge of the chest's creation. Indeed, it was a genuine surprise! (This part, at least, was not made up.) George also told Mabie that he was shipping the grand chest to California, his wife's new West Coast base, to ensure that any surviving and future keepsakes would last in any future fire.

Although some of Mabie's stories about Amelia, as provided by George, were considered overly sentimental by her editor, this "lifestyle" story touched the national readership of *The Christian Science Monitor*. While her article may have faded into obscurity, that inspired treasure chest endured the years and can be found in the Smithsonian's National Air and Space Museum.

In February 1936, alongside these grand gestures and carefully crafted appearances, other news stories captured the public's attention, offering a vivid snapshot of the era. Out in Ames, Iowa, a pair of parakeets named Amelia Earhart and George Putnam were causing quite a stir. Their peaceful coexistence was hilariously disrupted by a new parakeet named Al, whose shameless flirtations with Amelia left George in a sulk. It seemed that even parakeets couldn't escape the drama of love triangles, a whimsical reflection of the aviator's own tumultuous life.

On February 12, 1936, Hollywood buzzed with the premiere of Charlie Chaplin's *Modern Times* at Grauman's Chinese Theatre. The event drew a constellation of stars, including Douglas Fairbanks, Mary Pickford, Fred Astaire, Norma Shearer, and Helen Kane. Despite the rain, the glamorous evening was a spectacle of glistening umbrellas and gold paper programs. Among the distinguished guests were Amelia Earhart and George Palmer Putnam, who stood side by side, enjoying the evening's allure. Their presence at such high-profile events was a strategic move by George to maintain Amelia's public image amid the personal turbulence they were navigating. Nothing says "everything is fine" like rubbing elbows with Tinseltown's elite while your namesake parakeets steal headlines in the Midwest.

Yet despite these public displays of unity, George was acutely aware of the potential scandal brewing with Myrtle Mantz's impending divorce suit, an action that put Amelia at risk of being falsely implicated and her name at risk of being tarnished. To counter this, George may have strategically released even more flattering news stories about himself and Amelia, emphasizing their happy marriage. Having dined with Terry Minor many times in her apartment on Hollywood Way, both George and Amelia were well aware of Paul Mantz's secret affair with this other woman, the pretty thirty-four-year-old widow of the late stunt pilot Roy Minor, who had also been Paul's close friend. Though married, Paul had always flirted with Terry and wasted no time in passionately wooing her after Roy's death from an appendectomy gone wrong in 1935.

Amelia found herself entangled in the divorce case, as Myrtle had accused her of being the "other woman" involved with Paul. This accusation put Amelia in the uncomfortable position of having to sit through legal proceedings without publicly acknowledging her involvement or lack thereof. Myrtle's suspicions, though founded on the reality of her husband's infidelity, were misdirected at Amelia.

To get ahead of what would surely be horrific national headlines, George, without a secretary, furiously punched out a candid and unhinged letter to Dr. Elliott at Purdue. The poorly typed letter overflowed with typos and unrestrained anger, exposing George's intense need for control and his fiery temper.

> Elliott—
>
> This is a confidential note for you alone. There is a foolish woman out here who is suing her husband for divorce. The husband is Paul Mantz, our old friend and business associate and AE's technical advisor on her Pacific and Mexican flights.
>
> In the last year Mrs. Mantz has become insanely jealous of AE. I use the word insanely advisedly because they actually think she is borderline. Needless to say, there is of course not a mointilla [sic] of justice in any charges which she may make against AE, but unfortunately, she is in the hands of a publicity-seeking lawyer so that there is a chance some effort will be made to drag AE's name into the proceedings. With the circumstances there's always a chance of some dirty charges being made, no matter how baseless. That's the penalty of having a "front page name"... Frankly, there is nothing I would like more than to wring the slanderous lady's neck.

The coverage was just as bad as George had feared, and the salacious details were too irresistible for papers to hold back.

Mrs. Harriette Balsley, wife of Captain Clyde Balsley, a close friend of the Mantz couple, testified that Myrtle had confided in her about Amelia: "I know I am insanely jealous and upset, but I believe if Miss Earhart would take her clothes and leave our house, we would have a much better chance of getting along."

In court, Paul Mantz calmly explained that when Amelia stayed at their house—even when Myrtle was away—she paid her own way and was never alone with him. The sordid whispers of scandal, however, soon lost their heat, fading from public view to George's profound relief. For all his mastery of publicity, even he had no appetite for the kind of headlines that came with accusations of adultery.

Marguerite Martyn was another woman reporter who, like Janet Mabie, could always be counted on to keep things light and frothy. Amelia agreed to yet another new piece, which again positioned herself as nothing less than a modern happy wife: "I can't complain of any lack of cooperation on his part. We have just bought a little house in California. Mr. Putnam is looking forward as delightedly as I am to spend the summer remodeling it and running it alone when I am not there to do my part. His business is in motion pictures now. My headquarters remain in New York, and we'll keep an apartment there, but we can commute back and forth. We do it now, leaving New York at 3:30 in the afternoon and reaching Los Angeles at 7:30 the next morning. Soon, we'll be doing it in eight hours."

The photographer for the story piped up to say he was amazed that, up close, she had not become the least bit masculine from all her work in aviation. "Why should I?" she answered with what was said to be a rippling, birdlike laugh. She needed endurance, not muscle, to steer a plane. Flying, she added, took mental alertness, a good deal of technical knowledge and study, and keeping up with scientific developments. "I have one endowment for flying, a great love of physics, chemistry, and the mechanics of things. I have always been laboratory-minded. My early training was with being a doctor, you know."

George was usually adept at shaping Amelia's public persona with carefully curated stories, but when his grip loosened, rawer, less polished aspects of their relationship emerged. Around the time of the Mantz divorce trial, a notable example occurred. On April 18, a syndicated article titled "Amelia

Earhart and Her Husband Tell Why Their Marriage Clicks" provided a breezy account of their partnership, as needed during the blitz of lurid claims that Amelia was a wanton woman. However, while the reporter was working the story, she missed her interview subjects in the hotel lobby and hurried to their car, her photographer in tow, upon being alerted to their whereabouts by a staff member. George thundered, "Where were you? Mrs. Putnam is in the car! I doubt that she will give you an interview!" As his anger echoed down the street, Amelia blanched and emerged from the car, then graciously agreed to an impromptu interview. The reporter left the incident with contrasting views of Amelia and George: admiration for Amelia's calm demeanor and disapproval of George's combative stance. When she rushed to file her copy, this take was woven in among the niceties and further hinted at in the article's chosen photograph: George with a furrowed brow—sweet payback for being treated so poorly by him.

George's frequent outbursts were embarrassing—to all—and even gave Amelia pause, but unlike others, she had sound reasons for sticking with him through his strong-tempered bouts, especially as evidenced that very month when the newly launched Purdue Research Foundation announced that it would establish the Amelia Earhart Fund for Aeronautical Research, which contributed $50,000 toward the purchase of the Purdue Flying Laboratory. Additional funds came from wealthy alumni David E. Ross and Josiah K. Lilly, along with industrialist Vincent Bendix, bringing the total to $80,000—an extraordinary sum in 1936, equivalent to nearly $2 million today.

George's dogged negotiations had continued since his November meeting in DC. George and Amelia worked the room, even attending a black-tie Purdue fundraising gala as a team. Enabled by Purdue, George purchased a shiny, sleek twin-engine Lockheed Model 10-E Electra, a fast and reliable aircraft with a top altitude of twenty-seven thousand feet. Smaller contributions followed, and to help finance the Electra, Amelia sold her valuable stock in National Airways—stock that would one day be worth a small fortune, as the tiny airline eventually became the heavy hitter Northeast Airlines, which merged with Delta in 1972.

A former Lockheed executive present on the day of the sale had a story that veered sharply from Purdue's polished corporate narrative. According to him, George Palmer Putnam balked at the cost and gave a "great dissertation" on why he deserved a bargain on an Electra. The executive painted a vivid picture of how George declared that Amelia would elevate the entire field of aviation with this plane, emphasizing it was certainly not a moneymaking venture. George's impassioned plea made it sound like they were practically doing Lockheed a favor. However, Lockheed's top executive, the shrewd Robert Gross, wasn't buying it for a second. Gross had seen a few sales pitches in his time, and he could smell a self-serving scheme from a mile away. He guessed that Amelia and George had grand plans for the plane that had nothing to do with pushing the boundaries of aviation and everything to do with a glamorous world tour. After George had left the grounds, Gross reportedly turned to his staff and said, "Trust me, first they'll take it to Purdue, then they'll bring it back and ask for all sorts of upgrades, like long-range tanks and stuff."

Gross's skepticism was spot on. What George presented as an altruistic venture was, in reality, all about making a splash and, quite likely, a fair bit of money for the married couple. They hesitated to go along for this sort of ride.

In a private conversation, Amelia joked to her friends that her husband had found the "tree on which expensive airplanes grow." After the grand news of her plane purchase, Amelia, for her part, agreed to another two-year contract with Purdue as a teaching consultant. Of course, that was fine! There was a lot of excitement for both parties.

Frequently used in civil aviation by 1936, a Lockheed 10 could carry ten passengers and two pilots, and the 10-E was their newest model. Her custom-built aircraft was a one-off, with a rectangular tailpiece, orange scalloped patterns on the wings, and a horizontal stabilizer. Such adjustments would meet global safety standards for planes flying transatlantic routes, and it was thought that the orange would make it easier to find downed aircraft. By the time it was announced, it was already tinkered with inside Paul Mantz's hangars at Union Air Terminal, adjacent to Lockheed's factory. A Sperry autopilot and blind-flying instruments were among the special devices installed on Amelia's "Flying Laboratory," a hokey term George poached from Charles Lindbergh and the late Wiley Post.

Unbeknownst to many, Amelia's true ambition for the aircraft, as revealed in numerous discussions with George, was to turn it into a lucrative venture by flying it around the world—a plan potent enough to attract substantial media rights and, surely to George's mind, a bestselling book. Any official announcement of such grandiose plans was to be reserved for a formal press release when and if these plans materialized.

On her thirty-ninth birthday—July 24, 1936—Amelia Mary Earhart was formally presented with the seven-ton Electra at Burbank's Union Air Terminal. The plane's design dazzled all who saw it, with black, orange, and red pinstripes streaking across its wings and tail. The blue-gray metal sides shimmered in the light, engineered for enhanced visibility in jungle haze and early mornings. Gazing at the Electra, Amelia exclaimed, "I could write poetry about this plane!" More than just an aircraft, the Electra—named for a long-lost star—embodied Purdue's boldest statement of belief in a woman still doubted by many.

Shortly after, Bendix announced its sponsorship of various radio equipment to ensure Amelia's safety and that of any future navigators she might choose. As Gross had shrewdly predicted, the aircraft was due for yet another round of modifications. This time, the passenger windows were to be replaced with sleek aluminum panels, leaving only the navigator's windows clear. This wasn't just for aesthetics; it was a strategic move to reduce weight and enhance structural integrity, making room for more crucial additions—like extra gas tanks. With these modifications, the Electra's fuel capacity soared to twelve hundred gallons, extending its range to approximately twenty-seven hundred miles. The passenger seats were also removed, transforming the aircraft's interior into a more functional space. The real showstoppers, though, were the two Pratt & Whitney engines, each packing a hefty six hundred horsepower, allowing the Electra to cruise comfortably at speeds up to 205 miles per hour. It was a transformation befitting the grand ambitions of its pilot.

less, she hoped to earn something to pay some expenses. "But it's fun to be in the race."

Teamed with her friend Helen Richey, she came in fifth. Much more exciting was that two women, Louise Thaden and Blanche Noyes, came in first, beating out men in the second coed race. Amelia was close to both ladies and was thrilled about her friends' victory, even though she hadn't placed.

Later that fall, after securing her mother a short, affordable cruise abroad and getting one of her Germantown cousins to keep a relative's eye on her, Amelia had written her strict instructions that shed further light on her politics: "Please don't down the Roosevelt administration. It's all right to be reactionary inside, but it is out of step with the times to sound off about the chosen people who have inherited or grabbed the earth. You must think of me when you converse, and I believe the experiments carried on today point the way to a new social order when governments will be the voice of the proletariat far more than democracy ever can be."

"My parents and grandparents were very straightforward Republicans," Amelia's niece, Amy Kleppner, recalled at ninety-one in 2022 on her New England porch. "They always voted that way. It was nearly impossible to imagine anything that would have changed their minds. Amelia voted for the Democratic Party when she was married, even if her husband supported Republican candidates."

The world seemed to be at a tipping point. The drama unfolding within the British monarchy in December 1936—Edward VIII's shocking abdication for the love of an American divorcée, Wallis Simpson—reflected the volatility and uncertainty of the era. Edward's departure from royal duty marked a societal upheaval, as he was succeeded by George VI, who now had to navigate a throne during an identity crisis.

Amelia likely attended a private screening or perhaps a Hollywood premiere of *Crack-Up*, a Twentieth Century-Fox spy drama that marked another kind of departure the month of her erstwhile dance partner's abdication.

This transatlantic thriller starred Peter Lorre as the cunning brain behind an international spy ring targeting the top-secret plans of the Wild Goose Flying Laboratory—of course inspired by Amelia Earhart's remarkable Electra. With attention to detail, Paul Mantz, her trusted technical adviser, had helped recreate an aircraft that was nearly a carbon copy of her prized possession. The set designers captured the essence of the craft with astonishing accuracy, resulting in one-third of the film's scenes being set inside the cockpit. The Wild Goose Flying Laboratory met its tragic fate, and the star-crossed occupants sank into the unforgiving ocean abyss as they locked eyes in the cockpit. One can only wonder if Amelia, popcorn in hand, contemplated the perils and excitement of her profession and her love for those closest to her at that moment.

Sixteen

DEAD RECKONING

On a cold January day in 1937, twenty-six-year-old explorer Henry Bradford Washburn, director of Harvard's Institute of Geographical Exploration, received an unexpected invitation. It came from George Palmer Putnam, his former publisher and the husband of Amelia Earhart. Putnam invited Washburn to a private dinner at their estate in Rye, New York. Though Washburn had never met Earhart, his connection to Putnam was well established—three of his books had been published under Putnam's imprint, jump-starting his career as both a writer and explorer. The chance to meet the famed aviator was irresistible. Washburn accepted, intrigued to uncover what the famous couple had in mind.

Though Washburn was twelve years Amelia's junior, his credentials as an explorer, mapper, educator, and licensed pilot were evident that evening. After a warm cocktail reception, George unveiled the detailed plans for Amelia's forthcoming global expedition. Acknowledging Washburn's expertise, he hinted at Washburn as a potential navigator for Amelia. "He was the one who suggested me for the role, given my extensive experience in northern exploration and my current role teaching field astronomy," Washburn later recalled.

Washburn's notable contributions to an expedition cosponsored by

National Geographic and Pan Am, capturing aerial images of Mount McKinley (now Denali), underscored his suitability for Amelia's ambitious twenty-nine-thousand-mile global journey. It wasn't luck! His reputation for precision and scientific methods in exploration, coupled with the potential for increased publicity by using a former Putnam boy explorer, made him an ideal match for the project.

Washburn's skills were a stark contrast to Amelia's renowned self-confidence, at times frustrating but so often crucial for forging new paths. However, overconfidence comes with its own risks in the realm of exploration.

"I thought the idea was stupid to begin with," Washburn later said. "Not flying around the world, but flying around the world in a Lockheed Electra without a copilot. If she got sick on one of the legs, the copilot could hold the controls . . . while the pilot vomits. . . . So I thought it was a crazy idea."

After dinner, Amelia eagerly traced her route on a world map, highlighting how the difficult westward leg from Hawaii to Lae, on the island of New Guinea, necessitated a refueling stop at Howland Island, an uninhabited island covering a single square mile and located about seventeen hundred miles from Hawaii. Seizing the moment, Washburn aired his apprehensions about landing on such a remote speck of land. When queried about her navigational plan, Amelia responded, "We are going to do it by dead reckoning"—a method where the pilot calculates position based on estimated speed, time, and direction from a known location. Washburn, taken aback, exclaimed, "Holy smokes!" They were contemplating a voyage of under two thousand miles between Hawaii and Howland, with little room for navigational error.

Washburn saw their plan as delusional, with potentially fatal consequences. "I didn't feel she had anywhere near adequate equipment and preparation for a long overseas hop to Howland Island. I strongly urged her and her husband to send powerful radio equipment with Amelia." Meanwhile, Amelia remained supremely confident that all of this wouldn't be needed and she would hit the island right on the nose. "GP was just as confident in Amelia and her judgment—and this made a very difficult combination to argue with," he later reflected, still shocked decades after the evening's uncomfortable discussion.

Maintaining his composure, Washburn emphasized that while a complex radio setup was optional, some features were not. From his seasoned perspective, a continuous automatic signal or a locking mechanism for Amelia's RDF (radio direction finder) within a reasonable range was non-negotiable. An RDF, after all, helps pilots determine their position by receiving radio signals from known locations—a crucial tool when you're navigating over thousands of miles of empty ocean with nothing but your wits and a prayer. While Amelia and George pored over maps, George casually shrugged off Washburn's concerns with a dismissive wave. "All that effort," he quipped, "and we might miss the Christmas book release."

Washburn withdrew to one of the many guest rooms, perhaps the one with the colorfully painted underwater scene. By morning, he quickly departed, not realizing it would be his last encounter with them. As with others who would also be deemed obstacles, he'd just been junked from their inner sanctum.

"I've wanted to do this flight for a long time," Amelia said to the press around this same time. "I've worked hard and deserve one fling during my lifetime." But this was hardly a fling. Amelia and George, displaying devil-may-care confidence, seemed to disregard the detailed planning and risk assessments that Washburn considered vital.

After the gravity of Washburn's warnings fell on deaf ears, he was never formally offered the navigator position. Instead, Harry Manning, a figure from Amelia's past, was chosen for the coveted role. Manning's fame had grown since their flirtation during Amelia's transatlantic flight in 1928, further enhanced by a heroic sea rescue, and he'd scored his own Lucky Strike cigarette ads. A New York State Nautical School graduate with a passion for flying since 1930, Manning held expertise in radio operation and marine navigation. Over breakfasts and lounging sessions through the years, Amelia and Manning had often delved into discussions about celestial navigation, planting the seed for Manning's deep-seated desire to join

Amelia on a monumental flight. A decade later, Manning, taking leave from his captaincy at the United States Lines, was poised to navigate for Amelia up to Darwin, after which Amelia would continue alone.

On February 12, at New York's Barclay Hotel, Amelia made a significant announcement about the new Electra airplane. This location was strategically chosen for its substantial press presence, and it was at this event that Amelia unveiled her choice of navigator for the ambitious round-the-world trip: Harry Manning.

She emphasized Manning's critical skills, notably his proficiency in Morse code and telegraphy, which were essential for the over-ocean segments of the flight, on a route designed to hug the equator closely. Overcast conditions at sea could impede traditional celestial navigation, making Manning's expertise in radio communications pivotal. His plan involved using the radio to interact with ships, requesting their assistance in determining the Electra's position through their onboard radio compasses. This strategy would allow him to triangulate the aircraft's location accurately and track their progress according to the planned schedule.

A week after this conference, while on a test flight in the Electra from Cleveland to Burbank, Amelia, Manning, and the mechanic, Bo McNeeley, were grounded by a dust storm in Blackwell, Oklahoma. They had to stay overnight at the Larkin Hotel, a central hub in a region plagued by the Dust Bowl and economic hardships.

George, angered that he had not seen enough press coverage for the formal announcement, decided to best utilize his time and promptly cooked up some press. The first thing he did as part of his cringeworthy plan was borrow a Terraplane sedan from a local dealer, reminding the dealer of Amelia's role as the spokesperson for Terraplane. (This meant that Amelia never had to pay when George was around.) Then, with Amelia behind the wheel for a short drive to nearby Ponca City for lunch, he urged her to floor it. Why waste time? But soon they were unexpectedly stopped by a motorcycle officer. Amelia, the chronic speed freak, once again tried to charm her way out of the situation, noting the difficulty of slowing down after hitting high speeds. Manning also tried to explain that they were ticketing Amelia Earhart, but the officer was unmoved and insisted on taking the matter to court.

At the courthouse, Amelia requested that the hearing be held at 2:00 p.m. instead of the usual five o'clock because she was in a rush to keep on the flight home. She admitted to Judge Roy W. Cox that she was speeding, albeit not dangerously, and pleaded ignorance of the restricted district. The city officials, including the mayor, feared they had embarrassed a national figure. Amelia pleaded guilty to speeding at fifty miles per hour in a twenty-mile zone and was fined $2.50, which she promptly paid.

George Palmer Putnam's garish laughter echoed throughout the courtroom. It had all been a setup! Jester George had sneaked to a telephone and gotten an officer, Hiram Ragan, involved in his prank to have her arrested for speeding at fifty miles per hour as she entered the city limits. And, once again, he found the situation more amusing than anyone else. He later claimed, albeit falsely, that Judge Cox had been in on the prank—another all-too-easy lie fabricated for the benefit of the press. In response to the embarrassing situation, town executives quickly presented Amelia with a ten-foot paper key to the city. That afternoon, Amelia was warmly greeted by a crowd of three thousand locals. She spent over an hour signing autographs, injecting humor into the situation by inquiring about Blackwell's population. The Electra took off at 7:25 a.m., leaving behind a quirky and memorable episode in their journey. George's antics, designed to garner national press coverage, were successful, even if controversial.

CITY IN A DITHER AS AMELIA EARHART ARRESTED, BUT HUBBY JUST HAVING HIS FUN

Yet the overall expedition was far from trivial. It demanded detailed planning and strong connections. Key among the figures linked to the flight was William T. Miller, superintendent of airways for the Bureau of Air Commerce. Brought into the project by Gene Vidal, Miller was an experienced pilot and a lieutenant commander in the US Navy Reserve, with extensive knowledge of the Pacific Islands. Convinced of Miller's capabilities, Vidal tasked him in 1935 with overseeing the first global flight expedition. Based in Washington, DC, Miller was responsible for the colonization of Jarvis, Howland, and Baker Islands. He managed this with the help of four Hawaiian high school boys, hired for three dollars per day. Under his guidance, the American flag was raised on these islands, marking their annexation, and a small runway was completed on Howland Island by December 6, 1936.

Amelia had the backing of not only Miller but also his superior, Vidal. Additionally, she received endorsement from Eleanor Roosevelt at the White House. Miller, committed to both Amelia's success and his own career, painstakingly coordinated the flight logistics.

With Miller arriving in the new base office at Oakland's airport on February 25, George, for now, was only the "official flight manager." After a bit too much input, Amelia's husband was then advised by his wife and Miller to concentrate on the fundraising and financial aspects of the expedition. Even though Amelia now smartly relied primarily on Miller for the technical and navigational aspects of the flight, when they dismissed George's opinions and talked down to him, the new team of Earhart and Miller openly irritated him.

In the final weeks before Amelia's flying start, a young woman, Vivian Maata, was swiftly enlisted as the aviator's local secretary. Although George paid her salary, Maata primarily worked under Miller's direction; she rapidly familiarized herself with the flight team and found Amelia to be even more attractive in person, bursting with quiet energy and natural goodwill. As she later remembered, much of her time was spent absorbed in studying maps and charts at Miller's workspace.

On March 4, just before Amelia flew the Electra from Burbank to Oakland, she arranged a meeting with her friend Vidal in Los Angeles. Vidal had recently resigned as the director of the Bureau of Air Commerce, and with a call or two from George, Amelia and Vidal were photographed examining an emergency signal box kite gifted to Amelia by her pilot friend

Jackie Cochran. The *Los Angeles Times*, after another tip by George's office, hinted that Vidal, now a private citizen on vacation after leaving government employment, might even join Amelia and her husband in a business venture, potentially relating to transatlantic flights. Although Vidal neither confirmed nor denied the speculation, he was in on the publicity game. Vidal's return to Washington brought further attention to Amelia's flight when he voiced his confidence in Amelia's capabilities and joked, "What's easy for Amelia might be awfully difficult for the rest of us," a fun quote that went straight into the papers.

By March 1937, aviation had taken off—quite literally. Companies like Pan Am were making commercial transoceanic flights almost as routine as taking the bus. Yet flying around the globe remained a daunting feat, a challenge that separated the merely brave from the truly bold.

In 1933, Wiley Post accomplished the remarkable by becoming the first person to fly solo around the world. This adventurous endeavor took him precisely seven days, eighteen hours, and forty-nine minutes, a significant improvement on his previous record of eight days, set back in 1931 with his Australian navigator, Harold Gatty. During his fifteen-thousand-mile odyssey, Post made pit stops in cities such as Berlin, Moscow, Irkutsk, and Fairbanks to rest and refuel—both himself and his trusty plane.

Other aviators also tackled the globe in their unique styles. Clyde Pangborn and Hugh Herndon Jr., known for making the first nonstop flight across the Pacific Ocean in 1931, approached their flights with a different kind of daring. In 1932, German aviators had joined the round-the-world party, flying a Dornier Wal seaplane to prove that even flying boats could make the journey.

But Amelia Earhart had grander plans. Her globe-circling flight would be both the longest yet attempted and the first by a woman. Her route was a mindboggling twenty-nine thousand miles along the equator, ambitiously charted to include a stop at the incredibly remote Howland Island. This was no mere stroll in the sky; it was, as her proud husband told reporters, the "hard way."

Amelia's flight was as much about personal ambition as it was about commercial potential. The risks were extraordinary—long stretches over open ocean, unpredictable weather, and the sheer isolation of some of her stops. Yet the rewards promised to be substantial, with sponsorships, marketing opportunities, and media attention all waiting in the wings. The proposed journey would start in Oakland, California, with the last leg from Natal, Brazil, potentially touching down in Miami or Mexico before ending back in Oakland.

Amelia and George saw this flight, if successful, as their ticket to financial security and a way to cement her status as the Queen of the Air. In an industry evolving at breakneck speed, this daring circumnavigation was intended to keep Amelia soaring high above the rest.

During her extended stay at Oakland's airport hotel before this flight, Amelia was deeply involved in planning the complex journey. Amelia became a charismatic figure among the Boeing School of Aeronautics students staying extendedly at the hotel. She often engaged them over breakfast, igniting spirited discussions, and allowed a student named Harkness Davenport to capture interior photos of the Electra with his new thirty-five-millimeter camera. However, these lighter moments were abruptly interrupted when George stormed through the lobby after arriving from Hollywood with the subtlety of a blaring sousaphone. Later, as an old man, Davenport recalled George's outrageous ultimatums: "He'd go screaming through the lobby—the great George Putnam—and it was 'Out of the way, boys.'"

George Palmer Putnam now claimed to all covering the flight that he had gotten a month's leave from a nameless "motion picture concern" to oversee his wife's flight, a gigantic endeavor. Amelia sat comfortably in a plush divan within her airport hotel room, her lively conversation revolving solely around aviation. She enthusiastically reiterated her purpose of traveling for "scientific endeavors." Any possibility of an unfortunate mishap that would send their land plane into the Pacific Ocean, leaving her and her navigator, Captain Harry Manning, stranded on a rubber raft with only an orange kite to signal distress, remained a strictly taboo topic. Eavesdropping, George promptly inserted himself into one interview, interjecting to explain that he had rejected the idea of an amphibious aircraft due to concerns regarding weight and speed. However, the truth was that George had dismissed Paul Mantz's first suggestion of a much safer Sikorsky S-43 "Baby Clipper" amphibian for practical reasons. An amphibian would have provided significantly enhanced safety, but George had nixed that plane because Amelia wanted to use whatever gifted plane she acquired as her everyday aircraft upon her return, and with an amphibian, she would have "nothing to show for it" in the end.

When now questioned in front of George about his feelings regarding her latest extreme flight, Amelia responded with a mischievous smile and stated, "Well, he knew exactly who I was when he married me. Nevertheless, I consider myself incredibly fortunate to have his support, because I could never accomplish all of this without him."

There was much infighting away from the "happy family" interviews offered to the press, especially between Manning and George, who held sharply differing views on the fifty-five hundred stamp covers that would be housed in the airplane's nose, later to be sold through Gimbel Brothers to support the flight. George Putnam proposed removing them to reduce weight for extra fuel, with a plan to authenticate them differently afterward. Manning, now nationally recognized for his 1929 sea rescue, valued his unblemished reputation, and the idea of misrepresenting the stamp covers to potential buyers went against his principles. He held his ground, unwilling to jeopardize his integrity.

A poorly typed confidential letter was sent by George to Amelia's round-the-world adviser, William T. Miller, on March 1 (again without the help of a secretary so that he could keep his biggest secrets close to his chest). The letter requested that close contact be quietly established with a Pan Am navigator on the Pacific route.

> *Perhaps we could induce him to run down here as my guest for a talk with Manning, or if that doesn't work out, we will send Manning up for a visit with you, and them. Strictly between us, there doubtless is much Manning can go over with tnem [sic] to advatnage [sic]. Naturally his experience is limited in a job like this—and they might be able to help. GPP*

By March 11, Paul Mantz had rearranged his schedule to become a full-time dedicated flight coach and technical adviser. By March 13, after that secret letter, a fellow named Fred Noonan joined the crew. Noonan appeared on the scene four days before Amelia's scheduled departure from Oakland for Honolulu, as only then had she agreed to secure a backup navigator for Manning.

Noonan, a seasoned, broad-shouldered navigator with blue eyes and a rugged face, had amassed a wealth of Pacific knowledge through years of maritime experience. Born on April 4, 1893, in Chicago, he ran away from home at fifteen in 1908, working on windjammers and steamships—three times around Cape Horn! He further honed his aviation skills with Pan Am's Clipper flights, spanning South America and the Pacific region. Noonan also served as an airport manager in Port-au-Prince, Haiti, and was a licensed pilot, although he held only a limited commercial pilot's license. Noonan's career was notable except for one issue—his struggle with alcoholism. He was a good navigator, perhaps Pan Am's best, but Pan Am wanted to keep its public image pristine—and here was a man visibly plastered on off-duty hours. Noonan, off-the-record sources reveal, was also a great dancer with a notoriously superior appetite for women, one that left his Pan Am peers either impressed or exhausted. "Everyone knew he liked to drink, and his boss always kept an eye on him," the wife of a Pan Am Clipper captain recalled in the 1980s.

"Fred Noonan has been helping us on the navigation end," Amelia announced in a press interview. "With Pan American, he has done much pioneer Pacific flying. Paul Mantz will be [the] relief pilot as far as Honolulu. That will cut down the fatigue factor for me. . . . Manning, by the way, will handle the radio. He is an operator qualified in code sending and receiving, which none of the rest of us are."

Post-flight, Noonan hoped Amelia's fame would help him overcome the career slump due to his checkered past, and he could use good press to help get his own navigation school off the ground. There is trustworthy evidence that Amelia was against his selection, even though she had agreed to having a backup navigator. Insiders, such as Amelia's personal photographer, Albert Bresnik, a very young but strikingly accomplished man who had a secret terrible crush on her, claimed that despite shared experiences, such as attending Chicago's public schools, Amelia disliked Noonan because of his drinking habits. Bresnik further explained, "She didn't want him to go along." But as Bresnik recalled, George pushed for the deal, as Noonan came cheap.

Bresnik's claim is supported by another vital insider: While the Electra crew were still in Oakland, the *Los Angeles Times*' aviation editor, James Bassett Jr., witnessed a tipsy Noonan after he had gotten smashed in his hotel room. Amelia made a significant admission "off the record" to Bassett that she didn't like Noonan, but George insisted he was the cheapest option because of his alcoholism. Noonan, said Bassett, had assured Amelia that he had conquered his demons, but even Vivian Maata, the short-term secretarial hire for Oakland, hardly a confidante of Amelia's, noticed that she "had her doubts."

George Putnam, uneasy as the mission neared its start, pulled Mantz aside with a quiet but urgent proposition. Could Mantz join Amelia on her global flight, just in case complications arose with the crew? It was a reasonable request, born of worry, but Mantz waved it off with a characteristic confidence. Amelia was more than capable, he assured George. Besides, Mantz had his own reasons for staying put: his growing aviation business demanded his attention, and so did his new fiancée, Terry Minor. Leaving for months at a stretch seemed less like an adventure and more like a disruption to the life he was building.

Mantz, firm at first, began to yield under George's unrelenting persistence. Reluctantly, he agreed to join Amelia on the first leg of her journey, accompanying her as far as Honolulu. George, eager to ease his own worries, sweetened the deal. Mantz would come along—on one condition. George would foot the bill for Terry to join them for the trip. With that arrangement sealed, Mantz packed his bags, his mind still half on the skies and half on the life he was leaving behind, if only briefly.

As part of the deal, Mantz orchestrated a brief private retreat at the Christian Holmes mansion, a secluded Hawaiian hideaway perfect for catching their breath. Amelia would rest there after her arrival in Hawaii, joined by Mantz, her two navigators, and Terry. Once Amelia and her crew departed to continue the journey, Mantz and his fiancée planned to linger, savoring a few stolen days of tropical quiet before returning to their own realities.

Before the Electra's imminent departure, Amelia had a poignant conversation with C. B. Allen, her now close friend from the *New York Herald Tribune*. She confided in him: "I want to make way for the new generation before I'm feeble too. . . . I think there's just one more good flight left in me, and I'm hoping this trip is it. . . . As far as I know, I've only got one obsession, a small, probably typical feminine fear of growing old, so I won't feel totally cheated if I don't return." Allen, recognizing the significance of her words, wanted to publish the story, but Amelia requested that he hold off until after the flight.

On Saint Patrick's Day, at precisely 7:36 a.m., Amelia Earhart ascended into the sky from Oakland, California, beginning her historic attempt to circle the globe. At her side was Fred Noonan, her dapper navigator, who marked the occasion with a shamrock pinned to his sharply tailored suit—a nod to the holiday that didn't go unnoticed. Along with Noonan, Amelia was joined by Paul Mantz, her technical adviser and trusted instructor, whose sharp eye had guided her through months of rigorous training. Together, they had prepared for the perils of navigation, multi-engine maneuvers, and the nerve-testing demands of instrument flying, all skills that would soon be put to the ultimate test. Clarence Vellum, an Electra modification specialist, had determined the optimal range of their Lockheed Electra to be between twenty-five hundred and forty-three hundred miles. For this journey, the plane was heavily loaded, carrying over five thousand Gimbels cacheted covers in its cargo, meant to be stamped at various locations around the globe. To counterbalance the tail's heaviness, Manning and Noonan strategically sat on the fuel tanks.

Just before departure, Amelia and Mantz switched seats, allowing Mantz to handle the actual takeoff due to the challenging conditions: a short runway and muddy terrain. The Electra impressively covered 1,897 feet in twenty-five seconds, and Amelia's government adviser, Miller, praised "her" flawless takeoff in a telegram to the White House and other authorities.

George lingered at the airport after her departure, hawking his wife's autographs for six dollars each. To some onlookers, it was a tacky spectacle, but for the born promoter, every penny was essential.

Upon the Electra crew's arrival in Waikiki, they were greeted with a lavish display of leis and soon found themselves at the opulent home of Christian Holmes, a millionaire friend of Mantz's. Despite the luxurious setting, much of their time was spent indoors, captive to the relentless, disheartening drum of rain. Privately, Mantz expressed concern about the impact of the rain on Amelia's upcoming liftoff, particularly given the additional weight from the heavy load of fuel.

On March 20, amid warm wishes of aloha from those present, the crew prepared to embark on the second leg of their journey, and at Luke Field, Hawaii, they took to the runway, but almost immediately, a tire blew out at the far end of the strip, causing gasoline to leak from the heavily laden aircraft, which was significantly exceeding its gross design weight. As fuel sloshed unpredictably from side to side, the plane began to fishtail, struggling to stabilize and take off.

In 1937, pilots maneuvering two- and three-engine aircraft often leaned on intuition and extensive hands-on experience. Amelia's flight coach, Mantz, a stuntman renowned for his exacting preparation before risky flights, still harbored concerns about Amelia piloting the potent Electra, given her still relatively limited practice time. As the Electra readied for the ascent, Mantz calibrated the tachometer settings for each engine. However, Amelia, going against his repeated advice not to "jockey the throttles," decided to play it by ear, and the plane went into a ground loop, a perilous spin on the runway. Just as it was about to lift, everything went sideways—sparks flew, a wing bent, and the landing gear broke off. The plane came to a sudden stop in a belly flop. With 950 gallons of fuel on board, the only stroke of "good luck" was that it hadn't blown up. Though unharmed, Amelia and the team were plenty shaken up and now faced the wreckage of the $100,000 plane.

Amelia had faced danger many times before. But it was the public's criticism that weighed on her more. After this brutal setback, she confronted questions with a forced smile. This try had failed, but she'd be back. George claimed that the cause was that "a tire blew out" with no mention of ground looping.

It was necessary to ship the aircraft to California for extensive repairs at Lockheed's plant. Who would pay for this? Could there even be a second attempt after this bungle? Was their joint plan, which included a monetary windfall, in tatters? Amelia was afraid to ask George. Would she be allowed to try again?

After the crash in Hawaii, the disheartened Electra crew returned to California aboard the Matson Line. On the return trip to California aboard the SS *Malolo*, Harry Manning stayed isolated in his quarters, still distressed and shamefaced by the recent crash. Similarly, Amelia remained in her cabin, demoralized, with only her flight attire for company. As days passed, Amelia's absence at dinner became awkward and cumbersome for everyone on board. Worried, Terry visited her cabin, as she recalled in a 1970s interview (long after she had married Mantz and been widowed by him). "Amelia, I have three dinner dresses. If you'd like, you can choose one to wear," Terry remembered telling her. "She rejected the black and floral options, but when she saw the light-blue dress with a full skirt and a bolero-type jacket, she loved it." Terry even had a pair of blue shoes that perfectly matched the ensemble. On the fourth night, Amelia decided to wear the dress, and she looked stunning in it. On the final night, the captain's dinner, Amelia wore the same dress again.

After the returning gang cleared quarantine, George awaited them on a dock at the Los Angeles Harbor, where he had again decided to engage in a ruse. He approached Terry and informed her, "I have something to tell you. Myrtle [Paul's ex] is at the dock with a gun. . . . She's after Mrs. Minor." Shocked and frightened by this news, as Myrtle had actually threatened Paul with a gun before their divorce, Terry adamantly refused to disembark, declaring to those around her, "I am not getting off the ship." She remained on board until all other passengers had left. Finally, she stepped out, heavily disguised in a coat with a large fur collar, a droopy hat, and dark glasses. Upon seeing Terry, George couldn't contain his laughter and nearly collapsed in amusement as she set foot on the deck. It was sinister stuff, and if George or even Amelia found the prank harmlessly silly, years later Terry still bristled at his name, saying, "It was a harrowing afternoon. . . . I was intimidated, fearing his power. He was so cold."

For the official newspaper coverage, Manning stated he couldn't rejoin Amelia on her journey due to his leave constraints. Behind closed doors, though, Manning was clear that he wanted no further association with Amelia. "Oh, never again! I am going home," Terry recalled him stating. Surprisingly, Terry's wrath was not just reserved for George. Her opinion of Manning was less than glowing too; she found him outright unpleasant. Amelia's mechanic, Bo McNeeley, shared this sentiment, describing Manning as overly fussy and crude. But there was a contrasting view from Vivian Maata, the young secretary at the makeshift Oakland airport office; she perceived Manning as quite charming and gentlemanly, while finding Noonan to be a secret drunk and more than a bit off-putting.

Years later, in a recorded interview, Mildred Manning, Manning's second wife, shared a rather telling insight. According to her, Manning privately and repeatedly attributed the crash to Amelia's invincible attitude and disregard about her limitations. Her decision to add Noonan on the first flight left her husband feeling sidelined and worried about his future income. To add insult to injury, Amelia (and George) insisted that the men flying with her stay in the background, ensuring she could claim the lion's share of the glory. Manning had told his wife that Mantz had secretly piloted the Electra to Hawaii on the first leg of the journey to get some last-minute tutoring in—a juicy tidbit that wasn't widely known at the time.

When Manning returned to his job at United States Lines, he took a lower rank but quickly returned to his original position. Despite his frustration, he was concerned about Amelia's and Noonan's limited Morse code skills—chance favors the prepared. Why hadn't they knuckled down and learned the damn system? According to C. B. Allen, Noonan could send only ten to twenty-three words per minute using Morse code, even though Noonan had held a second-class commercial radiotelegraph license for two years. Manning knew that ships usually used a frequency of 3105 kilohertz at night and 6210 kilohertz during the day for Morse code communication. While CW (continuous wave, or Morse) was the norm, Amelia was now intent on using voice communication. If she was really going to try again, he wanted nothing to do with it, but why wouldn't she use a close call due to lack of technical skill as a valuable wake-up call? In Manning's opinion, Amelia should stop lecturing, fly more, and, while she was at it, learn Morse code when she had time, and he recommended keeping the equipment in case she tried again without him.

In the jagged days after her harrowing experience in Honolulu and subsequent return to the mainland, Amelia Earhart, feeling near collapse and not in the mood for George Palmer Putnam's potential reprimands, sought refuge at the Desert Ranch in Indio, California. This ranch, owned by two friends—the up-and-coming aviator Jackie Cochran and her husband, the multimillionaire Floyd Odlum—offered Amelia a much-needed escape hatch. Known then as the "Wizard of Wall Street," Odlum had so far navigated the Great Depression successfully. He had encouraged Cochran to learn to fly to promote her budding cosmetics company, a suggestion that led Cochran to become one of the most incredible fliers of the twentieth century.

At the Cochran-Odlum Ranch, Amelia could find solace and solitude, if she desired, with staff available to attend to her needs. She was a frequent guest here, having spent much of her last year at the ranch, often away from George for weeks. Cochran had previously urged her not to embark on the flight, once commenting, "I said, 'I think the whole damn flight is so screwy, Amelia, and doesn't make sense. You can do hundreds of things to get publicity if you want it—to prove your ability as a pilot—you already have a great reputation, and no one can take that away from you.'" Yet Amelia refused to be marked by cowardice.

The eight-hundred-acre property, located in the Coachella Valley and twenty-five miles from Palm Springs, was an idyllic retreat. It featured charming ranch-style guesthouses and a central swimming pool surrounded by citrus trees, date palms, vineyards, cultivated dates, tangerines, grapefruit, and grapes.

The Odlums had considerable resources and supported Amelia's flying endeavors. Cochran, a fiery personality and among the most notable female aviators of the 1930s, had been friends with Amelia since meeting her in New York City in 1935. Odlum found Amelia sweet, lovable, and forthright, recalling that she "smiled easily." Like many of Amelia's friends, though, he had less favorable thoughts on George. "We didn't like him or dislike him at the start," Odlum said. "But we came to dislike him because we thought he was taking advantage of Amelia. . . . She was his meal ticket. . . . He was the advance publicity agent, and she would run around so he could write stories about her and get pictures of her in the paper."

Cochran would later leave an indelible mark on aviation history, shattering gender barriers in competitive races and becoming the first woman to break the sound barrier. Amid World War II's tumult, she helped found and train the Women Airforce Service Pilots (WASP), preparing approximately eleven hundred women for flight duty. Although her aviation talent was unmatched by any woman of the twentieth century, her moral legacy is tinged with controversy. Archival records from her stint as the president of the Ninety-Nines show her active resistance to letting Black female aviators join the ranks. This exclusionary stance dims the shine of her other monumental contributions to women in aviation. Furthermore, her continued false narrative about being an orphan adds another disconcerting facet to her biography.

In stark contrast, Amelia's perspectives were continuously evolving and likely influenced by progressive stalwarts in her circle, such as Eleanor Roosevelt, who had outgrown any Jazz Age eugenic prejudices she might have once held. A particularly revealing moment, as narrated by Cochran, took place at the ranch. In the absence of her more conservative husband, Amelia fervently championed racial equality, impressively doing so in front of Assistant Attorney General Robert H. Jackson, who would later be involved with the Nuremberg Trials. Her impassioned advocacy for the rights of Black Americans was so compelling that Cochran later described it as the most intense display of conviction she had ever witnessed in Amelia. While Cochran personally didn't align with Amelia's beliefs, she simply adored her friend as a kind, authentic person.

Off the record, Cochran would tell one Hollywood screenwriter who was seeking to share Amelia's story: "I just disliked Putnam heartily." She was happy that Amelia had come alone after Hawaii, remembering all too well the time when Amelia gave a lecture titled "Aviation Adventures" in Redlands and then visited the ranch with George afterward. It was around eleven or twelve late at night, and Cochran offered some comforting milk toast as her thoroughly wrung-out friend gratefully sank into the chair, letting the day's tension melt away.

"She had slid down in this chair, one of those great big firm-back real lounging chairs," Cochran recalled, a tape recorder rolling. "So she had this stuck right on her chest, and she was eating, and he looked over and said, 'Nasty!' He said, 'You dressed like a lady. Why don't you sit up like one?!' I had an ashtray and threw an ashtray at him, and I said, 'You dirty bum! How dare you speak to your wife like that in my house! I won't stand for it! If you want to talk to her that way, get out of here. Too fond of her!'" Cochran said she didn't connect, and nobody laughed. "Unfortunately, he dodged. I said, 'If I were Amelia, I'd kick you right out the door, and you'd apologize in a hurry too. I thought she would cry. . . . She just looked so embarrassed and humiliated that night. There was no one there except Floyd, myself, Amelia, and George Putnam."

Despite it all, Cochran believed that Amelia loved George. Even if she often listened to him with blank distaste, she saw it in Amelia's face, which would light up whenever George called or when she looked at him. "You could tell when a woman is in love with a man." She couldn't understand it. To say she didn't like him would be an understatement. "He was a complete dope; he was the dullest person I've ever been around . . . a first-class bum."

On one of the nights Amelia requested to stay at the ranch, aviation entrepreneur Benny Howard and his wife, Maxine, were present. Amelia shared her story of the crash. Cochran expressed her concerns bluntly:

"The last thing I said was, 'You just don't have sufficient navigation and communication that I don't think you'll ever hit it.' The very last thing was, 'I wish you wouldn't go off and commit suicide, because that's exactly what you're doing, in my opinion.'" Years later, she criticized Amelia's lack of preparation, calling it foolish, even moronic. Cochran, trained in flying and planning to get a third-grade license in code, was frustrated by Amelia's refusal to prepare similarly. "If I am going to kill myself," Cochran said, "I'd like to do it myself. Have my own pleasure."

Shortly after the incident in Hawaii, while Amelia was still at the Odlum ranch, Fred Noonan stirred the aviation industry by divorcing Jo "Josie" Sullivan, whom he had been married to since 1927 and whom he had been unfaithful to. The couple, childless but sharing a melancholic white poodle named Pan Air, had garnered sympathy among the wives of Pan Am pilots, who favored Jo. Noonan finalized his divorce from Sullivan in Ciudad Juárez, Mexico, and within just two weeks, he married Mary Beatrice "Bea" Martinelli (née Passadori) from Oakland, a move that sparked much discussion within their social circles.

Back in Los Angeles, George quickly announced that Harry Manning would no longer serve as the navigator for any of Amelia's upcoming flights. The official reason? Manning had resigned to return to his responsibilities as a master mariner.

Freshly married and needing a steady income, Noonan was up for any role that could help. But a head-on collision on the Golden State Highway near Fresno, California, highlighted Fred's personal foibles. The crash occurred on April 4 while Fred was tooling down the highway with his new bride, Bea, who sustained slight injuries and cuts to her knee and scalp and spent some time recovering at the Burnett Sanitarium. Fred skinned his hand. More alarmingly, although the other car's driver was not hurt, two passengers, Marie Lorenz and her infant daughter, Catherine, were cut and bruised. Noonan was cited for driving in the wrong lane. In the 1960s, one author alleged (without offering any evidence) that on the bottom of the ticket, the officer had jotted down: "No injuries. Driver had been drinking."

Regardless of whether this scandalous claim was valid, Amelia well knew that the man who was to travel with her around the world was a drinker, but with her limited funds, what choice did she have if she wanted to proceed? As she had with Wilmer Stultz back in 1928, Amelia assured Noonan that she had deep faith in him, and Noonan told a friend that in Amelia, he had found a second chance.

Amelia eventually left the ranch and, at George's urging, made an appointment in New York with Harry Bruno, a leading aviation publicist who promoted aviators like Charles Lindbergh. She was more emotional than he'd ever seen her as she quietly asked if he could help with fundraising. In no time, Bruno drummed up some donations from notable figures like Admiral Richard Byrd, who loved Amelia. Despite past disagreements with George, Byrd matched the amount he'd previously given to Amelia's Lucky Strike ad campaign in 1928. Bruno tapped into his wealthy network, including Bernard Baruch, Roosevelt's wealthy adviser, to help Amelia; Baruch kicked in $1,000 to recognize Amelia's courage. Floyd Odlum, without asking Jackie Cochran, plunked down $5,000. With these funds and Amelia's lecture earnings, the repairs were finished in two months. Amelia then revised her flight strategy, planning to take off from Miami to circle the globe from west to east, sidestepping the monsoon season.

Despite the show of faith from some friends in high places, Amelia faced a breaking point in her already fraught marriage after the Hawaii crack-up. Love and companionship were at the core of Amelia and George's relationship, but the strain was inevitable.

Seventeen

WHISTLE IN THE DARK

In the spring of 1937, Amelia Earhart resurfaced in the public eye on April 1 during Bing Crosby's Kraft Music Hall broadcast over KFI. It was her first radio appearance since the disastrous Honolulu flight. With a nationwide audience glued to their sets, Amelia spoke about the "accident," while George Palmer Putnam and Paul Mantz, Amelia's technical adviser, discussed their ambitious plans for a new attempt to circumnavigate the globe. Bing Crosby, with his usual charm, jokingly suggested that Amelia should star in his next film. Amelia likably shot back, "You evidently haven't seen me in the newsreels."

During this period, Amelia and George were often away, leaving the final touches on their Toluca Lake house to an assistant. One of their trips took them to Callander, Ontario, ostensibly to observe the Dionne quintuplets at play. Quintland, a bizarre hybrid of medical facility and tourist attraction, housed the five girls taken from their parents, and had been drawing celebrities like James Cagney, Mae West, and Clark Gable since it opened to visitors in 1936. Amelia, the first major star to visit in 1937, found Annette, Émilie, Marie, Yvonne, and Cécile to be "lovely children." Yet her visit had a deeper purpose.

Quaker Oats, already featuring the quintuplets in their ads, offered Amelia a $5,000 donation for her renewed flight plans if she joined their sponsorship campaign. Drawing on her background in social work, Amelia agreed to serve as a youth reporter for the company, with an announcement planned after her return from the upcoming world flight. Meanwhile, George secured a modest deal with Harcourt, Brace & Company for a book "by" her to be called *World Flight*. This arrangement facilitated a form of double-dipping, whereby ghostwriters would transform her transmitted notes from various stops into American newspaper articles that, once aggregated at the journey's conclusion, could be seamlessly woven into a cohesive narrative for the forthcoming book.

Amelia had by now arranged for her mother, Amy, to fly from Boston to her new house in Toluca Lake, which overlooked a golf course. The plan was for Amy to live out her life here, with her own room and the help of Amelia and George's staff. After all, Amelia owned the house, not George. Despite her close relationship with her mother, Amelia often chose to dine alone, weary from her busy schedule and preferring to avoid her mother's well-intentioned but often critical comments. "No talkee, Mother, my cocoa, and goodnight," she would say in a little-girl voice before escaping to her upstairs bedroom.

Meanwhile, the fundraising for Amelia's flight continued relentlessly, often leaving her mother in the company of helpers or George. On May 6, from their California home, George's attempts to stir media interest in Amelia's endeavors were failing as the news cycle was dramatically overtaken by the tragic Hindenburg disaster, which claimed thirty-six lives at a naval air station in Lakehurst, New Jersey. At that very moment, David Binney Putnam, Amelia's stepson, was with his Binney relatives in Old Greenwich and had witnessed the airship overhead earlier that day before the catastrophe. After he shared this haunting experience with his father and stepmother in Los Angeles, they reflected on the enormity of the disaster and, perhaps, the looming reminder that Amelia, too, faced grave risks on her upcoming journey.

Under mounting financial pressures in early May, George took a drastic step by mortgaging his home in Rye. This gamble with his own money only worsened his already strained mood. Tensions soon escalated into a full-blown conflict with Mantz. The two men clashed over financial matters, their dispute degenerating into a stubborn standoff, with neither willing to back down.

Post-dispute, and with William T. Miller no longer involved after the Hawaii crash, decision-making fell to George. His lack of experience and tendency toward thriftiness led to Amelia making several questionable choices. By May 19, the refurbished Electra was ready at Lockheed's facility.

Two days later, Amelia was at Oakland Municipal Airport and watched quietly as her ground staff sneaked on the Gimbels stamp covers from the earlier journey to Honolulu. She then embarked on what she called a thorough "shakedown flight" to Miami to test her equipment, with George and her mechanic, Bo McNeeley, on board in this guise of a routine test. (In fact, she was embarking on a new eastward trip around the world and would leave American soil in Miami.)

Amelia, Fred, George, and Bo's initial stop was Burbank's Union Air Terminal to check the Electra's modifications. They landed in the evening and decided to stay overnight in Burbank due to necessary adjustments at a nearby hangar.

Having been tipped off about the Miami plan, C. B. Allen from the *New York Herald Tribune* was dispatched from Manhattan to Florida for first-hand updates.

Mantz was in St. Louis, engrossed in an aviation competition and oblivious to the latest developments. Anticipating his disapproval, Amelia had quietly slipped out of town without informing him. She was utterly fatigued by the incessant squabbles between George and Paul over finances, as well as by Paul's nitpicky safety concerns. Opting for a silent departure seemed the simplest solution to avoid further conflict. The Putnams kept the American leg of the journey tightly under wraps, using the secrecy to smooth out any issues before hitting Miami, where intense press coverage was expected. Despite the palpable tension between George and McNeeley, Amelia found comfort in having aboard her personal mechanic, whose loyalty was solely to her.

Blindsided by what he later termed "a sneak takeoff," as he had feared, Mantz was incensed at Amelia's departure without his checking of the equipment, and he had lingering fears about the skills she still needed to master. He was further angered that he learned about the journey through the radio, and he sat in his office fuming impotently on his own, speculating correctly that this was no test flight but a reverse route of her previously disastrous attempt at an around-the-world trip.

The four on board the Electra continued to Tucson for refueling, and then the plan was to fly on to Miami. However, a mishap occurred when they tried to restart the left engine in Arizona, leading to the emergency purchase of a "dandy big extinguisher" during an unplanned overnight stay.

Electing to bypass an impending sandstorm in El Paso, Amelia flew directly to New Orleans. By 4:00 p.m., she had swiftly checked into the Shushan Airport Inn. There, she reconnected with aviator Edna Gardner Whyte, her Ninety-Nines mentee and comrade, by now renowned as the "Flying Nurse of New Orleans"—a nod to her previous occupation.

Whyte, who ran the New Orleans Air College at Shushan Airport with her then husband, Ray Kidd, was delighted to see her old friend, and warmly invited Amelia, George, Fred, and Bo to dine at the inn as their guests. Kidd, a writer of sorts, was the person Whyte hoped could provide a publicity boost for her. When they had married two years prior, Kidd had promised to be her own George Palmer Putnam, and she wondered if George could offer some pointers. Whyte had never been a fan of Amelia's husband, but seeing how churlish and short-tempered he was with her friend that night cemented her disdain.

"I wondered if she wouldn't relish being off and away on the greatest adventure of her life," she later said. "He was so domineering and so pushy. We were to dinner, and she was saying something about the radio. He said, 'You had a chance to change, and it is too late now.' She turned her head down, and he looked at her and said, 'Stop your sniveling!' He was just as cruel as could be right in front of us all. Amelia was a striking contrast in virtue. We all loved her and disliked seeing what he was doing to her."

In Whyte's eyes, her friend's love for her husband had faded, leaving her trapped and immune to his relentless barking. Whyte also didn't want her friend, who lacked the necessary preparation and equipment, to undertake a slapdash flight over Howland Island. However, despite her efforts, she could not dissuade Amelia, a frustration Jackie Cochran had also experienced.

Later, and privately, Amelia acknowledged to Whyte that she and George had a significant financial stake in a successful flight. Whyte couldn't shake the feeling that only luck could guide Amelia and Noonan to a safe journey's end.

After their restful night in New Orleans, the four passengers aboard the Lockheed Electra smoothly landed in downtown Miami at the 36th Street Airport on the morning of May 23. Noonan skillfully—and soberly—guided the flight using dead-reckoning navigation.

David Binney Putnam was at the airport to welcome the plane, and he explained that Pan Am had received news of their coming just over an hour prior, leading George Hussey, chairman of Miami's reception committee, and R. V. Waters, president of the Greater Miami Airport Association, to quickly make their way to greet these esteemed visitors. They arranged for hangar space about nine miles away at aviation pioneer Karl Voelter's Curtiss-Wright flying school hangar, which he was managing at Miami Municipal Airport in Hialeah.

After securing the plane in the hangar, Amelia and her crew took a taxi back to downtown Miami, checking into the Columbus Hotel. With its Art Deco elegance, the hotel's rooms offered splendid views of Biscayne Bay, bathed in beautiful southern light, and the vibrant cityscape. George was delighted by the Miami media's coverage of their unexpected arrival. Amelia was even a last-minute addition to the guest list for a reception at Bayfront Park the following evening that was celebrating the return of a similar Electra piloted by Henry T. "Dick" Merrill and Jack Lambie. Along with George and her Ninety-Nines colleague Phoebe Omlie, Amelia was feted as an honored guest at the splendorous gala in the Bayfront Park Auditorium.

Omlie, one of the aviation world's true trailblazers, who had won the lighter-aircraft crown back at the famous 1929 Powder Puff Derby, was there to honor Merrill and his copilot, but she was tickled that she also got to spend unexpected alone time with Amelia, who, after swearing Omlie to secrecy, revealed her true plans. Omlie was the last of the Ninety-Nines to say goodbye to her face-to-face before her trip. Being a member of the NAA National Contest Board, Omlie was no stranger to scrutinizing and approving flight plans for record-breaking endeavors. Like so many others, her current concern lay with the challenging Pacific passage, an expansive realm where weather patterns and wind conditions were as unpredictable as they were unreliable. Yet Omlie acknowledged later that Amelia Earhart exuded confidence, assuring her that all possible contingencies had been considered.

"We're just on a shakedown trip," Amelia soon fibbed again to the *Miami Daily News*. "Miami wasn't on our route as originally planned, but on reaching New Orleans, we decided to continue the trip and visit David."

While the crew was still on American soil, they needed a low-cost temporary headquarters until any repairs needed or issues discovered could be made or addressed. Noonan remembered a rich business contact from a Miami Rotary Club meeting: W. Bruce MacIntosh was the president of the East Coast steam laundry and dry-cleaning empire called Mary MacIntosh, along with its local subsidiary, the Miami Laundry Company. When he heard about Amelia's financial struggles, MacIntosh agreed to help; while Amelia and Noonan worked with airport experts on any troubles, George could now operate his latest press push from a spare laundry office.

One day, George wanted a private word with Bo McNeeley, the mechanic. Expressing his worries about Amelia's safety on the upcoming trip, George asked McNeeley to accompany Amelia and Noonan. McNeeley recalled being taken aback by the unexpected request and explaining that he was close to his father, who had a heart condition, and feared the journey might be too arduous for him. Bo, who was known for his quiet competence and for bothering no one, seriously considered obtaining a passport despite his reservations. Eager to please and well connected, George assured McNeeley that he could arrange everything. Eventually, George let go of the idea when McNeeley decided his father had to come first, but it was a conversation that would haunt McNeeley for years to come.

On a sultry Sunday, Jane Wood, a fledgling Miami beat reporter, navigated to Hialeah Airfield during Florida's secretive nine-day aviation frenzy. She was unfamiliar with the aviation beat, so it was a daunting task to cover Amelia Earhart, and nerves and anticipation swirled inside her as she drove. For a rookie, landing a story on Amelia was a big deal. Her stomach fluttered with equal parts excitement and apprehension as she felt the gravity of the moment. One of the two men waiting in the airport office with her was Amelia's stepson David.

"Why, she's hard as nails, a real tough old girl," David told Wood. "You should hear her cuss!" Wood had heard she never cursed, and he answered with a "hyena grin," soon replaced by a loving glow. "But really, she is among the most wonderful people I have ever known. Really, she's wonderful." His beloved stepmom had attended football games, gifted him his first car, taken him up on planes, and even given him a first airplane lesson before introducing him to Paul Mantz, who trained him until he soloed. The conversation was interrupted by the arrival of Amelia's famous plane.

Wood gasped at the plane's bumpy landing. Nonetheless, Amelia appeared unfazed as she entered the airport with her navigator, Fred Noonan. Upon being introduced to the young reporter, Amelia, with a warm and disarming smile, greeted all by saying, "I certainly smacked it down hard that time."

Gathering her composure, Wood dived right into her interview. "Why are you taking this flight?" she asked Amelia directly. "Is there a scientific reason?"

George was nowhere to be seen, and Amelia was freer with her words than she had been when she claimed that she was off on a "laboratory flight" to provide data for an aviation research department at Purdue: "No, there's no scientific reason, no special reason," she said. "I'm doing it just for fun." A smile spread across her face, and with that caveat out of the way, she continued: "I'm going on vacation. Can you think of a better reason?"

Shortly after that interview, Amelia was again greeting her good old confidant C. B. Allen, who had been flown to Miami on the *New York Herald Tribune*'s dime. "In going over my list of the plane equipment on the Oakland–Honolulu flight," he later recalled in an unpublished document, "I asked Amelia as soon as I joined her group at the Miami airport to check the items. I read them all from my Oakland notes and then asked her to fill me in on any new equipment (if any) that had been added. This was accomplished quickly, but I noted the one item I considered quite important, particularly since it worked so well on the California–Hawaii flight in March, had been eliminated. 'Hey,' I said, 'what about your marine frequency radio for obtaining position fixes from ships at sea and shore safe stations operating at that band?' She replied, 'Oh! That was left off when Manning had to drop out of the flight. Both Fred Noonan and I know Morse code, but we're rank amateurs and probably never would be able to send and receive more than ten words a minute, and the professionals can't be bothered with ham operators who can't match their speed, so the marine frequency radio would have been just that much more dead weight carry, and we decided to leave it in California.'"

When she was in Miami, Amelia also admitted to C. B. Allen that she had left her Irvin parachutes in the hangar as she sneaked out of Oakland for Florida. "More dead weight," Amelia said. To her mind, parachutes could not help her over water. Allen was disgusted and knew that, unlike her husband, Mantz paid attention to vital details, and if Mantz had been on the scene at the departure in California, they would have been on board. C. B. Allen had weighed telling her how invaluable they might prove as shelter from the sun or insects should she come down in a jungle. He resisted because she was in such a "bizarre state" of mind, and her cavalier nature frustrated him. He didn't want to part with a fight between them.

While in what was already dubbed "the Magic City," Amelia also spoke privately with Alice Rogers Hager, another one of her favorite aviation reporters. According to Hager, aviation's major problem was that a pilot had to constantly keep track of the many instruments and calculations. Although it was impossible, it was an unavoidable "must," and she did not think Amelia up to this job. Hager knew that Amelia Mary Earhart would turn forty on July 24. Her epic trip would be wonderful to put behind her, a crowning achievement just before her fortieth birthday, and she could even be back on American soil for Independence Day.

From Miami, Amelia's next major stops would take her through the Caribbean to Venezuela, and then she would hop along the northeast shoulder of South America to Brazil. From there, her flight path would cross the Atlantic to Africa, skimming over the marshy floodplains of the Niger River basin, before continuing eastward through India's Ganges River delta and into Southeast Asia. Finally, she would make the pivotal leg over the vast Pacific back to the United States. This route had been selected to utilize favorable wind patterns and available airfields, forming a challenging yet feasible pathway around the globe.

As Allen and Hager both noticed, Amelia was in a strange mindset before her next big takeoff to Puerto Rico. Her business obligations were clear, and she was a woman of her word. Her only option would be to rely on her wits.

"After she returns, we'll settle down and enjoy life together . . . and I'll write some books," George told Harold McCracken, likely from Miami as McCracken was in New York looking over incoming mail. McCracken had watched his old friend shop and bargain for endorsements for Amelia's trip. In his later assessment, he concluded that George Palmer Putnam had low self-esteem and wanted to feel needed—a household-name wife's dependence on him gave him that feeling. Despite George's confidence, McCracken was most concerned about Amelia flying over two thousand miles of open water in a powerful plane to the "fantastically tiny" target of Howland Island.

He was also worried about their chronic cost cutting and well knew that the cheaper-model radio installed on board had a limited range of five hundred miles. Amelia and George had refused to upgrade the radio's antennae, despite experts' strong recommendations; they couldn't afford it.

Notwithstanding the documented stress and arguments between the couple, there were moments of lightness in Miami. A reporter Amelia befriended learned that she ate pompano (a delicious fish) three times a day and called her Madame Pompano, after Madame de Pompadour, chief mistress of Louis XV. This made her laugh hard.

Amelia, George, and Fred even got in a small getaway while they waited for mechanical repairs when the laundry king of Miami invited them aboard the *Brownie*, a thirty-seven-foot Chris-Craft yacht. No fish were caught, but Bruce and Lilly MacIntosh ensured that Amelia had more pompano for dinner. Sunburned from the tropical sun, she said, "I want to soak in some sunshine, not be fried by it."

Then the right side of her head was hurting, and she smartly declined George's request to visit the old Bayfront Park bandstand for one last promotional visit a day before the big flight. After they called Dr. Collins Sword for an emergency appointment, the local dentist diagnosed her with an impacted upper wisdom tooth. She couldn't travel with that risk, and it hurt like hell when he removed it. Come Monday afternoon, she only wanted to nap at the Columbus Hotel.

Later that day, George's youngest son, Junie, had his final encounter with his stepmother. Despite being based in Fort Pierce with his mother, he was thrilled he had a chance to say goodbye, and David was there, too, in a quiet meeting. Amelia warmly embraced and kissed her beloved stepsons.

Her last letter (dated June 1), to her mother, was scribbled out fast on Columbus Hotel stationery:

Hope to take off tomorrow A.M. to Puerto Rico. Here is three hundred bucks for me to put in household fund. Yr doter, A

On Tuesday, June 1, those lucky insiders connected with the flight had a wake-up call at 2:45 a.m. to get dressed for Amelia and Noonan's last night in America before their return in hopefully a month's time. At 3:15 a.m., Amelia's little posse headed to the airport, the star of the hour in frowsy trousers, a tan belt, and a brightly patterned Scotch plaid blouse with short sleeves.

George's friend and former client Eustace L. Adams, author of the Andy Lane series of juvenile flight adventure novels, had been roped into driving Amelia and George to the airport. A second car, driven by David Binney Putnam—now twenty-four years old and joined by his pregnant twenty-two-year-old wife, Nilla—followed them; these younger Putnams had driven over from their "starter apartment" in Fort Pierce.

But there was another in their privileged group: the gorgeous twenty-four-year-old Helen Louise Day, who drove the last car in Amelia Earhart's Miami procession with just her and Fred Noonan inside. Helen and Noonan had crossed paths in 1929, when Helen was sixteen, and Helen recalled a double date with two young men from Dinner Key, a landing spot in Biscayne Bay; seeing how young the possibly drunk men were, Noonan served as a gracious volunteer "chaperone" driver in a Chrysler. Noonan continued working at Dinner Key after its merger with Pan Am in 1930, but Helen lost touch with him during his stint on the West Coast. This time, the former chaperone returned to Miami on the Electra, called Helen up, invited her to dinner, and arranged for her to meet Amelia. He had been spending all his free time with her, and it was in this quasi-romantic stretch that Helen also met George Palmer Putnam, whom she described as "jittery and tense with rude manners," while Amelia was "curiously calm and genuinely kind." Upon learning that Helen's mother was blind, Amelia, the former social worker, had many questions. During their dinner, Noonan told Helen—perhaps trying to impress her—that he and Amelia were "just work pals." He conveyed optimism about the flight, and although Helen knew about Noonan's drinking habit, he assured her that it was behind him.

Although Noonan had remarried two months prior in California, his commitments seemed fickle, and he was likely having a sexual fling with Helen. He often wrote to his wife, referring to her as the "sweetest girl in the world," but he wrote flirtatious letters to Helen too. In one of his Miami missives, he humorously noted to a friend that he was meeting "too many blondes" and there weren't "enough brunettes available." Noonan's sister-in-law privately revealed that he had engaged in passionate romances all over the globe, irrespective of his marital status.

Surprisingly, it was Amelia who invited Helen to drive Noonan to the airport, sensing that Helen's presence calmed her navigator and also appreciating her working-girl status. Helen arrived at 3:30 a.m., skillfully evading the reporters stationed inside and outside the hotel. She met with the rest of the group upstairs, and they would soon head to the plane. Before arriving at the airfield, Amelia's entourage, now a party of seven, stopped to grab a bite at an all-night lunch stand. But only hot dogs and soda were available, which didn't suffice. Frustrated, they drove around until they found another spot, this one offering coffee, cocoa, fruit, doughnuts, and cereal.

The convoy arrived at the Miami Municipal Airport shortly after 4:00 a.m., and Amelia found Walter R. Davis alone on the night shift.

"What's the weather to San Juan?" she asked casually.

"Good."

A greasy spoon called the Atcher Airport Restaurant stood across the street from the aircraft. While her plane was being repaired, Amelia often ate lunch with a glass of buttermilk and told reporters the place had better food than downtown hotels. She joked that getting buttermilk at every stop might be critical to her success on the globe-trotting trip. Harry Andrews, the airport's night watchman, was the husband of the lady who ran Atcher's, and he was friendly with Amelia. He had a gift for her: his wife, Sarah, had stacked metal containers filled with home-cooked lunches for the pilot and her navigator. As she left the terminal for Puerto Rico, Amelia slipped up and over her head the black Bakelite whistle she used for getting Noonan's attention. "Here, Pop," she said, handing it to Harry, "I won't need this." (The prized gifted whistle remains in the Andrews family.)

Under the dim lights of the hangar, Bo McNeeley was fixing a critical component of the Electra—a broken thermocouple, essential for measuring temperature. Outside, Fred Noonan and Helen Louise Day exchanged words in hushed tones, their conversation a private interlude amid the morning's preparations.

Nearby, within the quiet confines of the hangar, a deeply emotional scene unfolded between George and Amelia as they shared a private moment away from the prying eyes of the world, a silent communion filled with unspoken understanding and sentiment. George later wrote: "In the dim chill, we perched briefly on cold concrete steps, and the feel of her hands in mine told more than the words we did not speak could have told."

At 4:30 a.m., the hangar doors were rolled open. At 5:15 a.m., Noonan and Amelia hopped into the cockpit, and Amelia adjusted her seat cushion. George climbed up on the wing to chat with his wife. Photographers took photos of him, and he whipped out his camera to snap pictures of them watching the Miami sunrise glow pink. A cheeky voice shouted out, "Extra! Man bites dog!"—a playful jab at the rare sight of George, usually the focus of photographers, turning the tables and capturing them instead.

But now the subtropical dawn had fragmented over Miami.

Amelia's trusty mechanic, Bo McNeeley, was speeding across the plane in white coveralls to clean up oil splattered on one of the propellers. In later years, the retired mechanic would remember Lockheed officials being concerned about the plane's 1,151 gallons of fuel, which weighed in at six pounds per gallon. Due to the heavy load, balance and center of gravity were significant concerns.

Amelia's new laundry millionaire pal, W. Bruce MacIntosh, was among a few lucky people invited to see Fred Noonan and Amelia Earhart off, and he shook Amelia's hand from her cockpit. Despite the gas tanks and tools in the middle of the plane, MacIntosh remembered Fred looking uncomfortable in the back of the fuselage. Despite carrying minimal personal items, Amelia made sure to pack a tiny camera—a Zeiss Ikon Ikonta 520/18, also known as a Baby Ikonta in the 1930s. Her young personal photographer, Albert Bresnik, had gifted it to her after a couple of lessons, hoping it would capture stunning images for her forthcoming book with Harcourt, Brace & Company.

Meanwhile, Amelia, crowded by equipment in the cockpit, told MacIntosh she couldn't eat anything in flight, even if she was famished. "Gas fumes make me nauseous."

Finally, at 5:40 a.m., the cockpit was closed, and the twin engines fired up.

"Better luck this time!" George called out, waving a hand as the plane soon taxied away, and Amelia's fair-haired stepson David ran down the runway waving before she waved back. McNeeley had a car with several fire extinguishers ready for any trouble with fuel overload at liftoff—as had happened in Hawaii.

No such problem occurred, but the wind shifted as Amelia taxied in the southwest area of the airport, so with Noonan's input, perhaps, she steered southwest. An airport worker named Eddy Jones jerked out the chocks, and she was off, making a wide arc around the west and south of Opa-Locka. After she took an elegant ascending turn, George and others watched, transfixed, from the roof of Miami Municipal Airport's administration building. At 5:57 a.m., the plane vanished from sight in a clear blue sky.

Godspeed.

Only one station was on the ground so early after dawn, but the WQAM amplifier acted up. Fortunately, there was a backup method, and a technician pointed out that the East Coast was just waking up. With blaring police escorts, Maurice Fink, the live broadcast control man, clocked eighty miles per hour rushing their on-wax description to studios. Amelia's voice was heard twenty-three minutes after she took off.

Fred Noonan and Amelia Earhart climbed to thirty-five hundred feet before embarking on their first flight as just two on board, maintaining a steady speed of 150 miles per hour. After seven hours and thirty-three minutes, they landed at Isla Grande Airport in San Juan. The quiet of their flight was only interrupted by George's voice over the radio. In San Juan, they were greeted by Clara Livingston's hospitality at her expansive sixteen-hundred-acre grapefruit and coconut plantation, situated just twenty miles from the city. Livingston, an accomplished aviator and the eleventh female helicopter pilot in the world, as well as the two-hundredth female pilot in history, was a close friend of Amelia's from the Ninety-Nines, and Livingston's nearby plantation offered a serene retreat. Respectful of their need for rest, Livingston let them sleep undisturbed. Recalling the events of that evening when George called and wanted to speak with his wife, Livingston shared, "I told him Amelia was sleeping, but I could wake her if the urgent call came." She remembered that he was not pleased with this and strongly told her so. Livingston, like many in Amelia's circle of women aviators, had a less-than-favorable view of him. She perceived his treatment of Amelia as dismissive and unpleasant.

Following the northeastern coast of South America, Amelia then flew the Electra 750 miles to Caripito, Venezuela, a red-roofed town surrounded by squat oil tanks. She refueled in Standard Oil's hangar, where the fliers were also served steak, grape juice, and fruitcake for lunch. They were joined by Henry Linam, president of Standard Oil in Venezuela, and the other lucky guests Linam had invited. It was the first time Amelia had seen a jungle from above. She was mentally fresh after landing in South America. She told devotees following along on her journey that she had never seen so many brown-eyed people, and she challenged herself to see how many had blue eyes.

On June 3, Amelia Earhart and her companion reached Paramaribo, the capital of what was then Dutch Guiana, now known as Suriname. To get there, they'd covered approximately 620 miles, and they were greeted with orange juice and sandwiches. During her stay, Amelia bartered with members of the Saramaka community in a vibrant marketplace, bustling with diverse aromas and a kaleidoscope of colors. This was the kind of travel she had always had in mind to expand her horizons, and she took more notes than usual. She was captivated by the Saramaka people, whose ancestors escaped from Dutch slavery.

Amelia's journalings (punched up by ghosts) offered colorful descriptions for her readers back home. She wrote about women adeptly balancing fruit on their heads and vendors selling unique items like softshell turtle eggs and elongated string beans. These observations were carefully jotted down for her upcoming articles and the book she had promised to Harcourt, Brace & Company, which was partially financing her epic flight.

In Paramaribo, Amelia and Noonan stayed at a modern hotel that showcased the city's blend of local traditions and contemporary advancements.

After another eleven hours in the sky, the fliers arrived in Fortaleza, Brazil. As they crossed the equator, Amelia was mesmerized by the stunning vista of the Amazon River unfurling below them. From the quaint airport, they embarked on a twenty-five-mile train journey to the bustling state capital. Their lodgings were at the Excelsior Hotel, a city marvel and its first skyscraper; the hotel exuded elegance with its Art Deco furniture, luxurious Irish linens, sparkling chandeliers, and a majestic grand piano punctuating the dining room.

On the terrace of the American Bar, the weary but spirited duo clinked glasses, savoring a well-earned drink. A mischievous grin spread across Noonan's face as he teased Amelia about his botched plan to surprise her with a bottle of cold water for crossing the equator. The absurdity of the moment sent them into fits of laughter. In this fleeting respite from the journey's pressures and George's meddling, their camaraderie sparkled—a bond that felt like their greatest asset on this daring global adventure.

With their spirits buoyed, Amelia and Noonan continued their journey. Covering nearly three hundred miles, they touched down in Natal, a picturesque coastal city in Brazil.

Setting out on their nineteen-hundred-mile journey across the southern Atlantic to Senegal's west coast, the scale of their adventure was undeniable. Following the Pan Am route, this leg brought its own challenges—thirteen relentless hours of flying, only slightly shorter than her fifteen-hour Atlantic crossing. Even the simplest task, like switching seats in the tight cockpit, became a feat of ingenuity, despite the rare luxury of an onboard bathroom.

Amelia and Noonan faced a much larger challenge during a monster storm as they sailed over the South Atlantic, testing their resilience and skill. As they neared Senegal, the storm abated. Their communication, while unconventional, was remarkably effective: To "speak" over the loud noises of the plane, Noonan would reel Amelia a note attached to a bamboo fishing pole they had jury-rigged to the ceiling, perhaps telling her to adjust their course or whatever he needed her to know. Due to the storm, they were diverted 136 miles from their original destination to Saint-Louis, Senegal. After reaching Dakar, they took a much-needed break to recuperate and service their aircraft before continuing their epic journey. On June 8, while resting in Dakar, Noonan wrote to his wife, expressing high regard for Amelia Earhart: "Amelia is a grand person for such a trip—she is the only woman flier I would care to make such a trip with. Because in addition to being a fine companion, she can take hardship as well as a man—and work like one."

Amelia and Noonan's nineteen-hundred-mile, thirteen-hour flight across the Atlantic would have made glowing headlines even a few years earlier. But the world's fascination with transatlantic flights had since diminished; while still perilous, such feats no longer captivated the public as they once had. Nevertheless, the *New York Herald Tribune* obtained an exclusive on Amelia's African stops. Yet their remarkable expedition was unexpectedly eclipsed by a more sensational news event—the untimely death of Jean Harlow, the platinum-blond film star, at age twenty-six from acute kidney failure. Her death seized the nation's attention, echoing the space given to the recent Hindenburg shock. Intriguingly, Harlow and Amelia, who both spent much of their youth in Kansas City, might have crossed paths within the Hollywood scene. Amelia and Noonan might have gotten wind of "Baby" Harlow's tragic end while on their flight.

A new continent immediately captivated Amelia's senses, and her American fans were soon updated on her adventures through notes she wired back to George. She was putting in her best effort under the pressure of delivering a contract. She once described Africa's aromas as "all kinds of different exciting smells" and a "sort of strong tang" of people. This cringeworthy remark, reflective of the dated anthropological perspectives of her time, was followed by a firsthand account of Amelia indulging in a bag of freshly roasted peanuts. The sight of a woman flier dressed in rumpled slacks and a button-down plaid shirt was so unexpected to Africans that someone in the community may have taken note of Amelia as well.

At a reception held in her honor in Dakar, Amelia was simply too zonked for formalities but dutifully wore the only dress she had brought to the governor-general's mansion.

She had readers everywhere, including one in the White House: Eleanor

Roosevelt. "All day I have been thinking of Amelia Earhart somewhere over the Atlantic Ocean and hoping she will make her flight safely," Roosevelt wrote in her popular column. "She is one of the most fascinating people I know, because . . . she never seems to think that any of the things she does require any courage."

After a few more hours of rest, Amelia faced the dangerous task of crossing Africa via less-established routes. Amelia and Noonan's continued journey, as chronicled in the logbook, tallied more dates and miles:

June 10—1,140 miles to the town of Gao in French West Africa (eight hours), on the upper branches of the Niger River.

June 11—1,000 miles to Fort Lamy, French Equatorial Africa—straight across the Sahara—six hours forty minutes. [From the sky, they spotted a herd of hippos. They also spent the night.]

June 12—900 miles to El Fasher, Anglo-Egyptian Sudan.

As Amelia wrote on June 13, after traveling five hundred miles to Khartoum, the desert capital of Sudan, heat waves danced up from the field—temperatures reached 110 degrees in the shade. Next Amelia and Fred traveled to two small towns in Eritrea, at that time an African colony of Italy, in the desert on the African coast of the Red Sea. The first stop was hot-as-hell Massawa. The language barrier was as tricky as the weather, since neither spoke Italian. Afterward, they headed for the similarly muggy port of Assab.

Amelia and Fred next flew from Africa to Karachi, now a part of Pakistan but part of British India back then. Her plane was thoroughly inspected on June 15 at the best airfield yet. Amelia put on a new white flight suit and smiled broadly. It was the first time anyone had flown to India from the Horn of Africa around Saudi Arabia's southern coast, which George proudly told her via phone. Half a world away, she said, "I'll cable you tomorrow; tell you then when I think we will get to Howland. Goodbye! See you in Oakland!" After George's urging, she sent more notes about her morning ride on a camel during her trip, which his staff edited into a piece for the *New York Herald Tribune*. "I climbed into the saddle and swung between his two humps. It was a startling takeoff as we rose . . . Camels should have shock absorbers."

From Karachi, Amelia wrote a short but tender letter to George: "I wish you were here. So many things you would enjoy. . . . Perhaps someday we could fly together to some of the remote places of the world—just for fun." As with many couples facing unexpected turmoil like financial difficulties, they had made arrangements for their marriage that provided safety. In a tumultuous decade when paychecks were uncertain, they were true partners. Some insiders would agree, including Putnam protégé Harold McCracken, who described their marriage as not overly passionate but one of mutual and genuine devotion.

During their stop in Karachi on June 16, Noonan took the opportunity to write to his wife, Bea, sharing insights into their mindset as they journeyed on the other side of the world. His letter sought to reassure her amid swirling rumors back home—both of romance and of disaster: "We should be back home in about two weeks from now. . . . We received word this morning that reports in the States said we had crashed. How such a rumor would materialize is beyond me because we have had no trouble whatsoever."

After his pleasant conversation with his wife, George was naturally in a better mood. He gave a brief, jovial interview from his fifteenth-floor office as the aviator's husband in Midtown Manhattan. He said his wife spent most of her time in the pilot's seat, which had over a hundred instruments: "She is kept very busy watching those instruments. In fact, she carries a small alarm clock to remind her when the petrol supply in one of the tanks is due to run out." He added that she "lives on tomato juice and carries cans in which she knocks a hole and inserts a straw. Occasionally, she eats a sandwich. She has emergency rations for a forced landing." That upbeat day, George even hinted at the potential of a film deal. Two of the biggest studios showed "strong interest" due to Amelia's significant popularity among female audiences. The film would be based on her soon-to-be-released book *World Flight*, which Harcourt, Brace & Company would expedite for a fall release, featuring her photos from the journey.

If the major studios lost interest, George had a backup plan. He had financial involvement in a smaller company, Major Pictures, led by his associate Emanuel Cohen. Once the vice president of production at Paramount, Cohen had been collaborating with George on various projects since the Lindbergh era. In 1935, Cohen had departed Paramount to establish his own production company, which roped in big names like Mae West and Bing Crosby. George, who had held the position of chairman of the editorial board at Paramount until his departure in December 1934, became an asset to Cohen. Recognizing George's impressive network and industry knowledge, Cohen hired him, granting him the impressive title of "Eastern Editorial Representative." (However, in practical terms, George's primary responsibility was to promote eight films for Cohen.)

The world flight had cost them $150,000—which was $30,000 more than expected, but it was entirely funded by Purdue and some "high-placed" friends. Amelia's daily dispatches were published under her name and edited by a *New York Herald Tribune* reporter—likely C. B. Allen. These articles were syndicated to thirty-six cities and brought in $15,000. Additionally, Amelia's commemorative stamps, carried in the nose of her plane, were sold through Gimbels, generating just over $12,000 for the flight. Stamp covers were priced at $2.50 for those not autographed by Amelia and $5.00 for those she signed. She autographed approximately half of these covers.

Even Amelia knew by now that the gamble they'd made together was finally starting to really pay off. A few trade publications tipped off by George reported that CBS and NBC were battling over who would land two exclusive Amelia Earhart broadcasts—one when she landed in Honolulu and the other when she was back on the mainland in San Francisco. "A breakfast cereal" could sponsor an Amelia Earhart radio series for youth. (George did not reveal the company, but it was Quaker Oats.) Did he mention that the NBC Artists' Bureau had agreed to a sixty-day contract with her? It was a pipeline to real money, and she would first be a guest on Cecil B. DeMille's popular Monday night talk show with forty million listeners.

Amelia and Noonan skillfully navigated 1,350 miles across central India through hazy skies, guided by the network of railway lines below; however, the two experienced a tense moment, narrowly avoiding a collision with black eagles soaring at five thousand feet. Amelia told Noonan that she wished they could have landed in Agra to see the Taj Mahal, the giant love letter to Mumtaz Mahal, the Mughal emperor Shah Jahan's beloved wife, who died giving birth to their fourteenth child.

Now flying from Karachi to Calcutta (now Kolkata), they passed over the vast and barren Thar Desert. "A great barren stretch," Earhart wrote. "A southerly wind whipped the sand into the air until the ground disappeared from view. We flew along until the ridges grew into mountains and poked their dark backs like sharks through a yellow sea. But the air cleared somewhat, so we could again see what we were flying over—dry river beds, a few roads connecting villages, and then a railroad." After they landed in Calcutta during monsoon season, the weather cleared, allowing the team of two to relax with a cup of tea while the mechanics worked on the aircraft. When Noonan became noticeably inebriated at a bar one night in Calcutta, Amelia became concerned about his behavior. As a result of Amelia's concerns about Noonan's drinking issues, she spoke in coded language to George, who was staying at the Hotel Seymour in Midtown Manhattan. During the prearranged call, Paul Collins and Gene Vidal were present in George's suite, and they were surprised by the excellent reception.

Amelia struggled to decide what to do as her confidence in Fred Noonan waned. Despite George's suggestion to halt the flight, Amelia wouldn't listen—what was the point of second-guessing now? There was only one challenging leg, or "bad hop," that she had to complete. George suggested she get in touch with him again once she landed in New Guinea. Despite her reservations, they took off from Calcutta's Dum Dum Airport on June 18. There were some malfunctions with their equipment, but they could not find repairs there. A brief stop in Akyab (now Sittwe) in Burma (now Myanmar) was made by Amelia and Noonan on June 19. On the ground, people waved hats at their plane from the rice paddies. During her stop, Amelia picked up some birthday bracelets for Amy, her niece, in Boston, and Noonan purchased a silver bowl for his new wife, but to save weight, they didn't collect other souvenirs.

Arriving in Rangoon (now called Yangon), Amelia and Noonan took in the sights, but Noonan's refusal to remove his shoes at a temple left Amelia with a miserable face on as she quietly went in as told. An initial run at Bangkok was foiled by a monsoon. When they finally left Rangoon on June 20, their plane skimmed over a sodden runway and adjacent trees. They covered three hundred miles to Bangkok, then flew to Singapore and Bandoeng in the Dutch East Indies. At the Grand Hotel Preanger in Bandoeng KLM techs serviced their Electra. Nearby Batavia (now Jakarta) was renowned for its java. Photos from Batavia show Amelia and Noonan smiling for cameras, but it was here where Amelia contracted dysentery, a severe gastrointestinal infection marked by diarrhea and dehydration—a potentially deadly condition in an era without advanced antibiotics. Francis "Fuzz" Furman, a young American mechanic for the Martin Company who was advising the duo during that difficult stretch of late June, was staying in the same fine hotel as the fliers and said they got plenty of rest. Noonan, who had "no more than one" shared beer, was worried about only one thing: hitting Howland Island.

From Bandung, as the unwell Amelia isolated in her hotel room, Noonan wrote yet another keep-your-chin-up letter to his wife. He must have been up all night, for he also managed to write a lengthy letter to Beverly Hunter, an attractive eighteen-year-old girl from Rockford, Illinois. Beverly had been his pen pal for two years, and Noonan maintained a polite and respectful tone in the letter. He mentioned the possibility of a lecture tour and said he would visit Rockford if he could. Although one could speculate about whether Fred would have written to Beverly if she weren't such an attractive young woman with a striking resemblance to Rita Hayworth, the letter, which is now held in a private collection in San Diego, contained nothing inappropriate; a careful read reveals that he mentioned the first round-the-world airmail they carried and offered an autograph from Amelia Earhart.

On June 25, George spoke again to the press, mentioning his conversation with Amelia from Surabaya. He hoped she would be home soon after completing her remaining stops in Howland, Hawaii, and, finally, Oakland. On June 27, Amelia and Noonan flew approximately 770 miles to Kupang, located on the southern tip of Timor in the Dutch East Indies.

The next day, a queasy Amelia Earhart and Fred Noonan zoomed five hundred miles to tropical Port Darwin in Australia, making a quick pit stop in East Timor for refueling. But due to a malfunctioning radio, Amelia arrived unannounced late Monday morning. When they heard her roaring motor and caught sight of the plane, swarms of excited onlookers rushed toward the Ross Smith Aerodrome. Oh, they knew exactly who had blown into town! Up popped Amelia from the hatch, her face bright with forced cheer as she took in the warm, steamy air. "I guess I'm late, but I am here just the same," she quipped. After giving a cheery hello to the greeting party, her first concern was whether the two Irvin Caterpillar chutes from the United States had arrived. (They had and were packed on board.)

She looked awful when she arrived and politely requested a quick bath and lunch before facing the media. (Besides exhaustion, the dysentery was another beast to tame.) They whisked her away to the aviator's room at the nearby Victoria Hotel, where every headline-grabbing visiting flier had once stayed. "We eat very little in the air, but when we land, we make up for it!" she confessed with a wink.

RAAF sergeant Stan Rose, the airport's radioman, was puzzled by Amelia's radio silence, as it was legally required to make contact. Approaching her, he inquired about the communication issue, and though reluctant, she allowed him to examine her equipment. Rose discovered that a blown power fuse had rendered the radio and transmitter nonfunctional in her Electra. Sheepishly, Amelia admitted that the equipment had not worked since they left the Americas, and the reports heard by amateur radio enthusiasts were merely wishful thinking. Reflecting on this later,

Rose remarked, "People tend to hear what they want to hear; their beliefs influence what they hear unintentionally." But then Rose thoroughly explained the situation and assured Amelia that it would be an easy fix, earning her gratitude. Though she warmed up to him and smiled more, Rose was surprised by her and Noonan's lack of training on rudimentary equipment, especially considering they had spare fuses on board that could have saved them from the trouble. When Amelia summoned Noonan, his responses were sparse. "Amelia was talkative when in the mood," Rose observed, but she wasn't one to chatter incessantly.

After the radio mishap, Amelia faced another hurdle with the quarantine officer. Her vaccination certificate needed the required government signature. She briefly considered flying to Canberra to get it sorted, but the idea was quickly shelved when someone highlighted the nearly two-thousand-mile distance and the ten-hour flight time. The ever-persistent quarantine officer, Dr. Carruthers, delayed the plane for ten hours until higher-ups intervened, granting Amelia the necessary pratique.

Before Amelia and Noonan departed Australia, workers gave the Electra a wash, and Sergeant Rose made an unusual gesture to his new friend. He volunteered to provide back bearings every fifteen minutes at five hundred kilocycles, a practice uncommon for most flights. Keeping his word, he offered three bearings until she was out of range, each one a crucial directional guide that charted her course over the expansive ocean, ensuring her safe departure from Australian soil. These periodic readings, essential for accurate navigation, helped Amelia maintain her intended path, and Rose continued to hear her perfectly until she blew out of range.

Days later, in newspaper syndication, Amelia regretted not getting to cradle a koala or meet the legendary New Zealander Jean Batten, who was then known as the first woman to fly solo from England to New Zealand. She hoped she would have another opportunity to visit the nation's "beauties."

On the day Amelia Earhart and Fred Noonan arrived in Lae, Papua and New Guinea were still separate territories under Australian control. Just past 4:00 p.m. on June 29, after twelve hundred miles, seven hours, and forty-three minutes, the plane touched down at its final stop before the "big hop" over the vast Pacific Ocean. The entire town turned out to welcome the Americans, who emerged from the hatch of their shiny Electra into a sauna bath of heat and humidity with big, tired smiles.

Amelia, showing signs of sleep deprivation and persistent diarrhea, looked far from her prime in the blurry wire images sent after her arrival. Her face was bloated, her skin had taken on a ghoulish tone, and she appeared all skin and bones. Though exhausted, she greeted the townspeople warmly, even as her primary focus remained on her plane.

Historically, Lae's importance to the West was forged by its gold mining industry. In 1920, the League of Nations mandated the Australians to replace the crushed Germans as the dominant European influence in the region. By 1928, the once-modest settlement was filled with Australians eager to mine and even a few Americans seeking to turn a fast dollar. Lae was a racially segregated company town for the upstart airliner Guinea Airways, whose cargo delivery in the mountainous region had fast transformed it into a connected economic engine. The town's tropical charm masked a darker reality in which native New Guinean workers were confined to the western side of town and faced daily hardships. Chinese immigrants arrived in the early 1930s, shamefully paid half the wages of white labor. Due to their own hateful experiences, they showed much more kindness toward the Melanesian community and established a handful of trade stores to earn extra income. Amelia Earhart likely purchased her only souvenir in Lae, a pidgin English dictionary, from one of these five stores in what was deemed Lae's "Chinatown."

Flora "Ma" Stewart, the locally famous widowed proprietress of Hotel Cecil, provided the Americans with the best (and only) accommodations in town. This square-shaped Art Deco building, built after the aviation boom and only a year old, had twelve upstairs rooms featuring glass sliding doors that opened out to a veranda with lounge chairs. In an era when outhouses were the norm in New Guinea, there were indoor bathrooms down the hall with separate hot-water showers for women and men. Downstairs was a large shared lounge with cooling fans, a dining room, and a well-equipped kitchen. And for the tipplers in town, the all-important bar. But after the (sleep-starved) Amelia walked into her well-appointed room without niceties at the front desk, Ma Stewart still remembered her manner years later as "rather fresh."

The local radioman for Guinea Airways was an Australian named Harry Balfour, who later recalled that "AE and Fred eventually settled into the hotel at Lae and would not see anyone but sent a message that she particularly wanted to see me. I went down to the hotel, and she wanted all the weather plus her private messages that had stacked up for her. I went over all these with her in detail, and she asked me if I could come to the hotel every day and bring her the weather reports and any other traffic. Fred trotted around quite a bit. I cannot remember everywhere he went, but AE was so enthusiastic over the flight that she did not want to go anywhere or be entertained by the local ladies (much to the anger of the local ladies)!"

By an earlier arrangement, she had another important ally in town to ease her stay: Guinea Airways' general manager, Eric Chater, a thirty-five-year-old English aviator with the swoony, rugged good looks of a British aviation film star. Chater said he would help her with anything she needed, and she told him she intended to leave the following morning at 10:00 a.m. Chater invited her to dine with him and his wife, Maisie, in his well-appointed (employer-owned) home, asking a few well-regarded locals to join them, including Jim Collopy, the regional aviation supervisor, who flew in from Salamaua to ensure that all went smoothly for her. Amelia was surprised to hear from Chater that Guinea Airways had operated a Lockheed Electra, just one serial number away from hers, for over twelve months in Lae. They had plenty to talk about.

Hotel Cecil's room for Collopy was next door to Noonan's, one down from Amelia's. Twenty-five-year-old Collopy was a famous scallywag in the area, a bachelor who enjoyed his beers and a good time. Noonan and Collopy met in the dimly lit hotel bar about an hour before the dinner at Chater's. Noonan had changed clothes and was drinking alone, so Collopy walked over to the navigator for a quick word. "Are you going to Chater's tonight, Fred?" he asked. Noonan (according to Collopy, at least) snapped, "The skinny bitch didn't invite me."

"Mr. Chater would have invited you, surely," Collopy said. He cheerfully added, "To hell with that nonsense!" And then he suggested that they sit together for a drink, after which Noonan's mood brightened. Noonan drank double Scotches, while Collopy drank beer. It was a very boozy night.

After more than a few Scotches with his newfound companion, Noonan seemed to relax quite a bit. In a moment of candor, he revealed that he had been unexpectedly "pitchforked" into this journey, that Amelia's original navigator, Harry Manning, had withdrawn after the Hawaii incident, effectively leaving the position vacant and thrusting him into the role almost by default. Amelia and George recognized Noonan's prowess as a navigator, but he had recently lost his job with Pan Am. The compensation from this assignment was crucial for his new marriage. From their conversation, it became clear to Collopy that Noonan had been reluctant to embark on this journey. Surprisingly, no love was lost between Noonan and Amelia. In Collopy's recollection, Noonan seemed relatively confident about navigating to Howland Island. But he did have concerns: the radio had posed challenges since their time in Darwin, Australia, and he was a tad nervous about the Electra's chronometers, essential tools for navigation.

Lae was a hard-drinking town in a hard-drinking era, and others wandered in and joined them for "a good session" at the bar, including Captain Bertie Heath, a Junkers pilot for Guinea Airways, and Bob Iredale, the assistant manager of Vacuum Oil Company, tasked with fueling Amelia's plane the following day. Eventually, Chater realized that Collopy had never made it to dinner.

Meanwhile, Amelia was drained and worried about the forthcoming flight to Howland Island. She only wanted to write up her diaries and go to bed early. She missed the sight of her tanked-up navigator, who had sworn blind after the incident in India that there wouldn't be any more slips with alcohol. Collopy put Noonan to bed around midnight, and Amelia, face creased with sleep, was awakened by the sounds of him getting the navigator straightened out after he got tangled up in the mosquito netting and fell to the floor.

Hearing this commotion from next door, Amelia called out through the thin walls, "Is that you, Fred?" Did he have people with him? Amelia asked, and Collopy responded, "Yes, me."

"Who is me?" Amelia demanded.

Noonan made such loud, drunken "shushing noises" to his new friend that Collopy couldn't help but laugh hard at the memory later. "I heard her get out of bed, and her light goes on . . ." Collopy quickly left the room but easily overheard harsh exchanges as she furiously reminded Fred of their upcoming flight.

"Fred, how could you be drinking?"

Noonan's breath reeked of Scotch as he defensively questioned her anger. "Well, I knew we wouldn't be leaving the next day."

Collopy later said he understood Amelia's rage at the navigator who'd pledged sobriety, but since Noonan never mentioned checking his chronometer that night, he did seem to understand that he had an extra day.

As Amelia decided what to do, George sent her a wire detailing the Fourth of July celebrations and a lucrative live radio broadcast opportunity, urging her to hasten her return. He certainly didn't tell her he was angry about recent press reports in America suggesting that Amelia was about to divorce him.

On the morning of June 30, after Collopy had replaced a faulty propeller and the airfield staff had checked the plane, Chater approached him: "Mate, what happened to you? Why didn't you come to dinner?"

"Oh, I got mixed up with Fred Noonan, who told me he wasn't invited." (This intel surprised Chater.)

In hindsight, Collopy regretted missing dinner with Amelia, which might have provided insight into the flight's perils.

More issues arose the next morning when Amelia met with Guinea Airways mechanics. She confirmed that Noonan had been hammered after a night at the bar and had forgotten a critical task the previous night—what aviators back then called the "time tick," which had to be done after daylight. When flying by the stars, precise time is vital. Think of a star as a marker in the sky. If you know the angle of that star at a specific moment—

for instance, precisely 23 degrees at 11:26 p.m.—you can determine your exact location. This was a big deal in 1937, when flying technology wasn't as advanced, and the "time tick" was a secret code that helped pilots determine their intended direction. Even a tiny mistake in Noonan's clock could disrupt their calculations and cause uncertainty about their location. Getting the time right was crucial, despite the possibility of a slight error of about five to ten miles, and Noonan had to complete this task at night. In 1937, different countries, such as Australia, Vietnam, and New Zealand, followed different time standards. Fortunately, during the night, they could rely on a strong and consistent signal for this job.

Amelia's irritation with Noonan grew by the hour, but she kept it to herself. She understood that if they were going to make it back, she'd need to watch him closely. Delaying their departure by a day served two purposes: it gave Chater's mechanics time to smooth out the final kinks and gave Noonan a chance to steady his footing.

An alarming telegram from Amelia reached George after she left her navigator's room: RADIO MISUNDERSTANDING AND PERSONNEL UNFITNESS. PROBABLY WILL HOLD ONE DAY.

She knew that George and his assistants back in New York required local insights to craft an article from her notes, and Chater devised a fascinating field trip for her and Noonan so she could keep him close and ensure his sobriety. Learning that the hotel driver was not feeling well, Amelia went ahead and borrowed Cecil's Bedford utility truck, and Noonan drove them eleven miles east to the outlying and Indigenous Sepik village of Butibum. Their jaunt to the "primitives" was just a few hours of sightseeing, but Amelia had Noonan close and managed to scribble notes. Although a ghostwriter would later polish her wired and mailed accounts, her observant and ever-curious nature shines through in what she managed to get down for her syndicated column, which paid for part of her flight: "The village was built more or less around a central open plaza. All huts were on stilts, and underneath the dogs and pigs held forth. We were told that the natives train pigs as 'watchdogs.' Fred said he would hate to come home late at night and admit being bitten by a pig! Some of the huts had carvings around under the eaves, grotesque-colored animals and crocodiles being the most numerous. They reminded me of the work encountered in some parts of Africa."

Amelia and Noonan went to bed early after dinner at the home of a local administrator named Allan Roberts, whose jurisdiction also included the mail. Thousands of Amelia's covers, stored in the nose of her plane in the baggage area, were franked overnight by Roberts and his postal assistant in response to a desperate request for assistance. (This proves that the covers were on board, and George Palmer Putnam had been shamed into honesty by Harry Manning after all.)

After sunup in Lae and breakfast at the Cecil on July 2, Amelia tested her aircraft following a documented tune-up, as detailed in a report Collopy sent to his superiors. In preparation, they shed any unnecessary weight. They prioritized additional fuel, ensuring they kept emergency rations, water, a two-person rubber raft, life belts, flares, a flare gun, and signaling equipment. Fully fueled, the Electra could hold 1,150 gallons of gasoline, providing a range of four thousand miles—though headwinds could reduce that significantly.

Amelia entrusted Guinea Airways' radio operator, Harry Balfour, with several personal items: her .32-caliber revolver, twenty rounds of ammunition, and, perhaps inadvertently, her radio facility books. These books were crucial, containing detailed instructions for communicating with the USCGC *Itasca* near Howland Island. The oversight in leaving these books behind, which may have been accidental, was notable, especially since Balfour's station operated solely on voice transmission and not CW, making the detailed information in the books even more essential. Additionally, to lighten the aircraft's load, Amelia sent several packages and clothing items back to George. These packages took six weeks to arrive. During this process, in a concerning oversight, smoke bombs intended for sea rescue were left under Noonan's bed at the Cecil and discovered only later during routine housekeeping.

Amelia must have had some last-minute panicking about her and Noonan's lack of radio skills, as she had an unusual and desperate request for Chater.

Could Lae's radio operator, Balfour, accompany them to Hawaii for radio support? She promised to arrange his return airfare to Lae, but Balfour had no desire to go, and Chater was equally reluctant to lose his only radio operator in an aviation town. Despite Amelia's willingness to drop some precious fuel to bring Balfour aboard and increase their safety, the answer was no. After that, she could only acquiesce.

After the Electra received mechanical tweaks from Guinea Airways' Herman Hotz and Ted Finn, Amelia completed a test flight. On her return, one of Noonan's new drinking buddies, Bob Iredale, had his Melanesian "boys" fill the plane to its almost capacity with gasoline —1,100 gallons of fuel and 64 gallons of oil—pushing the limits of the plane's takeoff clearance.

Amelia and Noonan were tragically unprepared for this last and most challenging leg of their trip. Amelia was sick and had lost considerable weight. The alcoholic Noonan was still recovering from a severe bender. Compounding their challenges, neither Amelia nor Noonan was adept at radio communication, and their radio, lacking the necessary antennae, was inadequately equipped. The crucial radio facility book, containing Amelia's communication arrangements with the *Itasca* and suggested frequencies, had been hastily and carelessly left behind. It was unlikely she could remember all the details from these papers—fat chance, really. The pilot and her navigator were not well versed in Morse code, their emergency smoke bombs had been forgotten under Noonan's bed, and their fuel was barely sufficient to reach their destination, assuming perfect conditions. This was the state of things as Amelia Earhart pointed her Electra toward a tiny speck in the earth's most yawning emptiness.

At Lae's airstrip, she gave a short speech, later wired to the world. "I set out to cruise the world, and up to now, it has been just that," she said. "The biggest experience is going to be when I peer through the Electra's windscreen over the Pacific and see the smudge of land that is America. . . . I shall be glad when we have the hazards of its navigation behind us."

In vintage footage of the moments before departure, Noonan springs up alongside her, meeting the camera's gaze. If he wasn't sufficiently sober, he concealed it deftly, and as they took off, he moved to his navigator's position in the back, behind the fuel tanks.

As the Electra taxied down the grass strip, a crowd cheered and waved goodbye. Amelia navigated the plane to the narrow runway's end, which abruptly dropped fifty feet to the ocean's edge. With its heavy fuel load, the plane disappeared as it sank toward the sea. The onlookers held their breath, unsure if it had crashed. Their anxiety quickly turned to awe when, moments later, the Electra reappeared, gracefully skimming the wave tops before steadily gaining altitude. The skillful pilot employed the "unsticking" technique, using a few intentional bounces to free the plane from the waves' grip. The aircraft headed eastward after a controlled dip and a deft maneuver around a steep overhang. With both admiration and concern, observers noted that Amelia's takeoff was a masterful yet daring feat, given the considerable fuel she carried. The Electra was filled with one thousand gallons of fuel; flight professionals would have called it "5,000 lbs. over gross." The seamless execution of the risky departure left a lasting impression on all who witnessed it.

"She had her hair cut short like a man, and wore trousers and checked shirt, and from a short distance looked like a slim, freckle-faced youth," Balfour, Lae's only radioman, would say. "But to talk to, she was very charming and seemed to take in all that was said to her. She was an excellent pilot and won the respect of our pilots for the way she handled the Lockheed."

After the Electra's departure, Collopy stayed in town another night to plot Amelia's course, keeping in touch with Balfour as he monitored the radio. As planned, Amelia communicated with him until she flew out of range. Allan Vagg, a radio operator at the nearby Bulolo station, was the fellow to hear the final message—that Amelia was flying at seventy-three hundred feet in heavy cloud cover, soon descending below. "Goodbye, Lae. I'm turning over to night frequency." That was the last anyone in Lae heard her voice.

Amelia settled into her seat, still dressed in the rumpled pants and plaid shirt that had been her uniform throughout the trip. As the Electra climbed to eight thousand feet, she prepared for the long cruise ahead. They were scheduled to arrive at Howland Island at 6:30 a.m. the following morning, Howland time, after an eighteen-hour flight. Before resuming their journey toward Hawaii, Amelia and Noonan had made a critical decision to leave behind the damaged trailing-wire antenna, which had proved problematic during takeoffs and landings. This choice was intended to simplify flight mechanics but inadvertently deprived them of crucial long-distance radio communications, significantly heightening the risks of navigating to the remote Howland Island.

Howland Island, a speck of earth barely the size of half of Central Park, floats alone in the vastness of the Pacific Ocean. Situated more than two thousand miles away from the nearest continents, it stands as a solitary outpost on the watery horizon. This island, no more than a raised coral atoll, was to be the Electra's last touch of solid ground before the leap across the open sea to Hawaii. Here, amid the immense isolation, surrounded by an endless expanse of blue, it promised a brief respite and crucial refueling stop for Amelia and her navigator before they would resume their ambitious flight across the globe's largest ocean.

Back in Burbank, Paul Mantz, Amelia's trusted adviser, was overwhelmed with anxiety as he chain-smoked in his office. The absence of the trailing antenna, crucial for navigation over vast ocean distances, filled him with dread. Without it, Amelia would only be able to spot Howland Island once directly overhead. Meanwhile, George Palmer Putnam, overwhelmed by his new responsibilities after William T. Miller's resignation in the wake of the Hawaii crash, was struggling to manage the expedition's logistics from his office. George's sporadic updates and the sudden decision for Amelia to take off from Oakland when Mantz wasn't present further unnerved him. George was now solely in charge of critical decisions, and his consolidation of control raised the stakes enormously—there were just a few more days to payday, but Amelia's safety hung in the balance.

While leaving behind the trailing-wire antenna was undeniably a grave error, it is challenging to place the blame entirely on Amelia and Noonan. They were also hindered by outdated navigational charts that Noonan had acquired in San Pedro, California. These maps erroneously positioned Howland Island about five and a half miles from its true location—a discrepancy known since 1937 but not updated in publications until 1941. Although this decision to forgo the antenna was indeed flawed, their reliance on these inaccurate charts was an equally significant and unfortunate misstep.

How was the mood inside the plane? Despite documented tensions due to Noonan's unseemly bender in Lae, they did not radio for assistance after crossing the international date line.

Meanwhile, at their isolated island pit stop, picket ships poised to assist were at the ready: the USCGC *Itasca*'s crew waited offshore; the USS *Ontario*, a seagoing tug, stayed between Lae and Howland to provide additional support; and the USS *Swan*, a minesweeper, patrolled midway between Howland and Hawaii.

Preparations were also in place on land. Since 1935, a group of mostly Hawaiian men had been helping settle equatorial islands for the United States, and these men were considered perfect cheap labor—receiving just three dollars a day. However, the underpaid men assigned to Howland diligently prepared for their renowned guest's arrival. Despite the presence of rats on the atoll, who rather unnervingly watched the settlers as they ate, the small, makeshift "government house" on the primarily deserted island where she'd be staying had amenities like a rainwater shower consisting of a canvas-enclosed fifty-gallon drum of fresh water, clean towels, and sheets. Hot-pink paint on the walls and curtains added a touch of femininity. A small, separate hut was set up for Noonan.

As Commander Warner K. Thompson told embedding AP and UPI wire reporters, preparation details were fine, but how hundreds of migratory birds were slaughtered on the island was to be kept secret: The *Itasca*'s crew worried about various seabirds (or gooneys, as they called them) that might collide with Amelia's propeller—terns and frigatebirds and grand albatrosses with eleven-foot wingspans. Sailors consider albatrosses lucky unless they meet unfortunate fates, like in Coleridge's poem "The Rime of the Ancient Mariner." The runway at Howland Island was blocked by birds, and TNT blocks were used to clear it temporarily. Despite the dynamite, many birds immediately flew back into position. Commander Thompson then ordered a larger group of his men ashore. "The day before she was to arrive," recalled mess cook Carl Panhorst, "the captain had us go out on the island with clubs and said, 'Kill as many of those birds as you can.'" (Wire service writers more pleasantly reported that they "scared the birds" away. And adding a further drain on George's wallet, the bill for this "cleanup" was on him.)

A few days before Amelia and Noonan's scheduled arrival, the crew of the *Itasca* set up an experimental portable direction finder under a tent. This last-minute addition was compact, lightweight, and smaller than a small television. As a precaution, the US Navy decided to leave this iffy device at the dock in Honolulu before departing. However, Tommy O'Hare, a third-class *Itasca* radioman, brought it on board while he was there having a smoke. The device, labeled with the model number T22, had a breadboard-style design with a loop on top. But Chief Radioman Leo Bellarts and his team were unfamiliar with it, since radio direction finding on this frequency (3105) was quite novel.

Despite being prepared for Amelia and Noonan's arrival under a hot equatorial sun, with the birds taken care of, the men on the *Itasca* had yet to hear from the pair for an extended period. It took much radio communication to finally confirm their departure from Lae. Richard Black's face brightened after hearing the good news. Black wasn't a regular member of the *Itasca*'s crew; he was a special guest sent by the government. Having served as an engineer under Admiral Byrd during two Antarctic expeditions, Black had landed a lucrative Depression-era gig overseeing the establishment of US territories on Pacific equatorial islands. Black pulled together a group of trusted friends he'd met during the long expedition to the island, including Lieutenant Commander Frank Kenner and UPI press representative Howard Hanzlick. "Amelia's on her way; let's toast her success. Any bourbon fans here?" Black proposed as he poured the spirit from the ship's four-case stash he had acquired en route from an island shop into scary big tumblers. Hanzlick wondered if he would be undone by the one glass.

As they toasted, the sky was pitch black with a new moon overhead. After Amelia made contact, nobody was overly concerned. If Noonan's celestial navigation failed to bring them within visual range, there was a backup plan: smoke signals. With an expert like Noonan on board, the very man who taught Pan Am's men celestial navigation, what could go wrong? Moreover, Amelia had promised the *Itasca* that she would listen to the radio frequency.

At least, that was the promise she had made.

At 4:30 p.m. Sydney time (6:30 a.m. Greenwich Civil Time, or GCT), Nauru Island's radio station picked up Amelia Earhart's Electra signals. Communication continued for five hours, until 9:30 p.m. Sydney time (11:30 a.m. GCT). By 8:30 p.m. Sydney time (10:30 a.m. GCT), Nauru Island reported that Amelia had spotted the British steamer *Myrtlebank*, which was en route to Nauru and arrived at the island at dawn. Based on this sighting, her position was estimated to be about sixty miles south of Nauru Island.

At 2:48 a.m. local Howland Island time (2:18 p.m. GCT), the U.S. Coast Guard cutter *Itasca*, stationed at Howland Island for plane-guard duty, made its first contact with Earhart. This contact, which occurred approximately two hours and forty-five minutes after Nauru's last reported signal, was faint and staticky. At 3:45 a.m., Earhart stated she would listen every hour and every half hour. At 4:43 a.m., the *Itasca* crew heard her say, "Overcast."

Why the cockeyed refusal to give up her position? She only inquired about the weather before tuning out and going incommunicado. Perhaps, like many accomplished pilots, she was proud and touchy about criticism. Repeated messages from the *Itasca* to stay online remained unanswered, and hearing this, Commander Warner K. Thompson was disgusted. "I screamed all night into that microphone," Tommy O'Hare recalled years later, adding that the signals she did give were too brief and weak to get a fix on her location. "But the shit hadn't hit the fan yet," O'Hare said. Chief Radioman Leo Bellarts was still asleep.

Around 6:00 in the morning, there were some puffy clouds above and blue skies all around. Richard Black put on his US Navy duck suit (white slacks, shirt, and necktie) with the embedded press photographers. As a man of high rank, Black had the privilege of taking refuge from the sun in the tiny government house where Amelia would stay.

When she next communicated over the radio at 6:14 a.m., she informed O'Hare that she was two hundred miles from Howland Island. She urgently requested a radio bearing and detailed her plan to whistle into the microphone. She believed the sound might help the cutter determine her and Noonan's location. Inside the radio room—one deck below the bridge and outfitted with seven receivers—the radiomen on duty exchanged puzzled glances. Whistling? They were used to seasoned pilots using CW, more commonly known as Morse code. These pilots would send long dashes, also called "dahs," to guide the receiving direction finders for fixes and navigational aid. It was later revealed that Amelia struggled with Morse code, despite being a two-time recipient of aviation's handsomest medal, the Harmon Trophy. If her original navigator, Harry Manning, had still been with her, it seems likely that his expertise in radio operations would have circumvented these issues. To their astonishment, even the seasoned Fred Noonan could transmit at a rate of only ten words per minute.

O'Hare found Amelia's lack of CW skills both perplexing and careless: "They gave her a license. I know she needed to pass the examination to obtain it, but believe me, she couldn't differentiate an *N* from an *A*. She overlooked one crucial detail: ships could have zeroed in on her. All she had to do was hold the key down; bearings could have been taken from around five hundred." He added, "How was she going to communicate on five hundred kilocycles when she didn't know the Morse code? She couldn't send and receive a dot." O'Hare emphasized that mastering Morse code requires dedication, whether one practices at school or home. These differences in channels and kilohertz are crucial, as they determine the method and effectiveness of communication. Amelia's inability to transmit Morse code effectively on five hundred kilocycles limited her ability to communicate with ships and potential rescuers. Without proficient Morse code skills, her distress signals may have gone unnoticed or misunderstood. Noonan might have caught more code, but he was stationed at the back of the plane with fuel tanks in between. They communicated by passing notes using a bamboo pole; he didn't have a headset.

However, what she emitted wasn't precisely a whistle, as Chief Radioman Leo Bellarts noted in a separate account. It lacked melody. "I jotted down 'whistling' because she mentioned it," Bellarts said. "She produced a shrill note."

At 6:15 a.m., she transmitted: "Please take [a] bearing on us and report in half [an] hour. I will make noise in mic."

At 7:18 a.m., the *Itasca* responded: "Cannot take bearing on 3105 very good, please send signals on 500 kHz or would you like to take a bearing on us? Go ahead." The message went unanswered.

At 7:43 a.m., the *Itasca* signaled to Earhart: "Received message.... Go ahead." There was silence on her end. But by 7:58 a.m., panic had set in. Amelia's voice came through on 3105 kilocycles, louder now, carrying an unmistakable edge of urgency: "KHAQQ calling *Itasca*. We are circling but cannot hear you. Go ahead on 7500 either now or at the scheduled time of half an hour." Despite the *Itasca*'s continuous transmissions, she had only received one message from them. The elusive Howland Island was nowhere in sight. Once Noonan completed his navigational duties and believed they were near the island, he likely moved to the front copilot seat to join Amelia as an additional lookout, having finished his tasks in the aircraft's rear. Amelia's frantic voice, clear near the radio room, reported their closing distance—first two hundred miles, then one hundred. Despite the strengthening radio signals, the island remained elusive. Howland Island's skies were tranquil, mirroring the calm sea, which posed a visibility challenge. On the ship's bridge, Commander Thompson commanded, "Make smoke!" The order was an effort to improve visibility. However, the light winds that day—normally twelve to fifteen knots during morning trade winds but only five to nine knots at Howland—meant that the smoke simply sank into a brown haze across the horizon, creating a smoke screen that more obscured than revealed the island's location. On a typical day near the atoll, ship smoke is visible from thirty to fifty miles away. Amelia might have easily spotted the smoke had she been approaching from the east to the west rather than the west to the east, as the revised plan dictated following the mishap in Hawaii.

But she was so loudly received that she had to be nearby. "Now she's blown my head off," O'Hare recalled. "I have her at a signal strength of five, which means she is overhead coming on us, and I physically put my head out the radio room door and looked in the sky for her. I was up there looking because we had an exceptionally long head coil—that you walk out of the radio shack with." During another interview, Bellarts paused to whistle. "We thought she'd crash right into our rigging. Oh man, she came in like a ton of bricks. I'll never forget her voice, just starting to crack. She was on the verge of going into hysterics."

At 8:00 a.m., the *Itasca* broadcast a series of *A* signals, to which Amelia responded promptly: "KHAQQ calling Itasca we received your sigs but unable to get a minimum. Please take bearing on us and answer 3105 with voice."

O'Hare and his colleagues were frustrated with Amelia's communication style. He explained that she would often end transmissions abruptly and fail to turn on her receiver to receive messages. This tendency continued until she faced critical situations, at which point she would realize the severity of her predicament and attempt to communicate more effectively. "That's what made us as operators disgusted with her," O'Hare said. "She would say something like that and then hang it up. It seemed like she didn't even bother to turn the receiver on to listen—whether it was to get her bearings, her off or on signals, or anything else. Until she got stuck, you know, when she realized, boy, her number was coming up, and then sure."

8:03 a.m.: "We received your signals," Amelia said, "but unable to get a minimum (for a bearing)."

At 8:14 a.m.: *Itasca* to Amelia—"Do you hear my sigs. . . . Please acknowledge with receipt on 3105." The communication was unreturned.

At 8:18 a.m., the men on board tried again: "Will you please acknowledge our sigs on 7500 or 3105." This also went unanswered.

Twenty hours and sixteen minutes post-departure from Lae, at precisely

8:43 a.m., the voice of Amelia Earhart crackled through the ether once again—this time tinged, unmistakably, with the high-pitched notes of fear: "We are on the line 157 337. We will repeat [this message] on 6210 kilocycles. Wait. . . . We are running north and south. Listening [on] 6210 kilocycles."

No one on board the *Itasca* knew precisely how they approached Howland. Spotting a small island becomes tricky when flying over the seas with a low, bright sun and cumulus clouds around. In a span of fifteen to twenty degrees with reflected sunlight, you're pretty much blinded by a dazzling path of silvery light. Seeing anything is impossible inside that area, and clouds appear like shaded islands. When flying at about a thousand feet, you are flying among the clouds and looking for the ocean through the gaps. Was the smoke obscuring her vision? Sun shadows could have obscured the tiny island too.

Without a radio bearing, pilots must use an offset approach. Instead of flying straight toward an island, they intentionally veer off course by a certain distance that they believe is reasonable. Then they fly upward until they intersect with a line they believe will lead them to that island. By following this line, they should eventually reach their destination, although there may be some deviation from the intended path. (An offset approach was used when Amelia crossed the Atlantic and flew into Dakar, Senegal.)

"That's barely a line of position!" Tommy O'Hare said to himself. "What's the use of a line of position? That's like saying, 'Meet me on Fifth Avenue.' Where?" At the time, the radio room was packed and alert, and the radiomen quickly switched to 6210 but didn't wholly abandon 3105. (It was unnecessary to search for 6210 on the receiver, because it had already been calibrated with pencil marks.) This was her last communication.

To a T, the men in the room felt she must have had no choice but to ditch the plane due to fuel exhaustion. "That's when she went down," O'Hare remembered, tears welling in his eyes as he was rereading his logbook. "She's through now, in the drink—the show was over now."

O'Hare clearly saw things differently from others, especially Bellarts, when it came to Amelia Earhart and Fred Noonan's final moments: "She knew better than the technicians what equipment she should carry, how to use it, et cetera. She was very casual about the communication system." He was frustrated with her, but he'd been on the horn with her, not Bellarts! As he recalled, she was rattled but not hysterical or anything of that nature; she was cool, calm, collected. "[Hysterical] is ridiculous; how [could] I copy her if she was screaming? I had no trouble slamming down what she was saying, so anyone that thinks that Amelia lost her cool is crazy, because she did not."

But Bellarts and O'Hare agreed that the Electra had crashed when they didn't hear a message on 6210 kilocycles. The US Navy and Coast Guard were used for low- or medium-frequency transmissions. That was their bread and butter; all their equipment and training was for that, as it's a predictable propagation over the saltwater ocean. High frequencies were all brand-new science—and not the best judgment. And why in the world 7500?! Today, that's no problem, but back then . . .

It was a heartache for both to even talk about it again. Chances of survival were minimal. Gravitational forces, often called g-forces, can exert a dragging effect in the water, and if they had been alert, which is unlikely, the experience would have been uncomfortable. Additionally, there are no food sources in the water, and on an island just fifty miles from the equator, the sweltering sun beats down at a relentless 110 degrees daily.

Perhaps, as aviator Grace McGuire and famed pilot and airline crash investigator Elgen Long independently calculated, part of the problem lay in the island's mislocation on maps. Based on outdated 1841 whaling data, these charts erroneously placed the island five and a half miles east of where it actually is. As they descended to the cloud line under the guidance of Noonan's sextant, a refraction miscalculation added an additional seven miles, putting them thirteen and a half miles off course. Noonan's decision to leave smoke bombs under his bed in Lae was driven by a need to lighten their load for the long, fuel-demanding flight. Unfortunately, without the smoke bombs, which would have been used to create visible signals for locating positions, Noonan found his options limited as he stared out at the water. Even his expertise wasn't enough; with everything that could go wrong having already gone wrong, discerning the right direction became impossible.

"She'd call and say the weather's overcast and then just hang up, not proceed," O'Hare recalled. "We could have caught her on five hundred kilocycles—all she had to do was hold down the key, and we could have taken a bearing with the ship's directional finder."

Later, Lockheed informed the distraught radio team that the plane couldn't float for more than fifteen minutes. Since they had aft tanks—extra fuel tanks positioned toward the back of the plane—they probably could have floated for five hours before sinking. The wind and current likely pushed them one and a half to one and three-quarter miles west. Even to this day, experts backed by the National Air and Space Museum's team agree that the plane rests on the ocean floor about thirty-five miles west-northwest of Howland Island, perfectly preserved at 16,800 feet. (None of the other theories are accepted.)

The *Itasca* remained near Howland Island until noon, diligently searching for any signs of survival. Then it headed northwest and east, combing the shark-infested waters for clues. Panhorst, the mess cook, had initially been dispirited that he would be in the galley and miss the action. When things started to boil up, he found himself listening near the transmitters and receivers in the radio room and was not shooed away. He later said that the captain called all men on deck when they lost contact with the plane. At this point, they still thought that Amelia may have ditched the plane, and that the ship could find her. "Each of us on the *Itasca* picked an hour of that day we would find her and put money in a pot." (The lottery was finally changed so that the seaman guessed the day of their arrival back in Hawaii.)

In Lae, Harry Balfour, already aware of the tragedy, knew that Amelia's radio equipment had been in good working order within New Guinea's range. Until that point, he could hear her clearly. In addition, Balfour held a negative view of Noonan because of his drinking, raising the tear-stained question of whether his hangover affected his seasoned judgment. Balfour had advised her and Noonan not to change the signal, but she'd done so and said, "Goodbye, Lae." Why had she done that? There was no static, and it was loud. At that point, perhaps she thought the *Itasca* would hear her better.

Further reminiscences in a private letter penned by Balfour might raise eyebrows: "At Lae, she spent most of her time between my radio room and the engine overhaul shop, and I was asked if I would have liked to go along with her, and that was the night before the takeoff. . . . Noonan arrived back in Lae the morning of the takeoff. He could not have done any flight planning. . . . Also, he had been up in the hills at Butibum all the time nibbling on the bottle."

As Amelia Earhart's radio signals fell eerily silent, newspapers across the nation featured a captivating story titled "A Candid Talk with George Palmer Putnam." The article was more photos than words and presented in the format of a photo essay; it showcased four flattering snapshots of George from an earlier, less fraught time. Each photo was accompanied by engaging captions, transforming the piece into a compelling narrative. Captured in each frame, the fifty-year-old Putnam was the picture of composed assurance, seated at his desk with a confident smile. "Flying, to me," he declared, "is just a quick way of getting from point A to B." He gestured toward a large-scale map, charting Amelia's path around the globe. "But to discover precisely where she is, I find myself asking the Associated Press, 'Can you tell me where my wife is this morning?'"

In this upbeat piece, placed before any bad news, George mentioned his role in fending off endorsement seekers and his habit of trying to be present during his wife's takeoffs and landings unless she beat him to it. He did not worry about Amelia, and he also emphasized her lack of worry for herself. They had started building a more spacious home together in Toluca Lake, California, three months before the flight—perhaps not for extended stays but to have a peaceful haven with a room for Amelia's mother, one bedroom upstairs, and a sundeck. George humorously noted their shared avoidance of playing bridge, saying, "So that saves us a lot of invitations." He added, "I just hope everything will come out all right with God."

Unfortunately, things didn't turn out all right.

A constant shadow of danger had always hovered over their relationship. When the harrowing news of Amelia Earhart's disappearance reached George via the US Coast Guard, time seemed to stand still, replaced by a numbing haze of shock and disbelief. The night before the official confirmation was excruciatingly sleepless: Amelia's plane was missing on her bold twenty-seven-thousand-mile quest. With George's tireless support, she had captivated the world for nearly a decade. Their partnership, marked by tremendous highs and some stark lows, now faced the unthinkable—the possibility of her being gone forever. This potential tragedy also threatened their imminent financial security. Yet even for George, financial concerns were momentarily secondary. Despite all his efforts to control and influence, George remained in awe of Amelia. This fiercely independent woman who kept her finances separate and retained her own name—she had chosen a life with him. The full weight of the situation was unbearable as George, trembling, prepared himself in Oakland to make the impossible call to Amelia's mother, who anxiously awaited her daughter's return.

Eighteen

SLOW CIRCLING DOWN

The world waited in suspense as Amelia Earhart's fate remained uncertain. When the grim news emerged, it sent waves of confusion and disbelief through the airwaves. Globally, people struggled with the shocking news: Amelia Earhart was missing. Unprepared, Lux Radio Theatre executives still aired their Amelia ads, now strikingly out of place.

Lawrence Ames, former chief of Lockheed's Burbank plant, would always remember the moment he first heard the news. A call from George Palmer Putnam followed shortly after, his voice tinged with panic, urgently pleading for Lawrence to help him find his wife.

As one of two embedded reporters on the *Itasca*, Howard Hanzlick looked back from a singular perspective, having witnessed Amelia's struggle with her radio—a struggle that, in his view, bordered on recklessness. He described a fatigued pilot, awake beyond twenty-four hours, hardly responding to *Itasca*'s signals. Hanzlick's notes captured a sense of mounting frustration among the radiomen as they desperately sought a response from Amelia. He watched, dismayed, as a seemingly inevitable tragedy unfolded, marked by Amelia's voice, weary yet determined, crackling through the radio.

Hanzlick's detailed accounts also shed light on the treacherous nature of the waters surrounding Amelia and Noonan's intended landing spot of

Howland Island. He recalled the shocking number of sharks in the area, a hazard that added another layer of danger to an already alarming situation. Yet his most scathing critique was directed toward George Palmer Putnam, whom he saw as motivated more by profit than by his wife's safety, a sentiment fueled by seeing cabled messages pressuring Amelia to hasten her journey for a lucrative radio deal.

The technical limitations of Amelia's onboard equipment soon became apparent. Inadequate equipment, an off-calibrated compass, and erroneous chart coordinates converged into a navigational catastrophe. These issues, worsened by unexpected headwinds and a major navigational deviation, led to a bleak conclusion: Amelia Earhart and Fred Noonan had vanished, possibly due to running out of fuel. Luck had been a lady before, but this time, she could no longer outrun fate.

Tommy O'Hare, one of the radio operators speaking directly with the missing flier, concisely yet movingly summarized: "Earhart ran out of gas and splashed." Although he blamed Amelia for some of her technical incompetence with Morse code and her unwise choice to leave needed equipment behind, his private reflections in the 1970s also hinted at a deeper issue with the radio equipment—specifically, the US Coast Guard's T-10 transmitter's erratic performance. These technical inadequacies and second-class radioman Frank Cipriani's inexperience hinted that both human and machine error played a role in the tragedy. O'Hare's frank 1970s interview—underscored by Leo Bellarts's later admission of secret slipups on the US Coast Guard end, which certainly did nothing to improve Amelia and Noonan's chances of survival—revealed a haunting layer of regret and unspoken truths among the rescue team.

Admiral Richard Black found Amelia's sporadic and brief radio transmissions especially baffling, a choice that seemed inexplicable given her dire circumstances. Similarly, Jim Collopy's report from Lae emphasized the crew's limited expertise in radio communication, a critical flaw in an age when Morse code and telephony were lifelines in the skies.

As the world continued to come to terms with the probable loss of one of its most intrepid aviators, a chorus of grief, regret, and unanswered questions echoed across continents. From Helen Louise Day's quiet weeping in Coconut Grove to Henry Bradford Washburn's deep sighs while tuning in to the radio in Alaska, and from the Ogontz students' shock to Jackie Cochran's retreat into solitude on an ocean liner in Europe, the news of Earhart's disappearance reverberated. But perhaps no one wept harder than Elinor Smith, Amelia's former rival and friend, her worst fears realized—Amelia's lack of practice had finally caught up with her.

Even as theories and speculations swirled, the search efforts continued, marked by a blend of wishful thinking and grim reality. George Palmer Putnam teetered between hope and despair. Amid the tumult, touching moments of humanity emerged—George's awkward yet sincere attempt to console Bea Noonan, Muriel Earhart's brave face despite her inner turmoil. Where was the hope beyond a miracle?

Rear Admiral Orin Gould Murfin, commander in chief of the Asiatic Fleet, led the US Navy's dragnet. The USCGC *Itasca*, leaving its guard at Howland, became the nucleus of the rescue operation. The battleship *Colorado* arrived under full steam, followed by the aircraft carrier *Lexington* with sixty-two planes on her flight deck. Not far behind were four destroyers, a minesweeper, and a seaplane. This impressive armada fanned out, and the military scoured the South Seas for sixteen days by sea and air; Japan even aided in a desperate search.

The stark reality set in as the days passed without any trace of Amelia Earhart or Fred Noonan. It was becoming increasingly clear that "America's premier lady flier" and her navigator had likely perished, their dicey journey culminating not in victory but in the enigmatic depths of the Pacific Ocean.

In the aftermath of Amelia's disappearance, executives at Quaker Oats were forced to confront the reality that their substantial financial backing of her international flight was irretrievably lost, and the fact that any attempt to recover this "donation" would likely lead to a PR disaster only compounded their woes. As Amelia's unutterable fate became increasingly clear, they opted to destroy several fully designed full-color advertisements—a prudent decision that would remain under wraps for decades. This aspect of the story only came to light years later through the examination of George Palmer Putnam's tax records, underscoring the complex financial stakes involved in Amelia's ill-fated journey.

This sense of loss and reflection was captured in the poignant strains of "Amelia Earhart's Last Flight," a folk ballad written by Red River Dave McEnery in July 1937, days after Earhart vanished, a song written so soon after her disappearance that it encapsulated the lingering hopes for her safe return. It gained further historical significance when it became the first song ever performed on commercial television during a 1939 broadcast at the New York World's Fair.

In the aftermath of Amelia's vanishing act, doubts about the wisdom of such daring escapades crept in. Several widely syndicated columnists suggested that Amelia's fate should serve as a sobering lesson for other audacious aviators. Their stances found support in public remarks from the US Navy and the Bureau of Air Commerce, alongside a chorus of editorials echoing concerns about the prudence of embarking on such hazardous flights.

Behind closed doors, criticism was just as pointed. It was in private that Gill Robb Wilson, editor and publisher of *Flying* magazine, shared his unsuccessful attempts to dissuade Amelia from undertaking her final flight. Wilson's objections were grounded in concerns over inadequate equipment and insufficient ground support, which he feared could not ensure a successful journey.

Harold McCracken, Putnam's close aide and confidant, agreed with Wilson's view that the primary objective of the flight was financial gain, driven by George's monetary struggles in 1937. McCracken's account painted a picture of a venture motivated more by profit than by the spirit of exploration.

Clarence L. "Kelly" Johnson, the renowned aeronautical expert at Lockheed, held a different view. Having personally trained the missing Earhart on the missing Electra, he understood both her capabilities and the limitations of the aircraft, and he believed that poor visibility due to overcast skies played a significant role in the aviators' inability to locate their navigational checkpoints.

The news deeply shook Bo McNeeley, Earhart's loyal mechanic, who rued missing a chance to join the search operation and felt that his presence during the flight, particularly in managing the aircraft's fuel, might have made a crucial difference.

In the immediate aftermath of Amelia's disappearance, her devoted assistant in Toluca Lake received a thick manila envelope from the renowned aviator, sent just days before her ambitious global flight commenced. The lost pilot's directive to her petite French Canadian aide, the daughter of the Putnams' housekeeper, was clear: should she not return, the contents were to be destroyed. "Amelia didn't want her private musings falling into others' hands," Margot DeCarie recalled years later, her hair still short and tousled, a nod to her admired employer. True to Amelia's wishes, after waiting a month, Margot set the papers alight. As the flames consumed the envelope, the delicate traces of Amelia's handwriting flickered momentarily before turning to ash. "It's hard to imagine destroying something from a daughter, sister, or wife," she reflected. "But Amelia trusted me to uphold her wishes."

Russell Owen, a Pulitzer Prize–winning journalist known for his expertise in Antarctic expeditions and a friend of Amelia's who knew concealed truths, provided a nuanced assessment of both Amelia and George in *The New York Times*. Despite his admiration for the aviator's spirit and skill, Owen saw her final journey as a needless gamble, a challenge against nature that was perhaps too ambitious.

Surrounded by diverse opinions, George confronted the harsh truth of Amelia's fate. On July 7, after receiving disheartening updates from naval sources at Fort Funston's USCG radio station, he announced his intention to return home, expressing doubt about unverified radio reports claiming contact with his missing wife. In a moment of rare public emotion, he broke down in tears, deeply grieving. However, during a later press conference in San Francisco, George's tone shifted. He firmly denied being overwhelmed by the situation and stated that if Amelia had indeed died, it was in a manner consistent with her adventurous nature, claiming, "I have not indulged in public sobbing." This strong denial stood in stark contrast to his earlier display of grief.

The US Navy's subsequent statement that sharks were a primary concern if Amelia and Noonan had survived soon fueled sensational tabloid stories, with one paper bluntly proclaiming that the pair were likely dead, victims of a shark attack in the Pacific. The article reflected a growing cynical view of Amelia's final journey, suggesting it was undertaken merely for enjoyment, a sentiment that belied the seriousness and ambition underpinning her aviation endeavors.

In response to these damning reports, George offered a softhearted (if well-crafted) reflection on his wife's character and philosophy: He believed that if she had met her end in the Pacific, it was in a manner surrounded by the mystery and romance she would have preferred. He recalled her frequent contemplations about death and her personal philosophy, which embraced such an end as part of an adventurous life.

Supporting George's statements, Amelia's poetic remnants, preserved at Purdue University, provide insights into her contemplative mind. Written during the late 1930s, they often dwell on themes of mortality, love, heartbreak, and the inexorable passage of time. One set of notes, for a poem she was translating called "Carrion," depicts death as a compassionate bird of prey, ending love's anguish.

> *Merciless life*
> *laughs in the burning sun*
> *and only Death*
> *slow-circling down,*
> *shadows the acrid flesh*
> *bruised by the panther-paws of love.*

Death's allure emerges again in another fragment found posthumously:

> *some meet death / with closed eyes of horror / dare infinitely / for another glimpse.*

Louise Thaden, the 1936 Bendix Trophy winner and an accomplished flier, shared her perspective: "I am a sissy; I have never flown over water, and I don't intend to.... Amelia had told me a little about her plans and was enthusiastic about the flight. Personally, I believe she is gone.... I am a fatalist, and I think most pilots are. When your time comes to go, you are going. That's all there is. I know she would have preferred to go out doing the thing she most wanted to do."

In a much later and far more candid interview, Thaden revealed insights into Amelia's personal life.

Amelia and GP weren't getting along very well. Amelia didn't see eye to eye with him. She didn't like all the exploitation that he was doing. But mainly he was pushing her to go ahead and pick up the flight in the other direction, which she didn't want to do. She wanted to wait (for the next year) and go the way they planned. And he kept bringing up the fact that they were in hock as much as they were. As much money as they had been able to raise, it still wasn't enough. They were counting on the book Amelia was going to write.

He was pushing her hard to go around the other way. Amelia was a very common-sense person. She kept her cool. She wasn't easily fazed by things. But GP really had her disturbed. GP was a very overbearing person with a tremendous ego. In a way, he dominated Amelia to a surprising degree. Amelia, being the kind of person she was, felt a great sense of loyalty to him and appreciation for everything he had done for her, which is why she married him in the first place. It was through pressure and a sense of obligation. It wasn't the kind of love that you normally get married for. She admired him and liked him, that kind of thing. Another factor, too, in her decision to marry him was she felt her position in the public eye was that she shouldn't marry just a nobody (or somebody without any stature). She talked to me one night. Well, we talked all night almost when she was trying to get her mind made up. It made it very difficult for her to resist his insistence that she go ahead and complete the flight in the other direction.

But Amelia has always weighed every flight she has made with great meticulousness. She can look at the pros and cons without bias or prejudice and weigh. And if the scales tip on the balance on the gold side, then she'd go. If they tipped the other way, then she wouldn't go. And she felt that by going west to east, at the time of the year it was, that the scales were balanced against her. And she didn't want to do it. Which is one reason I felt more badly than I normally would about what happened.

But on the other hand, Amelia, like most of us in those days, in particular, she was a fatalist. And she bore it, like I always have; it's all written down in the little black book. And when it's your time to go, you go. And I remember before her first attempt, which is in the book—I was just finishing it when Amelia was lost and added a chapter—we were sitting on the rubber life raft outside Paul Mantz's hangar, and I said to her I couldn't see the sense in her making the round-the-world flight. The navigational facilities were nothing in those days, and it was a hazardous flight. And particularly the one from Honolulu to Howland and Howland to Lae, although it wasn't much worse than some of that terrible country they flew over, but at least they weren't landing in the water.

This flight was just something she wanted to do—just for the heck of it. She said, "If I bop off"—and that's exactly the words she used—"you can carry on, you can all carry on."

So she knew the risks she was taking. But then this was going around the other way. And with the time very carefully picked, with the best weather, least hazardous. I don't know, but I've always had the feeling that Amelia kind of felt like she mightn't make this—she was very confident about the first one.

As details of Amelia and George's uneven relationship emerged, public fascination with her disappearance hit a fever pitch—a blend of heartfelt concern and intrusive curiosity. Predictably, the usual suspects surfaced: charlatan psychics and other attention-seekers spinning grandiose claims of insider knowledge. What began as a genuine quest for answers devolved into spectacle, transforming Amelia's life and legacy into fodder for a sensationalized narrative often far removed from the truth.

In the peculiar aftermath of Amelia Earhart's final flight, her enigmatic fate also served as a muse for the more opportunistic sectors of the artistic world. A rather tasteless yet bemusing example was the creation of "They Needed an Angel in Heaven So God Took the Queen of the Air" by two aspiring songwriters, evidently aspiring to hit the same emotional chord as the post–Great War classic "They Needed a Songbird in Heaven (So God Took Caruso Away)." Their attempt to blend sentimentality with opportunism, however, landed with a thud rather than a flourish. The discerning, and perhaps slightly more morose, arbiters of 1937's Tin Pan Alley unceremoniously showed them the door. It seems that even in an era of dramatic headlines, there was still a line drawn at serenading the lost with questionable taste.

Meanwhile, also with murderously bad timing, Beryl Markham, a notable English-born Kenyan aviator, discreetly explored opportunities in Hollywood for aviation film consulting just after Amelia's tragic demise. In 1936, Markham became the first to fly solo across the Atlantic from Britain to North America. She wanted to cross the Pacific solo in 1937. Amelia's death, however, led to the evaporation of financial support for Markham's Pacific endeavor. She remained near Hollywood, cautiously seeking consulting work without appearing opportunistic.

Alice Rogers Hager, who had proudly interviewed Amelia in Oakland and then in Miami before her final flight, secured an exclusive interview on July 10 with George. In her story, George maintained a hopeful vigil, refusing to let anyone see his pain. "You're looking very cheerful today, Mr. Putnam, and that must mean good news," Hager said. Struggling to maintain composure, George replied, "I'm feeling more cheerful. Perhaps this is a case of the wish being father to the thought, but the confidence is growing in me that they are safe. I think we'll find them, eventually, perched on a spit of sand or a reef edge, probably uncomfortable but otherwise all right. They have plenty of rations. . . . Unless one or both were seriously injured in the type of landing they would have had to make, and I can't believe that is the case, I think they are all right. Do you agree with me?"

On July 11, as newspapers reported the loss of the thirty-eight-year-old musical prodigy George Gershwin to a brain tumor, many also featured a touching photograph of George Palmer Putnam alongside his son David and erstwhile rival Paul Mantz. George was departing from his vigil for Amelia Earhart to return to Los Angeles. Born from shared grief, the temporary camaraderie between the usually-at-loggerheads George and Paul would be short-lived.

On July 14, as the investigation withered, even the ordinarily stoic Eleanor Roosevelt acknowledged that all chances were lost. And then, at 4:58 p.m., July 18, President Roosevelt knew facts had to be faced and issued a final order that read: "All search for Earhart terminated."

The US Navy hit the kill switch on its Amelia Earhart quest, ordering the aircraft carrier *Lexington* back to San Diego and ending the costly and fruitless search for the missing aviator. The facts were presented without drama: Amelia Earhart and Fred Noonan were deemed lost at sea by the government. Many now agreed she had run into headwinds stronger than expected and thought she had four extra hours of gas. She didn't. Ultimately, it was assumed that Amelia had run up against radio trouble and a weak knowledge of Morse code while also, simply and sadly, running out of gas. Several newspaper maps x-ed the spot near Howland Island where it was believed "America's premier lady flier" had met her end.

George was more than a little fragile when he spoke to reporters in Los Angeles: "I'm deeply grateful to the Navy for what it's done."

Despite previous disagreements, Mantz and George found common ground in their shared mourning for Amelia. Amelia's technical adviser felt that George was doing the right thing by listening to the US Navy. "No one, even if he had ten million dollars to spend, could do a more thorough job than has been done by the Navy."

In the wake of global grief following Amelia Earhart's disappearance, Bob Considine of New York's *Daily Mirror* provided a sharp analysis of the events. Considine, known for his swift and incisive reporting (as evidenced in his *Thirty Seconds over Tokyo*), likely tapped into insider knowledge from figures like Louise Thaden and Jackie Cochran, who were more informed than they could publicly admit. He critiqued the planning of Earhart's flight, suggesting it was mapped out by "uninformed friends" who prioritized economic motives over safety. Earhart, financially burdened, reluctantly agreed to their plan despite her preference for a different route. Considine noted that she had ignored warnings about dangerous waters and was driven by the need to secure her future, even admitting privately, "I really don't want to do it." He dismissed the supposed messages from her after the crash as "fantasies" conjured by those drawn to tragedy.

On July 19, in Los Angeles, George made a public declaration about his stance on the search efforts, announcing he had abandoned plans for any further search for his wife, stating his belief that additional searching would be futile and unwise, as it would take a yacht a year to achieve what the US Navy accomplished in just a few days. Despite this, he maintained hope and stressed that Amelia herself would be the last to give up.

After George's stoic announcement, another prominent reporter, Russell Owen, offered his insights on July 20. Known for his close relationship with Amelia, Owen often drew upon privileged information from those in her inner circle, such as Louise Thaden and Jackie Cochran. Writing for the Gray Lady, Owen, unlike his peer Considine, could not yet go on record about how Thaden and Cochran's dear friend Amelia had ignored their advice or about how much they also blamed George for her death. (After all, Owen's boss, Adolph S. Ochs, was great friends with George.) Nevertheless, his piece was a shiveringly honest epitaph that was widely reprinted worldwide: "Let us begin by saying the worst that can be said about Amelia Earhart. She was no feminine Lindbergh, flying oceans with the precision of a transport pilot. . . . She and her navigator, Frederick J. Noonan, had set out over the great wastes of the Pacific without the knowledge or the equipment which would have enabled them to ride into safety on the *Itasca*'s invisible beam. A little more careful preparation, and those two valiant souls might still be certainly in the land of the living. . . . But the qualities which involved Miss Earhart and her companion . . . were interwoven with her gay, luminous, self-confident personality. If she had not had a touch of recklessness, which arose, perhaps, out of a belief in her fortunate star, she would not have been Amelia Earhart."

When the *Itasca* docked in Honolulu, Richard Black traveled to Los Angeles for a dinner invitation at Amelia and George's recently renovated home in Toluca Lake. This occasion marked their first meeting, and after Black's arrival, George greeted him while preparing a drink, and his demeanor clearly reflected the burden of his wife's absence. He softly remarked, "Mrs. Earhart will be with us soon. Once she does, I ask that you refrain from discussing Amelia or the search. She hopes that Amelia might suddenly call or walk through the door."

The outlook was bleak.

Then came a day earmarked for dual celebrations—Amelia's fortieth birthday—now passed in subdued observation, with little celebration from the Earhart family, except for the flowers Muriel sent to her mother. On July 27, Amelia's niece, Amy Morrison, cherished a heartfelt birthday gift sent by her aunt. Amelia had been in India when she sent a package containing six gold-and-spun-glass bracelets to commemorate Amy's sixth birthday on July 30. Much later, at ninety-one, Amy would disclose that even these treasured keepsakes that once offered faint comfort mysteriously disappeared, echoing her aunt's fate.

Privately, George knew Amelia was lost, but publicly, he projected hope. As Amelia's disappearance fueled media frenzy, and sold papers, the press speculated that she and Noonan might still be alive, stranded and waiting for rescue. George's refusal to reject these theories served two purposes: it offered his inconsolable mother-in-law a slim hope, and it deepened the mystery of Amelia's disappearance, captivating the public's imagination when he already knew he would release a posthumous book by his wife in the fall. Marketing that was already in play.

It's difficult to fathom the depth of sorrow, guilt, and regret that must have consumed Gene Vidal, Amelia's closest friend, who withdrew from public engagements that summer. Deeply mourning the loss of his confidante, whom he had supported in her flight preparations, Vidal chose silence over sharing his grief in personal interviews.

Arriving in Newark, New Jersey, from California on July 29 to handle business in New York, George was immediately surrounded by a throng of

East Coast reporters. Despite his exhaustion, he knew he had to respond. With a careful choice of words, George offered a possibility that was as hopeful as it was haunting: "Sometimes people stranded on unknown isles live for years on just fish and fruits before they are found. Perhaps that's what happened to Captain Noonan and Amelia." His statement, a blend of hope and resignation, left the reporters momentarily silent, pondering the fate of the famed aviators.

Following George's arrival, Harold McCracken went to George's Midtown hotel suite at the Barclay Hotel and presented him with a stack of mail addressed to him and Amelia. This included hundreds of articles about her disappearance gathered by their press clipping service. One striking headline read SOLD DOWN THE RIVER. The devastating take on Amelia's end stressed the essentiality of reliable radio gear in high-risk flights and angrily declared that Amelia and Noonan had failed to find Howland because of an endorsement deal for faulty equipment that had been rushed. In essence, that George had caused her death.

As George read the story, McCracken observed his friend's bewildered expression, which he described later as "silent and stunned." After a tense silence, George tossed the newspaper clippings into the closest wastebasket.

In his tattered existence, a joyless shell of himself, George spoke of the rustic Wyoming retreat they had been constructing, detailing the belongings they had already sent for storage. McCracken offered his assistance, asking what George needed to retrieve. George expressed a desire to have Amelia's rifle from her personal possessions, and McCracken, understanding his friend's anguish, assured him that he would reach out to Carl Dunrud.

While lunching at the Algonquin, McCracken stood stiffly to bid his friend George goodbye, not realizing it would be their last meeting. Days later, George left for California, leaving McCracken among those he'd cast aside—people whom he resented over perceived wrongs or whom, in his constant quest for novelty, he'd simply tired of. As McCracken observed George in such a vulnerable state, still refusing to acknowledge any wrongdoing, George squirmed, perhaps feeling seen in ways he never wanted to be seen. It was only then that McCracken outlived his usefulness to his old friend. The end of the road was there, and like many dealing with George, McCracken would find himself left behind. Discarded.

In the ensuing days, George retreated to the Toluca Lake residence, now shared with his sorrowful mother-in-law, burdened by an indelible sense of haunting. Although he possessed the rifle, he could never revisit the desolate cabin, where decaying logs stood as the remnants of a forgotten past. Even his beloved hometown of Rye provided no peace, and he would never set again foot in the home he had shared with his first and second wives. Each of us harbors a haunted house, a secret space for our demons and unresolved conflicts, and these shadows whisper reminders of who we really are.

On August 3, the Earhart and Otis families held the first service for Amelia in Atchison, Kansas. It was a modest town with big memories, and the locals turned out in the hundreds, a quiet hum of chatter giving way to the solemn strains of a patriotic band playing "America" and "The Village Chapel." Her uncle Theodore Otis, fifty-nine, stepped to the front. He was not a polished speaker, hindered by intellectual challenges, but his voice quivered with unmistakable affection. The main address came from Dr. Burris Jenkins, a minister from Kansas City who had a talent for mixing scripture with sentiment. He read from a poem Amelia had once written for a magazine—lines that felt eerily prescient now—and let them linger in the air like a final echo of her presence.

How can life grant the boon of living,
Compensate for the dull, gray ugliness and pregnant hate,
Unless we dare?

"This is the very quality in Miss Earhart that lifted her above all petty rivalries, jealousies, criticisms, and condemnations," Jenkins told the mourners. "How do we know that this flight has failed? Or was it a great triumph?"

Reporters noted that George Palmer Putnam sanctioned the event yet opted not to attend; as a man in mourning, he wasn't in an emotional state to see these strangers. Seeking solace, he instead faced unending turmoil.

Almost immediately after her disappearance, the flood began: hoax phone calls with "clues." "Psychic" sightings. Sci-fi theories. Conspiracy theories. Loopy rants. Moneymaking schemes. And this flood has not slowed down in the twenty-first century.

On the same day, Walter Winchell had another item that seemed less mournful—George Palmer Putnam was back in New York, plowing ahead with life, and would soon announce an alliance with Floyd Odlum, Jackie Cochran's husband, in marketing a new color process for flickers.

He soon realized that this update did not sit well with Amelia's admirers; feigning ongoing search efforts, despite knowing their futility, kept him in better favor with the public. To George, the futility of those efforts was not a truth worth remembering.

Then came another press announcement; another one of the reasons for George's quick trip back East was revealed. He had been looking into a reported brown-and-white scarf, said to be Amelia's, found by a "sailor" on an illegal arms-running ship near New Guinea. Jo Berger, George's secretary, recognized the scarf. All of this was devised by Wilbur Rothar, alias Goodenough, a forty-two-year-old janitor and supposed sailor living modestly in the Bronx with his family of eight.

Rothar, claiming he was just onshore, produced a note that said, "We have your wife on the ship. I will call you Sunday." He claimed Amelia was ill and had been saved by a ship carrying arms to New Guinea. A Chinese doctor had treated her, and she required blood transfusions. They learned her identity when they reached Panama, read about her, and saw her photograph. She needed immediate medical attention and hospitalization.

The next day, George promptly informed the Federal Bureau of Investigation, and on Rothar's second visit to the Barclay Hotel, where George was staying, an FBI man posed as George's secretary. When the "sailor" produced the scarf, he demanded $2,000. Agents quickly discovered that the "sailor" had not been to sea for twenty-two years.

As ordered by J. Edgar Hoover, the Rothar/Goodenough case was turned over to Rhea Whitley, special agent in charge of the New York City division of the FBI, which commanded a team of 625 agents. (Having once worked undercover himself just after the Great War, George was familiar with the ways of the G-men.) When the grifter visited George's office, a fake secretary (a female FBI officer) gave him $1,000. The FBI's fake secretary walked Rothar to the bank for another $1,000. Following his exit, he was arrested on the street and held on a bond of $20,000. After a period at Bellevue, Rothar was committed by a judge to Beacon's Matteawan State Hospital on August 13.

There were many batty theories about Wilbur Rothar's true identity from so-called Earhart experts, and one even tried deciphering the letters of his name as spy code. But the son of Mary Fitzpatrick and Garrett Rothar was genuine, and his living grandniece revealed that Wilbur's brother was also a well-known scam artist and junk dealer in the Bronx; locals called him Harry the Junk Man.

At Amelia's Toluca Lake home, her mother, the heartbroken Amy Otis Earhart, glumly sifted through a daily stack of sympathetic letters hand-delivered to her room by Frederico "Fred" Tomas, a thirty-eight-year-old Filipino home aide and chef. During this emotionally challenging period, Tomas and his wife, Elstrude, became pillars of support for Amy. Occasionally, they entertained Amy's hopes for Amelia's potential return. Tomas was later hired as the chef at Disney's prestigious Penthouse Club atop the Animation Building and even became a good friend of Walt Disney.

Among the letters, one stood out: a note from Emily, the mother of Sam Chapman from Marblehead, Massachusetts. The Chapman and Earhart families had long-standing intricate connections. It's easy to imagine the thoughts that must have swirled in Amy's mind when she considered what might have been if Amelia had chosen a different path, especially since Amy had always considered her son-in-law a schemer and a liar, with whom she had only made peace to please her daughter. One poignant message from Emily read: "Sam wants to be remembered to you all, but is quite upset and is still waiting for good news. He is blue and won't talk about it, just waiting and waiting with the rest of us."

During Amelia's round-the-world flight, George had sent her several letters filled with affection. In contrast, her responses were more tempered and practical, list-like. At first blush, especially to some Putnam descendants keen on dispelling rumors about her disconnection from George, these letters might seem to fill in gaps around their undying passion. George's affectionate tone is evident in one letter that ends:

> *I have carefully analyzed our situation and appraised the last several days in your company. My considered conclusion is that I love you very much and would rather play and work with you than with anyone I have yet encountered or could imagine—comb that out of your carefully tousled hair.*
>
> G.

And he is just as affectionate in another:

> *Sunday evening.*
>
> *Dear Hon:*
>
> *I have been thinking a lot about your book. There is such a wealth of material. Probably the right thing for this book to concern solely "world flight," if or and when! Possibly it might embrace a chapter each on the Atlantic, first Pacific, and Mexico. These flights by themselves, with us as a background, or in between. Which would leave for another (and more important book) the rich material of these full five years ("A Full Five Years" is a possible title)—people, places, lecturing, Purdue . . .*
>
> *. . . Hon, I miss you.*
>
> *I alternate between spasms of contentment and of worry. I'm so happy with you, and we really do have such a swell time together, in all ways. And I wish this flight wasn't hanging over us. You know I sympathize fully with your ambition and will abet it, and 98% I know you'll get away with it. But we both recognize the hazards, and I love you dearly— I don't want to run the risk of perhaps having to go on without you—that*

makes me terribly sorry for myself? (Entirely disregarding your end of it!)

But gosh, once this is out of your hair, what a very happy interesting time we can have. We can have it, too, should you, for any reason, decide to quit.

Love you lots,
G

Were these syrupy, romantic letters to Amelia truly solid evidence of a private, loving relationship, or were they more examples of George's long and tangled history of using affectionate correspondence for manipulation, as he had with his first wife during financial struggles and subsequent relationships? This raises further doubts. Public speculation that Amelia was contemplating divorce, along with the tension preceding her departure from Miami, adds to this uncertainty. Jackie Cochran's remarks about Amelia's frequent absences from George, coupled with Floyd Odlum's observations—about the lack of affection between the couple and Amelia's apparent dissatisfaction with George, as documented at the Dwight D. Eisenhower Presidential Library and the University of Iowa—suggest a relationship more complex and strained than it appeared. Notably, there are no equivalent romantic letters from Amelia to George. Ultimately, the true nature of their marriage at its very end remains elusive, clouded by the contradictions and complexities of their interactions.

Following these events, life continued, marked by the marriage of Paul Mantz and Terry Minor on August 19, 1937, a mere six weeks after Amelia's mysterious disappearance.

According to the September 15 issue of *Variety*, George had tapped Janet Mabie of *The Christian Science Monitor* to complete Amelia's contracted book *World Flight*, which now hurtled to publication. After flying in from Boston, Mabie settled into one of the Putnams' four bedrooms. George proposed that, beyond dictating his insights, she reach out to those close to Amelia. He hoped their anecdotes would enrich the accelerated project, allowing Mabie to think expansively and finalize Amelia's book. With a memoir to market and mounting debts, any publicity was gold. Being back out on the hustle was a peculiar comfort, but it was terrain he knew well.

Reporters wondered how he could, during mourning, release such a book so quickly. Simple. She had sent George her logbooks from each landing site. Photographs and letters from New Guinea were the last received.

Rumors of a film based on Amelia's life didn't offend him. He'd even put out Hollywood feelers: "If the right story came along now, I'd approve."

Last Flight would make a wonderful holiday gift for Amelia fans, George offered. Keeping the "possibility of her return" in mind, he would write a biography after a year. "There is one chance in a thousand she is still alive," he said. "I will never get myself to believe she is dead. I've thought of sending out an expedition to hunt for her. I've offered a $2,000 reward for any information of her whereabouts. But it's like hunting for a needle in a haystack." One reporter asked after Amelia's mother—how was she holding up? "Mrs. Earhart, who lives with me now, puts fresh flowers on Amelia's dressing table every day," he said. "Her clothes are kept well pressed and hanging in their cupboards."

On September 24, George Palmer Putnam publicly revealed an excerpt from "his" memorial volume, primarily written by his hired ghostwriter, Janet Mabie. Notably, the release of this excerpt was strategically synchronized with the forthcoming Christmas launch of Amelia Earhart's posthumous book. George's habit of taking credit for others' work was evident, as newspapers nationwide published a serialized five-part snippet through the North American Newspaper Alliance, whose members included the *New York Herald Tribune*.

Plagued by rumors that he had a hand in Amelia's tragic end, George arranged for an article to be published on September 26 in which he stated, "We seriously thought about canceling the flight. But she didn't want to."

On October 18, Clyde Holley, Amelia's former lawyer, filed an application requesting that George be granted the authority to manage their estate. Amelia's assets, including stocks and properties, were valued at $25,000—a surprisingly modest sum to those who assumed the Putnams were rolling in wealth.

Weeks went by, and the pervasive gloom had taken its toll on George. He felt a public duty to search for Amelia, the icon he'd passionately promoted minutes after she walked into his office in 1928. With the growing frustrations of his mother-in-law, now referred to as Mother Earhart, life under his roof was becoming tense. He had been to literal hell, so how was he now meant to live? People hurt each other, deeply, and often in secret. Throughout the years, George had vanquished pain with the companionship of younger women. Before Amelia entered George's life, his languishing marriage to Dorothy had already been strained by infidelity. Yet with Amelia, it seemed there was an unspoken understanding of an open relationship. Thus, he likely believed that his wife, wherever she might be, would understand his yearning for companionship. One Los Angeles confidant described this aspect of George's nature: "He always had an affinity for younger women; he relished the vitality they brought into his life."

Then came Ione Reed, the effervescent "female Tarzan," whose strong Texas twang had doomed her career in talkies. This former minor actress in silent films had reinvented herself as a stuntwoman. How she crossed paths with George remains unclear, but it's easy to imagine an ambitious actress like Ione seizing the opportunity to connect with someone of George's influence. At thirty-four, the barely educated but vivacious Ione offered a stark contrast to Amelia's intellectual sophistication. Yet her sunny demeanor and daring career brought a refreshing verve to George's life. As a publisher always in search of exciting content, George found Ione's thrilling animal stunt stories revitalizing.

Seeking privacy with his pretty young stunt woman lover, the officially mourning George dreamed up a "scientific" expedition he would lead. He assembled a handpicked team, including his secretary as the director, for a small-animal collecting journey to the Galápagos and Cocos Islands in December. However, his deeper motive was to discreetly use a yacht as a sanctuary away from the public eye. With the intrepid Ione by his side, this oceanic adventure provided the emotional support George needed while offering a cover to indulge in the freshness of a new woman's touch.

Not one to be bogged down by remorse, George had hinted at a relationship with Ione in his October 22 letter to Marie "Missy" Mattingly Meloney, a close literary ally of Amelia's. In the letter, he sought Missy's recommendation for ten essential books for a "friend," a request that, in hindsight, was part of his preparations for this expedition. To lend his voyage an air of intellectual gravity, George enlisted a panel of prominent figures, many friends of Amelia, to select books for Ione's journey, including Lowell Thomas, Frederic Melcher, Alice Hager, Althea Warren, Roy Chapman Andrews, Tay Garnett, Mrs. Ogden Reid, John T. Frederick, and Gardner Cowles.

Most strikingly, Putnam secured the participation of Dr. Edward C. Elliott, the president of Purdue University—the very institution that had championed Amelia's career and funded her final flight. That one of Amelia's strongest institutional allies was now lending credibility—perhaps unknowingly—to a project that revolved around Putnam's secret lover adds a layer of irony to the endeavor.

In new articles running just before departure, George portrayed Ione as an archetypal American woman in her late twenties, from a humble town and armed mainly with high school "book learning." His careful curation of reading material for Ione was yet another layer of concealment, a literary smokescreen that involved Amelia's own circle advising his secret lover.

On November 21 at Floyd Bennett Field in Brooklyn, over two hundred people gathered for a memorial service to remember Amelia Earhart and Fred Noonan. The event had been organized by the Women's National Aeronautical Association, and a simple wooden platform served as its centerpiece. Mrs. Roosevelt sent a message from Washington, expressing her condolences, and Fannie Hurst attended on behalf of Mayor Fiorello La Guardia.

The day wasn't without disagreements, chiefly due to Viola Gentry, an aviator and a prominent figure in denial of Amelia's death. Gentry, who would later charge a speaker's fee for a controversial talk titled "Amelia Earhart Is Still Alive," stood firm in her belief that Amelia and Noonan were stranded on an island, waiting for rescue. This misguided viewpoint caused dismay among levelheaded aviators who knew, of course, that she was dead. As Gentry was leading the arrangements committee, the customary salute to the departed, "Taps," was noticeably absent from the service, indicating her denial of Amelia's fate.

Several notable figures besides Fannie Hurst spoke in honor of Amelia. Among them were test pilot Edwin Aldrin Sr. (father of astronaut Buzz Aldrin) and Jackie Cochran, who had recently set a new speed record in Detroit and struggled to express her grief before Gentry.

After the speeches, planes from the US Coast Guard and private entities flew overhead in tribute, circling three times and then dipping their wings above Hangar 6, where Amelia had once started a significant journey.

George Palmer Putnam was glaringly missing from the memorial, marking the second major event that the widower had skipped. Jane Terrell, a publicist from Harcourt, Brace & Company, publisher of Amelia's newly published posthumous book, spoke in his place.

George's subsequent days were marked by turmoil. Facing mounting bills and pressure from Amy, he reluctantly sold Amelia's beloved (gifted) 1936 Cord 810 Phaeton for $900 on November 21—a stark depreciation from its original worth of $2,195. Five days later, Harcourt, Brace & Company released *Last Flight* at $2.50 a copy.

On November 23, George admitted he was going on a yacht trip to rest, and he exhaled briefly until the very next day, when gossip columnist Louella Parsons's salacious scoop on an allegedly grieving widower was that he was already being comforted by his late wife's good friend Constance Garland, the thirty-year-old daughter of renowned memoirist Hamlin Garland. She had just divorced Joseph Harper, the great-grandson of the Joseph Harper who founded Harper & Brothers, which later became Harper & Row and is now known as HarperCollins. George was ten years older than Amelia but twenty years older than this new woman.

With the release of *Last Flight*, George shifted focus to his upcoming expedition to the Galápagos and Cocos Islands. Initially refuting any intent to search for Amelia, he later changed his tune.

"I have no intention of searching for Miss Earhart," he told reporters. "I would not stoop to such subterfuge as to claim she was the reason for the voyage. It's inconceivable that she could still be alive." Several scientists, he added, were invited.

On a brisk December afternoon in Los Angeles, George received the "posthumous" Order of the Aztec Eagle, honoring Amelia's daring 1935 flight. The following Sunday, December 12, at the bustling corner of Vineland Avenue, Lankershim Boulevard, and Camarillo Street, the North Hollywood Chamber of Commerce dedicated a one-and-a-half-ton redwood bole to the missing pilot. A bronze plaque proclaimed: AMELIA EARHART PUTNAM, CITIZEN OF NORTH HOLLYWOOD. Despite past frictions, Paul Mantz presided over the ceremony as master of ceremonies. In a moment of irony, George, once dismissive of Mantz's promotional skills, delivered a brief speech under the watchful eyes of Amelia's mother and close friends. This memorial was later replaced in 1954 by a more prominent stone monument, which remains today.

Before the year fizzled out, George arranged for the magazine *Look* to publish two significant spreads in February, while he would still be at sea on his "expedition." The first spread was to feature *Last Flight*. A few pages later, readers would find a four-page feature titled HOLLYWOOD STUNT GAL: HOW WOULD YOU LIKE HER JOB, centered on Ione Reed. Although she was already George's secret lover, the magazine portrayed her as a daring single stuntwoman. George selected dramatic photos of her performing with an elephant and showcasing other stunts. He planned to present his relationship with Ione as one that developed naturally at sea, allowing him to frame their connection in a light untouched by scandal upon his return.

On December 15, George finally embarked on his long-planned escape with Ione Reed, under the guise of expedition, aboard the 105-foot diesel yacht *Athene*, under the nominal leadership of movie director Tay Garnett, who stayed ashore. The voyage's crew included notable figures such as deep-water captain Asa Pitts Harris and George's trusted secretary, Jo Berger Greer, now dubbed "expedition secretary." Jo's role subtly shifted to chaperone, with Claire, her sister, accompanying her as a companion for Ione. Also on board were Winifred, Jo's zoologist husband, along with a skilled crew of nine who had previously sailed with Garnett around the world.

George devised yet another plan to captivate his audience: he would comb the equatorial seas, searching each atoll for news while continuing to portray Ione as a typical American girl—too preoccupied with supporting herself and her mother to indulge in meaningful literature. To further this image, he asked Amelia's friends to recommend books for what he called the "Magic Book Box." This box, filled with the suggested books, was intended for Ione to read on board, casting her as an uneducated girl whom readers might adopt and root for, thus deflecting attention from George's own relationship with her. The contents of the box would only be revealed once the yacht set sail. To engage the public further, he launched a contest for readers to guess the box's contents, with the actual books from the expedition and a bound edition offered as prizes. "Entries must be submitted by January 10," he announced with his usual public enthusiasm during interviews.

Jackie Cochran was so roiled that George had left his mother-in-law alone on her first Christmas without her daughter that she telegraphed Mrs. Earhart: WE WOULD LOVE TO HAVE YOU FOR THE HOLIDAYS.

On one of the last days of 1937, a national newspaper poll revealed the top ten stories that American women were most interested in; Amelia Earhart came third, behind the devastating story of the Ohio River flooding and the thousands of people forced out of their homes. Most men preferred stories about the Second Sino-Japanese War and Roosevelt's Supreme Court fight, in which he fought to increase the number of justices. Combining male and female responses, Earhart ranked fifth. Women and girls had looked up to her before her story was usurped by crafty men as tabloid fodder.

Meanwhile, ever resilient, George moved on—embracing the holiday spirit. Yet as 1937 closed, it was clear that the echoes of Amelia's disappearance would continue to shape his path, and no amount of distraction could erase the shadow she left behind.

Nineteen

WHO CAME TO DINNER

By February 1938, most people had accepted that Amelia Earhart and Fred Noonan were dead, but they were still legally alive until proven otherwise. This atmosphere of unresolved mystery sparked a unique tribute by Duane Bryers, a twenty-seven-year-old artist later renowned for his Hilda pinups. Not awaiting official confirmation to begin a memorial, Bryers dedicated over a week to crafting a majestic fourteen-foot-high snow bust of Amelia's head and neck. It was not long before this monument melted away, mirroring the dwindling hopes for any tangible trace of Amelia.

George returned from his sea expedition on March 29—unsurprisingly, without any news.

His mood plummeted when he entered his Los Angeles home. Amy, his resident mother-in-law, believed he had abandoned hopes of finding Amelia and quickly criticized his actions. While this was true, George reassured her otherwise and organized activities for Amy that might distract her from the debaucheries of his daily life.

By this time, George had turned his attention to new ventures, dead set on launching his own West Coast publishing house. It was during this period that he met Charles "Cap" Palmer—a determined Dartmouth graduate from the class of 1923—who was willing to assist him economically to gain some book writing experience. Once a sewer pipe salesman with an MBA, Cap had pivoted to writing due to the Depression's stagnation, and by thirty-five, he had stories featured in *Cosmopolitan* and *The Saturday Evening Post*. Recognizing Cap's talent and affordability, George invited him to join his fledgling publishing company in a cozy Sunset Boulevard office.

In a much later interview, Cap, the eventual screenwriter for Disney's *Lady and the Tramp*, humorously referred to himself as George's in-house hack wordsmith who, by his count, would ghostwrite twelve slapdash books for the former New York publisher. Cap soon became so involved in George's life and work that his family teased him about practically living there. On one occasion, he noticed a strange crate in the garage. A staff member mentioned that it had come from New Guinea before Amelia's last flight and held items removed to save weight, like extra clothes and lightweight curtains (probably for Amelia's privacy). All excess weight was swapped for fuel. Additionally, the crate contained an inflatable raft, which he initially gave little thought to, and he took the raft for his family when it was about to be thrown away. Later, he wondered if they'd left behind a piece of vital safety equipment. Sadly, this potential piece of history was lost in a family's move.

Full of ideas and always on the lookout, like a magpie attracted to shiny things, George often claimed that just a bit more effort could turn their modest book projects into gold mines. Their small office on Sunset Boulevard—humorously named "Menopause Manor" by the publisher due to its location above a teahouse frequented by middle-aged women—was a hub of activity. "I was supposed to earn fifty dollars a week. If George had it, he'd pay me, but more often than not, he didn't," Cap later noted, once again parsing the challenges of George's unpredictable nature and inconsistent payments. However, on a good day, George's charisma was irresistible, and his optimism about even the most outlandish ideas was contagious.

George's volatile temperament had damaged many of his previous relationships with colleagues like Harold McCracken, Richard Byrd, and Hilton Howell Railey. Following Amelia's death, he sought a new beginning, choosing to surround himself with younger friends and leaving old grudges behind. Cap found that a bit of flattery could often stabilize George's mood swings. He described George as a "go-go-go guy," always pushing forward. Their books weren't bestsellers, and George typically reinvested any profits into new ventures. Despite the challenges, Cap deeply valued their partnership, seeing George not as the unreliable type some believed him to be but as a tough, cherished family member. To those who knew him well, George was a unique source of confidence.

While George and his mother-in-law were often at odds, he couldn't ignore his obligation to care for her. And he wasn't the only target of Mother Earhart's critiques; Amy's surviving daughter, Muriel, despite her deep love for her mother, was long subjected to harsh judgments. With Amelia—the Earharts' perceived "brighter" daughter—gone, Muriel found an unlikely ally in George. Unlike her controlling and stingy husband, Albert, George offered her financial support for her loyalty. A handsome check here and there was a lifesaver for her, and a mutually beneficial relationship evolved, as underscored by a note discovered among George's papers, one penned after the big car accident that killed suffragette Benigna Green. In it, Muriel wrote, "What a pity it couldn't have been Mother instead." A rare and uncharacteristic moment of candid venting from the usually reserved Muriel. Remarkably, Muriel hardly knew George when Amelia was alive and barely saw them together. Muriel had never visited Amelia in any of the homes she shared with George—this camaraderie was new.

Finally reaching the end of his patience with his mother-in-law, George eventually moved her 370 miles north by "arranging" a living situation at the Berkeley Women's City Club. Yet the familial tension lingered across the miles, especially over money, as revealed in many bitter letters between the two, which were kept by his mother-in-law and his lawyer, Clyde Holley.

After months of in-depth research, Commander Thompson released a confidential report on May 12, highlighting Amelia Earhart's fatal errors, mainly her lack of preparation and her use of inadequate radio equipment that couldn't handle frequencies above 7500 kilocycles. Despite potential radio issues, Amelia and Noonan had departed from Lae after delays caused by Noonan's struggles to calibrate his chronometer. They likely would have survived if they had waited a few more days for repairs. A last-minute effort to secure a high-frequency direction finder proved futile, as the *Itasca* was given only eight hours' notice and couldn't arrange the necessary special radio equipment in time. Further complicating matters, George Palmer Putnam had incorrectly instructed the cutter on radio frequencies. Commander Thompson concluded, "I believe Miss Earhart passed north and west of Howland Island and missed it in the glare of the rising sun," damning both Amelia and George for their cavalier approach to vital radio communications.

On May 22, 1938, George Putnam, ever the charming widower, found himself as the guest of honor at a star-studded Hollywood salon tea party organized by Joanne Alderman. Joanne, well-known in Los Angeles for her no-charge celebrity gatherings in private homes, had once again pulled together fifty of her closest friends for an afternoon of mingling and tea. This time, George arrived not with a stuntwoman but with a different kind of daredevil—an accomplished and strikingly beautiful twenty-seven-year-old violinist from Oregon named Mildi Roberts.

Not long after their arrival, the room brightened with the entrance of a young blond socialite. She was a former schoolmate of Alderman's from the exclusive Marlborough School for Girls. At just twenty-six, Jean-Marie Consigny radiated an air of wholesome allure. Her creamy complexion, well-defined chin, and appealing lips were framed by neatly waved hair and animated eyes. George, despite being there with Mildi, couldn't resist the pull of curiosity. When the crisp, calculating hostess leaned in and discreetly whispered, "She's a Consigny!"—a name with significant clout in local banking circles—George's interest was piqued even further. It seemed his discreet quest for companionship and advantageous connections was far from over.

Consigny herself later recalled their sizzling chemistry: "When I first met GP, I fell for him like a ton of bricks. . . . My friends were saying hello, and then I walked into the living room. I saw this man sitting over there in a big chair in the corner, and I just took one look at him, and I was sunk; I was absolutely crazy about him without knowing anything about him whatsoever.... I didn't connect him with Amelia. But he pursued me as everyone was finishing their tea.... I don't remember exactly what we said. But, anyway, I said, 'Well, I was a garden editor for a magazine in Los Angeles,' and he said, 'Oh, you are?!' And then he went home."

Back in Toluca Lake, George's home was filled with activity. Janet Mabie, George's ghostwriter for the new *Soaring Wings* book project about Amelia, had come from New York to manage the detailed work, which Consigny described as "the nitty-gritty that bored GP." Amelia's sister, Muriel, was also present, collaborating with Mabie to infuse the upcoming book with intimate family tales that would be written under George's name. In the whirl of all this, George radiated an unexpected cheerfulness. Stealing a quiet moment with his closest secretary, Jo, he shared a secret: "I've met the girl I'm going to marry, so that's settled."

George Palmer Putnam had his own well-practiced brand of romantic pursuit and was laser-focused on winning Consigny's affection, much like he had been during his previous pursuits of Amelia and Dorothy. The second he had come home from the tea party, he had sent somebody to find out everything Consigny had ever written—even back to kid pieces she'd written for the Beverly Hills Grammar School. Soon he'd quiz her mother's Bel Air housekeeper about where mother and daughter were going for the day and then—voila!—mysteriously materialize at the same dining spot, even if it were in Santa Barbara or Palm Springs. If they drove down to the Hotel del Coronado, he'd be there. "It was just weird!" Consigny later recalled. As Dorothy and Amelia had experienced, the still-married Consigny was hunted prey, showered with affectionate messages daily, including very early together-forever talk. Far from finding this machinelike wooing unsettling, the young lady was intrigued. Imagine, the man who had won Amelia Earhart's heart was now fixated on her. Too fantastic! "I was just simply hook, line, and sinker for that man," Consigny recollected, "and I had never been that way before."

With Consigny in his crosshairs, George kept his distance from the other women in his mix: his violinist, his stuntwoman, and even the upcoming actress Greer Garson, who later became an Oscar winner. Others had cradled the hope of a bright future with the nationally known widower, and Consigny noticed the fierce competition for George's attention. She only later realized that Ione had once been close to George, and their breakup had deeply affected Ione—it hurts to be erased without a second thought. As a parting gesture, George helped Ione with a little-promoted ghostwritten novel, *Stunt Girl*, and secured some ad deals for her with Camel cigarettes.

Cap would marvel at how many beautiful ladies were drawn to George's charm, but they also knew he had extensive connections that could lead to significant roles in Hollywood. Among his other "avid admirers" were renowned women like dancer Irene Castle and columnist Hedda Hopper. Of them all, Greer Garson was the most notably infatuated. She not only wanted to marry George but also wished to portray Amelia Earhart in the film adaptation George was nursing along. This led to a controversial press release suggesting that a past lover might play his former wife.

However, with Consigny, who had no acting agenda and big eyes that stared at him in adoration, George found the peaceful companionship he longed for, especially after the intense spotlight following Amelia's disappearance. When Consigny felt she couldn't compete with George's glamorous past relationships, he reassured her, saying, "They scare the life out of me!" Although born in 1911, Consigny was unfazed by the twenty-four-year age difference. "But what I couldn't understand," she would later joke, "was how [George] could be working on a biography of Amelia Earhart and pursuing me relentlessly."

Fred Noonan's death was confirmed by Judge John J. Allen in Alameda Superior Court on June 20, 1938, at the request of his recent bride, Bea Martinelli. Judge Allen reached this verdict after examining a seven-page photostatic copy of communications between the US Coast Guard, Amelia Earhart, and Fred Noonan, along with subsequent radiograms. He then granted Bea, a beauty technician, letters of administration. Shortly after, Bea married the recently widowed Harry B. Ireland, a wealthy retired stockbroker from Santa Barbara whom she had met on a ship traveling from

Hawaii to Los Angeles. Her swift transition to a new marriage might have raised eyebrows among the more judgmental. But who were they to judge? Unless one has been through the hell she experienced, one shouldn't be so quick to cast stones. Circumstances often push people into corners where they must make hard choices.

And if Bea could get a judge to say Fred was dead, why couldn't George get one to say that Amelia was gone too? Why should he have to wait seven years just for a show? He was ready now to move on, and with a gorgeous young, unhappily married woman who wanted to marry him as soon as possible. And, in his opinion, she was marriage material—beautiful, with impeccable social standing (and, perhaps, he mistakenly thought, very rich).

Twenty

VEILED VENTURES

Eighteen months after Amelia Earhart's mysterious vanishing, a court declaration on January 5, 1939, pronounced her dead, bypassing the usual seven-year wait. This decision, influenced by the evidence and statements presented by her husband, George Palmer Putnam, and other key witnesses, corresponded with the Earhart family heirloom Bible that marked the pilot's death around July 2, the date of her disappearance.

In the wake of this legal ruling, George, though publicly appearing mournful, privately felt a sense of release. Judge Clarence "Elliot" Craig's expeditious handling of Amelia's 1932 legal will began a new chapter in his life. Now legally a widower, he could openly pursue relationships and manage the estate, including profiting from it without the lengthy wait. As the executor of Amelia's estate, intended to provide for her mother, Amy Otis, in later years, George found himself in a position of power. Amelia had envisioned her death, as any pilot does. She felt that George was perfectly capable of supporting himself without her money due to his work experience, age, and home ownership in Rye. Her sister was poor, and her half-deaf mother had nothing; she depended on Amelia financially and would depend on any money left to her if her daughter died. George wouldn't let her starve, but with this newfound authority, he resolved to strictly assist Amelia's mother and sister on his terms.

When the legal decision was announced, two of Amelia's closest associates, Jackie Cochran and Floyd Odlum, recalled their significant conversation with Amelia at their ranch in 1936. During this visit, Amelia had shared her concerns about ensuring financial security for her mother, Amy, if her world flight ended in tragedy. Cochran recalled their eye-opening discussion about a "holographic will"—a handwritten will that could supersede typed ones in California. Amelia had such a will drafted by Mabel Walker Willebrandt, a respected former assistant attorney general, at her home, done pro bono due to their mutual connection through Cochran and Odlum. With George presenting a different will for probate, Cochran suspected that a concealed, more favorable handwritten will might have been meant to better protect and provide for Amelia's mother. However, she questioned the benefit of making these suspicions public.

Not knowing any of this secret will business, Amelia's admirers across the world and even her detractors were already voicing plenty of skepticism about her husband's motives, outright puzzled by his rapid efforts to settle the estate of their hero.

After exiting the courtroom, George braced himself for an inevitable clash with his outspoken mother-in-law, who was still waiting for Amelia to show up. Despite her discernible fury, Amy, who was dealing with severe, ever-worsening hearing loss, was relegated to accepting whatever allowance George allocated, forced to rely on friends for any additional needs.

Financially unstable, George ignored his critics, including Amy, and pursued business ventures. His frustration peaked when a planned Howard Hawks film about Amelia, starring Katharine Hepburn, fell through. He then engaged with Hungarian director Gabriel Pascal about a potential film featuring Wendy Hiller and Paul Lukas. Concurrently, Amy weighed a $15,000 proposal to portray herself in a movie. Learning of this, an infuriated George insisted on collaboration, agitated by her intrusion into his domain. Ultimately, both film endeavors faltered, leaving George financially stranded as he considered remarrying.

Consigny, George's pretty Bel Air society girlfriend, who was embroiled in a divorce with a lawyering ex, grew apprehensive as the film projects collapsed, questioning the fiscal reality she might be entering with George, reputedly a millionaire publisher. George could read the writing on the wall. In a bid for financial recovery, he sold his lavish five-acre Rye estate to Dean Babbitt of Sonotone Corporation. This sale temporarily eased the strain and appeased Consigny, who was already unsettled by Amelia's lingering shadow in their relationship. To further alleviate those concerns, George had his house staff in Rye dispatch the life-size oil portrait of Amelia that hung in his property to Purdue University, where it still hangs.

Since Amelia's vanishing, George had steered clear of the Westchester property, reluctant to confront the memories and relics it harbored. The Rye residence was a painful and emotional trove filled with Amelia's portraits, souvenirs from George's two marriages to date, and exotic items like Peruvian shrunken heads from his Explorers Club friends—a history of a past self that George was hesitant to revisit.

With bills hidden from her, Consigny was still infatuated with this older, more worldly man and still under the impression of his substantial wealth. He joked it away with a mysterious word or two if she inquired about how he made most of his money. "Trade secrets!"

Though George had never been a paragon of virtue, Amelia's influence was often a moral compass, discouraging him from the more overtly deceptive practices up his sleeve (like fabricated death threats from Fascists). Yet in her absence, he reverted to his impulsive habits. After selling the house, George devised another disturbing scheme to further line his pockets, a plan that again hinged on generating free publicity to propel a book to bestseller status, with money going straight to him, not to a family firm. How much Consigny knew of this intricate web remains uncertain.

By April 1939, George Palmer Putnam's nascent publishing venture, George Palmer Putnam, Inc., was in full swing. Founded a year earlier with a focus on adapting books for film, the venture was based on Hollywood Boulevard and relied on Vail-Ballou Press for its printing needs. The bulk of its titles bore the unseen hand of Charles "Cap" Palmer, the young hired hand who viewed his work as a vocation, not a creative task.

Their first meeting revealed George's secret project, which he hoped would make him rich: *The Man Who Killed Hitler*, written by a ghostwriter named Dean Jennings but to be marketed under "by Anonymous" for added mystique. Cap elaborated that Jennings was a journeyman writer—akin to a skilled but unsung literary worker, much like a dependable plumber in the trades. Lacking the renown of celebrated authors, Jennings prioritized profit over praise and was eager to secure higher royalties through this project.

After working with Cap for a few weeks, George unveiled his extensive plans, first to the trade publications and then to the general press, to launch eight titles at his new California publishing house within the inaugural year. In his opinion, one title was so timely that postponing its release was a public disservice.

That alone would not get attention. But then, shortly after that, George revealed a forged letter warning against publishing his first book, a revealing novel on Hitler's inner world: "In a very short time, German will be the world's language. . . . You are hereby warned to stop the publication of *The Man Who Killed Hitler*. Heil Hitler. [Signed] Greater Germany."

George launched his most daring escapade yet by staging his own kidnapping, where he was dramatically found bound and gagged in Bakersfield, California, two hours from his Los Angeles home. After orchestrating this elaborate deception, he reported the bogus incident to the police, triggering a flurry of activity, including a statewide APB as investigators worked tirelessly to untangle his web of deceit. He then convened a press conference to detail his concocted ordeal. This audacious plot, riskier than any Jazz Age stunt he'd pulled, entangled his secretaries in a potentially criminal act, exposing them to the threat of imprisonment. Despite the potential fallout, George remained seemingly untroubled as reporters and photographers gathered on a lively Saturday evening at the Spanish colonial–style residence he once shared with Amelia Earhart.

Hair a mess, tie askew, George launched into his crackling tale, half panting, as the reporters braced themselves for yet another encounter with a tedious, talkative man known on both coasts for ploys. It began on April 22, when he received a threatening note and a bullet-riddled copy of *The*

Man Who Killed Hitler, "evidence" that he promptly submitted to the district attorney's office. "It is the third anonymous warning I've received!" he claimed, adding that little did he know two fearsome Germans would soon kidnap him, plunging his life into further disarray.

Lightbulbs flashed, and eyeballs rolled—Putnam was a known fabulist on both coasts—but those on assignment had been instructed to report the news straight, as their editors believed that the story of Amelia Earhart's kidnapped widower could sell papers.

"How did this happen?"

"Well, I'll tell you!" George said. "My secretary Jo Berger received a call at 5:00 p.m. from a woman claiming to work for actor Rex Cole's agent." He added, "Considering Cole is a trusted friend, I took the matter seriously."

"Sure you did," another reporter muttered sarcastically.

George stared at the reporter in disbelief. Was he questioning him? Yes, two Nazis had ambushed him while driving to Cole's house, and then they had bound and gagged him using tire tape after intimidating him with a weapon and blindfolding him. Despite their initial conversation in German, they switched to English inside the car. George reported that he maintained his silence when they demanded information about the anti-Nazi book. He was later shocked to learn they had driven him far from his home to Bakersfield. But he only found this out when he managed to free himself after a grueling couple of hours. A local resident named Roy Walker and his wife, Henrietta, came to his aid after hearing his yells.

Had anyone present heard of his upcoming book, *The Man Who Killed Hitler*? George then asked. Did they get the name of the book right? It was written by Anonymous because the writer was a true insider, George said. The story followed a Viennese doctor's wife persecuted by Nazis, with the protagonist seeking more than revenge—total annihilation. Yet the ending left Hitler's fate ambiguous . . .

But then it was back to his night of hell. If anyone had doubts about his watertight account, he offered to reenact the kidnapping, becoming more animated as he did so. And he challenged anyone who thought this was merely a publicity stunt for *The Man Who Killed Hitler* to say it to his face.

Captain Dalton Patton of the Bakersfield police planned to have George testify before a grand jury, but the jurors dismissed the idea as unworthy of their time. Everyone could see through this nonsense, at least in California, if not the rest of the gullible nation. Skepticism grew around George's credibility among the public and law enforcement. Local police had been duped, and an entire town had been put on lockdown in the search for the imaginary "Germans" George claimed were a threat.

While he'd achieved the nationwide headlines he'd sought, the move was just too mad, stupid, and pitiable. Days later, mocking laughter filled the room as his name was announced at a notable publishing event. The once-esteemed George Palmer Putnam, famous for publishing Lindbergh, had become a literal laughingstock in the industry. In his nationwide column, Walter Winchell pointed out that Nazis were "dragging a name" out of him, but before George's supposed kidnapping he had already revealed to many that the anonymous author was Dean Jennings. Winchell's competitor, Ed Sullivan, mentioned that journalists were left puzzled and actual book enthusiasts would simply prefer a good read.

Those well acquainted with George's life of shenanigans didn't hesitate to roast him. Heywood Broun, a revered member of the Algonquin Round Table, pilloried Putnam in his nationally syndicated column, suggesting that the two masked men who kidnapped his former publisher might have been Martians, stranded from the Halloween radio broadcast of Orson Welles's "The War of the Worlds." Broun tacked on: "There are times when even the most expeditious journalist should take occasion to count ten before he writes a single line."

Against these unseemly theatrics, *The Man Who Killed Hitler* quietly made its debut and quickly faded from public memory, much like the smoke and mirrors surrounding it.

David Binney Putnam and other direct descendants refute that documented pathological lying is at play here, and David angrily told one researcher that he believed his father possessed "an agile mind," a trait often misconstrued by reporters and screenwriters seeking to "do a job" on him. It was a professional promotion, not a "con kind of thing." (That attempt to sugarcoat the narrative is hard to reconcile with his father's faked attack by Fascists in 1930 and such 1939 headlines as AMELIA EARHART'S HUSBAND BOUND, GAGGED BY KIDNAPPERS.) George's grandiose ideas about his literary career often fueled such disturbing exaggerations, blurring the line between ambition and fiction.

In an interview given to the *Los Angeles Times Sunday Magazine* on May 14, George tried to rescue his reputation with one of the fluffier stories he always placed for Amelia when she was in a heck of a fix. This article portrayed him as a tireless professional surrounded by books, papers, and awards, and he amusedly described his home office setting, where he worked alongside two secretaries. "I'm like the fireman who won't retire," George said. "He scampers after flames. I chase manuscripts."

Just three days after Jean-Marie Consigny finalized her divorce from William James on May 19, she and fifty-two-year-old George tied the knot. Their quick nuptials on May 22 were held on a patio porch in Boulder City, Nevada. The haste of their union raised more than a few eyebrows again, including those belonging to Jackie Cochran, who felt that the marriage was disrespectful to Amelia. She stated that the couple had met "before Amelia was even cold in her grave" and also pointed out that Jean-Marie was "as young as a daughter would be, and very pretty."

For their honeymoon flight, George and Jean-Marie Putnam went incognito, reserving tickets under the names "Mr. and Mrs. Dean Drury"—a composite of George's very young and pretty part-time editor "Dory" Drury and Dory's recent lover, Dean Jennings, his ghostwriter on the Hitler novel. To a single reporter allowed on the scene for takeoff, George couldn't resist saying, "It's cheaper to marry one's authors and save royalties." This printed remark left Jean-Marie wondering what he meant. Since when was she an author?

The skepticism around their improbable marriage was something Jean-Marie had come to expect. Her more significant fear was that Amelia,

George's second wife, might resurface, invalidating their marriage, and the ghost of her past loomed large, threatening her newfound happiness. Jean-Marie was mighty spooked when, on June 25, four boys discovered a bottle in Boston's Bass River. Inside was a note, allegedly from Amelia Earhart, stating that she was stranded on Wake Island. The claim was taken seriously by Boston's Lieutenant Tobin, who triggered a spate of US Coast Guard communications. Amelia's sister, Muriel, called her in California and dismissed the note as far-fetched. Muriel and George knew it was nonsense but had to pretend to take it seriously for the court of public opinion.

Meanwhile, George was worried that his long-pampered wife, Jean-Marie, was idle, and he wanted her to be both happy and valuable. For help, he turned again to his underling Cap Palmer, who offered, "I had the quaint idea that maybe you could just have a nice wife to sit at the head of the table." George, however, had a different plan. "He came up with the idea that they could make Jeanie [Jean-Marie] a gardening expert.... I went to work and rounded up stuff," Cap said. Despite George's house sale in Rye, it was a lousy time to sell, and he was struggling financially, a fact he hid from Jean-Marie by living large and having staff and parties. Years later, she learned he was down to his last dollars; she confessed she had no idea they were broke.

Cap recalled that George "was always building something that he thought ought to be built and created and made useful. Now, this worked on every woman he was ever connected with; George abhorred waste—wasted brainpower, wasted human power—and a woman connected with him had to do something. She was conscious of societal norms, and he was doing things in this rough corncob fashion. George was letting the overt motive show too much."

Cap dutifully got to work and secretly began crafting a book called *Gardening for Fun in California*. Jean-Marie would not know about it until it appeared under her name as "coauthored" with Charles Palmer. (She would admit that she didn't write a word of any of the books George would put out under her name.)

Soon after, a nationally syndicated article appeared on July 4, painting

Jean-Marie as the epitome of a traditional, yet expert, wife. This was George's strategy for the book's surprise autumn release, and the article also indicated that George had softened his stance on working wives, lauding Jean-Marie's domesticity while emphasizing her gardening skills. The national piece left her perplexed. She had no idea it was part of George's more extensive plans for her. But she loved and appreciated him early in their marriage before the rot set in. "He was stronger than I was," she recalled years later. "He had more pep, more zing." Jean-Marie grew fond of their Toluca Lake home, initially Amelia's investment but now part of George's mother's estate. She appreciated its proximity to the Lakeside Golf Club, often using the club's pool, and marveled at having everyone who was anyone for dinner: "Hedda Hopper, Louella Parsons, Roy Chapman Andrews, William Beebe—it was exciting!"

However, the initially idyllic marriage didn't last; there were more dark and accusatory silences when George didn't get his way, and he'd already begun to shout, scream, and curse. Although Jean-Marie was attached to her dog, George would enter a new tirade whenever she brought it inside, even while encouraging her to interact with his pet bird, Red. The crazy-making.

George treated Jean-Marie like a treasured pet kitten, and Cap likened her to a little girl navigating a massive pool.

On August 10, George's Amelia Earhart biography, *Soaring Wings*, a blend of truth and much embellishment about his famous wife, hit the shelves to a mixed reception. Janet Mabie, his collaborator, who was unfairly left uncredited, was also shortchanged financially when George broke his promise to pay her. According to Mabie's letters, George conveniently picked a fight with her and critiqued her work, even though he had previously praised it as smoothly as expected.

Adding to the chorus of skeptics, even David Binney Putnam, who had deep affection for Amelia and his father, conceded that his dad was not a reliable narrator in his Amelia biography.

One reviewer sharply accused him of a lack of emotional distance and challenged his assertion that the flight was unselfish. "The disaster killed another person; it brought agony to others. It caused a disruption of life over a wide area." *The New Yorker*, never kind to Putnam, hit right for the jugular in its anonymous Briefly Noted column: "Mr. Putnam writes dully."

But there were essential champions too, like Eleanor Roosevelt, who received a book and mentioned it in her widely read column, My Day. Though Mrs. Roosevelt confessed that she had not yet read the book, she reckoned that she had read much of the material in serialized form in *Liberty* magazine. "There may be more in the book, however, and I am glad in any case to have it in permanent form, for this is the record of a friend one can never forget in a book to be treasured in one's library."

But a surprising nod of approval came from Katherine Woods, the first English translator of *The Little Prince*, who stated in the front-page story of *The New York Times Book Review* that George had portrayed Amelia first and foremost as a human being: "Mr. Putnam's book has the double value of giving his readers the record of her life as a whole and the feeling of her spirit. . . . Not even in its ending can this be a sad story. On the contrary, it is full of courage and determination."

Mabie, the ghost for the book, criticized the final biography as mostly well-known and inaccurate information, saying in private letters that George had heavily edited her manuscript to include "fanciful facts."

Soaring Wings secured respectable sales, yet it didn't reach bestseller status, and the oversanitized portrayal of Amelia might have been the limiting factor. Biographers with close ties to their subjects can occasionally prioritize a flattering narrative over an unvarnished truth.

Once hailed as the promoter of "America's Greatest Woman Pilot," George now hustled for "America's Greatest Gardening Expert." Although "her" book was produced gracefully on just $1,500 for two thousand copies, and though she was reluctantly thrust into this new role, Jean-Marie agreed to promotion, including a series of luncheon talks organized and successfully curated by George. His next chess move was tapping her significant societal ties. "He suggested sending pink notes about my book to our friends," Jean-Marie recalled, adding that they achieved regional success with hundreds of copies sold to their acquaintances alone.

By 1941, George's publishing venture was on shaky ground. But just when it seemed all was lost, Harcourt came through with an offer for a memoir deal, sweetened with an advance. George and his main secretary hastily patched together a manuscript from past articles, leading Cap to derisively dub it "literary chop suey." Ignoring Cap's reservations, George shipped it to his book editor, Sam Sloan, in New York. Sloan didn't hold back his disappointment over such sloppy work from a supposedly professional writer and editor, a sentiment shared by Jean-Marie, George's wife. Aware of George's explosive temperament, Sloan contacted Cap for counsel. After a loud chortle, Cap remarked, "George? Oh, he's a screamer. Just lay it out for him straight; it might be the kick he needs." Bracing himself, Sloan gave George the straightforward take of "not good," leading to a predictable George-sized explosion. Behind the scenes, Cap stealthily noted every anecdote George spilled, later nudging him to expand on those small vignettes. With Cap handling the heavy writing and injecting some much-needed humor—a trait he felt George sorely lacked—the result was published in *Cosmopolitan*'s December 1941 issue as "Autobiography of Other People." It later graced bookstores as *Wide Margins*. While it had its shining moments, it sometimes took liberties with the truth. Let's chalk it up as a solid gentleman's C.

In February 1942, sidelined and struggling for income, George sold three hundred of Amelia Earhart's books and personal items, for amounts ranging from thirty-five cents to fifty bucks, at Dawson's Book Shop. People were eager for a piece of Amelia's legacy.

By August 1942, with two sons already in the crosshairs of war, George Palmer Putnam yearned for action. Leaving behind the familiar hum of his publishing house and an eccentric plywood side hustle, he pivoted toward the call of duty. Friends were surprised; despite his ties with President Roosevelt, George had chosen the grit of basic training in Florida over an immediate officer's chair at fifty-five. Meanwhile, back home, Cap Palmer, the trusted confidant, kept the gears of George's empire turning, ensuring no single project missed a beat.

A few months earlier, in the spring of 1942, George Palmer Putnam had acquired a script titled *Stand By to Die*, authored by Horace McCoy and shelved since 1939 due to its overtly anti-Japanese sentiments. With its sappy plot about an aviatrix named Tonie Carter on a covert mission similar to Amelia Earhart's final flight, this script caught the eye of director Lothar Mendes and producer Fred Brisson, Rosalind Russell's husband. Recognizing its potential as wartime propaganda, the US government, which had previously dismissed spy-centric theories about Amelia, now supported the narrative to fuel enlistment and war bond sales.

Rosalind Russell was cast in the lead role, and the script was revised into a gold mine blending spy thriller elements with an Earhart-like biopic. Amid these developments, in the spring of 1942, *Variety* reported that RKO, directed by Floyd Odlum—Jackie Cochran's husband and a friend to Amelia—had acquired McCoy's script for $35,000. George, maintaining a public facade of indignation about exploiting Amelia's legacy, was in cahoots with Odlum, collaborating in secret and excluding Cochran from their plans.

Since he would profit if the film did well, George helped sell a *Skyways* magazine article crafted by Cap. The article speculated about Amelia's covert government ties and questioned her mission's purpose. This article mirrored the upcoming film's narrative, suggesting that Amelia might have been the first victim of Japanese aggression. Despite George's public distancing from the project, he was deeply involved in its success, manipulating public perception and fueling conspiracy theories for profit.

Flight for Freedom, reworked from earlier scripts to align with George's narrative, premiered in November 1942 at Radio City Music Hall. George expressed outrage at the film's liberties but was ultimately complicit, receiving a $7,000 payout disguised as a settlement for "material provided." This amount, which George later partially distributed to Amelia's family and Cap Palmer, was a prearranged payment, not a genuine legal settlement.

The film's ambiguous portrayal of Amelia Earhart's fate spurred further conspiracy theories post–World War II. Despite the official stance that any resemblance to real-life individuals was coincidental, the story, which blurred the lines between fact and fiction, left many Americans puzzled. This confusion was further propagated by Russell's portrayal of Tonie Carter in a Lux Radio play version of *Flight for Freedom* on September 20, 1943, amplifying the film's impact and popularity.

Additional sources of income for George included a $2,000 payment for a short novel based on the script, published in *Woman's Home Companion* to an audience of four million, further spreading the conspiracy-laden narrative.

His journey took another twist when he transitioned to a desk role in Washington's intelligence circles—ironically, the exact setting he once sought to escape. In April 1943, an interview surfaced with M. L. Brittain, the Georgia Tech president who participated in the search. Brittain speculated on Amelia's possible entanglement with the Japanese. When the spotlight turned to George for a comment, he was firm: "All of them are absolutely ridiculous. There was no prior understanding with the navy or anyone else. I oversaw all flight logistics—and I'm definitive. Amelia would never have undertaken such a venture."

He was grateful to receive the rank of major like his uncle, the old Major George Haven Putnam. He was sure to get press for himself on this unusual move. His service was the story, partly because of his age, and characteristically, even in wartime, he loved being asked about his military analysis by the press. "This is the most interesting job an older man can get in the air corps," he was quoted as saying in the papers. "I feel lucky to be associated with a crowd like this. With one exception, every man in this company is young enough to be my son. This keeps an old man like me on his toes."

Tensions between George and Jean-Marie, as documented in the "PUTNAM v. PUTNAM" folder held by George's lawyer, Clyde Holley, escalated quickly. Despite being away for eight months, George was shocked by Jean-Marie's cooled affections and intolerant of any dissent from her while he served his country. Meanwhile, she felt devalued by his lack of concern for her feelings, particularly as an older married man who had volunteered for service when he had a new, young wife at home. To Jean-Marie, all his military stories felt like a sunny account of abandonment. Was it genuinely selfless that he signed up, or was it partly for the glory? Legal records suggest Jean-Marie might have discovered affairs he dismissed as mere flirtations typical of military life. Their disputes climaxed on October 26 when, after a heated argument, George struck Jean-Marie. She fled to her car, only to discover that George, at his angry whim, had removed the keys. Defiantly, she retrieved a spare set, drove off with a visible mark from the slap, and sought refuge with a friend from her Christian Science church.

In his letters to his lawyer, George let his frustration spill out. He couldn't understand Jean-Marie's coldness toward his military service or, as he put it, her "unnatural" behavior. It ate at him, a slow burn that came through in every word he wrote. He plotted to publicly tarnish her reputation with a lawsuit for alienation of affection—not to win but to smear her publicly. Furious, he demanded that his lawyer secure a quick divorce before his potential deployment, ranting about his mistreatment and declaring his readiness to move on: "I want you to get it in the bag before I leave. I may leave in a month. I have been treated outrageously, and I'll be damned if I want to return with any strings remaining to tie me down. I might be in love with a China gal by then! At least she is not likely to be CS. GPP." Clyde Holley calmed him somewhat but eventually did as told—there was no arguing with a tornado.

Despite his public displays of faith and attendance at church events— a mirroring tactic Jean-Marie later said she believed—George privately mocked her Christian Science beliefs. He derisively dismissed the religion among friends, revealing a stark contrast between his public gestures and private sentiments.

As he had before with Dorothy (and possibly with Amelia), he now sent her sweet, manipulative notes that do not read like he took any blame: "Try a little to see the viewpoint of a guy who sees you for the first time in 8 months who is going away again at once. And even overseas, your first greeting is to reject his kiss of greeting. . . . I am sorry, as you well know, that I get cross. Never does any good, and it was foolish to try to make you what I'd call 'come to your senses' by kissing you and seeking to make you respond." (For some reason, he sent carbon copies of these very personal "heartfelt" letters to his lawyer too.)

Although California was more lenient than other states when it came to reasons women could divorce, the divorce was granted on the grounds of extreme cruelty. During the February 15, 1944, hearing, Jean-Marie testified about George's constant belittling and humiliation and the smack. By the end of their day in court, their marriage was legally dissolved. Cap Palmer, privy to George Palmer Putnam's worst marital indiscretions during the war (including sexual dalliances, which George, like many soldiers, viewed as reasonable indulgences during such tumultuous times), quietly felt relieved for the kind and naive gal he had known intimately while ghostwriting for her. He reflected: "As time passed, it wouldn't have been the happiest situation for her." Despite himself, Cap adored George and had fun with him, and in later years, he would share that admiration with his grandchildren, remembering how fine a man George could (sometimes) be. However, in private conversations, he would admit that "fate intervened, I think, happily in that situation."

New York's *Daily News*, known for openly disdaining George Palmer Putnam, gleefully ran the headline:

WIFE DIVORCES NAGGER EDITOR

Years later, Jean-Marie reflected, "I left him because I felt we no longer had anything in common." Though she was happily married by the 1970s, Jean-Marie admitted that she felt no one had ever loved her with such intensity, and despite the calm in her current marriage, she wondered if she had loused up by pushing him away. She kept returning to those exhilarating months when he chased her.

Awaiting a divorce, and while stationed near Smoky Hill Army Airfield in Salina, Kansas, George Palmer Putnam continued to quietly court women who would stay discreet. Now Major Putnam, he openly derided the conspiracy theories that continued to stem from *Flight for Freedom* and the widespread American hatred toward the Japanese that his own involvement with the film had helped stoke.

He was clear on his facts regarding Amelia's last flight, stating: "The last word came from a point near Howland Island, indicating she had thirty minutes left. It's logical to believe she perished somewhere near there."

Upon returning from war, after nine months of service with a Superfortress in the India-China theater, he moved briefly to the Silver Lake neighborhood of Los Angeles with Cap Palmer and Cap's wife. He began lecturing on his war experience—an officially divorced man who felt that something was amiss in his life without a wife.

Cap always perceived George as more of a strategic suitor than a true romantic. He believed George viewed a wife as just another item on his checklist: house, land, kitchen, wife—all part of the package in George's world. Cap recalled how George, filling the wife void, flipped open his little black book, landing on the name of a woman he had "dated" during the war while still married. "She'll do," George mused in front of his friend, though his patience wore thin after a few unsuccessful attempts to contact her. As Cap recounted in a taped 1981 interview for the National Air and Space Museum, George exclaimed, "To hell with this!" and dialed another number. This time, he was ringing USO hostess Margaret Haviland, known as Peg, who was five foot eight with blond hair and twenty-one years his junior. When his second-choice Peg answered, George wooed her with, "Oh, how I miss you!" All of it witnessed by Cap.

In June 1945, fifty-seven-year-old Major George Palmer Putnam married thirty-six-year-old Peg, an executive in the USO Mobile Service. Their wedding was held in a friend's garden in San Marino and officiated by Air Force chaplain Captain Willard Learned. Both donned their military uniforms for the ceremony and embarked on a cross-country honeymoon, starting in Santa Fe.

Despite the unromantic way he reached out to her (which she was never to know), Margaret Haviland Putnam, the last wife of George Palmer Putnam, Amelia Earhart's gruff and contentious widower, was perhaps his best match and understood him in ways that astounded him. In her later years, she shared candid insights into his complex personality. Off the record, she would describe him as brusque and frequently abrupt, often offending others with his impatience and constant busyness. George was always in a rush, with a callous sneer for those he deemed incompetent, greatly offending them. People's opinions of him were sharply divided—they either liked or disliked him—and he remained largely indifferent, consumed by his daily plan.

Even though he had given her a watered-down version of his old romantic self, she loved him anyway. He was a compulsive promoter whose mind raced with endless ideas to whip up interest in his projects, and she saw him as a mesmerizing raconteur, enchanting audiences of all ages. George's stories evoked sophisticated laughter from adults and brought delightful amusement to children, bridging the gap between generations. Although the subtleties might have eluded the young, the stories satisfied both age groups. George's unparalleled charm and storytelling prowess left an indelible mark on all who encountered him.

In a private letter, Peg revealed that her husband had grown weary of discussing the painful history of 1937 after their marriage. Instead, he delved into new and exciting ventures, including acquiring a charming historic inn in Death Valley, the Stovepipe Wells Hotel. With the help of a ghostwriter, George chronicled his new life, captivatingly diverging from the bustling pace of New York and Los Angeles. While overseeing the hotel's operations was not his primary focus, George found solace in his wife's budding painting hobby. He refrained from seeking book deals or speaking tours for her, but one guest remembered him signing and selling one of his books about Amelia.

Howard Hanzlick, one of the two young embeds on the *Itasca*, finally met George Palmer Putnam and recalled: "Years later, when I came to California, I took my mother and father on a trip. We went through Death Valley, but there's a place down there that I don't remember the name of.... We went into this café and general store, or whatever it was, and there was a man in there. I said, 'Are you George Putnam?' He said, 'Yes.' I told him, 'I was the United Press correspondent on the *Itasca* when your wife was lost.' His sole response was, 'Well, that's interesting. Can I help you?' He never pursued that thought, which really turned me off. I thought, 'Well, you son of a gun.'" The once-feared publisher was either embarrassed or no longer cared if he was relevant; Hanzlick could never decide which.

In October 1949, the Smithsonian hosted its first event honoring Amelia Earhart. However, a journalist from the Associated Negro Press questioned why there had been no formal celebration of pioneering Black aviators like Bessie Coleman, who died eleven years before Amelia, and Dorothy Darby, who flew nonstop from New York to California in 1936. Why were their groundbreaking contributions minimized and excluded from the canon? Among the chiefly white attendees was Amy Otis, Amelia's frail eighty-six-year-old mother. As she unveiled the display, her traumatic response to losing a daughter was evident, coupled with her buy-in to prejudicial propaganda; she remained convinced that the Japanese had taken, and perhaps even killed, her daughter. George was absent from the event, suffering from kidney failure. His still-living granddaughter, Cynthia Putnam, informed this author that the family believes he fell ill after consuming contaminated hog meat in Burma, which ultimately led to kidney failure. This is not noted in his medical records, and perhaps his kidney failure could be attributed to other causes, such as high blood pressure.

On January 4, 1950, after several harrowing weeks of illness, George Palmer Putnam died at sixty-two. By this point in his life, he had faded from the limelight, mostly remembered as Amelia Earhart's former spouse. In a twist of irony, he was also known for that 1939 Nazi kidnapping claim, which he never publicly acknowledged was a fabrication. Peg Putnam was by his side in his last moments, and his death coincided with a writing festival at his inn, the Stovepipe Wells. Reservations for the festival quickly vanished after the sorriest of news. Many of his dreams remained unfulfilled with his passing.

After the initial wave of conspiracy theories surrounding Amelia Earhart's disappearance quieted down in the 1940s, a resurgence occurred in the 1960s, sparked by Paul Briand, a young military man and new author who disseminated false information that came from a dental hygienist who claimed to have seen Amelia captured. A brief media frenzy ensued. In response to these recurring theories, Muriel Earhart, deeply frustrated, decided to set the record straight and present her version of her sister's life and character with Clara Studer, an old PR friend of Amelia's from the aviation world, the only nonflying member of the Ninety-Nines—who was happy to interview Muriel and serve as her ghostwriter. It is a stiff read but an important one, as much factual information first revealed by her was reused in later books on Amelia.

In a particularly reflective private letter written in the 1970s, Muriel offered a poignant view of Amelia, commenting on how she loved children and wanted her own yet chose not to become a mother because her life was "a syndrome of danger and the insatiable demands of the public." Her sister's life was, in her view, "the drama of a crusading spirit for women's equality." The detractors are the women who loved their female role—those who hated Amelia ("I suppose since you've cut off your hair, you smoke and drink while flying too") and those who were apathetic. On her side were the Neta Snooks and the Ninety-Nines, fellow adventurers like Eddie Rickenbacker, Roy Chapman Andrews, Will Rogers, and the thousands of ordinary earthbound people to whom she gave a bit of a vision as she "opened the door of the skies."

Appalled at the exploitation of her sister by obsessed men out to make a buck, Muriel scoffed at articles pushing the Japanese capture of Amelia. She was particularly struck by photos falsely showing Amelia wearing a Japanese kimono and her cherished lucky African elephant-toe bracelet—purported evidence of her capture. In reality, both the kimono and the bracelet were safe with Muriel. Amelia had explained that the bracelet—a hollowed-out African elephant toe bone intricately carved and inlaid with hammered silver—was a gift from George Schuyler. Schuyler had been sent to eastern Liberia's Loma country at the start of the decade by Brewer, Warren & Putnam to gather background material. He had informed Amelia that such bracelets were considered extremely lucky among the local tribes and were rarely given or sold.

Exhausted by the nonsense, Muriel refused to engage further with the men who exploited Amelia's name through these increasingly sensational theories. These stories, filled with tales of aliens, bondage, and other lurid tidbits, were published in pulpy men's magazines—the equivalent of clickbait in the Age of Aquarius. These magazines thrived on grotesque exaggeration and sensationalism, targeting a male audience seeking escapism and excitement.

Muriel felt helpless fighting the bunkum. The spreading of false history was not confined to obscure theorists; even the Pulitzer Prize–winning historian William Manchester bought into the nonsense, claiming that Amelia was murdered by the Japanese after catching a glimpse of their fortifications in the mandated Marianas.

When Peg Putnam was asked off the record in 1977 about George Palmer Putnam's thoughts on what happened to Amelia, she confirmed that he was convinced they had run out of gas and couldn't locate Howland Island. Regarding any theories about espionage, she dismissed them as "totally unbelievable," firmly stating that George believed nothing occurred beyond their plane plummeting into the ocean, floating briefly, and then sinking, the tragic end.

"I don't know that it was love the way we think of it," said George Palmer Putnam Jr., who was known as Junie growing up. In 2005, he was the last living person who had known her well. "But I think it was a happy, contented arrangement." She was "no-nonsense" and "full of enthusiasm," he said. He died convinced that his stepmother went down near Howland Island, adding in his last recorded interview: "There are no gas stations in the middle of the ocean."

With the death of George "Junie" Palmer Putnam Jr. in 2013, the last of the major players passed away, but not before he offered insightful thoughts on his father and Amelia. He liked his father, whom he spent quality time with after Amelia's death. As he remembered: "My father was rather nervous and agitated—short-tempered with people. Irritable. Arrogant. He annoyed a lot of people. He was under a lot of pressure, though. He wasn't a very healthy man—he always had trouble with his stomach. If you always got an ulcer, it's bound to act up." Like his brother, David, Junie had only the kindest thoughts about his stepmother, who had always been lovely to him. And to his mind, Amelia and his father had a good relationship. He never saw them kiss, but he noted, "My father was not very affectionate. I don't think either would like to display their emotions publicly. They weren't built that way. I don't think [there is] anything usual about them not kissing. People didn't do it then."

Amelia and George were more than mere partners; they were formidable figures who adeptly balanced their public personas with their private lives. Seeing both the positive and the negative simultaneously, Amelia, initially unsettled yet enchanted by George—a married man—fell in love despite friends' warnings. George, always captivated by innovation and new love, relentlessly pursued Amelia. Yet the deeper narrative reveals that Amelia was no innocent bystander. Leaving her quieter life and love in Boston behind for a dizzying array of opportunities, she recognized in George a strategic ally who could propel her stalled magnificent career ambitions forward and provide an escape from financial instability.

Their relationship, born in the vibrancy of the Jazz Age and tempered by the hardships of the Great Depression, was a complex mix of love, tension, and mutual ambition. Indubitably, he was a vital supporter of her career. Their final endeavor, planning a globe-circling flight motivated by shared profit, was a testament to their enduring spirit and the era's demanding pressures. While the motivations for their global flight and the issues they glossed over invite scrutiny, the legacy of Amelia Earhart and George Palmer Putnam's teamwork endures. Despite a final catastrophe of their own making, their daring ventures propelled aviation forward and laid a lasting foundation, inspiring generations to pursue their dreams against formidable odds and empowering women worldwide. In their union, they found not just love but a partnership that reshaped their lives—and ours.

EPILOGUE

In 1969, as the world watched a man walk on the moon, Muriel Earhart Morrissey thought of her sister, Amelia. "My sister used to tell her audiences that we would casually catch rockets to the moon one day. It is nice she went when she was at the crest of her career. She didn't accomplish all she would liked to have done, but she did a lot," Muriel said.

Beyond her many flight accomplishments, including a long list of record flights, Amelia Earhart showed a visionary spirit. She cofounded and lent her celebrity to the Ninety-Nines, an organization that fosters a community of women pilots. She left a lasting impact on aviation with this group, which is now an international beacon for women pilots. Amelia's strong advocacy for women in the field shaped the industry, serving as a rallying cry for gender equality and inspiring future generations. Muriel saw this part of her better than anyone.

Did Amelia envision women on the moon? While training to be one of the first women to join NASA's return to the lunar surface, American astronaut Jessica Meir told me she has come to deeply appreciate her predecessor's pioneering feminist impact. Amelia's advocacy for equal opportunities in aviation, with inspiration as her rocket fuel, has significantly influenced Meir's trajectory and accomplishments.

Meir further reflected on trailblazing female aviators: "I look forward to the day when space walks like mine with Christina Koch are mundane. Space is tough, but I'm not breaking new ground. I'm doing my job, just like any of my male colleagues. Remembering Amelia Earhart, she saw a future where skills beat out gender. That's the world I train for—a world where our achievements are the norm, not the novelty."

Amelia Earhart soared beyond her era, charting the course for women in science and engineering. She demonstrated the profound power of one individual to shape the future, envisioning a world free from gender constraints—a vision still unfolding. We remember Amelia not for the mystery of her disappearance but for the unyielding hope and determination that inspired girls to aim high—without needing a George Palmer Putnam to tell their story.

ACKNOWLEDGMENTS

Writing this book has been an exhilarating flight filled with high altitudes of inspiration and occasional turbulence. I am profoundly thankful to everyone who has provided lift and guidance along the way.

First and foremost, I am immensely grateful to my friend and agent, Peter Steinberg at UTA, who helped me pivot from a debut nonfiction work about an unknown Antarctic stowaway on Richard Byrd's first expedition to the daunting project of tackling the very well-known Amelia Earhart, a friend of Admiral Byrd. He saw clearly how the projects dovetailed and had unshakable belief in my ability to retell her story in new ways. Special thanks to Peter's assistants, Yona Levin and Harry Sherer, and to Peter's UK coagent, Sabhbh Curran. For foreign sales, I would like to again thank Yona Levin, as well as Emma Jamison, Melissa Chinchillo, and Ethan Schlatter.

My heartfelt thanks go to Emily Wunderlich, my charming, hip, meticulous editor at Viking. Together, we figured out the best editing style for me, and she had monthly meetings with me throughout the writing of the book—a true A+ editor! I'm indebted as well to Andrea Schulz, Viking's editor in chief, who championed this book alongside Emily. Their firm faith in this project made all the difference. Tremendous thanks are in order to Emily's assistant, Carlos Zayas-Pons, whose support, especially as I worked to finish the manuscript, was crucial to getting the job done. My gratitude also extends to more fine people at Viking, including a marvelous copyedit from Lauren Morgan Whitticom, proofreads from William Jeffries and Susan VanHecke, first serial sales handled by Bridget Gilleran, and publicist Sara DeLozier.

I am incredibly fortunate to have the unwavering support and guidance of my manager, Robin Budd of Viewfinder Management. Your insight, steady hand, and enduring friendship have been invaluable throughout this journey. Thank you for believing in me every step of the way.

Big, big love to my hero husband, Paul O'Leary, who has a great sense of humor and (famously) the patience of a saint—as exemplified by the day my computer died and I thought the current version of this book was lost. He sprang into action and got a MacBook data recovery expert on the phone while I was busy crying. And one more shout-out to my daughter, Violet O'Leary, your presence and encouragement mean the world to me.

I am incredibly fortunate to have marvelous writer friends like Eric Pomerance, who bravely waded through my first draft, delivering honest, razor-sharp feedback without a hint of sugarcoating. My most trusted reader, always. And a hearty thank-you to Corey S. Powell, my brilliant writer in arms and my other most-trusted reader, whose sharp insights and spirited feedback were indispensable.

My friend and fellow biographer Michelle Young whisked me away to a country retreat toward the end of my writing journey. Her generous gift provided a perfect sanctuary where I could recharge and finish the book after dealing with some unseemly nonsense. Everyone needs a Michelle—someone who knows just when to offer an escape hatch.

Special thanks to Adam Lawrence, my exceptional photo clearance expert, who worked tirelessly for weeks ensuring the accuracy and acquisition of the images used in this book. His dedication and professionalism were essential to this project.

Amy Rosenthal, initially a social-media-only friend, stepped up during the worst months of the pandemic to offer me her unused private office at a crazily cheap rate; even my beloved New York Public Library was shut then. There should be a Girl Scout badge for this wild act of generosity.

A week after signing my contract in November 2019, I flew to Indiana for my first long interview, prepandemic, with Sammie Morris, then head of archives and special collections at Purdue University. Purdue holds the bulk of

Amelia's documents, many donated by George Palmer Putnam and his family. Sammie, a treasure to the Amelia Earhart community, offered a wealth of knowledge and remained in constant communication throughout my research.

After wrapping up in West Lafayette, I jetted off to Boston to delve into what Harvard's Radcliffe Institute has on Amelia. The Radcliffe Institute boasts a significant collection, much of it generously donated by Amelia's sister, Muriel. My sincerest thanks go to Sarah Hutcheon, who guided me through that first month of intense reading. Her help was a lifesaver when I was drowning in a sea of documents, trying to make sense of it all.

With the main collections reviewed, I plunged into a deep panic—what if I had missed something crucial? In an admittedly unconventional move, I reached out to the most esteemed living Amelia biographers, some of whom who had done their research decades earlier, even before the internet. They had spoken to people who knew Amelia well, and I hoped to uncover anything hidden from the public, whether it had to do with sexuality, gender identity, or a sham marriage. Missing such biggies would mean missing a significant part of her interior life.

The biographers were understandably surprised by my audacity but graciously agreed to help. Sometimes I agreed with them, and sometimes I didn't, but I'm grateful for the civil discourse. In twenty years, I will gladly speak with future Amelia biographers who may not agree with my takes. You get as close as you can to the truth when you take a swing. Thank you, Mary Lovell, Susan Ware, Susan Butler, and Keith O'Brien.

I remain deeply grateful to Amy Kleppner (1931–2024), Amelia Earhart's accomplished niece, who generously shared family stories, insights, and treasured artifacts during our morning-long conversation in her Vermont home. Her deep connection to Amelia was unmistakable, and I feel fortunate to have learned from her.

Another key interview was with Dorothy Cochrane of the Smithsonian's National Air and Space Museum. From our first conversation, she proved to be an invaluable source, offering her expertise through countless emails over the years. We've met in person several times since, and I've come to think of her as the Voice of Reason. In a field often clouded by outlandish and improbable theories, Dorothy's clarity and grounded perspective are indispensable.

I am deeply beholden to the previously uninterviewed children of George Palmer Putnam's once headline-grabbing, now all-but-forgotten kid explorers.

These living sources hold a treasure trove of untapped stories and archives. Special thanks go to Mary Remsen North's kids, Rabbi Katy Z. Allen and David Allen, as well as two of Alison Barstow Murphy's children, Christopher K. Mathews and Ellie Mathews.

Eric Han dedicated many days to translating Fukiko Aoki's 1983 book, *Ameria o sagase* (*Searching for Amelia*), into English for me—a challenging task that he tackled with skill and precision.

Learning of my work after I wrote about Amelia Earhart's lost helmet for *The New York Times*, Robert Wilonsky of Heritage Auctions graciously invited me to Dallas to peruse a new Heritage auction. This was a massive sale of Amelia's belongings, which had been acquired by the recently deceased researcher Elgen Long and were about to be dispersed into private hands. Those two days in Texas were both a privilege and a treat—and let me tell you, the BBQ was off the charts.

Then there's David Viola, a US Navy intelligence officer, whom I swear I met randomly on the Williamsburg Bridge at the start of the pandemic while I was walking to Brooklyn for some fresh air. Though I was initially convinced he was spinning a tall tale, a few days later, there was a knock at my door, and I was greeted by a large box of declassified information about Amelia's disappearance. It was one of those moments that's so surreal you couldn't make it up if you tried.

I am thankful for the NYPL's Research Rooms and the use of the Frederick Lewis Allen Memorial Room—a special shout-out to Matt Knutzen, Melanie Locay, and Andy McCarthy, who were my main contacts while I was working there.

I am beyond appreciative of an incredible four-hour private tour of 20 Amelia Earhart Lane, courtesy of Angela and Ciro Chechile. This was Amelia and George's former home in Rye. I had initially shown up just to get a peek at the exterior while they were sunning themselves, but to my delight, they invited me inside and gave me an hours-long tour of every room. It was a real gift of time and an unforgettable experience.

Similarly, Paul R. Bates, who lives in the Noank home where Amelia was married, graciously gave me a personal tour. It felt like stepping back in time, with each room holding a story.

A shout-out to Josh and Amanda Schuler, the owners of Amelia's former house on 76 Brooks Street in West Medford. I was absolutely thrilled to meet them during a random visit while I was researching at Harvard. Their warm welcome made an ordinary research day extraordinary.

I made two delightful visits to Atchison, Kansas, where Amelia was born, and I owe a huge thanks to "my best friends in Kansas," Jacque Pregont and Karen Cray Seaberg. These two super-knowledgeable ladies not only gave me fantastic interviews but also made sure that, as a nondriver, I had rides everywhere. Their hospitality and kindness turned my research trips into memorable adventures.

My heartfelt thanks to Charles P. Fernyhough, a professor of psychology at Durham University. He is a steadfast scientist and compassionate skeptic who meticulously explores why some people believe they hear voices and consider themselves psychic, including, debatably, Amelia Earhart. Though this intriguing topic strayed from my book's central narrative and the section that covered it was ultimately mostly cut, it remains ripe for a stand-alone article—editors, feel free to reach out. Dr. Fernyhough provided fascinating insights during a terrific Zoom interview.

Likewise, much gratitude is due to Richard Wiseman, professor of the public understanding of psychology at the University of Hertfordshire and a preeminent scholarly skeptic. His profound insights, also dispensed via Zoom, illuminated the field of psychic studies, once given credence by the Duke University Parapsychology Laboratory. This institution, established in 1930 by Dr. J. B. Rhine and Dr. Louisa E. Rhine, continued its controversial research until its closure in 1965. Admirers of Duke's dubious studies, such as Floyd Odlum and Jackie Cochran, deftly exploited psychic claims to market their books. Similarly, figures like Eugenie "Gene" Dennis, the Atchison Wonder Girl—a friend of Amelia's who was managed by her former magician husband—capitalized on credulity during the Great Depression, perpetuating a legacy of exploitation that still resonates today.

Additional Interviews:

- ANN PELLEGRENO: Bravely flew and finished Amelia's route in 1967. She sent me by snail mail a cherished package of 1960s flight mementos.

ACKNOWLEDGMENTS

- CARL HOFFMAN: A seasoned journalist present on search expeditions with a conspiracy theory hogwash radar I deeply admire.

- CORNELIA GUEST AND DIANA PERKINS: Direct descendants of Amy Phipps Guest. Diana gave me the best picture of her amazing grandmother that is not in any history book.

- CYNTHIA PUTNAM: Granddaughter of George Palmer Putnam. What a gracious woman.

- DAVID JOURDAN: From the deep-sea exploration company Nauticos, David generously welcomed me into his Maine home for an in-depth interview and trusted me with his invaluable archive. His generosity and expertise were instrumental in my research, and he was always just an email away for any technical questions. Special thanks also to his wonderful wife, Lynn Jourdan, who helped scan the untapped archival treasures I discovered in their home. I'm deeply grateful to David, and to two more remarkable members of the Nauticos team, Rod Blocksome and Tom Vinson—retired engineers from Rockwell Collins (now Collins Aerospace, a division of Raytheon). These talented individuals have not only known and worked with each other for decades, but they've also dedicated over twenty years to Nauticos in the quest to find Amelia Earhart's airplane in the Pacific. I also had the pleasure of spending several days with the engineers at the 2024 Amelia Earhart Festival, where I watched them eagerly scribble notes during a presentation by their friendly rivals, the Romeo brothers, always more than happy to decipher them for me.

- DR. JESSICA MEIR: Astronaut and Amelia fangirl. I tried hard not to fangirl her.

- DUFFY JENNINGS: Son of both Dean Southern Jennings, secret author of *The Man Who Killed Hitler*, published by George Palmer Putnam, and Dori Jennings, George's young secretary, assistant to Jo Berger Greer, involved in Putnam's 1939 faked kidnapping ploy. Duffy had true insider stories.

- FRANKLIN DELANO ROOSEVELT III: Admittedly brief but fun interview on his grandparents' relationship with Amelia and George. I nervously cornered him at a play when I was seated near him! He affably said yes and had great insight.

- GARY MONTI: Director of museum operations at the Garden City's Cradle of Aviation Museum. He knew Elinor Smith very well. Flew with her, even.

"She was a straight talker, trust me! The stories about George Putnam were no fiction."

- GENEVIEVE TINA: In Trepassey, she is doing her all to preserve Amelia's heritage. We had a long, lovely lunch and tour of Amelia's temporary house in 1928 until the weather cleared. Her husband, John Devereaux, is a direct descendant of Amelia's hosts in the Jazz Age. Wow!

- GEORGE VECSEY: A retired *New York Times* aviation journalist who interviewed and also vetted Elinor Smith.

- HEATHER STEMP: Children's writer and granddaughter of Ginny Ross, featured in her delightful Amelia-themed kids' novels. Her grandmother really did meet Amelia Earhart just before she crossed the Atlantic solo! We had a delightful night sitting together during the fireworks at the Amelia Earhart Festival in Atchison.

- JAY PARINI: Biographer and close friend of Gore Vidal's. He assured me with a contagious laugh that Vidal often gave interviewers whatever facts they wanted and amped up stories for sport. He guffawed over the various "dubious" added details over the years.

- JOSHUA STOFF: The Cradle of Aviation Museum's expert on Jazz Age aviation.

- JULIA LAURIA-BLUM: Now a friend, she is the former women's aviation expert at the Cradle of Aviation Museum. She once gave me a hilariously zooming ride in her car at a shopping mall where Charles Lindbergh took off. It was like a history lesson on wheels, with a touch of roller coaster.

- KARLA JAY: A trailblazer in the field of lesbian and gay studies and general women's studies. Karla also researched some of the wishful thinking surrounding Amelia Earhart's fashion line that just isn't true. When I was nine in the 1970s, my mother was finishing a degree in women's studies and often took me along to do homework in her classes. Karla was one of her professors, and I still have the A that Karla gave me for my "report" on Susan B. Anthony.

- KATHLEEN ROTHAR WATSON: Grandniece of Wilbur Rothar, whom some conspiracy "experts" claim did not exist—news to his blood relative.

- LINDIE NAUGHTON: Biographer of the European aviator Lady Heath, who was bullied by George Palmer Putnam—we certainly had a lot to talk about.

- MARIKA PICKLES: Journalist and granddaughter of researchers Elgen and Marie Long. She also traveled on search missions and had much insider knowledge gleaned from her grandparents to share. The Longs were the original Voices of Reason in the Earhart world.

- MIRA NAIR: Director of the 2009 film *Amelia*, starring Hilary Swank. She graciously spoke to me on Zoom from India. (Another hero I also tried not to fangirl.)

- NANCY PORTER, JANE FEINBERG, JEAN JORDAN, MELANIE MCLAUGHLIN: All, interviewed separately, provided important background on what was cut from "Amelia Earhart," a 1992 *American Masters* special. They had much to say on Gore Vidal's reliability as a source, and on who pressured them to tone down George Palmer Putnam's behavior and more.

- NICHOLAS SPARK: Director of a film on Pancho Barnes with lots of info on Bobbi Trout too.

- NICOLE MACKINNEY: From Derry, Wales. Expert on Amelia Earhart's visit to Derry.

- PATRICIA SULLIVAN: Elinor Smith's eldest daughter, who had much to say about George Palmer Putnam. And she brought some incredible archives to our lunch at a Manhattan coffee shop.

- PROFESSOR PAUL A. LOMBARDO: Trusted eugenics expert at Georgia State University College of Law. He opened my eyes to some rather unsettling aspects of America's past.

- ROBERT BADER: Has a "Harpo Marx as Amelia's secret lover" theory that I thoroughly disagree with. But I like Robert! I also interviewed Marx Brothers expert Noah Wildman, who feels that Amelia was not Harpo's lover—a theory I agree with, as Amelia's husband set up her shots with Harpo.

- ROBIN SNOOK CAMPEAU: Granddaughter of Amelia's best friend, Virginia Parks. Terrific stories.

- RONALD KESSLER: A trusted expert on the early FBI and secret operations, indispensable for understanding the intrigues that Hilton Howell Railey and George Palmer Putnam were involved with during World War I. Incidentally, his high school teacher was Muriel Earhart Morrissey!

- SAM WOOD: Grandson of furniture maker Albert Wood, who knew a lot. Now a friend.

- SHERI JORDAN AND ALISON RELYEA: Rye Historical Society—lovely and very helpful. My very first interviews.

- STEPHANIE SUNDINE: Daughter of David Binney Putnam's girlfriend and then second wife, Patricia Sundine, who brought up George Palmer Putnam's infidelities on tape.

- STEPHAN WILKINSON: Aviation historian with a long interest in Amelia Earhart.

MORE THANKS TO PEOPLE WHO HELPED IN VARIOUS WAYS: Aaron Clifft, my deputized research assistant in Memphis; Acacia Ludwig, my talented web designer who also keeps my site running smoothly; Adam Penenberg, boss guy and champion at my NYU masters of journalism program where I am an adjunct professor; Allison Segura Balderrama; Amy Lutz, with keen insights on World War II propaganda about Amelia; Amy Dockser Marcus of *The Wall Street Journal*; Andrea Acosta, deputized NYU researcher (before I became an adjunct professor there) who rechecked her amazing work; Andrew Johnson, who pointed me to Toronto resources; Anthony Twiggs, whose mother owned the lost Amelia helmet and was the hero in my *New York Times* story on it; Barbara Kahn; Ben Yagoda; Beverly Bennett, archivist at Newfoundland's Provincial Archives Division, The Rooms; Bill Ferguson, an editor who has taught me a heck of a lot and championed me at *The New York Times*; Bob Ball, retired aviation reporter; Bob Johnston, my driver in Newfoundland and an instant friend; the Boston Biography Group, which let a New Yorker Zoom in; Bram Kleppner (Amelia's amiable grandnephew); Cait Coker, curator of rare books and manuscripts at the University of Illinois Urbana–Champaign; Captain Christopher LeGrow, an Air Canada pilot and proud Newfoundlander, whom I sat next to—of all people!—on my flight to St. John's, and who filled the ride with paper charts and his wealth of Newfoundland aviation knowledge; Cath Wilmott Sullivan, my college friend in Marblehead who drove this nondriver around Marblehead and visited Sam Chapman's grave; Charles Agvent, who let me pay off a rare book signed by

Amelia over YEARS—hero!; Chris Ivy and Samantha Sisler of Heritage Auctions; Chris Williamson from the Amelia podcast *Vanished!*; Christof W. Kheim, director of the Forney Museum; Claire Wyman Wengraf; Colleen Field, head of the Centre for Newfoundland Studies, Queen Elizabeth II Library; Daniel Briem of the Harrison Public Library; Daniel Zalewski, friend, mentor, and features editor of *The New Yorker*; Dr. Dawn Learsy for her keen insights into human behavior; Debbie Seracini of the San Diego Air & Space Museum; Elizabeth Borja, Smithsonian; Elizabeth Boucher, collections manager of the Noank Historical Society; Elizabeth Frank; Elizabeth Piwkowski, Cleveland State University librarian; Emeline Reynolds, University of New Hampshire librarian; Emily Schartz, University of Iowa; Erick Trickey; Erin Sawadzki of the Alice Paul Institute; Etta Maureen Madden, my friend and best bet for handwriting deciphering—Amelia's handwriting was the pits!; Franco Vogt and his daughter and assistant, Nora Vogt, for my author photo; Greg Ricci of the Harrison Historical Society; Harris Legome; J. Lincoln Hallowell Jr., ranger and historian at Floyd Bennett Field; Jay Boucher; Jennifer Boylan, PEN America president and Amelia Earhart expert; Joel Ebarb of Purdue University; Joe Maddalena; John Cahoon of the Seaver Center; John Granara (an expert on Medford); Juliet Wile, my friend who made an introduction to an astronaut; Karen Stone, minister of tourism for Newfoundland, who advised me on how to get around a gorgeous, daunting place without a driver's license; Kris LeBoutillier, my ex-boyfriend from college and, crazily enough, a Boots LeBoutillier relative; Lacey Flint, Explorers Club librarian; Lauren Cardillo; Lillian Hansberry, Ogontz Archive Room librarian; Linton Wells II, son of Amelia's friend Fay Gillis Wells; Lucy Beard and Erin Sawadzki of the Alice Paul Institute; Lynn Krantz of the Matson Archives, Hawaii; Margie Arnold; Mark Taylor, National Air and Space Museum; Meghan Anderson and Sara Fisher of the International Women's Air & Space Museum; Michelle Fanelli and Ralph C. Villecca Sr. of the NJ Hall of Fame; Nicole Norelli and Brian Chanes (also of Heritage Auctions in Dallas); Robert and Marie Whitman, friends who so kindly drove me to Amelia Miami sites; Russ Matthews; Scott and Elizabeth De Wolfe; Scott S. Taylor, Georgetown special collections librarian; Seth Kaller; Shaylyn Sawyer, 99s Museum of Women Pilots librarian; Siffy Torkildson of the Society of Women Geographers; the Sob Sisters women nonfiction group led by Abbott Kahler, Ada

Calhoun, and Susannah Cahalan; Stephen Novack, a young man who knows a heck of a lot about 1920s trains; Stuart Lutz, the last person to interview George "Junie" Putnam Jr.; Sydney Soderberg, who helped me research at the Eisenhower Library—she is the one to call; Teresa McAnerney; Tom Fitzsimmons of the Wings Club in New York City; Tula Goenka, my friend and a former documentary editor who connected me to Mira Nair; Vanessa Bonavia; Victoria Guest; Wayne Soini (my friend who, much to my shock, turned out to be related to Muriel's grandnephew and slipped me family papers); Wyman Wengraf.

Thank you, too, to my dear cousin Jackie Kutner for her support on some rough family-emergency days.

And to dear friends who offered emotional support along the way: Abbe Aronson; Adam Shrager; Adrianne Weremchuk; Alison Gilbert; Biz Mitchell; Bruce Tulgan and Debby Applegate; Burkhard Bilger; Debra Ramsey; Emily Nussbaum; Florence Eng; Ingrid Periz; Janet Rosen; Kevin Fitzpatrick; Leslie Camhi; Louise Bernikow; Lynn Hempel; Maria Smilios; Mark O'Leary; Melissa Caruso-Scott; Michelle Larsen; Pam Ito; Peter Lefkowitz and Lori Silver; Preeti Chawla; Robin Cembalest; Sarah Rose; Sylvia Schwartz; and Simone Weissman.

A heartfelt thank you to Dave Dolan, Steve Elkins, David Press, Mensun Bound, Dr. Laurie Marker, Nancy Nenow, and Rick Ridgeway—true living legends, world explorers, and new friends via the Explorers Club. Their boundless enthusiasm could steer me through the most uncharted territories, even though I can't drive.

Five people dear to me died while I wrote this book: World War II pilot Si Spiegel, who often talked with me about the day Amelia Earhart disappeared, and Malachy McCourt, who was a great cheerleader of telling the truth. I am especially thankful to my late friend Louisa McCune, who started as a random Facebook contact but soon became a true champion. We shared memorable adventures during my Oklahoma research, from visiting Wiley Post's grave to traveling a stretch of Route 66 together. And my beloved aunt, Paula Goldstein, born in 1923, also remembered the day of Amelia's disappearance in surprising detail. Aunt Paula was a nut about walking. She wore New Balance sneakers when she was one hundred. I walk everywhere too, and sometimes if I start getting tired, I think about her and revive. Gone but never forgotten.

Finally, I am eternally thankful to my cherished father, Julius Shapiro, who was old enough to be my grandfather and died in January 2020, weeks before the pandemic. He was sharp as a tack until his death and clearly remembered the day Amelia Earhart disappeared. He was thrilled that I sold the proposal for this book. When the end was near for him, he offered me the greatest gift of all by saying that the last thing he would want me to do was fall apart at his death. He died just short of his one hundredth birthday. He wanted me to finish for him. I did.

NOTES

For decades, biographers have relied on a dry but informative biography of Amelia Earhart's life written by her long-lived sister, Muriel, who was an esteemed high school English teacher. Incidentally, she taught both Paul and Alexander Theroux. According to her daughter, whom I interviewed in Vermont, Muriel had a tendency to "sweeten stories" to remove any ugliness, but she generally got the details right. Most Earhart biographies owe their accounts of Amelia's early life to Muriel's work.

After Amelia's tragic disappearance, Muriel stepped in to assist George Palmer Putnam, Amelia's husband, with his biography of her. This was after George's original ghostwriter left the project over a dispute. There is no record of Muriel meeting George before Amelia's death, and they were not particularly close. However, given the financial strains of the Depression, she accepted (after Amelia's death) his offer of a modest remuneration in exchange for her insights for a biography on his wife. She was willing to overlook any unseemliness associated with his professional ghostwriters, including her friend Janet Mabie.

In the 1960s, as conspiracy theories about Amelia's fate began to proliferate, Muriel wrote her own biography to combat these unfounded speculations.

For space considerations, I have added notes where there is information that may not have been seen before or lies off the radar of all but the most avid Earhart enthusiasts.

NEEDLE IN A HAYSTACK

2 **Miss Josephine "Jo" Berger:** "Yacht to Set Off on Search for Amelia Earhart; Mount Vernon Woman, Sister Members of Party," *Mount Vernon Argus*, December 15, 1937.

6 **it was undeniably "love":** Henry W. Clune, "No Soldier of Fortune," Seen and Heard (column), *Democrat and Chronicle*, July 13, 1937.

CHAPTER ONE: THE KINGMAKER

8 **our George's uncle:** "Obituary: George Peabody Putnam," *New-York Tribune*, December 21, 1872.

10 **fetch more than $14 million:** Robert Marchant, "Historic Binney Mansion Carries Price Tag of $14.95M," *Greenwich Time*, August 2, 2018.

10 **to suggest oiliness:** "Where Did the Brand Name Crayola Originate?," Crayola (website), accessed September 17, 2024, https://www.crayola.com/faq/your-history/where-did-the-brand-name-crayola-originate/.

10 **"A strenuous letter"**: Sally Putnam Chapman with Stephanie Mansfield, *Whistled Like a Bird: The Untold Story of Dorothy Putnam, George Putnam, and Amelia Earhart* (Warner Books, 1997), 17.
12 **a nationwide syndicated hit**: Information from the Bend Historical Society.
13 **at the family firm**: Hazel Reavis, "Perfect Lady Coming Back," *Sarasota Herald*, August 5, 1928; and Hilton Howell Railey, "The Bootleggers," *Saturday Evening Post*, August 28, 1920.
15 **an attractive brunette**: As recalled by Patricia Putnam Sundine, then David Binney Putnam's girlfriend, later his second wife, and eventually his ex-wife. See David Binney Putnam, oral history interview by Elgen Long, David Binney Putnam Tape 2 (Side-B), 28 December 1977, box 9, cassette 7, Amelia Earhart Project Recordings, National Air and Space Museum Archives, Smithsonian Institution, https://sova.si.edu/record/nasm.2020.0025/ref152?t=W&q=binney. (The tape shut off quickly, but not before a few seconds of the juicy bits!)
15 **demands in the bedroom**: Chapman with Mansfield, *Whistled Like a Bird*, 37.
16 **While the rush was on**: Harold McCracken, *Roughnecks and Gentlemen: Memoirs of a Maverick* (Doubleday, 1968), 378.
17 **George's eleven-year-old son**: "Dr. Beebe's Ship Silent 12 Days; No Radio Reply," *Brooklyn Daily Times*, April 10, 1925.
18 **"What I want to publish"**: McCracken, *Roughnecks and Gentlemen*, 377.
19 **One of the most dangerous**: Augusto Flores, *My Hike: Buenos Aires to New York* (G. P. Putnam's Sons, 1929).
20 **unchecked ambition and peril**: Boy explorer Halsey Fuller, accompanied by his "padre," Henry S. Whitehead—a horror writer with a murky reputation bolstered by strong but unproven rumors on Lovecraft fan sites—embarked on several wild adventures. Fuller's Siberian exploits are documented in Clarke Crichton Jr.'s *Frozen-In!: The Adventures of the "Nanuk's" Cabin Boy North of Siberia* (G. P. Putnam's Sons, 1930), which detailed their harrowing experience of getting stuck in ice on a Siberian fur-trapping boat. Newspapers of the time covered their dramatic rescue extensively.

For tales of volcanic peril, see Halsey Fuller, "When a Plane Nose-Dived at a Fiery Volcano," *Literary Digest*, December 12, 1931. The dramatic piece remains a gripping read.

Meanwhile, Dick Douglas's *A Boy Scout in the Grizzly Country* recounts his adventures on Kodiak Island, Alaska, where he hunted eleven-hundred-pound grizzly bears—quite a step up from the three-hundred-pound black bears back East. His narrative crescendos with an encounter involving his boat being attacked by a seventy-foot, seventy-ton blue whale, which towed the vessel for an hour, nearly leading to his demise. (Spoiler: He survived! Great for sales copy!) Additionally, Douglas faced real dangers, such as packs of wild dogs and the threat of African trypanosomiasis, also known as African sleeping sickness, spread by tsetse flies near their campsite.
23 **transatlantic flight longer than any**: Information cobbled together from multiple biographies and articles. See bibliography. Like many before me, I fell into this marvelous rabbit hole.
29 **her charismatic Yale boyfriend**: Chapman with Mansfield, *Whistled Like a Bird*, 43.
30 **"An evening never to be"**: Chapman with Mansfield, 57.
31 **visited during marital strain**: Debby Applegate, *Madam: The Biography of Polly Adler, Icon of the Jazz Age* (Anchor Books, 2021), 282.

CHAPTER TWO: SATURDAY'S CHILD

33 **stately home in Atchison**: Muriel Earhart's biography and oral interviews conducted with her in the 1970s by Elgen and Marie Long; many articles and books; and two personal pilgrimages to Atchison, Kansas, which included enthusiastic tours of the Amelia Earhart Birthplace Museum and the Amelia Earhart Hangar Museum.
34 **An adventurer in his own**: Personal section, *Atchison Daily Globe*, September 20, 1901.
37 **Virginia "Ginger" Park**: Author's phone interview with her granddaughter, Robin Snook Campeau.
38 **"I would think it would"**: Muriel Morrissey to Stewart Stern, letter, n.d., box 10, Stewart Stern Papers, University of Iowa Special Collections Repository.
41 **"Meek loveliness is round thee"**: *Aitchpe* (Hyde Park High School, 1915).

42 **elite founded in 1850:** Ogontz information comes from a daylong personal visit to Penn State Abington, which occupies the site of the former Ogontz School for Young Ladies. The school was sold to the university, and insights were gathered via archives I was guided through by library assistant Lillian Hansberry, as well as via subsequent independent article research.

42 **Among them was Gordon:** "Death of a Good Indian," *Kansas City Star*, March 12, 1899.

43 **confidence as a young woman:** Papers of Kenneth Griggs Merrill, 1918–1919, Schlesinger Library, Radcliffe Institute, Harvard University, Cambridge, MA. Research was conducted in person.

43 **She joined the field:** The Ogontz Archive Room, Penn State Abington Library, Abington, PA.

44 **legacy of such educational innovations:** Mac Daniel, "A Place to Remember a Private School Long Gone, But Not Forgotten," *Philadelphia Inquirer*, June 4, 1992. (This was new to the Ogontz librarian!)

47 **whose eloquent discourses:** "Canada's Future Depends on Girls of Today," *St. Catharines Standard*, February 24, 1922.

48 **The flu virus killed:** Much of this information is eloquently detailed in John M. Barry's *The Great Influenza: The Story of the Deadliest Pandemic in History* (Viking, 2014).

51 **"four small efforts":** Amelia Earhart, "Palm Tree," typed poem, George Palmer Putnam Collection of Amelia Earhart Papers, Purdue University Libraries, Archives and Special Collections, https://earchives.lib.purdue.edu/digital/collection/earhart/id/922.

CHAPTER THREE: THE GOLDEN TWENTIES

55 **made at Lake George:** Much of this Columbia information comes from Louise de Schweinitz Darrow and Columbia archivist Carrie E. Hintz. Stabler's memories are preserved in the Amelia Earhart: A Biography [Rich] Collection at the Smithsonian's National Air and Space Museum in Chantilly, Virginia. This collection contains material compiled by Doris Rich while she was conducting research for her 1989 book.

55 **"Don't think for an instant":** Fall 1919 letter from Amelia to her mother, as cited in Jean L. Backus, ed., *Letters from Amelia: An Intimate Portrait of Amelia Earhart* (Beacon Press, 1982), 51.

56 **This decision led Amelia:** Special thanks to train buff Stephen Novack for helping me figure out the routes and trains taken.

57 **shop in the market district:** Much of this information comes from Muriel Earhart Morrissey's memories, as recounted in her small-press biography of her sister, *Courage Is the Price* (McCormick-Armstrong Publishing, 1963). Many of her stories about Amelia therein have been retold in later biographies, not always with attribution.

59 **unexpectedly drawn to flying:** "Miss Earhart's Dad Talks," *Los Angeles Times*, June 18, 1928. "I told her that I was strongly against it, but that was about all I could do about it under the circumstances." Edwin Earhart was terrified he would lose his daughter to a Putnam publicity stunt.

60 **piercing Irish-blue eyes:** Insight into Amelia's early flying days comes mainly from Neta Snook Southern's self-published memoir, *I Taught Amelia to Fly* (Vantage Press, 1974). Some information comes from newspaper and radio interviews with Snook, as well as from a long oral interview conducted by Elgen and Marie Long at the Smithsonian's National Air and Space Museum.

61 **"fear the name":** Along with three others, this letter to Helen "Lev" Le Vesconte was auctioned off by Christie's in 1999. See "Lot 183," Christie's, accessed September 20, 2024, https://www.christies.com/en/lot/lot-1522486.

63 **Often seen kicking around:** Leland Brusse, oral history interview by Elgen Long, Tape 1 (Side-A), 19 July 1975, box 5, cassette 12, Amelia Earhart Project Recordings, National Air and Space Museum Archives, https://sova.si.edu/record/nasm.2020.0025/ref82?t=W&q=leland+brusse.

64 **In a recently rediscovered:** This audio gem can be found among the recently digitized Amelia Earhart Project Recordings in the Smithsonian's National Air and Space Museum Archives. See Muriel Earhart Morrissey, oral history interview by Elgen Long, 30 July 1975, Amelia Earhart Project Recordings, National Air and Space Museum Archives, https://sova.si.edu/record/nasm.2020.0025/search?q=muriel&t=W&o=doc_position. The Longs, who were obsessed, like many Earhart

researchers, with plane recovery rather than Amelia's interior life, often turned off the tape recorder when things got personal—exactly what a biographer is after. But with static removed and mumbled words amplified in the seconds before the off button was hit, I gleaned some real personal insights and did some detective work. Although Thomas Humphrey Bennett Varney, known to Amelia as "Fuzzy," isn't named, all clues point to him as the lover she preferred over Sam. I'm confident it's him, the real Powell Ramsdell—her sugar daddy of sorts—who also gifted her a sports car. In Neta Snook's book, Neta also notes that she changed names to prevent embarrassment.

66 **Even in her eighties:** Morrissey, oral history interview.

66 **a man Neta discreetly:** A questionnaire with Neta and this written refusal are held in box 2, folder 5, Series 1: Biographical Files, Amelia Earhart: A Biography [Rich] Collection, National Air and Space Museum Archives, Smithsonian Institution, https://sova.si.edu/record/nasm.1991.0003.

69 **"Amelia always wanted":** Neta Snook, oral history interview by Elgen Long, Tape 1 of 3 (Side-B), 12 July 1975, box 5, cassette 3, Amelia Earhart Project Recordings, National Air and Space Museum Archives, https://sova.si.edu/record/nasm.2020.0025/ref73?t=W&q=neta+snook.

72 **they would set down roots:** Murry Engle, "Sister Gives Insight on Amelia Earhart," *Honolulu Star-Bulletin*, June 27, 1980.

72 **She would later claim:** Morrissey, oral history interview.

73 **"The yellow boat rolled":** Letter to Helen "Lev" Le Vesconte, "Lot 183," Christie's.

75 **He helped her set up:** John K. Winkler, "The Golden Girl of the Air," *Smart Set*, October 1928, 82.

75 **dedication to a life together:** Winkler, "The Golden Girl of the Air," 82.

76 **"mannishly" crossing her legs:** Interview transcript, Amelia Earhart: A Biography [Rich] Collection, National Air and Space Museum Archives, Smithsonian Institution, https://sova.si.edu/record/nasm.1991.0003.

CHAPTER FOUR: AMELIA TAKES OFF

79 **The first lady to try:** "Plane Carrying Aged Princess May Be Lost," *Johnson City Staff-News*, September 1, 1927.

79 **The "eligible bachelorette":** "Florida Girl, Flier, Undaunted by Sea Tragedies," *Miami Daily News*, September 15, 1927.

80 **A Viennese film director:** "Actress Said to Be Flying Across Ocean," *Macon News*, October 4, 1927. Note that the spelling of Dillenz's first name varies.

80 **Mrs. Frances Wilson Grayson:** "No Word from Mrs. Grayson; Plane 29 Hours Overdue," *New York Times*, December 25, 1927.

80 **cultured thirty-four-year-old:** "Hinchliffe Takes Off for America with Daughter of Lord Inchcape; Passes Ireland and Heads Out to Sea," *New York Times*, March 14, 1928.

81 **"Regarding Fräulein Rasche":** Meyer Berger, *The Story of The New York Times, 1851–1951* (Simon & Schuster, 1951), 318.

81 **Rasche remained steadfast:** "Woman to Try Paris Flight," *Marysville Journal-Tribune*, March 19, 1928.

82 **On one cool mid-April:** Hilton Howell Railey to Paul Briand, box 2, Subseries A: Correspondence, Series 2: Daughters of the Sky, Paul Briand Papers (1920–1986), MC 120, Milne Special Collections and Archives, University of New Hampshire Library. Railey repeatedly spoke to Briand off the record in 1957 and 1958, conversations which, now that they're in a library, have become fair game. There are many biographies with varying takes on how George knew about the plane Byrd leased to Mrs. Guest, but Railey, who later helped lead the top-secret World War II Ghost Army and kept it secret to his death, is where my money is at. Although Briand later, for money, was first to push Japanese conspiracies in his error-riddled biography, *Daughter of the Sky*—all good until that far-fetched ending that Railey begged him not to invent—many documents from people who knew Amelia and George well are in his previously untapped collection. And, yes, legal demands for money from his star "witness" are in there too.

85 **As it happened:** John K. Winkler, "The Golden Girl of the Air," *Smart Set*, October 1928, 25, 82.

87 **"Why would you want"**: Dialogue without anyone alive to verify it is fraught with uncertainty, especially in the Jazz Age, when newspapers that sponsored flights often took liberties with the truth. Some of this comes from Amelia's ghostwritten writings, so she is one source, but it also appears in "Amelia Earhart," a 1961 episode of the documentary series *Biography*, hosted by Mike Wallace. Many of Amelia's friends were tapped as advisers and vouched for its relative accuracy. A shaky copy can be found at Harvard, and the University of New Hampshire holds a transcript of the twenty-six-minute episode in the Paul Briand Papers.

CHAPTER FIVE: THE RIGHT SORT OF GIRL

92 **George ached to be alone:** As revealed in Hilton Howell Railey to Paul Briand, 14 August 1957, box 2, Subseries A: Correspondence, Series 2: Daughters of the Sky, Paul Briand Papers (1920–1986), MC 120, Milne Special Collections and Archives, University of New Hampshire Library. Railey confessed that George always referred to Amelia as "the girl," which bothered Railey.

92 **Julia and Amelia dined:** John K. Winkler, "The Golden Girl of the Air," *Smart Set*, October 1928.

95 **She told George that:** This charming story, which George sort of remembered, traces to his 1937–1938 calls with Muriel Earhart Morrissey, who filled in more; after Amelia's death, she helped George and his ghostwriter Janet Mabie with their books.

96 **Coolidge also captured:** The perspective of Jake Coolidge and his son comes from personal interviews that Susan Butler conducted for her book *East to the Dawn: The Life of Amelia Earhart* (Da Capo Press, 1999).

96 **"I'm tired of being":** "Mabel Boll, Mysterious Diamond Queen, Anxious to Fly Across Atlantic," *Buffalo Sunday Times*, April 29, 1928.

97 **"A delicious soft rain":** Sally Putnam Chapman with Stephanie Mansfield, *Whistled Like a Bird: The Untold Story of Dorothy Putnam, George Putnam, and Amelia Earhart* (Warner Books, 1997), 92.

99 **Hooray for the last grand:** Amelia Earhart to E. S. Earhart, handwritten letter, 20 May 1928, George Palmer Putnam Collection of Amelia Earhart Papers, Purdue University Libraries, Archives and Special Collections, https://earchives.lib.purdue.edu/digital/collection/earhart/id/3559/rec/880.

99 **Even tho I have lost:** Amelia Earhart to Mrs. E. S. Earhart, handwritten letter, 20 May 1928, George Palmer Putnam Collection of Amelia Earhart Papers, Purdue University Libraries, Archives and Special Collections, https://earchives.lib.purdue.edu/digital/collection/earhart/id/3556/rec/881.

99 **I have tried to play:** As cited in "Miss Earhart Made Her Will Before Start," *New York Times*, June 5, 1928, https://timesmachine.nytimes.com/timesmachine/1928/06/05/91522312.html.

100 **"My regret is that":** As cited in Butler, *East to the Dawn*, 170.

102 **The newest entrant:** "Student, Worker, as Well as a Flier," *New York Times*, June 4, 1928, https://timesmachine.nytimes.com/timesmachine/1928/06/04/95581998.html.

104 **sketched out the shapes:** Amelia Earhart, *20 Hrs. 40 Min.: Our Flight in the Friendship* (G. P. Putnam's Sons, 1928). Though ghosted, this is undeniably true.

104 **"Where will you eat?":** Most of the color and facts in my Trepassey section were fact-checked in Trepassey with John Devereaux (a descendant of Richard and Fanny Devereaux), who shared family stories and mementos. Further research was conducted in extensive untapped collections at Memorial University's Queen Elizabeth II Library, which holds local coverage in newspapers and scrapbooks.

106 **In place of Stultz:** Information on Boots comes from his relative Kris LeBoutillier—my college boyfriend. Who knew my romantic past would come in handy for historical research?

107 **"Millie never thought of boys":** "Amelia Earhart, Flyer, Recalled as 'Millie' Who Went to West High Here," *Des Moines Register*, June 9, 1928.

107 **"She was just different":** "Amelia Earhart, Flyer."

108 **SUGGEST YOU GO INTO RETIREMENT:** All telegrams come from the George Palmer Putnam Collection of Amelia Earhart Papers at the Purdue University Archives and Special Collections.

109 **"Our competitors are gaining":** As cited in Butler, *East to the Dawn*, 184.

111 **to sit in the john:** Note that Cochran's once off-the-record thoughts on Amelia, as expressed to

NOTES

screenwriter Stewart Stern, are held at both the Eisenhower Presidential Library (in her donated papers) and the University of Iowa (within the Stewart Stern Papers). Cochran's candid reflections add a layer of complexity to our understanding of Amelia, offering a peek behind the curtain at the real dynamics between these aviation icons.

113 **leaked a letter:** Hilton Howell Railey to Paul Briand, 14 August 1957, box 2, Subseries A: Correspondence, Series 2: Daughters of the Sky, Paul Briand Papers (1920–1986), MC 120, Milne Special Collections and Archives, University of New Hampshire Library. The letter, brimming with George's anxieties, was inadvertently shared by a well-meaning friend, giving us a glimpse into the often turbulent mind of the man behind the publishing empire.

114 **after nearly twenty-one hours:** Although there is much newspaper coverage, what really happened in Wales is informed by Railey's written thoughts (held at the University of New Hampshire) and Welsh historian Jon Gower's *A Long Mile*.

116 **Now the impossible:** AP, "Flight Success Laid to Courage of Woman," *Washington Post*, June 19, 1928.

118 **"When Miss Earhart asks":** Wire service item, as exemplified by a run in *The Tacoma Daily Ledger*. See Frank Sullivan, "Miss Lindy Lands in Wales and Inquires Her Directions," *Tacoma Daily Ledger*, July 1, 1928. Sullivan, always quick with a quip, turned the unexpected landing into a moment of mirth, delighting readers on both coasts.

118 **"As was to be expected":** Guy Fawkes, "Good Old Days," The Wayward Press (column), *New Yorker*, June 30, 1928, 32. The ever-observant wags at *The New Yorker* couldn't resist weighing in, their sharp wit making the most of the *Friendship*'s landing and the ensuing spectacle.

119 **actively wrestling for her affections:** Hilton Howell Railey to Paul Briand, 14 August 1957, box 2, Subseries A: Correspondence, Series 2: Daughters of the Sky, Paul Briand Papers (1920–1986), MC 120, Milne Special Collections and Archives, University of New Hampshire Library.

119 **"foolhardy sporting adventure":** "Amelia's Dad Criticizes Her Ocean Attempt," *Coshocton Tribune*, June 5, 1928. Edwin Earhart, unable to reconcile his family pride with his fear for his daughter's safety, saw her flying as a reckless escapade rather than a pioneering pursuit.

CHAPTER SIX: LADY LINDY

122 **"Amelia was at ease":** Hilton Howell Railey to Paul Briand, 18 July 1957, box 2, Subseries A: Correspondence, Series 2: Daughters of the Sky, Paul Briand Papers (1920–1986), MC 120, Milne Special Collections and Archives, University of New Hampshire Library.

123 **His pen name:** Peter Cameron to Paul Briand, 31 August 1957, box 2, Subseries A: Correspondence, Series 2: Daughters of the Sky, Paul Briand Papers (1920–1986), MC 120, Milne Special Collections and Archives, University of New Hampshire Library.

124 **As the ship lurched:** Hilton Howell Railey to Paul Briand, 28 September 1957, box 2, Subseries A: Correspondence, Series 2: Daughters of the Sky, Paul Briand Papers (1920–1986), MC 120, Milne Special Collections and Archives, University of New Hampshire Library.

125 **"Why and wherefore!":** Dorothy's diary entries as cited in Sally Putnam Chapman with Stephanie Mansfield, *Whistled Like a Bird: The Untold Story of Dorothy Putnam, George Putnam, and Amelia Earhart* (Warner Books, 1997), 107, 112.

127 **Amelia's "three spinster friends":** A wire item, as exemplified in "Who Got Greater Welcome?," *Springfield Union*, July 11, 1928.

131 **"New York is used to big things":** "Miss Earhart Asks Globe to Thank Hub People for Congratulations," *Boston Globe*, July 6, 1928, https://www.newspapers.com/image/431081834/.

133 **feats over the waves:** "Amelia Quails at Speech," *Sunday Daily News*, July 8, 1928.

134 **"It is our deliberate judgment":** Of All Things (column), *New Yorker*, June 30, 1928, 26.

135 **"My status so far":** "Miss Earhart's Engagement Is Her Own Affair," *Hartford Courant*, July 8, 1928.

CHAPTER SEVEN: THE MITTEN

136 **"I'm so glad you're home"**: Muriel Earhart Morrissey to Stewart Stern, private correspondence, July 10, 1973, Stewart Stern Papers, University of Iowa Special Collections Repository.
138 **"I don't believe there is"**: Katherine Donovan, "Matrimony to Come Last for Amelia, Sea Flier," *Commercial Appeal*, July 11, 1928, https://www.newspapers.com/image/768541429.
140 **On a sheet of high-end**: Hilton Howell Railey to Paul Briand, 14 August 1957, box 2, Subseries A: Correspondence, Series 2: Daughters of the Sky, Paul Briand Papers (1920–1986), MC 120, Milne Special Collections and Archives, University of New Hampshire Library. All other private Boston conversations between Amelia and Railey in Boston, as well as their retrospective thoughts, are from the same 1957 file.
140 **"An obscure social worker"**: Hilton Howell Railey to Paul Briand, 14 August 1957, box 2, Subseries A: Correspondence, Series 2: Daughters of the Sky, Paul Briand Papers (1920–1986), MC 120, Milne Special Collections and Archives, University of New Hampshire Library.
141 **"Such an insight"**: As cited in Sally Putnam Chapman with Stephanie Mansfield, *Whistled Like a Bird: The Untold Story of Dorothy Putnam, George Putnam, and Amelia Earhart* (Warner Books, 1997), 111.
141 **"Sam opposed the Atlantic"**: Muriel Earhart Morrissey, oral history interview by Elgen Long, 30 July 1975, Amelia Earhart Project Recordings, National Air and Space Museum Archives, https://sova.si.edu/record/nasm.2020.0025/search?q=muriel&t=W&o=doc_position.
142 **his top ghostwriter**: This information is corroborated by Elinor Smith in her book *Aviatrix* (p. 239); Mary S. Lovell's *The Sound of Wings* (p. 107); a September 5, 1928, memorandum to George P. Putnam in the Georgetown University Library Special Archives; and a letter from Sidney Carroll to Paul Briand, box 2, Subseries A: Correspondence, Series 2: Daughters of the Sky, Paul Briand Papers (1920–1986), MC 120, Milne Special Collections and Archives, University of New Hampshire Library. Additionally, the author conducted a 2020 interview with Mary S. Lovell, who, writing two decades earlier, had access to more living witnesses, which further supports these findings.

CHAPTER EIGHT: UNDER WHOSE ROOFTREE

148 **Helen "Roses" Weber**: Marcia-Marie Canavello, interview by Doris L. Rich, transcript, December 21, 1984, folder 8, box 2, Series 1: Biographical Files, Amelia Earhart: A Biography [Rich] Collection, National Air and Space Museum Archives, Smithsonian Institution. Note: This folder exposes a prime example of the "You scratch my back, I scratch yours" mentality that drove much of Putnam's ventures. It reveals that Weber also ghostwrote a children's book about Amelia's flight coach, Bernt Balchen, titled *Viking of the Air* (Brewer, Warren & Putnam, 1931), for George Palmer Putnam's new company, under the pseudonym John Lawrence.
149 **"I cannot claim to be"**: As cited in Doris L. Rich, *Amelia Earhart: A Biography* (Smithsonian Institution, 1989), 44.
151 **worst childhood tantrums imaginable**: Hilton Howell Railey to Paul Briand, 1 September 1958, box 2, Subseries A: Correspondence, Series 2: Daughters of the Sky, Paul Briand Papers (1920–1986), MC 120, Milne Special Collections and Archives, University of New Hampshire Library.
151 **"George is absorbed in Amelia"**: As cited in Sally Putnam Chapman with Stephanie Mansfield, *Whistled Like a Bird: The Untold Story of Dorothy Putnam, George Putnam, and Amelia Earhart* (Warner Books, 1997), 120.
152 **Some hitherto unknown antlered creature**: Commander Richard Byrd's vivid musings, as quoted in J. Olin Howe, "The Bottom of the World," *Popular Mechanics*, February 1928, 196–97.
152 **"I'd like to dedicate"**: As cited in Chapman with Mansfield, *Whistled Like a Bird*, 6.
152 **"This was a surprise"**: Chapman with Mansfield, 6.
153 **Hidden from view**: As detailed in my book *The Stowaway: A Young Man's Extraordinary Adventure to Antarctica* (Simon & Schuster, 2018).
154 **The "charm" of suicide**: As cited in Chapman with Mansfield, *Whistled Like a Bird*, 130.

154 **"Lucky Strikes were the cigarette"**: American Tobacco Company, "Earhart Endorsement," newspaper ad, 1928, Foote, Cone & Belding Records (1906–1996), Wisconsin Historical Society Archives, https://www.wisconsinhistory.org/Records/Image/IM11754.

156 **a "pleasure flight"**: "Amelia Earhart Has First Crash, Unhurt," *Boston Daily Globe*, Sep 1, 1928.

156 **fueling the rumors**: Dorothy's diary entries, as discussed and cited in Chapman with Mansfield, *Whistled Like a Bird*, 134.

157 **a "passion-scalded pig"**: As cited in Chapman with Mansfield, 128.

157 **"Eight years ago"**: As cited in Chapman with Mansfield, 129.

158 **gone missing from the collection**: Elgen Long discusses a 1977 tape in which David Binney Putnam recalls his mother, Dorothy, claiming that she caught Amelia and George in bed. (See David Binney Putnam, oral history interview by Elgen Long, Tape 2, Side-B, 28 December 1977, box 9, cassette 7, Amelia Earhart Project Recordings, National Air and Space Museum Archives, https://sova.si.edu/record/nasm.2020.0025/ref152?t=W&q=david+binney+putnam.) David, interviewed with his then girlfriend, Patricia Sundine, in the room, is clearly uncomfortable, quietly saying "Maybe." After a bit of silence, he also says that his mother blamed her divorce on George's affair with Amelia. "Amelia and my father were what clean Americans should be," he says. "Both of them . . . no hanky-panky." When David's girlfriend interjects with "You thought [George] was having an affair with his secretary," the tape abruptly cuts off, leaving a beguiling hint of whitewashed scandal that strongly hints at Jo Berger when George was married to Dorothy. Although listed in Long's logs and delivered to the Smithsonian by David Jourdan after Long's death, the tape has since officially gone missing. Neither Jourdan, nor Long's granddaughter Marika Pickles, nor the Smithsonian knows its whereabouts. Was it removed on purpose? Likely.

158 **"the diametric opposite"**: Corey Ford, *The Time of Laughter* (Little, Brown and Company, 1967), 204–5.

159 **"Didn't you know?"**: Ford, *Time of Laughter*, 205.

159 **"begged him to leave"**: Jerry Kenion, "Amelia Earhart Is No Legend for a Winston-Salem Woman," *Greensboro Daily News*, October 24, 1976.

159 **"AE and GP left"**: Hilton Howell Railey to Paul Briand, 14 August 1958, box 2, Subseries A: Correspondence, Series 2: Daughters of the Sky, Paul Briand Papers (1920–1986), MC 120, Milne Special Collections and Archives, University of New Hampshire Library.

160 **records from Greenwich House**: Insider takes on Amelia, as reflected in material from the Greenwich House Records of the Tamiment Library / Robert F. Wagner Labor Archives at New York University, paint a far more nuanced—and, frankly, more intriguing—portrait of her activities and associations. It's a reminder that the truth often lies in the dusty archives, where the real stories wait to be unearthed.

161 **"just an ordinary person"**: Charles LeBoutillier, interview by Doris L. Rich, May 10, 1986, folder 12, box 1, Series 1: Biographical Files, Amelia Earhart: A Biography [Rich] Collection, National Air and Space Museum Archives, Smithsonian Institution. Note: Charles LeBoutillier is not a known relative of Oliver Colin "Boots" LeBoutillier, who flew with Mabel Boll.

161 **most eligible bachelors**: This revelation is openly discussed several times by Elgen Long on 1970s tapes that form part of the Amelia Earhart Project Recordings at the Smithsonian's National Air and Space Museum Archives. Loening's name is sometimes hard to make out but clearer other times. Elgen and Marie Long omitted this information from their book due to their greater focus on finding Amelia's plane. According to my interview with Marika Pickles, Elgen's granddaughter, who adored him and accompanied him on an expedition, Elgen found Amelia's personal life less interesting, and Marie preferred to leave private lives untouched. There are also numerous photos of Amelia and Loening together before the stock market crash, adding a visual layer to their intriguing relationship.

161 **Loening encouraged his**: Gillies has his own tapes in the Amelia Earhart Project Recordings and talks about dating Amelia as a ladies' man backup.

162 **a budding journalist**: Ella May Frazer to Doris L. Rich, February 26, 1983, folder 6, box 1, Series 1: Biographical Files, Amelia Earhart: A Biography [Rich] Collection, National Air and Space Museum Archives, Smithsonian Institution.

NOTES 461

164 **back to the office:** Harold McCracken, *Roughnecks and Gentlemen: Memoirs of a Maverick* (Doubleday, 1968), 378. Published in 1968, McCracken's account was muddled by a previous biography, which incorrectly stated that McCracken picked Amelia up for her first meeting with George Putnam. In reality, she was escorted by Hilton Howell Railey. It's likely the author did not have access to McCracken's hard-to-find book. Amelia's first cab ride with McCracken occurred months later, in winter, when he picked her up at Greenwich House.

165 **facade belied a darker reality:** Rudy Vallée reveals the horrific racism and antisemitism that permeated Putnam and Dickerman's Heigh-Ho Club in *Let the Chips Fall* and *My Time Is Your Time: The Rudy Vallée Story*. Vallée's accounts expose a dark underbelly of bigotry, showing that behind the glitz and glamour of Jazz Age high society, there was unsettling and pervasive prejudice.

165 **"Too much drinking":** As cited in Chapman with Mansfield, *Whistled Like a Bird*, 130.

166 **The pint-size dynamo:** Details on the long-lived Elinor Smith were sourced from her still-living daughter, Patricia Sullivan; Smith's own books; an interview with former *New York Times* aviation reporter George Vecsey; and staff at the Cradle of Aviation Museum who knew her well. Additionally, her newspaper articles and interviews are remarkably consistent, with no discrepancies found. In my strong opinion, she was a truth-teller.

166 **local law enforcement:** Information from an in-person interview with her daughter, Patricia Sullivan.

169 **"And tell your people":** All dialogue between Amelia and Dickinson comes from Blanche Taylor Dickinson, "Amelia Earhart Discusses the Negro: Transatlantic Woman Flier Believes in Race's Ability," *Pittsburgh Courier*, February 23, 1929.

172 **Jazz Age bacchanalia:** Marvelous details on this improbable secret Jazz Age club are drawn from the work of Bel Geddes biographer B. Alexandra Szerlip, including her May 2012 long-form article for *The Believer*, "Colossal in Scale, Appalling in Complexity," and her later 2017 book on Bel Geddes, *The Man Who Designed the Future*.

173 **"Does it mean that Amelia":** Allene Summer, The Woman's Day (column), *Whittier News*, December 13, 1928.

174 **As one of her Christmas:** "Takes Mother on Airplane Flight," *Boston Globe*, December 26, 1928.

174 **between mother and daughter:** Loose note, presumably by Paul Briand, undated, box 2, Subseries A: Correspondence, Series 2: Daughters of the Sky, Paul Briand Papers (1920–1986), MC 120, Milne Special Collections and Archives, University of New Hampshire Library.

CHAPTER NINE: SOMETHING HAD TO GIVE

177 **were "decidedly mediocre":** C. B. Allen's papers (and candid thoughts) are held at the Smithsonian's National Air and Space Museum, Chantilly, VA, in the Amelia Earhart Collection [Allen], Acc. XXXX-0520.

181 **He had a $25,000 check:** "First Lady of Flight: Capturing the Imagination of America, Elinor Smith Became a Pioneer of Aviation History," *Santa Cruz Sentinel*, October 11, 1998.

185 **"a lot of evil":** "First Lady of Flight," *Santa Cruz Sentinel*.

188 **affectionately called Chief:** "Amelia Earhart to Take Part in Her Sister's Wedding Today," *Boston Globe*, June 29, 1929.

189 **honor the fallen pilot:** "Associates Honor Wilmer Stultz at Funeral Services," *Brooklyn Daily Eagle*, July 3, 1929.

190 **notable plane manufacturer:** Dennis Parks, "Flying High Before the (Stock Market) Crash," *General Aviation News*, January 23, 2013, https://generalaviationnews.com/2013/01/23/flying-high-before-the-stock-market-crash/.

192 **"During our explanation":** Amelia Earhart, "The Fun of It," *Sunday Daily News*, June 19, 1932.

195 **Amelia and her shocked mother:** "Air Field Officials and Racer Killed," *Washington Post*, August 12, 1929.

CHAPTER TEN: PILOTS AND PLUNGES

199 **on the race's second day:** "Girl Flier in Air Race Found Dead Near Plane," *Napa Valley Register*, August 20, 1929. Much has been written about the Powder Puff Derby. Note that a marvelous nonfiction read on the race is Keith O'Brien's *Fly Girls*. Many hours in Oklahoma City at the archives of the Ninety-Nines added information to this already well-researched event.

200 **Blanche Noyes faced:** "Amelia Leading in Air Derby," *Alturas Plaindealer and Modoc County Times*, August 23, 1929.

200 **Another forced landing:** "Women Pilot Hurls Charges," *San Bernardino County Sun*, August 21, 1929.

203 **Irvin Air Chute's endorsement:** Elinor Smith, *Aviatrix* (Sullivan Family Press, 2016), 171–73.

205 **"suddenly realizing" the value:** As cited in Sally Putnam Chapman with Stephanie Mansfield, *Whistled Like a Bird: The Untold Story of Dorothy Putnam, George Putnam, and Amelia Earhart* (Warner Books, 1997), 162.

209 **"I could prevent":** As cited in Chapman with Mansfield, *Whistled Like a Bird*, 159.

211 **"I released him":** As cited in Chapman with Mansfield, 172.

212 **news he could dictate:** *New York Times* (wire), "'We'll Kill You!' Fascists Write U.S. Publisher," *Chicago Tribune*, December 31, 1929.

CHAPTER ELEVEN: THE TRUTH TO THE RUMOR

213 **With a poker face:** Dozens of news outlets worldwide covered Putnam's fake-bomb hoax. This narrative was drawn from a pastiche of topical articles, as exemplified by the straightforward *New York Times* wire piece "Black Shirts Threaten to Bomb Publishing House," January 1, 1930.

214 **After returning to his:** As cited in John William Tebbel, *A History of Book Publishing in the United States* (R. R. Bowker Co., 1972), 3:523–24.

215 **The untimely tragedy:** "Neva Paris, Aviatrix, Dies in Plane Crash," *Daily News*, January 10, 1930.

217 **wrote off the record:** Howard Cady to Paul Briand, 26 January 1957, box 2, Subseries A: Correspondence, Series 2: Daughters of the Sky, Paul Briand Papers (1920–1986), MC 120, Milne Special Collections and Archives, University of New Hampshire Library.

219 **"was financially ruined":** Harold McCracken, *Roughnecks and Gentlemen: Memoirs of a Maverick* (Doubleday & Company, 1968), 381.

219 **"It was a sad day":** McCracken, *Roughnecks and Gentlemen*, 381, 383.

223 **"I had to go":** Mary North Allen, *Falling Light and Waters Turning: Adventures in Being Human in Word and Image*, ed. Katy Z. Allen (Story Trust, 2016). Mary's grown-up thoughts on the trauma of being a Girl Explorer exploited by adults can be found in her journals, self-published after her death by her children.

225 **ghostwritten Amelia's debut book:** Elinor Smith, *Aviatrix* (Sullivan Family Press, 2016), 239.

226 **"I'm glad he has someone":** As cited in Sally Putnam Chapman with Stephanie Mansfield, *Whistled Like a Bird: The Untold Story of Dorothy Putnam, George Putnam, and Amelia Earhart* (Warner Books, 1997), 173.

231 **shook her head no:** Noank scenes are informed by a visit to the Noank Historical Society and the rest of the town. Although transcripts of the event are milder, the trauma is recounted in a recorded interview with the judge's son, Robert "Chip" Anderson, who was present that day. "And so she wept a great deal and kept shaking her head."

CHAPTER TWELVE: AN ATTRACTIVE CAGE

233 **There are some things:** Amelia Earhart to George Palmer Putnam, handwritten letter, 7 February 1931, George Palmer Putnam Collection of Amelia Earhart Papers, Purdue University Libraries, Archives and Special Collections, https://earchives.lib.purdue.edu/digital/collection/earhart/id/2998/rec/891.

NOTES

236 **Amelia sent a telegram:** As detailed in Muriel's Amelia biography, *Courage Is the Price* (McCormick-Armstrong Publishing, 1963).
237 **a petite upright piano:** Muriel Vernon, "Our Famous Neighbors," *New Rochelle Standard-Star*, October, 17, 1931.
238 **FLIT insecticide at George:** Fay Wray, *On the Other Hand: A Life Story* (St. Martin's Press, 1989), 118.
242 **"Amelia Earhart Putnam disappointed":** Howard Wolf, Good Evening! (column), *Akron Beacon Journal*, September 17, 1931.
244 **when she saw the flashing:** William Gaines, About New York (syndicated column), *Council Bluffs Nonpareil*, August 20, 1931.
244 **"mounted on her trusty":** Corey Ford, *Coconut Oil: June Triplett's Amazing Book Out of Darkest Africa!* (Brewer, Warren & Putnam, 1931), 14–15.

CHAPTER THIRTEEN: A KIND OF THE DITHERS

249 **visited the Putnams in Rye:** Marian Stabler interview with Doris L. Rich, transcript, June 16, 1984, folder 5, box 2, Series 1: Biographical Files, Amelia Earhart: A Biography [Rich] Collection, National Air and Space Museum Archives, Smithsonian Institution.
251 **"very aggressive person":** Eddie Gorski to Paul Briand, 15 October 1957, box 2, Subseries A: Correspondence, Series 2: Daughters of the Sky, Paul Briand Papers (1920–1986), MC 120, Milne Special Collections and Archives, University of New Hampshire Library.
259 **touchdown at Gallagher's Field:** All telegrams are part of Purdue University Libraries' George Palmer Putnam Collection of Amelia Earhart Papers and can be viewed online.
262 **"I had made up":** "Why Miss Earhart Flew Alone," *Western Morning News*, May 24, 1932.
265 **"We are about to":** Corisande, "The Prince Plays Yo-Yo at the Derby Ball," *Evening Standard*, July 1, 1932.
268 **"You remember that some":** Footage of this moment is easy to find online. It's lovely to watch, a real time travel for viewers, and a fine excuse to hear Amelia's charming voice. See, for example, British Pathé, "Miss Earhart's Wonderful Reception! (1932)," streamed on April 13, 2014, YouTube video, 1:57, https://youtu.be/FW7EXQUjKeE?si=i750bR7B_6B4GtuY.
273 **West Seventy-Second Street:** All details pertaining to the dinner for Amelia come from the Explorers Club's archives, which include the program from the evening.
275 **legal minds prevailed there:** This screwy plan is best recounted in Ben M. Hall, *The Best Remaining Seats: The Golden Age of the Movie Palace* (Crown, 1975).
278 **"It does mark an epoch":** "First Lady Rides Night Skies with Amelia Earhart as Pilot," *Baltimore Sun*, April 21, 1933.
282 **"Ban men all you want":** "Over 200 Fly with Aviatrix," *Bangor Daily News*, August 13, 1934.

CHAPTER FOURTEEN: CALL OF THE WILD

286 **The well-mannered Anne:** Anne Morrow Lindbergh to Amelia Earhart, letter, 26 January 1933, Missouri Historical Society.
286 **her "active living" ideas:** For more on the reality of her fashion line, see Karla Jay's interesting *No Bumps, No Excrescences: Amelia Earhart's Failed Flight into Fashions* (Rutgers University Press, 1994).
288 **a subtle hint:** "Miss Eve Bennett with Amelia Earhart Fashions," *Women's Wear Daily*, January 3, 1934.
288 **This astounding showdown:** Paul F. Collins, *Tales of an Old Air-Faring Man* (Foundation Press, 1983), 140.
289 **"Is she Black or white?":** Paul Briand, handwritten notes, 1957, box 3, Subseries B: Notes and Drafts, Series 2: Daughters of the Sky, Paul Briand Papers (1920–1986), MC 120, Milne Special Collections and Archives, University of New Hampshire Library; and notes from Briand's in-person interview with Henry Bradford Washburn.

290 **To further ease relations:** Doris L. Rich interview notes with David Binney Putnam, November 11, 1985, folder 4, box 7, Series 4: Book Correspondence, Amelia Earhart: A Biography [Rich] Collection, National Air and Space Museum Archives, Smithsonian Institution.
290 **Their lovely stay:** There is much to read on Amelia and George's special connection to Carl Dunrud in his memoir *Let's Go! 85 Years of Adventure* (WordsWorth Publishing, 1998). Additional information is drawn from various miscellaneous articles.
291 **The good people:** "Amelia Earhart, Husband, Returning from Vacation, Stop Overnight in Decatur," *Decatur Herald*, July 31, 1934.
292 **"I ushered upstairs":** "Amelia Earhart Here for a Night," *St. Joseph Gazette*, July 30, 1934.
295 **any scrap of news:** "'Mr. Amelia Earhart' Has Bad Time Trying to Remain Calm," *Imperial Valley Press*, January 12, 1935.
297 **Amelia was no stranger:** As detailed in Alec Nevala-Lee, *Inventor of the Future: The Visionary Life of Buckminster Fuller* (Dey Street Books, 2022). The anecdote is also covered in various articles and newsreels.
300 **While George's eruption:** L. L. Stevenson, Daily Lights of New York (column), *Binghamton Press*, May 28, 1935.
301 **"When you take a fast":** Will Rogers, Will Rogers Says (column), *Altoona Tribune*, May 9, 1935.
303 **a magazine the couple revered:** Karla Jay, "No Bumps, No Excrescences: Amelia Earhart's Failed Flight into Fashions," in *On Fashion*, ed. Shari Benstock and Suzanne Ferriss (Rutgers University Press, 1994), 87.
304 **Terry could still picture:** Theresa "Terry" Mantz, oral history interview by Elgen Long, 19 July 1975, box 5, cassette 13, Amelia Earhart Project Recordings, National Air and Space Museum Archives, https://sova.si.edu/record/nasm.2020.0025/ref83?t=W&q=mantz.
304 **gossip-mill darling Brown Derby:** "Stork Showers Imposing List," Marshall Kester, *Los Angeles Times*, June 29, 1935.
304 **as fundamentally platonic:** Gore Vidal to Paul Briand, handwritten letter, 22 July 1957, box 2, Subseries A: Correspondence, Series 2: Daughters of the Sky, Paul Briand Papers (1920–1986), MC 120, Milne Special Collections and Archives, University of New Hampshire Library.
305 **a different family dynamic:** Zoom interview with Jay Parini by the author.
305 **plane crash in Alaska:** James J. Haggerty, *Aviation's Mr. Sam* (Aero Publishers, 1974), 49.

CHAPTER FIFTEEN: MORNING BECOMES ELECTRA

311 **Thanks to another persuasive:** Albert Wood and Five Sons, Trophy Chest, Amelia Earhart, 1935, Burma teakwood, 51 1/4 × 23 1/4 × 24 in., National Air and Space Museum, Smithsonian, Washington, DC, object number A20030156000, https://airandspace.si.edu/collection-objects/chest-trophy-amelia-earhart/nasm_A20030156000.
312 **loss of Amelia's "peppers":** Interview with Sam Wood, Albert's grandson, by the author.
319 **Earhart's newly acquired plane:** "Joan Crawford Is Tricked into Ride in Plane," *Chicago Tribune*, September 3, 1936.
320 **"I hope to have":** All quotes from Amelia's conversation with Cooper are drawn from Lillian Cooper, "Amelia Earhart Says She'd Face Jail for Peace," *Daily Worker*, September 4, 1936.
320 **she was up against racers:** Cooper, "Amelia Earhart Says She'd Face Jail for Peace."
321 **"Please don't down":** Spring 1936 letter from Amelia to her mother, as cited in Jean L. Backus, ed., *Letters from Amelia: An Intimate Portrait of Amelia Earhart* (Beacon Press, 1982), 197.

CHAPTER SIXTEEN: DEAD RECKONING

324 **"I didn't feel she had":** Henry Bradford Washburn lived to ninety-seven, and his accounts of what happened at that private meeting in Rye are consistent over many years, starting with a letter found in the University of New Hampshire's Paul Briand Papers. Quotes come from many articles and interviews, as well as his own autobiography.

NOTES

327 **CITY IN A DITHER:** "City in a Dither as Amelia Earhart Arrested, but Hubby Just Having His Fun," Jack Austin, *Blackwell Journal-Tribune*, February 21, 1937.

328 **In the final weeks:** Vivian Maata Sims, oral history interview by Elgen Long, 10 March 1977, box 8, cassette 13, Amelia Earhart Project Recordings, National Air and Space Museum Archives, https://sova.si.edu/record/nasm.2020.0025/ref141?t=W&q=vivian.

330 **She often engaged:** Interview transcript with Harkness Davenport, September 22, 1985, folder 4, box 1, Series 1: Biographical Files, Amelia Earhart: A Biography [Rich] Collection, National Air and Space Museum Archives, Smithsonian Institution.

332 **years of maritime experience:** Noonan's backstory is gleaned from interviews and an unpublished essay ("Fred Noonan—the Forgotten Navigator") by amateur historian Winifred Wood. One particularly helpful article was "Noonan Seeks Juarez Divorce," *El Paso Times*, March 16, 1937. His birth date and city of birth come from ancestry.com.

332 **"Fred Noonan has been":** C. B. Allen, "'Hitch-Hikers' to Aid Amelia on First Legs of World Hop," *Buffalo Evening News*, March 13, 1937.

333 **as Noonan came cheap:** Albert Bresnik, oral history interview by Elgen Long, 17 June 1988, box 1, cassette 10, Amelia Earhart Project Recordings, National Air and Space Museum Archives, https://sova.si.edu/record/nasm.2020.0025/ref11?t=W&q=albert.

333 **smashed in his hotel room:** Interview transcript and notes with Mrs. James E. Bassett Jr. (Wilma, his widow), January 14, 1984, folder 8, box 6, Series 4: Book Correspondence, Amelia Earhart: A Biography [Rich] Collection, National Air and Space Museum Archives, Smithsonian Institution.

337 **"He was so cold":** Theresa "Terry" Mantz, oral history interview by Elgen Long, 19 July 1975, box 5, cassette 13, Amelia Earhart Project Recordings, National Air and Space Museum Archives, https://sova.si.edu/record/nasm.2020.0025/ref83?t=W&q=theresa.

337 **a rather telling insight:** Mildred Eisenhardt "Mil" Manning, oral history interview by Elgen Long, 1975, box 6, cassette 15, Amelia Earhart Project Recordings, National Air and Space Museum Archives, https://sova.si.edu/record/nasm.2020.0025/ref103?t=W&q=mildred.

340 **"She had slid down":** The transcript of screenwriter Stewart Stern's astounding recorded interview with Floyd Odlum and Jackie Cochran can be found at both the Eisenhower Library, in Abilene, Kansas, and in the Stewart Stern Papers, University of Iowa Special Collections Repository.

341 **at the Burnett Sanitarium:** "Sister of Salinas Woman Is Injured in Fresno Car Crash," *Californian*, April 5, 1937.

CHAPTER SEVENTEEN: WHISTLE IN THE DARK

343 **quintuplets at play:** "Amelia Travels to Visit Quints," *Ottawa Citizen*, April 22, 1937.

344 **before the catastrophe:** David Binney Putnam, oral history interview by Elgen Long, 28 December 1977, box 9, cassettes 6–8, Amelia Earhart Project Recordings, National Air and Space Museum Archives, https://sova.si.edu/record/nasm.2020.0025/search?q=david%20binney%20putnam&t=W&o=doc_position.

346 **her previous occupation:** Information and dialogue here are gleaned from Whyte's oral interview in the Edna Gardner Whyte Collection at the University of North Texas, as well as from several consistent articles and her autobiography, *Rising Above It: An Autobiography* (Crown, 1991).

348 **Omlie was the last:** Research conducted at the Memphis Public Libraries. See the Phoebe Omlie Collection, Memphis Public Libraries, Memphis, TN.

348 **"We're just on a shakedown":** "Earhart Plans Miami Takeoff on World Trip," *Miami Daily News*, May 30, 1937.

348 **Expressing his worries:** Ruckins "Bo" McNeeley tapes, tape 2, October 18, 1975, Amelia Earhart Project Recordings, National Air and Space Museum Archives.

350 **"In going over":** Unpublished document, C. B. Allen Papers, National Air and Space Museum Archives, Amelia Earhart Collection [Allen], Acc. XXXX-0520.

351 **looking over incoming mail:** George told Harold McCracken in New York. See Harold McCracken, *Roughnecks and Gentlemen: Memoirs of a Maverick* (Doubleday & Company, 1968), 383.

NOTES

352 **Her last letter:** Letter from Amelia to her mother, 1 June 1937, as cited in Jean L. Backus, ed., *Letters from Amelia: An Intimate Portrait of Amelia Earhart* (Beacon Press, 1982), 225–26.

353 **driver in a Chrysler:** Information comes from amateur historian Winifred Wood's unpublished essay ("Fred Noonan—the Forgotten Navigator"), as well as from letters received by Helen Louise Day and held by her son, Captain Jim Bible.

355 **"In the dim chill":** George Palmer Putnam, *Soaring Wings* (Harcourt, Brace & Co., 1939), 290.

363 **the excellent reception:** Paul F. Collins, *Tales of an Old Air-Faring Man* (Foundation Press, 1983), 147.

364 **hitting Howland Island:** Francis O. "Fuzz" Furman, oral history interview by Elgen Long, 22 March 1981, box 11, cassette 3, Amelia Earhart Project Recordings, National Air and Space Museum Archives, https://sova.si.edu/record/nasm.2020.0025/ref182?t=W&q=francis.

365 **required to make contact:** Stanley Rose, oral history interview by Elgen Long, 27–28 February 1976, box 7, cassette 9, Amelia Earhart Project Recordings, National Air and Space Museum Archives, https://sova.si.edu/record/nasm.2020.0025/ref119?t=W&q=+rose.

368 **as "rather fresh":** Flora "Ma" Stewart, oral history interview by Elgen Long, February 1976, box 7, cassette 8, Amelia Earhart Project Recordings, National Air and Space Museum Archives, https://sova.si.edu/record/nasm.2020.0025/ref118?t=W&q=flora.

368 **"AE and Fred eventually":** Harry Balfour, letter to conspiracy theorist Joe Gervais, March 4, 1961. The letter was first published in the *Amelia Earhart Society Newsletter* (July 1998) and is available online through multiple sources.

368 **"The skinny bitch":** James A. "Jim" Collopy, oral history interview by Elgen Long, 11 February 1976, box 7, cassette 5, Amelia Earhart Project Recordings, National Air and Space Museum Archives, https://sova.si.edu/record/nasm.2020.0025/ref115?t=W&q=collopy.

379 **miles from Howland Island:** Thomas J. "Tommy" O'Hare, oral history interview by Elgen Long, 20 May 1976, box 7, cassettes 13–16, Amelia Earhart Project Recordings, National Air and Space Museum Archives, https://sova.si.edu/record/nasm.2020.0025/search?q=o%27hare&t=W&o=doc_position. (Note that these are especially worth listening to, as O'Hare's account is unforgettable.)

380 **At 6:15 a.m., she transmitted:** The Coast Guard logs, available at the Library of Congress, contain heavy abbreviations. For the ease of the reader, these entries have been expanded and clarified here.

385 **As Amelia Earhart's radio:** "A Candid Talk with George Palmer Putnam" (syndicated), *Lock Haven Express*, July 3, 1937.

CHAPTER EIGHTEEN: SLOW CIRCLING DOWN

387 **first heard the news:** Lawrence Ames, oral history interview by Elgen Long, 17 March 1973, box 2, cassette 9, Amelia Earhart Project Recordings, National Air and Space Museum Archives, https://sova.si.edu/record/nasm.2020.0025/ref277?t=W&q=Lawrence.

387 **bordered on recklessness:** Howard Hanzlick, oral history interview by Elgen Long, 16 January 1981, box 10, cassettes 16–18, Amelia Earhart Project Recordings, National Air and Space Museum Archives, https://sova.si.edu/record/nasm.2020.0025/search?q=hanzlik&t=W&o=doc_position.

389 **no one wept harder:** "First Lady of Flight: Capturing the Imagination of America, Elinor Smith Became a Pioneer of Aviation History," *Santa Cruz Sentinel*, October 11, 1998.

389 **despite her inner turmoil:** "Putnam Tries to Cheer Up Mrs. Noonan," *Oakland Tribune*, July 4, 1937.

390 **spirit of exploration:** Harold McCracken, *Roughnecks and Gentlemen: Memoirs of a Maverick* (Doubleday & Company, 1968), 383.

391 **before turning to ash:** Margot DeCarie, oral history interview by Elgen Long, 29 March 1977, box 10, cassettes 8–9, Amelia Earhart Project Recordings, National Air and Space Museum Archives, https://sova.si.edu/record/nasm.2020.0025/ref171?t=W&q=margot. (Note that it is unclear whether this even happened. Her account changes over the years and sometimes veers into magical thinking. She's not always the most reliable narrator.)

393 **Amelia and GP weren't getting along:** Louise M. Thaden, oral history interview by Elgen Long, 10

January 1977, box 8, cassettes 10–11, Amelia Earhart Project Recordings, National Air and Space Museum Archives, https://sova.si.edu/record/nasm.2020.0025/ref138?t=W&q=louise+thaden.
395 **A rather tasteless:** Margaret Dale, column item, *Brooklyn Daily Eagle*, July 18, 1937.
395 **proudly interviewed Amelia:** "Putnam Keeps Vigil for His Wife," *Washington Evening Star*, July 10, 1937.
396 **provided a sharp analysis:** Louise M. Thaden, oral history interview by Elgen Long, 10 January 1977, box 8, cassettes 10–11, Amelia Earhart Project Recordings, National Air and Space Museum Archives, https://sova.si.edu/record/nasm.2020.0025/ref139?t=W&q=thaden; Bob Considine, "Miss Earhart Called Martyr to Friends," *Miami Herald*, July 19, 1937; and "The Untold Story of Amelia Earhart's Tragedy," *Atlanta Constitution*, August 8, 1937.
398 **echoing her aunt's fate:** Interview with Amy Morrison by the author.
399 **SOLD DOWN THE RIVER:** McCracken, *Roughnecks and Gentlemen*, 378.
402 **Harry the Junk Man:** Interview with Kathleen Rothar Watson by the author.
403 **letters filled with affection:** George Palmer Putnam to Amelia Earhart, undated, circa 1937, George Palmer Putnam Collection of Amelia Earhart Papers, Purdue University Libraries, Archives and Special Collections, https://earchives.lib.purdue.edu/digital/collection/earhart/id/1987/rec/.
405 **"There is one chance":** Sheilah Graham, "Putnam Clings to His Hope Amelia Earhart Lives," *Scranton Times*, September 20, 1937.
405 **his hired ghostwriter:** Papers of Janet Mabie (1912–1960), Schlesinger Library, Radcliffe Institute.
410 **"Magic Book Box":** "Putnam Sails; Mystery Veils Voyage Aims," *Hollywood Citizen-News*, December 16, 1937.

CHAPTER NINETEEN: WHO CAME TO DINNER

411 **his Hilda pinups:** "Amelia Earhart Sculptured in Snow," *Kansas City Star*, February 27, 1938.
412 **book writing experience:** "Movie Maker," *Dartmouth Alumni Magazine*, October 1966, 34.
414 **organized by Joanne Alderman:** Jean-Marie Consigny Putnam, oral history interview by Elgen Long, 3 January 1981, box 10, cassette 15, Amelia Earhart Project Recordings, National Air and Space Museum Archives, https://sova.si.edu/record/nasm.2020.0025/ref177?t=W&q=consigny.

CHAPTER TWENTY: VEILED VENTURES

419 **Amelia had such a will:** Discussion of the will can be found in a transcript of the taped interview by screenwriter Stewart Stern. Copies of the transcript can be accessed at the Eisenhower Library and in the Stewart Stern Papers at the University of Iowa Special Collections Repository.
420 **not a creative task:** Charles Albert "Cap" Palmer, oral history interview by Elgen Long, 5 March 1981, box 11, cassette 4, Amelia Earhart Project Recordings, National Air and Space Museum Archives, https://sova.si.edu/record/nasm.2020.0025/ref183?t=W&q=palmer.
421 **for added mystique:** Interview with Duffy Jennings, Dean's son, by the author.
421 **It began on April 22:** There are hundreds of articles about the faked kidnapping, downplayed as good sport by previous Amelia Earhart biographies, if mentioned at all. Articles with headlines like "Putnam Kidnaped [sic] by Germans" and "Found Gagged in House" were the gentler ones. Quite the deceit. Less good sport and more like the brainchild of someone who disturbingly fooled the police, wasted resources, and enlisted his employees in a criminal farce, all while thinking it was a jolly good lark.
424 **George tied the knot:** "Putnam Weds Young Divorcée," *Los Angeles Times*, May 22, 1939.
424 **"before Amelia was even":** Jacqueline Cochran Papers, Eisenhower Library; and Stewart Stern Papers, University of Iowa Special Collections Repository.
425 **The claim was taken:** AP, "'Earhart' Note Found in Bottle," *Spokesman-Review*, June 26, 1939.
428 **"the kick he needs":** Anecdote heard in Charles Albert "Cap" Palmer, oral history interview by Elgen Long.

433 **witnessed by Cap:** Another memorable tidbit heard in Charles "Cap" Palmer, oral history interview by Elgen Long.
434 **1937 after their marriage:** Peg Putnam to Paul Briand, 26 January 1976, box 2, folders 15 and 17, Subseries A, Series 2, Paul Briand Papers (1920–1986), MC 120, Milne Special Collections and Archives, University of New Hampshire Library.
436 **disseminated false information:** Interestingly, in his own papers, he kept correspondence that revealed he was secretly paying for supposedly "unbiased" information to support the claim that Amelia landed on Saipan. His lawyer, William W. Penaluna, even ramped up the pressure, demanding more money in exchange for "fair play," threatening that the cooked-up story would be sold to another biographer if they didn't pay up. This wild tale was labeled as "fantastic drool" by someone close to both Amelia and George at the time, who tried to warn Paul Briand, but to no avail. Hilton Howell Railey to Paul Briand, 31 August 1958, box 2, folder 2, Subseries A: Correspondence, Series 2: Daughters of the Sky, Paul Briand Papers (1920–1986), MC 120, Milne Special Collections and Archives, University of New Hampshire Library.

BIBLIOGRAPHY

ADULT LITERATURE

Adams, Jean, and Margaret Kimball. *Heroines of the Sky*. Doubleday & Co., 1942.
Albion, Michele Wehrwein. *The Quotable Amelia Earhart*. University of New Mexico Press, 2015.
Allen, Frederick Lewis. *Only Yesterday: An Informal History of the 1920s*. Harper & Row, 1931.
Allen, Mary North. *Falling Light and Waters Turning*. Edited by Katy Z. Allen. Story Trust Publishing, 2016.
Aoki, Fukiko. *Amelia o sagas*. Translated by Eric Han for the author. Bungei Shunjū, 1983. (Note: This book is only available in the original Japanese and has not been published in English translation.)
Arnold, Rebecca. *The American Look: Fashion, Sportswear and the Image of Women in 1930s and 1940s New York*. London: I. B. Tauris, 2009.
Asbury, Herbert. *The Great Illusion: An Informal History of Prohibition*. Doubleday, 1950.
Atkins, Annette. *We Grew Up Together: Brothers and Sisters in Nineteenth-Century America*. University of Illinois Press, 2001.
Backus, Jean. *Letters from Amelia*. Beacon Press, 1982.
Barry, John M. *The Great Influenza: The Story of the Deadliest Pandemic in History*. Viking, 2014.
Baxter, Carol. *The Fabulous Flying Mrs. Miller*. London: Scribe, 2019.
Bean Bower, Jennifer. *North Carolina Aviatrix Viola Gentry: The Flying Cashier*. Charleston, SC: The History Press, 2016.
Beebe, William. *The Arcturus Adventure*. G. P. Putnam's Sons, 1926.
Bel Geddes, Norman. *Miracle in the Evening: An Autobiography*. Edited by William Kelley. Doubleday, 1960.
Bell, Elizabeth S. *Sisters of the Wind: Voices of Early Women Aviators*. Trilogy Books, 1994.
Bell, Nevin. *Amelia Earhart*. Edito-Service, 1970.
Berg, A. Scott. *Lindbergh*. G. P. Putnam's Sons, 1998.
Berger, Meyer. *The Story of "The New York Times," 1851–1951*. Simon & Schuster, 1851.
Beyer, Rick, and Elizabeth Sayles. *The Ghost Army of WWII: How One Top-Secret Unit Deceived the Enemy with Inflatable Tanks, Sound Effects, and Other Audacious Fakery*. Princeton Architectural Press, 2015.
Boase, Wendy. *The Sky's the Limit: Women Pioneers in Aviation*. Macmillan, 1979.
Bokovoy, Matthew. *The San Diego World's Fairs and Southwestern Memory, 1880–1940*. University of New Mexico Press, 2006.

Boyer, Paul S., ed. *The Oxford Companion to United States History*. Oxford University Press, 2001.
Boyne, Walter J. *The Smithsonian Book of Flight*. Orion Books, 1987.
Briand, Paul L. Jr. *Daughter of the Sky*. Duell, Sloan & Pearce, 1960.
Brown, Dorothy M. *Setting a Course: American Women in the 1920s*. Twayne Publishers, 1987.
Bruno, Harry. *Wings Over America: The Story of American Aviation*. Halcyon House, 1942.
Bryson, Bill. *One Summer: America, 1927*. Doubleday, 2013.
Burke, John. *Winged Legend: The Story of Amelia Earhart*. G. P. Putnam's Sons, 1970.
Butler, Susan. *East to the Dawn: The Life of Amelia Earhart*. Addison-Wesley, 1997.
Cadogan, Mary. *Women with Wings: Female Flyers in Fact and Fiction*. Academy Chicago Publishers, 1992.
Carson, Gerard. *Cornflake Crusade: From the Pulpit to the Breakfast Table*. Rinehart & Co., 1957.
Chant, Christopher. *Pioneers of Aviation*. Barnes & Noble Books, 2001.
Chapin, Anna Alice. *Greenwich Village*. Dodd, Mead & Co., 1925.
Chapman, Sally Putnam. *Whistled Like a Bird: The Untold Story of Dorothy Putnam, George Putnam, and Amelia Earhart*. Warner Books, 1997.
Clarke, Basil. *Atlantic Adventure: A Complete History of Transatlantic Flight*. Allan Wingate, 1958.
Cochran, Jacqueline. *The Stars at Noon*. Little, Brown & Co., 1954.
Cochran, Jacqueline, and Maryanne Buckam Brinley. *Jackie Cochran: An Autobiography*. Bantam Books.
Collins, Paul F. *Tales of an Old Air-Faring Man*. University of Wisconsin–Stevens Point Foundation Press, 1983.
Cook, Blanche Wiesen. *Eleanor Roosevelt*. Vol. 2, *The Defining Years, 1933–1938*. Viking Penguin, 1999.
Corn, Joseph J. *The Winged Gospel: America's Romance with Aviation, 1900–1950*. Oxford University Press, 1983.
Corn, Joseph J., ed. *Into the Blue: American Writing on Aviation and Spaceflight*. Library of America, 2011.
Cott, Nancy F. *The Grounding of Modern Feminism*. Yale University Press, 1987.
Crowell, James LeRoy. *Frontier Publisher: A Romantic Review of George Palmer Putnam's Career at "The Bend Bulletin," 1910–1914*. Deschutes County Historical Society, 2008.
Dade, George C., and Frank Strand. *Picture History of Aviation on Long Island, 1908–1938*. Dover Publications, 1989.
Dalphin, Marcia. *Fifty Years of Rye, 1904–1954*. City of Rye, 1955.
Delegard, Kirstin Marie. *Battling Miss Bolsheviki: The Origins of Female Conservatism in the United States*. University of Pennsylvania Press, 2012.
Douglas, Ann. *Terrible Honesty: Mongrel Manhattan in the 1920s*. Farrar, Straus and Giroux, 1995.
Douglas, George H. *Women of the 20s*. Saybrook Publishers, 1986.
Douglas, Robert Dick Jr. *The Best 90 Years of My Life*. Vantage Press, 2007.
Dumenil, Lynn. *Modern Temper: American Culture and Society in the 1920s*. Hill and Wang, 1995.
Dunne, Colin, ed. *Rye in the Twenties*. Arno Press, 1978.
Dunrud, Carl M. *Let's Go!: 85 Years of Adventure*. WordsWorth, 1998.
Dwiggins, Don. *Hollywood Pilot: The Biography of Paul Mantz*. Doubleday & Co., 1967.
Earhart, Amelia. *The Fun of It*. Brewer, Warren & Putnam, 1932.
———. *Last Flight*. Harcourt, Brace and World, 1937.
———. *20 Hrs. 40 Min.: Our Flight in the Friendship*. Grosset & Dunlap, in arrangement with G. P. Putnam's Sons, 1928.
Erenberg, Lewis A. *Steppin' Out: New York Nightlife and the Transformation of American Culture, 1890–1930*. University of Chicago Press, 1981.
Erisman, Fred. *In Their Own Words: Forgotten Women Pilots of Early Aviation*. Purdue University Press, 2021.
Farmer, James H. *Celluloid Wings: The Impact of Movies on Aviation*. Tab Books, 1984.
Ford, Corey. *Coconut Oil: June Triplett's Amazing Book Out of Darkest Africa!* Brewer, Warren & Putnam, 1931.
———. *The Time of Laughter: A Sentimental Chronicle of the Twenties*. Little, Brown and Company, 1967.
Fowler, Gene. *Beau James: The Life and Times of Jimmy Walker*. Viking Press, 1949.

Fraser, Chelsea Curtis. *Famous American Flyers*. Thomas Y. Crowell, 1941.
French, Joseph Lewis, ed. *Conquerors of the Sky*. Introduction by Amelia Earhart. McLoughlin Bros., 1932.
Ganz, Cheryl R. *The 1933 Chicago World's Fair: A Century of Progress*. University of Illinois Press.
Gilroy, Shirley Dobson. *Amelia: Pilot in Pearls*. Link Press, 1985.
Glines, Carroll V. *Round-the-World Flights*. Van Nostrand Reinhold, 1982.
———. *Bernt Balchen: Polar Aviator*. Smithsonian Institution Press, 1999.
Goldstein, Donald M., and Katherine V. Dillon. *Amelia: The Centennial Biography of an Aviation Pioneer*. Brassey's, 1997.
Goldstein, Laurence. *The Flying Machine and Modern Literature*. Indiana University Press, 1986.
Gordon, Rose, with Ione Reed. *Stunt Girl: A Novel*. George Palmer Putnam, 1940.
Gould, Bruce. *Sky Larking: The Romantic Adventures of Flying*. Horace Liveright, 1929.
Gould, Carol Grant. *The Remarkable Life of William Beebe*. Island Press, 2004.
Gower, Jon. *A Long Mile*. Carmarthenshire County Council, 2004.
Greenspan, Ezra. *George Palmer Putnam: Representative American Publisher*. Pennsylvania State University Press.
Greenwood, Jim, and Maxine. *Stunt Flying in the Movies*. Tab Books, 1982.
Hackett, Alice Payne. *Fifty Years of Best Sellers 1895–1915*. R. R. Bowker Company, 1945.
Haggerty, James. *Aviation's Mr. Sam*. Aero Publishers, 1974.
Hale, Julian. *Women in Aviation*. Shire Publications, 2019.
Hall, David D, ed. *A History of the Book in America*. Vol. 4, *Print in Motion: The Expansion of Publishing and Reading in the United States, 1880–1940*, edited by Carl F. Kaestle and Janice A. Radway. University of North Carolina Press, 2009.
Hamelin, Joseph A. *Flight Fever*. Doubleday, 1971.
Hawks, Captain Frank. *Once to Every Pilot*. Stackpole Sons, 1936.
Henderson, Mary. *Famous Personalities of Flight Cookbook*. Smithsonian Institution Press, 1981.
Henriksen, Louise Levitas. *Anzia Yezierska: A Writer's Life*. Rutgers University Press, 1988.
Herrmann, Anne. *Queering the Moderns: Poses/Portraits/Performances*. Palgrave Macmillan, 2001.
Herrmann, Dorothy. *Anne Morrow Lindbergh: A Gift for Life*. Ticknor & Fields, 1993.
Hertog, Susan. *Anne Morrow Lindbergh: Her Life*. New York: Nan A. Talese, 1999.
History of the Ninety-Nines. The Ninety-Nines, International Organization of Women Pilots, 1979.
Hodgins, Eric, and F. Alexander Magoun. *Sky High: The Story of Aviation*. Little, Brown and Company, 1930.
Hodgman, Ann, and Rudy Djabbaroff. *Skystars: The History of Women in Aviation*. Atheneum, 1981.
Holden, Harry M. *Teterboro Airport*. Arcadia Publishing, 2009.
Horan, James D. *The Desperate Years: A Pictorial History of the Thirties*. Bonanza Books, 1962.
Jablonski, Edward. *Ladybirds: Women in Aviation*. Illustrated by Haris Petie. Hawthorn Books, 1968.
———. *Atlantic Fever: The Great Transatlantic Aerial Adventure*. Macmillan, 1972.
Jaros, Dean. *Heroes Without Legacy: American Airwomen 1912–1944*. University Press of Colorado, 1993.
Jennings, Duffy. *Reporter's Note Book*. Grizzly Peak Press, 2019.
Johnson, Osa. *I Married Adventure: The Lives of Martin & Osa Johnson*. J. B. Lippincott Company, 1940.
Jordan, Benjamin René. *Modern Manhood and the Boy Scouts of America*. University of North Carolina Press, 2016.
Josephy, Alvin M. Jr., ed. *American Heritage History of Flight*. Simon & Schuster, 1962.
Joslin, Les. *Legendary Locals of Bend*. Legendary Locals Press, 2016.
Jourdan, David W. *The Deep Sea Quest for Amelia Earhart*. Ocellus Productions, 2010.
Kennedy, David M. *Freedom from Fear: The American People in Depression and War, 1929–1945*. Oxford University Press, 1999. Ebook.
Klieger, P. Christiaan. *The Fleischmann Yeast Family*. Arcadia Publishing, 2004.
Knight, Clayton, and Robert C. Durham. *Hitch Your Wagon: The Story of Bernt Balchen*. Bell Publishing Co., 1950.
Kriebel, Robert C. *Ross-Ade: Their Purdue Stories, Stadium, and Legacy*. Purdue University, 2009.
Kyvig, David E. *Daily Life in the United States, 1920–1940*. Ivan R. Dee, 2002.

Landers, James. *The Improbable First Century of "Cosmopolitan" Magazine.* University of Missouri Press, 2010.
Lindbergh, Charles A. *"WE."* G. P. Putnam's Sons, 1927.
Lodeesen, Captain Marius. *Saying Goodbye to an Era.* Paladwr Press, 2004.
Long, Elgen M., and Marie K Long. *Amelia Earhart: The Mystery Solved.* Simon & Schuster, 1991.
Loth, David. *The City Within a City: The Romance of Rockefeller Center.* New York: William Morrow, 1966.
Lovell, Mary S. *Sound of Wings: The Life of Amelia Earhart.* St. Martin's Griffin, 1989.
Lutz, Stuart. *The Last Leaf: Voices of History's Last-Known Survivors.* Prometheus Books, 2010.
Mackworth-Praed, Ben. *Aviation: The Pioneer Years.* Chartwell Books, 1990.
Manchester, William. *The Glory and the Dream: A Narrative History of America, 1932–1972.* Little, Brown and Company, 1972.
Markel, Howard. *The Kelloggs: The Battling Brothers of Battle Creek.* Pantheon Books, 2017.
Maslin, Michael. *Peter Arno: The Mad, Mad World of The New Yorker's Greatest Cartoonist.* Regan Arts, 2016.
McCaughey, Robert A. *Stand, Columbia: A History of Columbia University in the City of New York, 1754–2004.* Columbia University Press, 2003.
McCracken, Harold. *Roughnecks and Gentlemen: Memoirs of a Maverick.* Doubleday, 1968.
Michaelis, David. *Eleanor.* Simon & Schuster, 2020.
Miller, Francis Trevelyan. *Lindbergh: His Story in Pictures.* G. P. Putnam's Sons, 1929.
Miller, Nathan. *New World Coming: The 1920s and the Making of Modern America.* Scribner, 2003.
Miller, Terry. *Greenwich Village and How It Got That Way.* Crown, 1990.
Milton, Joyce. *Loss of Eden: A Biography of Charles and Ann Morrow Lindbergh.* New York: Open Road Media, 2014.
Moolman, Valerie. *Women Aloft.* New York: Time-Life Books, 1981.
Moore-Smith, Rena "Beth." *Life in Owen's Valley!* Pine Tree Publishers, 2018.
Morrissey, Muriel Earhart. *Courage Is the Price: The Biography of Amelia Earhart.* McCormick-Armstrong Publishing, 1963.
Morrissey, Muriel Earhart, and Carol L. Osborne. *Amelia, My Courageous Sister.* Osborne Publisher, 1987.
Mosley, Leonard. *Lindbergh: A Biography.* Doubleday, 1976.
Nair, Mira. *Amelia: The Motion Picture.* Universe Publishing, 2019.
Naughton, Lindie. *Lady Icarus: The Life of Irish Aviator Lady Mary Heath.* Ashfield Press, 2004.
Nevala-Lee, Alec. *Inventor of the Future: The Visionary Life of Buckminster Fuller.* Dey Street Books, 2022.
Nichols, Ruth. *Wings for Life: The Life Story of the First Lady of the Air.* J. B. Lippincott Company, 1957.
Oakes, Claudia. *United States Women in Aviation 1930–1939.* Smithsonian Institution Press, 1985.
O'Brien, Edna V. *So I Went to Prison.* Frederick A. Stokes Company, 1938.
O'Brien, Keith. *Fly Girls: How Five Daring Women Defied All Odds and Made Aviation History.* Houghton Mifflin Harcourt, 2018.
Okrent, Daniel. *Great Fortune: The Epic of Rockefeller Center.* Viking, 2003.
———. *Last Call: The Rise and Fall of Prohibition.* Scribner, 2010.
Palmer, Henry R. Jr. *This Was Air Travel.* Bonanza Books, 1960.
Parrish, Michael E. *Anxious Decades: America in Prosperity and Depression, 1920–1941.* W. W. Norton, 1994.
Pauwels, Captain Linda. *Beyond Haiku: Women Pilots Write Poetry.* Fig Factor Media, 2021.
Phillips, Cabell. *"The New York Times" Chronicle of American Life: From the Crash to the Blitz, 1929–1939.* Macmillan, 1969.
Planck, Charles E. *Women with Wings.* Harper & Bros., 1942.
Prior, Rupert, comp. *Flying: The Golden Years: A Pictorial Anthology.* H. C. Blossom, 1991.
Putnam, George Haven. *Memoirs of a Publisher, 1865–1915.* G. P. Putnam's Sons, 1915.
Putnam, George Palmer. *The Southland of North America: Rambles and Observations in Central America During the Year 1912.* G. P. Putnam's Sons, 1913.
———. *Andrée: The Record of a Tragic Adventure.* Brewer & Warren, 1930.

———. *Soaring Wings: A Biography of Amelia Earhart.* Harcourt, Brace & Co., 1939. Ghostwritten and originally published serially as *Lady with Wings* in *Liberty* magazine.
———. *Wide Margins: A Publisher's Autobiography.* Harcourt, Brace & Co., 1942.
———. *Duration.* Doubleday, Doran, 1943.
Putnam, Jean-Marie (as Jean-Marie Consigny), with Charles Palmer. *Gardening for Fun in California.* G. P. Putnam, 1940.
Putnam, Jean-Marie, H. Britton Logan, and Lloyd C. Cosper. *Science in the Garden.* Duell, Sloan and Pearce, 1941.
Putnam, Jean-Marie, with Lloyd C. Cosper. *Gardens for Victory.* Harcourt, Brace & Co., 1942.
Quattrone, Frank D. *Penn State Abington and the Ogontz School.* Arcadia Publishing, 2016.
Railey, Hilton Howell. *Touch'd with Madness.* Carrick & Evans, 1938.
Rich, Doris L. *Amelia Earhart: A Biography.* Smithsonian Institution Press, 1989.
———. *Jackie Cochran: Pilot in the Fastest Lane.* University Press of Florida, 2007.
Roberts, David. *Escape from Luciana: An Epic Story of Survival.* Simon & Schuster, 2002.
Robinson, Cervin, and Rosemarie Haag Bletter. *Skyscraper Style: Art Deco New York.* Oxford University Press, 1975.
Roosevelt, Eleanor. *Eleanor Roosevelt's My Day: Her Acclaimed Columns, 1936–1945.* Edited by Rochelle Chadakoff. Pharos Books, 1989.
Ross, Walter S. *The Last Hero: Charles A. Lindbergh.* Harper & Row, 1964.
Safford, Captain Laurance, with Cameron A. Warren and Robert R. Payne. *Earhart's Flight into Yesterday: The Facts Without the Fiction.* Paladwr Press, 2003.
St. Clair, Mary Archer. *A Knock on the Door: Memories of Harry Manning.* Brandylane Publishers, 2001.
St. Johns, Adela Rogers. *Some Are Born Great.* New American Library, 1974.
Sann, Paul. *The Lawless Decade: A Pictorial History of a Great American Transition.* Bonanza Books, 1957.
Saunders, John Monk. *Wings.* Grosset & Dunlap, 1927. Based on the Paramount picture produced by Lucien Hubbard and directed by William A. Wellman.
Saunders, Lisa. *Mystic Seafarer's Trail.* CreateSpace Independent Publishing Platform, 2012.
Schultz, Barbra H. *Endorsed by Earhart: How Amelia Financed Her Flying.* Little Buttes Publishing Co., 2014.
Serling, Robert J. *Steel Rails and Silver Wings: The Lindbergh Line to the Birth of TWA.* Weekend Chief Publishing, 2006.
Simkhovitch, Mary Kingsbury. *Neighborhood: My Story of Greenwich House.* W. W. Norton, 1938.
Slung, Michele. *Living with Cannibals and Other Women's Adventures.* National Geographic Adventure Press, 2000.
Smith, Elinor. *Aviatrix.* Harcourt Brace Jovanovich, 1981.
Southern, Neta Snook. *I Taught Amelia to Fly.* Vantage Press, 1974.
Spick, Mike. *Milestones of Manned Flight: The Ages of Flight from the Wright Brothers to Stealth Technology.* Smithmark, 1994.
Stern, Robert A. M., Gregory Gilmartin, and Thomas Mellins. *New York 1930: Architecture and Urbanism Between the Two World Wars.* Rizzoli, 1994.
Stewart, Jules. *Gotham Rising: New York in the 1930s.* I. B. Tauris, 2016.
Stinson, Patrick M. *Around-the-World Flights: A History.* McFarland & Co., 2011.
Stoff, Joshua. *Charles A. Lindbergh: A Photographic Album.* Dover Publications, 1995.
———. *Long Island Airports.* Arcadia Publishing, 2004.
———. *Transatlantic Flight: A Picture History, 1873–1939.* Dover Publications, 2000.
Sullivan, Mark. *Our Times: America at the Birth of the Twentieth Century.* Vol. 1, *1900–1925.* Charles Scribner's Sons, 1996.
Sutherland, Abby A. *100 Years of Ogontz, 1850–1950.* Ogontz School, 1958.
Tate, Grover Ted. *The Lady Who Tamed Pegasus: The Story of Pancho Barnes.* Maverick Publishers, 1984.
Tebbel, John. *Between the Covers: The Rise and Transformation of American Book Publishing.* Oxford University Press, 1987.
———. *A History of Book Publishing in the United States.* Vol. 3, *The Golden Age Between Two Wars, 1920–1940.* R. R. Bowker Company, 1978.

Teitel, Amy Shira. *Fighting for Space: Two Pilots and Their Historic Battle for Female Spaceflight*. Grand Central Publishing, 2020.
Thaden, Louise. *High, Wide, and Frightened*. Stackpole Sons, 1938.
Tonsing, Ernest F. *Cousin Amelia: Stories of Amelia Earhart's Adventurous Family*. Luminare Press, 2021.
Vallée, Rudy. *Let the Chips Fall*. Stackpole Books, 1975.
Vallée, Rudy, and Gil McKean. *My Time Is Your Time: The Story of Rudy Vallée*. Ivan Obolensky, 1962.
Vargo, Dina. *Hidden History of Boston*. History Press, 2018.
Veca, Donna, and Skip Mazzio. *Just Plane Crazy: Biography of Bobbi Trout*. Osborne Publisher, 1987.
Vecsey, George, and George C. Dade. *Getting Off the Ground: The Pioneers of Aviation Speak for Themselves*. E. P. Dutton, 1979.
Vidal, Gore. *Palimpsest: A Memoir*. Random House, 1995.
———. *Point to Point Navigation: A Memoir*. Doubleday, 2006.
Wall, Robert. *Airliners*. Chartwell Books, 1980.
Waller, George. *Kidnap: The Story of the Lindbergh Case*. Dial Press, 1961.
Walsh, George. *Gentleman Jimmy Walker: Mayor of the Jazz Age*. Praeger, 1974.
Ware, Caroline F. *Greenwich Village, 1920–1930*. Octagon Books, 1935.
Ware, Susan. *Still Missing: Amelia Earhart and the Search for Modern Feminism*. W. W. Norton, 1993.
Washburn, Bradford, with Lew Freedman. *Bradford Washburn, an Extraordinary Life: The Autobiography of a Mountaineering Icon*. WestWinds Press, 2005.
Whyte, Edna Gardner, with Ann L. Cooper. *Rising Above It: An Autobiography*. Orion Books, 1991.
Wilson, Jan Doolittle. *The Women's Joint Congressional Committee and the Politics of Maternalism, 1920–1930*. University of Illinois Press, 2007.
Wilt, David. *Hardboiled in Hollywood: Five "Black Mask" Writers and the Movies*. Bowling Green State University Popular Press, 1991.
Winters, Kathleen C. *Amelia Earhart: The Turbulent Life of an American Icon*. Palgrave Macmillan, 2010.
———. *Anne Morrow Lindbergh: First Lady of the Air*. Palgrave Macmillan, 2006.
Wels, Susan. *Amelia Earhart: The Thrill of It*. Running Press, 2009.
Wosk, Julie. *Women and the Machine: Representations from the Spinning Wheel to the Electronic Age*. Johns Hopkins University Press, 2001.
Wray, Fay. *On the Other Hand: A Life Story*. Weidenfeld & Nicolson, 1990.
Wright, Monte Duane. *Most Probable Position: A History of Aerial Navigation to 1941*. University Press of Kansas, 1972.
Zeitz, Joshua. *Flapper: A Madcap Story of Sex, Style, Celebrity, and the Women Who Made America Modern*. New York: Crown Publishers, 2006.

CHILDREN'S LITERATURE

All True!: The Record of Actual Adventures That Have Happened to Ten Women of Today. Brewer, Warren & Putnam, 1931.
Bell, Betty Boyd. *Circus!: A Girl's Own Story of Life Under the Big Top*. Brewer, Warren & Putnam, 1931. (A girl's adventure story, likely suggested by Amelia.)
Cooper, Alice Cecilia, and Charles A. Palmer. *Twenty Modern Americans*. Harcourt, Brace & Co., 1942. (Includes a short chapter on Amelia written by Charles "Cap" Palmer, George's business partner, and likely informed by George.)
Crichton, Clarke Jr. *Frozen-In!: The Adventures of the "Nanuk's" Cabin Boy North of Siberia*. G. P. Putnam's Sons, 1930.
de Leeuw, Adele. *The Story of Amelia Earhart*. Illustrated by Harry Beckhoff. Grosset & Dunlap, 1955.
Douglas, Robert Dick Jr. *In the Land of the Thunder Mountains: Adventures with Father Hubbard Among the Volcanoes of Alaska*. Brewer, Warren & Putnam, 1932.
Douglas, Robert Dick Jr., David R. Martin Jr., and Douglas L. Oliver. *Three Boy Scouts in Africa*. G. P. Putnam's Sons, 1928.
Flores, Augusto. *My Hike: Buenos Aires to New York*. G. P. Putnam's Sons, 1929.
Fuller, Halsey Oakley. *Halsey in the West Indies*. G. P. Putnam's Sons, 1928.

Garst, Shannon. *Amelia Earhart: Heroine of the Skies*. Julian Messer, 1947.
Hawks, Frank. *Speed!* G. P. Putnam's Sons, 1931.
Murphy, Alison Barstow. *Every Which Way in Ireland*. G. P. Putnam's Sons, 1930.
North, Mary Remsen. *Down the Colorado by a Lone Girl Scout*. G. P. Putnam's Sons, 1930.
Nusbaum, Deric. *Deric in Mesa Verde*. G. P. Putnam's Sons, 1926.
———. *Deric with the Indians*. G. P. Putnam's Sons, 1927.
Parlin, John. *Amelia Earhart: Pioneer in the Sky*. Garrard Publishing Co., 1962.
Putnam, David Binney. *David Goes Voyaging*. G. P. Putnam's Sons, 1925.
———. *David Goes to Greenland*. G. P. Putnam's Sons, 1926.
———. *David Goes to Baffin Land*. G. P. Putnam's Sons, 1927.
Siple, Paul. *A Boy Scout with Byrd*. G. P. Putnam's Sons, 1931.
Stemp, Heather. *Amelia & Me*. Nimbus Publishing, 2020.
Washburn, Bradford. *Among the Alps with Bradford*. G.P. Putnam's Sons, 1927.

BOOKLETS

Brooks-Pazmany, Kathleen. *United States Women in Aviation, 1919–1929*. Smithsonian Institution Press, 1991.
Morrissey, Muriel Earhart. *The Quest of a Prince of Mystic: Henry Albert Morrissey, "The Chief."* Privately published for family only, 1983.
———. *Random Jottings from a Long Life with a Pen*. Privately published for family only, 1988.

COMIC BOOK

McCall, Felicity. *The Story of Amelia Earhart: The First Woman to Fly Solo across the Atlantic*. Illustrated by Joe Campbell. Shantallow Community Arts Project, 2007.

SELECTED ARTICLES

"A Round-the-World Flight Ends in the Pacific." *Life*, July 19, 1937.
"Aviation News." *World Progress*, April 1937.
Considine, Bob. "Amelia in Flight Against Will, Charge as Friends Are Blamed." Universal Wire Service, July 19, 1937.
"'Dog Tired' Bookman Relates Story of Hectic Night with Kidnapers [sic]; Indignantly Denies Hoax Talk." *Appeal-Democrat*, May 13, 1939.
Earhart, Amelia. "Flying the Atlantic." *American Magazine*, August 1932.
———. "My Flight from Hawaii." *National Geographic*, May 1935.
———. "Miss Earhart Goes to the Play." *Stage*, July 1935.
———. "My Lucky Turning Point." *This Week Magazine*, 1935.
Findley, Earl N. "Our Speedy Conquest of the Air." *Literary Digest*, August 19, 1933.
"Girl's Fiancé Is Anxious; But Boston Man Is Sure Miss Earhart Will Succeed." *New York Times*, June 9.
"Girls of the Flying Generation." *Everygirl's*, June 1929.
Hamill, Pete. "The Cult of Amelia Earhart." *Ms.*, September 1976.
Jennings, Dean S. "Is Amelia Earhart Still Alive?" Dean S. Jennings—who, according to his son Duffy Jennings, also ghostwrote *The Man Who Killed Hitler*—was commissioned by George Putnam to promote his new book on Amelia Earhart. Neither Putnam nor Jennings believed in the pseudoscience behind the three-part series that Jennings wrote, but they recognized its marketing potential. At the time, the Duke Parapsychology Lab, which opened in 1935, was stirring up interest with its dubious efforts to study extrasensory perception with Zener cards and other such bunkum, creating a significant market for this type of sensationalism. The series appeared in *Popular Aviation* in December 1939 and January 1940.
"Lady Lindy." *Pathfinder*, July 9, 1932.
McCoy, Horace. "Flight for Freedom." *Woman's Home Companion*, January 1943.

McMein, Neysa. Cover portrait of Earhart. *McCall's*, May 1937.
Mid-Week Pictorial. Numerous, 1928–1937. Predating *The New York Times Magazine* section, these are filled with historical photos, many of Amelia placed by George's team. The New York Public Library has paper copies of most years during the height of Amelia's fame. It is great fun to gently turn each page.
Moses, Phyllis R. "Keep Your Nose in the Turns" [Elinor Smith profile]. *Aviation History*, September 2003.
"Mrs. Putnam's Four Wreaths of Laurel." *Literary Digest*, June 4, 1932.
Palmer, Charles. "Was Amelia Earhart War's First Casualty? Was Famous Aviatrix Shot Down Exploring Jap Secret Bases?" *Skyways*, November 1942.
Pitman, Jack. "Amelia Earhart's Last Flight." *Coronet*, February 1956.
Putnam, David Binney. "From the Log of My Wonderful Voyage." *St. Nicholas*, September 1925.
"Putnam Denies Kern Kidnapping, Publicity Hoax to Sell Books." *Bakersfield Californian*, May 13, 1939.
"Putnam to Be Blown Up!" *Publishers Weekly*, January 18, 1930. This article stands out among the many documenting George Palmer Putnam's troubling claims of being targeted by Fascist bombing threats. The mocking tone of the piece was especially humiliating for George Haven Putnam, the head of the firm, who was appalled by his nephew's sensationalist antics.
"Putnam Weds at 42." *Pittsburgh Press*, April 21, 1934.
"Putnam Weds Young Divorcée: Publisher and Ex-Wife of Beverly Hills Man Fly to Boulder City." *Los Angeles Times*, May 22, 1939.
Sparling, Earl. "City Welcomes Miss Earhart, Ignores Pals." *New York World-Telegram*, July 6, 1928.
Steichen, Edward. "Miss Amelia Earhart." *Vanity Fair*, November 1931.
Strippel, Dick. "Flight into Eternity." *Air Classics*, July 1972.
"The Flapper Is Dead." *New York Times*, February 18, 1928.
"When a Plane Nose-Dived at a Fiery Volcano." *Literary Digest*, December 12, 1931.
White, D. Thompson. "Twenty-Five Years in the Cloud Since Man's First Successful Flight." *American Aviator*, January 1929.
Wilkinson, Stephan. "Amelia." *Aviation History*, January 2010.
Wilson, Florence Yoder. "What Women Can Do for Aviation." *Needlecraft*, May 1930.
Wilson, Juana, and Bill Wilson. "Amelia Earhart's Last Flight." *Modern Maturity*, June–July 1982.
Winchell, Walter. On Broadway: Notes of a New Yorker [column]. November 17, 1935. Winchell's syndicated column includes an interesting line: "On the office walls of George Putnam's place is displayed a telegram from Chapman Andrews, at that time in Peking, China—expressing regret over the death of his wife, Amelia Earhart."
Winfrey, Lee. "The Woman Who Flew Away." *Philadelphia Inquirer TV Week*, June 12, 1994.
Winkler, John. "The Golden Girl of the Air. What Is She Really Like? The First Intimate Picture of the Most Talked-About and Least-Known Heroine of Our Times." *Smart Set*, October 1, 1928.
Vidal, Gore. "On Flying." *New York Review of Books*, January 17, 1985.

MISCELLANEOUS SOURCES

Catalogs for G. P. Putnam books, 1924–1930.
Earhart, Amelia. "The Fun of It [radio broadcast]." London, 1932.
Hamill, Pete. "Amelia & Noonan," typescript, 1976. Performing Arts Research Collections. New York Public Library. (Note: Buckle up for this one—a wild conspiracy-theory screenplay from the legendary Pete Hamill. Back then, Hamill was romantically linked to Shirley MacLaine, who was lined up to star in this sensational narrative. Fast-forward and Hamill ties the knot with Japanese Earhart biographer Fukiko Aoki, whose meticulous research in Japan debunked those same capture theories. Talk about a plot twist!)
Aviation Project: Oral History Interviews. Charles Lindbergh, 1960. Harry A. Bruno, 1960. Jacqueline Cochran, 1960. Oliver C. LeBoutillier, 1976. Grover Cleveland Loening, 1967. Jerrie Cobb, 1960.

C. Blanche Noyes, 1960. Muriel Earhart Morrissey, 1960. Special Collections, Columbia University Libraries, New York, NY.

March of Time [radio program]. Produced by Time Inc. The July 9, 1937, episode of the radio series fictionalized Amelia Earhart's disappearance, causing many Americans to believe she was stranded on an island. Like the widespread panic caused by Orson Welles's "War of the Worlds" broadcast in 1938, this dramatization contributed to the mythos surrounding Earhart's fate.

Oral history of Edna Gardner Whyte, February 8, 1979. Edna Gardner Whyte Collection. Portal to Texas History. University of North Texas Libraries, Denton, TX.

Amelia Earhart Project Recordings (conducted by Elgen and Marie Long). Smithsonian National Air and Space Museum, Washington, DC. (As the first biographer to explore this priceless collection, donated by David W. Jourdan and Elgen Long's estate after Long's 2022 passing, I swooped in the moment it was available. Despite pandemic delays, years of hounding the patient librarians with emails finally paid off.)

Wood, Winifred. "Fred Noonan, the Forgotten Navigator: Unpublished Letters from His Famous Last Flight with Amelia Earhart," a thirteen-page unpublished article on Fred Noonan and his friendship with Helen Day. International Women's Air & Space Museum, Cleveland, OH.

Yearbook, *AITCHPE*, 1915. Hyde Park High School, Chicago, IL.

Harrison (NY) biography file, 1853–1988, 1922–1988 (bulk).

Charles Dawson History Center, White Plains, NY.

SELECTED ACADEMIC PIECES

Jay, Karla. "No Bumps, No Excrescences: Amelia Earhart's Failed Flight into Fashions." In *On Fashion*, edited by Shari Benstock and Suzanne Ferriss. Rutgers University Press, 1994.

Lieffers, Caroline. "Empires of Play and Publicity in G. P. Putnam's 'Boys' Books by Boys." *Diplomatic History* 43, no. 1 (January 2019): 31–56.

———. "What About Ireland? Alison Barstow Murphy and the Making of a Child Author." In *Home and Away: The Place of the Child Writer*, edited by David Owen and Lesley Peterson. Cambridge Scholars Publishing, 2016.

Lutz, Amy. "Amelia Earhart: Myth and Memory." Master's thesis, University of Missouri–St. Louis, 2020. https://irl.umsl.edu/thesis/365.

Morris, Sammie L. "What Articles Reveal: The Hidden Poems of Amelia Earhart." *Provenance, Journal of the Society of Georgia Archivists* 23, no. 1 (January 2005): 21–38. https://digitalcommons.kennesaw.edu/provenance/vol23/iss1/3/.

Smith, Sidonie. "Virtually Modern Amelia: Mobility, Flight, and the Discontents of Identity." In *Virtual Gender: Fantasies of Subjectivity and Embodiment*. University of Michigan Press, 1999.

SELECTED VIDEO

Amanda Pope, dir. *The Legend of Pancho Barnes and the Happy Bottom Riding Club*. Nick Spark Productions, 2009.

Kara Martinelli White, dir. *Beyond the Powder: The Legacy of the First Women's Cross-Country Air Race*. Hemlock Films and Western Reserve Public Media, 2015.

Lauren Cardillo, dir. and prod. *On a Wing and a Prayer*. 1982. A student project created by Lauren Cardillo during her academic studies, provided directly to the author by Cardillo for research purposes.

Lothar Mendes, dir. *Flight for Freedom*. RKO Radio Pictures, 1943.

Mike Wallace, dir. *Biography*. Episode "Amelia Earhart." Aired 1961 on A&E Networks. (Note: A shaky copy is available at the Harvard Radcliffe Institute's Schlesinger Library, and the University of New Hampshire holds the full transcript in its Paul Briand Papers. The episode can also be viewed online at the Internet Archive, https://archive.org/details/biography-amelia-earhart.)

Yves Simoneau, dir. *Amelia Earhart: The Final Flight*. Avenue Pictures Productions, 1994.

OTHER LOCATIONS AND REPOSITORIES

99s Museum of Women Pilots, Oklahoma City, OK
Alice Paul Institute, Mount Laurel, NJ
Amelia Earhart Birthplace Museum, Atchison, KS
Amelia Earhart Hangar Museum, Atchison, KS
American Geographical Society, Brooklyn, NY
American Museum of Natural History, New York, NY (Roy Chapman Andrews Papers)
Atchison Public Library, Atchison, KS
Aviation Hall of Fame and Museum of New Jersey, Teterboro, NJ
Barnard Archives and Special Collections, New York, NY
Bradford Washburn American Mountaineering Museum, Golden, CO (Zoom research)
Capitol Hill, Washington, DC (author present for the Amelia Earhart statue dedication with Nancy Pelosi and Mitch McConnell)
Centre for Newfoundland Studies, Queen Elizabeth II Library, Memorial University of Newfoundland, St. John's, NL, CAN
Cleveland State University, Cleveland, OH
Coffee House Club Archives, New York, NY
Columbia University Libraries' Special Collections, New York, NY
Cradle of Aviation Museum, Garden City, NY
Deschutes Historical Museum, Bend, OR (Zoom research)
Dinner Key Marina (now home to Miami City Hall, housed in the former Pan Am Terminal Building, once operations headquarters for overseas amphibious airline service to the Caribbean and South America), Miami, FL
Dwight D. Eisenhower Presidential Library, Museum & Boyhood Home, Abilene, KS
Elmer Holmes Bobst Library's Special Collections Center, New York, NY
Explorers Club Library, New York, NY
Forney Museum of Transportation History, Denver, CO (Zoom research of the archives)
Frontiers of Flight Museum, Dallas, TX
Greenwich House, New York, NY
Harvard University, Cambridge, MA (Papers of Janet Mabie, 1912–1960; Papers of Amy Otis Earhart, 1884–1987; Papers of Clarence Strong Williams, 1907–1971; Papers of Kenneth Griggs Merrill, 1918–1919; Denison House Records, 1890–1984)
Henry Ford Museum of American Innovation, Dearborn, MI (Zoom research)
Heritage Auctions, Dallas, TX
Hialeah Airport, Hialeah, FL
Indianapolis Public Library's Special Collections, Indianapolis, IN
International Women's Air and Space Museum, Cleveland, OH
Library of Congress, Washington, DC (Society of Woman Geographers Records, 1905–2015)
Matson Corporate Archives, Honolulu, HI
Memphis Public Library, Memphis, TN (Phoebe Omlie Collection)
Miami Airport, Miami, FL
Miami Municipal Airport, Miami, FL (formerly, now a Miami Dade College campus built over the runways; Dinner Key corresponds to the City Hall / Pan Am location)
New England Air Museum, Windsor Locks, CT
New Jersey Hall of Fame, Newark, NJ
New York Public Library's Special Collections, New York, NY (including the Karla Jay Papers)
New York University's Special Collections, New York, NY
Newark Liberty International Airport, Newark, NJ
Noank's Square House, Noank, CT
Ogontz Archive Room, Penn State, University Park, PA
Old Burial Hill Cemetery, Marblehead, MA
Old Rhinebeck Aerodrome, Red Hook, NY

Princeton University Library, Princeton, NJ (Bernard M. Baruch Papers)
Private Collection of David W. Jourdan (gifted via Elgen Long's estate), Cape Porpoise, ME
Purdue University Archives and Special Collections, West Lafayette, IN
Rye Historical Society, Rye, NY
San Diego Air and Space Museum Library and Archives, San Diego, CA (Fred Noonan Collection researched via email exchange)
San Diego History Center, San Diego, CA (Jean-Marie Consigny Putnam Collection)
Seaver Center for Western History Research, Natural History Museum of Los Angeles County, Los Angeles, CA
Smithsonian National Air and Space Museum, Washington, DC
Smithsonian National Air and Space Museum's Steven F. Udvar-Hazy Center, Chantilly, VA
Smithsonian's National Postal Museum Archives, Washington, DC
The Rooms Archives, St. John's, NFL, CAN
University of Illinois Urbana–Champaign, Urbana and Champaign, IL (Papers of G. P. Putnam's Sons researched via Zoom)
University of Iowa, Iowa City, IA (Papers of Stewart Stern)
University of New Hampshire, Durham, NH (Papers of Paul L. Briand Jr.)
University of North Texas, Denton, TX (Edna Gardner Whyte Collection, 1966–1983, researched via Zoom and email)
University of Texas at Dallas, Richardson, TX (Joseph Gervais Papers researched via email; reviewed entire Earhart holdings of a conspiracy theorist)
University of Wyoming, Laramie, WY (Interlibrary exchange of documents in the Eugene L. Vidal Papers)
Wings Club Archives, New York, NY

IMAGE CREDITS

Insert 1, p. 1; p. 2: Schlesinger Library, Harvard Radcliffe Institute.

Insert 1, p. 3, bottom right; p. 5, center right; insert 2, p. 6, top right: Hagley Museum and Library.

Insert 1, p. 3, top left; p. 8; p. 16; insert 2, p. 1, top; p. 3, top left; p. 7; p. 8, top; p.10, top; p. 10, bottom left: Courtesy of Purdue University Libraries, Karnes Archives and Special Collections.

Insert 1, p. 4, top left: *Letters from Amelia: An Intimate Portrait of Amelia Earhart* by Jean L. Backus.

Insert 1, p. 4, bottom right: "Thomas Humphrey Bennett Varney," Find a Grave, August 20, 2012, findagrave.com/memorial/95685024/thomas-varney.

Insert 1, p. 5, top left; p. 14, top; insert 2, p. 8, top left; p. 8, center right: San Diego Air & Space Museum Library & Archives.

Insert 1, p. 5, bottom left; insert 2, p. 1, center left: From the collection of the author.

Insert 1, p. 6, top: Deschutes County Historical Society.

Insert 1, p. 6, bottom left; p. 7, top left: Photos by Adam Lawrence. From the collection of the author.

Insert 1, p. 7, bottom right: *My Hike* by Augusto Flores.

Insert 1, p. 9, top left: *20 Hrs. 40 Min.* by Amelia Earhart.

Insert 1, p. 9, bottom: Photos by Adam Lawrence. Special thanks to the New Jersey Aviation Hall of Fame.

Insert 1, p. 10, top right: Library of Congress [sn83045462].

Insert 1, p. 10, bottom: National Portrait Gallery, Smithsonian Institution; gift of George R. Rinhart, in memory of Joan Rinhart.

Insert 1, p. 11, top left: Tekniska museets arkiv (Technical Museum Archive), Harald Martin Samling (Harald Martin Collection), via CC PDM 1.0.

Insert 1, p. 11, bottom: Photo by Staff/mirrorpix Daily Mirror/Mirrorpix via Getty Images.

Insert 1, p. 12, top left: Library of Congress [sn83045462].

Insert 1, p. 12, top right: Library of Congress [sn84026749].

IMAGE CREDITS

Insert 1, p. 12, bottom left: Library of Congress [sn87055779].

Insert 1, p. 12, bottom right: Library of Congress [sn86063730].

Insert 1, p. 13, top right: *20 Hrs. 40 Min.* by Amelia Earhart.

Insert 1, p. 13, bottom; insert 2, p. 5: National Portrait Gallery, Smithsonian Institution; gift of George R. Rinhart, in memory of Joan Rinhart. Via CC0.

Insert 1, p. 14, bottom left: Courtesy of the Delaware Public Archives.

Insert 1, p. 15, top left: Courtesy of the General Mills Archives.

Insert 1, p. 15, bottom right: Wikimedia.

Insert 1, p. 15, center left: From the Collections of the Henry Ford.

Insert 2, p. 1, bottom right: International News Photos / Wikimedia Commons.

Insert 2, p. 2: Schlesinger Library, Harvard Radcliffe Institute.

Insert 2, p. 3, bottom right: C. V. Glines, Jr. Papers, History of Aviation Collection, Special Collections and Archives Division, Eugene McDermott Library, The University of Texas at Dallas.

Insert 2, p. 4, top center: Courtesy of the Seth Kaller Collection.

Insert 2, p. 4, bottom: Stock media provided by Retrofootage/Pond5.

Insert 2, p. 6, bottom right: Messmore and Damon Company Records, Archives Center, National Museum of American History, Smithsonian Institution.

Insert 2, p. 8, bottom: Amelia Earhart, George P. Putnam and Paul Mantz inspecting Earhart's new home in Los Angeles, Calif., 1935, Los Angeles Times Photographic Archive, UCLA Library Special Collections via CC by 4.0 (creativecommons.org/licenses/by/4.0/).

Insert 2, p. 9, bottom right: Amelia Earhart in a Kimono Robe, Reading a Book, Waikiki, 1935, Matson Archives, Lynn Blocker Krantz, matsonvintageart.com.

Insert 2, p. 11, top left: National Archives, Eisenhower Presidential Library, Abilene, Kansas.

Insert 2, p. 11, center right: Photograph by J. C. Allen. Courtesy of Purdue University Libraries, Karnes Archives and Special Collections, and courtesy of Smithsonian Institute National Air and Space Museum.

Insert 2, p. 11, bottom left: Media News Group/Oakland Tribune via Getty Images.

Insert 2, p. 12, top right: Library of Congress [LC-USZ62-135361].

Insert 2, p. 12, bottom: From the collection of Santa Clarita Valley Historical Society. SCVhistory.com.

Insert 2, p. 13, top: Bettmann Archive/Getty Images.

Insert 2, p. 13, bottom left; p. 14, bottom left: AP Photo.

Insert 2, p. 14, top: Courtesy Nauticos.

Insert 2, p. 15, top: Photo by Adam Lawrence. From the collection of Laurie Gwen Shapiro (left); Adam Lawrence (right).

Insert 2, p. 15, bottom left: Courtesy of Amy Kleppner.

Insert 2, p. 16: Photo by Edward Steichen/Condé Nast via Getty Images.

INDEX

Adams, Eustace L., 353
Air League of the British Empire, 119
airships, 80, 201–2, 344
Akeley, Carl, 16
Alderman, Joanne, 414
Aldrin, Edwin, Sr., 408
Algonquin Round Table, 118, 150, 158, 245, 260, 423
Allan, Scotty, 97
Allen, C. B., 177, 178, 185, 203–4, 224, 228, 334, 337, 345, 350, 362
Allen, Cecil, 306
Allen, John J., 416–17
All Quiet on the Western Front (Remarque), 16, 176, 216
Alsterlund, Norah, 182, 192, 239
Amelia Earhart Fashions, 284–88, 293
Amelia Earhart Fund for Aeronautical Research, 316
Amelia Earhart Project, 158, 307, 455n64, 460n161
American Museum of Natural History, 88, 220
American Society for the Promotion of Aviation, 225
American Woman's Association, 182
Ames, Lawrence, 387
Anderson, Arthur P., 230, 234–35
Anderson, Robert "Chip," 231, 234–36, 240
Anderson, Sherwood, 43
Andrée, Salomon August, 230
Andrews, Harry, 354
Andrews, Roy Chapman, 16, 273, 407, 426, 436

Antarctic expeditions, 82, 90, 94, 102, 152–53, 194–95, 391
Archibald, Harry, 253
Archibald, Rose, 253–54
Arctic expeditions, 30, 34, 230
Arcturus Expedition, 17
Arden Galleries, 312
Argles, Arthur, 106
Atchison, Kansas, 32–39, 291–92, 302, 400
Atchison and Topeka Railroad Company, 33
autogiros, 234–35, 240–47
Avro Avian Moth, 123, 147, 153, 156, 186, 188, 194
Aylesworth, Merlin, 203

Babbitt, Dean, 420
Baer, Paul F., 178
Baffin Land expedition, 30, 93, 210
Bailey, Henry L., 230
Balbo, Italo, 267
Balch, Walter, 218
Balchen, Bernt, 90, 242, 244, 250–51, 253
Baldwin–Ziegler expedition, 34
Balfour, Harry, 368, 372, 373, 374, 384–85
Balis, Margaret Otis, 36, 39, 42, 44, 236
Balsley, Clyde, 314
Balsley, Harriette, 314
Barber, Frederick A., 248
Barnes, Florence Lowe "Pancho," 197, 198–99
barnstorming, 22, 61, 67–68, 240
Barton, Ernest Victor, 265
Baruch, Bernard, 342
Bassett, James, Jr., 319, 333

Batten, Jean, 366
Battle Creek Sanitarium, 245–47
Beebe, William, 17, 426
Beech-Nut, 240–41, 245
Belknap, Reginald Rowan, 85–86, 92
Bell, Alexander Graham, 169
Bellanca, Giuseppe Mario, 179, 185, 187
Bellanca Aircraft Company, 109, 180–85
Bellarts, Leo, 377–78, 380–83, 388
Bend, Oregon, 11–15, 156
Bendix, Vincent, 316, 318
Bendix Trophy, 306, 320, 392–93
Bennett, Floyd, 82
Berger, Josephine "Jo," 2–3, 15, 89, 184, 219, 236, 401, 409, 422, 460n158
Binney, Dorothy. *See* Putnam, Dorothy
Binney, Edwin, 9–11
Birchall, Fred, 24, 25
Black, Richard, 377, 379, 388, 398
Blumenthal, Ralph, 264
Boeing School of Aeronautics, 330
Boll, Mabel "Mibs," 81–83, 96, 101, 103, 106, 109–10, 116, 122, 253
Boston and Maine Railroad, 279
Boston Chamber of Commerce, 137
Boston–Maine Airways, 279–80, 281
Bow, Clara, 22
Boys' Books by Boys series, 19
A Boy Scout in the Grizzly Country (Douglas), 454n20
Bresnik, Albert, 333, 355
Brewer, Warren & Putnam, 219, 230, 244, 248–49, 260, 436–37
Briand, Paul, 436, 456n82, 468n436
Brisson, Fred, 429
Brittain, M. L., 430
Broun, Heywood, 260, 423
Brownsville, Texas, 178
Bruce, Alisa Mellon, 264
Bruce, Ann, 143, 145
Bruno, Harry, 342
Brusse, Leland, 63
Bryers, Duane, 411
Bureau of Air Commerce, 284, 304, 327–28, 390
Burry Port, Wales, 114, 116
Byrd, Marie, 97
Byrd, Richard
  Antarctic expeditions, xi–xii
  and Black's background, 377
  and Earhart's circumnavigation attempt, 342
  and Earhart's return from Europe, 126–27
  and Earhart's solo Atlantic flight, 250
  and events celebrating Earhart's aviation achievements, 131–32, 135–37
  and *Friendship*'s transatlantic flight, 5, 89–92, 94, 96–98, 100, 106
  and mural at Roxy Theatre, 276
  National Geographic Society award, 269
  and origins of transatlantic flight, 83–84
  and polar expeditions, 82–83, 89–90, 152–53, 155, 194–95, 258
  and Putnam's temperament, 412

Cady, Howard, 217–18
Cameron, Peter, 123
Campbell, Alan, 302
Cantor, Eddie, 169, 271
Cárdenas, Lázaro, 299
Carlsbad Caverns, 177
Carter, Howard, 1, 16
Cedars of Lebanon Hospital, 302
celestial navigation, 325–26, 378
Challis, Lucy, 232, 236
Chamberlin, Clarence, 131, 158, 179
Chaplin, Charlie, 172, 274, 313
Chapman, Samuel "Sam"
  background, 57–58
  and Earhart's death, 402
  and Earhart's fame, 134–35, 137, 140–43, 147, 188, 225
  and Earhart's first Atlantic flight, 98, 100, 102, 107–8, 121, 125
  and Earhart's intellectual interests, 58
  and Earhart's romantic interests, 64–68
  and Earhart's social work, 75
  engagement ended, 169, 174
  engagement to Earhart, 70, 72–73, 107–8
  and Putnam's interest in Earhart, 127, 129, 145–46, 155, 161, 237
Charlebois, John, 50
Chater, Eric, 368–73
Chater, Maisie, 368
Chautauqua lecture series, 186
Chevalier of the Order of Leopold award, 268
Chicago, Burlington & Quincy Railroad Co., 40
Chicago Air Show, 169–70, 171, 180
Christian Science, 56–57, 71, 227, 431
chronometers, 369–70, 414
Churchill, Winston, 83, 122
Clarke, Irwin Napier Colin, 265
Cleveland National Air Races, 169, 202
Cochran, Jacqueline "Jackie"
  and concerns about circumnavigation attempt, 347
  and Earhart's will and estate, 419
  and *Friendship*'s transatlantic flight, 112
  hosting Earhart at Desert Ranch, 338–42

INDEX

hosting Earhart's mother for holidays, 410
and memorial services for Earhart, 408
and publicity for Earhart's circumnavigation flight, 329
Putnam and Earhart's marriage, 404
and Putnam's marriage to Consigny, 424
reaction to Earhart's disappearance, 389
and speculation on causes of lost flight, 396–97
WASPs service, 308
Coe, Charles Frances, 309
Coffee House Club, 174, 292
Cohan, George M., 271
Cohen, Emanuel, 95, 260, 297, 362
Cole, Rex, 422
Coleman, Bessie, 168, 269–70, 435
Collins, Paul F. "Dog," 226, 279, 288–89, 363
Collopy, Jim, 368–70, 372, 374, 388
Columbia University, 4, 53–55, 59, 61–62, 74
Communist Party, 319–20
Conference on Current Problems, 292
Considine, Bob, 396
Consigny, Jean-Marie, 414–16, 419–20, 424, 427–28, 430–32
Coolidge, Jake, 95–96, 100
Cooper, Lillian, 319–20
Cosmopolitan, 154–55, 160–63, 182, 243, 412, 428
Cowles, Gardner, 407
Cox, Roy W., 327
Craig, Clarence "Elliot," 418
Crawford, Joan, 319
Crosby, Bing, 303, 343
Cross, Mark, 303
Crosson, Marvel, 199
Curtiss, Glenn, 60, 173

Daily News, 103, 146, 167, 209, 300, 432
Daniels, John, 114–15
Darby, Dorothy, 435
Daughter of the Sky (Briand), 456n82
Davenport, Harkness, 330
Davis, Marjorie B., 174, 225
Davis, Walter R., 354
Day, Helen Louise, 353–54, 389
dead reckoning navigation, 324
DeCarie, Margot, 303, 391
DeMille, Cecil B., 274, 363
Denison House, 74–76, 85–86, 90, 98, 100, 135, 138, 141–42
Dennison, Harold, 75–76, 174
Desert Ranch, 338–42
Devereaux, Richard and Fanny, 104
Dewey, John, 288
Dickens, Charles, 43

Dickerman, Don, 165, 171, 207, 219–20
Dickinson, Blanche Taylor, 168
Dickinson, Emily, vii
Dietrich, Marlene, 304
Dillenz, Lilli, 80
Disney, Walt, 402
Distinguished Flying Cross, 272
Doe, Thomas, 277
Doolittle, Jimmy, 211, 225
Double Dee Guest Ranch, 290–91
Douglas, Robert "Dick," Jr., 20–21, 167, 454n20
Douglas Aircraft Company, 68, 300
Down the Colorado (by a Lone Girl Scout) (North), 222–23
Du Bois, W. E. B., 169
Dudley, Binney, 159
Dunhill, Alfred, 288
Dunrud, Carl, 153, 290, 399
du Pont, Henry B., 181
Dymaxion vehicle, 297

Earhart, Amelia
Atlantic solo flight, 249–50, 254–58
autogiro flights, 240–47
aviation competitions, 194–202, 272, 296, 306, 348
awards and honors, 267–68, 270, 272, 409
birth, 32
circumnavigation flight lost, 373–86
declared dead, 418
education, 4, 37–39, 40–45, 53–55, 59, 61–62, 74
engagement to Chapman, 70, 72, 169
events celebrating aviation achievements, 130–37, 140–45, 270
fame and publicity, 142, 164
family background, 32–37, 39–41
feminism and progressive politics, 37, 46, 54, 75, 134, 149–50, 236, 251–52, 273, 309, 319–21, 439
financial pressures, 297–98, 344–45, 397, 438
first aviation job, 68–69
first meeting with Putnam, 1–6
flying lessons, 59–63, 65, 67, 70–71
and *Friendship*'s transatlantic flight, 91–117
health troubles from influenza, 49–50, 73, 101, 245, 302
intellectual and literary interests, 41, 50–52, 55–58, 62, 75
introduction to aviation, 45–48
lectures and speaking engagements, 155, 164, 171, 173, 182, 292, 298, 308–9
lost pilot's directive, 391
marriage to Putnam, 230–33

485

Earhart, Amelia (*cont.*)
  memorials and commemorative events, 407, 435
  Pacific solo flight, 295–97
  pacifism, 50, 57, 248–49, 278, 319–20
  and pilot license requirements, 67, 71, 88, 139–40, 178–79, 186, 197, 223–24
  relationships and romantic interests, 63–68, 124–25, 143 (*see also* Chapman, Samuel "Sam"; Putnam, George Palmer)
  and scams/conspiracy theories on lost flight, 401, 407–8, 425, 429–30, 433, 435–37, 453, 456n82, 468n436
  social work and settlement house job, 74–76, 85–86, 90, 141–42, 160, 164, 344
  wartime service, 45–49
  White House visits, 277–78, 297
  will and estate, 98–100, 405–6
Earhart, Amy Otis
  accommodations at Greenwich House, 160
  and aircraft purchase, 69
  and Amelia's disappearance, 385
  and Amelia's education, 42–43, 54–55
  and Amelia's engagement, 70
  and Amelia's family background, 34–41
  and Amelia's financial success, 164
  and Amelia's health troubles, 302
  and Amelia's intellectual interests, 62
  and Amelia's lost flight, 398
  and Amelia's marriage to Putnam, 236–37, 239
  and Amelia's plane acquisitions, 273
  and Amelia's progressive politics, 320–21
  and Amelia's return from Europe, 127
  and Amelia's romantic interests, 65–66
  and Amelia's speaking engagements, 155
  and Amelia's transatlantic flight, 259, 262–63
  and Amelia's wartime service, 45–48
  and Amelia's will and estate, 418–19
  birth of daughters, 32–33
  divorce, 71–72
  and Edwin's death, 227–28
  and events celebrating Amelia's aviation achievements, 135, 136, 435
  and family finances, 57
  and *Friendship*'s transatlantic flight, 92, 94, 99–100, 102–3, 117, 119
  and health problems, 56
  hosted by Cochran for holidays, 410
  life after Amelia's death, 400, 406, 408, 410–11, 413
  move to Boston, 182
  move to Toluca Lake house, 344
  and Putnam's interest in Amelia, 174, 224–26

  and scams/conspiracy theories on lost flight, 402
  social conservatism, 68
  and Stephens's death, 195
Earhart, Edwin
  alcoholism, 38–39
  and Amelia's engagement, 70
  and Amelia's family background, 32–41
  and Amelia's flying lessons, 59–60
  and Amelia's letters before flights, 99
  and Christian Science, 56–57, 71, 227
  divorce, 71–72
  and Earhart family's finances, 57
  and events celebrating Amelia's aviation achievements, 144
  and *Friendship*'s transatlantic flight, 119–20
  illness and death, 227–28
  marital troubles, 71
Earhart, Grace Muriel. *See* Morrissey, Grace Muriel
Earhart, Helen ("Annie"), 157, 226, 236
Earhart–Mantz Flying School, 306
Eastern Air Lines, 301, 309
Edward VIII, King of England, 321
Eisenhower, Dwight, 218
Elder, Ruth, 79–80, 180, 197, 199
Elliott, Edward C., 292, 307, 314, 407
Ellsworth, Lincoln, 250
Equal Rights Amendment, 149, 150, 319
Escape (Nitti), 212, 214–15
eugenics, 21, 169, 246, 339
Every Which Way in Ireland (Murphy), 220–21
Explorers Club, 18, 188, 220, 221, 238, 258, 272–73, 283, 420

Fahy, Claire May, 200
Fahy, Herbert, 200
Fairbanks, Douglas, 172, 276, 313
Fairey, Charles Richard, 266
Fascism, 163–64, 212–14, 217–18, 267
Faulkner, Charles, 234
Federal Aviation Administration, 67
Federal Bureau of Investigation, 401–2
Fédération Aéronautique Internationale, 67, 71, 139
Fields, W. C., 166, 303
Fink, Maurice, 356
Finn, Ted, 373
Fitzgerald, F. Scott, xiii, 27–28, 43, 158
Fitzgerald, Zelda, 63, 207
Fitzpatrick, Mary, 402
flapper era, 4, 63, 154–55, 207

Flores, Augusto, 19–20
Floyd Bennett Field, 320, 407
Ford, Corey, 158–59
Ford, Henry, 149
Franklin Institute, 273
Frazer, Ella May, 162–63, 182
Frederick, John T., 407
Fried, George, 113
Frogge, John, 186
Fuller, Buckminster, 297
Fuller, Halsey, 454n20
Fuller, Hector, 131
The Fun of It (Earhart), 269–70
Furman, Francis "Fuzz," 364

Gable, Clark, 319
Gallagher, Robert and Isobel, 256–57
Gardener, Helen Hamilton, 45
Garland, Constance, 408
Garland, Hamlin, 408
Garnett, Tay, 407, 409
Garson, Greer, 416
Gates Flying Circus, 84
Geddes, Norman Bel, 172–73
gender norms and equality
   Earhart's feminism and progressive politics, 36–37, 46, 54, 75, 134, 149–50, 236, 251–52, 273, 309, 319–21, 439
   and Earhart's legacy, 436, 439
   and Equal Rights Amendment, 149–50, 319
   and flying competitions, 339
   misogyny in aviation world, 106–7, 198, 200
   and prior research on Earhart, xii
   and Putnam's wife, 12
   and traditional wife/mother roles, 72
   women's military service, 300
   women's suffrage, 56
   and World War I, 53
Gentry, Viola, 228–29, 407
George Palmer Putnam, Inc., 420
Gershwin, George, 396
Gill, Fred, 104
Gillies, Bud, 161–62
Gimbel Brothers, 331, 345, 362
Girl Explorer books, 221–23
Gordon, Louis Edward "Slim"
   and Earhart's endorsements, 154
   and Earhart's reception in Europe, 122
   and events celebrating Earhart's aviation achievements, 136, 143–45
   and *Friendship*'s transatlantic flight, 101–2, 104–5, 111–12, 114, 116
   and media coverage of Earhart, 130
   planning for transatlantic flight, 87, 91, 96
   and Stultz's death, 189
Gore, Nina, 277
Gorski, Edward "Eddie," 250–51, 253
Gould, Laurence "Larry" McKinley, 152–53, 258
Gower, Lou, 100, 109, 189
G. P. Putnam's Sons
   and Beebe's writing, 17
   and Julia Railey's writing, 92
   London office, 113–15
   and publication of Nitti's book, 213–15
   and Putnam and Earhart's first meeting, 2
   Putnam's final days with, 213–19, 221–22
   and Putnam's PR efforts, 212
   Putnam's publishing background, 16–22
   and young adventurer publications, 19–21, 221–22, 454n20
Grabiner, Harry, 306
Grayson, Frances Wilson, 80
Great Northern Railway, 255
Green, Benigna, 309, 413
Green, Fitzhugh, 142–43, 148, 225
Greenwich House, 159, 164, 174, 182, 225
Grimm, Ruth, 308
Gross, Robert, 317–18
Guest, Amy Phipps
   and Earhart's reception in Europe, 122
   and Earhart's return from Europe, 125–26
   and *Friendship*'s transatlantic flight, 4–5, 83–84, 87–88, 91, 94, 96, 98, 102–3, 105, 111, 117–19
Guest, Frederick Edward, 83
Guinea Airways, 367–68, 370, 372–73

Hager, Alice Rogers, 350–51, 395, 407
Haldeman, George, 180, 181–82
ham radio, 295, 350
Hanzlick, Howard, 377, 387–88, 434–35
Harbour Grace, Newfoundland, 104, 109–11, 122, 252–53, 255
Harcourt, Brace & Company, 344, 355, 357, 362, 408
Harlem Renaissance, 207–8
Harper, Joseph, 408
Harres, Amelia, 33–35, 37, 39, 41
Harris, Asa Pitts, 409–10
Harvard Club, 238
Hawks, Frank, 59, 211, 272
Hawks, Howard, 306, 419
Hearst, William Randolph, 131, 163
Heath, Bertie, 369

Heath, Sophie (Lady Heath), 123, 139, 153, 179–80, 183–86, 211, 229
Heigh-Ho Club, 164–65, 171, 219–20
Hemingway, Ernest, 43
Henderson, Cliff, 196
Hepburn, Katharine, 419
Herndon, Hugh, Jr., 329
Herrick, Myron T., 27
Hickok, Lorena, 244
Hindenburg, Paul von, 276
Hindenburg disaster, 344
Hitler, Adolf, 44, 276
Holley, Clyde, 405, 413, 430–31
Holmes, Christian R., 295, 333–35
Hoover, Herbert, 259, 269, 277
Hoover, J. Edgar, 401–2
Hopper, Hedda, 416, 426
Hotz, Herman, 373
Howard, Benny and Maxine, 340–41
Howland Island
  and likely location of Earhart's lost plane, 384, 414, 433
  and navigation concerns about Earhart's flight, 347, 364, 369, 375–80, 382
  and planning for Earhart's circumnavigation flight, 324
  runway construction, 328
  and speculation on causes of lost flight, 388–89, 394, 396, 399, 433, 437
Hunter, Beverly, 364
Hurst, Fannie, 407–8
Hussey, George, 347
Hutchinson, A. S. M., 231
Hutchinson, Myron, 194

Industrial Workers of the World (IWW), 58, 320
influenza pandemic (1918–1920), 14, 48–49, 71–72
instrument navigation, 251, 254
Iredale, Bob, 369, 373
Ireland, Harry B., 416–17
Irvin Air Chute, 187, 202–3, 350, 365
Irving, Washington, 13, 293
USCGC *Itasca*, 372–73, 376–78, 380–82, 384–85, 387, 389, 397–98, 414, 434–35

Jackman, Mike, 104, 112
Jackson, Robert H., 339
James, William, 424
Jenkins, Burris, 400
Jennings, Dean, 421, 423–24
Johnson, Amy, 256
Johnson, Clarence L. "Kelly," 390
Johnson, Evelyn, 76

Johnson, Kendrick, 209
Johnson, Martin, 167
Jones, Eddy, 356
Jourdan, David, 460n158
Julian, Hubert, 168

Kahn, Otto Hermann, 274
Kane, Helen, 313
Kellogg, John Harvey, 245–47
Kenner, Frank, 377
Khayyam, Omar, 62
Kidd, Ray, 346
Kilgallen, Dorothy, 258
Kimball, Doc, 106, 111, 299
Kinner, Bert, 63, 65, 75
Kinner, Cora, 65–66
Kleppner, Amy, 308–9, 321, 364
Koch, Christina, 440
Kopchovsky, Annie Cohen, 37
Kunz, Opal, 201, 210, 215

Labrot, Sylvester, 162
Lae, Papua and New Guinea, 324, 366–67, 374, 394
La Guardia, Fiorello, 292, 407
Lake, Simon, 193
Lamb, Thomas W., 275–76
Lambie, Jack, 347
Lamour, Dorothy, 303
Lancaster, Bill, 165, 180, 182, 185, 194
Landis, Reed, 144
Last Flight (Earhart), 405, 408–9
Law, Bernard, 178
Law, Ruth Bancroft, 300
Lawrence, J. M., 11
Layman, David, 83–85, 87–88, 94, 96, 98, 100, 105
Learned, Willard, 433
LeBoutillier, Oliver Colin "Boots," 106, 109–11, 122
Le Gallienne, Eva, 97
Le Vesconte, Helen Primrose, 61
Levine, Charles, 106
Lighton, Louis D., 22, 302
Lilly, Josiah K., 316
Linam, Henry, 357
Lindbergh, Anne Morrow, 192, 259, 268–69, 286
Lindbergh, Charles
  and Earhart's Lockheed 10 modifications, 318
  and Earhart's motivations, 216
  and Earhart's public image, 4
  and Earhart's return from transatlantic flight, 268–69
  and Earhart's transatlantic flight, 259

and events celebrating Earhart's aviation achievements, 131
extramarital affairs, 244–45
and *Friendship*'s transatlantic flight, 83, 103
Lindbergh Line ownership, 190–91
and media coverage of Earhart, 138
memorabilia lost in house fire, 293
Mexico City flight, 178
and public interest in aviation, 22, 78–79, 342
and Putnam's career, 1
and Putnam's promotion of Earhart, 107
transatlantic flight and book deal, 3, 22–28, 173
Livingston, Clara, 356
Lockheed, 195, 230, 384, 387
Loening, Grover, 161–62, 460n161
Londonderry, Annie, 37
Long, Elgen, 66, 158, 383, 455n64, 460n161
Long, Marie, 158, 455n64
Loomis, Hiram B., 144
Lorenz, Catherine, 341
Lorenz, Marie, 341
Loring, Hope, 22, 302
Lorre, Peter, 321–22
Los Angeles Times, 66, 70, 71, 319, 329, 333
Low, Juliette Gordon, 221
Löwenstein-Wertheim-Freudenberg, Anne (Lady Anne Saville), 79
Loy, Myrna, 271
Luce, Irene L., 99
Luce, Oscar B., 99
Lucky Strike, 154, 325
Ludington Line, 226, 240, 279, 283
Lux Radio Theatre, 387, 429
Lyman, Lauren D. "Deac," 181, 184, 187, 203–4, 224, 228
Lyon, Henry "Harry," 165

Maata, Vivian, 328, 333, 337
Mabie, Janet, 311, 315, 404–5, 415, 426–27
MacCracken, William P., Jr., 178
MacDonald, J. Carlisle, 26–27
MacDonald, Jeanette, 270
MacDonald, Ramsay, 264
MacIntosh, W. Bruce, 348, 355
Mackay, Elsie ("Poppy Wyndham"), 80–81
Maddux, Jack, 192, 212, 293
Madison Square Garden, 142, 164
Manning, Harry
  and Earhart's first circumnavigation attempt, 336–37
  Earhart's interest in, 124–25, 143
  and Earhart's navigation and radio shortcomings, 337–38, 341, 350, 369, 379
  and Earhart's return from Europe, 124–25
  and first circumnavigation attempt, 330–32, 334
  and planning for Earhart's circumnavigation flight, 325–27
  and Putnam's interest in Earhart, 161
  on stamp covers in Earhart's plane, 372
Manning, Mildred, 337
Manship, Paul, 311–12
Mantz, Myrtle, 293, 313–15
Mantz, Paul
  and Bendix Trophy race, 306
  divorce, 314–15
  and Earhart's autogiro flights, 242
  and Earhart's first circumnavigation attempt, 334–37
  and Earhart's "shakedown flight," 345–46, 349–50
  and Earhart's solo Pacific flight, 294–95
  flying school, 306–7
  and Hollywood productions, 271, 319, 321–22
  Lockheed 10 modifications, 317–18
  marriage to Minor, 404
  and navigation concerns about Earhart's flight, 375
  and planning for Earhart's circumnavigation flight, 332, 343
  and posthumous awards for Earhart, 409
  and speculation on causes of lost flight, 394, 396
  and Terry Minor, 303–4
The Man Who Killed Hitler (anonymous), 421–24
Markham, Beryl, 395
Martin, Glenn, 60
Martinelli, Mary Beatrice "Bea," 341, 416–17
Martyn, Marguerite, 315
Maxwell, Lucia, 149
McCallion, Dan, 256
McClure, Francis, 257, 263
McCoy, Horace, 429
McCracken, Harold
  and biographies of Earhart, 461n164
  and concerns about circumnavigation attempt, 351
  and Earhart's autogiro flights, 241
  and Earhart's fashion line, 293
  and Earhart's return from transatlantic flight, 268
  and Earhart's speaking engagements, 164
  and events celebrating Earhart's aviation achievements, 270
  and *Friendship*'s transatlantic flight, 107
  and publishing business, 219–20
  on Putnam and Earhart's marriage, 361
  and Putnam's life after Earhart's death, 412
  and reactions to Earhart's disappearance, 390
  and speculation on causes of lost flight, 399–400
  and young adventurer publications, 18–20

McCrory, Herbert, 167
McEnery, David "Red River Dave," 390
McGeady, James, 256
McGuire, Grace, 383
McIntyre, O. O., 154
McKee, Joseph, 131
McLaughlin, Hughie, 256
McMein, Neysa, 171
McNeeley, Bo, 326, 337, 345, 348–49, 354–56, 391
McQueen, Elizabeth Lippincott "Queenie," 196
McVaugh, Eddie, 240–41
Meière, Hildreth, 281
Meir, Jessica, 439
Melcher, Frederic, 407
Mellon, Andrew, 263–64
Meloney, Marie "Missy" Mattingly, 407
Mendes, Lothar, 429
Merrill, Henry T. "Dick," 347
Merrill, Kenneth Griggs, 43
Miller, Grace, 74
Miller, Jessie "Chubbie," 165, 197
Miller, Johnny, 240, 241
Miller, William T., 327–28, 331, 345, 375
Mills, A. K., 112
Minor, Roy, 313
Minor, Terry, 303–4, 313, 333, 336–37, 404
Monroe, Harriet, 51–52
Montijo, John, 70
Morden, William J., 273
Morgan, Anne, 182
Morgan, J. Pierpont, 182
Morley, Maynard, 69
Morrison, Amy, 398
Morrissey, Albert, 188, 309, 413
Morrissey, Grace Muriel
  and divorce of parents, 71
  and Earhart's family background, 33, 34–41
  and Earhart's fashion line, 285
  and Earhart's interest in poetry, 50
  and Earhart's legacy, 439
  and Earhart's plane acquisitions, 273
  and Earhart's progressive politics, 320
  and Earhart's relationship with stepson, 289
  and Earhart's romantic interests, 64–67, 72
  and Earhart's speaking engagements, 308–9
  and Earhart's sponsorships, 243
  and Earhart's transatlantic flight, 257, 259, 262–63
  and Earhart's wartime service, 47–48
  education, 45, 50
  and events celebrating Earhart's aviation achievements, 136, 141
  and *Friendship*'s transatlantic flight, 99, 102–3, 119
  and key source for biographers, 453n
  life after Earhart's death, 413
  marriage, 188, 413
  and mother's move to Greenwich House, 160
  and posthumous books on Earhart, 415, 453n
  and Putnam and Earhart's marriage, 231–32, 236–39
  and Putnam's interest in Earhart, 224–25
  and Putnam's marriage proposals to Earhart, 230
  reaction to Earhart's disappearance, 389
  and scams/conspiracy theories on lost flight, 425, 436–37
Murfin, Orin Gould, 389
Murphy, Alison Barstow, 220–21
Murphy, Grace E., 220
Murphy, Robert Cushman, 220
Mussolini, Benito, 163–64, 212, 267

National Aeronautic Association, 85, 139, 348
National Air and Space Museum, 27, 158, 274, 313, 384, 433, 460n161
National Air Races, 155–57, 169, 196, 198, 245, 306
National Airways, 279, 281–83, 288–89, 305, 316
National Geographic Society, 269, 324
National League of Women Voters, 149
National Woman's Party, 150, 319
Naughton, Lindie, 185, 186
Nauru Island, 378
navigation
  celestial navigation, 325–26, 378
  and concerns about circumnavigation attempt, 366, 368–85
  dead reckoning, 324
  instrument navigation, 251, 254
  offset approach, 382
  outdated charts of Howland Island, 375–76, 383, 388
  and planning for Earhart's circumnavigation flight, 341
  and radio direction finding, 325, 377
  and report on lost flight, 413–14
  and speculation on causes of lost flight, 390–91, 394
  and "time ticks," 370–71
Nazism, 276–77
New Deal, 309
New York Herald Tribune
  and Earhart's circumnavigation flight, 359, 361, 362
  and Earhart's first circumnavigation attempt, 334

INDEX

and Earhart's "shakedown flight," 345, 350
and Earhart's speaking engagements, 292
and posthumous books on Earhart, 405, 453n
and Putnam's sabotage of Smith's career, 203
New York State Fair, 155
New York State Nautical School, 325
New York Stock Exchange, 205
The New York Times
　coverage of women's aviation, 184–85
　and Earhart's autogiro flights, 240
　and Earhart's deep-sea dive, 194
　and Earhart's endorsements and PR, 155
　and Earhart's speaking engagements, 171
　and flapper era, 4
　and *Friendship*'s transatlantic flight, 93, 107–8, 112, 115, 117–18
　and Lindbergh's transatlantic flight, 24
　and New York's publishing district, 2
　and public interest in women aviators, 81
　and Putnam's sabotage of Smith's career, 203
　and speculation on causes of lost flight, 391
Nichols, Malcolm, 137
Nichols, Ruth
　aviation achievements, 121–22, 140, 179
　and competition among women aviators, 176, 225
　and *Defender* christening, 201
　and Earhart's progressive politics, 149, 150
　and Earhart's public image, 135
　and Earhart's transatlantic flight, 251–52, 257–58, 259
　and events celebrating Earhart's aviation achievements, 131
　and onset of Great Depression, 206
　and public interest in women aviators, 81
　and Putnam's social circle, 4
Nineteenth Amendment, 56
The Ninety-Nines
　and Black female aviators, 339
　Earhart elected president, 245
　and Earhart's fashion line, 287
　and Earhart's legacy, 439
　and Earhart's "shakedown flight," 346, 347–48
　and Earhart's transatlantic flight, 253
　and Livingston, 356
　origin of, 211
　and Paris's death, 215
　promotion of women's aviation, 215–16
　and Putnam's marriage proposals to Earhart, 229
　and scams/conspiracy theories on lost flight, 436
　and Smith's transport license, 224

Nitti, Francesco Fausto, 212–15
Noonan, Bea, 361
Noonan, Fred
　alcoholism, 341–42
　and circumnavigation flight, 356–61, 363–66, 368–80, 383–85
　declared dead, 416–17
　divorce and remarriage, 341
　and Earhart's "shakedown flight," 347–50, 352–61
　memorial service for, 407
　planning and preparations for circumnavigation flight, 332–34, 337, 341–42
　and scams/conspiracy theories on lost flight, 407–8
　and speculation on causes of lost flight, 387–89, 396–99, 411, 414
North, Mary Remsen, 221–23
Northeast Airlines, 316
North Pole expeditions, 34, 82, 90, 230
Northrop, John Knudsen, 197
Noyes, Blanche, 200–201, 229, 321
Noyes, Dewey, 229
Nusbaum, Deric, 19
Nusbaum, Jesse, 19
Nutshell Jockey Club, 172

O'Brien, Edna, 229
Ochs, Adolph S., 81, 93, 117, 185
Odlum, Floyd, 338–42, 401, 404, 419, 429
O'Donnell, Gladys, 200, 201
Ogontz School for Young Ladies, 42–46, 285, 389, 454n42
O'Hare, Tommy, 377, 378–79, 381–85, 388
Omlie, Phoebe, 179, 201, 347–48
Orteig, Raymond, 22
Orteig Prize, 22, 28, 106
Otis, Alfred, 32–35, 37, 39, 41
Otis, Mark, 34, 39, 41
Ott, George, 165
Owen, Russell, 391, 397

Paderewski, Ignacy Jan, 15
Palmer, Charles "Cap," 411–13, 420–21, 425, 428–29, 432–33
Pan Am, 178, 186, 324, 329, 331–32, 341, 347, 353, 358, 369, 378
Pangborn, Clyde, 329
Panhorst, Carl, 377, 384
Paramount, 260, 270, 297, 302
Parini, Jay, 305
Paris, Neva, 210–11, 215

Park, Virginia "Ginger," 37
Parker, Dorothy, 134, 171, 260, 302
Parsons, Louella, 408, 426
Pascal, Gabriel, 419
Patterson, Margaret, 46
Patton, Dalton, 423
Paul, Alice, 54
Payre, Andree, 69
Penaluna, William W., 468n436
Perkins, Frances, 288
Perkins, Marion, 75, 86, 90, 94, 98
Perkins, Max, 158
Phipps, John, 84–85, 87
Pickford, Mary, 276, 313
Pickles, Marika, 460n158, 460n161
Pitcairn Aircraft Company, 234, 240
Pollock, Gordon, 42–43
Porter, Cole, 172
Post, Emily, 292
Post, Wiley, 195, 299, 305, 318, 329
Potter, Beatrix, 95
Pratt & Whitney engines, 251, 318
SS *President Roosevelt*, 123–24, 140, 152
Progress of Women (Meière), 281
Prohibition, 54, 85–86, 109, 191, 264, 277, 284
Pulitzer Prizes, 181, 437
Purdue University, 292, 307–8, 311, 314, 316–19, 392, 407, 420
Putnam, Binney, 302
Putnam, Cynthia, 435
Putnam, David Binney
  and Arcturus Expedition, 17–18
  and Earhart at Rye estate, 148
  and Earhart's departure on circumnavigation flight, 352–53, 356
  and Earhart's "shakedown flight," 347, 349
  and Earhart's speaking engagements, 155
  and the Explorers Club, 258
  and father's fake kidnapping plot, 423–24
  and father's Hollywood career, 270
  flight training and license, 272, 280
  and George and Amelia's marriage, 239
  and the Hindenburg disaster, 344
  life in Bend, Oregon, 12
  and National Airways, 288–89
  and parents' marital troubles, 158, 207, 209–10, 460n158
  and posthumous books on Earhart, 426
  South American expedition, 280
  and speculation on causes of lost flight, 396
  and Weymouth's tutelage, 30
  and Women's Day aviation event, 283
  young adventurer titles, 18, 30
Putnam, Dorothy
  affairs, 187–88
  and Arcturus Expedition, 17–18
  and *City of New York* christening, 191–92
  courtship and marriage to George, 9–12
  divorce from George, 209–12, 218, 460n158
  and Earhart's deep-sea dive, 193–94
  and Earhart's public image, 148–49
  and events celebrating Earhart's aviation achievements, 133, 136–37, 140–41, 143, 145
  and events honoring Earhart, 150, 153
  and *Friendship*'s transatlantic flight, 117
  and George's financial difficulties, 229
  and George's PR stunts, 174–75
  and life at Rye home, 147–48, 150
  marital troubles, 15–16, 29–31, 89, 93–94, 97–98, 100, 108, 125–26, 156–59, 164–66, 169–71, 174, 177, 187–88, 206–7, 288–89
  marriage to Upton, 216
  at Nutshell Jockey Club, 172
  and onset of Great Depression, 204–5
  and Putnam and Earhart's marriage, 238–40
  and Putnam's interest in Earhart, 151–54, 226
  and Stultz's death, 189
Putnam, Frances, 151, 230–31, 234–36, 249
Putnam, George Haven ("the Major"), 8–9, 13–16, 176, 214, 216–18, 430
Putnam, George Palmer
  and Arcturus Expedition, 17–18
  background of Earhart's story, xi–xiii
  correspondence with Earhart, 403–4
  courtship and marriage to Dorothy, 9–12
  death, 435
  divorces, 431–32, 460n158
  and Earhart declared dead, 418
  and Earhart's first transatlantic flight, 82–90, 91–120
  family background, 7–9
  first meeting with Earhart, 1–6
  innovations in publishing business, 12–22, 28–30
  interview after lost flight, 395
  and Jazz Age interests, 28–29
  kidnapping staged by, 421–24, 435, 467n421
  and Lindbergh's flight and book deal, 22–28
  marital troubles with Dorothy, 15–16, 29–31, 89, 93–94, 97–98, 100, 108, 125–26, 156–59, 164–66, 174, 187–88, 206–7
  marriages after Earhart, 424–25, 433–34
  marriage to Earhart, 230–33
  name treatment for text, xv–xvi
  nicknames, xv–xvi, 27, 94
  promotion of women pilots, 82

volatile temperament, 217–18, 289, 314–16, 346–47, 412–13, 428, 437–38
and young explorer publications, 17–21
Putnam, George Palmer, I, 7–8, 123
Putnam, George Palmer, III ("Junie"), 14, 148, 155, 210, 281, 352, 437–38
Putnam, Irving, 216–18
Putnam, Israel, 7
Putnam, John Bishop, 8, 13
Putnam, Margaret Haviland "Peg," 433–35, 437
Putnam, Nina Wilcox, 14
Putnam, Palmer Cosslett, 8, 217–18
Putnam, Robert Faulkner, 13, 14

Quaker Oats, 343–44, 362, 389–90
Quiet Birdmen, 189

racism and racial dynamics, 21, 165–66, 168–69, 246, 270, 339–40
Radio City Music Hall, 274–75
radio communication
    advertising, 176
    and *City of New York* christening, 191
    and competition among women aviators, 187
    and concerns about circumnavigation attempt, 351, 356, 362, 365–66, 368–85
    Earhart's radio appearances, 343
    and Earhart's "shakedown flight," 346
    and Earhart's solo Pacific flight, 295
    and Earhart's speaking engagements, 173, 182
    equipment sponsored for Earhart's plane, 318
    and events celebrating Earhart's aviation achievements, 270
    and Flaming Youth culture, 78
    and *Friendship*'s transatlantic flight, 103, 106, 112–14, 121
    ham operators, 295, 350
    and Lindbergh's flight, 23–25
    Morse code, 326, 337–38, 350, 372, 373, 379–80, 388, 396
    and planning for Earhart's circumnavigation flight, 324–26, 332
    radio direction finding, 377
    Smith's announcing job, 197–98, 203
    and speculation on causes of lost flight, 375–76, 387–89, 391, 399, 413–14, 416
    Welles's "The War of the Worlds," 423
    and the Women's Air Derby, 197–98
Ragan, Hiram, 327
Raiche, Bessie, 44
Railey, Hilton Howell
    discovery of Earhart, 77
    and Earhart's first meeting with Putnam, 1–3, 5–6

and Earhart's media image, 92
and Earhart's reception in Europe, 122–27
and Earhart's transatlantic flight, 257–58, 260
and events celebrating Earhart's aviation achievements, 132, 137
and *Friendship*'s transatlantic flight, 82–96, 108–9, 111–19, 142–43
and posthumous books on Earhart, 456n82
and Putnam's background, 13
and Putnam's interest in Earhart, 140, 151–56, 158–59
and Putnam's life after Earhart's death, 412
and Putnam's marriage proposals to Earhart, 229
and young adventurer publications, 21
Railey, Julia, 92, 94
Rasche, Thea, 81–82, 109–10, 135, 150, 197, 199–200, 201, 259
Rasmussen, Knud, 16
Raven, Henry, 273
Raymond, Allen, 112
Red Cross, 44, 46, 162
Redwood Aviation School, 64
Reed, Ione, 406–7, 409–10, 416
Rex, Peggy, 201
Rich, Doris, 65
Richey, Helen, 321
Richthofen, Manfred, Freiherr von, 106
Rickenbacker, Eddie, 301, 436
Roberts, Allan, 372
Roberts, Mildi, 414
Roberts, Ossie, 114–15
Rogers, Will, 197, 300–301, 305, 436
Roosevelt, Eleanor
    and Conference on Current Problems, 292
    and Earhart's circumnavigation flight, 359–60
    and Earhart's progressive politics, 309, 339
    and Earhart's White House visits, 277–78
    and Fuller's Dymaxion car, 297
    and Hickok, 244
    and planning for Earhart's circumnavigation flight, 328
    and posthumous books on Earhart, 427
    and termination of search for Earhart, 396
Roosevelt, Franklin D.
    and Earhart's progressive politics, 304, 319, 321
    and Earhart's solo Pacific flight, 296
    and Earhart's White House visits, 277
    and end of Prohibition, 284
    and labor activism, 58
    letter to Orville Wright, 294
    and Putnam's enlistment in military, 428
    and Putnam's marital troubles, 31

INDEX

Roosevelt, Franklin D. (*cont.*)
   and Putnam's publishing career, 222
   termination of search for Earhart, 396
Roosevelt, Hall, 277
Roosevelt, Theodore, 42–43
Rose, Stan, 365–66
Ross, David E., 316
Ross, Harold, 172
Rossetti, Christina, 62
Rossetti, Dante Gabriel, 51
Rothafel, Sam "Roxy," 274–75
Rothar, Wilbur, 401–2
Rouff, Maggy, 288
Royer, Lloyd, 67–68
Russell, Rosalind, 429–30

Sandburg, Carl, 62
Sanger, Margaret, 169
Sarnoff, David, 203
Saunders, John Monk, 22, 237–38
Savage, Sam, 183
Schiaparelli, Elsa, 286
Schleman, Helen, 308
Schuyler, George, 436
Selfridge, Harry Gordon, 264
Seventh-day Adventists, 246
Shapiro, Laurie Gwen, xiii
Shearer, Norma, 313
Shields, Nilla Ruth, 289–90, 302, 353
Sikorsky, Igor, 173
Simkhovitch, Mary Kingsbury, 160–61
Simpson, Wallis, 265, 321
Skyward (Byrd), 89–90, 98
Sloan, Sam, 428
Smith, Charles Kingsford, 297
Smith, Elinor
   background, 166–67
   and the Chicago Air Show, 170–71
   and competition among women aviators, 176, 179–87
   and Earhart's transatlantic flight, 252, 259
   and endurance flying records, 203–4
   and Irvin Air Chute endorsement, 202–3
   and Putnam's marriage proposals to Earhart, 228–29
   reaction to Earhart's disappearance, 389
   and safety concerns in women's aviation, 211, 216, 224–25
   transport license, 223–24
   and the Women's Air Derby, 197, 201
Smith, Harry H., 266
Smithsonian Institution, 27, 158, 179, 187, 313, 435, 460n161

Snook, Neta, 60–70, 156, 211, 436
Soaring Wings (Putnam), 234, 415, 426–27
social work, 164, 344. *See also* Denison House; Greenwich House
Society of Woman Geographers, 243
Solomon, Samuel, 279, 282, 305
Sopwith, Thomas, 46
Southern, Bill, 63, 66–67
Spadina Military Hospital, 49
Spanish-American War, 43
Stabler, Marian, 50–51, 55, 216, 249–50
Steichen, Edward, 276
Stephens, Orville, 194–95
Stewart, Flora "Ma," 367–68
St. Louis World's Fair (1904), 35
Stovepipe Wells Hotel, 434–35
Strandenaes, Brynjulf, 107
Studer, Clara, 215, 436
Stultz, Wilmer
   alcoholism, 100, 109–10, 112, 123–24, 133, 144, 189
   death, 189–90
   and Earhart's endorsements, 154
   and Earhart's reception in Europe, 122–24
   and Earhart's return from Europe, 126
   and events celebrating Earhart's aviation achievements, 132, 136, 143–45
   and *Friendship*'s transatlantic flight, 84, 91–92, 96, 100–101, 104–6, 109–17
   and media coverage of Earhart, 128–30
Sullivan, Frank, 118, 423
Sullivan, Jo ("Josie"), 341
Sundine, Patricia, 460n158
Sutherland, Abby, 58
Swanson, Gloria, 191
Switlik, Stanley, 301
Sword, Collins, 352

Tata, Mithan, 45
television, 243–44
Terrell, Jane, 408
Thaden, Louise, 200, 208, 215, 241, 253, 296, 321, 392–94, 396–97
Third Street Music School Settlement, 55
Thomas, Lowell, 407
Thompson, Warner K., 376–78, 380, 413–14
Three Boy Scouts in Africa (Douglas), 20–21, 167, 221
ticker-tape parades, 20, 25–26, 49, 130–35, 137, 188, 268–69
"time ticks," 370–71
Tin Pan Alley, 395
Tissot, Ernest "Ernie," 294
Tomas, Frederico "Fred," 402
Toynbee Hall, 123

INDEX

Tracy, Arthur, 268
Transcontinental Air Transport (TAT), 190–92, 195, 202, 204, 212, 226–27, 304
Travel Air, 200
Travis, June, 306
Treadwell, Sarah, 43
Trepassey, Newfoundland, 101–5, 109–11, 114, 122, 253
Trianon Ballroom, 145
Trout, Evelyn "Bobbi," 179, 200–201, 203
Truman, Harry, vii
Turbyfill, Mark, 50–52
Turner, Roscoe, 211
20 Hrs. 40 Min. (Earhart), 114, 157
Twenty-First Amendment, 284

Ulm, Charles, 294
Ulsvois, Mary, 239
Underhill, Jackson, 69
United States Lines, 326, 337
Upton, Frank, 187–88, 204, 216, 288
US Coast Guard, 383, 386, 388, 408, 416, 425
US Department of Commerce, 242, 254
US Navy, 377, 383, 390, 391–92, 396

Vagg, Allan, 374
Vallée, Rudy, 165
Vanderbilt, William K., 182
Van Dyke, W. S., 319
Varney, Ella, 64
Varney, Thomas Humphrey Bennett, 63–68, 70, 73, 456n64
Varney, Walter, 64
Vellum, Clarence, 334
Vidal, Eugene "Gene," 226, 259, 277, 284, 293, 304, 327–29, 363, 398
Vidal, Gore, 269, 279, 284, 304–5
Voelter, Karl, 347
Voluntary Aid Detachment (VAD), 46
Volunteer (blimp), 202
Vultee, Gerard, 197

Waggener, Balie, 35
Walker, Henrietta, 422
Walker, Jimmy, 19–20, 131–32, 167, 170, 172, 191, 268–69
Walker, Roy, 422
"The War of the Worlds" (Welles), 423
Warren, Althea, 407
Washburn, Henry Bradford, 19, 289, 323–25, 389
Waters, R. V., 347

"We" (Lindbergh), 3, 27
Weatherdon, Edward, 177
Weber, Helen "Roses," 148
Weissmuller, Johnny, 246
Welles, Orson, 423
Wells, Fay Gillis, 216
Weymouth, George, 29–30, 93
Whalen, Grover, 131, 191
Whitehead, Henry S., 20, 454n20
White House, 277–78, 297
Whitley, Rhea, 402
Whitney, Richard, 205
Whyte, Edna Gardner, 215–16, 346
Wide Margins (Putnam), 428
Wiese, Otis, 154
Wilderness Society, 238
Wiley and Putnam, 8
Willebrandt, Mabel Walker, 419
Williams, Helen, 202
Wilson, Gill Robb, 390
Winchell, Walter, 401, 423
Withycombe, James, 13
Womack, Lyle, 79
Women Airforce Service Pilots (WASP), 308, 339
Women's Air Derby, 194–201, 272, 296, 348
Women's Committee for the British Empire, 122
Women's Day, 281–83
Women's Educational and Industrial Union, 74
Women's International Association of Aeronautics, 196
Women's National Aeronautical Association, 201, 407
women's rights and equality. *See* gender norms and equality
Wood, Jane, 349
Woods, Katherine, 427
Woodward, Donald, 83, 177
Woollcott, Alexander, 172
World Flight (Earhart), 344, 362, 404–5
World War I, 22, 43, 45–46, 53, 57, 59, 68, 144, 189, 220, 300
World War II, 6, 206, 308, 339
Wray, Fay, 22, 238
Wright, Orville, 6, 28, 173, 273–74, 294
Wright, Wilbur, 28, 173

Yeats, William Butler, 220
Young, Joe, 266
Young, Owen, 203

Ziegfeld, Flo, 133

100 YEARS of PUBLISHING

Harold K. Guinzburg and George S. Oppenheimer founded Viking in 1925 with the intention of publishing books "with some claim to permanent importance rather than ephemeral popular interest." After merging with B. W. Huebsch, a small publisher with a distinguished catalog, Viking enjoyed almost fifty years of literary and commercial success before merging with Penguin Books in 1975.

Now an imprint of Penguin Random House, Viking specializes in bringing extraordinary works of fiction and nonfiction to a vast readership. In 2025, we celebrate one hundred years of excellence in publishing. Our centennial colophon features the original logo for Viking, created by the renowned American illustrator Rockwell Kent: a Viking ship that evokes enterprise, adventure, and exploration, ideas that inspired the imprint's name at its founding and continue to inspire us.

For more information on Viking's history, authors, and books, please visit penguin.com/viking.